Secret ORACLE

Unleashing the Full Potential of the ORACLE DBMS
by Leveraging Undocumented Features

Norbert Debes

ORADBPRO Publishing

Secret ORACLE

Unleashing the Full Potential of the ORACLE DBMS by Leveraging Undocumented Features

ISBN 978-1-4357-0551-7

Library of Congress Control Number: 2007909938

Publisher:
Lulu Enterprises Inc.
860 Aviation Parkway
Suite 300
Morrisville, NC 27560
United States of America

This book is dedicated to Arthur Janov, Michel Odent, and Aletha Solter, whose work has the potential to render mankind more human and more feeling.

About the Author

Norbert Debes has more than eleven years of experience as an ORACLE database administrator. He holds a master's degree in computer science from the University of Erlangen, Germany and is an Oracle8, Oracle8*i*, and Oracle9*i* Certified Professional ORACLE Database Administrator. For well over six years, he held different positions in technical roles at Oracle Germany, among them team leader in Oracle Support Services and technical account manager in Strategic Alliances. In his last role at Oracle, he was responsible for promoting Real Application Clusters on a technical level. During his tenure, he contributed to the Oracle9*i* SQL Reference and Real Application Clusters manuals as well as Real Application Clusters training materials.

As early as 2000, he published an article on performance diagnosis with extended SQL trace event 10046 by using a logon trigger and writing session statistics from `V$SESSTAT` and `V$SESSION_EVENT` to a trace file with the package `DBMS_SYSTEM`. This article appeared in the DOAG News magazine of the German Oracle User Group. Additional publications include articles in trade journals as well as two books on Oracle9*i*, which he coauthored. He has given numerous presentations on the ORACLE DBMS at trade fairs, such as Cebit and the annual German Oracle Users Conference.

Since 2002, he has been working as an independent consultant for large corporations in the industrial, financial, automotive, and services sectors. His assignments include topics such as Real Application Clusters, Data Guard, Streams, performance tuning, migration, Advanced Queuing, PL/SQL development, and Perl DBI scripting as well as RMAN backup and recovery. On most of his assignments, he has the role of an administrator, performance engineer, or architect. However, he occasionally does software development and serves as a trainer too. He was featured in the *Peer to Peer* section of the January/February 2005 edition of Oracle Magazine.

Right from the beginning of his quest into the ORACLE DBMS, he always wanted to know exactly how things work. He would not be satisfied with superficial explanations, but demand evidence. The passion to dig deeper served him well in acquiring extensive knowledge of the ORACLE DBMS and occasionally makes him a restless researcher who may be working on a topic from dusk until dawn when captured by the flow.

In his spare time, he likes to go hiking, play basketball, or read non–fiction on topics such as the emotional brain. Furthermore he is a passionate analog and digital photographer and recently—having been intrigued by the vibrancy of stereoscopic capture for twenty years—added a stereoscopic (3D) camera to his lineup.

Table of Contents

Introduction ix

Part I	**Initialization Parameters**	
Chapter 1	Partially Documented Parameters	19
	AUDIT_SYSLOG_LEVEL	19
	PGA_AGGREGATE_TARGET	23
	EVENT	32
	OS_AUTHENT_PREFIX	33
Chapter 2	Hidden Initialization Parameters	37
	Trace File Permissions and _TRACE_FILES_PUBLIC	38
	ASM Test Environment and _ASM_ALLOW_ONLY_RAW_DISKS	39

Part II	**Data Dictionary Base Tables**	
Chapter 3	Introduction to Data Dictionary Base Tables	47
Chapter 4	IND$, V$OBJECT_USAGE and Index Monitoring	51

Part III	**Events**	
Chapter 5	Event 10027 and Deadlock Diagnosis	61

Chapter 6   Event 10046 and Extended SQL Trace...64
Chapter 7   Event 10053 and the Cost Based Optimizer 66
Chapter 8   Event 10079 and Oracle Net Packet Contents 84

Part IV   X$ Fixed Tables

Chapter 9   Introduction to X$ Fixed Tables..89
Chapter 10   X$BH and Latch Contention 98
Chapter 11   X$KSLED and Enhanced Session Wait Data..104
Chapter 12   X$KFFXP and ASM Metadata..109

Part V   SQL Statements

Chapter 13   ALTER SESSION/SYSTEM SET EVENTS 117
Chapter 14   ALTER SESSION SET CURRENT_SCHEMA 121
Chapter 15   ALTER USER IDENTIFIED BY VALUES..126
Chapter 16   SELECT FOR UPDATE SKIP LOCKED 130

Part VI   Supplied PL/SQL Packages

Chapter 17   DBMS_BACKUP_RESTORE 143
Chapter 18   DBMS_IJOB...150
Chapter 19   DBMS_SCHEDULER..156
Chapter 20   DBMS_SYSTEM 167
Chapter 21   DBMS_UTILITY 179

Part VII   Application Development

Chapter 22   Perl DBI and DBD::Oracle 187
Chapter 23   Application Instrumentation and End to End Tracing 207

Part VIII   Performance

Chapter 24   Extended SQL Trace File Format Reference...223
Chapter 25   Statspack 249
Chapter 26   Integrating Extended SQL Trace and AWR 274
Chapter 27   ESQLTRCPROF Extended SQL Trace Profiler..278
Chapter 28   The MERITS Performance Optimization Method......................................294

Part IX   Oracle Net

Chapter 29   TNS Listener IP Address Binding and IP=FIRST.....................................317
Chapter 30   TNS Listener TCP/IP Valid Node Checking..325
Chapter 31   Local Naming Parameter ENABLE=BROKEN...330

Chapter 32   Default Host Name in Oracle Net Configurations..333

Part X   **Real Application Clusters**
Chapter 33   Session Disconnection, Load Rebalancing, and TAF..337
Chapter 34   Removing the RAC Option without Reinstalling 348

Part XI   **Utilities**
Chapter 35   OERR..359
Chapter 36   Recovery Manager Pipe Interface..364
Chapter 37   ORADEBUG SQL*Plus Command 373

Part XII   **Appendixes**
Appendix A   Glossary 385
Appendix B   Enabling and Disabling DBMS Options 389
Appendix C   Bibliography 391
Index **393**

Introduction

This book brings together a wealth of information on undocumented as well as incompletely documented features of the ORACLE database management system (DBMS). It has been my goal to combine many of the hidden features of the ORACLE database server into a single source. The reader will be hard–pressed in finding the same density of material on advanced undocumented topics in another book. Certain topics addressed may also be found in articles on the Internet, but I have striven to provide more background information and in–depth examples than is usually available on the Internet. The book also contains a significant amount of original material, such as the inclusion of think time in resource profiles for performance diagnosis, an emergency procedure for the conversion of a RAC installation to a single instance installation as well as the integration of Statspack, Active Workload Repository, and Active Session History with SQL trace.

The book is intended to complement the vast documentation from Oracle Corp. as well as articles found on Oracle's Metalink support platform. Arguably, the omission of some features from Oracle's documentation might be considered a documentation bug. Many features, especially among those for troubleshooting (e.g. events) and tracing, remain undocumented on purpose and for good reason, since Oracle Corp. rightfully suspects that they might backfire when used in the wrong situation or without fully understanding the implications of their use. Such features are not the subject of this book either. Instead, this text is centered on those undocumented features that provide significant benefit without compromising the integrity or availability of databases.

In this book, a certain feature is said to be undocumented if the full text search of the documentation provided at the Oracle Technology Network[1] web site does not yield any hint on the existence of the feature. A feature is said to be partially documented if the full text search does reveal that the feature exists, but significant aspects of the feature are undocumented, thus limiting the usefulness of the feature. Incomplete documentation often causes the need to investi-

---

1. http://otn.oracle.com

gate a feature, which constitutes a significant investment in time and thus money, to reveal the undocumented aspects through trial and error, searching the Internet, or Oracle's Metalink support platform. A significant number of undocumented aspects unveiled in this text are not addressed by Metalink articles.

This book is a highly technical book. I have spared no effort in making the material as easily accessible as possible by not assuming too much previous knowledge by the reader, adopting a clear writing style, and presenting many examples. An occasional humorous remark serves to intermittently stimulate the right brain and perhaps even trigger a grin, allowing the left analytical brain to rest for a moment before tackling more technicalities.

Although this book is not expressly an ORACLE DBMS performance optimization book, it has been my intention to offer a solid performance diagnostic method based on the analysis of extended SQL trace data. To the best of my knowledge, this is the first book which covers the Oracle10*g* and Oracle11*g* extended SQL trace file formats, which differs in several important aspects from the format used by Oracle9*i*. I sincerely hope that the free extended SQL trace profiler ESQLTRCPROF provided with the book will help to quickly diagnose and solve difficult performance problems the reader might face. As far as I know ESQLTRCPROF is the only profiler that classifies the wait event *SQL*Net message from client* into unavoidable latency due to client/server communication and think time due to non database–related processing by the client. This configurable feature of the profiler alone is immensely valuable in situations where proof is needed that the ORACLE DBMS is not the cause of a performance problem. Since think time cannot be optimized, except by recoding the application or other applications waited for, proper identification of think time will also aid in estimating the maximum speedup attainable by tuning interactions between client and DBMS instance.

In situations where it's appropriate for an ORACLE database administrator to see past the end of his or her nose, I include background information on operating systems, networking, and programming. I have also devoted some sections to operating system tools, which are useful for troubleshooting or investigation. I hope the reader will agree with me that this leads to a broader understanding of the features discussed than could be attained by exclusively focusing on ORACLE DBMS software and leaving interactions with the operating system on which it runs aside.

Given the vast amount of hidden parameters, undocumented events, and X\$ fixed tables, it is impossible to cover all of these. It would keep me busy for the rest of my lifetime and I could never share the insights with my readers. It has been my goal to explain how these undocumented features integrate into the ORACLE DBMS and most of all to present a structured approach for dealing with them. Thus, after assimilating the knowledge conferred, the reader will be able to make his or her own discoveries of valuable undocumented features.

ORACLE Database Server Releases

When I started working on this book in 2007, Oracle9*i* Release 2 was still fully supported, while Oracle10*g* had been adopted by a significant portion of users. In the fall of 2007, Oracle11*g* was released. Error correction support for Oracle9*i* Release 2 ended in July 2007. However, Oracle9*i* Release 2 was still in widespread use. I decided that the best way to deal with these three software releases was to incorporate some new material on Oracle11*g* and to repeat some of the tests with Oracle11*g*. Repeating each and every test with Oracle11*g* would have caused unacceptable delays in the production of this book. Generally, most of the material is rather release independent. Events, ORADEBUG, ASM, extended SQL trace, Statspack and AWR have not changed tremendously in Oracle11*g*. Of course, the latest release has additional wait and diagnostic events. The extended SQL trace format has changed slightly, but remains undocumented. There are also lots of new documented features like the result cache, Real Application Testing, additional partitioning strategies (interval, reference, system, list–list, list–hash, list–range, range–range), PIVOT/ UNPIVOT, and Secure Files, which I have not included in this book on undocumented features.

The MERITS performance optimization method, which is presented in Chapter 28, applies equally to all three releases. I have incorporated support for the Oracle11*g* SQL trace file format into the ESQLTRCPROF extended SQL trace profiler (see Chapter 27). Since the TKPROF release shipped with Oracle11*g* still does not calculate a resource profile, I recommend using ESQLTRCPROF instead of TKPROF, no matter which ORACLE release your company is running. For the reader who is interested in quickly locating material pertaining to Oracle11*g*, I have included a separate entry in the index, which refers to all the pages with material on Oracle11*g*.

Intended Audience of the Book

This book was written for advanced database administrators, who have gained a solid understanding of the ORACLE DBMS over the course of several years. It is not intended for the ORACLE DBMS novice. Having made this clear, it is obvious that I will not dwell much on introductory material. Where necessary and appropriate, discussions of undocumented features start by presenting an overview of the respective feature to establish a starting point for the ensuing discussion. Yet, these overviews are no substitute for reading the documentation on the feature and previous experience with the documented aspects of the feature discussed is recommended. By no means is it my intention to deter the novice DBA from reading this book. As long as he or she is willing to draw on other sources, such as the extensive ORACLE documentation to acquire prerequisite knowledge, then please be my guest.

Organization of the Book

This book is organized into twelve major parts. The denotations of the parts (e.g. Initialization Parameters, Utilities) are inspired by documentation on the ORACLE DBMS, such that the reader will immediately be familiar with the overarching structure of the book. Each part is mostly self–contained. Accordingly, there is no need to read the book from cover to cover. Instead, it can be used like a reference manual by picking chapters that might assist with the current workload of the reader—be it performance optimization or troubleshooting. Whenever material in different chapters is interrelated, this is indicated by cross references.

Material in the individual parts is organized into chapters. Each chapter starts with a status and a benefits section. The status section sets out which ORACLE database manual (if any) contains information on the topic of the chapter. If you have not yet worked with the feature discussed, it is a good idea to read the documentation in addition to the respective chapter. The benefits section points out why the chapter is a worthwhile read and under which circumstances the knowledge conferred is valuable. Chapters in the parts on SQL statements, supplied PL/SQL packages, application development, Oracle Net, Real Application Clusters, and Utilities may be read in any order. Chapters in the remaining parts on initialization parameters, data dictionary base tables, events, performance, and X$ fixed tables should be read in the order in which they appear in the text, since later chapters build on the foundation laid in earlier chapters within the same part.

- Part I, *Initialization Parameters*, deals with partially documented and undocumented initialization parameters. Among the parameters covered, `PGA_AGGREGATE_TARGET` is the most widely used. Chapter 1 explains the inner workings of work area sizing and the hidden parameters that it is based on. The remaining documented parameters addressed are `AUDIT_SYSLOG_LEVEL`, `EVENT` and `OS_AUTHENT_PREFIX`. Chapter 2 presents the hidden parameters `_TRACE_FILES_PUBLIC` and `_ASM_ALLOW_ONLY_RAW_DISKS`.
- Part II, *Data Dictionary Base Tables*, is a look under the hood of data dictionary views. After introducing the reader to data dictionary base tables in Chapter 3, Chapter 4 on index usage monitoring details how to build a better view for finding used indexes than the built–in view `V$OBJECT_USAGE`.
- Part III, *Events*, presents events for performance diagnosis (Chapter 6), tracing the cost based optimizer (Chapter 7), dumping Oracle Net packet contents (Chapter 8), etc. It also demonstrates how to find undocumented events supported by a certain DBMS release.
- Part IV, *X$ Fixed Tables*, addresses X$ tables, which are the foundation of GV_$ and V_$ views. The latter views are documented as dynamic performance views. X$ tables contain information that goes beyond dynamic performance views. This part unveils how to find hidden parameters along with descriptions in X$ tables (Chapter 9), how to get additional information on the buffer cache and latches (Chapter 10), and how to retrieve wait event timings at microsecond resolution instead of the centisecond resolution offered by `V$SESSION_WAIT` (Chapter 11). Chapter 12 explains Automatic Storage Management (ASM) metadata and the mapping between database file extents and ASM allocation units. Again, a structured approach for dealing with undocumented features is emphasized. An example of this is a method that generates a document with dependencies between V$ views and X$ tables and vice versa.
- Part V, *SQL Statements*, talks almost exclusively about undocumented SQL statements. The statements may be used to set events at session or instance level (Chapter 13), change the parsing schema identifier (Chapter 14), temporarily change a user's password (Chapter 15), and enhance scalability in concurrent processing (Chapter 16). Examples for the usefulness of each statement are provided.

- Part VI, *Supplied PL/SQL Packages*, focuses on three undocumented as well as two partially documented packages. Chapter 17 on DBMS_BACKUP_RESTORE explains how to restore a database, which was backed up with Recovery Manager (RMAN), in a disaster scenario, i.e. after the loss of the RMAN catalog and all database files including the most recent copy of the control file, which contains the directory of the most recent backups. The remaining packages covered address topics such as performance diagnosis and tracing (DBMS_SYSTEM), jobs (DBMS_IJOB), undocumented aspects of the Oracle10g and Oracle11g database scheduler (DBMS_SCHEDULER), and database object name resolution (DBMS_UTILITY).
- Part VII, *Application Development*, consists of two chapters. Chapter 22 is an introduction to Perl DBI and DBD::Oracle—a Perl interface for accessing ORACLE databases built with Oracle Call Interface. It is undocumented that each Oracle10g and Oracle11g ORACLE_HOME includes a Perl installation with the DBI. Scripting in Perl and the DBI is much more powerful than using a combination of a (UNIX) shell and SQL*Plus. Development time is also reduced. Oracle Corporation's documentation is lacking a document which explains the benefits and effects of JDBC end to end metrics. This is what Chapter 23 does. It brings together all the information on performance diagnosis and monitoring, which relates to application instrumentation, end to end tracing (DBMS_MONITOR), extended SQL trace, and the TRCSESS utility.
- The goal of Part VIII, *Performance*, is to acquaint the reader with a solid performance optimization method, based for the most part on the assessment of extended SQL trace files. This part covers the undocumented extended SQL trace file format (Chapter 24) as well as how to get the most out of Statspack (Chapter 25) and AWR (Chapter 26). Chapter 27 presents the free extended SQL trace profiler ESQLTRCPROF provided with this book. Chapter 28 on the MERITS performance optimization method is the culmination of this part. The MERITS method is a tested, proven framework for diagnosing and solving performance problems.
- Part IX, *Oracle Net*, addresses undocumented and partially documented Oracle Net parameters, which may be used to configure the TNS Listener and certain Oracle Net features. Chapter 29 explains the setting IP=FIRST, which was introduced, but not documented, in Oracle10g. Chapter 30 explains how to use the fully dynamic valid node checking feature of the listener to set up a simple form of a firewall to protect ORACLE instances from intruders. Chapter 31 discusses the parameter ENABLE=BROKEN. Chapter 32 talks about the default host name feature.
- Part X, *Real Application Clusters*, discusses undocumented aspects of Transparent Application Failover (TAF) and database services (DBMS_SERVICE), which may be used for load re–balancing after a cluster node has failed and subsequently re–joined the cluster (Chapter 33). Chapter 34 presents a quick procedure for converting an ORACLE RAC installation with or without ASM to an ORACLE single instance installation. The procedure is intended for disaster scenarios where hardware failure or software defects make it impossible to run the DBMS in multi–instance mode (i.e. with RAC enabled).
- Part XI, *Utilities*, includes chapters on the OERR utility (Chapter 35), the RMAN pipe interface (Chapter 36) and ORADEBUG (Chapter 37). Among these, ORADEBUG is presumably the most useful. It may be used to control processes of an instance, enable and disable SQL trace, retrieve the SQL trace file name, generate diagnostic dumps for hang analysis, and much more.
- Part XII, *Appendixes*, contains a glossary and a bibliography. You may wish to read the glossary first, to acquaint yourself with the terms used in this book. Throughout the book, four letter strings and the year of publication in angle brackets (e.g. [ShDe 2004]) refer to sources in the bibliography. This part also contains an appendix, which lists make targets for enabling and disabling DBMS options, such as RAC or Partitioning.

Source Code Depot

Source code shown in listings is downloadable as a zip archive from the web page of ORADBPRO Consulting Services & Publishing at http://www.oradbpro.com. Each listing exceeding approximately a dozen lines is identified by a unique file name. At the end of most chapters, there is a section titled *Source Code Depot*. This section lists all the source files of the respective chapter and their functionality. To download the source code depot of the entire book, browse to http://www.oradbpro.com/publications.html and click on the link *Source Code Depot*. You will be asked for a user name and password. Please enter the user name "secretoracle" and use the first eight digits of the ISBN reproduced on page ii as the password.

Conventions and Terms

In my understanding, the designation Oracle refers to the company Oracle Corporation and its international subsidiaries. I adhere to the convention concerning the designations Oracle and ORACLE that Oracle Corporation proposes[1]. Oracle Corp. refers to the company, whereas ORACLE refers to the database server product. ORACLE_HOME (or the environment variable $ORACLE_HOME on UNIX; %ORACLE_HOME% on Windows) designates the directory where the database server software is installed. Contrary to most authors, I refrain from using the designation Oracle to refer to any software manufactured by Oracle Corp. Instead, I use the term ORACLE DBMS (database management system) to refer to the database server software Oracle Corp. offers.

Database vs. Instance

On page 1–8, the manual *Oracle Database Concepts 10g Release 2* explains "the physical database structures of an Oracle database, including data files, redo log files, and control files". Thus, an ORACLE database is made up of data files (grouped into tablespaces), redo log files, and control files—a collection of files residing on disk. On page 1–13, the same manual goes on to say that:

> *Every time a database is started, a system global area (SGA) is allocated and Oracle background processes are started. The combination of the background processes and memory buffers is called an ORACLE instance.*

I'm a strong advocate of stating things clearly and using terms consistently. Unfortunately, the term database is often used incorrectly. If we take the definition of a database as consisting of data files, redo log files and control files literally, then it is obvious that a database cannot be started. It is the ORACLE DBMS instance, which consists of processes and memory structures, such as the SGA, that breathes life into an ORACLE database. I invite the reader to adopt the wording concerning database and instance in Table 1. In this book, I have made every effort to use the terms database and instance in the sense defined above, to avoid confusion.

Table 1: Instance vs. Database

Wording	*Action*	*SQL*Plus command*
To start an ORACLE DBMS instance	The instance reads the parameter file, starts processes (SMON, PMON, etc.), and creates the SGA (system global area) in memory.	STARTUP NOMOUNT
To mount a database	Certain processes of the DBMS instance open the control file(s) of the database. No other files are accessed at this time.	STARTUP MOUNT
To open a database	The DBMS instance opens the online redo logs and one or more tablespaces (at least the tablespace called SYSTEM, which contains the data dictionary).	STARTUP or STARTUP OPEN
To shut down an instance	The DBMS instance first closes the data files and online redo logs (message "Database closed" in SQL*Plus), then closes the control file(s) (message "Database dismounted"), and finally removes the SGA and terminates all processes (message "ORACLE instance shut down"). The SQL statements ALTER DATABASE CLOSE and ALTER DATABASE DISMOUNT may also be used to accomplish the first two steps.	SHUTDOWN

Instance Service Name vs. Net Service Name

To disambiguate the term service name, I use the denomination *Net* (from Oracle Net) *service name* for services defined in tnsnames.ora or a directory service such as LDAP. I call the service names an instance registers with a listener *instance service names*. Instance service names are defined either through the parameter SERVICE_NAMES or

---

1. See line 234 of $ORACLE_HOME/rdbms/mesg/oraus.msg

with the package DBMS_SERVICE in Oracle10*g* and Oracle11*g*. The command tnsping accepts Net service names, whereas the list of services returned by the command lsnrctl services contains instance service names. Connect strings, such as ndebes/secret@ten.oradbpro.com contain Net service names. The body of a Net service name definition includes either an instance service name or an ORACLE_SID (SID=*oracle_sid*). A Net service name definition in tnsnames.ora has the following format:

net_service_name =
```
  (DESCRIPTION =
    (ADDRESS_LIST =
      (ADDRESS = (PROTOCOL = TCP)(HOST = host_name)(PORT = 1521))
    )
    (CONNECT_DATA =
      (SERVICE_NAME = instance_service_name)
    )
  )
```

Mind the keyword SERVICE_NAME in the body of the DESCRIPTION section. The setting of SERVICE_NAME is an instance service name and in Oracle10*g* it is reflected in the column V$SESSION.SERVICE_NAME and in SQL trace files. In Oracle10*g*, all configured instance service names are in DBA_SERVICES.NETWORK_NAME. Why NETWORK_NAME? These are the instance service names registered with an Oracle Net listener (parameters LOCAL_LISTENER and REMOTE_LISTENER)[1].

Client sessions that connect by using a Net service name definition, which contains SID=*oracle_sid* instead of SERVICE_NAME=*instance_service_name*, have the service name SYS$USERS in V$SESSION.SERVICE_NAME. This is also true for local sessions established without specifying a Net service name. These latter sessions use the so called bequeath protocol adapter, which takes the setting of SID from the environment variable ORACLE_SID.

Typographical Conventions

The typographical conventions used in this book are summarized in Table 2.

Table 2: Typographical Conventions

Convention	Meaning
italic	Italic type indicates book titles, quotes, emphasis, or placeholder variables for which particular values have to be supplied.
monospace	Monospace type indicates operating system, SQL, or SQL*Plus commands as well as file or code excerpts.
GUI ITEM	Small caps designate items in graphical user interfaces, e.g. CONTROL PANEL.
...	One or more lines omitted. Used in log file or code excerpts.
<placeholder>	The expression <placeholder> is used in syntax descriptions and represents a placeholder that needs to be replaced by an actual value. Angle brackets surround the placeholder and include the string that must be replaced by an actual value. Here's an example syntax: CONNECT <username>/<password>. With actual values filled in, it might become: CONNECT ndebes/secret.
$	Marks commands entered at a UNIX shell prompt (Bourne or Korn Shell).

---

1. To immediately register instance service names with a listener, e.g. after a listener restart, the command ALTER SYSTEM REGISTER is provided.

Table 2: Typographical Conventions

Convention	Meaning
`C:>`	Marks commands entered at the prompt of a Windows command interpreter (`cmd.exe`).
`SQL>`	Marks commands entered in a SQL*Plus database session.
`{value1|…|valueN}`	Range of acceptable values, e.g. `INSTANCE_TYPE={ASM|RDBMS}`. Vertical bars separate alternatives.

Table 3 contains a list of abbreviations used throughout the book.

Table 3: Abbreviations

Abbreviation	Meaning
ASCII	American Standard Code for Information Interchange
ASH	Active Session History
AWR	Active Workload Repository
ADDM	Automatic Database Diagnostic Monitor
DBA	Database Administrator
DBMS	Database Management System
GCS	Global Cache Service
GES	Global Enqueue Service
I/O	input/output from/to a device
IP	Internet Protocol
LOB	Large Object (`BLOB`, `CLOB`, `NCLOB`)
LUN	Logical unit number
OCI	Oracle Call Interface
PGA	Program Global Area
RAC	Real Application Clusters
SCN	System Change Number
SGA	System Global Area
TCP	Transmission Control Protocol
UDP	User Datagram Protocol
a.k.a.	also known as
e.g.	for example (from Latin: exempli gratia)
et al.	and others (from Latin: et alteri)
i.e.	that is (from Latin: id est)
n/a	not applicable

Send Us Your Comments

The author and technical reviewers have verified and tested the information in this book to the best of their capability. Please inform the author of any issues you may find in spite of our efforts to make this book as reliable a source as possible. You may reach the author by e–mail (norbert.debes@oradbpro.com) or post by writing to:

ORADBPRO Publishing
Norbert Debes
Zaubzerstrasse 57
D-81677 Munich
Germany

An errata pertaining to this publication is maintained at http://www.oradbpro.com/publications.html.

Acknowledgments

I am indebted to the following persons for their comments, suggestions, and encouragement (in alphabetical order): Helga Debes, Lise Andreasen, Pete Finnigan, and William Kehoe. I would also like to thank all of my clients for the privilege of fulfilling assignments for them and the trust placed in me.

Part I

Initialization Parameters

Chapter 1

Partially Documented Parameters

AUDIT_SYSLOG_LEVEL

Status: AUDIT_SYSLOG_LEVEL is partially documented. There are several inaccuracies in the documentation, which suggest that the parameter is less useful than it actually is.

Benefit: Database actions by SYS and/or database administrators or operators may be audited to operating system syslog log files owned by the UNIX user root. This prevents such privileged users from removing audit records that contain a log of their activities. The default setting is to audit CONNECT, STARTUP, and SHUTDOWN with SYSDBA or SYSOPER privileges to files owned by the ORACLE software owner, while not auditing SQL, PL/SQL statements, and other actions with these privileges or other privileges, such as the role DBA, at all. As a consequence, there will be no trace of many activities performed by privileged users. Enabling auditing to operating system files owned by the ORACLE software owner (AUDIT_TRAIL=OS) or to the database table SYS.AUD$ (AUDIT_TRAIL=DB) is inappropriate, since DBAs normally have access to the ORACLE software owner's UNIX account as well as to SYS.AUD$, allowing them to easily remove audit records generated for their actions. Auditing via the UNIX syslog facility is also useful for detecting intrusions by hackers or manipulations by malevolent insiders.

Syslog Facility

A new feature of Oracle10g is the ability to write audit trails using the syslog facility on UNIX systems. This facility consists of a daemon process named syslogd (see man syslogd) that accepts log messages from applications via the syslog C library function (see man syslog). The configuration file for syslogd is usually /etc/syslog.conf and log messages go to files in /var/log or /var/adm depending on the UNIX variant. The log file name is determined by a string that consists of a facility name and a priority or level. Most of these may be used when setting AUDIT_SYSLOG_LEVEL. Each entry in /etc/syslog.conf assigns a log file name to a certain combination of facility and priority. By placing the entry user.notice /var/log/oracle_dbms into the file syslog.conf and telling syslogd to reread the configuration file by sending it a hang–up signal with the command kill[1], any subsequent log entries from an ORACLE instance with the setting AUDIT_SYSLOG_LEVEL=user.notice will be recorded in the file /var/log/oracle_dbms.

Introduction to Auditing

On UNIX systems, CONNECT, STARTUP, and SHUTDOWN of an ORACLE instance with SYSDBA or SYSOPER privileges are unconditionally audited to files with extension .aud in $ORACLE_HOME/rdbms/audit or a directory specified with the parameter AUDIT_FILE_DEST[2]. Oracle9i was the first release that had the capability of auditing actions other than CONNECT, STARTUP, and SHUTDOWN performed with SYSDBA or SYSOPER privileges by setting AUDIT_SYS_OPERATIONS=TRUE.

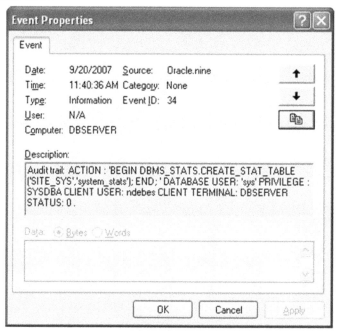

Figure 1: Event Details in Windows Event Viewer

When AUDIT_SYSLOG_LEVEL and AUDIT_SYS_OPERATIONS are combined, any SQL and PL/SQL run as user SYS may be audited using the syslog facility. Since the files used by syslog are owned by root, and a DBA usually does not have access to the root account, DBAs will not be able to remove traces of their activity. Of course, this also applies to intruders who have managed to break into a machine and have gained access to the account of the ORACLE software owner, but not to the root account. The same applies to hackers who have cracked the password of a privileged database user and are able to connect via Oracle Net.

On Windows, the parameters AUDIT_SYSLOG_LEVEL and AUDIT_FILE_DEST are not implemented, since the Windows event log serves as the operating system audit trail. Just like on UNIX, CONNECT, STARTUP, and SHUTDOWN are unconditionally logged. When AUDIT_SYS_OPERATIONS=TRUE is set, operations with SYSDBA or SYSOPER privilege are also written to the Windows event log, which may be viewed by navigating to START > CONTROL PANEL > ADMINISTRATIVE TOOLS > EVENT VIEWER. The logging category used is APPLICATION and the source is named ORACLE.ORACLE_SID. Events for a certain DBMS instance may be filtered by choosing VIEW > FILTER.

The *Oracle Database Reference 10g Release 2* manual explains AUDIT_SYSLOG_LEVEL as follows (page 1–22):

AUDIT_SYSLOG_LEVEL enables OS audit logs to be written to the system via the syslog utility, if the

---

1. Use kill -HUP `cat /var/run/syslogd.pid` on Red Hat Linux
2. AUDIT_FILE_DEST is used as soon as an instance has started. When connecting as SYSDBA or SYSOPER while an instance is down, the default audit file destination $ORACLE_HOME/rdbms/audit is used.

AUDIT_TRAIL parameter is set to os. The value of facility can be any of the following: USER, LOCAL0-LOCAL7, SYSLOG, DAEMON, KERN, MAIL, AUTH, LPR, NEWS, UUCP or CRON. The value of level can be any of the following: NOTICE, INFO, DEBUG, WARNING, ERR, CRIT, ALERT, EMERG.

Tests of the new feature on a Solaris 10 and a Red Hat Linux system showed that the documentation is inaccurate on three counts:

1. AUDIT_SYSLOG_LEVEL is independent of AUDIT_TRAIL. When AUDIT_SYSLOG_LEVEL is set and AUDIT_TRAIL has the default value NONE, CONNECT, STARTUP, and SHUTDOWN are logged via syslog.
2. Setting the parameters AUDIT_SYSLOG_LEVEL and AUDIT_SYS_OPERATIONS=TRUE causes any actions such as SQL and PL/SQL statements executed with SYSDBA or SYSOPER privilege to be logged via syslog, even if AUDIT_TRAIL=NONE.
3. Only certain combinations of facility and level are acceptable. Inacceptable combinations cause the error "ORA-32028: Syslog facility or level not recognized" and prevent DBMS instances from starting.

If the documentation were accurate, it would not be possible to audit actions performed with SYSDBA or SYSOPER privileges to the system log, while auditing actions by other users to the data dictionary base table SYS.AUD$. However, such a limitation does not exist.

Using AUDIT_SYSLOG_LEVEL

As stated earlier, the string assigned to AUDIT_SYSLOG_LEVEL must consist of a facility name and a priority or level. Surprisingly, when doing a SHOW PARAMETER or a SELECT from V$PARAMETER, merely the facility is visible and the dot as well as the level are suppressed[1]. For example, with the entry *.audit_syslog_level='USER.NOTICE' in the SPFILE used to start the instance, SHOW PARAMETER yields:

```
SQL> SHOW PARAMETER audit_syslog_level
NAME                                 TYPE        VALUE
------------------------------------ ----------- -----
audit_syslog_level                   string      USER
SQL> SELECT value FROM v$parameter WHERE name='audit_syslog_level';
VALUE
-----
USER
```

Yet, when executing CONNECT / AS SYSDBA, the facility and level logged in /var/adm/messages on Solaris is "user.notice":

```
Feb 21 11:45:52 dbserver Oracle Audit[27742]: [ID 441842 user.notice] ACTION :
'CONNECT'
Feb 21 11:45:52 dbserver DATABASE USER: '/'
Feb 21 11:45:52 dbserver PRIVILEGE : SYSDBA
Feb 21 11:45:52 dbserver CLIENT USER: oracle
Feb 21 11:45:52 dbserver CLIENT TERMINAL: pts/3
Feb 21 11:45:52 dbserver STATUS: 0
```

If an SPFILE is used, the full setting is available by querying V$SPPARAMETER:

```
SQL> SELECT value FROM v$spparameter WHERE name='audit_syslog_level';
VALUE
-----------
user.notice
```

Auditing Non–Privileged Users

Of course, you may also direct audit records pertaining to non–privileged users to the system log by setting AUDIT_TRAIL=OS in addition to AUDIT_SYSLOG_LEVEL. Non–privileged users cannot delete audit trails logging their actions. The search for perpetrators with queries against auditing views, such as DBA_AUDIT_STATEMENT or DBA_AUDIT_OBJECT, is easier than searching the system log. For these reasons, keeping the audit trails of non-privileged users inside the database with AUDIT_TRAIL=DB is preferred. With the latter setting, audit trails are written to

---

1. Test performed with ORACLE DBMS version 10.2.0.3.

the table `SYS.AUD$` and may be queried through the aforementioned data dictionary views. Setting `AUDIT_TRAIL=NONE` switches off auditing of actions by non–privileged users.

After enabling auditing for database connections established by non–privileged users, e.g. as in:

```
SQL> AUDIT CONNECT BY appuser /* audit_trail=os set */;
```

Entries similar to the following are written to the syslog facility (example from Solaris):

```
Feb 21 11:41:14 dbserver Oracle Audit[27684]: [ID 930208 user.notice] SESSIONID: "15"
ENTRYID: "1" STATEMENT: "1" USERID: "APPUSER" USERHOST: "dbserver" TERMINAL: "pts/3"
ACTION: "100" RETURNCODE: "0" COMMENT$TEXT: "Authenticated by: DATABASE" OS$USERID:
"oracle" PRIV$USED: 5
```

Another entry is added to `/var/adm/messages` when a database session ends:

```
Feb 21 11:44:41 dbserver Oracle Audit[27684]: [ID 162490 user.notice] SESSIONID: "15"
ENTRYID: "1" ACTION: "101" RETURNCODE: "0" LOGOFF$PREAD: "1" LOGOFF$LREAD: "17"
LOGOFF$LWRITE: "0" LOGOFF$DEAD: "0" SESSIONCPU: "2"
```

Note that additional data provided on the actions LOGON (100) and LOGOFF (101) conforms to the columns of the view `DBA_AUDIT_SESSION`. Translation from action numbers to action names is done via the view `AUDIT_ACTIONS` as in the example below:

```
SQL> SELECT action, name FROM audit_actions WHERE action IN (100,101)
ACTION NAME
------ ------
   100 LOGON
   101 LOGOFF
```

When `AUDIT_SYSLOG_LEVEL=AUTH.INFO`, `AUDIT_SYS_OPERATIONS=FALSE` and `AUDIT_TRAIL=NONE`, CONNECT, STARTUP, and SHUTDOWN are logged via syslog. With these settings, an instance shutdown on Solaris writes entries similar to the following to `/var/adm/messages`:

```
Feb 21 14:40:01 dbserver Oracle Audit[29036]:[ID 63719 auth.info] ACTION:'SHUTDOWN'
Feb 21 14:40:01 dbserver DATABASE USER: '/'
Feb 21 14:40:01 dbserver PRIVILEGE : SYSDBA
Feb 21 14:40:01 dbserver CLIENT USER: oracle
Feb 21 14:40:01 dbserver CLIENT TERMINAL: pts/3
Feb 21 14:40:01 dbserver STATUS: 0
```

When `AUDIT_SYSLOG_LEVEL=AUTH.INFO`, `AUDIT_SYS_OPERATIONS=TRUE` and `AUDIT_TRAIL=NONE`, SQL and PL/SQL statements executed with `SYSDBA` or `SYSOPER` privilege are also logged via syslog. Dropping a user after connecting with `/ AS SYSDBA` results in a syslog entry similar to the one shown below:

```
Feb 21 14:46:53 dbserver Oracle Audit[29170]: [ID 853627 auth.info] ACTION : 'drop user
appuser'
Feb 21 14:46:53 dbserver DATABASE USER: '/'
Feb 21 14:46:53 dbserver PRIVILEGE : SYSDBA
Feb 21 14:46:53 dbserver CLIENT USER: oracle
Feb 21 14:46:53 dbserver CLIENT TERMINAL: pts/3
Feb 21 14:46:53 dbserver STATUS: 0
```

Lessons Learned

CONNECT, STARTUP, and SHUTDOWN with `SYSDBA` or `SYSOPER` privilege are logged to `*.aud` files by default in spite of an `AUDIT_TRAIL=NONE` setting. If `AUDIT_SYSLOG_LEVEL` is set, the SQL*Plus STARTUP command is logged to a `*.aud` file in `$ORACLE_HOME/rdbms/audit`, whereas `ALTER DATABASE MOUNT` and subsequent commands as well as SHUTDOWN are logged via syslog, since a running instance is required for using the syslog facility and the instance is not yet running when STARTUP is issued.

Setting `AUDIT_SYSLOG_LEVEL` and `AUDIT_SYS_OPERATIONS=TRUE` produces additional auditing trail records covering all actions performed with `SYSDBA` or `SYSOPER` privileges in the configured `syslog` log file irrespective of the setting of `AUDIT_TRAIL`. Intruders who have not managed to break into the account of the UNIX user root, will not be able to remove these audit trail records.

Of course, an intruder who is aware of these features might remove the setting of `AUDIT_SYSLOG_LEVEL`, but at least the change of the parameter would be logged if an SPFILE is used and the change would not be in effect immediately since it is a static parameter. You may wish to set `AUDIT_SYS_OPERATIONS=FALSE` during maintenance operations such as an upgrade, which have to be run as user `SYS`, to avoid generating large syslog log files.

PGA_AGGREGATE_TARGET

Status: `PGA_AGGREGATE_TARGET` is documented in the *Oracle9i Database Performance Tuning Guide and Reference Release 2* and in *Oracle Database Performance Tuning Guide 10g Release 2*. The Oracle9i manual states that the parameters `SORT_AREA_SIZE` and `HASH_AREA_SIZE` for manual PGA memory management should not be used, except in Shared Server environments, since Oracle9i Shared Server cannot leverage automatic PGA memory management (pages 1-57 and 14-50). The algorithm that governs sizing of individual work areas for serial and parallel execution is undocumented.

Benefit: Knowing the undocumented restrictions imposed on work area sizing, allows DBAs to set the most appropriate value for `PGA_AGGREGATE_TARGET`, thus avoiding expensive spilling of work areas to disk and allowing operations to run entirely in memory realizing significant performance gains. Under rare circumstances, it may be desirable to override automatic settings of hidden parameters affected by `PGA_AGGREGATE_TARGET`.

Introduction to Automatic PGA Memory Management

The program global area (PGA) is a private memory region where server processes allocate memory for operations such as sorts, hash joins, and bitmap merges. Consequently, the PGA is a memory region separate from the SGA (system global area). There is even a third memory region, the UGA (user global area), which holds session and cursor state information. Dedicated server processes allocate UGA memory inside the PGA, whereas shared server processes place the UGA inside the SGA, since it must be accessible to all shared server processes. If the SGA contains a large pool (parameter `LARGE_POOL_SIZE`), shared server processes place the UGA inside the large pool. In Oracle10g, the shared pool, large pool, java pool, streams pool, and the default buffer pool with standard block size[1] can be sized automatically and dynamically with Automatic Shared Memory Management (parameter `SGA_TARGET`).

In releases prior to Oracle9i, several `*_AREA_SIZE` parameters had to be used to adjust the sizes for various PGA memory regions. Examples of these parameters are `SORT_AREA_SIZE` and `HASH_AREA_SIZE`. On UNIX, where the ORACLE DBMS is implemented as a multi–process architecture, PGA memory could not always be returned to the operating system after a memory–intensive operation. It lingered within the virtual address space of the server process and may have caused paging. Memory thus allocated was also not available to other server processes. There was also no instance–wide limit on PGA memory regions. Since each server process was allowed to allocate memory for an operation up to the limits imposed by `*_AREA_SIZE` parameters, the instance–wide memory consumption could become extensive in environments with several hundred server processes. Note also that the `*_AREA_SIZE` parameters enforce a per operation limit, not a per session limit. Since a query may open several cursors simultaneously and each might execute an expensive `SELECT` that includes an `ORDER BY` or a hash join, there is no limit on overall memory consumption with the old approach now called manual PGA memory management.

To address these shortcomings, automatic PGA memory management was introduced with Oracle9i. On UNIX, it is based on the modern technology of memory mapping, which enables a process to allocate virtual memory and to map it into its virtual address space. Once the memory is no longer needed, it can be returned to the operating system by removing the mapping into the virtual address space. On Solaris, the UNIX system calls used are `mmap` and `munmap`. Calls to memory mapping routines by the ORACLE kernel may be traced using `truss` (Solaris) or `strace` (Linux)[2]. Another interesting utility is `pmap` (Solaris, Linux). It displays information about the address space of a process, which includes anonymous memory mapped with `mmap`. Back in the old days of 32–bit computing, this tool provided precisely the information needed to relocate the SGA base address to allow mapping of a larger shared memory segment into the limited virtual address space of a 32–bit program (see Metalink note 1028623.6). Using `pmap` while a process sorts, reveals how many regions of anonymous memory it has mapped and what their cumulative size is.

---

1. Oracle10g supports up to seven buffer pools: five buffer pools varying in block size between 2 KB and 32 KB; additionally, there can be a keep and a recycle cache with standard block size, i.e. the block size set with the parameter `DB_BLOCK_SIZE`.

2. The web page titled *Rosetta Stone for UNIX* at http://bhami.com/rosetta.html lists system call tracing utilities for common UNIX systems.

Here's an example (29606 is the UNIX process id of the server process found in V$PROCESS.SPID). The relevant column is "Anon" (anonymous mapped memory):

```
$ pmap -x 29606 | grep Kb
        Address      Kbytes        RSS        Anon     Locked Mode    Mapped File
        total Kb     934080      888976      63008     806912
```

With automatic PGA memory management, so called work areas are used for operations such as sorts or hash joins. The target for the cumulative size of all active work areas is specified with the parameter PGA_AGGREGATE_TARGET (PAT). A single process may access several work areas concurrently. Information on automatic PGA memory management and work areas is available by querying dynamic performance views such as V$PGASTAT, V$PROCESS, V$SQL_WORKAREA, and V$SQL_WORKAREA_ACTIVE.

Misconceptions about PGA_AGGREGATE_TARGET

The parameter name PGA_AGGREGATE_TARGET is a name well chosen. What I'm trying to say is that it is what it sounds like—a target, not an absolute limit, merely a target. This means that the actual amount of memory consumed under high load may constantly, or at least intermittently, be higher than the target value. But the implementation of automatic PGA memory management is so well crafted that processes will then release memory, such that the total memory consumption will soon drop below the target, if at all possible. Especially when PL/SQL, which allocates a lot of memory, e.g. for collections such as index–by tables, is executed, the target may be permanently exceeded. Whereas sort memory requirements can be reduced by using temporary segments, PL/SQL memory requirements cannot.

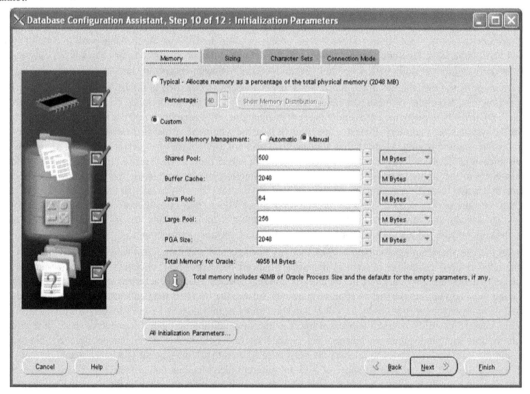

Figure 2: PGA Sizing in Database Configuration Assistant

When creating a database with the database configuration assistant (DBCA), there is a memory configuration page for customizing most of the aforementioned pools as well as the PGA. On this page, DBCA adds the sizes of all pools as well as the PGA and reports the resulting figure as TOTAL MEMORY FOR ORACLE. This lead some people to believe that this amount of memory (4956 MB in the screenshot) will be allocated when the ORACLE instance is started. Knowing that the SGA is allocated on instance startup, they implied that the same must be true for the PGA. However, this is not the case. PGA memory is allocated on demand. Even the *_AREA_SIZE parameters do not cause a memory allocation of the designated size. These too are allocated on an as needed basis.

Since the documentation does not address the details of work area sizing, many database administrators assume that the entire memory set aside with PGA_AGGREAGTE_TARGET is available to a single session as long as it does not have to compete for the memory with other sessions. In case you're curious what the real deal is, please read on.

Researching PGA_AGGREGATE_TARGET

The research presented in this section was done with Oracle10g Release 2. Results show that the algorithms used by Oracle9i and Oracle10g are different. Due to space constraints, no example or evidence concerning Oracle9i is included[1].

Creating a Large Table with a Pipelined Table Function

For starters, we need a table that is large enough to cause disk spilling during sort operations. The next few paragraphs show how to code a pipelined table function that returns an arbitrary number of rows (see file row_factory.sql in the source code depot). This function may then be used in conjunction with the package DBMS_RANDOM to create arbitrarily sized tables with random data. Since pipelined table functions return a collection type, we start by creating an object type for holding a row number:

```
SQL> CREATE OR REPLACE TYPE row_nr_type AS OBJECT (row_nr number);
  /
```

The pipelined table function will return a collection type made up of individual row_nr_types.

```
SQL> CREATE OR REPLACE TYPE row_nr_type_tab AS TABLE OF row_nr_type;
  /
```

The function row_factory returns any number of rows—within the limits of the ORACLE NUMBER data type, of course. It has the two parameters first_nr and last_nr, which control how many rows will be returned.

```
CREATE OR REPLACE FUNCTION row_factory(first_nr number, last_nr number)
RETURN row_nr_type_tab PIPELINED
AS
    row_nr row_nr_type:=NEW row_nr_type(0);
BEGIN
    FOR i IN first_nr .. last_nr LOOP
        row_nr.row_nr:=i;
        PIPE ROW(row_nr);
    END LOOP;
    return;
END;
/
```

When last_nr is larger than first_nr, row_factory returns last_nr - first_nr + 1 rows. The result is very much like SELECT ROWNUM FROM *table*, except that the argument values and not the number of rows in a table control how many rows are returned. Here's an example:

```
SQL> SELECT * FROM TABLE(row_factory(1,2));
    ROW_NR
- - - - - - - - - -
         1
         2
```

The classical approach for generating a large table consists of selecting from a real table, possibly using a Cartesian join to arrive at a very large number of rows. Beyond requiring less coding for the CREATE TABLE statement, this novel approach using a pipelined table function has the additional benefit of not causing any consistent or physical reads on a segment. By calling row_factory with a first_nr and last_nr setting of 1 and 1000000, we can now create a table with one million rows:

```
CREATE TABLE random_strings AS
SELECT dbms_random.string('a', 128) AS random_string FROM TABLE(row_factory(1,1000000))
```

---

1. For research on Oracle9i, see Jonathan Lewis' article at http://www.jlcomp.demon.co.uk/untested.html

```
NOLOGGING;
```

The first argument (opt) tells DBMS_RANDOM to generate random mixed case strings consisting solely of letters. The second argument (len) controls the length of the random string. Note that in releases prior to Oracle11g, arguments to PL/SQL routines cannot be passed by name from SQL[1].

In my test database with db_block_size=8192, the above CTAS (create table as select) resulted in a segment size of about 150 MB. DBMS_RANDOM is also capable of generating random alphanumeric strings in lower, upper or mixed case as well as random numbers[2].

V$SQL_WORKAREA_ACTIVE

A good way to monitor PGA memory management at session level is to query the dynamic performance view V$SQL_WORKAREA_ACTIVE. It has the following columns:

```
SQL> DESC v$sql_workarea_active
 Name                                      Null?    Type
 ----------------------------------------- -------- ------------
 WORKAREA_ADDRESS                                   RAW(4)
 OPERATION_TYPE                                     VARCHAR2(20)
 OPERATION_ID                                       NUMBER
 POLICY                                             VARCHAR2(6)
 SID                                                NUMBER
 QCINST_ID                                          NUMBER
 QCSID                                              NUMBER
 ACTIVE_TIME                                        NUMBER
 WORK_AREA_SIZE                                     NUMBER
 EXPECTED_SIZE                                      NUMBER
 ACTUAL_MEM_USED                                    NUMBER
 MAX_MEM_USED                                       NUMBER
 NUMBER_PASSES                                      NUMBER
 TEMPSEG_SIZE                                       NUMBER
 TABLESPACE                                         VARCHAR2(31)
 SEGRFNO#                                           NUMBER
 SEGBLK#                                            NUMBER
```

I wrote a small Perl DBI program for closely monitoring the use of PGA work areas. The Perl program executes a SELECT on V$SQL_WORKAREA_ACTIVE once per second and prints the results to the screen. In addition to the session identifier, which corresponds to V$SESSION.SID, the current and maximum work area sizes, and the size of temporary segments, the query also retrieves a timestamp. All sizes are reported in MB. The SELECT statement used by the Perl program is:

```
SELECT sid, to_char(sysdate,'mi:ss') time, round(work_area_size/1048576, 1)
work_area_size_mb,
round(max_mem_used/1048576, 1) max_mem_used_mb, number_passes, nvl(tempseg_size/
1048576, 0) tempseg_size_mb
FROM v$sql_workarea_active
ORDER BY sid;
```

Now we have a large table and a monitoring tool. So we're all set to run some actual tests. Since I'm the only tester using the instance, I might assume that the entire memory set aside with PGA_AGGREGATE_TARGET will be available to me. As stated before, the segment size of the table is about 150 MB, such that a PGA_AGGREGATE_TARGET setting of 256 MB should be more than sufficient for an in–memory sort. So this is the value we will use:

```
SQL> ALTER SYSTEM SET pga_aggregate_target=256m;
System altered.
```

---

1. In Oracle11g, SELECT * FROM TABLE(row_factory(first_nr => 1, last_nr => 3)) is syntactically correct. In prior releases this statement causes ORA-00907.
2. The document *A Security Checklist for Oracle9i* lists DBMS_RANDOM among a list of packages that might be misused and recommends to revoke execute permission on DBMS_RANDOM from PUBLIC (see http://www.oracle.com/technology/deploy/security/oracle9i/pdf/9i_checklist.pdf)

To start monitoring, set the `ORACLE_SID` and DBI environment variables (see also Chapter 22), then run `sql_workarea_active.pl`. The example below is from Windows. On UNIX, use `export` to set environment variables.

```
C:> set ORACLE_SID=ORCL
C:> set DBI_USER=ndebes
C:> set DBI_PASS=secret
C:> set DBI_DSN=DBI:Oracle:
C:> sql_workarea_active.pl
   SID  TIME WORK_AREA_SIZE MAX_MEM_USED PASSES TEMPSEG_SIZE
```

The Perl program does not display any data until one or more work areas are allocated. We will use the script `sort_random_strings.sql` to run `SELECT ... ORDER BY` in SQL*Plus. The contents of the script are:

```
set timing on
set autotrace traceonly statistics
SELECT * FROM random_strings ORDER BY 1;
exit
```

The SQL*Plus command `SET AUTOTRACE` with the options `TRACEONLY STATISTICS` is very useful in this context, since it executes the statement without printing the result set to the screen. Furthermore it collects execution statistics from `V$SESSTAT` and displays them. In a separate window from the one running `sql_workarea_active.pl`, execute the script `sort_random_strings.sql` with SQL*Plus:

```
C:> sqlplus ndebes/secret @sort_random_strings.sql
Connected to:
Oracle Database 10g Enterprise Edition Release 10.2.0.1.0 - Production
1000000 rows selected.
Elapsed: 00:00:18.73
Statistics
--------------------------------------------------
        133  recursive calls
          7  db block gets
      18879  consistent gets
      16952  physical reads
          0  redo size
  138667083  bytes sent via SQL*Net to client
     733707  bytes received via SQL*Net from client
      66668  SQL*Net roundtrips to/from client
          0  sorts (memory)
          1  sorts (disk)
    1000000  rows processed
```

Surprisingly, the available memory was insufficient and the sort spilled to disk. Below is the output from `sql_workarea_active.pl`, which shows that the session performed a one–pass sort, since it only got a work area size of 51.2 MB:

```
SID  TIME WORK_AREA_SIZE MAX_MEM_USED PASSES TEMPSEG_SIZE
148 31:38           51.2         51.2      0           16
148 31:39           51.2         51.2      0           48
148 31:40           51.2         51.2      1           73
148 31:41           21.4         51.2      1          100
148 31:42           25.8         51.2      1          130
...
148 31:56            2.9         51.2      1          133
```

The timestamps confirm that the statement completed after 18 seconds. The temporary segment grew to 133 MB, somewhat less than the table's segment size. Obviously the entire memory set aside with PAT is not available to a single session. Accordingly, additional undocumented restrictions must be in place. Searching the Internet using the words "pga_aggregate_target tuning undocumented", one quickly realizes that several hidden parameters impact automatic PGA memory management. The names of the hidden parameters are `_PGA_MAX_SIZE`, `_SMM_MAX_SIZE` and `_SMM_PX_MAX_SIZE`. Of these, `_PGA_MAX_SIZE` is in bytes and the other two in kilobytes (KB). Descriptions and current values of these parameters are available by querying the X$ fixed tables `X$KSPPI` and `X$KSPPCV` (see also Part IV). The script `auto_pga_parameters.sql`, which queries these X$ fixed tables and normalizes all four relevant parameters to kilobytes, is reproduced below:

```
SELECT x.ksppinm name,
CASE WHEN x.ksppinm like '%pga%' THEN to_number(y.ksppstvl)/1024
ELSE to_number(y.ksppstvl)
END AS value,
x.ksppdesc description
FROM x$ksppi x, x$ksppcv y
WHERE x.inst_id = userenv('Instance')
AND y.inst_id = userenv('Instance')
AND x.indx = y.indx
AND x.ksppinm IN ('pga_aggregate_target', '_pga_max_size', '_smm_max_size',
'_smm_px_max_size');
```

With the current settings, the script gives the result below:

```
C:> sqlplus -s / as sysdba @auto_pga_parameters
NAME                    Value (KB) DESCRIPTION
--------------------    ---------- -------------------------------------------------
pga_aggregate_target        262144 Target size for the aggregate PGA memory
                                   consumed by the instance
_pga_max_size               204800 Maximum size of the PGA memory for one
                                   process
_smm_max_size                52428 maximum work area size in auto mode (serial)
_smm_px_max_size            131072 maximum work area size in auto mode (global)
```

I prepared the script `pga_aggregate_target_iterator.sql`, which varies `PGA_AGGREGATE_TARGET` between its minimum value of 10 MB up to a maximum value of 32 GB and calls `auto_pga_parameters.sql` for each setting, to investigate how changes of PAT affect these hidden parameters. Shutting down and restarting the DBMS is not necessary, since all three parameters are recalculated dynamically within certain limits. The results are presented in Table 4. Results beyond 8 GB are omitted, since no change in policy is seen beyond this value.

Table 4: PGA_AGGREGATE_TARGET (PAT) and Dependent Hidden Parameters

PAT	*_pga_max_size* (% of PAT)	*_smm_max_size* (% of _pga_max_size)	*_smm_max_size* as % of PAT	*_smm_px_max_size* (% of PAT)
10 MB	200 MB (2000%)	2 MB (1%)	20%	5 MB (50%)
32 MB	200 MB (625%)	6.4 MB (3.2%)	20%	16 MB (50%)
64 MB	200 MB (320%)	12.8 MB (6.4%)	20%	32 MB (50%)
128 MB	200 MB (156%)	25 MB (12%)	20%	64 MB (50%)
256 MB	200 MB (78%)	51 MB (25%)	20%	128 MB (50%)
512 MB	200 MB (39%)	100 MB (50%)	19.5%	256 MB (50%)
1 GB	204 MB (20%)	102 MB (50%)	10%	512 MB (50%)
2 GB	410 MB(20%)	205 MB (50%)	10%	1 GB (50%)
3 GB	416 MB (13.5%)	208 MB (50%)	6.8%	1536 MB (50%)
4 GB	480 MB (11.7%)	240 MB (50%)	5.8%	2 GB (50%)
8 GB	480 MB (5.8%)	240 MB (50%)	2.9%	4 GB (50%)

Looking at Table 4, a few patterns emerge. These are addressed in the sections that follow. Note that when overriding the settings of _SMM_MAX_SIZE or _SMM_PX_MAX_SIZE by putting them into a parameter file, these are no longer dynamically adjusted as PGA_AGGREGATE_TARGET is modified. Since both parameters are static, the ability to change them at runtime, albeit indirectly, is lost.

_PGA_MAX_SIZE

The parameter _PGA_MAX_SIZE limits the maximum size of all work areas for a single process. For values of PAT below 1 GB, _PGA_MAX_SIZE is 200 MB. For values of PAT between 1 GB and 2 GB, _PGA_MAX_SIZE is 20% of PAT. At values beyond 2 GB, _PGA_MAX_SIZE keeps on growing as PAT is increased, but at a lower rate, such that _PGA_MAX_SIZE is less than 20% of PAT. There is a limit of 480 MB on _PGA_MAX_SIZE, which takes effect at a PAT value of 4 GB. Increasing PAT beyond 4 GB does not result in higher values of _PGA_MAX_SIZE than 480 MB. In Oracle9*i*, _PGA_MAX_SIZE had a limit of 200 MB. Just like PGA_AGGREGATE_TARGET, _PGA_MAX_SIZE is a dynamic parameter that can be modified with ALTER SYSTEM. Changing _PGA_MAX_SIZE increases _SMM_MAX_SIZE in a similar way that modifying PGA_AGGREGATE_TARGET does. However, the rule that _SMM_MAX_SIZE is 50% of _PGA_MAX_SIZE does not hold for manual changes of _PGA_MAX_SIZE. Below is an example that increases _PGA_MAX_SIZE beyond the limit of 480 MB that can be reached by modifying PGA_AGGREGATE_TARGET:

```
SQL> @auto_pga_parameters
NAME                    Value (KB) DESCRIPTION
-------------------- ---------- --------------------------------------------
pga_aggregate_target    1048576 Target size for the aggregate PGA memory
                                consumed by the instance
_pga_max_size            209700 Maximum size of the PGA memory for one
                                process
_smm_max_size            104850 maximum work area size in auto mode (serial)
_smm_px_max_size         524288 maximum work area size in auto mode (global)
SQL> ALTER SYSTEM SET "_pga_max_size"=500m;
System altered.
SQL> @auto_pga_parameters
NAME                    Value (KB) DESCRIPTION
-------------------- ---------- --------------------------------------------
pga_aggregate_target    1048576 Target size for the aggregate PGA memory
                                consumed by the instance
_pga_max_size            512000 Maximum size of the PGA memory for one
                                process
_smm_max_size            209715 maximum work area size in auto mode (serial)
_smm_px_max_size         524288 maximum work area size in auto mode (global)
```

By increasing _PGA_MAX_SIZE, the work area size(s) available can be increased, without extending the memory allowance for the whole instance. When memory is scarce, this might avoid some paging activity. As long as very few sessions concurrently request large work areas, i.e. competition for PGA memory is low, this may lead to better response time for operations involving large sorts. By altering _PGA_MAX_SIZE, _SMM_MAX_SIZE can be dynamically set to values larger than the normal limit of 240 MB.

_SMM_MAX_SIZE

The parameter _SMM_MAX_SIZE limits the maximum size of an individual work area for a single process. For values of PAT below 512 MB, _SMM_MAX_SIZE is 20% of PGA_AGGREGATE_TARGET. For PAT values of 512 MB and beyond, _SMM_MAX_SIZE is always 50% of _PGA_MAX_SIZE. In Oracle9*i*, _SMM_MAX_SIZE had a limit of 100 MB. Below is an example of a session that had two simultaneously active work areas when the following parameters were in effect:

```
NAME                    Value (KB)
-------------------- ----------
pga_aggregate_target    1536000
_pga_max_size            307200
_smm_max_size            153600
_smm_px_max_size         768000

C:> sql_workarea_active_hash.pl
SID  TIME HASH_VALUE         TYPE  WORK_AREA_SIZE MAX_MEM_USED PASSES TMP_SIZE
159 57:46 1705656915  SORT (v2)             133.7         133.7      0        0
159 57:46 3957124346  HASH-JOIN              16.2          15.7      0      105
...
```

```
159 57:52 1705656915  SORT (v2)        133.7        133.7      0         0
159 57:52 3957124346  HASH-JOIN        108.3         96.1      1       138
```

Output from the Perl script `sql_workarea_active_hash.pl` includes the columns HASH_VALUE and TYPE from V$SQL_WORKAREA_ACTIVE. Both work areas combined exceeded _SMM_MAX_SIZE, but not _PGA_MAX_SIZE.

_SMM_PX_MAX_SIZE

The setting of _SMM_PX_MAX_SIZE is always 50% of PGA_AGGREGATE_TARGET. There is no limit on _SMM_PX_MAX_SIZE (at least not within the tested range of PGA_AGGREGATE_TARGET of 10 MB to 32 GB). In Oracle9*i*, _SMM_PX_MAX_SIZE was 30% of PGA_AGGREGATE_TARGET.

Shared Server

In Oracle10*g*, Shared Server was recoded to use automatic PGA memory management. Oracle9*i* Shared Server uses the *_AREA_SIZE Parameters, i.e. it behaves as if ALTER SESSION SET WORKAREA_SIZE_POLICY=MANUAL had been executed. Hence it is valid to leave SORT_AREA_SIZE inside an Oracle9*i* PFILE or SPFILE and to set it to a more useful value, such as 1048576, than the default 65536. Of course it is still valid to set meaningful values for SORT_AREA_SIZE, HASH_AREA_SIZE, etc. in Oracle10*g*, for sessions that might run with manual work area sizing (WORKAREA_SIZE_POLICY=MANUAL).

Parallel Execution

The hidden parameter _SMM_PX_MAX_SIZE applies to parallel execution, but how exactly needs to be revealed by further tests. Regarding parallel execution (PX), it is important to bear in mind that a parallel full scan of a table at degree *n* divides the work among *n* parallel execution processes, such that the volume of data handled by each process equates approximately one *n*–th of the entire data volume. The figure *n* is commonly called the degree of parallelism or DOP.

Each parallel execution process allocates his own work area(s). Since each process handles merely a fraction of the data, the work areas required by individual processes in parallel mode are smaller than a single work area in serial mode.

It turns out that _SMM_PX_MAX_SIZE places an additional restriction on the maximum work area size, which is exercised on parallel execution processes. Each PX process may not use more than _SMM_PX_MAX_SIZE/DOP memory. The per process restriction of _SMM_MAX_SIZE remains in effect for PX, such that the available memory is the lesser of _SMM_MAX_SIZE and _SMM_PX_MAX_SIZE/DOP. To sort entirely in memory, two conditions must be met:

* The data volume per PX process must be less than _SMM_MAX_SIZE.
* The data volume per PX process must be less than _SMM_PX_MAX_SIZE/DOP.

Let's run some examples. The previous tests revealed that the SELECT from the test table has a data volume of about 133 MB. Thus, at a DOP of four, each PX process requires a work area size of around 133 MB divided by 4 or approximately 34 MB for an optimal sort. Rounding up slightly to 40 MB to allow for fluctuations of the data volume among PX processes, we will set _SMM_MAX_SIZE=40960, since the unit of _SMM_MAX_SIZE is KB. To avoid PGA_AGGREGATE_TARGET or _SMM_PX_MAX_SIZE becoming the limiting factor, we also set both parameters to DOP times _SMM_MAX_SIZE or 160 MB. To set these parameters, place the following three lines into a parameter file and restart the instance with STARTUP PFILE:

```
pga_aggregate_target=160m
_smm_px_max_size=163840 # in KB
_smm_max_size=40960 # in KB
```

Verifying the settings with the script `auto_pga_parameters.sql` gives:

```
NAME                  Value (KB) DESCRIPTION
--------------------  ---------- --------------------------------------------
pga_aggregate_target      163840 Target size for the aggregate PGA memory
                                 consumed by the instance
_pga_max_size             204800 Maximum size of the PGA memory for one
                                 process
_smm_max_size              40960 maximum work area size in auto mode (serial)
_smm_px_max_size          163840 maximum work area size in auto mode (global)
```

Next, a FULL and a PARALLEL hint must be added to the SELECT statement to enable parallel execution:

```
SQL> SELECT /*+ FULL(r) PARALLEL(r, 4) */ * FROM random_strings r ORDER BY 1;
```

Running the parallel query at DOP four and monitoring it with `sql_workarea_active.pl` gives:

SID	TIME	WORK_AREA_SIZE	MAX_MEM_USED	PASSES	TEMPSEG_SIZE
143	06:36	1.7	1.6	0	0
144	06:36	1.7	1.6	0	0
145	06:36	2.6	2.1	0	0
146	06:36	1.7	1.6	0	0
...					
145	06:43	32.3	39.6	0	0
...					
146	06:46	31.6	31.6	0	0
...					
144	06:48	31.4	31.4	0	0
...					
143	06:50	31.2	31.2	0	0

As expected, an optimal sort was performed. The response time is 14 s. Halving DOP results in only two processes sharing the workload and the following measurements:

SID	TIME	WORK_AREA_SIZE	MAX_MEM_USED	PASSES	TEMPSEG_SIZE
140	23:48	3.1	2.7	0	0
147	23:48	3.8	3.1	0	0
...					
147	24:03	1.2	40	1	71
...					
140	24:08	1.2	40	1	63

Here, _SMM_MAX_SIZE lead to a degradation of response time to around 20 s, since at DOP two, each process requires a work area size of around 75 MB, but only 40 MB were available, resulting in one–pass sorts and spilling to disk. Back to the original DOP four. A reduction of _SMM_PX_MAX_SIZE below the data volume divided by DOP also results in spilling to disk. Below are the results at DOP four with these settings:

```
pga_aggregate_target=160m
_smm_px_max_size=122880 # in KB
_smm_max_size=40960 # in KB
```

This time, _SMM_PX_MAX_SIZE is the limiting factor.

SID	TIME	WORK_AREA_SIZE	MAX_MEM_USED	PASSES	TEMPSEG_SIZE
143	33:27	1.7	1.7	0	0
...					
145	33:41	1.2	30	1	40
...					
146	33:44	1.2	30	1	32
...					
144	33:46	1.2	30	1	32
...					
143	33:49	1.2	30	1	31

All slaves spilled their work areas to disk, since work areas were limited to 120 MB / DOP = 40 MB and the query completed in 22 s.

Lessons Learned

When using automatic PGA memory management, three hidden parameters work behind the scenes to enforce restrictions on memory consumption. The parameter _PGA_MAX_SIZE limits the size of all work areas in use by a single process. The size of an individual work area is limited by _SMM_MAX_SIZE for both serial and parallel execution. When parallel execution is used, an additional restriction on the total size of all work areas in use by the processes involved is in place. This limit is controlled with the parameter _SMM_PX_MAX_SIZE. Within certain limits, all three parameters are recalculated at runtime as a result of modifying PAT. All three parameters may be set manually to override the result of this calculation.

EVENT

Status: The parameter EVENT is partially documented in the *Oracle Database Reference* manual. The parameter syntax as well as which events may be set are undocumented. The manual states that the parameter must not be used except under the supervision of Oracle Support Services.

Benefit: The parameter EVENT may be used to set one or more events at instance level. Events set in this way are enabled for the entire lifetime of an instance. All other approaches for setting events, such as DBMS_SYSTEM, do not cover the entire lifetime of an instance. The parameter is appropriate for situations where other means for setting events are not feasible or events must be set right when a process starts. Processing of a technical assistance request by Oracle Support Services may involve setting certain events. A DBA who is familiar with the parameter EVENT is less dependent on Oracle Support and may find a workaround without needing to ask for assistance.

Syntax

The events that may be set with the parameter EVENT are the same events that can be set by other means, such as ALTER SESSION, ALTER SYSTEM, and ORADEBUG. The commonalities go even further, since the event specification syntax for the aforementioned methods and the parameter EVENT is identical. Multiple events may be set by entering several event specifications separated by colons. The syntax is:

    event='event_specification1 [:event_specificationN] * '

Brackets indicate that an element is optional. The asterisk indicates that the preceding element may be repeated. The syntax for an individual event specification is:

    event_number trace name context forever, level event_level

The placeholders *event_number* and *event_level* are both integers. Most event numbers are in the range 10000 to 10999[1]. On UNIX systems, these events are listed in the file $ORACLE_HOME/rdbms/mesg/oraus.msg along with a description. The supported event level is unspecified for most of the events in the file, such that it may be necessary to involve Oracle Support to determine the correct level. The OERR utility may be used to retrieve the description for a certain event. Below is an example for an event that switches off a cost based optimizer (CBO) access path:

```
$ oerr ora 10196
10196, 00000, "CBO disable index skip scan"
// *Cause:
// *Action:
```

It is also possible to request a diagnostic dump when an ORA-*nnnnn* error occurs. The syntax for this is identical to the syntax that has to be used with ALTER SESSION/SYSTEM SET EVENTS and is covered in Chapter 13. Further information on events is in Part III.

Leveraging Events at Instance–Level

Several scenarios mandate setting events at instance level. These are:

- enabling or disabling bug fixes
- enabling or disabling features, such as cost based optimizer access paths
- tracing certain code paths or features in all processes of an instance
- enabling or disabling certain checks
- writing a diagnostic dump whenever an ORACLE error (ORA-*nnnnn*) is raised in any database session

Consider the parameter EVENT whenever events must be set right when a process starts or for all processes of an instance. While it is absolutely feasible to obtain SQL trace files for multiple processes, such as those originating from a connection pool by setting event 10046 with parameter EVENT, I am a strong opponent of such a procedure, since more sophisticated approaches, such as using a logon trigger or DBMS_MONITOR exist. Setting event 10046 at level 8 or 12 with the parameter EVENT is better than setting SQL_TRACE=TRUE at instance level, since wait events and binds may be included, however both incur the unnecessary overhead of tracing each and every process of the instance. I certainly wouldn't be willing to sift through dozens or even hundreds of trace files to find a few relevant ones when other features allow tracing just the processes of interest.

---

1. Events 14532 (enable bug fix for excess use of shared pool memory during DDL on partitioned objects in 10.2.0.3) and 38068 (CBO enable override of guess impact on index choice) are example exceptions to this rule.

Case Study

Recovery Manager (RMAN) supports writing backups to file systems and to third party media managers. Writing backups to a file system works out of the box and does not incur additional expenses. Since writing to a local file system does not protect against the failure of the database server hardware as a whole, writing to remote file systems or network attached storage (NAS) arrays via NFS is supported too. RMAN has several undocumented requirements concerning NFS mount options. If the mount options `hard,rsize=32768,wsize=32768` are not used, RMAN will refuse to write to an NFS file system. However, certain releases of RMAN still throw an error when these requirements are met. Under these circumstances, Oracle Support has suggested setting event 10298 at level 32 as a temporary workaround until the underlying issue is resolved.

This is a case for setting an event at instance level with parameter `EVENT`. With other methods for setting events, such as `ORADEBUG` or `DBMS_SYSTEM`, it is impossible to set the event in time for the multiple processes that RMAN spawns. Furthermore it would be too cumbersome to set the event after each instance startup with `ALTER SYSTEM SET EVENTS`.

OS_AUTHENT_PREFIX

Status: `OS_AUTHENT_PREFIX` is documented in the *Oracle Database Reference* manual. It is undocumented that a database user name which is prefixed by the string `OPS$` allows for local authentication through the operating system and password authentication when connecting over a network.

Benefit: Since `REMOTE_OS_AUTHENT=FALSE` should be set for security reasons, it's impossible to use externally identified users to connect to an instance over a network, e.g. using Oracle Net and the TCP/IP protocol adapter. Creating `OPS$` users with password authentication allows the convenience of omitting the user name and password when connecting locally using the Oracle Net bequeath adapter, while being able to connect over a network using password authentication.

OPS$ Database Users and Password Authentication

Operating system authentication is intended for local connections. The *Oracle Database SQL Reference 10g Release 2* manual states the following on externally identified users:

EXTERNALLY Clause

Specify EXTERNALLY to create an external user. Such a user must be authenticated by an external service, such as an operating system or a third–party service. In this case, Oracle Database relies on authentication by the operating system or third–party service to ensure that a specific external user has access to a specific database user.

In the same way that a user who belongs to the DBA group (usually the UNIX group dba) can connect with `SYSDBA` privileges without entering a password using `CONNECT / AS SYSDBA`, an externally identified user can connect using `CONNECT /`. When verifying credentials for an externally identified user, the value of the ORACLE initialization parameter `OS_AUTHENT_PREFIX` is prepended to the operating system user name. If the resulting username exists in the data dictionary and `DBA_USERS.PASSWORD=EXTERNAL` for this user, then the user may connect without entering a password. The syntax for creating an externally identified user is:

```
CREATE USER <os_authent_prefix><os_user_name> IDENTIFIED EXTERNALLY;
```

It is undocumented that operating system authentication also works for users created with password authentication as long as `OS_AUTHENT_PREFIX` is left at its default setting of `ops$`. That is, users created with the syntax `CREATE USER ops$os_user_name IDENTIFIED BY password` may connect locally without entering a password as long as `OS_AUTHENT_PREFIX=ops$`. In a way, this approach combines the best of both worlds. The need to enter passwords for interactive database sessions as well as storing passwords for batch jobs running locally is dispelled and the same user name may be used to connect over the network.

Case Study

The environment for this case study is a UNIX system, where the DBA group name is "dba", the OPER group name is "oper" and the ORACLE software owner group is "oinstall". Furthermore a password file is used. In a moment, you will see how a user who is not a member of any of the aforementioned three special groups may be granted the

SYSOPER privilege, allowing him to start and stop an instance, while not being able to change parameters or to modify the ORACLE software installation. This is an additional option that may be implemented with the undocumented approach discussed in the previous section.

First of all, we verify that the parameter OS_AUTHENT_PREFIX has the default value ops$:

```
SQL> SHOW PARAMETER os_authent_prefix
NAME                                     TYPE         VALUE
------------------------------------- ----------- -----
os_authent_prefix                        string       ops$
```

Next, we create a database user whose name is formed by prepending the string ops$ to the operating system user name, in this case "ndebes", and grant the privileges CONNECT and SYSOPER to the new user.

```
SQL> CREATE USER ops$ndebes IDENTIFIED BY secret;
User created.
SQL> GRANT CONNECT, SYSOPER TO ops$ndebes;
Grant succeeded.
SQL> SELECT * FROM v$pwfile_users;
USERNAME                         SYSDBA SYSOPER
----------------------------- ------ -----
SYS                              TRUE   TRUE
OPS$NDEBES                       FALSE  TRUE
```

As evidenced by Figure 3, the database user OPS$NDEBES can connect via the Oracle Net TCP/IP adapter from a windows system. Password authentication is required, since REMOTE_OS_AUTHENT=FALSE is set.

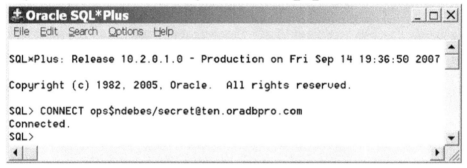

Figure 3: SQL*Plus Session via the Oracle Net TCP/IP Adapter

Back on UNIX, the operating system user "ndebes" can connect without entering a password:

```
$ id
uid=500(ndebes) gid=100(users) groups=100(users)
$ sqlplus /
SQL*Plus: Release 10.2.0.3.0 - Production on Wed Sep 5 08:02:33 2007
Connected to:
Oracle Database 10g Enterprise Edition Release 10.2.0.3.0 - Production
SQL> SHOW USER
USER is "OPS$NDEBES"
```

Thanks to password authentication and a password file, connecting AS SYSOPER works too:

```
SQL> CONNECT ops$ndebes/secret AS SYSOPER
Connected.
SQL> SHOW USER
USER is "PUBLIC"
SQL> SELECT * FROM session_privs;
PRIVILEGE
---------------------------------------
CREATE SESSION
RESTRICTED SESSION
SYSOPER
```

Due to the SYSOPER privilege, the database user "OPS$NDEBES" can stop and restart the instance:

```
SQL> SHUTDOWN IMMEDIATE
Database closed.
Database dismounted.
ORACLE instance shut down.
SQL> STARTUP
ORACLE instance started.
Database mounted.
Database opened.
```

Contrary to SYSDBA, the SYSOPER privilege does not include access to data dictionary views or tables, but allows the use of ARCHIVE LOG LIST for monitoring. Merely database objects accessible to PUBLIC may be accessed with the SYSOPER privilege.

```
SQL> SELECT startup_time FROM v$instance;
SELECT startup_time FROM v$instance
                         *
ERROR at line 1:
ORA-00942: table or view does not exist
SQL> ARCHIVE LOG LIST
Database log mode              No Archive Mode
Automatic archival             Disabled
Archive destination            /opt/oracle/product/db10.2/dbs/arch
Oldest online log sequence     18
Current log sequence           19
```

The combined benefits of operating system authentication and password authentication become unavailable with a non–default setting of OS_AUTHENT_PREFIX. The SYSDBA privilege can merely be granted to database users created with password authentication, but obviously such users must enter the correct password when connecting. The problem is that the undocumented check for operating system authentication in spite of an assigned password is not done when OS_AUTHENT_PREFIX has a non–default value.

```
SQL> ALTER SYSTEM SET os_authent_prefix='' SCOPE=SPFILE;
System altered.
```

Since OS_AUTHENT_PREFIX is now a zero–length string, operating system user name and database user name are identical:

```
SQL> CREATE USER ndebes IDENTIFIED BY secret;
User created.
SQL> GRANT CONNECT, SYSOPER TO ndebes;
Grant succeeded.
```

To allow the changed value of OS_AUTHENT_PREFIX to take effect, the instance must be restarted. Clearly, the operating system user "ndebes" will not be able to connect as database user "ndebes" without entering the password "secret".

```
$ sqlplus -s /
ERROR:
ORA-01017: invalid username/password; logon denied
```

When setting the authentication method for the user to operating system authentication, the string "EXTERNAL" instead of an encrypted password is stored in DBA_USERS.PASSWORD:

```
SQL> ALTER USER ndebes IDENTIFIED externally;
User altered.
SQL> SELECT password FROM dba_users WHERE username='NDEBES';
PASSWORD
------------------------------
EXTERNAL
```

Now the operating system user "ndebes" is able to connect without entering the password:

```
$ id
uid=500(ndebes) gid=100(users) groups=100(users)
$ sqlplus /
```

```
Connected to:
Oracle Database 10g Enterprise Edition Release 10.2.0.3.0 - Production
SQL> CONNECT ndebes/secret as SYSOPER
ERROR:
ORA-01031: insufficient privileges
```

However the ability to connect as SYSOPER using the password stored in the password file is lost for the now externally identified database user. The same applies to the privilege SYSDBA.

Lessons Learned

There is an undocumented code path that enables operating system authentication for database users whose user name starts with OPS$, even when these users are created with password authentication. This combines the best aspects of the otherwise mutually exclusive approaches of operating system and password authentication. To leverage the undocumented feature, the initialization parameter OS_AUTHENT_PREFIX must have the default value ops$. The feature may also be used to set up a single database user with SYSDBA or SYSOPER privilege who does not belong to the DBA or OPER operating system groups and who can connect locally without entering a password. Such a user must only enter the password when connecting over the network or when needing a session with SYSDBA or SYSOPER privilege. Separate database users are required without the undocumented feature or if a non–default setting of OS_AUTHENT_PREFIX is in effect. If you are dealing with a security sensitive environment and need to make sure that an intruder cannot exploit this feature, then you should disable it by assigning a non–default value to the parameter OS_AUTHENT_PREFIX.

Source Code Depot

Table 5: Partially Documented Parameters Source Code Depot

File Name	Functionality
auto_pga_parameters.sql	Retrieves all the documented and undocumented parameters that affect SQL work area sizing.
pga_aggregate_target_iterator.sql	This script varies PGA_AGGREGATE_TARGET between 10 MB and 32 GB and calls auto_pga_parameters.sql at each iteration.
row_factory.sql	Creates a pipelined table function that returns an arbitrary number of rows.
sort_random_strings.sql	This script enables SQL*Plus AUTOTRACE and selects rows from the test table RANDOM_STRINGS.
sql_workarea_active.pl	This perl script monitors work areas by querying the dynamic performance view V$SQL_WORKAREA_ACTIVE.
sql_workarea_active_hash.pl	This perl script monitors work areas by querying the dynamic performance view V$SQL_WORKAREA_ACTIVE. The output includes SQL statement hash values.

Chapter 2

Hidden Initialization Parameters

Introduction to Hidden Initialization Parameters

The view V$PARAMETER provides access to documented initialization parameters. This view is built on top of the X$ fixed tables X$KSPPI and X$KSPPCV (more on X$ fixed tables in Part IV). All hidden parameters start with one or two underscores (_). V$PARAMETER is built in such a way that it lists documented parameters only. There are 540 undocumented parameters in Oracle9*i* Release 2, 1124 in Oracle10*g* Release 2 and 1627 in Oracle11*g*. Their names and a short description may be retrieved with the query below (file hidden_parameters.sql):

```
SQL> SELECT ksppinm name,
ksppstvl value,
ksppdesc description
FROM x$ksppi x, x$ksppcv y
WHERE (x.indx = y.indx)
AND x.inst_id=userenv('instance')
AND x.inst_id=y.inst_id
AND ksppinm LIKE '\_%' ESCAPE '\'
ORDER BY name;
```

The source code depot contains a complete list of undocumented parameters in Oracle9*i*, Oracle10*g*, and Oracle11*g*. Due to the large amount of undocumented parameters, it is impossible to investigate what they all do and to document the results. I have chosen _TRACE_FILES_PUBLIC and _ASM_ALLOW_ONLY_RAW_DISKS as examples of two useful hidden parameters and discuss both in detail in this chapter. Of course there are many more, which may be useful under certain circumstances. Some may be set to work around bugs (e.g. _DISABLE_RECOVERABLE_RECOVERY), while others may have an effect on performance (e.g. _ROW_CACHE_CURSORS, _ASM_AUSIZE). Still others may be used to salvage data from a database when the documented recovery procedures fail due to invalid backup procedures

Secret ORACLE

or the loss of the current online redo log (_ALLOW_RESETLOGS_CORRUPTION, _OFFLINE_ROLLBACK_SEGMENTS). Normally hidden parameters should only be set under the supervision of Oracle Support Services.

Trace File Permissions and _TRACE_FILES_PUBLIC

Trace files are created either on request, e.g. with ALTER SYSTEM SET SQL_TRACE=TRUE or when internal errors occur. Trace files from foreground processes are located in the directory set with the parameter USER_DUMP_DEST, whereas trace files from background processes take the directory setting from the initialization parameter BACKGROUND_DUMP_DEST. In any case, the file name extension is .trc. By default, trace files are readable only for the owner of the ORACLE installation (normally "oracle") or members of the installation group (normally "oinstall"). If a database administrator does not belong to the installation group, even he or she cannot read trace files.

Since trace files may contain sensitive information, either as bind variable values or literals, it is appropriate that the default permissions are restrictive. On a test system however, where developers enable SQL trace and need to analyze the output with TKPROF, it's much more convenient to allow anyone with access to the system to read trace files. A hidden parameter called _TRACE_FILES_PUBLIC may be used to make newly created trace files readable by everyone. As shown by running the script hidden_parameter_value.sql below, the default setting of the static parameter is FALSE.

```
$ cat hidden_parameter_value.sql
col name format a33
col value format a36
set verify off
SELECT x.ksppinm name, y.ksppstvl value
FROM x$ksppi x, x$ksppcv y
WHERE x.inst_id = userenv('Instance')
AND y.inst_id = userenv('Instance')
AND x.indx = y.indx
AND x.ksppinm='&hidden_parameter_name';
$ sqlplus -s / as sysdba @hidden_parameter_value.sql
Enter value for hidden_parameter_name: _trace_files_public
NAME                              VALUE
-------------------------------   ------------------------------------
_trace_files_public               FALSE
```

Let's have a look at the permissions of files in the user dump destination:

```
SQL> SHOW PARAMETER user_dump_dest
NAME                          TYPE          VALUE
----------------------------  -----------   ------------------------------------
user_dump_dest                string        /opt/oracle/obase/admin/TEN/udump
SQL> !cd /opt/oracle/obase/admin/TEN/udump; ls -l
total 68
-rw-r-----  1 oracle oinstall 1024 Jul 21 21:26 ten1_ora_11685.trc
-rw-r-----  1 oracle oinstall  874 Jul 24 02:56 ten1_ora_13035.trc
-rw-r-----  1 oracle oinstall  737 Jul 24 02:56 ten1_ora_13318.trc
```

As expected, read permission is granted solely to the owner of the file and the group "oinstall"[1]. If a server parameter file (SPFILE) is used, _TRACE_FILES_PUBLIC must be changed with an ALTER SYSTEM command. Double quotes around the parameter name are mandatory, since it starts with an underscore (_):

```
SQL> ALTER SYSTEM SET "_trace_files_public" = TRUE SCOPE=SPFILE;
```

---

1. The format, in which the UNIX command ls displays permissions, is {r|-}{w|-}{x|-}. This sequence of characters is repeated three times. The left part applies to the owner of the file, group permissions are in the middle, and permissions for anyone (a.k.a. world) on the right. A minus sign means that the permission represented by the position in the string is not granted. For example, rwxr-xr-x means that the owner may read, write and execute, the group may read and execute and anyone may read and execute.

Double quotes around the parameter are not required when a text parameter file (PFILE) is used. Since the parameter is static, the instance must be shut down and restarted for the new setting to take effect. Using ORADEBUG (see Chapter 37) we can quickly verify that read permission for others is now granted on newly created trace files:

```
SQL> ORADEBUG SETMYPID
Statement processed.
SQL> ALTER SESSION SET SQL_TRACE=TRUE;
Session altered.
SQL> SELECT sysdate FROM dual;
SYSDATE
---------
25-JUL-07
SQL> ORADEBUG TRACEFILE_NAME
/opt/oracle/obase/admin/TEN/udump/ten1_ora_18067.trc
SQL> !cd /opt/oracle/obase/admin/TEN/udump;ls -l ten1_ora_18067.trc
-rw-r--r-- 1 oracle oinstall 1241 Jul 25 20:53 ten1_ora_18067.trc
```

As you would expect by looking at the parameter name, _TRACE_FILES_PUBLIC has no effect on permissions of the alert log.

ASM Test Environment and _ASM_ALLOW_ONLY_RAW_DISKS

Automatic Storage Management is essentially a volume manager and a file system for exclusive use by ORACLE instances. The volume management capabilities include mirroring and striping. ASM implements the S.A.M.E. (stripe and mirror everything[1]) approach. ASM uses a number of raw devices[2], concatenates them into a large pool of storage, and offers the storage space as a kind of file system to ORACLE instances. Raw disks (e.g. LUNs in a SAN) are grouped into disk groups. ASM can rely on RAID storage arrays for mirroring (external redundancy) or it can do its own mirroring (normal/high redundancy). If necessary, disks in a disk group may be assigned to failure groups, which indicate the storage system topology to ASM, such that mirrored copies can be placed on different storage arrays or may be accessed using different host bus adapters.

For readers who would like to familiarize themselves with ASM, but do not have access to a SAN or cannot create raw devices on a local disk due to space constraints or lack of privileges, this chapter demonstrates how to set up a test environment for automatic storage management on Windows with *cooked files* and _ASM_ALLOW_ONLY_RAW_DISKS. Old school UNIX jargon distinguished raw files from cooked files. Cooked files are simply the opposite of raw devices–files in a file system. After all, something that's not raw has to be cooked, right?

ASM Hidden Parameters

Undocumented parameters pertaining to ASM may be retrieved by running the following query as user SYS:

```
SQL> SELECT x.ksppinm name, y.ksppstvl value, x.ksppdesc description
FROM x$ksppi x, x$ksppcv y
WHERE x.inst_id = userenv('Instance')
AND y.inst_id = userenv('Instance')
AND x.indx = y.indx
AND x.ksppinm LIKE '\_asm%' ESCAPE '\'
ORDER BY name;
NAME                             VALUE      DESCRIPTION
-------------------------------- ---------- ----------------------------------
_asm_acd_chunks                  1          initial ACD chunks created
_asm_allow_only_raw_disks        TRUE       Discovery only raw devices
_asm_allow_resilver_corruption   FALSE      Enable disk resilvering for
                                            external redundancy
_asm_ausize                      1048576    allocation unit size
```

---

1. See http://www.oracle.com/technology/deploy/availability/pdf/OOW2000_same_ppt.pdf
2. Oracle10g Release 2 on Linux supports block devices too. These are opened with O_DIRECT to eliminate caching by the Linux operating system kernel as with raw devices. Performance is the same as that of raw devices, which have been deprecated on the Linux platform.

_asm_blksize	4096	metadata block size
_asm_disk_repair_time	14400	seconds to wait before dropping a failing disk
_asm_droptimeout	60	timeout before offlined disks get dropped (in 3s ticks)
_asm_emulmax	10000	max number of concurrent disks to emulate I/O errors
_asm_emultimeout	0	timeout before emulation begins (in 3s ticks)
_asm_kfdpevent	0	KFDP event
_asm_libraries	ufs	library search order for discovery
_asm_maxio	1048576	Maximum size of individual I/O request
_asm_stripesize	131072	ASM file stripe size
_asm_stripewidth	8	ASM file stripe width
_asm_wait_time	18	Max/imum time to wait before asmb exits
_asmlib_test	0	Osmlib test event
_asmsid	asm	ASM instance id

These parameters unveil some of the inner workings of ASM. The default settings indicate that ASM divides an allocation unit (_ASM_AUSIZE) into chunks of 128 KB (_ASM_STRIPESIZE) and places each of those chunks on up to eight different disks (_ASM_STRIPEWIDTH). Very large databases may benefit from increasing _ASM_AUSIZE, but this is beyond the scope of this book[1]. This chapter merely addresses _ASM_ALLOW_ONLY_RAW_DISKS.

Setting up Oracle Clusterware for ASM

To start an ASM instance, a stripped down version of Oracle Clusterware must be running on the same system. This is accomplished with the command %ORACLE_HOME%\bin\localconfig add. It creates an ORACLE cluster registry (OCR) in %ORACLE_HOME%\cdata\localhost\local.ocr. It also creates a new Windows service for the OCSSD Clusterware daemon. OCSSD logging goes to the file %ORACLE_HOME%\log\<host name>\cssd\ocssd.log.

```
C:> localconfig add
Step 1:  creating new OCR repository
Successfully accumulated necessary OCR keys.
Creating OCR keys for user 'ndebes', privgrp ''..
Operation successful.
Step 2:  creating new CSS service
successfully created local CSS service
successfully added CSS to home
```

The service that implements OCSSD is called OracleCSService. You can verify that the service is functional by running the command net start in a Windows command interpreter. This command lists all running services:

```
C:> net start
...
OracleCSService
OracleDB_10_2TNSListener
...
```

The Clusterware command for checking OCSSD's status is crsctl check css:

```
C:> crsctl check css
CSS appears healthy
```

By running crsctl check crs, it becomes apparent that only a subset of Clusterware daemons are active in a local–only configuration. The CRS and EVM daemons required for RAC are not needed.

```
C:> crsctl check crs
CSS appears healthy
Cannot communicate with CRS
Cannot communicate with EVM
```

---

1. See http://h20331.www2.hp.com/ERC/downloads/4AA0-9728ENW.pdf and Metalink note 368055.1

ASM Instance Setup

Next, we will create some cooked files for ASM storage. ASM will use these files instead of raw disks. I use the UNIX command dd, which is included in Cygwin[1], to create four files which will serve as "disks". Each file has a size of 512 MB and is initialized with binary zeros by reading from /dev/zero.

```
C:\> mkdir \oradata
C:\> cd \oradata
C:\oradata> dd if=/dev/zero bs=1048576 count=512 of=ARRAY1_DISK1
512+0 records in
512+0 records out
536870912 bytes (537 MB) copied, 20.914 s, 25.7 MB/s
```

Repeat the command dd with the file names ARRAY1_DISK2, ARRAY2_DISK1 and ARRAY2_DISK2 to create three more files. These files will be used to simulate two disk arrays (ARRAY1 and ARRAY2) with two logical units (LUNs) each. We will then setup ASM to mirror across the two arrays. Striping occurs within the array boundaries.

```
C:\oradata>ls -l
total 2463840
-rw-rw-rw-  1 ndebes        mkpasswd   536870912 Nov  2 13:34 ARRAY1_DISK1
-rw-rw-rw-  1 ndebes        mkpasswd   536870912 Nov  2 13:38 ARRAY1_DISK2
-rw-rw-rw-  1 ndebes        mkpasswd   536870912 Nov  2 13:40 ARRAY2_DISK1
-rw-rw-rw-  1 ndebes        mkpasswd   536870912 Nov  2 13:38 ARRAY2_DISK2
```

To start an ASM instance, a parameter file which contains INSTANCE_TYPE=ASM is required. The parameter ASM_DISKSTRING is used to indicate where ASM should search for disks. Create a file called pfile+ASM.ora with the following contents in %ORACLE_HOME%\database:

```
instance_type = ASM
asm_diskstring = 'c:\oradata\*'
```

Next, create a Windows service for the ORACLE ASM instance with oradim:

```
C:> oradim -new -asmsid +ASM -syspwd secret -startmode manual -srvcstart demand
Instance created.
```

The command oradim creates and starts a Windows service called OracleASMService+ASM. You may verify that the service is running with net start:

```
C:> net start | grep -i asm
   OracleASMService+ASM
```

Now we are ready to start the ASM instance:

```
C:> set ORACLE_SID=+ASM
C:> sqlplus / as sysdba
SQL*Plus: Release 10.2.0.3.0 - Production on Tue Aug 14 16:17:51 2007
Copyright (c) 1982, 2005, Oracle.  All rights reserved.
Connected to an idle instance.
SQL> STARTUP NOMOUNT PFILE=?\database\pfile+ASM.ora
ASM instance started
Total System Global Area   79691776 bytes
Fixed Size                  1247396 bytes
Variable Size              53278556 bytes
ASM Cache                  25165824 bytes
```

Next, we create a server parameter file (SPFILE), such that ASM will be able to store disk group names it should mount at instance startup in the SPFILE:

```
SQL> CREATE SPFILE FROM PFILE='?\database\pfile+ASM.ora';
File created.
```

This creates an SPFILE called spfile+ASM.ora. Let's see whether ASM recognizes the cooked files as disks:

```
SQL> SELECT path, header_status FROM v$asm_disk;
no rows selected
```

---

1. Cygwin is free software available at http://www.cygwin.com

ASM does not see any disks that it might use. This is not surprising, since the default setting of the parameter _ASM_ALLOW_ONLY_RAW_DISKS is FALSE. We need to shutdown the instance and restart it before we can change the parameter in the SPFILE that we created:

```
SQL> SHUTDOWN IMMEDIATE
ORA-15100: invalid or missing diskgroup name
ASM instance shutdown
SQL> STARTUP NOMOUNT
ASM instance started
...
SQL> SHOW PARAMETER SPFILE
NAME      TYPE        VALUE
--------  ----------- -----------------------------------------------------
spfile    string      C:\ORACLE\PRODUCT\DB10.2\DATABASE\SPFILE+ASM.ORA
```

Since _ASM_ALLOW_ONLY_RAW_DISKS is a static parameter, another instance restart is required after changing it:

```
SQL> ALTER SYSTEM SET "_asm_allow_only_raw_disks"=FALSE SCOPE=SPFILE SID='*';
System altered.
SQL> SHUTDOWN IMMEDIATE
ORA-15100: invalid or missing diskgroup name
ASM instance shutdown
SQL> STARTUP NOMOUNT
ASM instance started
...
SQL> SELECT path, header_status, library, total_mb, free_mb FROM v$asm_disk;
PATH                     HEADER_STATUS LIBRARY   TOTAL_MB   FREE_MB
----------------------   ------------- -------   ---------- ----------
C:\ORADATA\ARRAY1_DISK1  CANDIDATE     System         512         0
C:\ORADATA\ARRAY2_DISK2  CANDIDATE     System         512         0
C:\ORADATA\ARRAY2_DISK1  CANDIDATE     System         512         0
C:\ORADATA\ARRAY1_DISK2  CANDIDATE     System         512         0
```

This time ASM did recognize the cooked files as disks for use in a disk group, so we may go ahead and create a disk group with external redundancy. By assigning the failure group array1 to the disks in the first disk array (files ARRAY1_DISK1 and ARRAY1_DISK2) and the failure group array2 to the second disk array (files ARRAY2_DISK1 and ARRAY2_DISK2), ASM is instructed to mirror across the two disk arrays. It will automatically stripe the data within each disk array.

```
SQL> CREATE DISKGROUP cooked_dg NORMAL REDUNDANCY
FAILGROUP array1
DISK
'C:\ORADATA\ARRAY1_DISK1' NAME array1_disk1,
'C:\ORADATA\ARRAY1_DISK2' NAME array1_disk2
FAILGROUP array2
DISK
'C:\ORADATA\ARRAY2_DISK1' NAME array2_disk1,
'C:\ORADATA\ARRAY2_DISK2' NAME array2_disk2;
Diskgroup created.
```

The disks that were formerly candidates are now members of a disk group:

```
SQL> SELECT path, header_status, library, total_mb, free_mb FROM v$asm_disk;
PATH                     HEADER_STATUS LIBRARY   TOTAL_MB   FREE_MB
----------------------   ------------- -------   ---------- ----------
C:\ORADATA\ARRAY1_DISK1  MEMBER        System         512       482
C:\ORADATA\ARRAY1_DISK2  MEMBER        System         512       489
C:\ORADATA\ARRAY2_DISK1  MEMBER        System         512       484
C:\ORADATA\ARRAY2_DISK2  MEMBER        System         512       487
```

As you can see by comparing the columns TOTAL_MB and FREE_MB, ASM uses quite a bit of space for internal purposes. The view V$ASM_DISKGROUP gives access to information on disk groups. If you have read the overview of hidden ASM parameters at the beginning of this chapter attentively, you will recognize the settings of two hidden parameters in the output below:

```
SQL> SELECT name, block_size, allocation_unit_size, state, type, total_mb,
usable_file_mb
FROM v$asm_diskgroup;
NAME       BLOCK_SIZE ALLOCATION_UNIT_SIZE STATE       TYPE   TOTAL_MB USABLE_FILE_MB
---------- ---------- -------------------- ----------- ------ ---------- --------------
COOKED_DG       4096              1048576 MOUNTED     NORMAL     2048            715
```

The value in column BLOCK_SIZE is derived from the parameter _ASM_BLKSIZE, while ALLOCATION_UNIT_SIZE is derived from _ASM_AUSIZE. You may now use DBCA to create a database in the disk group. Make sure you choose ASM storage for all data files.

Disk Failure Simulation

Chances are high that you have never had to deal with disk failure in an ASM environment. To prepare yourself for such a case, you may wish to use the environment set up in this chapter to simulate disk failure and gain experience with repairing an ASM setup. Disk failure may be simulated by placing cooked files on an external FireWire disk drive, USB disk drive or USB stick and pulling the cable to the disk or the stick. In a SAN environment, disk failure might by simulated by pulling cables, changing the zoning configuration, or logical unit number (LUN) access rights in a storage array. The term zoning is used to describe the configuration whereby a storage area network administrator separates a SAN into units and allocates storage to those units. Each disk or LUN in a SAN has a unique identification called worldwide number (WWN). If a WWN is made invisible to a system by changing the zoning configuration, neither ASM nor RDBMS instances will be able to use the LUN.

Source Code Depot

Table 6: Hidden Parameters Source Code Depot

File Name	Functionality
10g_hidden_parameters.html	Complete list of undocumented parameters in Oracle10g with default values and descriptions
11g_hidden_parameters.html	Complete list of undocumented parameters in Oracle11g with default values and descriptions
9i_hidden_parameters.html	Complete list of undocumented parameters in Oracle9i with default values and descriptions
hidden_parameters.sql	SELECT statement for retrieving all hidden parameters with their values and descriptions
hidden_parameter_value.sql	SELECT statement for retrieving the value of a single hidden parameter

Part II

Data Dictionary Base Tables

Chapter 3

Introduction to Data Dictionary Base Tables

Status: The script `sql.bsq`, which creates the tablespace SYSTEM and data dictionary base tables, is mentioned by a few manuals, e.g. *Oracle Database Security Guide 10g Release 2*. The section *Using LogMiner to Analyze Redo Log Files* in the *Oracle Database Utilities 10g Release 2* manual shows how creating database objects causes the execution of SQL statements against data dictionary base tables, such as `SYS.OBJ$` and `SYS.TAB$`.

Benefit: Knowing how to leverage data dictionary base tables allows a DBA to accomplish tasks that cannot be completed by accessing data dictionary views built on top of dictionary base tables. This includes scenarios where dictionary views lack required functionality as well as workarounds for defects in data dictionary views.

Data Dictionary

Each ORACLE database contains a data dictionary, which holds metadata, i.e. data about the database itself. The data dictionary objects are mostly clusters, tables, indexes, and large objects. The data dictionary is like the engine of a car. If it doesn't ignite (or rather bootstrap using `SYS.BOOTSTRAP$`), then all the other fancy features are quite useless. Traditionally, all data dictionary objects were stored in the tablespace SYSTEM. With the release of Oracle10g, the additional tablespace SYSAUX was introduced. This new tablespace contains the Workload Repository base tables (`WRI$*` and `WRH$*` tables) and other objects.

The data dictionary is created behind the scenes when the SQL statement CREATE DATABASE is executed. It is created by running the script `$ORACLE_HOME/rdbms/admin/sql.bsq`. Except for some placeholders, `sql.bsq` is a regular SQL*Plus script. Oracle9i contains 341 data dictionary base tables, Oracle10g 712 and Oracle11g 839.

Database administrators and users seldom access the data dictionary base tables directly. Since the base tables are normalized and often rather cryptic, the data dictionary views with prefixes DBA_*, ALL_* and USER_* are provided for convenient access to database metadata. Some data dictionary views do not have one of these three prefixes (e.g.

AUDIT_ACTIONS). The well known script `catalog.sql` creates data dictionary views. By looking at view definitions in `catalog.sql`, it becomes apparent which base table column corresponds to which dictionary view column.

For optimum performance, data dictionary metadata are buffered in the dictionary cache. To further corroborate the saying that well designed ORACLE DBMS features have more than a single name, the dictionary cache is also known as the row cache. The term row cache stems from the fact that this cache contains individual rows instead of entire blocks like the buffer cache does. Both caches are in the SGA. The dictionary cache is part of the shared pool, to be precise.

The role DBA includes read only access to data dictionary base tables through the system privilege SELECT ANY DICTIONARY. This privilege should not be granted frivolously to non–DBA users. This is especially true for Oracle9*i* where the dictionary base table SYS.LINK$ contains unencrypted passwords of database links, whereas the dictionary view DBA_DB_LINKS, which is accessible through the role SELECT_CATALOG_ROLE, hides the passwords. Passwords for database links are encrypted during the upgrade process to Oracle10*g*. Table 7 lists some dictionary tables which are related to prominent database objects.

Table 7: Data Dictionary Base Tables

Object	*Data Dictionary Base Table*	*Associated DBA_ * View(s)*
Clusters	CLU$	DBA_CLUSTERS, DBA_SEGMENTS
Database links	LINK$	DBA_DB_LINKS
Data files	FILE$	DBA_DATA_FILES, DBA_FREE_SPACE
Free extents	FET$	DBA_FREE_SPACE
Indexes	IND$	DBA_INDEXES
Large objects	LOB$	DBA_LOBS
Database objects	OBJ$	DBA_OBJECTS, DBA_LOBS, DBA_TYPES
Segments	SEG$	DBA_SEGMENTS
Tables	TAB$	DBA_TABLES, DBA_LOBS
Tablespaces	TS$	DBA_TABLESPACES, DBA_DATA_FILES, DBA_LOBS
Types	TYPE$	DBA_TYPES
Used extents	UET$	DBA_SEGMENTS, DBA_FREE_SPACE
Users	USER$	DBA_USERS, DBA_DB_LINKS, DBA_LOBS

Of course, dictionary base tables should never be changed directly, as this may easily cause database corruption. Querying dictionary base tables should be considered when data dictionary views do not expose enough information to solve a task. Sometimes dictionary views have bugs, which can be worked around by accessing the base tables directly. The script `sql.bsq` is well commented, such that reading this script may aid in understanding the structure of the dictionary base tables.

Large Objects and PCTVERSION vs. RETENTION

An example of leveraging direct access to dictionary base tables is an issue with the data dictionary view DBA_LOBS in Oracle9*i* and Oracle10*g* Release 1. The view fails to correctly report the versioning setting for LOB segments. Since Oracle9*i*, multi–version read consistency for LOBs is done either by setting aside a certain percentage of storage in the LOB segment (SQL keyword PCTVERSION; old approach) or with undo segments (SQL keyword RETENTION; new approach). The default for an Oracle9*i* database with automatic undo management is PCTVERSION. For an Oracle10*g* database in automatic undo management mode, the default is RETENTION. The setting of RETENTION cannot be specified with SQL syntax and is copied from the parameter UNDO_RETENTION. Here's an example that uses both approaches within a single table:

```
SQL> CREATE TABLE blog (
   username VARCHAR2(30),
   date_time DATE,
   text CLOB,
   img BLOB)
LOB (text) STORE AS blog_text_clob (RETENTION),
LOB (img) STORE AS blog_img_blob (PCTVERSION 10);
Table created.
SQL> SELECT pctversion, retention FROM user_lobs WHERE table_name='BLOG';
PCTVERSION  RETENTION
----------  ----------
        10      10800
        10      10800
SQL> SHOW PARAMETER undo_retention
NAME                               TYPE        VALUE
---------------------------------- ----------- ------------------------
undo_retention                     integer     10800
```

The result of querying the data dictionary view USER_LOBS is obviously incorrect. Looking at sql.bsq, there's unfortunately no comment that says which column is used to discern PCTVERSION and RETENTION, though it appears likely that the column FLAGS holds the required information. Here's the relevant excerpt of sql.bsq:

```
create table lob$                                 /* LOB information table */
( obj#           number not null,        /* object number of the base table */
  ...
  lobj#          number not null,          /* object number for the LOB */
  ...
  pctversion$    number not null,                    /* version pool */
  flags          number not null,                /* 0x0000 = CACHE */
                                         /* 0x0001 = NOCACHE LOGGING */
                                       /* 0x0002 = NOCACHE NOLOGGING */
  ...
  retention      number not null,        /* retention value = UNDO_RETENTION */
```

The PCTVERSION settings is stored in the column PCTVERSION$ and the RETENTION settings is stored in the column by the same name. Since LOB$.LOBJ# corresponds to DBA_OBJECTS.OBJECT_ID (see definition of DBA_LOBS in the file catalog.sql), we can query LOB$.FLAGS for our table by joining DBA_OBJECTS and LOB$:

```
SQL> SELECT object_name, flags
FROM sys.lob$ l, dba_objects o
WHERE l.lobj#=o.object_id
AND o.object_name IN ('BLOG_TEXT_CLOB', 'BLOG_IMG_BLOB');
OBJECT_NAME              FLAGS
-------------------- ----------
BLOG_IMG_BLOB               65
BLOG_TEXT_CLOB              97
```

There's the missing piece of information: if retention is specified, then LOB$.FLAGS, which is obviously a bit vector, is incremented by 32. So the bit which represents 2^5 is set if RETENTION is used. Leveraging our finding, we can write the following query, which uses the function BITAND to detect whether RETENTION is enabled:

```
SQL> SELECT owner, object_name,
CASE WHEN bitand(l.flags, 32)=0 THEN l.pctversion$ ELSE NULL END AS pctversion,
CASE WHEN bitand(l.flags, 32)=32 THEN l.retention ELSE NULL END AS retention
FROM sys.lob$ l, dba_objects o
WHERE l.lobj#=o.object_id
AND o.object_type='LOB'
AND OWNER='NDEBES';
OWNER                        OBJECT_NAME             PCTVERSION  RETENTION
---------------------------- ----------------------- ----------  ----------
NDEBES                       BLOG_IMG_BLOB                   10
NDEBES                       BLOG_TEXT_CLOB                              10800
```

The result of this query is in line with the CREATE TABLE statement executed earlier. Direct access to the dictionary base table SYS.LOB$ resolved the issue.

Chapter 4

IND$, V$OBJECT_USAGE and Index Monitoring

Status: The view V$OBJECT_USAGE is partially documented in the *Oracle Database Reference* manual and in the *Oracle Database Administrator's Guide*. It is undocumented that the view can only be queried for information on indexes within a single schema at a time while logged in as the user corresponding to the schema. Furthermore, it is undocumented that ALTER INDEX REBUILD switches off index monitoring and marks the index rebuilt as used. Last but not least, it is undocumented that there is a performance penalty for index monitoring, since it causes the execution of recursive SQL statements each time a monitored index is used. The *Oracle Database SQL Reference* manual incorrectly states that the MONITORING USAGE clause of ALTER INDEX may only be used on indexes owned by the user who executes ALTER INDEX. Additional undocumented aspects are that index usage monitoring cannot be used for primary key indexes of index organized tables (the error "ORA-25176: storage specification not permitted for primary key" would be raised) and domain indexes ("ORA-29871: invalid alter option for a domain index" would result).

Benefit: Provide a better view to the DBA by accessing data dictionary base tables. The enhanced view removes the restriction of merely retrieving information on indexes owned by the current user. It takes the effects of ALTER INDEX REBUILD into account and designates only those indexes as used, which were accessed by DML, and not an index rebuild operation.

Schema Restriction

V$OBJECT_USAGE is a misnomer for a view, which is based only on data dictionary tables in schema SYS and not on X$ fixed tables. The prefix V$ suggests that it is a dynamic performance view, but it is not. The lack of a column called "OWNER" might send you wondering how the DBA is supposed to find out which indexes in an application schema have been used. After all, views such as DBA_INDEXES and DBA_SEGMENTS have a column "OWNER" and dynamic performance views such as V$ACCESS and V$SEGMENT_STATISTICS also have a column called "OWNER", such that the DBA can view information for any schema he or she chooses. If you thought you as the almighty DBA could do the same with index usage information and retrieve information for other schemas than your own DBA schema—think again. Seriously, the only way to get index usage information for a foreign schema is to connect to that schema, which requires knowledge of the password or a temporary change of the password as discussed in Chapter 15. The temporary password change is risky, since any connect attempt by an application will fail while the changed password is in effect. When done properly, the window where this can happen is small, but nonetheless it may cause problems. ALTER SESSION SET CURRENT_SCHEMA (see Chapter 14) won't help, since it affects only the current schema name but not the logon user name.

Below are the column definitions of V$OBJECT_USAGE:

```
SQL> DESCRIBE v$object_usage
 Name                                      Null?    Type
 ----------------------------------------- -------- ------------
 INDEX_NAME                                NOT NULL VARCHAR2(30)
 TABLE_NAME                                NOT NULL VARCHAR2(30)
 MONITORING                                         VARCHAR2(3)
 USED                                               VARCHAR2(3)
 START_MONITORING                                   VARCHAR2(19)
 END_MONITORING                                     VARCHAR2(19)
```

Take a closer look at the columns START_MONITORING and END_MONITORING. Their data type is VARCHAR2. I think I vaguely remember that Oracle Corp. recommends using DATE columns and not VARCHAR2 to store date and time information. Well, maybe the design concept for this view was approved on April Fools' Day. Let's have a look at the view's definition:

```
SQL> SET LONG 0815
SQL> SELECT text FROM dba_views WHERE owner='SYS' and
view_name='V$OBJECT_USAGE';
TEXT
------------------------------------------------------------
select io.name, t.name,
       decode(bitand(i.flags, 65536), 0, 'NO', 'YES'),
       decode(bitand(ou.flags, 1), 0, 'NO', 'YES'),
       ou.start_monitoring,
       ou.end_monitoring
from sys.obj$ io, sys.obj$ t, sys.ind$ i, sys.object_usage ou
where io.owner# = userenv('SCHEMAID')
  and i.obj# = ou.obj#
  and io.obj# = ou.obj#
  and t.obj# = i.bo#
```

There's the culprit. The view uses the undocumented parameter SCHEMAID in a call of the function USERENV. Called in this way, it returns the numeric user identification in the same way as the query SELECT user_id FROM all_users WHERE username=user would. The numeric identifier is used to filter SYS.OBJ$, the data dictionary base table underlying views such as DBA_OBJECTS. As a consequence, a DBA cannot retrieve information on indexes in foreign schemas.

Index Usage Monitoring Case Study

We will use the sample schema HR (see *Oracle Database Sample Schemas* manual) as our playground for the case study. First, I will enable index usage monitoring on all indexes in schema HR. For this purpose, the source code depot contains the function MONITOR_SCHEMA_INDEXES (file monitor_schema_indexes.sql), which may be used to switch index usage monitoring on all indexes in a schema on or off. Before proceeding, I will acquaint the reader with this function.

Function MONITOR_SCHEMA_INDEXES

The syntax of function MONITOR_SCHEMA_INDEXES is:

```
FUNCTION site_sys.monitor_schema_indexes (
   ownname VARCHAR2 DEFAULT NULL,
```

```
     failed_counter OUT NUMBER,
     monitoring BOOLEAN DEFAULT TRUE
) RETURN INTEGER AUTHID CURRENT_USER;
```

Parameters

Parameter	Description
ownname	Schema name on which to operate. If NULL, the current schema is used.
failed_counter	Returns the number of times an ALTER INDEX statement failed due to "ORA-00054 resource busy and acquire with NOWAIT specified". This happens when another session holds an incompatible lock on the base table of an index, such as when a transaction on the table is open.
monitoring	Used to switch monitoring on (TRUE) or off (FALSE)

Usage Notes

The function returns the number of indexes that were successfully altered. If the value of FAILED_COUNTER is larger than zero, it is best to wait until open transactions have completed and to rerun the procedure until FAILED_COUNTER=0 is returned, i.e. no objects to be altered remain.

Examples

Switch on index monitoring on all indexes in schema SH:

```
SQL> VARIABLE success_counter NUMBER
SQL> VARIABLE failed_counter NUMBER
SQL> EXEC :success_counter:=site_sys.monitor_schema_indexes(ownname=>'SH',
failed_counter=>:failed_counter);
```

Switch off index monitoring on all indexes in the current schema:

```
SQL> EXEC :success_counter:=site_sys.monitor_schema_indexes(
failed_counter=>:failed_counter, monitoring=>false);
```

Enabling Index Monitoring on Schema HR

To enable index usage monitoring on all indexes in schema HR, connect as user HR and run SITE_SYS.MONITOR_SCHEMA_INDEXES. Before doing so, you may wish to query V$OBJECT_USAGE to confirm that none of the indexes in schema HR have ever been monitored:

```
SQL> CONNECT hr/secret
SQL> SELECT * FROM v$object_usage;
no rows selected
SQL> VARIABLE success_counter NUMBER
SQL> VARIABLE failed_counter NUMBER
SQL> SET AUTOPRINT ON
SQL> EXEC :success_counter:=site_sys.monitor_schema_indexes(
failed_counter=>:failed_counter);
PL/SQL procedure successfully completed.
FAILED_COUNTER
--------------
             0
SUCCESS_COUNTER
---------------
            18
SQL> SELECT table_name, index_name, monitoring, used, start_monitoring, end_monitoring
FROM v$object_usage ORDER BY 1, 2;
TABLE_NAME   INDEX_NAME          MONITORING USED START_MONITORING     END_MONITORING
-----------  ------------------- ---------- ---- -------------------- ---------------
DEPARTMENTS  DEPT_ID_PK          YES        NO   10/04/2007 17:21:54
DEPARTMENTS  DEPT_LOCATION_IX    YES        NO   10/04/2007 17:21:55
```

```
EMPLOYEES    EMP_DEPARTMENT_IX  YES        NO   10/04/2007 17:21:55
EMPLOYEES    EMP_EMAIL_UK       YES        NO   10/04/2007 17:21:55
EMPLOYEES    EMP_EMP_ID_PK      YES        NO   10/04/2007 17:21:55
EMPLOYEES    EMP_JOB_IX         YES        NO   10/04/2007 17:21:55
EMPLOYEES    EMP_MANAGER_IX     YES        NO   10/04/2007 17:21:55
EMPLOYEES    EMP_NAME_IX        YES        NO   10/04/2007 17:21:55
...
```

The SQL*Plus setting SET AUTOTRACE TRACEONLY EXPLAIN tells SQL*Plus to merely run EXPLAIN PLAN on the statements entered, without actually executing them or fetching any rows in case of a SELECT statement. May I ask the reader to cast a vote: Will EXPLAIN PLAN mark indexes indicated by a plan as used, or is it necessary to actually access an index by fetching rows? Please cast your vote before you read on.

```
SQL> SET AUTOTRACE TRACEONLY EXPLAIN
SQL> SELECT emp.last_name, emp.first_name, d.department_name
FROM hr.employees emp, hr.departments d
WHERE emp.department_id=d.department_id
AND d.department_name='Sales';
Execution Plan
-----------------------------------------------------------
Plan hash value: 2912831499
---------------------------------------------------------------------------------
| Id | Operation                    | Name            | Rows | Bytes | Cost (%CPU)|
---------------------------------------------------------------------------------
|  0 | SELECT STATEMENT             |                 |   10 |   340 |    4   (0)|
|  1 |  TABLE ACCESS BY INDEX ROWID | EMPLOYEES       |   10 |   180 |    1   (0)|
|  2 |   NESTED LOOPS               |                 |   10 |   340 |    4   (0)|
|* 3 |    TABLE ACCESS FULL         | DEPARTMENTS     |    1 |    16 |    3   (0)|
|* 4 |    INDEX RANGE SCAN          | EMP_DEPARTMENT_IX |  10 |      |    0   (0)|
---------------------------------------------------------------------------------

Predicate Information (identified by operation id):
-----------------------------------------------------
   3 - filter("D"."DEPARTMENT_NAME"='Sales')
   4 - access("EMP"."DEPARTMENT_ID"="D"."DEPARTMENT_ID")
```

The execution plan[1] indicates that the index EMP_DEPARTMENT_IX would be used if the query were executed. Let's take a look at V$OBJECT_USAGE:

```
SQL> SELECT table_name, index_name, monitoring, used, start_monitoring, end_monitoring
FROM v$object_usage
WHERE table_name IN ('EMPLOYEES', 'DEPARTMENTS');
TABLE_NAME   INDEX_NAME         MONITORING USED START_MONITORING     END_MONITORING
-----------  -----------------  ---------- ---- -------------------- --------------
DEPARTMENTS  DEPT_ID_PK         YES        NO   10/04/2007 17:21:54
DEPARTMENTS  DEPT_LOCATION_IX   YES        NO   10/04/2007 17:21:55
EMPLOYEES    EMP_DEPARTMENT_IX  YES        YES  10/04/2007 17:21:55
EMPLOYEES    EMP_EMAIL_UK       YES        NO   10/04/2007 17:21:55
...
```

The index EMP_DEPARTMENT_IX is indeed marked as used (column USED=YES), even though merely EXPLAIN PLAN was executed.

Index Rebuild

It is undocumented that an index rebuild affects V$OBJECT_USAGE. It sets V$OBJECT_USAGE.USED=YES and V$OBJECT_USAGE.MONITORING=NO, i.e. it terminates index monitoring:

```
SQL> ALTER INDEX dept_id_pk REBUILD;
Index altered.
SQL> SELECT * FROM v$object_usage WHERE table_name='DEPARTMENTS';
```

---

1. To improve legibility, the column TIME was omitted from the execution plan.

```
INDEX_NAME        TABLE_NAME   MONITORING USED START_MONITORING     END_MONITORING
----------------  -----------  ---------- ---- -------------------  ---------------
DEPT_ID_PK        DEPARTMENTS  NO          YES 10/04/2007 17:21:54
DEPT_LOCATION_IX  DEPARTMENTS  YES         NO  10/04/2007 17:21:55
```

This behavior is a bit surprising, since an index rebuild is not the kind of index usage a DBA would be interested in. Other DDL statements, such as ANALYZE INDEX index_name VALIDATE STRUCTURE or ANALYZE TABLE table_name VALIDATE STRUCTURE CASCADE have no influence on the index status in V$OBJECT_USAGE, although they do access index segments.

Indexes Used by DML

Finding out which indexes were used by DML statements is what really counts. Several factors make this more intricate than one might suspect. We haven't yet considered the case where index monitoring on an index that was marked as used is switched off. By calling MONITOR_SCHEMA_INDEXES with the parameter MONITORING set to FALSE, we switch off index monitoring for all indexes in schema HR.

```
SQL> EXEC :success_counter:=site_sys.monitor_schema_indexes(monitoring=>false,
failed_counter=>:failed_counter);
FAILED_COUNTER
--------------
             0
SUCCESS_COUNTER
---------------
            17
```

Since the index rebuild already switched off monitoring on one of the indexes and the function only considers indexes which do not yet have the desired status, the value of the variable SUCCESS_COUNTER is 17. Let's take a look at the contents of V$OBJECT_USAGE:

```
SQL> SELECT table_name, index_name, monitoring, used, start_monitoring, end_monitoring
FROM v$object_usage
WHERE table_name IN ('EMPLOYEES', 'DEPARTMENTS');
TABLE_NAME  INDEX_NAME        MONITORING USED START_MONITORING     END_MONITORING
----------- ----------------- ---------- ---- -------------------  -------------------
DEPARTMENTS DEPT_ID_PK        NO          YES 10/04/2007 17:21:54
DEPARTMENTS DEPT_LOCATION_IX  NO          NO  10/04/2007 17:21:55  10/04/2007 18:17:58
EMPLOYEES   EMP_DEPARTMENT_IX NO          YES 10/04/2007 17:21:55  10/04/2007 18:17:58
EMPLOYEES   EMP_EMAIL_UK      NO          NO  10/04/2007 17:21:55  10/04/2007 18:17:58
...
```

What we're seeing now is that as expected MONITORING=NO for all indexes. Note the subtle difference between the index DEPT_ID_PK, which had index monitoring switched off due to an ALTER INDEX REBUILD, and the index EMP_DEPARTMENT_IX, which had index monitoring switched off with ALTER INDEX index_name NOMONITORING by the function MONITOR_SCHEMA_INDEXES. The former has END_MONITORING set to NULL, whereas the latter has the point in time when index monitoring was switched off. This is a clue for distinguishing between an index rebuild and a genuine index usage due to DML.

Taking all of the findings into account, three cases have to be considered:

- Rebuilt indexes are marked as used and monitoring on them is switched off, while leaving the value END_MONITORING set to NULL. Since we are only interested in index usage due to DML, we need to exclude this case.
- Indexes which were used by DML retain the settings of MONITORING (YES) and END_MONITORING (NULL).
- Indexes on which monitoring was switched off after they have been used by DML retain the setting MONITORING=YES, but have an actual timestamp instead of NULL in END_MONITORING

The following query retrieves only indexes which were marked as used by DML, but not by an index rebuild:

```
SQL> SELECT * FROM v$object_usage
WHERE (monitoring='YES' AND used='YES') OR
(used='YES' AND end_monitoring IS NOT NULL)
ORDER BY index_name;
```

INDEX_NAME	TABLE_NAME	MONITORING	USED	START_MONITORING	END_MONITORING
EMP_DEPARTMENT_IX	EMPLOYEES	NO	YES	10/04/2007 17:21:55	10/04/2007 18:17:58

This essentially solves the issue of index monitoring, apart from the annoyance that a DBA cannot retrieve information on foreign schemas, except by connecting with the user name that is identical to the schema name. This is the time for data dictionary base tables to make their appearance on stage. After dwelling on the definition of V$OBJECT_USAGE in the file catalog.sql for a moment, it is not hard to write an enhanced version of the view, which deserves the name DBA_INDEX_USAGE, i.e. a view that allows access to index usage information for all indexes in a database, not just within the current schema. Since I don't intend to cause confusion by imitating Oracle Corporation's naming convention, I will simply call the view INDEX_USAGE. The script view_index_usage.sql to create it is reproduced below. It adds the column OWNER, which it retrieves from SYS.USER$. USER$ has to be joined with OBJ$ using OBJ$.OWNER#=USER$.USER# to retrieve the names of index owners. I'm creating database objects in schema SITE_SYS to prevent interference with the data dictionary in schema SYS:

```
SQL> CONNECT / AS SYSDBA
SQL> GRANT SELECT ON obj$ TO site_sys WITH GRANT OPTION;
SQL> GRANT SELECT ON ind$ TO site_sys WITH GRANT OPTION;
SQL> GRANT SELECT ON object_usage TO site_sys WITH GRANT OPTION;
SQL> GRANT SELECT ON user$ TO site_sys WITH GRANT OPTION;
SQL> CREATE OR REPLACE VIEW site_sys.index_usage
    (owner,
     INDEX_NAME,
     TABLE_NAME,
     MONITORING,
     USED,
     START_MONITORING,
     END_MONITORING)
AS
SELECT u.name, io.name index_name, t.name table_name,
       decode(bitand(i.flags, 65536), 0, 'NO', 'YES'),
       decode(bitand(ou.flags, 1), 0, 'NO', 'YES'),
       ou.start_monitoring,
       ou.end_monitoring
FROM sys.obj$ io, sys.obj$ t, sys.ind$ i, sys.user$ u, sys.object_usage ou
WHERE io.owner# = t.owner#
AND io.owner# = u.user#
AND i.obj# = ou.obj#
AND io.obj# = ou.obj#
AND t.obj# = i.bo#;
-- have to grant to public, to allow non DBAs access to the view
-- used by function MONITOR_SCHEMA_INDEXES, which runs with AUTHID CURRENT_USER
GRANT SELECT ON site_sys.index_usage TO PUBLIC;
```

Still connected as SYS or any other user with the required privileges, we may now retrieve index usage information on any foreign schema such as HR:

```
SQL> SELECT owner, table_name, index_name, monitoring, used
FROM site_sys.index_usage
WHERE owner='HR'
AND ((monitoring='YES' AND used='YES')
OR (used='YES' AND end_monitoring IS NOT NULL));
```

OWNER	TABLE_NAME	INDEX_NAME	MONITORING	USED
HR	EMPLOYEES	EMP_DEPARTMENT_IX	NO	YES

Lessons Learned

This wraps up the case study on index monitoring. With the function MONITOR_SCHEMA_INDEXES and the view INDEX_USAGE, a DBA has the required tools to monitor index usage in any schema. Indexes which were not used over a period of time that covers the complete code paths of applications using a database may be dropped to reduce index maintenance costs. The issue here lies with complete code path. You may never be certain that the entire code path of an application has been exercised. As a consequence, it is best to use the functionality in the early stages of development and test instead of taking the risk to drop an index in a production database, that later turns out to be required for end of business year processing.

A less intrusive way of finding used indexes, which does not cause a performance penalty due to recursive SQL, is using Statspack at level 6 or higher (see Chapter 25). However, this approach is significantly more risky, since Statspack samples SQL statements and their execution plans, such that you may not have any data on the usage of certain indexes, simply since the Statspack snapshots were taken at a time when no execution plans indicating these indexes were cached in the shared pool.

Source Code Depot

Table 8: Index Monitoring Source Code Depot

File Name	*Functionality*
`monitor_schema_indexes.sql`	Contains function `MONITOR_SCHEMA_INDEXES` for switching index usage monitoring on all indexes in a schema on or off. Calls the script `view_index_usage.sql` to create the view `INDEX_USAGE`, since it is used by the function.
`view_index_usage.sql`	Contains the view `INDEX_USAGE` for accessing index usage information for an entire database instead of merely for the current schema as with `V$OBJECT_USAGE`.

Part III

Events

Chapter 5

Event 10027 and Deadlock Diagnosis

Status: Event 10027 is undocumented.

Benefit: A trace file is written whenever an ORACLE instance detects a deadlock and signals the error "ORA-00060 deadlock detected while waiting for resource". Event 10027 gives the DBA control over the amount and type of diagnostic information generated.

Deadlocks

A deadlock occurs when two or more sessions hold locks and another lock request, which would result in a circular chain of locks, is issued. If this new lock request were granted, the sessions would deadlock and none of them would ever finish. Hence, the ORACLE DBMS detects circular chains pertaining to interdependent locks, signals ORA-00060, and rolls back one of the sessions involved in the would–be deadlock. Figure 4 depicts a deadlock situation among two database sessions. Session 1 locks the row with EMPLOYEE_ID=182 at time t_1. At time t_2, session 2 locks the row with EMPLOYEE_ID=193. At t_3, session 1 requests a lock on the row with EMPLOYEE_ID=193, which is already locked by session 2. Hence, session 1 has to wait on the event *enq: TX - row lock contention*. At t_4, session 2 requests a lock on the row that session 1 locked at t_1. Since granting this lock would lead to a circular chain, the DBMS signals "ORA-00060: deadlock detected while waiting for resource" at t_5. The UPDATE statement executed by session 1 at t_3 is rolled back. At this point, session 2 is still waiting for the lock on the row with EMPLOYEE_ID=182, which session 1 continues to hold. Session 1 should ROLLBACK in response to ORA-00060, releasing all its locks and allowing session 2 to complete the update of employee 182.

To avoid deadlocks, rows need to be locked in the same order by all database sessions. If this is not feasible, deadlocks and the overhead associated with writing trace files may be avoided by executing SELECT FOR UPDATE NOWAIT prior to an UPDATE. If this returns ORA-00054, then the session needs to roll back and reattempt the entire transac-

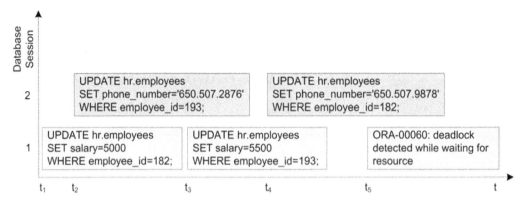

Figure 4: Deadlock Detection

tion. The ROLLBACK will allow other transactions to complete. The downside of this approach is the additional processing. Below is an example, which is tailored to the scenario presented above:

```
SQL> SELECT rowid FROM hr.employees WHERE employee_id=182 FOR UPDATE NOWAIT;
SELECT rowid FROM hr.employees WHERE employee_id=182 FOR UPDATE NOWAIT
       *
ERROR at line 1:
ORA-00054: resource busy and acquire with NOWAIT specified
SQL> ROLLBACK;
Rollback complete.
SQL> SELECT rowid FROM hr.employees WHERE employee_id=182 FOR UPDATE NOWAIT;
ROWID
------------------
AAADNLAAEAAAEi1ABb
SQL> UPDATE hr.employees SET phone_number='650.507.9878'
WHERE rowid='AAADNLAAEAAAEi1ABb';
1 row updated.
```

Event 10027

Event 10027 gives the DBA control over the amount and type of diagnostic information generated in response to ORA-00060. At default settings, an ORA-00060 trace file contains cached cursors, a deadlock graph, process state, current SQL statements of the sessions involved, and session wait history (in Oracle10*g* and subsequent releases). Except for the current SQL statements and the deadlock graph, all the information pertains merely to the session which received ORA-00060. Event 10027 may be used to achieve two oppositional goals:

- Reduce the volume of trace information generated in response to ORA-00060, e.g. when there is no way to fix the issue.
- Augment the trace information with a system state dump or call stack, hoping to find the root cause of the deadlocks.

The smallest amount of trace information is written at level 1. At this level, the trace file merely contains a deadlock graph and the current SQL statements of the sessions involved. An example ORA-00060 trace file with event 10027 at level 1 is below:

```
*** ACTION NAME:() 2007-09-08 05:34:52.373
*** MODULE NAME:(SQL*Plus) 2007-09-08 05:34:52.373
*** SERVICE NAME:(SYS$USERS) 2007-09-08 05:34:52.373
*** SESSION ID:(159.5273) 2007-09-08 05:34:52.372
DEADLOCK DETECTED ( ORA-00060 )
[Transaction Deadlock]
The following deadlock is not an ORACLE error. It is a
deadlock due to user error in the design of an application
or from issuing incorrect ad-hoc SQL. The following
```

```
information may aid in determining the deadlock:
Deadlock graph:
                      ---------Blocker(s)--------  ---------Waiter(s)---------
Resource Name         process session holds waits  process session holds waits
TX-0007000f-000002a4     20       159    X            16      145          X
TX-000a0013-000002a3     16       145    X            20      159          X
session 159: DID 0001-0014-0000004B    session 145: DID 0001-0010-0000004E
session 145: DID 0001-0010-0000004E    session 159: DID 0001-0014-0000004B
Rows waited on:
Session 145: obj - rowid = 0000334B - AAADNLAAEAAAEi1ABb
  (dictionary objn - 13131, file - 4, block - 18613, slot - 91)
Session 159: obj - rowid = 0000334B - AAADNLAAEAAAEi2AAE
  (dictionary objn - 13131, file - 4, block - 18614, slot - 4)
Information on the OTHER waiting sessions:
Session 145:
  pid=16 serial=1880 audsid=210018 user: 34/NDEBES
  O/S info: user: oracle, term: pts/5, ospid: 24607, machine: dbserver1.oradbpro.com
          program: sqlplus@dbserver1.oradbpro.com (TNS V1-V3)
  application name: SQL*Plus, hash value=3669949024
  Current SQL Statement:
  UPDATE hr.employees SET phone_number='650.507.9878' WHERE employee_id=182
End of information on OTHER waiting sessions.
Current SQL statement for this session:
UPDATE hr.employees SET salary=5500 WHERE employee_id=193
```

The system state dump included in the trace file at event level 2 may aid in diagnosing the cause of a deadlock. A system state dump includes cached SQL and wait history of all sessions, not just the current SQL statements of the sessions involved in the deadlock. Thus, it may be possible to reconstruct the scenario that lead to a deadlock.

The call stack trace included in the trace file at event level 4 is less useful. It shows which C function an ORACLE server process was in at the time when a deadlock was detected. If you encounter deadlocks in an application for the first time, it is a good idea to temporarily set event 10027 at level 2 with ALTER SYSTEM as below:

```
SQL> ALTER SYSTEM SET EVENTS '10027 trace name context forever, level 2';
```

This will increase your chances of finding the root cause of deadlocks. If the setting shall persist across instance start-ups, you need to use the initialization parameter EVENT:

```
EVENT="10027 trace name context forever, level 2"
```

As soon as you have obtained enough system state dumps for further analysis, you may reduce the event level to 1. Since locks are released after an ORA-00060 trace file is written, event 10027 at level 1 makes sure that sessions can respond more quickly. In my testing, I observed that trace files at this level were one hundred times smaller than trace files with default settings. The supported event levels and the trace information included at each level is summarized in Table 9.

Table 9: Event 10027 and Trace File Contents

Contents/Level	Default	Level 1	Level 2	Level 4
Cached cursors	yes	no	yes	yes
Call stack trace	no	no	no	yes
Deadlock graph	yes	yes	yes	yes
Process state	yes	no	yes	yes
SQL statements	yes	yes	yes, for all sessions[a]	yes
Session wait history	yes	no	yes, for all sessions	yes
System state	no	no	yes	no

a. SQL statements for all sessions are in the system state dump section.

Chapter 6

Event 10046 and Extended SQL Trace

Status: It is documented in *Oracle Database Performance Tuning Guide 10g Release 2* that event 10046 at level 8 may be used to enable logging of wait events to a SQL trace file. Additional supported event levels are undocumented.

Benefit: Event 10046 is ideal for enabling extended SQL trace. When combined with ALTER SESSION, event 10046 is the only way to enable extended SQL trace that does not require DBA or SYSDBA privileges. This event is useful for building self–tracing capability into applications.

Event 10046

Event 10046 is used in the context of performance diagnosis in several places in this book. Part VIII contains numerous examples of leveraging event 10046. This chapter is intended as a brief reference for the event and its levels. The event is most useful at session and process level. Examples of using the event at session level are in Chapter 13. Please refer to Chapter 37 for instances of using the event at process level.

Table 10: SQL Trace Levels

SQL Trace Level	Database Calls	Bind Variable Values	Wait Events
1	yes	no	no
4	yes	yes	no
8	yes	no	yes
12	yes	yes	yes

The supported event levels are detailed in Table 10. The term *database call* refers to the parse, execute, and fetch stages of executing SQL statements. The following example illustrates how to use event 10046 to trace SQL statements, bind variables, and wait events. The trace file is from Oracle11g Release 1. Note the new Oracle11g parameter sqlid, which corresponds to V$SQL.SQL_ID, in the PARSING IN CURSOR entry:

```
SQL> ALTER SESSION SET EVENTS '10046 trace name context forever, level 12';
Session altered.
SQL> VARIABLE id NUMBER
SQL> INSERT INTO customer(id, name, phone) VALUES (customer_id_seq.nextval, '&name',
'&phone') RETURNING id INTO :id;
Enter value for name: Deevers
Enter value for phone: +1 310 45678923
1 row created.
```

Excerpts of the resulting SQL trace file are reproduced below:

```
*** ACTION NAME:() 2007-11-28 22:02:15.625
*** MODULE NAME:(SQL*Plus) 2007-11-28 22:02:15.625
*** SERVICE NAME:(SYS$USERS) 2007-11-28 22:02:15.625
*** SESSION ID:(32.171) 2007-11-28 22:02:15.625
...
WAIT #6: nam='SQL*Net message to client' ela= 6 driver id=1111838976 #bytes=1 p3=0
obj#=15919 tim=230939271782
*** 2007-11-30 09:45:33.828
WAIT #6: nam='SQL*Net message from client' ela= 235333094 driver id=1111838976 #bytes=1
p3=0 obj#=15919 tim=231174604922
=====================
PARSING IN CURSOR #4 len=122 dep=0 uid=32 oct=2 lid=32 tim=231174605324 hv=798092392
ad='6b59f600' sqlid='96032xwrt3v38'
INSERT INTO customer(id, name, phone) VALUES (customer_id_seq.nextval, 'Deevers', '+1
310 45678923') RETURNING id INTO :id
END OF STMT
PARSE #4:c=0,e=111,p=0,cr=0,cu=0,mis=0,r=0,dep=0,og=1,tim=231174605317
BINDS #4:
 Bind#0
  oacdty=02 mxl=22(22) mxlc=00 mal=00 scl=00 pre=00
  oacflg=03 fl2=1000000 frm=00 csi=00 siz=24 off=0
  kxsbbbfp=07a7e7a0  bln=22  avl=04  flg=05
  value=370011
WAIT #4: nam='SQL*Net message to client' ela= 7 driver id=1111838976 #bytes=1 p3=0
obj#=15919 tim=231174606084
EXEC #4:c=15625,e=673,p=0,cr=0,cu=3,mis=0,r=1,dep=0,og=1,tim=231174606139
STAT #4 id=1 cnt=0 pid=0 pos=1 obj=0 op='LOAD TABLE CONVENTIONAL  (cr=0 pr=0 pw=0
time=0 us)'
STAT #4 id=2 cnt=1 pid=1 pos=1 obj=15920 op='SEQUENCE  CUSTOMER_ID_SEQ (cr=0 pr=0 pw=0
time=0 us)'
*** 2007-11-30 09:45:39.015
WAIT #4: nam='SQL*Net message from client' ela= 5179787 driver id=1111838976 #bytes=1
p3=0 obj#=15919 tim=231179786085
```

For details on how to interpret extended SQL trace files and how to automatically generate a resource profile for performance diagnosis, please refer to Part VIII.

Chapter 7

Event 10053 and the Cost Based Optimizer

Status: Event 10053 is undocumented.

Benefit: There is no better way to comprehend decisions and cost calculations of the cost based optimizer (CBO) than to read an optimizer trace generated with event 10053. Oracle Support will request such a trace file if you intend to file a technical assistance request against the optimizer.

Event 10053

Essentially, the CBO is a mathematical model for calculating estimates of SQL statement response times. It receives initialization parameters, object statistics pertaining to tables and indexes as well as system statistics, which represent the capabilities of the hardware, as input. According to *Oracle9i Database Performance Tuning Guide and Reference Release 2*, the cost calculation formula for serial execution used by the optimizer is:

$$\frac{\text{SRds} \cdot \text{sreadtim} + \text{MRds} \cdot \text{mreadtim} + \dfrac{\text{CPU Cycles}}{\text{cpuspeed}}}{\text{sreadtim}}$$

Thus, the unit of cost is the time it takes to complete a single block read. Table 11 explains the placeholders used in the formula. In case you are familiar with system statistics gathering using DBMS_STATS.GATHER_SYSTEM_STATS, the three placeholders sreadtim, mreadtim and cpuspeed will be familiar. All three are part of so called workload statistics, which are derived from measurements of the system on which the DBMS runs. The documented interfaces for setting these parameters (and a few more) are the packaged procedures DBMS_STATS.SET_SYSTEM_STATS and DBMS_STATS.IMPORT_SYSTEM_STATS. The current settings may be retrieved with a call to the packaged procedure DBMS_STATS.GET_SYSTEM_STATS. System statistics were optional in Oracle9i. Oracle10g uses so called *nowork-*

load statistics if actual measurements have not been imported into the data dictionary table SYS.AUX_STATS$ by one of the interfaces cited above.

Table 11: CBO Cost Calculation Placeholders

Placeholder	Meaning
SRds	Single block reads
sreadtim	Single block read time
MRds	Multi block reads
mreadtim	Multi block read time, i.e. the time it takes for a multi block read request to complete. The number of blocks requested in a multi block read request is limited by the parameter DB_FILE_MULTIBLOCK_READ_COUNT
CPU Cycles	Number of CPU cycles required to execute a statement
cpuspeed	Number of instructions per second[a]

a. Event 10053 trace files from Oracle10*g* Release 2 contain lines such as the one below:
   CPUSPEED: 839 millions instructions/sec
   This seems to indicate that the DBMS measures CPU speed by calculating how many instructions complete per second. The kind of instruction used for this purpose is undocumented.

The query result below is from a system where all workload statistics parameters, except SLAVETHR, the parallel execution slave throughput, were set:

```
SQL> SELECT * FROM sys.aux_stats$;
SNAME           PNAME          PVAL1 PVAL2
-------------  ----------  -------  ----------------
SYSSTATS_INFO STATUS                 COMPLETED
SYSSTATS_INFO DSTART                 11-29-2007 13:49
SYSSTATS_INFO DSTOP                  11-29-2007 13:49
SYSSTATS_INFO FLAGS           1
SYSSTATS_MAIN CPUSPEEDNW 841.336
SYSSTATS_MAIN IOSEEKTIM      10
SYSSTATS_MAIN IOTFRSPEED   4096
SYSSTATS_MAIN SREADTIM        4
SYSSTATS_MAIN MREADTIM       10
SYSSTATS_MAIN CPUSPEED      839
SYSSTATS_MAIN MBRC           14
SYSSTATS_MAIN MAXTHR     8388608
SYSSTATS_MAIN SLAVETHR
```

Workload parameters are reproduced in bold. MBRC is the actual multi block read count derived from statistics collected in X$ fixed tables. MBRC is limited by the parameter DB_FILE_MULTIBLOCK_READ_COUNT and is usually somewhat lower than this parameter. DB_FILE_MULTIBLOCK_READ_COUNT had the value 16 on the system used for the example and the actual MBRC was 14. MAXTHR is the maximum I/O throughput. SLAVETHR is the average parallel execution slave I/O throughput.

There are three noworkload statistics parameters:

- CPUSPEEDNW (noworkload CPU speed)
- IOSEEKTIM (I/O seek time in ms)
- IOTFRSPEED (I/O transfer speed in KB/s)

The unit of CPU speed is not MHz, but rather some undocumented measure proprietary to Oracle Corp. Clearly, the output of the CBO is an execution plan. But this is not the only output from the optimizer. Additionally, it provides the following items:

- the estimated number of rows in the statement's results set

- the estimated number of bytes processed
- query block names
- filter predicates
- access predicates
- column projection information

A subset of the additional information may also be retrieved with DBMS_XPLAN.DISPLAY_CURSOR. An Oracle10g 10053 trace file contains a full set of hints, which describe the chosen execution plan with the lowest cost. These hints include query block names and are an ideal basis for testing alternative plans with hints.

Trace File Contents

A 10053 trace file is a protocol of the optimizer's inputs, calculations, and outputs. The correct event level to use is 1. Higher levels do not produce additional output. Be warned that the trace file contents as well as the costing formulas used by the CBO are subject to change without notice. The main sections of an Oracle10g Release 2 trace file are:

- query blocks and object identifiers (DBA_OBJECTS.OBJECT_ID) of the tables involved in an optimized statement
- query transformations considered (predicate move–around, subquery unnesting, etc.)
- legend (abbreviations used)
- results of bind variable peeking
- optimizer parameters (documented and hidden)
- system statistics (workload or noworkload)
- object statistics for tables and indexes
- single table access path and cost for each table
- list of join orders and cost of each
- execution plan
- predicate information
- a full set of hints including query block names, which would be used to define a stored outline

If, after enabling event 10053, you do not find the aforementioned sections in a trace file, the CBO may have used a cached execution plan instead of optimizing a statement from scratch. You can force a cursor miss by inserting a comment into the statement.

Case Study

In the subsequent section, we will generate a 10053 trace file for a five–way join on tables of the sample schema HR:

```
SQL> VARIABLE loc VARCHAR2(30)
SQL> EXEC :loc:='South San Francisco'
SQL> ALTER SESSION SET EVENTS '10053 trace name context forever, level 1';
SQL> SELECT emp.last_name, emp.first_name, j.job_title, d.department_name, l.city,
    l.state_province, l.postal_code, l.street_address, emp.email,
    emp.phone_number, emp.hire_date, emp.salary, mgr.last_name
FROM hr.employees emp, hr.employees mgr, hr.departments d, hr.locations l, hr.jobs j
WHERE l.city=:loc
AND emp.manager_id=mgr.employee_id
AND emp.department_id=d.department_id
AND d.location_id=l.location_id
AND emp.job_id=j.job_id;
SQL> ALTER SESSION SET EVENTS '10053 trace name context off';
```

The query used in the case study is available in the file hr_5way_join.sql in the source code depot. The trace file excerpts below are from Oracle10g Release 2.

Query Blocks and Object Identifiers

This section lists all the query blocks along with the tables in each. Since the query executed did not contain any sub-selects, there is but a single query block:

```
Registered qb: SEL$1 0x4aea6b4 (PARSER)
  signature (): qb_name=SEL$1 nbfros=5 flg=0
    fro(0): flg=4 objn=51905 hint_alias="D"@"SEL$1"
    fro(1): flg=4 objn=51910 hint_alias="EMP"@"SEL$1"
    fro(2): flg=4 objn=51908 hint_alias="J"@"SEL$1"
    fro(3): flg=4 objn=51900 hint_alias="L"@"SEL$1"
    fro(4): flg=4 objn=51910 hint_alias="MGR"@"SEL$1"
```

The object identifiers (objn) may be used to determine the owner(s) of the tables:

```
SQL> SELECT owner, object_name, object_type
FROM dba_objects WHERE object_id IN (51905, 51910);
OWNER OBJECT_NAME OBJECT_TYPE
----- ----------- -----------
HR    DEPARTMENTS TABLE
HR    EMPLOYEES   TABLE
```

Query Transformations Considered

The optimizer considers several query transformations. Note the SQL identifier "2ck90xfmsza4u" in the unparsed query subsection, which may be used to retrieve past execution plans for the statement with the packaged procedure DBMS_XPLAN.DISPLAY_AWR or Statspack (see Chapter 25).

```
***************************
Predicate Move-Around (PM)
***************************
PM: Considering predicate move-around in SEL$1 (#0).
PM:   Checking validity of predicate move-around in SEL$1 (#0).
CBQT: Validity checks failed for 2ck90xfmsza4u.
CVM: Considering view merge in query block SEL$1 (#0)
Query block (04AEA6B4) before join elimination:
SQL:******* UNPARSED QUERY IS *******
SELECT "EMP"."LAST_NAME" "LAST_NAME","EMP"."FIRST_NAME" "FIRST_NAME","J"."JOB_TITLE"
"JOB_TITLE","D"."DEPARTMENT_NAME" "DEPARTMENT_NAME","L"."CITY"
"CITY","L"."STATE_PROVINCE" "STATE_PROVINCE","L"."POSTAL_CODE"
"POSTAL_CODE","L"."STREET_ADDRESS" "STREET_ADDRESS","EMP"."EMAIL"
"EMAIL","EMP"."PHONE_NUMBER" "PHONE_NUMBER","EMP"."HIRE_DATE"
"HIRE_DATE","EMP"."SALARY" "SALARY","MGR"."LAST_NAME" "LAST_NAME" FROM
"HR"."EMPLOYEES" "EMP","HR"."EMPLOYEES" "MGR","HR"."DEPARTMENTS" "D","HR"."LOCATIONS"
"L","HR"."JOBS" "J" WHERE "L"."CITY"=:B1 AND "EMP"."MANAGER_ID"="MGR"."EMPLOYEE_ID" AND
"EMP"."DEPARTMENT_ID"="D"."DEPARTMENT_ID" AND "D"."LOCATION_ID"="L"."LOCATION_ID" AND
"EMP"."JOB_ID"="J"."JOB_ID"
Query block (04AEA6B4) unchanged
CBQT: Validity checks failed for 2ck90xfmsza4u.
***************
Subquery Unnest
***************
SU: Considering subquery unnesting in query block SEL$1 (#0)
**************************
Set-Join Conversion (SJC)
**************************
SJC: Considering set-join conversion in SEL$1 (#0).
***************************
Predicate Move-Around (PM)
***************************
PM: Considering predicate move-around in SEL$1 (#0).
PM:   Checking validity of predicate move-around in SEL$1 (#0).
PM:     PM bypassed: Outer query contains no views.
FPD: Considering simple filter push in SEL$1 (#0)
FPD:   Current where clause predicates in SEL$1 (#0) :
```

```
        "L"."CITY"=:B1 AND "EMP"."MANAGER_ID"="MGR"."EMPLOYEE_ID" AND
"EMP"."DEPARTMENT_ID"="D"."DEPARTMENT_ID" AND "D"."LOCATION_ID"="L"."LOCATION_ID" AND
"EMP"."JOB_ID"="J"."JOB_ID"
kkogcp: try to generate transitive predicate from check constraints for SEL$1 (#0)
constraint: "MGR"."SALARY">0
constraint: "EMP"."SALARY">0
predicates with check contraints: "L"."CITY"=:B1 AND
"EMP"."MANAGER_ID"="MGR"."EMPLOYEE_ID" AND "EMP"."DEPARTMENT_ID"="D"."DEPARTMENT_ID"
AND "D"."LOCATION_ID"="L"."LOCATION_ID" AND "EMP"."JOB_ID"="J"."JOB_ID" AND
"MGR"."SALARY">0 AND "EMP"."SALARY">0
after transitive predicate generation:
"L"."CITY"=:B1 AND "EMP"."MANAGER_ID"="MGR"."EMPLOYEE_ID" AND
"EMP"."DEPARTMENT_ID"="D"."DEPARTMENT_ID" AND "D"."LOCATION_ID"="L"."LOCATION_ID" AND
"EMP"."JOB_ID"="J"."JOB_ID" AND "MGR"."SALARY">0 AND "EMP"."SALARY">0
finally: "L"."CITY"=:B1 AND "EMP"."MANAGER_ID"="MGR"."EMPLOYEE_ID" AND
"EMP"."DEPARTMENT_ID"="D"."DEPARTMENT_ID" AND "D"."LOCATION_ID"="L"."LOCATION_ID" AND
"EMP"."JOB_ID"="J"."JOB_ID"
apadrv-start: call(in-use=744, alloc=0), compile(in-use=47988, alloc=0)
kkoqbc-start
            : call(in-use=756, alloc=0), compile(in-use=49312, alloc=0)
```

The optimizer retrieves check constraints from the data dictionary to generate additional predicates (AND "MGR"."SALARY">0 AND "EMP"."SALARY">0).

Legend

The legend section lists abbreviations used in the trace file:

```
Legend
The following abbreviations are used by optimizer trace.
CBQT - cost-based query transformation
JPPD - join predicate push-down
FPD - filter push-down
PM - predicate move-around
CVM - complex view merging
SPJ - select-project-join
SJC - set join conversion
SU - subquery unnesting
OBYE - order by elimination
ST - star transformation
qb - query block
LB - leaf blocks
DK - distinct keys
LB/K - average number of leaf blocks per key
DB/K - average number of data blocks per key
CLUF - clustering factor
NDV - number of distinct values
Resp - response cost
Card - cardinality
Resc - resource cost
NL - nested loops (join)
SM - sort merge (join)
HA - hash (join)
CPUCSPEED - CPU Speed
IOTFRSPEED - I/O transfer speed
IOSEEKTIM - I/O seek time
SREADTIM - average single block read time
MREADTIM - average multiblock read time
MBRC - average multiblock read count
MAXTHR - maximum I/O system throughput
```

```
SLAVETHR - average slave I/O throughput
dmeth - distribution method
  1: no partitioning required
  2: value partitioned
  4: right is random (round-robin)
  512: left is random (round-robin)
  8: broadcast right and partition left
  16: broadcast left and partition right
  32: partition left using partitioning of right
  64: partition right using partitioning of left
  128: use hash partitioning dimension
  256: use range partitioning dimension
  2048: use list partitioning dimension
  1024: run the join in serial
  0: invalid distribution method
sel - selectivity
ptn - partition
```

Results of Bind Variable Peeking

This section contains all the bind variables used in the query, their data types (`oacdty`), and values. The output is identical to the format of an extended SQL trace with event 10046 at levels 4 or 12.

```
**********************************************
Peeked values of the binds in SQL statement
**********************************************
kkscoacd
 Bind#0
  oacdty=01 mxl=32(30) mxlc=00 mal=00 scl=00 pre=00
  oacflg=03 fl2=1000000 frm=01 csi=178 siz=32 off=0
  kxsbbbfp=04c3ae00  bln=32  avl=19  flg=05
  value="South San Francisco"
```

Optimizer parameters

This section holds a listing of 184 documented and hidden parameters, which affect the optimizer's calculations and decisions. It consists of three subsections:

1. Parameters with altered values
2. Parameters with default values
3. Parameters supplied with the hint `OPT_PARAM` (e.g. `OPT_PARAM('optimizer_index_cost_adj' 30)`). This undocumented hint may be part of stored outlines.

Subsections 1 and 3 from the example trace file are empty, since all parameters had default values.

```
******************************************
PARAMETERS USED BY THE OPTIMIZER
******************************************
  ******************************************
  PARAMETERS WITH ALTERED VALUES
  ******************************************
  ******************************************
  PARAMETERS WITH DEFAULT VALUES
  ******************************************
  optimizer_mode_hinted           = false
  optimizer_features_hinted       = 0.0.0
  parallel_execution_enabled      = true
  parallel_query_forced_dop       = 0
  parallel_dml_forced_dop         = 0
  parallel_ddl_forced_degree      = 0
  parallel_ddl_forced_instances   = 0
  _query_rewrite_fudge            = 90
```

```
optimizer_features_enable          = 10.2.0.1
_optimizer_search_limit            = 5
cpu_count                          = 2
active_instance_count              = 1
parallel_threads_per_cpu           = 2
hash_area_size                     = 131072
bitmap_merge_area_size             = 1048576
sort_area_size                     = 65536
sort_area_retained_size            = 0
_sort_elimination_cost_ratio       = 0
_optimizer_block_size              = 8192
_sort_multiblock_read_count        = 2
_hash_multiblock_io_count          = 0
_db_file_optimizer_read_count      = 16
_optimizer_max_permutations        = 2000
pga_aggregate_target               = 119808 KB
_pga_max_size                      = 204800 KB
_query_rewrite_maxdisjunct         = 257
_smm_auto_min_io_size              = 56 KB
_smm_auto_max_io_size              = 248 KB
_smm_min_size                      = 128 KB
_smm_max_size                      = 23961 KB
_smm_px_max_size                   = 59904 KB
_cpu_to_io                         = 0
_optimizer_undo_cost_change        = 10.2.0.1
parallel_query_mode                = enabled
parallel_dml_mode                  = disabled
parallel_ddl_mode                  = enabled
optimizer_mode                     = all_rows
sqlstat_enabled                    = false
_optimizer_percent_parallel        = 101
_always_anti_join                  = choose
_always_semi_join                  = choose
_optimizer_mode_force              = true
_partition_view_enabled            = true
_always_star_transformation        = false
_query_rewrite_or_error            = false
_hash_join_enabled                 = true
cursor_sharing                     = exact
_b_tree_bitmap_plans               = true
star_transformation_enabled        = false
_optimizer_cost_model              = choose
_new_sort_cost_estimate            = true
_complex_view_merging              = true
_unnest_subquery                   = true
_eliminate_common_subexpr          = true
_pred_move_around                  = true
_convert_set_to_join               = false
_push_join_predicate               = true
_push_join_union_view              = true
_fast_full_scan_enabled            = true
_optim_enhance_nnull_detection     = true
_parallel_broadcast_enabled        = true
_px_broadcast_fudge_factor         = 100
_ordered_nested_loop               = true
_no_or_expansion                   = false
optimizer_index_cost_adj           = 100
optimizer_index_caching            = 0
```

```
_system_index_caching                    = 0
_disable_datalayer_sampling              = false
query_rewrite_enabled                    = true
query_rewrite_integrity                  = enforced
_query_cost_rewrite                      = true
_query_rewrite_2                         = true
_query_rewrite_1                         = true
_query_rewrite_expression                = true
_query_rewrite_jgmigrate                 = true
_query_rewrite_fpc                       = true
_query_rewrite_drj                       = true
_full_pwise_join_enabled                 = true
_partial_pwise_join_enabled              = true
_left_nested_loops_random                = true
_improved_row_length_enabled             = true
_index_join_enabled                      = true
_enable_type_dep_selectivity             = true
_improved_outerjoin_card                 = true
_optimizer_adjust_for_nulls              = true
_optimizer_degree                        = 0
_use_column_stats_for_function           = true
_subquery_pruning_enabled                = true
_subquery_pruning_mv_enabled             = false
_or_expand_nvl_predicate                 = true
_like_with_bind_as_equality              = false
_table_scan_cost_plus_one                = true
_cost_equality_semi_join                 = true
_default_non_equality_sel_check          = true
_new_initial_join_orders                 = true
_oneside_colstat_for_equijoins           = true
_optim_peek_user_binds                   = true
_minimal_stats_aggregation               = true
_force_temptables_for_gsets              = false
workarea_size_policy                     = auto
_smm_auto_cost_enabled                   = true
_gs_anti_semi_join_allowed               = true
_optim_new_default_join_sel              = true
optimizer_dynamic_sampling               = 2
_pre_rewrite_push_pred                   = true
_optimizer_new_join_card_computation     = true
_union_rewrite_for_gs                    = yes_gset_mvs
_generalized_pruning_enabled             = true
_optim_adjust_for_part_skews             = true
_force_datefold_trunc                    = false
statistics_level                         = typical
_optimizer_system_stats_usage            = true
skip_unusable_indexes                    = true
_remove_aggr_subquery                    = true
_optimizer_push_down_distinct            = 0
_dml_monitoring_enabled                  = true
_optimizer_undo_changes                  = false
_predicate_elimination_enabled           = true
_nested_loop_fudge                       = 100
_project_view_columns                    = true
_local_communication_costing_enabled     = true
_local_communication_ratio               = 50
_query_rewrite_vop_cleanup               = true
_slave_mapping_enabled                   = true
```

```
_optimizer_cost_based_transformation = linear
_optimizer_mjc_enabled                = true
_right_outer_hash_enable              = true
_spr_push_pred_refspr                 = true
_optimizer_cache_stats                = false
_optimizer_cbqt_factor                = 50
_optimizer_squ_bottomup               = true
_fic_area_size                        = 131072
_optimizer_skip_scan_enabled          = true
_optimizer_cost_filter_pred           = false
_optimizer_sortmerge_join_enabled     = true
_optimizer_join_sel_sanity_check      = true
_mmv_query_rewrite_enabled            = true
_bt_mmv_query_rewrite_enabled         = true
_add_stale_mv_to_dependency_list      = true
_distinct_view_unnesting              = false
_optimizer_dim_subq_join_sel          = true
_optimizer_disable_strans_sanity_checks = 0
_optimizer_compute_index_stats        = true
_push_join_union_view2                = true
_optimizer_ignore_hints               = false
_optimizer_random_plan                = 0
_query_rewrite_setopgrw_enable        = true
_optimizer_correct_sq_selectivity     = true
_disable_function_based_index         = false
_optimizer_join_order_control         = 3
_optimizer_cartesian_enabled          = true
_optimizer_starplan_enabled           = true
_extended_pruning_enabled             = true
_optimizer_push_pred_cost_based       = true
_sql_model_unfold_forloops            = run_time
_enable_dml_lock_escalation           = false
_bloom_filter_enabled                 = true
_update_bji_ipdml_enabled             = 0
_optimizer_extended_cursor_sharing    = udo
_dm_max_shared_pool_pct               = 1
_optimizer_cost_hjsmj_multimatch      = true
_optimizer_transitivity_retain        = true
_px_pwg_enabled                       = true
optimizer_secure_view_merging         = true
_optimizer_join_elimination_enabled   = true
flashback_table_rpi                   = non_fbt
_optimizer_cbqt_no_size_restriction   = true
_optimizer_enhanced_filter_push       = true
_optimizer_filter_pred_pullup         = true
_rowsrc_trace_level                   = 0
_simple_view_merging                  = true
_optimizer_rownum_pred_based_fkr      = true
_optimizer_better_inlist_costing      = all
_optimizer_self_induced_cache_cost    = false
_optimizer_min_cache_blocks           = 10
_optimizer_or_expansion               = depth
_optimizer_order_by_elimination_enabled = true
_optimizer_outer_to_anti_enabled      = true
_selfjoin_mv_duplicates               = true
_dimension_skip_null                  = true
_force_rewrite_enable                 = false
_optimizer_star_tran_in_with_clause   = true
```

```
   _optimizer_complex_pred_selectivity = true
   _gby_hash_aggregation_enabled       = true
   ***************************************
   PARAMETERS IN OPT_PARAM HINT
   ****************************
```

When changing DB_FILE_MULTIBLOCK_READ_COUNT at session level, this is reflected as the undocumented parameter _DB_FILE_OPTIMIZER_READ_COUNT in the subsection on altered values:

```
   ***************************************
   PARAMETERS WITH ALTERED VALUES
   ****************************
   _db_file_optimizer_read_count      = 64
```

The excerpt below illustrates the effect of adjusting OPTIMIZER_INDEX_COST_ADJ at statement level with the hint OPT_PARAM on the third subsection:

```
   ***************************************
   PARAMETERS IN OPT_PARAM HINT
   ****************************
   optimizer_index_cost_adj           = 30
```

A small subset of these parameters, pertaining to the SELECT statement used as an example, may be retrieved with the following query:

```
SQL> SELECT name FROM V$SQL_OPTIMIZER_ENV WHERE sql_id='2ck90xfmsza4u';
```

System statistics

On the system where the case study was performed, workload statistics had been set in the data dictionary with the following anonymous PL/SQL block (file set_system_stats.sql):

```
SQL> BEGIN
   dbms_stats.set_system_stats('sreadtim', 4);
   dbms_stats.set_system_stats('mreadtim', 10 );
   dbms_stats.set_system_stats('cpuspeed', 839);
   dbms_stats.set_system_stats('mbrc', 14);
   dbms_stats.set_system_stats('maxthr', 8 * 1048576);
END;
/
```

This is reflected in the 10053 trace as reproduced below:

```
   ****************************
   SYSTEM STATISTICS INFORMATION
   ****************************
   Using WORKLOAD Stats
   CPUSPEED: 839 millions instructions/sec
   SREADTIM: 4 milliseconds
   MREADTIM: 10 milliseconds
   MBRC: 14.000000 blocks
   MAXTHR: 8388608 bytes/sec
   SLAVETHR: -1 bytes/sec
```

These system statistics were derived by averaging the results of several system statistics gatherings with DBMS_STATS.GATHER_SYSTEM_STATS. The value of CPUSPEED depends on the hardware used and fluctuates with the apportionment of CPU time to the DBMS. I have included the script gather_get_system_stats.sql in the source code depot of this chapter. The script collects system statistics during several subsequent intervals and stores them in a statistics table outside of the data dictionary. By default, it uses four intervals of 15 minutes each. It also includes PL/SQL code for retrieving system statistics. The script does not affect any optimizer parameters or decisions. Workload statistics must be imported into the data dictionary to affect execution plans generated by the CBO.

When noworkload statistics are used, the 10053 system statistics trace file section looks as below:

```
   ****************************
   SYSTEM STATISTICS INFORMATION
   ****************************
```

```
Using NOWORKLOAD Stats
CPUSPEED: 485 millions instruction/sec
IOTFRSPEED: 4096 bytes per millisecond (default is 4096)
IOSEEKTIM: 10 milliseconds (default is 10)
```

The value of CPUSPEED depends on the hardware used, whereas the parameters IOTFRSPEED and IOSEEKTIM have identical values on any UNIX or Windows port of Oracle10*g*.

Object Statistics for Tables and Indexes

This section comprises statistics from DBA_TABLES, DBA_TAB_COL_STATISTICS and DBA_INDEXES. If the statement accesses partitioned objects, statistics from DBA_TAB_PARTITIONS and DBA_IND_PARTITIONS would be present. In case histograms have been created for some columns, statistics from DBA_TAB_HISTOGRAMS would be displayed. In the excerpt below, the column LOCATION_ID has a histogram with seven buckets, whereas column DEPARTMENT_ID does not have a histogram. Merely columns that are candidates for filter or access predicates are listed. Abbreviations used in this section and their meanings are depicted in Table 12.

```
*****************************************
BASE STATISTICAL INFORMATION
***********************
Table Stats::
  Table: JOBS  Alias:  J
    #Rows: 19 #Blks:  5  AvgRowLen:  33.00
  Column (#1): JOB_ID(VARCHAR2)
    AvgLen: 8.00 NDV: 19 Nulls: 0 Density: 0.052632
Index Stats::
  Index: JOB_ID_PK  Col#: 1
    LVLS: 0  #LB: 1  #DK: 19  LB/K: 1.00  DB/K: 1.00  CLUF: 1.00
Table Stats::
  Table: DEPARTMENTS  Alias:  D
    #Rows: 27 #Blks:  5  AvgRowLen:  20.00
  Column (#1): DEPARTMENT_ID(NUMBER)
    AvgLen: 4.00 NDV: 27 Nulls: 0 Density: 0.037037 Min: 10 Max: 270
  Column (#4): LOCATION_ID(NUMBER)
    AvgLen: 3.00 NDV: 7 Nulls: 0 Density: 0.018519 Min: 1400 Max: 2700
    Histogram: Freq  #Bkts: 7  UncompBkts: 27  EndPtVals: 7
Index Stats::
  Index: DEPT_ID_PK  Col#: 1
    LVLS: 0  #LB: 1  #DK: 27  LB/K: 1.00  DB/K: 1.00  CLUF: 1.00
  Index: DEPT_LOCATION_IX  Col#: 4
    LVLS: 0  #LB: 1  #DK: 7  LB/K: 1.00  DB/K: 1.00  CLUF: 1.00
...
```

Table 12: Abbreviations Used in the Section "Base Statistical Information"

Abbreviation	Meaning	Dictionary View (and Column)
#Bkts	Number of histogram buckets	DBA_TAB_HISTOGRAMS
#Blks	Number of table blocks below the high water mark	DBA_TABLES.BLOCKS
#DK	Distinct keys	DBA_INDEXES.DISTINCT_KEYS
#LB	Number of index leaf blocks	DBA_INDEXES.LEAF_BLOCKS
#Rows	Number of table rows	DBA_TABLES.NUM_ROWS
AvgLen	Average column value length	DBA_TAB_COLUMNS.AVG_COL_LEN
AvgRowLen	Average row length	DBA_TABLES.AVG_ROW_LEN
EndPtVals	Histogram end point values	DBA_TAB_HISTOGRAMS

Table 12: Abbreviations Used in the Section "Base Statistical Information"

Abbreviation	Meaning	Dictionary View (and Column)
CLUF	Clustering factor	DBA_INDEXES.CLUSTERING_FACTOR
DB/K	Average number of index data blocks per key	DBA_INDEXES.AVG_DATA_BLOCKS_PER_KEY
LB/K	Average number of index leaf blocks per key	DBA_INDEXES.AVG_LEAF_BLOCKS_PER_KEY
LVLS	B–tree level	DBA_INDEXES.BLEVEL
NDV	Number of distinct values	DBA_TAB_COLUMNS.NUM_DISTINCT
UncompBkts	Uncompressed buckets	n/a

The clustering factor is an indication of how clustered (beneficial) or randomly distributed (detrimental) data is in a table's segment. Indexes are always sorted. When individual index blocks point to many table blocks, data pertaining to a range of index keys is randomly distributed within a table's segment and a high clustering factor, which renders index access unattractive, results.

When histograms are absent, the following holds for density:

$$\text{Density} = \frac{1}{\text{NDV}}$$

Missing Statistics

As soon as one of the objects referenced in a SQL statement has object statistics, the CBO is used to calculate the best execution plan. When statistics for one or more tables, indexes, or partitions thereof are missing, the calculation may go awry. The 10053 trace file points out which objects lack statistics and contains the default values CBO uses instead of actual values computed with DBMS_STATS:

```
Table Stats::
  Table: LOCATIONS  Alias:  L  (NOT ANALYZED)
    #Rows: 409  #Blks:  5  AvgRowLen:  100.00
  Column (#1): LOCATION_ID(NUMBER)  NO STATISTICS (using defaults)
    AvgLen: 22.00 NDV: 13 Nulls: 0 Density: 0.07824
Index Stats::
  Index: LOC_CITY_IX  Col#: 4    (NOT ANALYZED)
    LVLS: 1  #LB: 25  #DK: 100  LB/K: 1.00  DB/K: 1.00  CLUF: 800.00
```

Single Table Access Path and Cost

The optimizer ignores join conditions in the single table access path section. Solely access predicates, which were supplied a value with a literal or bind variable, are considered. In the absence of such predicates, merely a full table scan or index fast full scan are considered for a table. The optimizer estimates how many rows will be retrieved and calculates the cheapest alternative for getting them. In the excerpt below, it determines that it is cheaper to use the index LOC_CITY_IX than to perform a full table scan.

```
SINGLE TABLE ACCESS PATH
  Column (#4): CITY(VARCHAR2)
    AvgLen: 9.00 NDV: 23 Nulls: 0 Density: 0.043478
  Table: LOCATIONS  Alias: L
    Card: Original: 23  Rounded: 1  Computed: 1.00  Non Adjusted: 1.00
  Access Path: TableScan
    Cost:  3.01  Resp: 3.01  Degree: 0
      Cost_io: 3.00  Cost_cpu: 41607
      Resp_io: 3.00  Resp_cpu: 41607
  Access Path: index (AllEqRange)
    Index: LOC_CITY_IX
    resc_io: 2.00  resc_cpu: 14673
```

```
            ix_sel: 0.043478  ix_sel_with_filters: 0.043478
         Cost: 2.00  Resp: 2.00  Degree: 1
       Best:: AccessPath: IndexRange   Index: LOC_CITY_IX
             Cost: 2.00  Degree: 1  Resp: 2.00  Card: 1.00  Bytes: 0
     ****************************************
   SINGLE TABLE ACCESS PATH
     Table: JOBS  Alias: J
       Card: Original: 19  Rounded: 19  Computed: 19.00  Non Adjusted: 19.00
     Access Path: TableScan
        Cost:  3.01  Resp: 3.01  Degree: 0
          Cost_io: 3.00  Cost_cpu: 38837
          Resp_io: 3.00  Resp_cpu: 38837
     Best:: AccessPath: TableScan
             Cost: 3.01  Degree: 1  Resp: 3.01  Card: 19.00  Bytes: 0
     ****************************************
```

According to Jonathan Lewis ([Lewi 2005]), the CBO calculates the cost of a B–tree index access with the formula below:

$$\text{LVLS} + \text{ceiling}(\#\text{LB} \cdot \text{ix\_sel}) + \text{ceiling}(\text{CLUF} \cdot \text{ix\_sel\_with\_filters})$$

The values for ix_sel (index selectivity) and ix_sel_with_filters (effective table selectivity) are found in the trace file. The values for LVLS (B–tree level), #LB (number of leaf blocks), and CLUF (clustering factor) are in the section entitled "BASE STATISTICAL INFORMATION" presented earlier. When the formula is applied to the index LOC_CITY_IX, it does yield the same result as in the optimizer trace:

$$0 + \text{ceiling}(1 \cdot 0.043478) + \text{ceiling}(1 \cdot 0.043478) = 2$$

The formula also gives correct results when applied to more complicated cases.

Dynamic Sampling

Dynamic sampling is a feature of the CBO introduced with Oracle9i. Dynamic sampling is the capability of the CBO to calculate statistics based on a small sample of rows as it optimizes a query. The feature is controlled by the parameter OPTIMIZER_DYNAMIC_SAMPLING and is enabled by default in Oracle9i Release 2 and subsequent versions. The excerpt below depicts the SELECT statement the optimizer used to dynamically sample the table LOCATIONS, after object statistics for the table had been deleted:

```
   ** Generated dynamic sampling query:
      query text :
   SELECT /* OPT_DYN_SAMP */ /*+ ALL_ROWS opt_param('parallel_execution_enabled', 'false')
   NO_PARALLEL(SAMPLESUB) NO_PARALLEL_INDEX(SAMPLESUB) NO_SQL_TUNE */ NVL(SUM(C1),0),
   NVL(SUM(C2),0), NVL(SUM(C3),0) FROM (SELECT /*+ NO_PARALLEL("L") INDEX("L" LOC_CITY_IX)
   NO_PARALLEL_INDEX("L") */ 1 AS C1, 1 AS C2, 1 AS C3  FROM "LOCATIONS" "L" WHERE
   "L"."CITY"=:B1 AND ROWNUM <= 2500) SAMPLESUB
   *** 2007-11-30 16:44:25.703
   ** Executed dynamic sampling query:
      level : 2
      sample pct. : 100.000000
      actual sample size : 23
      filtered sample card. : 1
      filtered sample card. (index LOC_CITY_IX): 1
      orig. card. : 23
      block cnt. table stat. : 5
      block cnt. for sampling: 5
      max. sample block cnt. : 4294967295
      sample block cnt. : 5
      min. sel. est. : 0.01000000
      index LOC_CITY_IX selectivity est.: 0.04347826
```

Join Orders

This section depicts all the join orders the CBO has scrutinized. There are *n*! (*n* factorial) join orders for an *n*–way join. Thus, a 5–way join has 120 join orders and a 6–way join has 720. For higher order joins, it would be a waste of CPU resources to try all possible join orders. Hence, the CBO does not consider them all and stops examining join orders that exceed the cost of the best plan found so far.

```
******************************************
OPTIMIZER STATISTICS AND COMPUTATIONS
******************************************
GENERAL PLANS
******************************************
Considering cardinality-based initial join order.
************************
Join order[1]:  LOCATIONS[L]#0  JOBS[J]#1  DEPARTMENTS[D]#2  EMPLOYEES[EMP]#3
EMPLOYEES[MGR]#4
***************
Now joining: JOBS[J]#1
***************
NL Join
  Outer table: Card: 1.00  Cost: 2.00  Resp: 2.00  Degree: 1  Bytes: 48
  Inner table: JOBS  Alias: J
  Access Path: TableScan
    NL Join:  Cost: 5.02  Resp: 5.02  Degree: 0
       Cost_io: 5.00  Cost_cpu: 53510
       Resp_io: 5.00  Resp_cpu: 53510
  Best NL cost: 5.02
          resc: 5.02 resc_io: 5.00 resc_cpu: 53510
          resp: 5.02 resp_io: 5.00 resp_cpu: 53510
Join Card:  19.00 = outer (1.00) * inner (19.00) * sel (1)
Join Card - Rounded: 19 Computed: 19.00
Best:: JoinMethod: NestedLoop
       Cost: 5.02  Degree: 1  Resp: 5.02  Card: 19.00  Bytes: 75
...
***************
Now joining: DEPARTMENTS[D]#2
***************
...
***************
Now joining: EMPLOYEES[EMP]#3
***************
...
***************
Now joining: EMPLOYEES[MGR]#4
***************
...
************************
Best so far: Table#: 0  cost: 2.0044  card: 1.0000  bytes: 48
             Table#: 1  cost: 5.0159  card: 19.0000  bytes: 1425
             Table#: 2  cost: 6.0390  card: 73.2857  bytes: 6862
             Table#: 3  cost: 9.5672  card: 15.1429  bytes: 2400
             Table#: 4  cost: 11.6050  card: 15.0013  bytes: 2580
************************
Join order[2]:  LOCATIONS[L]#0  JOBS[J]#1  DEPARTMENTS[D]#2  EMPLOYEES[MGR]#4
EMPLOYEES[EMP]#3
***************
Now joining: EMPLOYEES[MGR]#4
...
************************
```

For each potential join order, the optimizer evaluates the cost of three join methods:

- nested loops (NL) join
- sort–merge (SM) join
- hash join (HA)

At the end of each section entitled "Now joining", CBO reports the best join method (e.g. "Best:: JoinMethod: NestedLoop").

```
Join order[8]:  LOCATIONS[L]#0  DEPARTMENTS[D]#2  EMPLOYEES[EMP]#3  JOBS[J]#1
EMPLOYEES[MGR]#4
***************
Now joining: EMPLOYEES[EMP]#3
***************
NL Join
   Outer table: Card: 3.86  Cost: 3.01  Resp: 3.01  Degree: 1  Bytes: 67
   Inner table: EMPLOYEES  Alias: EMP
   Access Path: TableScan
     NL Join:  Cost: 8.09  Resp: 8.09  Degree: 0
       Cost_io: 8.00  Cost_cpu: 316513
       Resp_io: 8.00  Resp_cpu: 316513
   Access Path: index (AllEqJoinGuess)
     Index: EMP_DEPARTMENT_IX
     resc_io: 1.00  resc_cpu: 13471
     ix_sel: 0.091767  ix_sel_with_filters: 0.091767
     NL Join: Cost: 4.65  Resp: 4.65  Degree: 1
       Cost_io: 4.63  Cost_cpu: 52993
       Resp_io: 4.63  Resp_cpu: 52993
   Best NL cost: 4.65
           resc: 4.65 resc_io: 4.63 resc_cpu: 52993
           resp: 4.65 resp_io: 4.63 resp_cpu: 52993
Join Card:  15.14 = outer (3.86) * inner (107.00) * sel (0.036691)
Join Card - Rounded: 15 Computed: 15.14
SM Join
   Outer table:
     resc: 3.01  card 3.86 bytes: 67  deg: 1  resp: 3.01
   Inner table: EMPLOYEES  Alias: EMP
     resc: 3.02  card: 107.00  bytes: 66  deg: 1  resp: 3.02
     using dmeth: 2  #groups: 1
     SORT resource      Sort statistics
       Sort width:          138 Area size:       131072 Max Area size:     24536064
       Degree:               1
       Blocks to Sort:      1 Row size:            84 Total Rows:            4
       Initial runs:        1 Merge passes:        0 IO Cost / pass:        0
       Total IO sort cost: 0     Total CPU sort cost: 3356360
       Total Temp space used: 0
     SORT resource      Sort statistics
       Sort width:          138 Area size:       131072 Max Area size:     24536064
       Degree:               1
       Blocks to Sort:      2 Row size:            83 Total Rows:          107
       Initial runs:        1 Merge passes:        0 IO Cost / pass:        0
       Total IO sort cost: 0     Total CPU sort cost: 3388500
       Total Temp space used: 0
   SM join: Resc: 8.04  Resp: 8.04  [multiMatchCost=0.00]
   SM cost: 8.04
     resc: 8.04 resc_io: 6.00 resc_cpu: 6842201
     resp: 8.04 resp_io: 6.00 resp_cpu: 6842201
HA Join
   Outer table:
     resc: 3.01  card 3.86 bytes: 67  deg: 1  resp: 3.01
```

```
Inner table: EMPLOYEES  Alias: EMP
  resc: 3.02  card: 107.00  bytes: 66  deg: 1  resp: 3.02
  using dmeth: 2  #groups: 1
  Cost per ptn: 0.50  #ptns: 1
  hash_area: 0 (max=0)  Hash join: Resc: 6.53  Resp: 6.53  [multiMatchCost=0.00]
HA cost: 6.53
   resc: 6.53 resc_io: 6.00 resc_cpu: 1786642
   resp: 6.53 resp_io: 6.00 resp_cpu: 1786642
Best:: JoinMethod: NestedLoop
    Cost: 4.65  Degree: 1  Resp: 4.65  Card: 15.14  Bytes: 133
***************
Now joining: JOBS[J]#1
***************
NL Join
...

***********************
Best so far: Table#: 0  cost: 2.0044  card: 1.0000  bytes: 48
            Table#: 2  cost: 3.0072  card: 3.8571  bytes: 268
            Table#: 3  cost: 4.6454  card: 15.1429  bytes: 1995
            Table#: 1  cost: 5.6827  card: 15.1429  bytes: 2400
            Table#: 4  cost: 7.7205  card: 15.0013  bytes: 2580
...
Join order[76]:  EMPLOYEES[MGR]#4  EMPLOYEES[EMP]#3  DEPARTMENTS[D]#2  LOCATIONS[L]#0
JOBS[J]#1
***************
Now joining: DEPARTMENTS[D]#2
...
Join order aborted: cost > best plan cost
***********************
(newjo-stop-1) k:0, spcnt:0, perm:76, maxperm:2000
Number of join permutations tried: 76
*********************************
(newjo-save)    [1 2 4 0 3 ]
Final - All Rows Plan:  Best join order: 8
  Cost: 7.7205  Degree: 1  Card: 15.0000  Bytes: 2580
  Resc: 7.7205  Resc_io: 7.6296  Resc_cpu: 305037
  Resp: 7.7205  Resp_io: 7.6296  Resc_cpu: 305037
```

At the end of the report for a particular join sequence, the CBO prints the best join order detected so far along with its cost, cardinality, and data volume (bytes). All three figures displayed under the heading "Best so far" are cumulative in the same way that the cost of a row source in an execution plan includes the cost of dependent row sources.

The CBO has decided that the join order 8, which joins the tables in the sequence LOCATIONS, DEPARTMENTS, EMPLOYEES (alias EMP), JOBS, and EMPLOYEES (alias MGR), has the lowest cost. This join order is reflected in the execution plan and the LEADING hint in the next sections.

Execution Plan

This section contains a nicely formatted execution plan. Besides DBMS_XPLAN.DISPLAY_CURSOR, V$SQL_PLAN, AWR and Statspack, the 10053 trace file is another reliable source for execution plans. Remember that EXPLAIN PLAN is notoriously unreliable and should never be used in optimization projects. Oracle Corp. cautions DBAs that "with bind variables in general, the EXPLAIN PLAN output might not represent the real execution plan" (*Oracle Database Performance Tuning Guide 10g Release 2*, page 19–4). It is a good idea to check the cardinalities (column "Rows") in the plan table. Suboptimal plans may result whenever these are grossly incorrect.

```
============
Plan Table
============
```

Id	Operation	Name	Rows	Bytes	Cost	Time
0	SELECT STATEMENT				8	
1	NESTED LOOPS		15	2580	8	00:00:01
2	NESTED LOOPS		15	2400	6	00:00:01
3	NESTED LOOPS		15	1995	5	00:00:01
4	NESTED LOOPS		4	268	3	00:00:01
5	TABLE ACCESS BY INDEX ROWID	LOCATIONS	1	48	2	00:00:01
6	INDEX RANGE SCAN	LOC_CITY_IX	1		1	00:00:01
7	TABLE ACCESS BY INDEX ROWID	DEPARTMENTS	4	76	1	00:00:01
8	INDEX RANGE SCAN	DEPT_LOCATION_IX	4		0	
9	TABLE ACCESS BY INDEX ROWID	EMPLOYEES	4	264	1	00:00:01
10	INDEX RANGE SCAN	EMP_DEPARTMENT_IX	10		0	
11	TABLE ACCESS BY INDEX ROWID	JOBS	1	27	1	00:00:01
12	INDEX UNIQUE SCAN	JOB_ID_PK	1		0	
13	TABLE ACCESS BY INDEX ROWID	EMPLOYEES	1	12	1	00:00:01
14	INDEX UNIQUE SCAN	EMP_EMP_ID_PK	1		0	

Predicate Information

The output in the predicate and plan sections is nearly identical to the output you would get from running SELECT * FROM table (DBMS_XPLAN.DISPLAY_CURSOR()) immediately after the statement you are investigating:

```
Predicate Information:
---------------------
6 - access("L"."CITY"=:LOC)
8 - access("D"."LOCATION_ID"="L"."LOCATION_ID")
10 - access("EMP"."DEPARTMENT_ID"="D"."DEPARTMENT_ID")
12 - access("EMP"."JOB_ID"="J"."JOB_ID")
14 - access("EMP"."MANAGER_ID"="MGR"."EMPLOYEE_ID")
```

Hints and Query Block Names

This section comprises a full set of hints including query block names. The hints would be used to define a stored outline, which fixes the plan chosen by the CBO. The data is displayed with correct syntax for hints:

```
Outline Data:
/*+
  BEGIN_OUTLINE_DATA
    IGNORE_OPTIM_EMBEDDED_HINTS
    OPTIMIZER_FEATURES_ENABLE('10.2.0.1')
    ALL_ROWS
    OUTLINE_LEAF(@"SEL$1")
    INDEX(@"SEL$1" "L"@"SEL$1" ("LOCATIONS"."CITY"))
    INDEX(@"SEL$1" "D"@"SEL$1" ("DEPARTMENTS"."LOCATION_ID"))
    INDEX(@"SEL$1" "EMP"@"SEL$1" ("EMPLOYEES"."DEPARTMENT_ID"))
    INDEX(@"SEL$1" "J"@"SEL$1" ("JOBS"."JOB_ID"))
    INDEX(@"SEL$1" "MGR"@"SEL$1" ("EMPLOYEES"."EMPLOYEE_ID"))
    LEADING(@"SEL$1" "L"@"SEL$1" "D"@"SEL$1" "EMP"@"SEL$1" "J"@"SEL$1" "MGR"@"SEL$1")
    USE_NL(@"SEL$1" "D"@"SEL$1")
    USE_NL(@"SEL$1" "EMP"@"SEL$1")
    USE_NL(@"SEL$1" "J"@"SEL$1")
    USE_NL(@"SEL$1" "MGR"@"SEL$1")
  END_OUTLINE_DATA
*/
```

Source Code Depot

Table 13: Event 10053 Source Code Depot

File Name	*Functionality*
hr_5way_join.sql	Five–way join of tables in the sample schema HR
set_system_stats.sql	This script sets workload system statistics in the data dictionary
gather_get_system_stats.sql	This script collects system statistics during several subsequent intervals (default: 4 intervals, 15 minutes each) and stores them in a statistics table outside of the data dictionary
hr.dmp	Conventional export dump file which contains tables from the sample schema HR (created with Oracle10g Release 2)

Chapter 8

Event 10079 and Oracle Net Packet Contents

Status: Event 10079 and applicable levels are undocumented.

Benefit: Event 10079 may be used to dump Oracle Net packet contents to a trace file. It is useful for quickly determining which SQL statements, PL/SQL calls, or SQL*Plus commands send sensitive data such as passwords unencrypted.

Event 10079

Similar to Oracle Net tracing, event 10079 may be used to dump Oracle Net network packets. It is more convenient than changing `sqlnet.ora` to enable dumping of Oracle Net packet contents. Unlike `trace_level_client` in `sqlnet.ora` it may also be used to enable packet dumps for database sessions which are already established. Table 14 lists the supported event levels.

Table 14: Supported Levels of Event 10079

Level	Purpose
1	Trace network operations to/from client
2	In addition to level 1, dump data
4	Trace network operations to/from database link
8	In addition to level 4, dump data

Case Study

The subsequent sections assume that the Advanced Security Option for the encryption of Oracle Net traffic is not used. The *SQL*Plus User's Guide and Reference* does not state whether passwords are sent encrypted or not when modified with the SQL*Plus command PASSWORD. Event 10079 may be used to find out:

```
SQL> CONNECT / AS SYSDBA
Connected.
SQL> ALTER SESSION SET EVENTS '10079 trace name context forever, level 2';
Session altered.
SQL> PASSWORD ndebes
Changing password for ndebes
New password:
Retype new password:
Password changed
SQL> ORADEBUG SETMYPID
Statement processed.
SQL> ORADEBUG TRACEFILE_NAME
/opt/oracle/obase/admin/TEN/udump/ten1_ora_20364.trc
```

The resulting trace file contains the following packet dump:

```
C850BD0 FFD668BF 646E06BF 73656265 00000030  [.h....ndebes0...]
C850BE0 54554110 454E5F48 53415057 524F5753  [.AUTH_NEWPASSWOR]
C850BF0 0000C044 31384000 39314642 38373930  [D....@81BF190978]
C850C00 41323232 39363642 45453539 42303242  [222AB66995EEB20B]
C850C10 46323546 30324343 30313239 39453434  [F52FCC20921044E9]
C850C20 34423130 32353232 45423332 44393431  [01B4225223BE149D]
C850C30 30304542 00003245 00270000 410D0000  [BE00E2....'....A]
C850C40 5F485455 53534150 44524F57 00000000  [UTH_PASSWORD....]
```

Obviously, the password was sent encrypted. Thus, the SQL*Plus PASSWORD command is a safe way to change passwords, whereas ALTER USER *user_name* IDENTIFIED BY *new_password* is not, since it sends the password unencrypted along with the SQL statement text. By the way, the encryption is different from the one used in DBA_USERS.PASSWORD, such that eavesdropping a communications link cannot be used to glean encrypted passwords stored in the dictionary base table USER$.

Some applications use roles, which are protected by a password, to enable certain privileges only when a user connects with the application. This is intended to restrict the privileges of users who connect with SQL*Plus or other applications. Event 10079 may be used to prove that both the SQL statement SET ROLE *role_name* IDENTIFIED BY *password* as well as DBMS_SESSION.SET_ROLE send the role's password unencrypted to the DBMS server. This means that any user who knows enough about Oracle Net, can get the unencrypted role password from a packet dump. Since an end user cannot add an ALTER SESSION statement to an application, an alternative way to dump Oracle Net packets is needed. All that is necessary is to copy tnsnames.ora and sqlnet.ora to the user's home directory and to set TNS_ADMIN to the same directory. Then, after adding the following two lines to sqlnet.ora:

```
trace_level_client=support
trace_directory_client=<user's home directory>
```

and restarting the application, the clear text password may be retrieved from the trace file[1]:

```
[28-NOV-2007 23:10:54:156] nspsend: 00 2E 42 45 47 49 4E 20  |..BEGIN.|
[28-NOV-2007 23:10:54:156] nspsend: 64 62 6D 73 5F 73 65 73  |dbms_ses|
[28-NOV-2007 23:10:54:156] nspsend: 73 69 6F 6E 2E 73 65 74  |sion.set|
[28-NOV-2007 23:10:54:156] nspsend: 5F 72 6F 6C 65 28 3A 72  |_role(:r|
[28-NOV-2007 23:10:54:156] nspsend: 6F 6C 65 5F 63 6D 64 29  |ole_cmd)|
[28-NOV-2007 23:10:54:156] nspsend: 3B 20 45 4E 44 3B 0A 00  |;.END;..|
[28-NOV-2007 23:10:54:156] nspsend: 01 00 00 00 01 00 00 00  |........|
[28-NOV-2007 23:10:54:156] nspsend: 00 00 00 00 00 00 00 00  |........|
[28-NOV-2007 23:10:54:156] nspsend: 00 00 00 00 00 00 00 00  |........|
[28-NOV-2007 23:10:54:156] nspsend: 00 00 00 00 08 00 00 00  |........|
```

---

1. The naming convention for Oracle Net trace files is cli_*spid*.trc, where *spid* is the client process identifier.

```
[28-NOV-2007 23:10:54:156] nspsend: 00 00 00 00 00 00 00 00  |........|
[28-NOV-2007 23:10:54:156] nspsend: 00 00 00 00 00 00 00 00  |........|
[28-NOV-2007 23:10:54:156] nspsend: 00 00 00 00 01 01 03 00  |........|
[28-NOV-2007 23:10:54:156] nspsend: 00 32 00 00 00 00 00 00  |.2......|
[28-NOV-2007 23:10:54:156] nspsend: 00 00 00 00 00 00 00 00  |........|
[28-NOV-2007 23:10:54:156] nspsend: 00 00 00 00 00 B2 00 01  |........|
[28-NOV-2007 23:10:54:156] nspsend: 00 00 00 00 00 07 1F 61  |.......a|
[28-NOV-2007 23:10:54:156] nspsend: 70 70 72 6F 6C 65 20 69  |pprole.i|
[28-NOV-2007 23:10:54:156] nspsend: 64 65 6E 74 69 66 69 65  |dentifie|
[28-NOV-2007 23:10:54:156] nspsend: 64 20 62 79 20 74 6F 70  |d.by.top|
[28-NOV-2007 23:10:54:156] nspsend: 73 65 63 72 65 74        |secret  |
```

The safe way to implement privileges, which are only available when connecting with an application, is to use proxy authentication in conjunction with Oracle Internet Directory and secure application roles.

Of course, the same vulnerability also applies to CREATE USER *user_name* IDENTIFIED BY *password*. This statement also sends the password in clear text:

```
[08-SEP-2007 09:28:23:864] nspsend: 08 23 43 52 45 41 54 45  |.#CREATE|
[08-SEP-2007 09:28:23:864] nspsend: 20 55 53 45 52 20 68 72  |.USER.hr|
[08-SEP-2007 09:28:23:864] nspsend: 20 49 44 45 4E 54 49 46  |.IDENTIF|
[08-SEP-2007 09:28:23:864] nspsend: 49 45 44 20 42 59 20 73  |IED.BY.s|
[08-SEP-2007 09:28:23:864] nspsend: 65 63 72 65 74 01 00 00  |ecret...|
```

Hence you should create users as externally identified and then change the password with the SQL*Plus command PASSWORD.

Part IV

X$ Fixed Tables

Chapter 9

Introduction to X$ Fixed Tables

Status: A few X$ tables are mentioned by the documentation, but the vast majority is undocumented. For example X$BH is mentioned in the *Oracle9i Performance Tuning Guide* as well as the *Oracle10g Performance Tuning Guide*. The *Oracle10g Warehouse Builder Installation and Administration Guide* contains a procedure for resolving locking issues pertaining to the library cache by accessing X$KGLLK[1].

Benefit: Many X$ tables hold much more information than the GV$ views built on top of them. In instances where information provided by GV$ or V$ views is insufficient, the underlying X$ table may be scrutinized. Numerous X$ tables do not serve as the basis for GV$ views at all.

X$ Fixed Tables and C Programming

At least a significant part, if not all of the code for the ORACLE DBMS kernel, is written in the C programming language. A lot of data is maintained in two–dimensional arrays. On UNIX systems, C arrays located in the SGA may be read by commercial third party performance diagnostic utilities, that attach one or more shared memory segments, which hold the SGA[2]. Personally, although I have great respect for the developers who reverse engineer internal data structures in the SGA, I am not an advocate of such SGA sampling tools. After all they are mere sampling tools and may miss relevant data. In my view, extended SQL trace data combined with Statspack (or AWR) snapshots provide sufficient database performance diagnostic data that is not collected by sampling.

---

1. The manual shows how to access X$KGLLK for resolving the error "ORA-04021 time–out occurred while waiting to lock object".
2. See *Oracle Wait Interface: A Practical Guide to Performance Diagnostics and Tuning* by Richmond Shee et al. ([ShDe 2004])

The basic idea behind V$ views is to expose information in C data structures to database administrators. This is done by mapping V$ views to C data structures through some intermediate layers. X$ tables are one of the intermediate layers. They are the layer closest to C, to be precise. Of course the word *table* in X$ table has a meaning that is almost entirely different from the meaning in a SQL context. It goes without saying that none of the X$ tables have a segment in DBA_SEGMENTS associated with them. Additional evidence for the uniqueness of X$ tables comes from the fact that the row source for accessing them is FIXED TABLE FULL. To speed up access, indexes on X$ tables are maintained. The row source associated with index access to a fixed table is called FIXED TABLE FIXED INDEX. Along the same lines, there are no metadata on V$ views in DBA_VIEWS. Conversely, metadata on V_$ views, which are used for granting access to V$ views, is available through DBA_VIEWS.

Some X$ tables are linked to disk storage. For example, the column DCNAM of the X$ fixed table X$KCCDC holds path names of data file copies created with the RMAN command COPY DATAFILE. The disk storage for these path names is within the control file. By looking at V$CONTROLFILE_RECORD_SECTION or its foundation X$KCCRS, you will be able to identify a section called "DATAFILE COPY". This is the control file section represented by X$KCCDC (KCCDC is short for Kernel Cache Control file Data file Copy).

There is an old saying about the ORACLE DBMS which maintains that any well designed feature has more than a single denomination. The synonymous terms V$ dynamic performance view and V$ fixed view are an example of this. Another example is automatic undo management, which is also known as system managed undo (SMU) or the System Change Number (SCN), which is occasionally referred to as the System Commit Number.

Layered Architecture

X$ fixed tables are accessed in a layered manner as depicted in Figure 5. A public synonym by the same name exists for each V$ or GV$ fixed view. These synonyms refer to V_$ and GV_$ views owned by SYS. These are true views with metadata in DBA_VIEWS. DDL for these views is in catalog.sql. It is of the form:

```
CREATE OR REPLACE VIEW {g|v}_$<view_name> AS
SELECT * FROM {g|v$}<fixed_view_name>;
```

SELECT on these V_$ and GV_$ views is then granted to SELECT_CATALOG_ROLE. All V$ dynamic performance views hold information pertaining to the current instance, i.e. the instance the user has connected to. V$ fixed views are based on GV$ fixed views, which are built on top of on one or more X$ fixed tables. On systems running Real Application Clusters, GV$ fixed views provide access to information about other instances that have mounted the same database. Array offsets in C start at 0, whereas a minimum index of 1 is preferred in SQL, e.g. the value of the pseudo–column ROWNUM starts at 1. This is why you see that 1 is added to some columns of X$ tables in the definition of the GV$ view.

Note that V$OBJECT_USAGE is the only view—a true view with metadata in DBA_VIEWS—that is not based on a GV$ view. Instead, it retrieves information from data dictionary tables in tablespace SYSTEM owned by user SYS. Since it violates the aforementioned rules for V$ views, it doesn't deserve the prefix V$. Apparently no knight armored by a valid Oracle customer service number dares to dispute the undeserved prefix by opening a service request.

V$ Public Synonyms
SYS.V_$ Views
SYS.V$ Fixed Views
GV$ Public Synonyms
SYS.GV_$ Views
SYS.GV$ Fixed Views
SYS.X$ Fixed Tables

Figure 5: Layered Architecture of V$ Fixed Views, GV$ Fixed Views, and X$ Fixed Tables

Many X$ table names follow a strict naming convention, where the first few letters represent a layer or module in the ORACLE kernel. For example KC means Kernel Cache and KT Kernel Transaction. Table 15 has some more abbreviations used by X$ tables and their presumed meaning.

Table 15: Abbreviations used in X$ Fixed Table Names

Abbreviation	*Presumed Meaning*
K	Kernel
KC	Kernel Cache
KCB	Kernel Cache Buffer
KCBW	Kernel Cache Buffer Wait
KCC	Kernel Cache Control file
KCCB	Kernel Cache Control file Backup
KCCCF	Kernel Cache Copy Flash recovery area
KCCDC	Kernel Cache Control file Data file Copy
KCP	Kernel Cache transPortable tablespace
KCR	Kernel Cache Redo
KCT	Kernel Cache insTance
KG	Kernel Generic
KGL	Kernel Generic Library cache
KGLJ	Kernel Generic Library cache Java
KS	Kernel Service
KSB	Kernel Service Background
KSM	Kernel Service Memory
KSU	Kernel Service User
KSUSE	Kernel Service User SEssion
KSUSECON	Kernel Service User SEssion COnnection
KSUSEH	Kernel Service User SEssion History
KT	Kernel Transaction
KTU	Kernel Transaction Undo
KX	Kernel eXecution
KXS	Kernel eXecution Sql

Granting Access to X$ tables and V$ views

For users other than SYS, the role SELECT_CATALOG_ROLE is sufficient to access V$ views in SQL statements and anonymous blocks. Since roles are disabled inside stored PL/SQL routines such as packages, users who require access to V$ or GV$ views from PL/SQL must be granted SELECT on the corresponding V_$ or GV_$ view directly, rather than indirectly through a role. Another option is to grant the system privilege SELECT ANY DICTIONARY. The latter option should be used with caution, since it grants access to unencrypted passwords in SYS.LINK$ in Oracle9*i*. If security is a concern, you might not even want to give access to encrypted passwords in DBA_USERS with SELECT_CATALOG_ROLE, since an intruder might try to crack them.

Contrary to V$ fixed views and corresponding V_$ views, there are no X_$ views on X$ fixed tables. Hence there is no quick way to grant access to X$ tables to users other than SYS. The preferred way to implement this access, is to mimic the approach taken with V$ views, by creating true views on X$ tables owned by SYS and granting access to these. Following the naming conventions, these views might be given the prefix X_$. Except for the prefix, this is precisely the approach taken in the implementation of Statspack. The Statspack installation script creates three such views. Their names and purpose are summarized in Table 16. Access to these views is granted to user PERFSTAT only, but grants to other users are in order.

Table 16: Statspack Views on X$ Fixed Tables

Public Synonym	View	X$ base table	Associated V$ views
STATSXKSPPI	STATS$X_$KSPPI	X$KSPPI (Parameter names and descriptions)	V$PARAMETER, V$PARAMETER2, V$SGA_CURRENT_RESIZE_OPS, VSGA_RESIZE_OPS, VSYSTEM_PARAMETER2, V$SYSTEM_PARAMETER,
STATSXKSPPSV	STATS$X_$KSPPSV	X$KSPPSV (Parameter values at system level)	V$SYSTEM_PARAMETER, V$SYSTEM_PARAMETER2
STATSXKCBFWAIT	STATS$X_$KCBFWAIT	X$KCBFWAIT (Wait time and number of waits at data file level)	n/a

Drilling Down From V$ Views to X$ Fixed Tables

The next few sections present an approach for drilling down from a V$ view—via its underlying GV$ view—all the way to one or more X$ tables at the lowest level. This approach is suitable whenever the information exposed by a V$ view is a limiting factor in a troubleshooting or performance diagnosis effort. Although Oracle Corp. has exposed more and more information in X$ tables over the last few releases, it may occasionally be necessary to glean additional information from X$ tables. Of course, due to their undocumented nature, X$ tables are subject to change without notice.

Some articles endorsing X$ tables found on the Internet overlook that in many cases equally useful information can be pulled from V$ views. As an example, instead of turning to X$BH to detect contention and hot blocks, one might also access V$SEGMENT_STATISTICS, which was introduced in Oracle9*i*. Statspack reports at level 7 or higher include data captured from V$SEGMENT_STATISTICS. Personally, I have never needed information from X$ tables to resolve a performance problem. Resolving hanging issues is a different matter, since the documented view DBA_BLOCKERS does not consider library cache pins. Under such circumstances, knowing about X$KGLLK is truly advantageous.

Drilling Down from V$PARAMETER to the Underlying X$ Tables

The best known X$ tables are probably X$KSPPI and X$KSPPCV. This section shows how to uncover both by drilling down from V$PARAMETER. Likely, any DBA has used or heard of one or the other undocumented (or hidden) parameter. Undocumented parameters start with an underscore character (_). Such parameters are not found in V$PARAMETER. In Oracle10*g*, you may have noticed double underscore parameters in the server parameter files of instances with enabled automatic shared memory management (e.g. __db_cache_size). The columns of the view V$PARAMETER are:

```
SQL> DESCRIBE v$parameter
 Name                                      Null?    Type
 ----------------------------------------- -------- -------------
 NUM                                                NUMBER
 NAME                                               VARCHAR2(80)
 TYPE                                               NUMBER
 VALUE                                              VARCHAR2(512)
 DISPLAY_VALUE                                      VARCHAR2(512)
 ISDEFAULT                                          VARCHAR2(9)
 ISSES_MODIFIABLE                                   VARCHAR2(5)
```

```
ISSYS_MODIFIABLE                                    VARCHAR2(9)
ISINSTANCE_MODIFIABLE                               VARCHAR2(5)
ISMODIFIED                                          VARCHAR2(10)
ISADJUSTED                                          VARCHAR2(5)
ISDEPRECATED                                        VARCHAR2(5)
DESCRIPTION                                         VARCHAR2(255)
UPDATE_COMMENT                                      VARCHAR2(255)
HASH                                                NUMBER
```

In a few moments, you will learn how to generate a list of all undocumented parameters along with the default value and a description for each. The documented V$ view V$FIXED_VIEW_DEFINITION will serve as our starting point. This V$ view is the repository for all V$ and GV$ views as well as X$ tables of an instance. Inquiring this view about V$PARAMETER gives:

```
SQL> COLUMN view_definition FORMAT a80 WORD_WRAPPED
SQL> SELECT view_definition FROM v$fixed_view_definition
WHERE view_name='V$PARAMETER';
VIEW_DEFINITION
-------------------------------------------------------------------------
select  NUM , NAME , TYPE , VALUE , DISPLAY_VALUE, ISDEFAULT ,
ISSES_MODIFIABLE, ISSYS_MODIFIABLE , ISINSTANCE_MODIFIABLE, ISMODIFIED,
ISADJUSTED, ISDEPRECATED, DESCRIPTION, UPDATE_COMMENT, HASH
from GV$PARAMETER where inst_id = USERENV('Instance')
```

We learn that V$PARAMETER is based on GV$PARAMETER and that the former removes the cross–instance information found in the latter by filtering rows from other instances. No surprises here. Except for the additional column INST_ID, GV$PARAMETER has the same structure as V$PARAMETER.

```
SQL> DESC gv$parameter
 Name                                    Null?     Type
 -------------------------------------- -------- ------------
 INST_ID                                          NUMBER
 NUM                                              NUMBER
 NAME                                             VARCHAR2(80)
 TYPE                                             NUMBER
 VALUE                                            VARCHAR2(512)
 DISPLAY_VALUE                                    VARCHAR2(512)
 ISDEFAULT                                        VARCHAR2(9)
 ISSES_MODIFIABLE                                 VARCHAR2(5)
 ISSYS_MODIFIABLE                                 VARCHAR2(9)
 ISINSTANCE_MODIFIABLE                            VARCHAR2(5)
 ISMODIFIED                                       VARCHAR2(10)
 ISADJUSTED                                       VARCHAR2(5)
 ISDEPRECATED                                     VARCHAR2(5)
 DESCRIPTION                                      VARCHAR2(255)
 UPDATE_COMMENT                                   VARCHAR2(255)
 HASH                                             NUMBER
```

Further tapping V$FIXED_VIEW_DEFINITION gives:

```
SQL> SELECT view_definition FROM v$fixed_view_definition
WHERE view_name='GV$PARAMETER';
VIEW_DEFINITION
-------------------------------------------------------------------------
select x.inst_id,x.indx+1,ksppinm,ksppity,ksppstvl, ksppstdvl, ksppstdf,
decode(bitand(ksppiflg/256,1),1,'TRUE','FALSE'),
decode(bitand(ksppiflg/65536,3),1,'IMMEDIATE',2,'DEFERRED',
3,'IMMEDIATE','FALSE'),  decode(bitand(ksppiflg,4),4,'FALSE',
decode(bitand(ksppiflg/65536,3), 0, 'FALSE', 'TRUE')),
decode(bitand(ksppstvf,7),1,'MODIFIED',4,'SYSTEM_MOD','FALSE'),
decode(bitand(ksppstvf,2),2,'TRUE','FALSE'),  decode(bitand(ksppilrmflg/64, 1), 1,
'TRUE', 'FALSE'),  ksppdesc, ksppstcmnt, ksppihash
```

```
from x$ksppi x, x$ksppcv y where (x.indx = y.indx) and   ((translate(ksppinm,'_','#')
not like '##%') and ((translate(ksppinm,'_','#') not like '#%') or (ksppstdf = 'FALSE')
or (bitand(ksppstvf,5) > 0)))
```

The well–known X$ tables X$KSPPI and X$PSPPCV have come to the fore. Looking at the where–clause, it is very obvious that parameters that start with one or two underscores are hidden from the prying eyes of DBAs thirsty for knowledge.

Next, we need to make sense out of the cryptic column names. Since the column sequence of GV$PARAMETER is known, we can add the well understandable column names of GV$PARAMETER as column aliases to the view definition, by traversing the select–list of the view from top to bottom. This yields:

```
select
x.inst_id AS inst_id,
x.indx+1 AS num, -- C language arrays start at offset 0, but SQL stuff usually starts at
offset 1
ksppinm AS name,
ksppity AS type,
ksppstvl AS value,
ksppstdvl AS display_value,
ksppstdf AS isdefault,
decode(bitand(ksppiflg/256,1),1,'TRUE','FALSE') AS isses_modifiable,
decode(bitand(ksppiflg/65536,3),1,'IMMEDIATE',2,'DEFERRED',
3,'IMMEDIATE','FALSE') AS issys_modifiable,
decode(bitand(ksppiflg,4),4,'FALSE', decode(bitand(ksppiflg/65536,3), 0, 'FALSE',
'TRUE')) AS isinstance_modifiable,
decode(bitand(ksppstvf,7),1,'MODIFIED',4,'SYSTEM_MOD','FALSE') AS ismodified, -- vf
might mean value flag
decode(bitand(ksppstvf,2),2,'TRUE','FALSE') AS isadjusted,
decode(bitand(ksppilrmflg/64, 1), 1, 'TRUE', 'FALSE') AS isdeprecated,
ksppdesc AS description,
ksppstcmnt AS update_comment,
ksppihash AS hash
from x$ksppi x, x$ksppcv y
where (x.indx = y.indx)
and (
   (translate(ksppinm,'_','#') not like '##%')
   and
   (
      (translate(ksppinm,'_','#') not like '#%')
      or (ksppstdf = 'FALSE') or (bitand(ksppstvf,5) > 0)
   )
);
```

Thus, we obtain a mapping from the cryptic column names of X$KSPPI and X$KSPPCV to the well understandable column names of the view GV$PARAMETER. The mappings for X$KSPPI and X$KSPPCV are in Table 17 and Table 18 respectively.

Table 17: Columns of X$KSPPI

X$ Table Column	GV$ View Column
X$KSPPI.ADDR	n/a
X$KSPPI.INDX	GV$PARAMETER.NUM
X$KSPPI.INST_ID	GV$PARAMETER.INST_ID
X$KSPPI.KSPPINM	GV$PARAMETER.NAME
X$KSPPI.KSPPITY	GV$PARAMETER.TYPE
X$KSPPI.KSPPDESC	GV$PARAMETER.DESCRIPTION

Table 17: Columns of X$KSPPI

X$ Table Column	GV$ View Column
X$KSPPI.KSPPIFLG	GV$PARAMETER.ISSES_MODIFIABLE, GV$PARAMETER.ISSYS_MODIFIABLE, GV$PARAMETER.ISINSTANCE_MODIFIABLE
X$KSPPI.KSPPILRMFLG	GV$PARAMETER.ISDEPRECATED
X$KSPPI.KSPPIHASH	GV$PARAMETER.HASH

The column X$KSPPI.KSPPIFLG is a flag that is expanded to three separate columns in GV$PARAMETER using BITAND and DECODE.

Table 18: Columns of X$KSPPCV

X$ Table Column	GV$ View Column
X$KSPPCV.ADDR	n/a
X$KSPPCV.INDX	GV$PARAMETER.NUM
X$KSPPCV.INST_ID	GV$PARAMETER.INST_ID
X$KSPPCV.KSPPSTVL	GV$PARAMETER.VALUE
X$KSPPCV.KSPPSTDVL	GV$PARAMETER.DISPLAY_VALUE
X$KSPPCV.KSPPSTDF	GV$PARAMETER.ISDEFAULT
X$KSPPCV.KSPPSTVF	GV$PARAMETER.ISMODIFIED
X$KSPPCV.KSPPSTCMNT	GV$PARAMETER.UPDATE_COMMENT

To retrieve undocumented parameters, we need to modify the where–clause in such a way that only underscore parameters satisfy the predicates. We substitute LIKE ESCAPE in place of the awkward TRANSLATE used in the original GV$ view definition (file hidden_parameters.sql):

```
SELECT ksppinm name,
ksppstvl value,
ksppdesc description
FROM x$ksppi x, x$ksppcv y
WHERE (x.indx = y.indx)
AND x.inst_id=userenv('instance')
AND x.inst_id=y.inst_id
AND ksppinm LIKE '\_%' ESCAPE '\'
ORDER BY name;
```

Running this query on Oracle10*g* Release 2 retrieves an impressive amount of 1124 undocumented parameters (540 in Oracle9*i* Release 2 and 1627 in Oracle11*g*). A small excerpt of the query result, which includes the double underscore parameters introduced in Oracle10*g*, is below:

```
NAME                     VALUE         DESCRIPTION
------------------------ ------------- -------------------------------------
_4031_dump_bitvec        67194879      bitvec to specify dumps prior to 4031
                                       error
...
_PX_use_large_pool       FALSE         Use Large Pool as source of PX buffers
__db_cache_size          473956352     Actual size of DEFAULT buffer pool for
                                       standard block size buffers
__dg_broker_service_names orcl_XPT     service names for broker use
__java_pool_size         4194304       Actual size in bytes of java pool
__large_pool_size        4194304       Actual size in bytes of large pool
__shared_pool_size       117440512     Actual size in bytes of shared pool
```

```
__streams_pool_size       4194304      Actual size in bytes of streams pool
_abort_recovery_on_join   FALSE        if TRUE, abort recovery on join
                                       reconfigurations
...
_yield_check_interval     100000       interval to check whether actses
                                       should yield
1124 rows selected.
```

Relationships between X$ tables and V$ views

Wouldn't it be convenient to consult a document that contains the underlying X$ fixed table for any V$ view and vice versa? Such a document would facilitate the drill down process presented in the previous section. Such a document may be generated automatically. Four facts are paramount to coding the generation of such a document:

1. The column PREV_HASH_VALUE of the dynamic performance view V$SESSION holds the hash value of the previous SQL statement executed by a database session.
2. The execution plan for a SQL statement, which is identified by its hash value, is available in V$SQL_PLAN
3. A cached execution plan contains the names of the objects accessed in V$SQL_PLAN.OBJECT_NAME.
4. All row sources pertaining to X$ tables contain the string "FIXED TABLE".

Based on this information, an algorithm that executes SELECT statements on V$ views and pulls the names of underlying X$ tables from V$SQL_PLAN may be devised. The final task is to store the associations between V$ views and X$ tables found in a table, such as the one below:

```
CREATE TABLE x_v_assoc (
    x_id number,
    v_id number);
```

Instead of storing the fixed table or view names, the table X_V_ASSOC saves their object identifiers. The names may be retrieved by joining either column with V$FIXED_TABLE.OBJECT_ID.

Pseudo–code of the aforementioned algorithm is below:

LOOP over all V$ view names and their OBJECT_ID in V$FIXED_TABLE

Parse and execute SELECT * FROM *view_name* using dynamic SQL (DBMS_SQL)

Get the value of V$SESSION.PREV_HASH_VALUE for the current session

LOOP over all object names from the execution plan for the previous SQL statement in V$SQL_PLAN, considering only row sources that contain the string "FIXED TABLE"

Translate the object name to the fixed table number V$FIXED_TABLE.OBJECT_ID

Insert the object identifier of the X$ table and the object identifier of the associated V$ view into the table X_V_ASSOC

END LOOP

END LOOP

The full source code is too long to reproduce here, but it is available in the file x_v_assoc.sql in the source code depot. Once the table X_V_ASSOC is populated, the following query retrieves X$ fixed tables and the V$ views, which are based on them:

```
SQL> SELECT
f1.name x_name,
f2.name v_name
FROM x_v_assoc a, v$fixed_table f1, v$fixed_table f2
WHERE a.x_id=f1.object_id
AND a.v_id=f2.object_id
ORDER BY x_name;
```

In Oracle10g Release 2, 727 rows are returned by this query. To get a list of X$ fixed tables underlying V$ views, run the following query:

```
SQL> SELECT
f1.name v_name,
f2.name x_name
```

```
FROM x_v_assoc a, v$fixed_table f1, v$fixed_table f2
WHERE a.v_id=f1.object_id
AND a.x_id=f2.object_id;
```

Table 19 depicts a tiny subset of the associations returned by the latter query.

Table 19: Some V$ Views and their Underlying X$ Fixed Tables

V$ View	Underlying X$ table
V$ARCHIVED_LOG	X$KCCAL
V$BH	X$BH
V$CONTROLFILE	X$KCCCF
V$DATAFILE	X$KCCFN
V$DB_PIPES	X$KGLOB
V$INSTANCE	X$KVIT, X$QUIESCE, X$KSUXSINST
V$LATCH	X$KSLLD
V$MYSTAT	X$KSUSGIF, X$KSUMYSTA
V$PROCESS	X$KSUPR
V$RECOVER_FILE	X$KCVFHMRR
V$SEGMENT_STATISTICS	X$KTSSO, X$KSOLSFTS
V$SESSION	X$KSLED, X$KSUSE
V$SQL	X$KGLCURSOR_CHILD
V$SQL_BIND_DATA	X$KXSBD
V$SQL_PLAN	X$KQLFXPL

By spooling the output of the script x_v_assoc.sql, a text document that contains all the associations between V$ views and X$ tables may be generated.

Source Code Depot

Table 20: X$ Fixed Tables Source Code Depot

File Name	Functionality
hidden_parameters.sql	Lists hidden parameters from X$KSPPI and X$KSPPCV
x_v_assoc.sql	Generates associations between V$ fixed views and X$ fixed tables

Chapter 10

X$BH and Latch Contention

Status: X$BH is partially documented in *Oracle Database Performance Tuning Guide 10g Release 2.*

Benefit: This chapter provides additional information on X$BH. Contrary to what the reader might expect, I will show that scrutinizing undocumented X$ tables such as X$BH is not necessarily the royal road to optimum system performance.

Latch Contention

A latch is a low–level locking mechanism used by the ORACLE DBMS to protect memory structures. The wait event *latch free* is used to account for the wait time a process incurs when it attempts to get a latch, and the latch is unavailable on the first attempt. In Oracle10g, there are several dedicated latch–related wait events for latches, which are usually affected by contention. For those events, the name of the latch appears in the name of the wait event. The wait events *latch: library cache* or *latch: cache buffers chains* may serve as examples. The additional wait events in Oracle10g dispel the requirement to find out which latch a generic *latch free* wait pertains to. In Oracle9i, V$SESSION_WAIT.P2 contains the latch number waited for. The latch number corresponds to V$LATCH.LATCH#. By joining V$SESSION_WAIT and V$LATCH, the latch name in V$LATCH.NAME may be retrieved.

The cache buffers chains latches are used to protect a buffer list in the buffer cache. These latches are used when searching for, adding, and removing a buffer from the buffer list. Contention on this latch usually indicates that there is contention for the blocks protected by certain latches. Contention may be detected by looking at the column MISSES of the fixed view V$LATCH_CHILDREN. The query below identifies child latches with the highest miss count:

```
SQL> SELECT name, addr, latch#, child#, misses, sleeps
FROM v$latch_children
WHERE misses > 10000
ORDER BY misses;
```

```
NAME                  ADDR     LATCH# CHILD# MISSES SLEEPS
--------------------- -------- ------ ------ ------ ------
cache buffers chains  697ACFD8    122    190  11909    125
session idle bit      699B2E6C      7      2  13442     75
library cache pin     68BC3C90    216      2  30764     79
library cache         68BC3B58    214      2 178658    288
```

The cache buffers chains child latch with address 697ACFD8 is among the latches with the highest miss count. Counters in V$LATCH_CHILDREN are since instance startup. I chose the predicate MISSES > 10000 simply since this restricted the result of the query to four rows. Of course, one should look at figures from an interval where a performance problem was observed, not figures since instance startup.

Applying the procedure for making sense out of cryptic X$ column names from the previous chapter, yields the column mapping between GV$BH and X$BH shown in Table 21. Note that only a subset of X$BH columns, which includes all columns of GV$BH, are shown. Approximately half of the columns in X$BH are not externalized by GV$BH. Table 21 contains n/a under the heading "GV$BH Column Name" for columns not externalized by GV$BH.

Table 21: Mapping of GV$BH Columns to X$BH

X$BH Column Name	GV$BH Column Name	Meaning
ADDR	n/a	Buffer header address
INDX	n/a	Buffer header index (0–n)
INST_ID	INST_ID	Instance number, corresponds to GV$INSTANCE.INSTANCE_NUMBER
HLADDR	n/a	Child latch address
BLSIZ	n/a	Block size
FLAG	DIRTY, TEMP, PING, STALE, DIRECT	Flag for the type and status of the block
TS#	TS#	Tablespace number; corresponds to V$TABLESPACE.TS#
FILE#	FILE#	File number; corresponds to V$DATAFILE.FILE#
DBARFIL	n/a	Relative file number
DBABLK	BLOCK#	Block number from data block address
CLASS	CLASS#	Class number
STATE	STATUS	Block status (free, xcur, cr, etc.)
LE_ADDR	LOCK_ELEMENT_ADDR	Lock element address
OBJ	OBJD	Dictionary object number of the segment that contains the object
CR_SCN_BAS	n/a	Consistent read SCN base
CR_SCN_WRP	n/a	Consistent read SCN wrap
TCH	n/a	touch count
TIM	n/a	touch time

By joining X$BH and DBA_OBJECTS, we may find out to which database objects the blocks protected by the child latch belong (script latch_vs_blocks.sql):

```
SQL> SELECT bh.file#, bh.dbablk, bh.class,
decode(bh.state,0,'free',1,'xcur',2,'scur',3,'cr',
4,'read',5,'mrec',6,'irec',7,'write',8,'pi', 9,'memory',10,'mwrite',11,'donated') AS
status, decode(bitand(bh.flag,1), 0, 'N', 'Y') AS dirty, bh.tch,
```

```
    o.owner, o.object_name, o.object_type
FROM x$bh bh, dba_objects o
WHERE bh.obj=o.data_object_id
AND bh.hladdr='697ACFD8'
ORDER BY tch DESC;
FILE# DBABLK CLASS STATUS DIRTY TCH OWNER  OBJECT_NAME        OBJECT_TYPE
----- ------ ----- ------ ----- --- ------ ------------------ -----------
    4    476    1 xcur    N      24 NDEBES SYS_IOT_TOP_53076  INDEX
    1  48050    1 xcur    N       4 SYS    SYS_C00651         INDEX
    1   7843    1 xcur    N       2 SYS    ICOL$              TABLE
    1   7843    1 xcur    N       2 SYS    IND$               TABLE
    1   7843    1 xcur    N       2 SYS    COL$               TABLE
    1   7843    1 xcur    N       2 SYS    CLU$               TABLE
    1   7843    1 xcur    N       2 SYS    C_OBJ#             CLUSTER
```

The index SYS_IOT_TOP_53076 has the highest touch count among all objects protected by the child latch[1]. This index is the segment underlying an index organized table:

```
SQL> SELECT table_name, table_type
FROM dba_indexes
WHERE index_name='SYS_IOT_TOP_53076';
TABLE_NAME                     TABLE_TYPE
------------------------------ -----------
CUSTOMER                       TABLE
```

The big question is, whether this whole investigation deserves the DBA's time and energy or whether he is about to become afflicted by CTD? Compulsive tuning disorder (CTD) is a term coined by Gaja Krishna Vaidyanatha, co–author of *Oracle Performance Tuning 101* ([VaDe 2001]). Of course, CTD is a pun on the designation of the serious psychiatric disorder OCD (obsessive compulsive disorder). Looking at a Statspack report that quantifies the workload, which caused the latch contention, it turns out that the wait event *latch: cache buffers chains* is insignificant. I modified the Statspack report parameter top_n_events to include the top ten timed events in the report (default is five). In spite of this, the cache buffers chains wait event did not make the cut:

```
Snapshot        Snap Id   Snap Time          Sessions Curs/Sess Comment
~~~~~~~~        --------- ------------------ -------- --------- -------------------
Begin Snap:     662 15-Oct-07 20:20:20         16      5.1 contention customer
  End Snap:     663 15-Oct-07 20:24:30         17      6.1 contention customer
   Elapsed:               4.17 (mins)

...

Top 10 Timed Events                                           Avg %Total
~~~~~~~~~~~~~~~~~~~                                           wait   Call
Event                                Waits    Time (s)  (ms)  Time
-----------------------------------  -------- --------- ----- ------
db file sequential read               3,109       89    29    39.7
CPU time                                          59          26.3
control file sequential read            532       23    43    10.1
db file parallel write                  191       17    87     7.4
db file scattered read                  580        9    15     3.8
buffer busy waits                    12,530        7     1     3.2
read by other session                   420        4     8     1.6
os thread startup                         5        3   597     1.3
log file sync                            59        3    48     1.3
SQL*Net more data to client          88,397        3     0     1.2
...

Wait Events  DB/Inst: TEN/ten  Snaps: 662-663
...
```

---

1. It's also possible to join X$BH with DBA_EXTENTS by using the where–clause WHERE bh.file#=e.file_id AND bh.dbablk BETWEEN e.block_id AND e.block_id+e.blocks-1.
However, the response time of such a query is quite long.

Event	Waits	%Time -outs	Total Wait Time (s)	Avg wait (ms)	Waits /txn
db file sequential read	3,109	0	89	29	97.2
...					
latch: cache buffers chains	53	0	0	5	1.7
...					

In the five minute interval covered by the Statspack report, a meager 165 ms were spent waiting for the cache buffers chains latch. What about individual sessions which are affected by this wait event? These are identified by querying V$SESSION_EVENT:

```
SQL> SELECT s.sid, s.serial#, p.spid, e.event, e.total_waits, e.time_waited
FROM v$session s, v$process p, v$session_event e
WHERE s.paddr=p.addr
AND s.sid=e.sid
AND s.type='USER'
AND e.event LIKE 'latch%'
ORDER BY time_waited;
SID SERIAL# SPID EVENT                          TOTAL_WAITS TIME_WAITED
--- ------- ---- ------------------------------ ----------- -----------
 27     769 4400 latch: cache buffers chains             49           0
 27     769 4400 latch: library cache pin                 3           0
 32    1921 5232 latch: library cache pin                29           0
 32    1921 5232 latch: cache buffers chains            129           1
 32    1921 5232 latch: library cache                    86           1
 27     769 4400 latch: library cache                    35           1
SQL> ORADEBUG SETOSPID 5232
Oracle pid: 18, Windows thread id: 5232, image: ORACLE.EXE (SHAD)
SQL> ORADEBUG EVENT 10046 trace name context forever, level 8
Statement processed.
SQL> ORADEBUG TRACEFILE_NAME
c:\programs\oracle\product\admin\ten\udump\ten_ora_5232.trc
```

Since session (SID) 32 with operating system process identifier (SPID) 5332 had the highest amount of waits for *latch: cache buffers chains*, I decided to trace this session at level 8 using ORADEBUG (see Chapter 37). Then I generated a resource profile from the trace file using the free extended SQL trace profiler ESQLTRCPROF, included with this book:

```
C:> esqltrcprof.pl ten_ora_5232.trc
ORACLE version 10.2 trace file. Timings are in microseconds (1/1000000 sec)
Resource Profile
================

Response time: 43.387s; max(tim)-min(tim): 58.216s
Total wait time: 26.738s
--------------------------

Note: 'SQL*Net message from client' waits for more than 0.005s are considered think
time
Wait events and CPU usage:
 Duration    Pct        Count   Average Wait Event/CPU Usage/Think Time
 --------  ------  ------------ --------- ---------------------------------
  22.439s  51.72%        188693 0.000119s SQL*Net message from client
  16.250s  37.45%        188741 0.000086s total CPU
   1.124s   2.59%             2 0.561751s log file switch (checkpoint incomplete)
   0.774s   1.78%             3 0.257905s think time
   0.642s   1.48%           362 0.001774s enq: TX - index contention
   0.625s   1.44%          4543 0.000138s buffer busy waits
   0.569s   1.31%        188696 0.000003s SQL*Net message to client
```

```
  0.399s   0.92%                          unknown
  0.329s   0.76%          4   0.082256s log file switch completion
  0.170s   0.39%          5   0.034085s log buffer space
  0.057s   0.13%          4   0.014250s db file sequential read
  0.005s   0.01%          1   0.004899s log file sync
  0.002s   0.00%         20   0.000093s latch: library cache
  0.001s   0.00%         13   0.000056s latch: cache buffers chains
  0.001s   0.00%         10   0.000054s latch free
  0.000s   0.00%         28   0.000015s buffer deadlock
  0.000s   0.00%         10   0.000022s latch: cache buffers lru chain
  0.000s   0.00%          1   0.000101s latch: library cache pin
--------- ------- --------------------------------------------------------------
 43.387s 100.00% Total response time
```

```
Total number of roundtrips (SQL*Net message from/to client): 188696


CPU usage breakdown
-----------------------
parse CPU:     0.00s (12 PARSE calls)
exec  CPU:    16.25s (188707 EXEC calls)
fetch CPU:     0.00s (22 FETCH calls)
...
```

The most expensive SQL statement was an INSERT statement on the table CUSTOMER identified earlier by accessing X$BH:

```
Statements Sorted by Elapsed Time (including recursive resource utilization)
===========================================================================

Hash Value: 1256130531 - Total Elapsed Time (excluding think time): 42.608s

INSERT INTO customer(id, name, phone) VALUES (customer_id_seq.nextval, :name, :phone)
        RETURNING id INTO :id
```

DB Call	Count	Elapsed	CPU	Disk	Query	Current	Rows
PARSE	0	0.0000s	0.0000s	0	0	0	0
EXEC	188695	19.6005s	16.2344s	4	4241	581188	188695
FETCH	0	0.0000s	0.0000s	0	0	0	0
Total	188695	19.6005s	16.2344s	4	4241	581188	188695

Wait Event/CPU Usage/Think Time	Duration	Count
SQL*Net message from client	22.439s	188692
total CPU	16.234s	188695
think time	0.774s	3
enq: TX - index contention	0.642s	362
buffer busy waits	0.625s	4543
SQL*Net message to client	0.569s	188694
log file switch completion	0.329s	4
log buffer space	0.170s	5
db file sequential read	0.023s	2
latch: library cache	0.002s	20
latch: cache buffers chains	0.001s	13
latch free	0.001s	10
buffer deadlock	0.000s	28
latch: cache buffers lru chain	0.000s	10
latch: library cache pin	0.000s	1

Again, the contribution of the wait event *latch: cache buffers chains* is negligible. The problem is elsewhere: 51% of the response time are due to *SQL*Net message from client*, the most significant contributor to overall response time. Look at the columns "Count" and "Rows" of the statistics for the INSERT statement. The figures are identical. Furthermore the number of executions is almost identical to the number of network round–trips (*SQL*Net message from client*). This means that the application does single row inserts, i.e. one network round–trip per INSERT statement executed. This observation is confirmed by looking at the row count r of EXEC entries in the trace file. These consistently have the value 1:

```
WAIT #3: nam='SQL*Net message to client' ela= 3 driver id=1413697536 #bytes=1 p3=0
obj#=-1 tim=347983945867
EXEC #3:c=0,e=79,p=0,cr=0,cu=2,mis=0,r=1,dep=0,og=1,tim=347983945892
WAIT #3: nam='SQL*Net message from client' ela= 109 driver id=1413697536 #bytes=1 p3=0
obj#=-1 tim=347983946105
```

A major reduction in response time could be achieved by recoding the application to use array inserts. I caution the reader against following advice on the Internet to search for latch contention by accessing X$ tables. Such advice may lead you on the road to compulsive tuning disorder, rather than paving the way to a solution for performance problems. Always use a response time based approach. Never drill down to some perceived anomalies or ratios that you deem to be too high unless you have convincing evidence that these contribute significantly to response time. Several years ago, I had the opportunity to talk to the renowned neuroscientist Jaak Panksepp. To this date, I remember him asking "what data do you have in support of this claim?" More often than not, unsubstantiated assertions may be dismissed by asking this question. Instead of prematurely attributing symptoms to causes and haphazardly implementing hypothetical solutions, we as DBAs would be better advised to adopt scientific approaches resembling those used by the medical community.

Source Code Depot

Table 22: X$BH Source Code Depot

File Name	Functionality
latch_vs_blocks.sql	Retrieves database objects protected by a child latch.

Chapter 11

X$KSLED and Enhanced Session Wait Data

Status: X$KSLED is an undocumented X$ fixed table. V$SESSION_WAIT is based on X$KSLED and X$KSUSECST. X$KSLED contributes the wait event name to V$SESSION_WAIT whereas X$KSUSECST holds timing information. Neither Oracle9*i* nor Oracle10*g* have a V$ view that provides more than centisecond resolution for a single wait event at session level[1]. There is also no view which integrates information on operating system processes found in V$PROCESS with wait information. It's a bit cumbersome to correctly interpret the columns WAIT_TIME and SECONDS_IN_WAIT of the view V$SESSION_WAIT depending on the value of the column STATE.

Benefit: Direct access to X$ fixed tables makes it possible to get microsecond resolution for wait events without the need to enable SQL trace. Furthermore, an enhanced version of V$SESSION_WAIT, which combines information from V$SESSION, V$SESSION_WAIT and V$PROCESS and is easier to interpret, may be built. Note that V$SESSION in Oracle9*i* does not include information on wait events, whereas wait event information has been incorporated into V$SESSION in Oracle10*g*. The enhanced session wait view presented in this chapter is compatible with both Oracle9*i* and Oracle10*g*.

Drilling Down From V$SESSION_WAIT

By drilling down from V$SESSION_WAIT, as presented in Chapter 9, it becomes apparent that this view is based on X$KSLED and X$KSUSECST. Adding column alias names, which correspond to the column names of GV$SESSION, to the view definition retrieved from V$FIXED_VIEW_DEFINITION, yields the following SELECT statement:

```
SELECT s.inst_id AS inst_id,
s.indx AS sid,
```

---

1. In Oracle11*g*, the dynamic performance view V$SESSION_WAIT has the following new columns: WAIT_TIME_MICRO, TIME_REMAINING_MICRO, and TIME_SINCE_LAST_WAIT_MICRO.

```
s.ksussseq AS seq#,
e.kslednam AS event,
e.ksledp1 AS p1text,
s.ksussp1 AS p1,
s.ksussp1r AS p1raw,
e.ksledp2 AS p2text,
s.ksussp2 AS p2,
s.ksussp2r AS p2raw,
e.ksledp3 AS p3text,
s.ksussp3 AS p3,
s.ksussp3r AS p3raw,
decode(s.ksusstim,0,0,-1,-1,-2,-2,   decode(round(s.ksusstim/10000),0,-
1,round(s.ksusstim/10000))) AS wait_time,
s.ksusewtm AS seconds_in_wait,
decode(s.ksusstim, 0, 'WAITING', -2, 'WAITED UNKNOWN TIME',  -1, 'WAITED SHORT TIME',
'WAITED KNOWN TIME') AS state
FROM x$ksusecst s, x$ksled e
WHERE bitand(s.ksspaflg,1)!=0
and bitand(s.ksuseflg,1)!=0
and s.ksussseq!=0
and s.ksussopc=e.indx
```

Note how the microsecond resolution in X$KSUSECST is artificially reduced to centisecond resolution through the division by 10000. At reduced resolution, it is impossible to learn how long short wait events such as *db file sequential read*, *db file scattered read*, or global cache related wait events in Real Application Clusters (RAC) were. Wait times shorter than 1 centisecond are displayed as -1 by V$SESSION_WAIT. At this resolution, it is impossible to see disk access times at session level. Peaks in I/O service time also remain unnoticed, as long as the duration of the wait events stays below 1 centisecond, which it normally will. Below is an example:

```
SQL> SELECT event, wait_time, seconds_in_wait, state
FROM v$session_wait
WHERE (state='WAITED KNOWN TIME' or state='WAITED SHORT TIME')
AND event !='null event';
EVENT                         WAIT_TIME SECONDS_IN_WAIT STATE
----------------------------- --------- --------------- -----------------
db file sequential read              -1               0 WAITED KNOWN TIME
SQL*Net message from client          -1               0 WAITED KNOWN TIME
SQL*Net message to client            -1               0 WAITED KNOWN TIME
```

An Improved View

Now that the restrictions of V$SESSION_WAIT have become apparent, we may set goals for an improved view. The goals are to:

- provide wait event duration at microsecond resolution
- integrate process, session and session wait information
- present the wait status and wait time in a readily accessible format without requiring further decoding by users of the view

Information on processes and sessions is available from the X$ tables underlying V$PROCESS and V$SESSION. These are X$KSUSE and X$KSUPR respectively. It requires some perseverance to construct the largish view, which meets the goals set above. Below is the DDL to create the view, which I have called X_$SESSION_WAIT (script file name x_session_wait.sql):

```
CREATE OR REPLACE view x_$session_wait AS
SELECT s.inst_id AS inst_id,
s.indx AS sid,
se.ksuseser AS serial#,
-- spid from v$process
p.ksuprpid AS spid,
-- columns from v$session
```

```
se.ksuudlna AS username,
decode(bitand(se.ksuseidl,11),1,'ACTIVE',0,
decode(bitand(se.ksuseflg,4096),0,'INACTIVE','CACHED'),2,'SNIPED',3,'SNIPED',
'KILLED') AS status,
decode(ksspatyp,1,'DEDICATED',2,'SHARED',3,'PSEUDO','NONE') AS server,
se.ksuseunm AS osuser,
se.ksusepid AS process,
se.ksusemnm AS machine,
se.ksusetid AS terminal,
se.ksusepnm AS program,
decode(bitand(se.ksuseflg,19),17,'BACKGROUND',1,'USER',2,'RECURSIVE','?') AS type,
se.ksusesqh AS sql_hash_value,
se.ksusepha AS prev_hash_value,
se.ksuseapp AS module,
se.ksuseact AS action,
se.ksuseclid AS client_identifier,
se.ksuseobj AS row_wait_obj#,
se.ksusefil AS row_wait_file#,
se.ksuseblk AS row_wait_block#,
se.ksuseslt AS row_wait_row#,
se.ksuseltm AS logon_time,
se.ksusegrp AS resource_consumer_group,
-- columns from v$session_wait
s.ksussseq AS seq#,
e.kslednam AS event,
e.ksledp1 AS p1text,
s.ksussp1 AS p1,
s.ksussp1r AS p1raw,
e.ksledp2 AS p2text,
s.ksussp2 AS p2,
s.ksussp2r AS p2raw,
e.ksledp3 AS p3text,
s.ksussp3 AS p3,
s.ksussp3r AS p3raw,
-- improved timing information from x$ksusecst
decode(s.ksusstim,
-2, 'WAITED UNKNOWN TIME',
-1,'LAST WAIT < 1 microsecond', -- originally WAITED SHORT TIME
0,'CURRENTLY WAITING SINCE '|| s.ksusewtm || 's',
'LAST WAIT ' || s.ksusstim/1000 || ' milliseconds (' || s.ksusewtm || 's ago)')
wait_status,
to_number(decode(s.ksusstim,0,NULL,-1,NULL,-2,NULL, s.ksusstim/1000)) AS
wait_time_milli
from x$ksusecst s, x$ksled e , x$ksuse se, x$ksupr p
where bitand(s.ksspaflg,1)!=0
and bitand(s.ksuseflg,1)!=0
and s.ksussseq!=0
and s.ksussopc=e.indx
and s.indx=se.indx
and se.ksusepro=p.addr;
```

The unit of wait time in the column WAIT_TIME_MILLI is 1 millisecond. Fractional milliseconds are preserved, yielding microsecond resolution. The column WAIT_STATUS indicates whether the session is currently waiting or not. In case the session is waiting, it displays for how many seconds it has already been waiting. For sessions that are not currently waiting, the duration of the last wait event and the time which has elapsed since the last wait event began, are reported. The query below confirms that wait events are actually timed with microsecond resolution:

```
SQL> SELECT sid, serial#, spid, username, event, wait_status, wait_time_milli
FROM x_$session_wait
```

```
WHERE wait_time_milli > 0 and wait_time_milli <10;
SID SERIAL# SPID     USERNAME EVENT           WAIT_STATUS        WAIT_TIME_MILLI
--- ------- -------- -------- --------------- ------------------ ---------------
 24   58259 1188090  SYS      db file         LAST WAIT 6.541 ms           6.541
                              sequential read (0 s ago)
 22   48683 966786   SYS      SQL*Net message LAST WAIT .003 ms             .003
                              to client       (0 s ago)
```

I have included the operating system process identifier SPID, represented by the column KSUPRPID from the X$ fixed table X$KSUPR, in the view. This column corresponds to V$PROCESS.SPID. It is useful for enabling SQL trace with ORADEBUG SETOSPID and ORADEBUG EVENT (see Chapter 37). In a scenario where operating system tools, such as top, prstat, or nmon are used to identify resource intensive processes (e.g. high I/O wait percentage), the column SPID provides instant access to wait information based on the process identifier displayed by these tools.

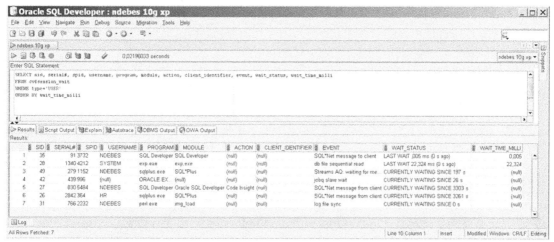

Figure 6: Result of a Query on the Enhanced Session Wait View CV_$SESSION_WAIT

Users other than SYS may be given access to x_$SESSION_WAIT by granting SELECT privilege on the view and creating a public synonym. Below are some DDL statements that mimic the hierarchical approach of the built–in V$ and GV$ views. Additional database objects are created in schema SITE_SYS, to avoid cluttering the data dictionary with site–specific objects. Privileges on the views in schema SITE_SYS are then granted to SELECT_CATALOG_ROLE. The letter C for custom in the view and synonym names is used to distinguish these views from the built–in dynamic performance views. Use the public synonyms CV$SESSION_WAIT and CGV$SESSION_WAIT to access enhanced versions of the views V_$SESSION_WAIT and GV_$SESSION_WAIT respectively.

```
SQL> GRANT SELECT ON x_$session_wait TO site_sys WITH GRANT OPTION;
Grant succeeded.
SQL> CREATE OR REPLACE VIEW site_sys.cgv_$session_wait AS SELECT * FROM
sys.x_$session_wait;
View created.
SQL> CREATE OR REPLACE VIEW site_sys.cv_$session_wait AS SELECT * FROM
sys.x_$session_wait WHERE inst_id=userenv('instance');
View created.
SQL> GRANT SELECT ON site_sys.cgv_$session_wait TO select_catalog_role;
Grant succeeded.
SQL> GRANT SELECT ON site_sys.cv_$session_wait TO select_catalog_role;
Grant succeeded.
SQL> CREATE OR REPLACE PUBLIC SYNONYM cgv$session_wait FOR site_sys.cgv_$session_wait;
Synonym created.
SQL> CREATE OR REPLACE PUBLIC SYNONYM cv$session_wait FOR site_sys.cv_$session_wait;
Synonym created.
```

Source Code Depot

Table 23: X$KSLED Source Code Depot

File Name	Functionality
x_session_wait.sql	This script contains enhanced views for accessing session wait events. In addition to columns from V$SESSION_WAIT, the views include information from V$PROCESS and V$SESSION. Wait time has microsecond resolution. The script includes grants and public synonyms.

Chapter 12

X$KFFXP and ASM Metadata

Status: The X$ fixed table X$KFFXP is undocumented in Oracle10*g* and Oracle11*g*.

Benefit: ASM metadata concerning mirroring and the assignment of ASM file extents to allocation units in ASM disks is available through X$KFFXP. An understanding of X$KFFXP enables a DBA to directly access database and server parameter files stored in ASM with operating system commands. Beyond educational purposes, an understanding of ASM file layout may prove useful for salvaging data or troubleshooting.

X$KFFXP

Each ASM file consists of one or more extents. Extents are striped across disks within the disk group where the file resides. The size of an extent and the size of an ASM allocation unit (parameter _ASM_AUSIZE) are identical. Due to striping, a mapping table between contiguous ASM file extents and non–contiguous storage of files in ASM disks must be maintained.

An ORACLE segment consists of one or more extents. Each extent consists of a contiguous set of blocks at a certain offset (block number) from the beginning of a data file. The locations and sizes of a segment's extents within a data file are available by querying the dictionary view DBA_EXTENTS. This applies to all the storage options for a data file, such as file system, raw device, or ASM file.

The X$ fixed table X$KFFXP holds the mapping between ASM file extents and allocation units within ASM disks. It keeps track of the position of striped and mirrored extents for each ASM file. You must be connected to an ASM instance to retrieve rows from this view. Given a block number within a segment from DBA_EXTENTS, it is possible to find out which block of an ASM disk holds the data in the block.

Each file in an ASM disk group is identified by a file number and an incarnation. Both numbers are part of the file name in V$ASM_ALIAS. V$ASM_ALIAS is built on top of X$KFFIL and not X$KFFXP. Actually, there is no V$ fixed view, which is based on X$KFFXP. ASMCMD, a command line utility which presents ASM disk groups as if they were file systems, displays the file number and incarnation when the command ls -l is used. The alias name spfileTEN.ora in the example below points to the ASM file with file number 265 and incarnation 632700769:

```
$ asmcmd
ASMCMD> cd DG/TEN
ASMCMD> ls -l spfileTEN.ora
Type Redund Striped Time Sys Name
                          N spfileTEN.ora => +DG/TEN/PARAMETERFILE/spfile.265.632700769
```

X$KFFXP also contains the file number and incarnation. Since the view must keep track of all the striped and mirrored extents, it includes a number of other columns that hold information on disk groups, disks, and ASM files. Table 24 lists the columns of X$KFFXP.

Table 24: X$KFFXP Columns

X$KFFXP Column Name	Meaning
ADDR	Address
INDX	Row index
INST_ID	Instance identifier (1 for single instance, 1..*n* for RAC)
GROUP_KFFXP	Disk group number; corresponds to V$ASM_DISKGROUP.GROUP_NUMBER
NUMBER_KFFXP	File number; corresponds to V$ASM_FILE.FILE_NUMBER
COMPOUND_KFFXP	Compound index; corresponds to V$ASM_FILE.COMPOUND_INDEX
INCARN_KFFXP	Incarnation; corresponds to V$ASM_FILE.INCARNATION
PXN_KFFXP	Unknown
XNUM_KFFXP	Extent number
LXN_KFFXP	Logical extent number (0=primary, 1=mirrored copy)
DISK_KFFXP	Disk number; corresponds to V$ASM_DISK.DISK_NUMBER
AU_KFFXP	Offset within the device in multiples of the allocation unit size (V$ASM_DISKGROUP.ALLOCATION_UNIT_SIZE)
FLAGS_KFFXP	Unknown
CHK_KFFXP	Unknown

Salvaging an SPFILE

Presumably I am not the only DBA who has had to face the issue of a server parameter file (SPFILE) that had undergone a modification with ALTER SYSTEM, which rendered the file unsuitable to start up an instance. This may manifest itself by several different errors. An example is below:

```
SQL> STARTUP
ORA-00821: Specified value of sga_target 356M is too small, needs to be at least 564M
ORA-01078: failure in processing system parameters
```

The SPFILE, which is a binary file, cannot be modified, except by performing an ALTER SYSTEM command against a running instance. However, in this case the instance refuses to start up with the SPFILE. If the SPFILE is stored in a file system, it can easily be converted to a text parameter file with a text editor by removing non ASCII characters. However, if the SPFILE is an ASM file and you do not have a recent RMAN backup of it, you are stuck. Unless of course you know how to retrieve the SPFILE directly from an ASM disk, which is what you will learn shortly.

Run against an ASM instance, the five–way join below retrieves all the information that is required to retrieve an SPFILE from ASM storage with the UNIX command dd[1]. The query receives the name of the SPFILE as input (not the absolute path within the disk group, which would be assigned to the parameter SPFILE). The example below is

from a disk group with external redundancy. Thus, there is merely the primary allocation unit and no second allocation unit for mirroring:

```
SQL> SELECT a.name, a.group_number AS group#, a.file_number AS file#, f.bytes,
allocation_unit_size AS au_size, au_kffxp AS au#, decode(x.lxn_kffxp, 0, 'PRIMARY', 1,
'MIRROR') AS type, d.failgroup AS failgrp, d.path
FROM v$asm_alias a, v$asm_file f, x$kffxp x, v$asm_disk d, v$asm_diskgroup dg
WHERE lower(a.name)=lower('spfileTEN.ora')
AND a.group_number=f.group_number
AND a.file_number=f.file_number
AND f.group_number=x.group_kffxp
AND f.file_number=x.number_kffxp
AND x.disk_kffxp=d.disk_number
AND f.group_number=dg.group_number;
NAME           GROUP# FILE# BYTES AU_SIZE AU# TYPE    FAILGRP PATH
------------- ------ ----- ----- ------- --- ------- ------- ----------------------
spfileTEN.ora      1   265  2560 1048576 240 PRIMARY SDA9    /dev/oracleasm/disks
                                                             /SDA9
```

With normal redundancy, i.e. two–way mirroring by ASM, you would see a primary and a secondary allocation unit,
which are assigned to different disks belonging to disjoint fail groups:

```
NAME           GROUP# FILE# BYTES AU_SIZE AU# TYPE    FAILGRP PATH
------------- ------ ----- ----- ------- --- ------- ------- ----------------------
spfileten.ora      1   257  2560 1048576  23 PRIMARY DC1     /dev/rlv_asm_dc1_dsk09
spfileten.ora      1   257  2560 1048576  26 MIRROR  DC2     /dev/rlv_asm_dc2_dsk09
```

The column AU# in the query output (X$KFFXP.AU_KFFXP) is the offset of an allocation unit from the first block of an
ASM disk. The default size of an ASM allocation unit is 1048576 bytes (1 MB). Taking this into consideration, the
SPFILE with a size of 2560 bytes, which is stored in allocation unit 240, may be retrieved with the following com-
mand pipeline:

```
$ dd if=/dev/oracleasm/disks/SDA9 bs=1048576 skip=240 count=1 | dd bs=2560 count=1 |
strings > spfile.txt
1+0 records in
1+0 records out
1+0 records in
0+0 records out
```

The dd options bs, skip and count indicate the block size, number of blocks to skip from the beginning of a file, and
the number of blocks to read respectively. The strings command near the end of the command pipeline removes all
non–ASCII characters. Hence, the resulting file spfile.txt is an ASCII text file, ready for editing. The commands
head and tail, which display the beginning and end of the file, confirm that the entire contents of the SPFILE were
retrieved:

```
$ head -3 spfile.txt
*.audit_file_dest='/opt/oracle/obase/admin/TEN/adump'
*.background_dump_dest='/opt/oracle/obase/admin/TEN/bdump'
*.compatible='10.2.0.3.0'
$ tail -3 spfile.txt
TEN1.undo_tablespace='UNDOTBS1'
TEN2.undo_tablespace='UNDOTBS2'
*.user_dump_dest='/opt/oracle/obase/admin/TEN/udump'
```

Mapping Segments to ASM Storage

Now that we have successfully completed the warm–up exercise, we are ready to tackle the more difficult task of
mapping a block in a database segment to the corresponding block in an ASM disk. Beyond the mapping to the correct allocation unit in an ASM disk, this requires finding the correct block within the allocation unit. A single ASM
allocation unit may contain blocks from several database segments. Remember that the smallest extent size in a

---

1. On Windows, use the dd command that ships with Cygwin.

locally managed tablespace with AUTOALLOCATE option is 64 KB. The case study that follows uses the segment LOCATIONS in tablespace USERS as an example. We repeat the query from the previous section, however this time pass the single data file of tablespace USERS as input:

```
SQL> SELECT x.xnum_kffxp AS extent, a.group_number AS grp#, a.file_number AS file#,
f.bytes, allocation_unit_size AS au_size, au_kffxp AS au, decode(x.lxn_kffxp, 0,
'PRIMARY', 1, 'MIRROR') AS type, d.failgroup AS failgrp, d.path
FROM v$asm_alias a, v$asm_file f, x$kffxp x, v$asm_disk d, v$asm_diskgroup dg
WHERE lower(a.name)=lower('USERS.263.628550085')
AND a.group_number=f.group_number
AND a.file_number=f.file_number
AND f.group_number=x.group_kffxp
AND f.file_number=x.number_kffxp
AND x.disk_kffxp=d.disk_number
AND f.group_number=dg.group_number
ORDER BY x.xnum_kffxp;
```

The size of the file USERS.263.628550085 is 175 MB. The result of the query, which is depicted below, shows how ASM has striped the file across five disks. By default, ASM stripes across eight disks (parameter _ASM_STRIPEWIDTH), given that the disk group contains enough disks to accomplish this.

EXTENT	GRP#	FILE#	BYTES	AU_SIZE	AU	TYPE	FAILGRP	PATH
0	1	263	183508992	1048576	123	PRIMARY	SDA11	/dev/oracleasm/disks/SDA11
1	1	263	183508992	1048576	126	PRIMARY	SDA6	/dev/oracleasm/disks/SDA6
2	1	263	183508992	1048576	123	PRIMARY	SDA9	/dev/oracleasm/disks/SDA9
3	1	263	183508992	1048576	125	PRIMARY	SDA10	/dev/oracleasm/disks/SDA10
4	1	263	183508992	1048576	125	PRIMARY	SDA5	/dev/oracleasm/disks/SDA5
5	1	263	183508992	1048576	124	PRIMARY	SDA11	/dev/oracleasm/disks/SDA11
6	1	263	183508992	1048576	127	PRIMARY	SDA6	/dev/oracleasm/disks/SDA6
7	1	263	183508992	1048576	124	PRIMARY	SDA9	/dev/oracleasm/disks/SDA9
8	1	263	183508992	1048576	126	PRIMARY	SDA10	/dev/oracleasm/disks/SDA10
9	1	263	183508992	1048576	126	PRIMARY	SDA5	/dev/oracleasm/disks/SDA5
10	1	263	183508992	1048576	125	PRIMARY	SDA11	/dev/oracleasm/disks/SDA11

...

The next step consists of locating the right database block among all those ASM file extents. The package DBMS_ROWID may be used to retrieve the block within a segment, where a certain row resides. The block number returned by DBMS_ROWID.ROWID_BLOCK_NUMBER must subsequently be mapped to the correct extent within the ASM file. We will use the row in table LOCATIONS, which contains the name of the city of angels, as an example:

```
SQL> SELECT f.file_name, e.relative_fno AS rel_fno, e.extent_id, e.block_id AS "1st
BLOCK", e.blocks, dbms_rowid.rowid_block_number(l.ROWID) AS block_id
FROM locations l, dba_extents e, dba_data_files f
WHERE l.city='Los Angeles'
AND f.relative_fno=e.relative_fno
AND e.relative_fno=dbms_rowid.rowid_relative_fno(l.ROWID)
AND dbms_rowid.rowid_block_number(l.ROWID)
BETWEEN e.block_id AND e.block_id + e.blocks -1;
```

FILE_NAME	REL_FNO	EXTENT_ID	1st BLOCK	BLOCKS	BLOCK_ID
+DG/ten/datafile/users.263.628550085	4	0	21793	8	21798

The row where LOCATIONS.CITY='Los Angeles' is in file 4, block 21798 (column BLOCK_ID in the query result). Block 21798 is in extent 0 of the segment, which starts at block 21793. Extent 0 has a total of 8 blocks. The name of file 4 indicates that it is an ASM file. Next, we need to locate the ASM allocation unit, which contains this database block. The BLOCK_ID is the offset from the beginning of the database file. The following query takes into consideration that the database block size is 8192 bytes and the ASM allocation unit size is 1048576 bytes. Offsets in a segment are measured in database blocks (DB_BLOCK_SIZE or the tablespace's block size), whereas offsets in ASM disks are measured in allocation units. The extent in the ASM file, which contains the block, is thus:

$$\text{floor}\!\left(\frac{21798 \cdot 8192}{1048576}\right) = 170$$

The query below returns the ASM disk and the sought after allocation unit within the disk:

```
SQL> SELECT x.xnum_kffxp AS extent, a.group_number AS grp#, a.file_number AS file#,
f.bytes, allocation_unit_size AS au_size, au_kffxp AS au#,
decode(x.lxn_kffxp, 0, 'PRIMARY', 1, 'MIRROR') AS type, d.failgroup, d.path
FROM v$asm_alias a, v$asm_file f, x$kffxp x, v$asm_disk d, v$asm_diskgroup dg
WHERE lower(a.name)=lower('USERS.263.628550085')
AND a.group_number=f.group_number
AND a.file_number=f.file_number
AND f.group_number=x.group_kffxp
AND f.file_number=x.number_kffxp
AND x.disk_kffxp=d.disk_number
AND f.group_number=dg.group_number
AND x.xnum_kffxp=trunc(21798*8192/1048576);
EXTENT GRP# FILE#     BYTES AU_SIZE AU# TYPE    FAILGROUP PATH
------ ---- ----- --------- ------- --- ------- --------- ------------------------
   170    1   263 183508992 1048576 238 PRIMARY SDA9      /dev/oracleasm/disks/SDA9
```

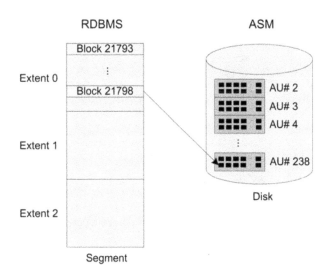

Figure 7: Mapping of a Block in a Database Segment to a Block within an Allocation Unit of an ASM Disk

Finally, we need to find the right block within the 1 MB sized allocation unit. The following formula calculates the offset of a database block from the beginning of an ASM disk:

$$\frac{\text{AU\#} \cdot \text{AU Size} + \text{Block\#} \cdot \text{DB\_BLOCK\_SIZE} - (\text{ASM Extent\#} \cdot \text{AU Size})}{\text{DB\_BLOCK\_SIZE}}$$

In the above formula, AU# is the allocation unit (offset) in an ASM disk (X$KFFXP.AU_KFFXP), AU size is the ASM allocation unit size, Block# is the block number in the database segment, DB_BLOCK_SIZE is the database block size (or tablespace block size, if different) and ASM Extent# is the ASM extent number (X$KFFXP.XNUM_KFFXP) in the ASM file. The offset thus obtained is in multiples of the database (or tablespace) block size. Entering the figures from the query result above into the formula yields:

$$\frac{238 \cdot 1048576 + 21798 \cdot 8192 - (170 \cdot 1048576)}{8192} = 30502$$

The database block, which contains the string "Los Angeles" is at an offset of 30502 blocks from the beginning of the disk, where each block has a size of 8192 bytes. To extract this block, we need to use the dd command below:

```
$ dd if=/dev/oracleasm/disks/SDA9 bs=8192 skip=30502 count=1 | strings | \
grep "Los Angeles"
1+0 records in
1+0 records out
Los Angeles
```

Of course, I did not cheat by creating a table that contains the string "Los Angeles" in each and every row. Adjacent blocks do not contain this string:

```
$ dd if=/dev/oracleasm/disks/SDA9 bs=8192 skip=30501 count=1 | strings | \
grep "Los Angeles"
1+0 records in
1+0 records out
$ dd if=/dev/oracleasm/disks/SDA9 bs=8192 skip=30503 count=1 | strings | \
grep "Los Angeles"
1+0 records in
1+0 records out
```

Figure 7 depicts the mapping of block 21978 in extent 0 of the database segment LOCATIONS to allocation unit 238 in the ASM disk. This block is 38 blocks past the first block in allocation unit 238. Since the segment's extent consists of 8 blocks, the ASM allocation unit contains additional extents, possibly belonging to different segments.

Part V

SQL Statements

Chapter 13

ALTER SESSION/SYSTEM SET EVENTS

Status: ALTER SESSION SET EVENTS and ALTER SYSTEM SET EVENTS are undocumented in the Oracle9*i* and Oracle10*g* *Oracle Database SQL Reference* manuals as well as in *Oracle Database SQL Language Reference 11g Release 1*. The manual *Oracle Database Performance Tuning Guide 10g Release 2* contains an ALTER SESSION statement for the presumably best known event 10046 at level 8. Yet, it is undocumented how to switch event 10046 off. The remaining levels of event 10046, which are also very useful, are undocumented too. Furthermore, there are hundreds of other undocumented events that may be set with ALTER SESSION and ALTER SYSTEM, some of which may be very useful too.

Benefit: Still today, for a database user who has the privilege ALTER SESSION but was not granted the role DBA, ALTER SESSION SET EVENTS is the only way to enable extended SQL trace in his own session in such a way that wait events and/or bind variables are included in the SQL trace file. Both ALTER SESSION SET EVENTS and ALTER SYSTEM SET EVENTS may also be used to request diagnostic dumps when a certain ORA-*nnnnn* error occurs.

Tracing Your Own Session

Supposedly every DBA and developer is aware of the SQL statement ALTER SESSION SET SQL_TRACE=TRUE. This statement creates a trace file, which logs all the SQL statements of the session that executed the command. Actually it logs much more than that, e.g. session identification information, application instrumentation entries, and timestamps, to mention a few. For details, please refer to Chapter 24. What is lacking are wait events and information on bind variables[1]. Both are needed for reliable performance diagnoses and the reproduction of performance problems.

---

1. Wait events and bind variables are equally missing when SQL trace is enabled with the packaged procedure DBMS_SESSION.SET_SQL_TRACE(TRUE).

Oracle10*g* was the first release that offered a documented interface to enable tracing of bind variables. This is possible with the package DBMS_MONITOR. DBMS_MONITOR also supports tracing of wait events. But execute permission on DBMS_MONITOR is solely granted to the role DBA (see $ORACLE_HOME/rdbms/admin/dbmsmntr.sql). The same applies to the undocumented package DBMS_SYSTEM, which is capable of setting events, such as 10046. The undocumented package DBMS_SUPPORT, which also provides tracing of wait events and bind variables in addition to database calls (parse, execute, fetch) is not even granted to the role DBA. All three are too powerful to allow normal database users to execute them. Last but not least, there is the SQL*Plus command ORADEBUG, which is merely available to SYS. So the average database user who is proficient in performance diagnosis is still at a loss when it comes to creating trace files without bothering a DBA—if it weren't for ALTER SESSION SET EVENTS.

ALTER SESSION SET EVENTS

ALTER SESSION SET EVENTS is ideal for building self–tracing capability into applications and for enabling SQL trace in a logon trigger. By self–tracing, I mean the ability of an application to enable SQL trace depending on an environment variable or a menu item in a graphical user interface. The syntax for switching an event on is:

    ALTER SESSION SET EVENTS 'event_number TRACE NAME CONTEXT [FOREVER,] LEVEL lvl'

The kind of event is determined by the integer *event_number*. The level, which often controls the verbosity, is set with the integer *lvl*. By including the keyword FOREVER, the event remains on, whereas without it, the event is only switched on momentarily. Normally, an event must remain switched on for a longer period of time, hence FOREVER is almost always used. If, for example, you were to execute ALTER SESSION SET EVENTS '10046 trace name context level 1', then the resulting SQL trace file would record the ALTER SESSION statement and tracing would be switched off when it finishes. Not very useful. Instead, you will want to use ALTER SESSION SET EVENTS '10046 trace name context forever, level 12' to trace wait events and bind variables of all subsequent statements.

The syntax for switching events off is:

    ALTER SESSION SET EVENTS 'event_number trace name context off'

The usual approach is to first enable event 10046, then exercise a code path that requires optimization, and finally to switch off event 10046. Performance diagnosis may then be done with TKPROF or with an extended SQL trace profiler such as ESQLTRCPROF, which is included in this book (see Chapter 27). In case you suspect or already know that the optimizer picks suboptimal execution plans for some of the traced statements, you should also enable event 10053 with the same syntax and for the same interval as event 10046. Event 10053 instructs the cost–based optimizer to write a log of its decision making process to a trace file. Level 1 is the right level for this event.

Using ALTER SESSION SET EVENTS, it's also possible to obtain all of the name–based dumps, such as system state, library cache, heap, control file, and many more. The SQL*Plus command ORADEBUG DUMPLIST prints a list of all available dumps. A while ago, Pete Finnigan has pointed out that a library cache dump may be used to glean passwords, which were used in ALTER USER statements against Oracle8. This issue is fixed in Oracle10*g*, as the test below proves:

```
SQL> ALTER USER hr IDENTIFIED BY secret;
User altered.
SQL> ALTER SESSION SET EVENTS 'immediate trace name library_cache level 10';
Session altered.
```

The resulting trace file contains asterisks instead of the password:

```
BUCKET 76429:
  LIBRARY OBJECT HANDLE: handle=6c15e8e8 mutex=6C15E99C(1)
  name=ALTER USER hr IDENTIFIED BY ******
```

There might be other similar exploits, such that you may feel that granting ALTER SESSION is too risky. The free instrumentation library for ORACLE (ILO) from Hotsos[1] contains the package HOTSOS_ILO_TIMER, which may be used to enable and disable tracing of database calls, wait events, and bind variables without providing access to events or dumps. Be warned however that you should revoke execute privilege from PUBLIC on HOTSOS_SYSUTIL, which is installed with ILO. Otherwise any database user could write to the alert log with the procedure WRITE_TO_ALERT.

---

1. ILO is available for download at http://sourceforge.net/projects/hotsos-ilo

Of course, you may also build your own wrapper around DBMS_SUPPORT or DBMS_MONITOR, but ILO also provides interesting functionality for application instrumentation with module, action and client identifier (see Chapter 28).

ALTER SYSTEM SET EVENTS

ALTER SYSTEM SET EVENTS is the instance level counterpart to ALTER SESSION SET EVENTS. It sets events for all future database sessions. Events set in this way do not persist across instance restarts. If an event must be set each time an instance starts, use the parameter EVENT (see page 32).

Here's a scenario for using an event at instance level, which you will hopefully never have to face. Let's assume that there are several block corruptions in a table segment. Unfortunately, the database is in no archive log mode, so neither data file nor block level recovery are an option. Importing the last export dump would result in data loss. There is an undocumented event that enables skipping of corrupt blocks during a full table scan[1]:

```
$ oerr ora 10231
10231, 00000, "skip corrupted blocks on _table_scans_"
// *Cause:
// *Action: such blocks are skipped in table scans, and listed in trace files
```

You may be able to salvage most of the changes since the last export was done by a table level export with this event. Yet, there is no way to instruct the export utility exp to set an event after it has connected. This is where ALTER SYSTEM SET EVENTS comes in handy. By using DBMS_SYSTEM.READ_EV, we may confirm that events thus set really are picked up by new database sessions:

```
SQL> CONNECT / AS SYSDBA
Connected.
SQL> VARIABLE lev NUMBER
SQL> SET AUTOPRINT ON
SQL> ALTER SYSTEM SET EVENTS '10231 trace name context forever, level 10';
System altered.
SQL> EXECUTE sys.dbms_system.read_ev(10231, :lev)
       LEV
----------
         0
SQL> CONNECT / AS SYSDBA
Connected.
SQL> EXECUTE sys.dbms_system.read_ev(10231, :lev)
       LEV
----------
        10
```

Event 10231 was not enabled in the database session that ran ALTER SYSTEM SET EVENTS. After starting a new database session, the event is set. At this point the export utility might be started to salvage the data. As soon as it finishes, the event may be switched off:

```
SQL> ALTER SYSTEM SET EVENTS '10231 trace name context off';
System altered.
SQL> CONNECT / AS SYSDBA
Connected.
SQL> EXECUTE sys.dbms_system.read_ev(10231, :lev)
       LEV
----------
         0
```

ALTER SESSION/SYSTEM SET EVENTS and Diagnostic Dumps

ALTER SESSION SET EVENTS and ALTER SYSTEM SET EVENTS may also be used to request certain diagnostic dumps in the event of an ORA-*nnnnn* error. The resulting trace files could be sent to Oracle Support for analysis. Usually,

---

1. The documented procedure DBMS_REPAIR.SKIP_CORRUPT_BLOCKS provides the same functionality in Oracle9*i* and subsequent releases.

such trace files document the state of an instance at the time when an error occurred. Thus, they may prove useful in pinpointing the cause of a defect. The syntax for requesting a dump when an ORA-*nnnnn* error occurs is:

```
ALTER {SESSION|SYSTEM} SET EVENTS 'error_code TRACE NAME dump_name LEVEL lvl'
```

To print a list of available dumps, use the command ORADEBUG DUMPLIST in SQL*Plus. The syntax for disabling a dump in the event of an ORACLE error is:

```
ALTER {SESSION|SYSTEM} SET EVENTS 'error_code TRACE NAME dump_name OFF'
```

Let's assume that several sessions have encountered the error ORA-04031, for example "ORA-04031: unable to allocate 4096 bytes of shared memory ("java pool","unknown object","joxs heap","Intern")". To create a heap dump each time any database session receives the ORACLE error 4031, you would run the following ALTER SYSTEM statement[1]:

```
SQL> ALTER SYSTEM SET EVENTS '4031 trace name heapdump level 536870914';
System altered.
```

Valid levels for this event are 1, 2, 3, 32 and 536870912 plus one of the levels between 1 and 32. Among others, the resulting trace file contains a call stack trace and the SQL statement, which was active at the time when the error occurred:

```
ioc_allocate (size: 4096, heap name: *** SGA ***, flags: 110009) caught 4031
*** 2007-11-12 16:20:54.359
ksedmp: internal or fatal error
ORA-04031: unable to allocate 4096 bytes of shared memory ("java pool","unknown
object","joxs heap","Intern")
Current SQL statement for this session:
SELECT SYNNAM, DBMS_JAVA.LONGNAME(SYNNAM), DBMS_JAVA.LONGNAME(SYNTAB),
TABOWN, TABNODE, PUBLIC$, SYNOWN, SYNOWNID, TABOWNID, SYNOBJNO    FROM    SYS.EXU9SYN
WHERE   SYNOWNID = :1      ORDER  BY SYNTIME
----- Call Stack Trace -----
calling              call       entry                   argument values in hex
location             type       point                   (? means dubious value)
...
```

After collecting sufficient diagnostic data, the dump event may be disabled with:

```
SQL> ALTER SYSTEM SET EVENTS '4031 trace name heapdump off';
System altered.
```

Immediate Dumps

It is also possible to request that a dump be taken immediately. The syntax for requesting an immediate dump is:

```
ALTER SESSION SET EVENTS 'IMMEDIATE TRACE NAME dump_name LEVEL lvl'
```

If you suspect that an instance is hanging, you might take a system state dump like this:

```
SQL> ALTER SESSION SET EVENTS 'immediate trace name systemstate level 10';
Session altered.
```

The header of a system state dump looks as below:

```
SYSTEM STATE
------------
System global information:
     processes: base 6ED426BC, size 50, cleanup 6ED47FF4
     allocation: free sessions 6ED60D60, free calls 00000000
     control alloc errors: 0 (process), 0 (session), 0 (call)
     PMON latch cleanup depth: 0
     seconds since PMON's last scan for dead processes: 21
     system statistics:
166 logons cumulative
18 logons current
1082648 opened cursors cumulative
25 opened cursors current
```

---

1. Oracle10*g* automatically writes a trace file when an ORA-4031 error is raised.

Chapter 14

ALTER SESSION SET CURRENT_SCHEMA

Status: ALTER SESSION SET CURRENT_SCHEMA was undocumented in Oracle8 and prior releases. It is partially documented in the Oracle8*i*, Oracle9*i* and Oracle10*g* SQL Reference manuals. There are undocumented restrictions concerning certain database objects. Restrictions apply to Advanced Queuing and database links.

Benefit: The CURRENT_SCHEMA session parameter offers a convenient way to perform operations on objects in a schema other than that of the current user without having to qualify the objects with the schema name. It does not affect the privileges of a session.

Privilege User vs. Schema User

The ORACLE DBMS distinguishes between a schema user identity and a privilege user identity. The privilege user identity determines which permissions are available to create or access database objects, while the schema user identity provides the context for statement parsing and execution. After logging into a DBMS instance, say as database user SYSTEM, the privileges granted to user SYSTEM are available and any unqualified database objects referred to are expected in schema SYSTEM. One might say that by default the current schema of the user SYSTEM is the schema SYSTEM. The DBMS responds as if the database objects used had been qualified by the schema name SYSTEM. But since the default current schema of user SYSTEM is SYSTEM, the DBMS does not require qualification by a schema name.

The user name and the current schema need not always be equal. This is evident from the columns PARSING_USER_ID, PARSING_SCHEMA_ID, and PARSING_SCHEMA_NAME of the view V$SQL as well as from SQL trace files, which distinguish between user identity (uid) and logical identity (lid) in the PARSING IN CURSOR entry.

This functionality is similar to UNIX systems, which discern an effective user identity from a real user identity. The omnipotent UNIX user root may switch to another user through the command su (switch user). Processes spawned thereafter have an effective user identity of the user switched to and a real user identity of root.

In circumstances where it is sufficient to change the parsing schema identifier, ALTER SESSION SET CURRENT_SCHEMA is a less intrusive alternative to a temporary change of the password and subsequent reset with ALTER USER IDENTIFIED BY VALUES (see Chapter 15).

The following query retrieves SQL statements run by user HR from the shared pool by selecting from the view V$SQL. Note that there are no SQL statements where the parsing user identity differs from the parsing schema identity:

```
SQL> SELECT s.parsing_user_id, u.username, s.parsing_schema_id, s.parsing_schema_name,
substr(s.sql_text,1,15) sql_text
FROM v$sql s, dba_users u
WHERE s.parsing_user_id=u.user_id
AND s.parsing_schema_name='HR';
PARSING_USER_ID USERNAME PARSING_SCHEMA_ID PARSING_SCHEMA_NAME SQL_TEXT
--------------- -------- ----------------- ------------------- ---------------
             38 HR                      38 HR                  SELECT USER FRO
             38 HR                      38 HR                  BEGIN DBMS_OUTP
```

After importing some tables into schema HR by running the IMPORT utility (imp) as SYSTEM, the same query on V$SQL shows that some statements were executed with parsing user identity SYSTEM, while the parsing schema identity was HR.

```
PARSING_USER_ID USERNAME PARSING_SCHEMA_ID PARSING_SCHEMA_NAME SQL_TEXT
--------------- -------- ----------------- ------------------- ---------------
             38 HR                      38 HR                  BEGIN   sys.dbm
             38 HR                      38 HR                  ALTER SESSION S
             38 HR                      38 HR                  ALTER SESSION S
              5 SYSTEM                  38 HR                  BEGIN   SYS.DBMS
              5 SYSTEM                  38 HR                  BEGIN   SYS.DBMS
```

If we trace the SQL statements issued by the IMPORT utility, we will find an ALTER SESSION SET CURRENT_SCHEMA statement in the SQL trace file. To set SQL_TRACE=TRUE in the import session, use the undocumented command line option TRACE=TRUE:

```
imp trace=true
Import: Release 10.2.0.1.0 - Production on Tue Jun 19 10:09:40 2007
Copyright (c) 1982, 2005, Oracle.  All rights reserved.
Username:
```

By the way, Data Pump Export (expdp) and Import (impdp) have the same undocumented TRACE switch. The resulting SQL trace file contains lines such as these:

```
PARSING IN CURSOR #5 len=38 dep=0 uid=5 oct=42 lid=5 tim=63968187622 hv=886929406
ad='6786940c'
ALTER SESSION SET CURRENT_SCHEMA= "HR"
END OF STMT
PARSE #5:c=0,e=523,p=0,cr=0,cu=0,mis=1,r=0,dep=0,og=1,tim=63968187614
EXEC #5:c=0,e=63,p=0,cr=0,cu=0,mis=0,r=0,dep=0,og=1,tim=63968187802
XCTEND rlbk=0, rd_only=1
====================
PARSING IN CURSOR #5 len=113 dep=0 uid=38 oct=13 lid=5 tim=63968189065 hv=0
ad='8eaf7d4'
CREATE SEQUENCE "LOCATIONS_SEQ" MINVALUE 1 MAXVALUE 9900 INCREMENT BY 100 START WITH
3300 NOCACHE NOORDER NOCYCLE
END OF STMT
PARSE #5:c=0,e=711,p=0,cr=0,cu=0,mis=1,r=0,dep=0,og=1,tim=63968189057
```

The trace file shows that the statement ALTER SESSION SET CURRENT_SCHEMA="HR" was parsed with parsing user identity 5 (lid=5; SYSTEM) and parsing schema identity 5 (uid=5). This ALTER SESSION statement sets the parsing schema name to HR, as evidenced by the subsequent statement CREATE SEQUENCE, which was parsed with a parsing schema identity of 38 (uid=38), which corresponds to the schema HR.

Creating Database Objects in a Foreign Schema

Let's assume that a software developer working with the account HR needs a large quantity of new tables for testing purposes. The database user HR does not have the privilege CREATE TABLE, since the developer is only allowed to work with existing tables in the schema HR. Thus, the developer is unable to create the tables in schema HR himself. The developer sent a script for creating the tables, but the database object names in the script are not prefixed by a schema name.

This scenario is an example for putting the ALTER SESSION SET CURRENT_SCHEMA statement to use. Without the statement, one of the following solutions must be chosen:

1. The DBA has to temporarily grant CREATE TABLE to the database user HR, such that the developer can create the tables himself.
2. The DBA has to ask the developer to prefix each and every object name in the script with the schema name HR, such that the DBA can run the script.

The DBA may run the script unchanged by leveraging CURRENT_SCHEMA. Below is a single CREATE TABLE statement executed after ALTER SESSION SET CURRENT_SCHEMA. The example illustrates that database objects are created under the parsing schema identifier, not the privilege schema identifier:

```
SQL> SHOW USER
USER is "SYSTEM"
SQL> ALTER SESSION SET current_schema=hr;
Session altered.
SQL> CREATE TABLE country (
    country_id char(2),
    country_name varchar2(40),
    region_id number,
    CONSTRAINT pk_country PRIMARY KEY (country_id)
);
Table created.
SQL> SELECT owner, object_type FROM dba_objects WHERE object_name IN ('COUNTRY',
'PK_COUNTRY');
OWNER OBJECT_TYPE
----- -----------
HR    TABLE
HR    INDEX
```

The database objects were created in schema HR. It is undocumented that restrictions pertaining to certain database objects apply when using ALTER SESSION SET CURRENT_SCHEMA.

Restrictions of ALTER SESSION SET CURRENT_SCHEMA

Switching to a different parsing schema identifier cannot be used with Advanced Queuing. Furthermore it is impossible to create a private database link in a foreign schema. It is possible to create a stored outline in a foreign schema. The next sections provide the details on these restrictions.

Advanced Queuing

ALTER SESSION SET CURRENT_SCHEMA has no effect on name resolution by the Advanced Queuing (AQ) packages DBMS_AQADM and DBMS_AQ. It is documented that synonyms cannot be used with advanced queues. Hence, the only way to use queue tables and queues in a foreign schema in conjunction with the PL/SQL packages DBMS_AQ and DBMS_AQADM, is to qualify the object names with the schema name, in the same way that a table in a foreign schema needs to be qualified as long as there is no synonym in the current schema. The following code sample assumes that the queue created in Chapter 16 resides in schema NDEBES.

```
$ sqlplus / as sysdba
Connected to:
Oracle Database 10g Enterprise Edition Release 10.2.0.1.0 - Production
SQL> SELECT owner FROM dba_queues WHERE name='CAUGHT_IN_SLOW_Q_AGAIN';
OWNER
---------
```

```
NDEBES
SQL> ALTER SESSION SET CURRENT_SCHEMA=ndebes;
Session altered.
SQL> EXEC dbms_aqadm.stop_queue('CAUGHT_IN_SLOW_Q_AGAIN')
BEGIN dbms_aqadm.stop_queue('CAUGHT_IN_SLOW_Q_AGAIN'); END;
*
ERROR at line 1:
ORA-24010: QUEUE SYS.CAUGHT_IN_SLOW_Q_AGAIN does not exist
ORA-06512: at "SYS.DBMS_AQADM_SYS", line 4913
ORA-06512: at "SYS.DBMS_AQADM", line 240
ORA-06512: at line 1
SQL> CONNECT ndebes/secret
Connected.
SQL> EXEC dbms_aqadm.stop_queue('CAUGHT_IN_SLOW_Q_AGAIN')
PL/SQL procedure successfully completed.
```

The reason for the failure of STOP_QUEUE executed by SYS is not a lack of privileges. When SYS qualifies the queue name with the correct schema name, STOP_QUEUE works flawlessly:

```
SQL> CONNECT / AS SYSDBA
Connected.
SQL> EXEC dbms_aqadm.stop_queue('NDEBES.CAUGHT_IN_SLOW_Q_AGAIN')
PL/SQL procedure successfully completed.
```

Private Database Links

It is impossible to create a private database link in a foreign schema, since a database link cannot be prefixed with a schema name. This restriction remains, even when ALTER SESSION SET CURRENT_SCHEMA is used:

```
SQL> CONNECT / AS SYSDBA
Connected.
SQL> ALTER SESSION SET CURRENT_SCHEMA=ndebes;
Session altered.
SQL> CREATE DATABASE LINK lnk CONNECT TO remote_user IDENTIFIED BY pwd USING
'dbserver1.oradbpro.com';
CREATE DATABASE LINK lnk CONNECT TO remote_user IDENTIFIED BY pwd USING
'dbserver1.oradbpro.com'
                          *
ERROR at line 1:
ORA-01031: insufficient privileges
```

The error message makes sense, since there is no privilege such as CREATE ANY DATABASE LINK. If you really do need to create a database link in a foreign schema, then you may use the trick with a stored procedure below:

```
CREATE OR REPLACE PROCEDURE ndebes.create_db_link
IS
BEGIN
   EXECUTE IMMEDIATE 'CREATE DATABASE LINK lnk CONNECT TO remote_user IDENTIFIED BY pwd
USING ''dbserver1.oradbpro.com''';
END;
/
Procedure created.
SQL> EXEC ndebes.create_db_link
PL/SQL procedure successfully completed.
SQL> SELECT owner, db_link, username, host FROM dba_db_links WHERE db_link LIKE 'LNK%';
OWNER  DB_LINK          USERNAME     HOST
------ ---------------- ----------- ----------------------
NDEBES LNK.ORADBPRO.COM REMOTE_USER dbserver1.oradbpro.com
```

Since stored procedures are run with owner's rights by default, the CREATE DATABASE LINK statement is executed as privilege user NDEBES and parsing user NDEBES, such that the database link is created in the same schema as the procedure. Analogous to database links, a directory name in a CREATE DIRECTORY statement cannot be prefixed with a schema name. However, all directories are owned by SYS, so it's irrelevant which user creates a directory.

Stored Outlines

Stored outlines may be used to fix an execution plan for a SQL statement, such that the optimizer always uses the plan from the stored outline instead of optimizing the statement in the current environment. It is possible to create a stored outline in a foreign schema, although there is no privilege CREATE ANY OUTLINE:

```
SQL> CONNECT system/secret
Connected.
SQL> ALTER SESSION SET CURRENT_SCHEMA=ndebes;
Session altered.
SQL> CREATE OUTLINE some_outline ON
SELECT emp.last_name, emp.first_name, d.department_name
FROM hr.employees emp, hr.departments d
WHERE emp.department_id=d.department_id;
Outline created.
SQL> SELECT node, stage, join_pos, hint FROM dba_outline_hints
WHERE owner='NDEBES'
AND name='SOME_OUTLINE'
ORDER by node, join_pos;
NODE STAGE JOIN_POS HINT
---- ----- -------- ------------------------------------------------------------
   1     1        0 USE_NL(@"SEL$1" "D"@"SEL$1")
   1     1        0 LEADING(@"SEL$1" "EMP"@"SEL$1" "D"@"SEL$1")
   1     1        0 OUTLINE_LEAF(@"SEL$1")
   1     1        0 ALL_ROWS
   1     1        0 IGNORE_OPTIM_EMBEDDED_HINTS
   1     1        0 OPTIMIZER_FEATURES_ENABLE('10.2.0.1')
   1     1        1 FULL(@"SEL$1" "EMP"@"SEL$1")
   1     1        2 INDEX(@"SEL$1" "D"@"SEL$1" ("DEPARTMENTS"."DEPARTMENT_ID"))
```

User NDEBES is the owner of the outline. Outlines consist of hints, which fully describe the execution plan for a statement.

Chapter 15

ALTER USER IDENTIFIED BY VALUES

Status: ALTER USER IDENTIFIED BY VALUES is undocumented. It is used internally by import utilities to store an encrypted password, which was previously saved with an export utility, in the data dictionary base table SYS.USER$.

Benefit: In situations where a DBA needs to connect as a certain user, but does not or must not know the password of that user, the capability saves time and spares the DBA from annoyance asking around for passwords.

The Password Game

Regularly, DBAs are asked to create database objects in a foreign schema or to investigate malfunctions which manifest themselves only when working with a certain user. Often, a DBA does not know the password to connect as a particular user. Company policy may not even allow him to obtain the password from a colleague or none of the colleagues on–shift know the password. In situations like these, the DBA will often be able to complete a task much more quickly if he or she has access to the schema involved. As a solution, the DBA can record the encrypted password of the schema, change the password, connect using the changed password, and reset the password. This chapter explains the approach made possible by the undocumented SQL statement ALTER USER IDENTIFIED BY VALUES. Some tasks can only be accomplished by connecting to the schema in question, rendering the approach presented here the only path to a solution. Some examples are querying the view V$INDEX_USAGE or running third party scripts, that do not prefix database objects with schema names, without changing the code.

The example below uses the user SYSTEM, which has DBA privileges, and the application schema HR. The first step is to connect as a DBA and to save the current unknown password:

```
SQL> CONNECT system
Enter password:
Connected.
SQL> SPOOL pwd.log
```

```
SQL> SELECT password FROM dba_users WHERE username='HR';
PASSWORD
------------------------------
2AB46277EE8215C4
SQL> SPOOL OFF
```

The file pwd.log now contains the encrypted password of the schema HR. Next, edit pwd.log, such that it contains a SQL statement suitable for resetting the password to its original value. The syntax is ALTER USER *username* IDENTIFIED BY VALUES '*encrypted_password*', where *encrypted_password* is the password obtained above. After editing, the file pwd.log should contain the following line:

```
ALTER USER hr IDENTIFIED BY VALUES '2AB46277EE8215C4';
```

Now the password may be changed temporarily:

```
SQL> ALTER USER hr IDENTIFIED BY secret;
User altered.
```

Note that the above statement will send the temporary password to the DBMS instance unencrypted. Use the SQL*Plus command PASSWORD, if this concerns you. The encrypted password stored in the data dictionary has now changed:

```
SQL> SELECT password FROM dba_users WHERE username='HR';
PASSWORD
------------------------------
D370106EA83A3CD3
```

Next, start one or more applications suitable for diagnosing and/or solving the issue at hand. To minimize the interval while the changed password is in effect, proceed to restore the original password immediately after the application has connected to the DBMS instance.

```
$ sqlplus hr/secret
Connected to:
Oracle Database 10g Enterprise Edition Release 10.2.0.1.0 - Production
SQL>
```

Now, reset the password to its original value by running the ALTER USER command in file pwd.log:

```
SQL> SET ECHO ON
SQL> @pwd.log
SQL> ALTER USER hr IDENTIFIED BY VALUES '2AB46277EE8215C4';
User altered.
```

The original password has now been restored and it is no longer possible to connect with the temporary password "secret":

```
SQL> SELECT password FROM dba_users WHERE username='HR';
PASSWORD
----------------
2AB46277EE8215C4
SQL> CONNECT hr/secret
ERROR:
ORA-01017: invalid username/password; logon denied
Warning: You are no longer connected to ORACLE.
```

The password encryption depends on the username, i.e. the same password used for different users yields different encrypted passwords. Here's an example:

```
SQL> CREATE USER U1 IDENTIFIED BY "Rattle And Hum";
User created.
SQL> CREATE USER U2 IDENTIFIED BY "Rattle And Hum";
User created.
SQL> SELECT username, password FROM dba_users WHERE username IN ('U1', 'U2');
USERNAME                         PASSWORD
------------------------------   ------------------------------
U1                               07A31E4964AEAC50
U2                               31019CA688540357
```

Locking Accounts with ALTER USER IDENTIFIED BY VALUES

By following Oracle Corporation's recommendation to lock the accounts of internal schemas such as CTXSYS, MDSYS, XDB, OLAPSYS, etc., you allow an attacker to find out which components are installed and to specifically exploit vulnerabilities in these components. The error "ORA-28000: the account is locked" tells the attacker that a certain schema does exist. You might prefer leaving the account open, while setting an impossible encrypted password with ALTER USER IDENTIFIED BY VALUES. Attempts to connect will then result in "ORA-01017: invalid username/password; logon denied", such that the attacker will not gain information on which user names exist. Since it is impossible to specify a matching password for the incorrect encryption, such an account is effectively locked, even without an expired password.

```
SQL> ALTER USER ctxsys IDENTIFIED BY VALUES 'LOCKED' ACCOUNT UNLOCK;
User altered.
SQL> SELECT password FROM dba_users WHERE username='CTXSYS';
PASSWORD
--------
LOCKED
SQL> CONNECT ctxsys/impossible_to_crack_incorrectly_encoded_password
ERROR:
ORA-01017: invalid username/password; logon denied
```

No matter which approach you prefer, you may always audit failed connect attempts by setting AUDIT_TRAIL=DB and enabling auditing for connect failures with AUDIT CONNECT WHENEVER NOT SUCCESSFUL. The following query will then yield failed connect attempts:

```
SQL> SELECT username, os_username, userhost, terminal, timestamp, returncode
FROM dba_audit_trail
WHERE action_name='LOGON'
AND returncode!=0;
USERNAME OS_USERNAME       USERHOST              TERMINAL  TIMESTAMP       RETURNCODE
-------- ---------------- -------------------- --------- -------------- ----------
CTXSYS   DBSERVER\ndebes   WORKGROUP\DBSERVER    DBSERVER  28.09.07 20:22        1017
MDSYS    DBSERVER\ndebes   WORKGROUP\DBSERVER    DBSERVER  28.09.07 20:37       28000
```

In the context of security, it is worth mentioning that Oracle10*g* databases, which were created based on a seed database such as GENERAL PURPOSE or TRANSACTION PROCESSING with DBCA, contain a new undocumented profile called MONITORING_PROFILE, which is assigned to the user DBSNMP. This profile allows an unlimited number of failed login attempts, whereas the standard profile DEFAULT, which also exists in Oracle9*i* and prior releases, allows ten failed login attempts in Oracle10*g*, before locking an account:

```
SQL> SELECT profile, limit FROM dba_profiles
WHERE resource_name='FAILED_LOGIN_ATTEMPTS';
PROFILE                          LIMIT
-------------------------------- ----------------------------------------
DEFAULT                          10
MONITORING_PROFILE               UNLIMITED
```

This setting makes the account DBSNMP a likely target for password cracking routines. This vulnerability does not apply to databases which were created manually or using CUSTOM DATABASE in DBCA.

ALTER USER and Unencrypted Passwords

In case you are concerned about sending unencrypted passwords across a network—after all this is one of the reasons why telnet and ftp have been abandoned in favor of secure shell (SSH)—you should be aware of the fact that ALTER USER IDENTIFIED BY does just that, unless your site has licensed and installed the Advanced Security Option, which encrypts all Oracle Net traffic. It's fairly easy to demonstrate this, since the undocumented Oracle Net trace file format contains an ASCII dump of the network packages transmitted by a database client when the highest trace level support is enabled. After setting the parameters below in sqlnet.ora on a Windows client system, trace files will be written to C:\temp:

```
trace_level_client=support
trace_directory_client=c:\temp
```

After running the SQL statement ALTER USER ndebes IDENTIFIED BY secret, the trace file contains the unencrypted password:

```
[28-SEP-2007 18:07:38:305] nspsend: 00 26 41 4C 54 45 52 20   |.&ALTER.|
[28-SEP-2007 18:07:38:305] nspsend: 55 53 45 52 20 6E 64 65   |USER.nde|
[28-SEP-2007 18:07:38:305] nspsend: 62 65 73 20 49 44 45 4E   |bes.IDEN|
[28-SEP-2007 18:07:38:305] nspsend: 54 49 46 49 45 44 20 42   |TIFIED.B|
[28-SEP-2007 18:07:38:305] nspsend: 59 20 73 65 63 72 65 74   |Y.secret|
```

This vulnerability does not apply to the SQL*Plus command PASSWORD, as is evident from the Oracle Net trace file. After changing a password in the following manner:

```
SQL> PASSWORD ndebes
Changing password for ndebes
New password:
Retype new password:
Password changed
```

You will notice an encrypted password in the trace file:

```
[28-SEP-2007 18:12:17:602] nspsend: 06 6E 64 65 62 65 73 10   |.ndebes.|
[28-SEP-2007 18:12:17:602] nspsend: 00 00 00 10 41 55 54 48   |....AUTH|
[28-SEP-2007 18:12:17:602] nspsend: 5F 4E 45 57 50 41 53 53   |_NEWPASS|
[28-SEP-2007 18:12:17:602] nspsend: 57 4F 52 44 40 00 00 00   |WORD@...|
[28-SEP-2007 18:12:17:602] nspsend: 40 44 38 36 38 43 39 36   |@D868C96|
[28-SEP-2007 18:12:17:602] nspsend: 41 42 34 43 42 37 39 39   |AB4CB799|
[28-SEP-2007 18:12:17:602] nspsend: 36 41 44 34 31 36 36 31   |6AD41661|
[28-SEP-2007 18:12:17:602] nspsend: 32 44 43 41 36 46 42 37   |2DCA6FB7|
[28-SEP-2007 18:12:17:602] nspsend: 43 46 44 39 35 41 35 33   |CFD95A53|
[28-SEP-2007 18:12:17:602] nspsend: 34 35 33 41 45 35 34 39   |453AE549|
[28-SEP-2007 18:12:17:602] nspsend: 35 36 39 34 46 45 37 36   |5694FE76|
[28-SEP-2007 18:12:17:602] nspsend: 36 33 31 38 44 43 43 43   |6318DCCC|
[28-SEP-2007 18:12:17:602] nspsend: 31 00 00 00 00 0D 00 00   |1.......|
[28-SEP-2007 18:12:17:602] nspsend: 00 0D 41 55 54 48 5F 50   |..AUTH_P|
[28-SEP-2007 18:12:17:602] nspsend: 41 53 53 57 4F 52 44 00   |ASSWORD.|
```

Chapter 16

SELECT FOR UPDATE SKIP LOCKED

Status: SELECT FOR UPDATE SKIP LOCKED is undocumented in Oracle9*i* and Oracle10*g*. It is used behind the scenes by Advanced Queuing, a reliable messaging service built into the ORACLE DBMS. Oracle11*g* Release 1 is the first DBMS release that includes documentation on SELECT FOR UPDATE SKIP LOCKED.

Benefit: SELECT FOR UPDATE SKIP LOCKED improves the scalability of applications, which attempt to concurrently update the same set of rows in a table. It eliminates wait time for TX locks. Consistency and isolation are preserved. The DBMS server assigns a fair share of the rows to each database client, which is interested in an overlapping result set.

Advanced Queuing

Advanced Queuing (AQ) is Oracle's implementation of a reliable messaging service, which is integrated into the ORACLE DBMS. AQ has been available since Oracle8. With the advent of Oracle10*g*, it was renamed Streams AQ (see *Streams Advanced Queuing User's Guide and Reference Oracle10g Release 2*), since Streams—an alternative replication mechanism to Advanced Replication—is built on top of message queuing and message propagation with AQ. Streams is based on redo log mining (Log Miner), whereas Advanced Replication is trigger–based.

AQ messages are usually made up of a user defined *abstract data type* (ADT; see *Application Developer's Guide—Advanced Queuing*) built with CREATE TYPE. The latter is called the *payload* of a message. In its simplest form, the payload is merely a BLOB instead of an ADT. Messages may be created by calling DBMS_AQ.ENQUEUE, propagated from one queue to another (even from one database to another or to another messaging system from a different vendor), and consumed with DBMS_AQ.DEQUEUE. The details are beyond the scope of this book. Please keep in mind though that AQ ships with all editions of the ORACLE DBMS at no additional cost, is highly reliable, since it benefits from the infrastructure of the ORACLE DBMS server, which provides crash and media recovery, and has

Java, PL/SQL, and C/C++ interfaces. So if you do need message queuing functionality in an upcoming project, AQ might be the right choice for you.

If you have ever taken a closer look behind the scenes of AQ, you may have noticed the undocumented SELECT FOR UPDATE SKIP LOCKED statement. In case you weren't among the lucky ones who were able to obtain a backstage pass, the well kept secret will be unveiled instantly.

AQ uses SKIP LOCKED when removing messages from a queue with DBMS_AQ.DEQUEUE to ensure scalability by preventing waits for TX locks. In a situation where several processes dequeue from the same queue simultaneously, locking would severely limit the scalability of applications that want to use concurrent processes for dequeuing. To be precise, this applies only when applications ask for any message, which is ready for dequeuing, which is the predominant approach. When concurrent processes ask for specific messages, the probability for contention is lower.

The following example shows how to obtain a SQL trace file that illustrates the use of the clause SKIP LOCKED by AQ. Before running the code below, make sure you have sufficient privileges to execute the package DBMS_AQADM that is needed to create queue tables and queues.

```
SQL> EXEC dbms_aqadm.create_queue_table('post_office_queue_table', 'raw');
SQL> EXEC dbms_aqadm.create_queue('caught_in_slow_q_again',
'post_office_queue_table');
SQL> EXEC dbms_aqadm.start_queue('caught_in_slow_q_again');
SQL> ALTER SESSION SET SQL_TRACE=TRUE;
Session altered.
SQL> DECLARE
    dequeue_options dbms_aq.dequeue_options_t;
    message_properties dbms_aq.message_properties_t;
    payload blob;
    msgid raw(16);
BEGIN
    dequeue_options.wait:=dbms_aq.no_wait; -- default is to patiently wait forever
    DBMS_AQ.DEQUEUE (
        queue_name => 'caught_in_slow_q_again',
        dequeue_options => dequeue_options,
        message_properties => message_properties,
        payload => payload,
        msgid => msgid);
END;
/
DECLARE
*
ERROR at line 1:
ORA-25228: timeout or end-of-fetch during message dequeue from
NDEBES.CAUGHT_IN_SLOW_Q_AGAIN
ORA-06512: at "SYS.DBMS_AQ", line 358
ORA-06512: at "SYS.DBMS_AQ", line 556
ORA-06512: at line 8
```

In the SQL trace file, you will see an example of a SELECT with the FOR UPDATE SKIP LOCKED clause:

```
PARSING IN CURSOR #27 len=367 dep=0 uid=30 oct=47 lid=30 tim=69919173952 hv=3830655786
ad='6771d48c'
DECLARE
    dequeue_options dbms_aq.dequeue_options_t;
    message_properties dbms_aq.message_properties_t;
    payload blob;
    msgid raw(16);
BEGIN
    dequeue_options.wait:=dbms_aq.no_wait;
    DBMS_AQ.DEQUEUE (
        queue_name => 'caught_in_slow_q_again',
        dequeue_options => dequeue_options,
```

```
        message_properties => message_properties,
        payload => payload,
        msgid => msgid);
END;
END OF STMT
PARSE #27:c=0,e=123,p=0,cr=0,cu=0,mis=0,r=0,dep=0,og=1,tim=69919173943
=====================
PARSING IN CURSOR #26 len=565 dep=1 uid=0 oct=3 lid=0 tim=69919341626 hv=319671114
ad='674e3128'
select  /*+ FIRST_ROWS(1) */   tab.rowid, tab.msgid, tab.corrid, tab.priority,
tab.delay,   tab.expiration, tab.retry_count, tab.exception_qschema,
tab.exception_queue, tab.chain_no, tab.local_order_no, tab.enq_time,
tab.time_manager_info, tab.state, tab.enq_tid, tab.step_no,   tab.sender_name,
tab.sender_address, tab.sender_protocol,   tab.dequeue_msgid, tab.user_prop,
tab.user_data  from "NDEBES"."POST_OFFICE_QUEUE_TABLE" tab  where q_name = :1 and
(state = :2  )  order by q_name, state, enq_time, step_no, chain_no, local_order_no for
update skip locked
END OF STMT
EXEC #26:c=0,e=168,p=0,cr=0,cu=0,mis=0,r=0,dep=1,og=2,tim=69919341618
FETCH #26:c=0,e=139,p=0,cr=3,cu=0,mis=0,r=0,dep=1,og=2,tim=69919363741
EXEC #27:c=0,e=38468,p=0,cr=12,cu=0,mis=0,r=0,dep=0,og=1,tim=69919378626
ERROR #27:err=25228 tim=0
```

Contention and SELECT FOR UPDATE SKIP LOCKED

Let's pretend the SKIP LOCKED extension did not exist. To investigate what happens when several processes attempt to consume messages simultaneously (any available message), we need to first enqueue some messages:

```
SQL> SET SERVEROUTPUT ON
SQL> DECLARE
    enqueue_options dbms_aq.enqueue_options_t;
    message_properties dbms_aq.message_properties_t;
    payload blob;
    msg raw(64);
    msgid raw(16);
BEGIN
    dbms_lob.createtemporary(payload, true);
    msg:=utl_raw.cast_to_raw('message in a bottle');
    dbms_lob.writeappend(payload, utl_raw.length(msg), msg);
    DBMS_AQ.ENQUEUE (
        queue_name => 'caught_in_slow_q_again',
        enqueue_options => enqueue_options,
        message_properties => message_properties,
        payload => payload,
        msgid => msgid);
    dbms_output.put_line(rawtohex(msgid));
END;
/
89A118C42BFA4A22AE31932E3426E493
PL/SQL procedure successfully completed.
SQL> COMMIT;
Commit complete.
```

Let's see which messages, except the one with MSGID=89A118C42BFA4A22AE31932E3426E493 we just enqueued, are in the queue:

```
SQL> SELECT tab.msgid, tab.state
FROM "NDEBES"."POST_OFFICE_QUEUE_TABLE" tab
WHERE q_name='CAUGHT_IN_SLOW_Q_AGAIN';
```

```
MSGID                                    STATE
--------------------------------------  ----------
3DB7BE5A803B4ECB91EF7B021FB223F4             1
00E146F0560C4760886B7AEEEDCF7BF2             1
34F01D98AF0444FF91B10C6D00CB5826             0
54783A999BB544419CDB0D8D44702CD3             0
B78950028B3A4F42A5C9460DDDB9F9D7             0
89A118C42BFA4A22AE31932E3426E493             0
25CC997C9ADE48FFABCE33E62C18A7F3             0
353D44D753494D78B9C5E7B515263A6D             0
2544AA9A68C54A9FB9B6FE410574D85A             0
F7E0192C2AEF45AEAEE5661F183261CC             1
10 rows selected.
```

There are currently 10 messages in the queue (each row represents one message). STATE=0 means the message is ready for dequeue, while STATE=1 means the message was enqueued with a delay for deferred dequeue (message_properties.delay>0; the delay is in seconds).

What happens when two processes dequeue concurrently? Let's take a simplified version of the SELECT FOR UPDATE we found in the SQL trace file of the dequeue operation and run it in session 1 without SKIP LOCKED while retaining the bind variables:

```
SQL> VARIABLE q_name VARCHAR2(30)
SQL> VARIABLE state NUMBER
SQL> BEGIN
    :q_name:='CAUGHT_IN_SLOW_Q_AGAIN';
    :state:=0;
END;
/
PL/SQL procedure successfully completed.
SQL> ALTER SESSION SET SQL_TRACE=TRUE;
Session altered.
SQL> SELECT userenv('sid') FROM dual;
USERENV('SID')
--------------
           134
SQL> SET ARRAYSIZE 1
SQL> SET PAGESIZE 1
SQL> SET TIME ON
23:41:04 SQL> SET PAUSE "Hit return to continue"
23:41:04 SQL> SET PAUSE ON
23:41:04 SQL> SELECT tab.msgid FROM "NDEBES"."POST_OFFICE_QUEUE_TABLE" tab WHERE
q_name=:q_name and (state=:state) FOR UPDATE;
Hit return to continue
```

Session 1 has retrieved one row up to this point, even though SQL*Plus does not yet display that row. The SQL trace output, which contains a FETCH call with r=1 (r is short for rows), proves it:

```
$ tail -f ten_ora_1724.trc
=====================
PARSING IN CURSOR #2 len=112 dep=0 uid=30 oct=3 lid=30 tim=78932802402 hv=2531579934
ad='6792e910'
SELECT tab.msgid
FROM "NDEBES"."POST_OFFICE_QUEUE_TABLE" tab
WHERE q_name=:q_name  and (state=:state)
FOR UPDATE
END OF STMT
PARSE #2:c=0,e=115,p=0,cr=0,cu=0,mis=0,r=0,dep=0,og=1,tim=78932802391
EXEC #2:c=0,e=1290,p=0,cr=16,cu=9,mis=0,r=0,dep=0,og=1,tim=78932838870
FETCH #2:c=0,e=459,p=0,cr=12,cu=0,mis=0,r=1,dep=0,og=1,tim=78932843524
```

In theory, this leaves 6 rows worth of messages with STATE=0 for session 2. Let's see what happens in session 2:

```
SQL> ALTER SESSION SET EVENTS '10046 trace name context forever, level 8';
Session altered.
SQL> SELECT userenv('sid') FROM dual;
USERENV('SID')
--------------
           158
SQL> SET ARRAYSIZE 1
SQL> SET PAGESIZE 1
SQL> SET TIME ON
23:45:28 SQL> SET PAUSE "Hit return to continue"
23:45:28 SQL> SET PAUSE ON
23:45:28 SQL> SELECT tab.msgid FROM "NDEBES"."POST_OFFICE_QUEUE_TABLE" tab WHERE
q_name=:q_name  and (state=:state) FOR UPDATE;
```

The second session is unable to retrieve any data. Here's the level 8 SQL trace output from that session:

```
*** 2007-07-10 23:45:40.319
WAIT #1: nam='enq: TX - row lock contention' ela= 2999807 name|mode=1415053318 usn<<16
| slot=327721 sequence=660 obj#=16567 tim=79706625648
WAIT #1: nam='enq: TX - row lock contention' ela= 3000541 name|mode=1415053318 usn<<16
| slot=327721 sequence=660 obj#=16567 tim=79709637248
WAIT #1: nam='enq: TX - row lock contention' ela= 2999946 name|mode=1415053318 usn<<16
| slot=327721 sequence=660 obj#=16567 tim=79712642844
WAIT #1: nam='enq: TX - row lock contention' ela= 3000759 name|mode=1415053318 usn<<16
| slot=327721 sequence=660 obj#=16567 tim=79715649132
*** 2007-07-10 23:45:52.347
WAIT #1: nam='enq: TX - row lock contention' ela= 2999721 name|mode=1415053318 usn<<16
| slot=327721 sequence=660 obj#=16567 tim=79718655012
```

We see repeated waits for a TX lock, due to a lock (enqueue) request constantly being reattempted. A look at V$LOCK confirms that session 1 with SID=134 blocks session 2 with SID=158:

```
SQL> SELECT sid, type, id1, id2, lmode, request, block
FROM v$lock
WHERE sid IN (134,158)
ORDER BY 1;
SID TYPE    ID1 ID2 LMODE REQUEST BLOCK
--- ---- ------ --- ----- ------- -----
134 TM   16567   0     3       0     0
134 TX   458764 657    6       0     1
158 TM   16567   0     3       0     0
158 TX   458764 657    0       6     0
```

The TYPE and LMODE in V$LOCK are represented as name|mode=1415053318 in the extended SQL trace file. This is a decimal number with the upper two bytes representing the enqueue name as ASCII encoded letters and the lowest byte representing the lock mode. Name and mode are equivalent to V$SESSION_WAIT.P1 when the wait in V$SESSION_WAIT.EVENT is for a TX enqueue. Oracle9*i* uses the generic wait event name *enqueue*, whereas Oracle10*g* uses *enq: TX - row lock contention*. Oracle10*g* provides the same information in V$SESSION.EVENT and V$SESSION.P1 as well.

You have two options for converting name and mode into a more human readable format. The first one uses decimal to hexadecimal and decimal to ASCII conversion, whereas the second relies entirely on SQL. The UNIX utility bc (an arbitrary precision calculator) may be used to convert between decimal and hexadecimal numbers (most implementations of bc do not support comments (#), but the one by the Free Software Foundation does). Here's the output of a bc session, which accomplished the conversion.

```
$ bc 1.06
Copyright 1991-1994, 1997, 1998, 2000 Free Software Foundation, Inc.
obase=16 # ask for hexadecimal output, i.e. output base 16
1415053318 # convert name and mode to hexadecimal
54580006
# lock mode is 6 (exclusive) and enqueue name is hex 5458, let's convert that to decimal
```

```
obase=10 # ask for output in decimal, i.e. base 10
ibase=16 # input will be hexadecimal
54 # hex
84
# is 84 decimal
58 # hex
88
# is 88 decimal
```

Now we can use the function CHR in SQL*Plus to convert from decimal to ASCII:

```
SQL> SELECT chr(84)||chr(88) AS name FROM dual;
NAME
----
TX
```

Alternatively, a SELECT statement, that incorporates the function BITAND, may be used to extract the information from the decimal name and mode:

```
SQL> VARIABLE p1 NUMBER
SQL> EXEC :p1:=1415053318
SQL> SELECT chr(to_char(bitand(:p1,-16777216))/16777215)||
    chr(to_char(bitand(:p1, 16711680))/65535) "Name",
    to_char( bitand(:p1, 65535) ) "Mode"
FROM dual;
Name Mode
---- ----
TX   6
```

Let's go back to session 1 and hit the return key, such that it can continue:

```
23:41:04 SQL> SELECT tab.msgid FROM "NDEBES"."POST_OFFICE_QUEUE_TABLE" tab WHERE
q_name=:q_name  and (state=:state) FOR UPDATE;
Hit return to continue
34F01D98AF0444FF91B10C6D00CB5826
Hit return to continue
```

The row previously fetched by SQL*Plus session 1 is now displayed and the SQL trace file shows that another FETCH call was done:

```
FETCH #1:c=0,e=158,p=0,cr=12,cu=0,mis=0,r=1,dep=0,og=1,tim=79430535911
*** 2007-07-10 23:48:01.833
FETCH #1:c=0,e=19466,p=0,cr=1,cu=0,mis=0,r=2,dep=0,og=1,tim=79848141763
```

SQL*Plus pauses again after displaying one row, since PAGESIZE=1 is set. Switching back to session 2 there is still no progress. Even though I prevented SQL*Plus from fetching all the relevant rows with a single FETCH call by reducing ARRAYSIZE from its default of 15 to just 1, the whole process is single threaded and thus there's no room for benefiting from a multiprocessor system.

Finally, after fetching all rows and committing in session 1, session 2 can retrieve the matching rows. In the real world though, there would be no rows left for session 2 to process, since session 1 would have changed the status to a value other than 0 after finishing its job. Here's the COMMIT in session 1:

```
Hit return to continue
2544AA9A68C54A9FB9B6FE410574D85A
7 rows selected.
23:56:03 SQL>
23:56:05 SQL> COMMIT;
Commit complete.
23:56:17 SQL>
```

Now session 2 wakes up:

```
Hit return to continue
34F01D98AF0444FF91B10C6D00CB5826
...
```

```
2544AA9A68C54A9FB9B6FE410574D85A
7 rows selected.
```

Even though the normal processing of SQL*Plus was altered, the result of this test is disappointing. However, taking locking strategies of relational databases into account, the behavior observed is exactly what one should expect. Let's investigate what happens when we add SKIP LOCKED to the picture.

Session 1:

```
00:50:41 SQL> ALTER SESSION SET EVENTS '10046 trace name context forever, level 8';
Session altered.
00:50:51 SQL> SET ARRAYSIZE 1
00:50:51 SQL> SET PAGESIZE 1
00:50:51 SQL> SET TIME ON
00:50:51 SQL> SET PAUSE "Hit return to continue"
00:50:51 SQL> SET PAUSE ON
00:50:51 SQL> SELECT tab.msgid
00:50:51 FROM "NDEBES"."POST_OFFICE_QUEUE_TABLE" tab
00:50:51 WHERE q_name=:q_name  and (state=:state)
00:50:51 FOR UPDATE SKIP LOCKED;
Hit return to continue
```

Session 2:

```
00:50:44 SQL> ALTER SESSION SET EVENTS '10046 trace name context forever, level 8';
Session altered.
00:51:00 SQL> SET FEEDBACK ON
00:51:00 SQL> SET ARRAYSIZE 1
00:51:00 SQL> SET PAGESIZE 1
00:51:00 SQL> SET TIME ON
00:51:00 SQL> SET PAUSE "Hit return to continue"
00:51:00 SQL> SET PAUSE ON
00:51:00 SQL> SELECT tab.msgid FROM "NDEBES"."POST_OFFICE_QUEUE_TABLE" tab WHERE
q_name=:q_name  and (state=:state) FOR UPDATE SKIP LOCKED;
Hit return to continue
```

Both sessions are waiting for input in order to display the first row. Note how session 2 now prints "Hit return to continue". This was not the case in the first test, since the FETCH call of session 2 could not complete due to the wait for a TX enqueue. Now hit return in session 2:

```
...
Hit return to continue
54783A999BB544419CDB0D8D44702CD3
Hit return to continue
```

Session 2 succeeded in retrieving a row, even though session 1 issued SELECT FOR UPDATE SKIP LOCKED first. Now hit return in session 1:

```
...
Hit return to continue
34F01D98AF0444FF91B10C6D00CB5826
Hit return to continue
```

Session 1 also retrieved a row. Hitting the return key alternatingly in both sessions, shows that both get a fair share of the rows. Looking at V$LOCK confirms that this time neither session is blocked:

```
SQL> SELECT sid, type, id1, id2, lmode, request, block
FROM v$lock WHERE sid IN (134,158)
ORDER BY 1;
SID TYPE    ID1 ID2 LMODE REQUEST BLOCK
--- ---- ------ --- ----- ------- -----
134 TM   16567   0     3       0     0
134 TX  196644 644     6       0     0
158 TX   65539 666     6       0     0
158 TM   16567   0     3       0     0
```

Table 25 illustrates the whole sequence chronologically. Rows further down in the table correspond to a later point in time. The timestamps (format is HH24:MI:SS) printed by SQL*Plus due to SET TIME ON, serve to further document the sequence of events.

Table 25: Concurrent SELECT FOR UPDATE SKIP LOCKED

Session 1	*Session 2*

`00:50:51 SQL> SELECT tab.msgid`
`FROM "NDEBES"."POST_OFFICE_QUEUE_TABLE" tab`
`WHERE q_name=:q_name AND (state=:state) FOR`
`UPDATE SKIP LOCKED;`
`Hit return to continue`	

	`00:51:00 SQL> SELECT tab.msgid`
	`FROM "NDEBES"."POST_OFFICE_QUEUE_TABLE"`
	`tab WHERE q_name=:q_name AND (state=:state)`
	`FOR UPDATE SKIP LOCKED;`
	`Hit return to continue`

`34F01D98AF0444FF91B10C6D00CB5826` `Hit return to continue`	
	`54783A999BB544419CDB0D8D44702CD3` `Hit return to continue`
`25CC997C9ADE48FFABCE33E62C18A7F3` `Hit return to continue`	
	`B78950028B3A4F42A5C9460DDDB9F9D7` `Hit return to continue`

`353D44D753494D78B9C5E7B515263A6D`
`3 rows selected.`
`00:57:43 SQL>`	

	`89A118C42BFA4A22AE31932E3426E493`
	`Hit return to continue`
	`2544AA9A68C54A9FB9B6FE410574D85A`
	`4 rows selected.`
	`00:57:45 SQL>`

This time the results are excellent. Both sessions fetched a fair share of the rows, no row was fetched by more than one session, and no rows were skipped. Both sessions were properly isolated from each other due to locking, yet no session blocked the other. The level 8 extended SQL trace files for both sessions confirm this in that they do not contain a single wait for a TX lock during the whole sequence of FETCH calls. The approach works just as well with three or more sessions.

At the beginning of this chapter, I recommended the use of AQ for good reason. As we learned in this chapter, it is inherently scalable, since it uses the undocumented SKIP LOCKED clause when dequeuing messages. Another compelling reason for using AQ is that it has no requirement for polling to find out whether messages are available or not. I have seen several systems which were under high load due to applications that asked the DBMS instance several dozen times a second whether there was work to do. In AQ parlance, one would say that these applications were looking for messages to consume. The poor implementation resulted in one CPU being almost 100% busy all the time.

A closer look at how DBMS_AQ.DEQUEUE is implemented reveals that it is possible to wait one or more seconds for a message to arrive. Database sessions which request a message do not keep a CPU busy while they are waiting. Instead, the session is put to sleep on the wait event *Streams AQ: waiting for messages in the queue* (in Oracle10g). The first parameter of this wait event (V$SESSION_EVENT.P1) is the object identifier of the queue in the data dictionary (DBA_OBJECTS.OBJECT_ID). V$SESSION_EVENT.P3 holds the time (in seconds) which was used in the call to DBMS_AQ.DEQUEUE.

```
SQL> SELECT p1, p1text, p2, p2text, p3, p3text
FROM v$session_wait
WHERE event='Streams AQ: waiting for messages in the queue';
   P1 P1TEXT              P2 P2TEXT    P3 P3TEXT
----- -------- ---------- -------- --- ---------
16580 queue id 1780813772 process# 120 wait time
SQL> SELECT object_name, object_type FROM dba_objects WHERE object_id=16580;
OBJECT_NAME              OBJECT_TYPE
--------------------- -----------
CAUGHT_IN_SLOW_Q_AGAIN QUEUE
```

By the way, if you are merely trying to protect a shared resource from being used simultaneously by different processes, consider using DBMS_LOCK instead of implementing a sort of mutual exclusion or semaphore mechanism with a table. I'm addressing this point, since I have seen postings on the Internet, that suggest using SELECT FOR UPDATE SKIP LOCKED to implement a resource control table, i.e. a dedicated table, that has one row per resource and a status column. The value of the status column would indicate whether the resource was available or not. Obviously, frequent concurrent accesses to such a table will incur waits for TX locks, unless the undocumented SKIP LOCKED clause is used.

DBMS_LOCK – A Digression

DBMS_LOCK allows you to request and release locks in shared as well as exclusive mode. What's more, locks can even be converted between modes. With regards to redo generation, calling DBMS_LOCK is also preferable over implementing a locking mechanism based on a table, which needs to be updated in order to reflect the status of locks. The use of DBMS_LOCK.REQUEST/RELEASE to obtain and release locks does not generate any redo. DBMS_LOCK is fully documented in the PL/SQL Packages and Types Reference, but a small example for its use is in order.

Lock names or numbers must be agreed upon by all components of an applications. To make sure different applications do not interfere witch each other by accidentally using the same lock number, DBMS_LOCK provides a way to convert a name for a lock to a lock handle, which then replaces the rather meaningless lock number. All sessions wishing to use the same lock (e.g. MYAPP_MUTEX1 in the example below) must call DBMS_LOCK.ALLOCATE_UNIQUE once, to convert the lock name to a lock handle.

```
SQL> VARIABLE lockhandle VARCHAR2(128)
SQL> BEGIN
   -- get a lock handle for the lockname that was agreed upon
   -- make sure you choose a unique name, such that other vendors' applications
   -- won't accidentally interfere with your locks
   DBMS_LOCK.ALLOCATE_UNIQUE(
      lockname => 'MYAPP_MUTEX1',
      lockhandle => :lockhandle
   );
END;
/
print lockhandle
LOCKHANDLE
---------------------
10737418641073741864187
```

There's now a new row in table SYS.DBMS_LOCK_ALLOCATED:

```
SQL> SELECT * FROM sys.dbms_lock_allocated /* no public synonym */;
NAME                                      LOCKID EXPIRATION
----------------------------------------- ---------- --------------
DROP_EM_USER:SYSMAN                       1073741824 13.03.07 17:45
ORA$KUPV$MT-SYSTEM.SYS_EXPORT_SCHEMA_01   1073741844 09.03.07 15:51
ORA$KUPV$JOB_SERIALIZE                    1073741845 09.03.07 15:51
ORA$KUPM$SYSTEM$SYS_EXPORT_SCHEMA_01      1073741846 09.03.07 15:48
MYAPP_MUTEX1                              1073741864 20.07.07 19:52
```

As is obvious from the other entries above, the ORACLE DBMS uses DBMS_LOCK for internal purposes.

```
SQL> VARIABLE result NUMBER
SQL> BEGIN
    -- request the lock with the handle obtained above in exclusive mode
    -- the first session which runs this code succeeds
    :result:=DBMS_LOCK.REQUEST(
        lockhandle => :lockhandle,
        lockmode => DBMS_LOCK.X_MODE,
        timeout => 0,
        release_on_commit => TRUE /* default is false */
    );
END;
/
SELECT decode(:result,0,'Success',
    1,'Timeout',
    2,'Deadlock',
    3,'Parameter error',
    4,'Already own lock specified by id or lockhandle',
    5,'Illegal lock handle') Result
FROM dual;
RESULT
-------
Success
```

The second session (the initial call to DBMS_LOCK.ALLOCATE_UNIQUE is omitted) may then run the same code:

```
SQL> VARIABLE result NUMBER
SQL> BEGIN
    :result:=DBMS_LOCK.REQUEST(
        lockhandle => :lockhandle,
        lockmode => DBMS_LOCK.X_MODE,
        timeout => 0,
        release_on_commit => TRUE /* default is false */
    );
END;
/
SQL> SELECT decode(:result,1,'Timeout') Result FROM dual;
RESULT
-------
Timeout
```

The second session was unable to obtain the lock held by the first session in exclusive mode. The time spent waiting for the lock is accounted for by the wait event *enqueue* in Oracle9*i* and *enq: UL - contention* in Oracle10*g*. The abbreviation UL means user lock. After session 1 has committed, session 2 is able to obtain the lock, since session 1 had specified RELEASE_ON_COMMIT=TRUE in its lock request.

Session 1:

```
SQL> COMMIT;
Commit complete.
```

Session 2:

```
BEGIN
    :result:=DBMS_LOCK.REQUEST(
        lockhandle => :lockhandle,
        lockmode => DBMS_LOCK.X_MODE,
        timeout => 0,
        release_on_commit => TRUE /* default is false */
    );
END;
/
```

```
SQL> SELECT decode(:result,0,'Success') Result FROM dual;
RESULT
-------
Success
```

As you can see, very little code is required to lock resources for exclusive use with DBMS_LOCK. Just like with AQ, there is no need for any resource intensive polling, since a non–zero time–out may be used when waiting for a lock. Waiting sessions sleep on the event *enq: UL - contention*, in case another session holds the requested lock in an incompatible mode. The second parameter of this wait event (V$SESSION_WAIT.P2) is the user lock identifier (LOCKID) in the dictionary view SYS.DBMS_LOCK_ALLOCATED:

```
SQL> SELECT p1, p1text, p2, p2text, wait_class, seconds_in_wait, state
FROM v$session_wait
WHERE event='enq: UL - contention';
        P1 P1TEXT             P2 P2TEXT WAIT_CLASS  SECONDS_IN_WAIT STATE
---------- --------- ---------- ------ ----------- --------------- -------
1431044102 name|mode 1073741864 id     Application             121 WAITING
SQL> SELECT name
FROM sys.dbms_lock_allocated la, v$session_wait sw
WHERE sw.event='enq: UL - contention'
AND la.lockid=sw.p2;
NAME
------------
MYAPP_MUTEX1
```

At the end of the day, DBMS_LOCK is no more, but also no less, than the ORACLE database server's powerful enqueue mechanism externalized through a PL/SQL interface.

Source Code Depot

Table 26: SELECT FOR UPDATE SKIP LOCKED Source Code Depot

File Name	*Functionality*
create_queue_deq.sql	Creates an AQ queue table and attempts to dequeue a message
aq_enq.sql	Enqueues a message into a queue
dbms_lock.sql	Illustrates how to use the package DBMS_LOCK

Part VI

Supplied PL/SQL Packages

Chapter 17

DBMS_BACKUP_RESTORE

Status: DBMS_BACKUP_RESTORE is undocumented in the *Oracle9i Supplied PL/SQL Packages and Types Reference* as well as in *Oracle Database PL/SQL Packages and Types Reference* of Oracle10g and subsequent releases.

Benefits: DBMS_BACKUP_RESTORE makes a restore without RMAN in a disaster scenario possible. Such a scenario is characterized by the loss of all current control files and the lack of or unavailability of a recovery catalog or control file backup, which contains records of the most recent data file and archived redo log backups.

Recovery Manager

Recovery Manager (RMAN) is a backup and recovery utility that was introduced with Oracle8. RMAN is a database client just like SQL*Plus, Data Pump Export/Import, SQL*Loader, or any other program that can interact with an ORACLE instance through Oracle Call Interface (OCI).

RMAN itself does not back up or restore any part of an ORACLE database. If you recall that RMAN can run on any machine within a network, connect to an ORACLE instance on a remote database server, and perform backup and recovery, it is quite clear that RMAN neither needs to nor has the capability to read or write any database files. Instead, RMAN uses the undocumented package DBMS_BACKUP_RESTORE to instruct an ORACLE instance to perform backup and restore operations.

The ORACLE DBMS supports mounted file systems and so called media managers for storage of backups. A media manager is software that integrates with an ORACLE instance through the SBT (System Backup to Tape, see *Oracle Database Backup and Recovery Basics 10g Release 2*) interface and is capable of controlling tape devices for storing backups. The SBT interface is a specification by Oracle Corporation. The specification is disseminated to software companies wishing to support RMAN–based backup and recovery. The SBT interface is not documented in ORACLE DBMS documentation and is usually implemented as a shared library (a.k.a. dynamic link library or DLL), which is used by the program $ORACLE_HOME/bin/oracle (or oracle.exe on Windows) that implements an ORACLE instance. Oracle Corp. provide an implementation of the SBT interface that is linked with the executable oracle[.exe] by default. Usually, this executable is relinked with a shared library shipped with media management software, to enable an ORACLE instance to talk to a media manager.

Oracle Corp. recently entered the circle of companies that provide media management software by offering Oracle Secure Backup (see *Oracle Secure Backup Administrator's Guide*). Other well known players are Hewlett Packard with OmniBack, Symantec with NetBackup and Tivoli Software with Tivoli Storage Manager.

DBMS_BACKUP_RESTORE makes extensive use of the control file to keep track of what was backed up, when, and how. Here, *when* means at what time the backup started and when it ended. *What* means what type of file such as control file, data file, or archived redo log file. *How* refers to the medium that holds the backup, such as a file system mounted on the database server or a media manager as well as the incremental level at which the backup was taken. Note that Oracle10*g* only supports incremental levels 0 and 1, whereas Oracle9*i* and previous releases supported levels 0 to 4. Considering that there are cumulative backups on top of the default differential backups, there is no truly compelling argument for more than two levels.

In what follows, the data inside the control file representing the *when, what, and how* will be called backup metadata. Please refer to Table 27 for an overview of some of the V$ views which provide access to the metadata.

Table 27: Backup–related V$ Views

V$ View	*Purpose*	*Related RMAN Command*
V$ARCHIVED_LOG	Archived redo log files, their thread number, sequence number, and status (available, deleted, expired, or unavailable)	BACKUP ARCHIVELOG, DELETE ARCHIVELOG, CATALOG ARCHIVELOG,
V$BACKUP_DATAFILE	Backups of data files (FILE# > 0) and control files (CONTROLFILE_TYPE IS NOT NULL); both types of files may be present in the same backup piece, since a backup of file 1, which belongs to tablespace SYSTEM, also backs up the control file, unless automatic control file backups are enabled (AUTOBACKUP).	BACKUP DATABASE, BACKUP TABLESPACE, BACKUP DATAFILE, BACKUP CURRENT CONTROLFILE
V$BACKUP_PIECE	Backup pieces with creation time, device type, status, and path name (column HANDLE)	BACKUP
V$BACKUP_SET	Backup sets consist of one or more backup pieces, in case the files contained in a backup set exceed the maximum piece size	BACKUP
V$BACKUP_SPFILE	Backups of the server parameter file	BACKUP SPFILE
V$BACKUP_REDOLOG	Backups of archived redo logs	BACKUP ARCHIVELOG

ORACLE DBMS releases up to Oracle8*i* release 3 (8.1.7) had a considerable vulnerability due to the fact that the database—the control file to be precise—is used to keep track of backups. Of course, RMAN supported a recovery catalog for duplicating recovery–related information in the control file right from the first release with Oracle8. The recovery catalog enables restore operations when no control file is available. Contrary to the control file, backup metadata in a recovery catalog are exempt from overwrites (parameter CONTROLFILE_RECORD_KEEPTIME). This left the architecture with two vulnerabilities:

1. Metadata on backups that were taken without connecting to a catalog (NOCATALOG command line switch) and were never propagated by a subsequent run of RMAN are not registered in the recovery catalog. Let's say a backup script is smart enough to check the availability of the catalog and to run RMAN with the NOCATALOG option, should the availability test fail. Should you lose the most recent control file before the catalog and control file are resynchronized, you would not be able to restore the most recent archived redo log files, even if the recovery catalog outage was already over.

2. After the loss of the most recent control file, recovery will not be possible while there is an outage of the recovery catalog.

No special action is required to resynchronize backup metadata from the control file with the recovery catalog. If needed, RMAN automatically propagates metadata records from the control file to the recovery catalog whenever an RMAN command is run while connected to a catalog. This feature may be leveraged to synchronize the control file metadata with two or more recovery catalogs on different database servers, thus achieving higher availability of the catalog without resorting to clustering or replication technologies. Merely run RMAN one more time after the backup has finished, connect to an additional recovery catalog (e.g. with CONNECT CATALOG), and execute the RMAN command RESYNC CATALOG.

The aforementioned vulnerabilities could be worked around by creating a control file copy (ALTER DATABASE BACKUP CONTROLFILE TO '*path*') and backing up that copy with a file system backup utility. The downside of this approach is that the administrator performing the restore will need to be familiar with and privileged for use of both RMAN and file system restore utilities. Often, privileges for file system restores are available only to privileged operating system users such as root on UNIX systems or the group Administrators on Windows systems. Thus, a DBA would need assistance from a system administrator to perform restore operations.

Oracle9*i* RMAN shipped with the new automatic control file backup functionality[1], which addresses the issues discussed above. Automatic backup of the control file after each backup makes sure that the most recent copy of the control file, i.e. the only copy which contains all the bookkeeping information required to restore the last backup, is either backed up to disk or to a media manager. However, this feature is disabled by default, such that databases remain vulnerable, unless the DBA enables this new feature.

For the first time, thanks to automatic control file backup, the most recent control file can be restored without accessing a recovery catalog. An example of how to restore a control file from an automatic control file backup is shown below. The database identifier (V$DATABASE.DBID), which is stored inside the control file, is required by restore operations. To restore an automatic control file backup after the loss of all current control files, the database identifier needs to be set with the command SET DBID[2].

```
C:> rman target /
Recovery Manager: Release 10.2.0.1.0 - Production on Mon Jul 2 18:32:08 2007
connected to target database: TEN (not mounted)
RMAN> SET DBID 2848896501;
executing command: SET DBID
RMAN> RUN {
   RESTORE CONTROLFILE FROM AUTOBACKUP;
}
Starting restore at 02.07.07 18:32
using target database control file instead of recovery catalog
allocated channel: ORA_DISK_1
channel ORA_DISK_1: sid=156 devtype=DISK
channel ORA_DISK_1: looking for autobackup on day: 20070702
channel ORA_DISK_1: autobackup found: c-2848896501-20070702-02
channel ORA_DISK_1: control file restore from autobackup complete
output filename=C:\ORADATA\TEN\CONTROL01.CTL
Finished restore at 02.07.07 18:32
```

The default format for automatic control file backups is %F. This translates to c-*database_id*-*YYYYMMDD*-*QQ*, where *QQ* represents a hexadecimal sequence number between 0 and FF (0–256 in decimal). The remaining format string adheres to the well known SQL date and time format models. In case a custom format has been configured—which I strongly discourage—a RESTORE command for an automatic control file backup must be preceded by the command SET CONTROLFILE AUTOBACKUP FORMAT FOR DEVICE TYPE *device_type* TO '*autobackup_format*', to let RMAN know the non–default format. By the way, it is undocumented how RMAN uses the hexadecimal sequence number *QQ*. It serves to generate unique file names for automatic control file backups within a single day. Remember

---

1. See documentation on the commands CONFIGURE CONTROLFILE AUTOBACKUP ON, CONFIGURE CONTROLFILE AUTOBACKUP FORMAT FOR DEVICE TYPE in [OL92 2002].
2. In Oracle10*g*, it is possible to embed the database identifier in the backup piece name by using the placeholder %I in the FORMAT specification. Thus, even if no log files from past backups remain, the database identifier may be derived from the backup piece names in the media manager repository.

that due to the date format "YYYYMMDD" without a time component, all automatic control file backups within a single day would have the same filename or handle (V$BACKUP_PIECE.HANDLE). As the clock strikes 12 and a new day is about to dawn, RMAN begins using the new value of "YYYYMMDD" and resets QQ to zero. But what if more than 256 automatic control file backups were written within a single day? Then RMAN leaves QQ at FF and overwrites the backup piece with sequence FF (QQ=FF). Here is the proof:

```
SQL> SELECT completion_time, handle
FROM v$backup_piece
WHERE handle LIKE '%FF';
COMPLETION_TIME HANDLE
--------------- ------------------------
02.07.07 22:04  C-2848896501-20070702-FF
```

After another automatic control file backup on the same day, the backup piece name has been reused and the query yields:

```
SQL> SELECT completion_time, handle
FROM v$backup_piece
WHERE handle LIKE '%FF';
COMPLETION_TIME HANDLE
--------------- ------------------------
02.07.07 22:30  C-2848896501-20070702-FF
```

The first control file autobackup one day later again uses the hexadecimal sequence number 00:

```
SQL> SELECT completion_time, handle
FROM v$backup_piece
WHERE handle like '%00';
COMPLETION_TIME HANDLE
--------------- ------------------------
02.07.07 17:17  C-2848896501-20070702-00
03.07.07 22:51  C-2848896501-20070703-00
```

This is the only situation that I am aware of, where RMAN overwrites existing backup pieces with new data. Under all other circumstances, RMAN refuses to overwrite existing files and aborts the command BACKUP with "ORA-19506: failed to create sequential file, name="*string*", parms="*string*" for device type SBT_TAPE" or "ORA-19504: failed to create file "*string*" for device type disk" and "ORA-27038: created file already exists".

This behavior sheds some light on the algorithm RMAN uses to generate backup piece handles in its quest for a control file from an automatic control file backup. Among others, the settings of the optional parameters MAXDAYS and MAXSEQ in the command RESTORE CONTROLFILE FROM AUTOBACKUP determine the handle names RMAN generates. If MAXSEQ is not set, RMAN uses the default of 256, translates it to hexadecimal FF, and builds a handle name according to the %F format presented earlier. If no such backup piece exists, the sequence number (QQ) is decremented by 1 until it reaches 0. If no control file backup is found during this process, RMAN moves on to the previous day and recommences the process with a hexadecimal sequence number of FF. The default for MAXDAYS is 7 with a permissible range between 1 and 366. If, after MAXDAYS days before the current day have been tried, RMAN still fails to locate a suitable backup piece, the RESTORE command terminates with the error "RMAN-06172: no autobackup found or specified handle is not a valid copy or piece". The search may be accelerated somewhat by using a lower MAXSEQ such as 10 in cases where it is known that no more than 10 BACKUP commands get executed per day due to data file and archived log backups.

The new automatic control file backup functionality—which also backs up the server parameter file (SPFILE), if present—is *disabled* by default (page 2–69 *Oracle Database Backup and Recovery Reference 10g Release 2*). There certainly are production systems, which are still vulnerable, since no backup—automatic or not—of the control file with the most recent recovery–related metadata exists.

Undoubtedly, the likelihood of scenarios 1 and 2 above is low. Nonetheless it is reassuring to learn that even on systems where the quality of backup scripts is insufficient, the road to full recovery is still open when following the advice on the undocumented package DBMS_BACKUP_RESTORE that I will present shortly.

Disaster Recovery Case Study with Tivoli Data Protection for Oracle

Tivoli Data Protection for ORACLE (TDPO) is software that conforms to Oracle Corporation's SBT specification and enables integration of RMAN–based backup and recovery with Tivoli Storage Manager (TSM) through a shared library (see http://www.tivoli.com). It supports the client platforms AIX, HP–UX, Solaris, Linux and Windows.

From the perspective of the TSM server, an ORACLE instance is a backup client. Using the TSM utility dsmadmc, it is possible to retrieve the names of backup pieces. If a control file were available, these would match the backup piece names in V$BACKUP_PIECE.HANDLE. The TSM server accepts SQL statements for retrieving files backed up by a client. The column NODE_NAME stores the name of the TSM client used by the database server host. If you have given different file name prefixes to control file, data file, and archived log backups, it will pay off now:

```
dsmadmc> SELECT * FROM backups WHERE node_name='DBSERVER'
ANR2963W This SQL query may produce a very large result table, or may require a
significant amount of time to compute.
Do you wish to proceed? (Yes (Y)/No (N)) y
NODE_NAME: DBSERVER
FILESPACE_NAME: /adsmorc
FILESPACE_ID: 1
STATE: ACTIVE_VERSION
TYPE: FILE
HL_NAME: //
LL_NAME: CF-DB-NINE-20071010-vsiu61og
OBJECT_ID: 201461790
BACKUP_DATE: 2007-10-10 14:43:27.000000
DEACTIVATE_DATE:
OWNER: oraoper
CLASS_NAME: DEFAULT
```

In the output from dsmadmc, you would look for the most recent control file backup or the most recent backup piece, which contains a control file. Control files are backed up whenever file 1, the first file of tablespace SYSTEM, is backed up. The script dbms_backup_restore_cf_tdpo.sql, which is reproduced below, may be used to restore a control file without mounting a database and accessing a catalog or automatic control file backup. The LL_NAME found in the TSM repository is used as the piece name in the call to DBMS_BACKUP_RESTORE:

```
variable type varchar2(10)
variable ident varchar2(10)
variable piece1 varchar2(513)
begin
    :type:='SBT_TAPE';
    :ident:='channel1';
    :piece1:='CF-DB-NINE-20071010-vsiu61og';
end;
/
set serveroutput on
DECLARE
    v_devtype    VARCHAR2(100);
    v_done       BOOLEAN;
    v_maxPieces NUMBER;
    TYPE t_pieceName IS TABLE OF varchar2(513) INDEX BY binary_integer;
    v_piece_name_tab t_pieceName;
BEGIN
    -- Define the backup pieces (names from the RMAN Log file or TSM repository)
    v_piece_name_tab(1) := :piece1;
    --v_piece_name_tab(2) := '<backup piece name 2>';
    v_maxPieces    := 1;
    -- Allocate a channel (Use type=>null for DISK, type=>'sbt_tape' for TAPE)
    v_devtype := DBMS_BACKUP_RESTORE.deviceAllocate(
        type=>:type,
        ident=> :ident,
```

```
            params => 'ENV=(TDPO_OPTFILE=/usr/tivoli/tsm/client/oracle/bin64/tdpo.opt)'
    );
    dbms_output.put_line('device type '||v_devtype);
    -- begin restore conversation
    DBMS_BACKUP_RESTORE.restoreSetDataFile(check_logical=>false);
    -- set restore location with CFNAME parameter
    DBMS_BACKUP_RESTORE.restoreControlFileTo(cfname=>'/tmp/control.ctl');
    FOR i IN 1..v_maxPieces LOOP
        dbms_output.put_line('Restoring from piece '||v_piece_name_tab(i));
        DBMS_BACKUP_RESTORE.restoreBackupPiece(handle=>v_piece_name_tab(i),
            done=>v_done, params=>null);
        exit when v_done;
    END LOOP;
    -- Deallocate the channel
    DBMS_BACKUP_RESTORE.deviceDeAllocate(:ident);
    EXCEPTION WHEN OTHERS THEN
        DBMS_BACKUP_RESTORE.deviceDeAllocate(:ident);
    RAISE;
END;
/
```

Of course, an instance must be running to be able to execute PL/SQL, but STARTUP NOMOUNT is sufficient to run the script in SQL*Plus. Normal PL/SQL packages can only be executed when the database is open, since the so called PL/SQL mpcode in the data dictionary is read. Some kind of undocumented "magic" makes it possible to execute DBMS_BACKUP_RESTORE without even mounting a database. Below is a sample run of the control file restore script dbms_backup_restore_cf_tdpo.sql:

```
$ sqlplus "/ as sysdba"
SQL*Plus: Release 9.2.0.8.0 - Production on Wed Oct 10 21:33:44 2007
Connected to:
Oracle9i Enterprise Edition Release 9.2.0.8.0 - 64bit Production
SQL> @dbms_backup_restore_cf_tdpo.sql
PL/SQL procedure successfully completed.
device type SBT_TAPE
Restoring from piece CF-DB-NINE-20071010-vsiu61og
PL/SQL procedure successfully completed.
SQL> !ls -l /tmp/control.ctl
-rw-r-----   1 oracle   dba          1413120 Oct 10 21:33 /tmp/control.ctl
```

The control file was restored as file /tmp/control.ctl. If this control file contains the backup piece names of the most recent data file and archived log backups, the database should be mounted and the restore continued with RMAN in the usual manner. However, if no control file backup with the most recent backup piece names exists, simply since the control file was not backed up after the last backup (e.g. since automatic control file backup is disabled), data files and archived logs must also be restored by calling DBMS_BACKUP_RESTORE. For these purposes, the source code depot contains the scripts dbms_backup_restore.sql and dbms_backup_restore_arch_tdpo.sql.

Source Code Depot

Table 28: DBMS_BACKUP_RESTORE Source Code Depot

File Name	*Functionality*
dbms_backup_restore.sql	Disaster recovery script for restoring a control file and multiple data files using a disk channel
dbms_backup_restore_arch_tdpo.sql	Disaster restore script for restoring archived redo logs from a backup set, which may consist of several backup pieces, using TDPO (device type SBT_TAPE)

Table 28: DBMS_BACKUP_RESTORE Source Code Depot

File Name	Functionality
`dbms_backup_restore_cf_tdpo.sql`	Disaster restore script for restoring a control file using TDPO (device type `SBT_TAPE`)

Chapter 18

DBMS_IJOB

Status: DBMS_IJOB is undocumented. This package is called internally by DBMS_JOB.

Benefit: By using DBMS_IJOB directly, the limitations inherent in DBMS_JOB may be overcome. Using DBMS_IJOB, it is possible to create and drop jobs in other schemas, to export jobs as PL/SQL scripts, and to change the NLS environment of jobs as well as the database user who runs a job.

Introduction to DBMS_JOB

The package DBMS_JOB submits PL/SQL procedures, which shall be run at regular intervals, to the job queue. The job queue is enabled by setting the initialization parameter JOB_QUEUE_PROCESSES to a value larger than zero. The job queue is handled by the job queue coordinator process CJQ0 and job queue slave processes (JNNN). The documented interface to the job queue is the package DBMS_JOB. This package does not allow a database administrator to create, modify, and drop jobs in foreign schemas.

DBMS_JOB calls the undocumented package DBMS_IJOB to accomplish its tasks. Using DBMS_IJOB directly, allows a database administrator to overcome the aforementioned limitations. Changes to the job queue with DBMS_IJOB take effect when COMMIT is issued (same as with DBMS_JOB). The data dictionary table underlying DBA_JOBS is SYS.JOB$.

DBMS_JOB and DBMS_IJOB have the procedures BROKEN, REMOVE and RUN in common. These procedures have identical arguments in both packages. For each of them I provide an example that illustrates how DBMS_IJOB gives the DBA full control of all jobs in the database.

BROKEN Procedure

This procedure may be used to change the status of a job in any schema, thus overcoming the limitation of DBMS_JOB.BROKEN. Jobs with status broken (DBA_JOBS.BROKEN=Y) are not run automatically, but may be run manually with DBMS_JOB.RUN.

Syntax

```
DBMS_IJOB.BROKEN (
    job IN BINARY_INTEGER,
    broken IN BOOLEAN,
    next_date IN DATE DEFAULT SYSDATE);
```

Parameters

Parameter	Description
job	Job number; corresponds to DBA_JOBS.JOB
broken	TRUE: mark job as broken, FALSE: mark job as not broken
next_date	Next time and date to run job

Usage Notes

There is no public synonym for DBMS_IJOB, so you need to qualify the package name with the schema name SYS. For jobs with status BROKEN=Y the column NEXT_DATE always has the value January 1st, 4000.

Examples

Here's an example of marking a job in a foreign schema as broken. It fails with DBMS_JOB, but succeeds with DBMS_IJOB.

```
SQL> SHOW USER
USER is "NDEBES"
SQL> SELECT role FROM session_roles WHERE role='DBA';
ROLE
------------------------------
DBA
SQL> SELECT job, what, broken FROM dba_jobs WHERE priv_user='PERFSTAT';
JOB WHAT            BROKEN
--- -------------- ------
  1 statspack.snap; N
SQL> EXEC dbms_job.broken(1,true)
BEGIN dbms_job.broken(1,true); END;
*
ERROR at line 1:
ORA-23421: job number 1 is not a job in the job queue
ORA-06512: at "SYS.DBMS_IJOB", line 529
ORA-06512: at "SYS.DBMS_JOB", line 245
SQL> EXEC sys.dbms_ijob.broken(1, true)
PL/SQL procedure successfully completed.
SQL> COMMIT;
Commit complete.
SQL> SELECT job, what, broken FROM dba_jobs WHERE priv_user='PERFSTAT';
JOB WHAT            BROKEN
--- -------------- ------
  1 statspack.snap; Y
```

FULL_EXPORT Procedure

This procedure returns strings, which hold PL/SQL calls to recreate a job. It may be used to export job definitions.

Syntax

```
DBMS_IJOB.FULL_EXPORT(
    job IN BINARY_INTEGER,
    mycall  IN OUT VARCHAR2,
    myinst IN OUT  VARCHAR2);
```

Parameters

Parameter	Description
job	Job number; corresponds to DBA_JOBS.JOB
mycall	After a successful call of the procedure, the return value holds a string that represents a call to DBMS_IJOB.SUBMIT.
myinst	After a successful call of the procedure, the return value holds a string that represents a call to DBMS_JOB.INSTANCE.

Examples

The script dbms_ijob_full_export.sql exports the definition of a single job in a format that is suitable for recreating the job. The main part of the script is reproduced below:

```
variable job number
variable submit_call varchar2(4000)
variable instance_call varchar2(4000)
exec :job:=&job_number;
begin
    dbms_ijob.full_export(:job, :submit_call, :instance_call);
end;
/
print submit_call
print instance_call
```

Below is an example of running the script to export a job, which takes Statspack snapshots:

```
$ sqlplus -s / as sysdba @dbms_ijob_full_export.sql
       JOB WHAT
---------- ------------------------------------------------
        21 statspack.snap;
Enter value for job_number: 21
sys.dbms_ijob.submit(job=>21,luser=>'PERFSTAT',puser=>'PERFSTAT',cuser=>'PERFSTAT',
next_date=>to_date('2007-12-07:21:00:00','YYYY-MM-DD:HH24:MI:SS'),
interval=>'trunc(SYSDATE+1/24,''HH'')',
broken=>FALSE,what=>'statspack.snap;',nlsenv=>'NLS_LANGUAGE=''AMERICAN''
NLS_TERRITORY=''AMERICA'' NLS_CURRENCY=''$'' NLS_ISO_CURRENCY=''AMERICA''
NLS_NUMERIC_CHARACTERS=''.,'' NLS_DATE_FORMAT=''dd.mm.yyyy hh24:mi:ss''
NLS_DATE_LANGUAGE=''AMERICAN'' NLS_SORT=''BINARY''',env=>'0102000200000000');
dbms_job.instance(job=>21, instance=>1, force=>TRUE);
```

Job 21 may be recreated by executing the PL/SQL calls generated by DBMS_IJOB.FULL_EXPORT.

REMOVE Procedure

Use this procedure to remove jobs in any schema.

Syntax

```
DBMS_IJOB.REMOVE(
```

```
    job IN BINARY_INTEGER);
```

Parameters

Parameter	Description
job	Job number

Examples

Below is an example of deleting a job in a foreign schema.

```
SQL> SHOW USER
USER is "NDEBES"
SQL> SELECT priv_user FROM dba_jobs WHERE job=29;
PRIV_USER
------------------------------
PERFSTAT
SQL> EXEC sys.dbms_ijob.remove(29)
PL/SQL procedure successfully completed.
SQL> COMMIT;
Commit complete.
```

RUN Procedure

This procedure may be used to run jobs in any schema, irrespective of their status (BROKEN=Y/N). The job is run by the foreground process of the user executing DBMS_IJOB instead of by a job queue process. This facilitates trouble-shooting or performance diagnosis of the job, since the session to trace or monitor is known. DBA_JOBS.NEXT_DATE is recalculated.

Syntax

```
DBMS_IJOB.RUN(
    job IN BINARY_INTEGER,
    force IN BOOLEAN DEFAULT FALSE);
```

Parameters

Parameter	Description
job	Job number
force	If TRUE, DBMS_IJOB.RUN ignores the instance affinity setting of the job specified with the parameters INSTANCE and FORCE=TRUE to DBMS_JOB.SUBMIT. If FORCE=TRUE when calling DBMS_IJOB.RUN, then the job may be run in any instance, thereby ignoring instance affinity.

Usage Notes

In a scenario where a database user approaches a DBA and asks the DBA to diagnose a failing job, the DBA would normally need to start a database session as the owner of the job to reproduce the problem. Using DBMS_IJOB, the DBA can run and diagnose the job without knowing the password of the job owner or asking the job owner to log him in.

Contrary to the Oracle10g scheduler (DBMS_SCHEDULER), which records the reason for a job's failure in the data dictionary view DBA_SCHEDULER_JOB_RUN_DETAILS, the DBMS_JOB job queue does not record errors from job runs in the database. Errors from failed DBMS_JOB jobs are recorded in job queue slave process trace files in the background dump destination (parameter BACKGROUND_DUMP_DEST). Job developers are expected to implement their own error logging. Three undocumented PL/SQL metadata variables are available to DBMS_JOB jobs. Their variable names, data types, and descriptions are in Table 29.

Table 29: DBMS_JOB Metadata

Variable Name	Data Type	Description
job	BINARY_INTEGER	Job number of the job currently being executed
next_date	DATE	Date and time of the next scheduled job run; this variable may be used to override the repeat interval of a job.
broken	BOOLEAN	The value of this variable is initially FALSE, irrespective of the current job status. It may be used to mark a job as broken. If this variable is assigned the value TRUE and the job completes without raising an exception, the job is marked as broken (ALL_JOBS.BROKEN='Y').

The variable broken is provided for jobs that catch exceptions. The job queue cannot detect failing jobs if a job catches exceptions internally. Setting broken=TRUE in an anonymous PL/SQL block, which implements a job, allows a job developer to mark the job as broken if an exception is caught. Thus, he may set the job's status according to his own strategy. Jobs that do raise exceptions are marked as broken after 16 failures. Job queue processes use an exponential backoff strategy for calculating the next scheduled run date of failed jobs. Jobs are reattempted one minute after the initial failure. The wait interval is doubled after each additional failure. The next scheduled run of a job may be overridden by assigning a tailored value to the variable next_date. This may be used to implement a custom strategy for reattempting failed jobs. The source code depot contains the file dbms_job_metadata.sql with a sample implementation of a job, which uses the three PL/SQL metadata variables in Table 29.

Examples

Below is a scenario for debugging a failing job in a foreign schema by running it in a foreground process with DBMS_IJOB.RUN.

```
SQL> SHOW USER
USER is "SYS"
SQL> SELECT job, priv_user, failures FROM dba_jobs WHERE job=1;
       JOB PRIV_USER       FAILURES
---------- ------------ ----------
         1 PERFSTAT               1
SQL> EXEC dbms_job.run(1)
BEGIN dbms_job.run(1); END;
*
ERROR at line 1:
ORA-23421: job number 1 is not a job in the job queue

SQL> EXEC sys.dbms_ijob.run(1)
BEGIN sys.dbms_ijob.run(1); END;
*
ERROR at line 1:
ORA-12011: execution of 1 jobs failed
ORA-06512: at "SYS.DBMS_IJOB", line 406
ORA-06512: at line 1
SQL> ORADEBUG SETMYPID
Statement processed.
SQL> ORADEBUG TRACEFILE_NAME
/opt/oracle/obase/admin/TEN/udump/ten1_ora_19365.trc
SQL> !tail -4 /opt/oracle/obase/admin/TEN/udump/ten1_ora_19365.trc
ORA-12012: error on auto execute of job 1
ORA-00376: file 3 cannot be read at this time
ORA-01110: data file 3: '+DG/ten/datafile/sysaux.261.628550067'
```

```
ORA-06512: at "PERFSTAT.STATSPACK", line 5376
```

Source Code Depot

Table 30: DBMS_IJOB Source Code Depot

File Name	*Functionality*
dbms_ijob_full_export.sql	Generates PL/SQL code to recreate a job by retrieving its metadata from DBA_JOBS (or rather SYS.JOB$)
dbms_job_metadata.sql	This script creates a table for implementing custom logging of DBMS_JOB jobs in a database table. The job definition uses PL/SQL job metadata variables to record the job number and the next scheduled run date. If an exception occurs, the job catches it, records the error in the logging table, and marks itself as broken.

Chapter 19

DBMS_SCHEDULER

Status: The database scheduler is an advanced job scheduling capability built into Oracle10g and subsequent releases. The package DBMS_SCHEDULER is the interface to the job scheduler. It is extensively documented in the *Oracle Database Administrator's Guide* and the *PL/SQL Packages and Types Reference*. Important aspects concerning the execution of external jobs, such as exit code handling, removal of environment variables, details of program argument passing, requirements to run external programs owned by users other than SYS, and default privileges of external jobs defined by the configuration file externaljob.ora are undocumented.

Benefit: This chapter provides all the details on the subject of external jobs: how they are run, which environment variables and privileges are available to them, how to signal success and failure, and how to integrate custom logging with the scheduler's own logging.

Running External Jobs with the Database Scheduler

The database scheduler is an advanced job scheduling capability, which ships with Oracle10g and subsequent releases. The PL/SQL package DBMS_SCHEDULER is the interface to a rich set of job scheduling features. Oracle10g Release 1 was the first ORACLE DBMS release, which had the capability to run jobs outside of the database. The scheduler supports three types of jobs:

- stored procedures
- PL/SQL blocks
- executables, i.e. external programs, which run outside of the database engine

Job chains are another new feature introduced with Oracle10g. Chains consist of several jobs. Rules are used to decide which job within a chain to execute next. Since the scheduler supports jobs that run within as well as outside of the database engine, it makes sense to use it for controlling complex processing that involves job steps at operating system level as well as within the database. Another option for running jobs at operating system level is the Enterprise Manager job system. In my own experience, the database scheduler has worked flawlessly, whereas I witnessed several failures of the Enterprise Manager job system. Hence I recommend using the database scheduler in favor of the Enterprise Manager job system. Enterprise Manager Grid Control includes a web–based interface for both. Enterprise Manager Database Control has a web–based interface for the database scheduler.

In a high availability environment, such as a failover cluster or Real Application Clusters, the scheduler solves the issue that jobs need to run in spite of a node or instance failure. Since high availability solutions ensure that at least one instance in a cluster is up (exactly one instance per database in a failover cluster), this instance is available to execute jobs. Thus, for the sake of scheduling, it is unnecessary to protect an Enterprise Manager agent (and its job system) or a third party scheduling solution by clustering software.

Certain undocumented aspects of the database scheduler apply to both windows and UNIX, whereas others are platform specific. Generic aspects are covered in the next two sections. Platform specific scheduler features are addressed in separate sections, which pertain to UNIX and Windows. An interesting generic feature of the scheduler, which is documented in the *Oracle Database Administrator's Guide*, is that it captures and saves up to 200 bytes of standard error output in the column ADDITIONAL_INFO of the dictionary view DBA_SCHEDULER_JOB_RUN_DETAILS.

Exit Code Handling

On UNIX systems as well as Windows programs signal success or failure by returning an exit code to the parent process. The exit code zero signals successful execution, whereas an exit code between 1 and 255 indicates a failure or at least a warning. In the Bourne, Korn, and Bash shells, the 8 bit exit code is available in the variable $?. If a program is terminated by a signal, the exit code is $128+n$, where n is the number of the signal, which terminated the program. On UNIX, signal numbers are defined in the C programming language include file /usr/include/sys/signal.h. Here's an example. Start the UNIX program sleep and while sleep is still running interrupt the process with Ctrl+C:

```
$ sleep 10
$ echo $?
130
```

The echo statement retrieves the exit code from sleep. Since $130 - 128$ is 2, we need to look for signal 2 in signal.h:

```
#define SIGINT  2       /* interrupt */
```

Signal 2 is the interrupt signal, which may also be sent to a process with kill -INT *pid*, where *pid* is the process identifier.

In Perl $? provides information on which signal, if any, had a role in ending the child process as well as whether or not a core dump was generated in addition to the exit code. Thus $? is a 16 bit value in Perl. How does the database scheduler fare in this respect? It is undocumented how the scheduler decides whether an external job succeeded or failed.

On Windows, %ERRORLEVEL% has the same purpose as $? on UNIX systems. Below is an example, which calls the programs true.exe and false.exe shipped with Cygwin, a highly recommended, free, UNIX–like environment for Windows systems, which provides all the UNIX utilities, such as bash, find, awk, grep, vim (Vi iMproved), and even X11 to redirect the output of X11 clients on UNIX systems (such as the Oracle Universal Installer) to a bitmapped display on a Windows machine.

```
C:> false.exe
C:> echo %ERRORLEVEL%
1
C:> true.exe
C:> echo %ERRORLEVEL%
0
```

Back to the database scheduler. Successful execution of a job is characterized by the value "SUCCEEDED" in the column STATUS of the view DBA_SCHEDULER_JOB_LOG. Failure is signaled by the value "FAILED" (not "FAILURE" as stated in the *Oracle Database Administrator's Guide 10g Release 2* on page 2–27). But how does this relate to the exit code of the executable? Except signaling success or failure, the exit code might also indicate why the external job failed. Could it be available in DBA_SCHEDULER_JOB_LOG.ADDITIONAL_INFO or in any of the columns STATUS, ERROR#, or ADDITIONAL_INFO of the view DBA_SCHEDULER_JOB_RUN_DETAILS? Some tests reveal that:

- Executables which return exit code zero are assigned the job status "SUCCEEDED". All other exit codes result in the status "FAILED".
- The exit code itself is not available.
- The column DBA_SCHEDULER_JOB_RUN_DETAILS.STATUS, which has an undocumented range of values in the *Oracle10g Release 2 Database Reference*, has the same range of values as the column STATUS of the view DBA_SCHEDULER_JOB_LOG ("SUCCEEDED" or "FAILED").

Standard Error Output

UNIX shell scripts and windows command–line scripts support the same output redirection syntax. Both environments provide three default file handles. These are summarized in Table 31.

Table 31: Input and Output Handles

Handle Designation	Numeric Equivalent	Description
STDIN	0	Keyboard input
STDOUT	1	Output to the terminal window
STDERR	2	Error output to the terminal window

By default, the UNIX command echo prints its arguments to standard output (STDOUT). To redirect an error message to standard error (STDERR), use a command such as the one below:

```
$ echo Command failed. 1>&2
Command failed.
```

This works in exactly the same way on Windows:

```
C:> echo Command failed. 1>&2
Command failed.
```

Evidence for the findings reported so far comes from running a small command–line script, which terminates with exit code 1. The subsequent example is coded for Windows, but the results apply equally to UNIX. The source code of the Windows command–line script (file failure.bat) is reproduced below:

```
echo This is script %0.
echo About to exit with exit code 1. 1>&2
exit 1
```

The following PL/SQL block creates an external job, which runs the above script. The supplied calendaring expression "FREQ=MINUTELY;INTERVAL=3" schedules the job to run every three minutes. Note that the job is created and run as user SYS.

```
C:> sqlplus / as sysdba
Connected to:
Oracle Database 11g Enterprise Edition Release 11.1.0.6.0 - Production
SQL> BEGIN
    DBMS_SCHEDULER.CREATE_JOB(
        job_name => 'failure_test',
        job_type => 'EXECUTABLE',
        job_action => 'C:\home\ndebes\bin\failure.bat',
        start_date => systimestamp,
        repeat_interval => 'FREQ=MINUTELY;INTERVAL=3',
        enabled=>true /* default false! */
    );
END;
/
PL/SQL procedure successfully completed.
```

The job may be run manually by calling the procedure DBMS_SCHEDULER.RUN_JOB:

```
SQL> EXEC dbms_scheduler.run_job('failure_test')
```

```
BEGIN dbms_scheduler.run_job('failure_test'); END;
*
ERROR at line 1:
ORA-27369: job of type EXECUTABLE failed with exit code: Incorrect function.
ORA-06512: at "SYS.DBMS_ISCHED", line 154
ORA-06512: at "SYS.DBMS_SCHEDULER", line 450
ORA-06512: at line 1
```

Due to the non–zero exit code, the job is classified as "FAILED". After the above manual job execution and a single scheduled execution, querying DBA_SCHEDULER_JOB_LOG and DBA_SCHEDULER_JOB_RUN_DETAILS yields the results below:

```
SQL> SELECT jl.log_id, jl.status, jl.additional_info AS log_addtl_info, jd.status,
jd.additional_info AS details_addtl_info
FROM dba_scheduler_job_log jl, dba_scheduler_job_run_details jd
WHERE jl.job_name='FAILURE_TEST'
AND jl.log_id=jd.log_id
ORDER BY jl.log_id;
LOG_ID STATUS LOG_ADDTL_INFO            STATUS DETAILS_ADDTL_INFO
------ ------ -------------------- ------ ----------------------------------
   245 FAILED                            FAILED ORA-27369: job of type EXECUTABLE
                                                failed with exit code: Incorrect
                                                function.
                                                STANDARD_ERROR="About to exit with
                                                exit code 1. "
   246 FAILED REASON="manually run" FAILED ORA-27369: job of type EXECUTABLE
                                                failed with exit code: Incorrect
                                                function.
                                                STANDARD_ERROR="About to exit with
                                                exit code 1. "
```

The results of the test presented above as well as additional tests are summarized below:

- The column ADDITIONAL_INFO of the view DBA_SCHEDULER_JOB_RUN_DETAILS captures standard error output for external jobs irrespective of their exit codes. This column is a CLOB, such that it could theoretically capture up to 8 TB or 128 TB depending on the setting of the parameter DB_BLOCK_SIZE (see Database Reference 10g Release 2, page A1).
- There is a size limitation of 200 bytes on DBA_SCHEDULER_JOB_RUN_DETAILS.ADDITIONAL_INFO.
- Standard output is never captured in DBA_SCHEDULER_JOB_RUN_DETAILS.ADDITIONAL_INFO.
- The column ADDITIONAL_INFO of the view DBA_SCHEDULER_JOB_LOG is NULL for jobs that are run based on a schedule and has the value REASON="manually run" for jobs that were run manually by a call to the procedure DBMS_SCHEDULER.RUN_JOB.

To drop the job named "FAILURE_TEST", execute the call to DBMS_SCHEDULER.DROP_JOB reproduced below:

```
SQL> EXEC dbms_scheduler.drop_job('failure_test')
```

External Jobs on UNIX

Wouldn't it be nice to teach a database how to back itself up by running RMAN as an external job? The unsuspecting DBA might think that all that needs to be done is to run RMAN through the scheduler with exactly the same command line options as from a shell. Actual tests however reveal that matters are more intricate. Environment variables and argument passing are two of the issues which pose undocumented obstacles and must be overcome.

In the source code depot, I provide a prototype of a job, which controls RMAN through the pipe interface discussed in Chapter 36 (file rman_backup.sql). It creates an external job, which runs RMAN through the scheduler, and a job of type PLSQL_BLOCK. This latter job starts RMAN by manually executing the aforementioned external job and passes commands to RMAN through the pipe interface. Thus, the database has been taught to back itself up. There is no longer any need for scheduling backups outside of the DBMS instance. In a high availability environment, guarding the DBMS instance against failure automatically protects the backup job too.

The scheduler provides several metadata attributes to jobs of type PLSQL_BLOCK. Oracle10g and Oracle11g support the same attributes (see page 114–61 in *Oracle Database PL/SQL Packages and Types Reference 11g Release 1*). Unfortunately, the value of the sequence SYS.SCHEDULER$_INSTANCE_S, which is used for numbering the column LOG_ID in the views DBA_SCHEDULER_JOB_LOG and DBA_SCHEDULER_JOB_RUN_DETAILS is not among them. It would be very useful for integrating custom logging in a database table with the scheduler's own logging. Yet, there is a workaround. After a scheduled job run, the value of DBA_SCHEDULER_JOBS.NEXT_RUN_DATE is copied to DBA_SCHEDULER_JOB_RUN_DETAILS.REQ_START_DATE (requested start date). A job of type PLSQL_BLOCK, which selects NEXT_RUN_DATE and incorporates it into a custom logging table, solves the integration issue. After the job has completed, the custom logging table may be joined with DBA_SCHEDULER_JOB_RUN_DETAILS using the column REQ_START_DATE. A sample implementation is included in the file rman_backup.sql in the source code depot.

Removal of Environment Variables

It is undocumented that the scheduler removes all environment variables before it starts a UNIX process, which implements an external job. Evidence for this trait is easily collected by having the scheduler run a shell script that calls the program env. On UNIX systems, if called without arguments, env prints out all the environment variables that it inherited. Below is the code of a shell script that prints a sorted list of all environment variables on standard error output and saves a copy of the output to the file /tmp/env.out by using the command tee. Execute permission on the file env.sh is required and is set using chmod.

```
$ more env.sh
#!/bin/sh
env | sort | tee /tmp/env.out 1>&2
exit 0
$ chmod +x env.sh
```

To have the database scheduler run this shell script, we create the following scheduler program called "ENV":

```
SQL> BEGIN
    DBMS_SCHEDULER.CREATE_PROGRAM(
        program_name=>'env',
        program_action=>'/home/oracle/env.sh',
        program_type=>'EXECUTABLE',
        number_of_arguments=>0,
        comments=>'environment variables',
        enabled=>true);
end;
/
```

Then we create a job, which uses the program above:

```
SQL> BEGIN
    sys.dbms_scheduler.create_job(
        job_name => 'env_job',
        program_name => 'env',
        auto_drop => FALSE,
        enabled => false);
END;
/
```

The job was defined as disabled, which dispels the requirement to supply a schedule. We are now ready to run the job manually:

```
SQL> EXEC dbms_scheduler.run_job(job_name => 'env_job')
PL/SQL procedure successfully completed.
SQL> SELECT status, error#, additional_info
FROM dba_scheduler_job_run_details
WHERE job_name='ENV_JOB'
AND owner='SYS';
STATUS           ERROR# ADDITIONAL_INFO
--------- ---------- ----------------------
SUCCEEDED          0 STANDARD_ERROR="PWD=/
```

```
SHLVL=1
_=/bin/env"
```

Thanks to terminating the shell script with exit code 0, the job is considered successful ("SUCCEEDED"). The job scheduler saved the standard error output of the job in the column ADDITIONAL_INFO of the view DBA_SCHEDULER_JOB_RUN_DETAILS. There are merely three environment variables and these are certainly not the ones you would expect. PATH, ORACLE_HOME, and ORACLE_SID are missing. PWD—the process's working directory—is a familiar one. SHLVL and "_" are present due to the fact that the test was performed on a Linux system, where /bin/sh is a symbolic link to /bin/bash. SHLVL (shell level) is incremented by one each time bash starts another instance of bash as a child process. Bash places the full path of each command it runs in the environment variable "_" (underscore), which is then inherited by child processes.

If we insist on implementing a database that can back itself up, we must run RMAN through the scheduler in such a way that the environment variables ORACLE_HOME and ORACLE_SID are visible. NLS_DATE_FORMAT should also be set, since it controls the date and time format used by RMAN. Several approaches come to mind:

1. Run /usr/bin/env through the scheduler, set environment variables with the command line arguments to env, and then have env run RMAN as in the example below:

```
$ /usr/bin/env ORACLE_HOME=/opt/oracle/product/db10.2 ORACLE_SID=TEN \
NLS_LANG=dd.Mon.yy-hh24:mi:ss /opt/oracle/product/db10.2/bin/rman target / \
cmdfile /opt/oracle/admin/scripts/backup.rcv msglog /opt/oracle/admin/log/rman.log
```

2. Write a shell script that sets the required environment variables and then calls RMAN. Have the scheduler run the shell script.

3. Write a general purpose shell script wrapper, which receives the name of a file with environment variables to set as well as the program to run as input.

The third approach should be the most promising, since some reuse is possible and the wrapper script could print the exit code of the program on standard error for later retrieval through the view DBA_SCHEDULER_JOB_RUN_DETAILS. A sample implementation of such a wrapper script is in the file extjob.sh in the source code depot.

Command Line Processing

Another undocumented aspect concerns how the scheduler runs the PROGRAM_ACTION specified with one of the procedures DBMS_SCHEDULER.CREATE_PROGRAM or DBMS_SCHEDULER.CREATE_JOB. The *Oracle Database PL/SQL Packages and Types Reference 10g Release 2* informs us that "the PROGRAM_ACTION for a program of type EXECUTABLE is the name of the external executable, including the full path name and any command–line arguments" (page 93–35, [OL10 2005]). The first part of this statement is correct, since the attempt to run an external program without specifying the full path name fails with "ORA-27369: job of type EXECUTABLE failed with exit code: No such file or directory". After a job failure, scheduler error messages may be retrieved from the column ADDITIONAL_INFO of the data dictionary view DBA_SCHEDULER_JOB_RUN_DETAILS.

The second part however, solely applies to Windows. On UNIX, arguments to external programs must be defined with the procedure DBMS_SCHEDULER.DEFINE_PROGRAM_ARGUMENT instead of adding them to the PROGRAM_ACTION. Otherwise jobs based on the program fail with "ORA-27369: job of type EXECUTABLE failed with exit code: No such file or directory". External jobs, which are not based on programs, cannot receive arguments.

On UNIX, the program $ORACLE_HOME/bin/extjobo is responsible for running external jobs owned by SYS. Using a system call trace utility such as truss or strace reveals that extjobo uses the UNIX system call access to verify that the program action is executable. A program action which includes arguments, fails this test with the UNIX error ENOENT (No such file or directory). System call tracing also reveals that the executable is run directly with the system call execve. This implies that characters such as ? or * within program arguments, which have special meaning to shells, must not be escaped.

Another implication is that the pseudo comment #!/bin/sh (or #!/bin/ksh, #!/bin/bash, etc.), which specifies an interpreter for running text files, must be present in the first line of shell scripts. If the specification of a command interpreter is missing, the error "ORA-27369: job of type EXECUTABLE failed with exit code: 255" is reported and DBA_SCHEDULER_JOB_RUN_DETAILS.ADDITIONAL_INFO contains STANDARD_ERROR="execve: Exec format error".

Likewise, perl must be specified as the command interpreter in order to run Perl scripts as external jobs. Thus, the first line of a Perl script might specify the absolute path to the perl interpreter as in:

```
#!/opt/oracle/product/db10.2/perl/bin/perl
```
The more portable approach is to use /usr/bin/env, which has the same absolute path on all UNIX systems, to run perl as in:
```
#!/usr/bin/env perl
```
The disadvantage of this latter approach in the context of the database scheduler is that the environment variable PATH is removed by extjobo. Thus, some mechanism that sets PATH before the Perl script is run must be in place. Once more /usr/bin/env may be used for this purpose, by defining a program which calls env and sets PATH in a program argument. Below is an example. The Perl script test.pl, which shall be executed by the scheduler, contains the code below:
```
#!/usr/bin/env perl
printf STDERR "This is perl script $0 executed by UNIX process $$.\n";
exit 0;
```
The PL/SQL block below creates a program with two arguments for running the Perl script test.pl. To enable a program, which includes arguments, all arguments must be defined with separate calls to the packaged procedure DBMS_SCHEDULER.DEFINE_PROGRAM_ARGUMENT:
```
begin
    dbms_scheduler.create_program(
        program_name=>'perl_program',
        program_type=>'EXECUTABLE',
        program_action=> '/usr/bin/env',
        number_of_arguments=>2,
        enabled=>false
    );
    dbms_scheduler.define_program_argument(
        program_name=>'perl_program',
        argument_position=>1,
        argument_name=>'env',
        argument_type=>'VARCHAR2',
        default_value=>'PATH=/opt/oracle/product/db10.2/perl/bin:/home/oracle'
    );
    dbms_scheduler.define_program_argument(
        program_name=>'perl_program',
        argument_position=>2,
        argument_name=>'script',
        argument_type=>'VARCHAR2',
        default_value=>'test.pl'
    );
    dbms_scheduler.enable('perl_program');
    dbms_scheduler.create_job(
        job_name=>'perl_job',
        program_name=>'perl_program',
        enabled=>false,
        auto_drop=>false
    );
  end;
  /
```
The job succeeds, since the environment variable PATH, which is removed by the scheduler, is supplied explicitly as a program argument. The file test.pl must be located in one of the directories assigned to PATH:
```
SQL> EXEC dbms_scheduler.run_job('perl_job')
PL/SQL procedure successfully completed.
SQL> SELECT status, additional_info
FROM dba_scheduler_job_run_details
WHERE log_id=(SELECT max(log_id) FROM dba_scheduler_job_run_details);
```

```
STATUS     ADDITIONAL_INFO
---------  -----------------------------------------------------------
SUCCEEDED  STANDARD_ERROR="This is perl script /home/oracle/test.pl
           executed by UNIX process 5387."
```

External Jobs and Non–privileged Users

On UNIX, external jobs owned by the privileged user SYS are run with the privileges of the ORACLE software owner—usually the UNIX user oracle. The execution of external jobs owned by database users other than SYS is enabled by default. It is undocumented which UNIX user is used to run these external jobs. Users which have neither the privilege SYSDBA nor the role DBA require the system privileges CREATE JOB and CREATE EXTERNAL JOB to successfully create and run external jobs. Thus, to create a new user EXTJOB with just enough privileges to run external jobs, the following SQL statements may be used:

```
SQL> CREATE USER extjob IDENTIFIED BY secret;
SQL> GRANT CONNECT TO extjob;
SQL> GRANT CREATE JOB TO extjob;
SQL> GRANT CREATE EXTERNAL JOB TO extjob;
```

When called without arguments, the UNIX program id displays the user name and group set of the current user. This program may be used to find out which UNIX user is used to run external programs by non–privileged users. Calling a shell script which redirects the output of id to standard error for capture by the scheduler yields:

```
SQL> SELECT additional_info
FROM all_scheduler_job_run_details
WHERE log_id=(SELECT max(log_id) FROM all_scheduler_job_run_details);
ADDITIONAL_INFO
-----------------------------------------------------------------------
STANDARD_ERROR="uid=99(nobody) gid=99(nobody) groups=800(oinstall),801(dba)"
```

The UNIX user and group nobody are used. For this reason, the existence of the UNIX user nobody is an installation prerequisite mentioned in installation guides for the ORACLE DBMS. Oracle10g Release 2 UNIX installation guides incorrectly state that the program $ORACLE_HOME/bin/extjob must be owned by nobody. When this is the case, external jobs fail with the error message below in ALL_SCHEDULER_JOB_RUN_DETAILS.ADDITIONAL_INFO:

```
ADDITIONAL_INFO
-----------------------------------------------------------------------
ORA-27369: job of type EXECUTABLE failed with exit code: 274662
STANDARD_ERROR="Oracle Scheduler error: Config file is not owned by root or is
writable by group or other or extjob is not setuid and owned by root"
```

The "config file" mentioned in the error message refers to the file externaljob.ora, which is located in the directory $ORACLE_HOME/rdbms/admin. This file is undocumented in Oracle10g and is partially documented in *Oracle Database Administrator's Guide 11g Release 1*. It must be owned by root and must be writable only by the owner:

```
$ ls -l $ORACLE_HOME/rdbms/admin/externaljob.ora
-rw-r-----  1 root oinstall 1534 Dec 22  2005 /opt/oracle/product/db10.2/rdbms/admin/externaljob.ora
```

Contents of the file externaljob.ora are reproduced below[1]:

```
# This configuration file is used by dbms_scheduler when executing external
# (operating system) jobs. It contains the user and group to run external
# jobs as. It must only be writable by the owner and must be owned by root.
# If extjob is not setuid then the only allowable run_user
# is the user Oracle runs as and the only allowable run_group is the group
# Oracle runs as.
run_user = nobody
run_group = nobody
```

---

1. The error "ORA-27369: job of type EXECUTABLE failed with exit code: 274668 STANDARD_ERROR="Oracle Scheduler error: Invalid or missing run_group in configuration file."" may be raised in spite of a correct configuration due to a line in externaljob.ora that exceeds 100 characters.

The correct permissions for `extjob` are setuid root:

```
$ ls -l $ORACLE_HOME/bin/extjob
-rwsr-x---  1 root oinstall 64920 Jul 21 17:04 /opt/oracle/product/db10.2/bin/extjob
```

Setuid permissions are required to allow the program `extjob` to change its effective user id to that of the user nobody by calling the C library function `seteuid`. The effective group id is set by a call to `setegid`. Since both the effective user and group id are changed to nobody before using `execve` to run the external program, merely the permissions of user and group nobody are available to external jobs not owned by SYS. This mechanism must be in place to prevent external jobs from connecting as SYS, which would pose a serious security threat.

Metalink note 391820.1 suggests setting `run_user=oracle` and `run_group=oinstall` as part of resolving the errors "ORA-27369: job of type EXECUTABLE failed with exit code: Operation not permitted" and "ORA-27369: job of type EXECUTABLE failed with exit code: 274662". From a security perspective, this is very problematic. Normally, the UNIX user oracle is a member of the OSDBA group (usually group dba) and may connect as SYS without supplying a password. By allowing users other than SYS to execute external jobs as a member of the OSDBA group, those users may connect as SYS in their external jobs! Thus, any user who has the privileges CREATE JOB and CREATE EXTERNAL JOB can connect as SYS! The correct solution would have been to create and run the job as SYS. Jobs owned and run by SYS are always executed as the ORACLE software owner. The program `$ORACLE_HOME/bin/extjobo`, which runs these jobs, does not use the configuration file `externaljob.ora`. Setuid permission for `extjobo` is not required either, since this program does not alter effective user or group identifiers.

External Jobs on Windows

The implementation of the database scheduler on Windows differs from the UNIX implementation in three respects. These are:

- command line argument handling
- environment variables
- execution of external jobs by non-privileged users

The next three sections address these topics in detail.

Command Line Argument Handling

Contrary to UNIX, scheduler programs or job actions on Windows may contain command line arguments. The source code depot contains a complete prototype for taking RMAN backups with the scheduler (zip file `exec_rman.zip`). The prototype includes the backup script `exec_rman.bat`, which requires two arguments:

- a batch script with configuration variables, such as a directory for log files (`LOG_DIR`) and a connect string for the RMAN catalog (`CATALOG_CONNECT`)
- the name of an RMAN script to run, e.g. for database or archived redo log backup

The script `exec_rman.bat` calls the configuration batch file (e.g. `TEN_config.bat`) to read the configuration and then runs the requested RMAN script. It checks RMAN's exit code and prints it to standard error output, such that it may be retrieved from the view `DBA_SCHEDULER_JOB_RUN_DETAILS`. In case RMAN terminates with a non–zero exit code, `exec_rman.bat` terminates with a non–zero exit code too, thus signaling success or failure of the backup to the scheduler.

Below is an example of a job, which uses `exec_rman.bat`, and supplies the required command line arguments:

```
SQL> BEGIN
  DBMS_SCHEDULER.CREATE_JOB(
      job_name => 'rman_online_backup',
      job_type => 'EXECUTABLE',
      job_action => 'c:\home\ndebes\bin\exec_rman.bat
C:\home\ndebes\rman\TEN_config.bat backup_online.rcv',
      start_date => systimestamp,
      repeat_interval => 'FREQ=DAILY;BYHOUR=22',
      enabled=>true /* default false! */
  );
END;
/
```

On Windows, the Process Explorer[1] is the right tool to visualize relationships among processes. Figure 8 shows that the scheduler uses `%ORACLE_HOME%\bin\extjobo.exe` and a Windows command interpreter (`cmd.exe`) to run the batch script defined in the job's action. The option `/C` instructs `cmd.exe` to execute the string passed as a command and to exit as soon as the command has finished.

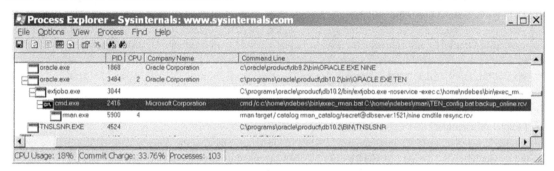

Figure 8: An External Job in Process Explorer

Windows Environment Variables

In the previous section, we saw that `cmd /c` is used to run external jobs on Windows. Since `cmd.exe` retrieves and sets system–wide as well as user–specific environment variables, we should expect that environment variables are available to external jobs. A quick test confirms that this assumption is correct. By default, the service which implements an ORACLE instance, runs as user SYSTEM. Thus, only system–wide environment variables are available. If however, the service is run as a specific user, environment variables set by that user are also available. The batch script below (file `environment.bat`) may be run as an external job to check environment variables:

```
echo PATH=%PATH% > c:\temp\environment.log
echo ORACLE_HOME=%ORACLE_HOME% >> c:\temp\environment.log
echo ORACLE_SID=%ORACLE_SID% >> c:\temp\environment.log
echo NLS_DATE_FORMAT=%NLS_DATE_FORMAT% >> c:\temp\environment.log
echo TNS_ADMIN=%TNS_ADMIN% >> c:\temp\environment.log
echo PERL5LIB=%PERL5LIB% >> c:\temp\environment.log
```

An interesting result is that ORACLE_SID, which is normally not defined as an environment variable, is set to the same value as V$INSTANCE.INSTANCE_NAME. This behavior of the DBMS on Windows is just the opposite of what we saw on UNIX. Whereas `extjob` and `extjobo` on UNIX remove all environment variables, the same programs on Windows appear to set ORACLE_SID (or at least they don't remove it after inheritance from another process).

External Jobs and Non–privileged Users

External jobs owned by the database user SYS run as Windows user SYSTEM. SYSTEM is a member of the group Administrators. From a security perspective, this is as if external jobs were run as root on UNIX. Care must be taken that scripts or executables run by external jobs cannot be modified by potential intruders.

After a default installation, jobs owned by users other than SYS fail with the errors below:

```
SQL> EXEC dbms_scheduler.run_job('id')
BEGIN dbms_scheduler.run_job('id'); END;
*
ERROR at line 1:
ORA-27370: job slave failed to launch a job of type EXECUTABLE
ORA-27300: OS system dependent operation:accessing execution agent failed with status: 2
ORA-27301: OS failure message: The system cannot find the file specified.
ORA-27302: failure occurred at: sjsec 6a
ORA-27303: additional information: The system cannot find the file specified.
```

---

1. Process Explorer is available at no charge at http://www.sysinternals.com. It may be used to find out which process has opened a DLL or file. I recommend two other tools from Sysinternals: Regmon for monitoring registry access and Filemon for monitoring file access.

```
ORA-06512: at "SYS.DBMS_ISCHED", line 150
ORA-06512: at "SYS.DBMS_SCHEDULER", line 441
ORA-06512: at line 1
```

Services Created by the ORADIM Utility

ORADIM is a command line utility for creating Windows services, which implement RDBMS and ASM instances. In case you have ever taken a close look at the services, which ORADIM creates, you may have noticed that it creates two services in Oracle10*g* and subsequent releases. If, for example, you create an RDBMS instance called TEST as below:

```
C:> oradim -new -sid TEST -syspwd secret -startmode manual -srvcstart demand
```

You will see two new services:

- OracleServiceTEST
- OracleJobSchedulerTEST

The service OracleServiceTEST implements the RDBMS instance. Opening the registry with `regedit.exe` reveals that the service HKEY_LOCAL_MACHINE\SYSTEM\CurrentControlSet\Services\OracleServiceTEST is based on the executable `oracle.exe`. The service OracleJobSchedulerTEST has status disabled and is implemented by `extjob.exe`. This service must be started for external jobs owned by database users other than SYS to complete successfully.

OracleJobScheduler Service

The new service OracleJobScheduler*ORACLE_SID*, where *ORACLE_SID* is the name of an instance created with `oradim.exe`, is undocumented in Oracle10*g*. It is documented in *Oracle Database Platform Guide 11g Release 1 for Microsoft Windows*. The Oracle11*g* documentation points out that the service must be configured to run as a user with low privileges before enabling it. By default, OracleJobScheduler*ORACLE_SID* is configured to run as user SYSTEM. For security reasons, this setting must be modified. Otherwise, any database user with enough privileges to execute external jobs might use operating system authentication to connect as SYS and take control of databases on the local system. The account used to run OracleJobScheduler*ORACLE_SID* should not be a member of the groups Administrators or ORA_DBA.

Source Code Depot

Table 32: DBMS_SCHEDULER Source Code Depot

File Name	*Functionality*
`environment.bat`	Saves Windows environment variable settings available to external jobs in a file.
`exec_rman.zip`	Prototype for taking RMAN backups on Windows with the database scheduler
`extjob.sh`	Shell script wrapper for running external jobs through the database scheduler. Sets environment variables before running the proper job.
`failure.bat`	Windows command–line script for simulating job failure
`perl_job.sql`	Scheduler program and job for running the perl script `test.pl` on UNIX
`rman_backup.sql`	Creates an external job, which runs RMAN with the pipe interface enabled. A second job of type PLSQL_BLOCK passes commands to RMAN through the pipe interface. The pipe messages sent to and received by RMAN are logged in a custom database table. This table is integrated with the scheduler's own logging. The package `RMAN_PIPE_IF`, presented in Chapter 36, is required.
`test.pl`	Perl script which writes the script name and the process identifier of the process that executes the script to standard error output

Chapter 20

DBMS_SYSTEM

Status: The package DBMS_SYSTEM is installed by default in Oracle9i and subsequent releases. Execute permission on this package is only available to the user SYS. There are a few references to the package DBMS_SYSTEM in manuals, but it is undocumented in the *Oracle9i Supplied PL/SQL Packages and Types References* as well as in the *Oracle Database PL/SQL Packages and Types Reference* of Oracle10g Release 2 and Oracle11g Release 1.

Benefit: DBMS_SYSTEM provides a wide array of useful functionality, such as enabling SQL trace at all supported levels in any database session, setting events, generating dumps without using the SQL*Plus command ORADEBUG, writing custom entries to the alert log or trace files, getting environment variable values, and changing parameters in running sessions. Since the package DBMS_SUPPORT is not installed by default, DBMS_SYSTEM is an alternative to using DBMS_SUPPORT for tracing sessions.

GET_ENV Procedure

This procedure gives read only access to environment variables of the process servicing a database client. In case you have ever been desperately seeking for a way to ask a DBMS instance which ORACLE_HOME it is running in, look no further. While the machine a DBMS instance is running on (V$INSTANCE.HOST_NAME) as well as the ORACLE_SID of the instance (V$INSTANCE.INSTANCE_NAME) are available through the view V$INSTANCE, none of the V$ views tell what the setting of ORACLE_HOME is. The procedure GET_ENV is not available in Oracle9i.

Syntax

```
DBMS_SYSTEM.GET_ENV(
    var IN VARCHAR2,
    val OUT VARCHAR2);
```

Parameters

Parameter	Description
var	Name of an environment variable
val	Value of the environment variable

Usage Notes

When there is no environment variable that matches the name passed in parameter var, an empty string is returned in val. If the maximum length of val is insufficient to hold the value of the environment variable, the error "ORA-06502: PL/SQL: numeric or value error: character string buffer too small" is thrown. To avoid this, I recommend that you always declare val as large as possible. In SQL*Plus the maximum size is VARCHAR2(4000) as opposed to VARCHAR2(32767) in PL/SQL. Environment variable names on UNIX systems are case-sensitive, whereas they are not case-sensitive on Windows system.

Examples

The following PL/SQL code may be used to retrieve the value of the environment variable ORACLE_HOME in SQL*Plus:

```
SQL> SET AUTOPRINT ON
SQL> VARIABLE val VARCHAR2(4000)
SQL> BEGIN
   dbms_system.get_env('ORACLE_HOME', :val);
END;
/
PL/SQL procedure successfully completed.
VAL
-----------------------------------------------
/opt/oracle/product/10.2
```

KCFRMS Procedure

This procedure resets the maximum wait time for each event (V$SESSION_EVENT.MAX_WAIT), the maximum read time for a data file (V$FILESTAT.MAXIORTM), and the maximum write time for a data file (V$FILESTAT.MAXIOWTM) to zero. This procedure might be useful in an environment where peaks in file access (V$FILESTAT) or wait events (V$SESSION_EVENT) are observed. By saving the values from these V$ views just before calling DBMS_SYSTEM.KCFRMS on an hourly basis, it would be possible to determine at which times during the day and to what extent peaks occur.

Syntax

```
DBMS_SYSTEM.KCFRMS();
```

Usage Notes

The values are set to zero for all sessions in V$SESSION_EVENT, not solely the session which calls the procedure DBMS_SYSTEM.KCFRMS.

Examples

Below are some sample rows of V$SESSION_EVENT, before calling DBMS_SYSTEM.KCFRMS (all timings are in seconds; the value of the column MAX_WAIT is natively in centiseconds):

```
SQL> SELECT sid, wait_class, event, round(time_waited_micro/1000000,3) AS
time_waited_sec, max_wait/100 AS max_wait_sec
FROM v$session_event WHERE sid in(140, 141)
ORDER BY sid, wait_class, event;
```

```
SID WAIT_CLASS   EVENT                           TIME_WAITED_SEC MAX_WAIT_SEC
--- -----------  ----------------------------    --------------- ------------
140 Application  enq: TX - row lock contention             4.929            3
140 Commit       log file sync                              .009          .01
140 Idle         SQL*Net message from client              53.167        29.72
140 Network      SQL*Net message to client                     0            0
140 System I/O   control file sequential read               .006          .01
140 User I/O     db file scattered read                     .208          .13
140 User I/O     db file sequential read                    .603          .04
140 User I/O     direct path write temp                        0            0
141 Application  SQL*Net break/reset to client              .022            0
141 Commit       log file sync                               .04          .01
141 Idle         SQL*Net message from client            2432.647       171.39
141 Network      SQL*Net message to client                  .001            0
141 Other        events in waitclass Other                 1.042         1.04
141 System I/O   control file sequential read             2.166            0
141 User I/O     db file sequential read                    .267          .02
```

After calling DBMS_SYSTEM.KCFRMS, the same query on V$SESSION_EVENT gave the results below:

```
SID WAIT_CLASS   EVENT                           TIME_WAITED_SEC MAX_WAIT_SEC
--- -----------  ----------------------------    --------------- ------------
140 Application  enq: TX - row lock contention             4.929            0
140 Commit       log file sync                              .009            0
140 Idle         SQL*Net message from client             379.432            0
140 Network      SQL*Net message to client                     0            0
140 System I/O   control file sequential read               .006            0
140 User I/O     db file scattered read                     .208            0
140 User I/O     db file sequential read                    .603            0
140 User I/O     direct path write temp                        0            0
141 Application  SQL*Net break/reset to client              .022            0
141 Commit       log file sync                               .04            0
141 Idle         SQL*Net message from client            2460.816        28.17
141 Network      SQL*Net message to client                  .001            0
141 Other        events in waitclass Other                 1.042            0
141 System I/O   control file sequential read             2.166            0
141 User I/O     db file sequential read                    .267            0
```

As you can see above, the values in column MAX_WAIT (column MAX_WAIT_SEC) have been set to zero for all columns. For session 141 the value of MAX_WAIT has become non-zero again, since it had become active after DBMS_SYSTEM.KCFRMS had finished.

The contents of V$FILESTAT before calling DBMS_SYSTEM.KCFRMS were:

```
SELECT file#, phyrds, phywrts, readtim, writetim, maxiortm, maxiowtm
FROM v$filestat;
FILE# PHYRDS PHYWRTS READTIM WRITETIM MAXIORTM MAXIOWTM
----- ------ ------- ------- -------- -------- --------
    1   8194     845   36635      810        6        8
    2     26    1655      88     1698        0        1
    3    720    1324    3060     1534        4        0
    4    213      10     997        0        8        0
    5      5       1      23        1        0        0
```

After calling DBMS_SYSTEM.KCFRMS, querying V$FILESTAT returned the following data:

```
SELECT file#, phyrds, phywrts, readtim, writetim, maxiortm, maxiowtm
FROM v$filestat;
FILE# PHYRDS PHYWRTS READTIM WRITETIM MAXIORTM MAXIOWTM
----- ------ ------- ------- -------- -------- --------
    1   8194     849   36635      812        0        0
    2     26    1655      88     1698        0        0
    3    720    1324    3060     1534        0        0
```

| 4 | 213 | 10 | 997 | 0 | 0 | 0 |
| 5 | 5 | 1 | 23 | 1 | 0 | 0 |

KSDDDT Procedure

This procedure writes a timestamp into a SQL trace file. The format of the timestamp as represented by ORACLE DBMS date and time format models (see chapter 2 of *Oracle Database SQL Reference 10g Release 2*) is YYYY-MM-DD HH24:MI:SS.FF3.

Syntax

```
DBMS_SYSTEM.KSDDDT();
```

Usage Notes

If the process servicing the current database session does not yet have a trace file, e.g. from an execution of the statement ALTER SESSION SET sql_trace=TRUE, then a trace file is created. The timestamp's format does not depend on the session's national language support (NLS) settings, i.e. NLS_DATE_FORMAT and related parameters do not influence the format of the timestamp.

Examples

```
C:> sqlplus / as sysdba
SQL*Plus: Release 10.2.0.1.0 - Production on Mon Jun 25 13:17:07 2007
SQL> ORADEBUG SETMYPID
Statement processed.
SQL> ORADEBUG TRACEFILE_NAME
Statement processed.
SQL> EXEC dbms_system.ksdddt();
PL/SQL procedure successfully completed.
SQL> ORADEBUG TRACEFILE_NAME
c:\programs\admin\ten\udump\ten_ora_4588.trc
SQL> $type c:\programs\admin\ten\udump\ten_ora_4588.trc
Dump file c:\programs\admin\ten\udump\ten_ora_4588.trc
Mon Jun 25 13:17:25 2007
...
Windows thread id: 4588, image: ORACLE.EXE (SHAD)
...
*** SERVICE NAME:(SYS$USERS) 2007-06-25 13:17:25.923
*** SESSION ID:(147.755) 2007-06-25 13:17:25.923
*** 2007-06-25 13:17:25.923
```

The last line above is the timestamp written by DBMS_SYSTEM.KSDDDT. As you can see, when ORADEBUG TRACEFILE_NAME was first called, it did not return the path of a trace file, since no trace file existed at that point in time. By running DBMS_SYSTEM.KSDDDT a trace file was created and its path was returned by the second call to ORADEBUG TRACEFILE_NAME.

KSDFLS Procedure

This procedure flushes any pending output to the target file (alert log and/or trace file).

Syntax

```
DBMS_SYSTEM.KSDFLS();
```

Usage Notes

Personally, I have never found a situation where it was necessary to call DBMS_SYSTEM.KSDFLS.

Examples

```
SQL> EXEC dbms_system.ksdfls
```

KSDIND Procedure

This procedure indents the next string written to a SQL trace file with DBMS_SYSTEM.KSDWRT by placing one or more colons (:) as specified by parameter lvl at the beginning of the line.

Syntax

```
DBMS_SYSTEM.KSDIND(
    lvl IN BINARY_INTEGER);
```

Parameters

Parameter	Description
lvl	Indentation level

Usage Notes

This procedure has no effect when writing to the alert log with DBMS_SYSTEM.KSDWRT.

Examples

```
SQL> BEGIN
    sys.dbms_system.ksdind(3);
    sys.dbms_system.ksdwrt(1, 'indented string');
END;
/
```

The above anonymous block writes the following line to the trace file:

```
:::indented string
```

KSDWRT Procedure

This procedure writes a string to the SQL trace file of the server process servicing the database client, the alert log of the instance or both. If SQL_TRACE has not been enabled (through ALTER SESSION, DBMS_SYSTEM, DBMS_SUPPORT[1], etc.) in the server process and thus no trace file exists yet, a trace file is created. Thus it is possible to write transcripts of sessions to trace files without enabling SQL trace.

Syntax

```
DBMS_SYSTEM.KSDWRT(
    dest IN BINARY_INTEGER,
    tst IN VARCHAR2);
```

Parameters

Parameter	Description
dest	Destination file, 1=SQL trace file, 2=alert log, 3=both
tst	String to write to destination file

Usage Notes

When writing to a SQL trace file, a timestamp such as the one written by DBMS_SYSTEM.KSDDT is automatically placed on the line preceding the string written, given that the session has been inactive for more than 10 seconds. To

---

1. The package DBMS_SUPPORT may be installed with the script $ORACLE_HOME/rdbms/admin/dbmssupp.sql. Tracing of a foreign session is initiated with the procedure START_TRACE_IN_SESSION and terminated with the procedure STOP_TRACE_IN_SESSION.

make sure the string written is always preceded by a timestamp, explicitly call DBMS_SYSTEM.KSDDT before calling DBMS_SYSTEM.KSDWRT.

When writing to the alert log, the string written is unconditionally preceded by a timestamp and the format is "Dy Mon DD HH24:MI:SS YYYY" (e.g. "Mon Jun 25 15:17:37 2007").

Since the package DBMS_SYSTEM has functionality that should only be accessible to privileged sessions, it is advisable to provide access to DBMS_SYSTEM through wrapper procedures. Such wrapper procedures are part of the open source ORACLE instrumentation library ILO by Hotsos[1]. Their names are HOTSOS_SYSUTIL.WRITE_DATESTAMP and HOTSOS_SYSUTIL.WRITE_TO_TRACE. Execute permission on these packages is granted to PUBLIC.

Examples

The following anonymous block shows how timing information for expensive tasks can be written to a trace file. The string '===' at the beginning of the line serves to make sure that the line is ignored by the TKPROF utility. DBMS_UTILITY.GET_CPU_TIME is not available in Oracle9*i*.

```
SQL> DECLARE
    elapsed_time_t1 number;
    elapsed_time_t2 number;
    cpu_time_t1 number;
    cpu_time_t2 number;
BEGIN
    elapsed_time_t1:=dbms_utility.get_time;
    cpu_time_t1:=dbms_utility.get_cpu_time;
    dbms_stats.gather_schema_stats(user); -- do something expensive
    elapsed_time_t2:=dbms_utility.get_time;
    cpu_time_t2:=dbms_utility.get_cpu_time;
    sys.dbms_system.ksdddt;
    sys.dbms_system.ksdwrt(1, '=== Elapsed time: ' ||
        to_char((elapsed_time_t2 - elapsed_time_t1)/100)||
    ' sec CPU: ' || to_char((cpu_time_t2 - cpu_time_t1)/100) || ' sec');
END;
/
```

This anonymous block writes entries such as these into a trace file:

```
*** 2007-06-25 16:23:12.316
=== Elapsed time: 1.15 sec CPU: .68 sec
```

Another example for leveraging DBMS_SYSTEM.KSDWRT might be to record errors that are not normally logged to the alert log by creating a SERVERERROR trigger which calls KSDWRT. For example, Oracle9*i* does not write entries to the alert log when "ORA-01555 snapshot too old" occurs (Oracle10*g* does). By implementing a SERVERERROR trigger that checks for error code 1555, this error and the statement that failed could be written to the alert log of an Oracle9*i* instance. Many monitoring tools such as Enterprise Manager or Tivoli TEC are able to parse the alert log of an instance and to relay errors found to a management console. By writing custom errors such as ORA-20000 to the alert log, a simple yet efficient integration may be built.

READ_EV Procedure

This procedure reads the level at which an event has been enabled. It returns zero for disabled events.

Syntax

```
DBMS_SYSTEM.READ_EV(
    iev IN BINARY_INTEGER,
    oev OUT BINARY_INTEGER);
```

---

1. See http://www.hotsos.com

Parameters

Parameter	Description
`iev`	Event number; usually between 10000 and 10999
`oev`	Level at which the event is set; level=0 means the event is disabled

Usage Notes

`DBMS_SYSTEM.READ_EV` works as expected when SQL trace has been enabled by setting event 10046, e.g. with `ALTER SESSION`, `DBMS_MONITOR.SESSION_TRACE_ENABLE` or `DBMS_SYSTEM.SET_EV`.

`DBMS_SYSTEM.READ_EV` does not work in conjunction with `ALTER SESSION SET SQL_TRACE=TRUE` in Oracle10*g* and Oracle11*g*, since the `oev` returned by `DBMS_SYSTEM.READ_EV` remains 0 when this statement is executed (in Oracle9*i* `oev`=1 is returned, i.e. it works as expected in Oracle9*i*). In the latter case, `SELECT value FROM v$parameter WHERE name='sql_trace'` can be used to find out whether SQL trace is switched on or not in both releases.

Examples

The example below shows that using `DBMS_MONITOR` in Oracle10*g* to enable tracing of SQL statements and wait events, sets event 10046 at level 8.

```
SQL> VARIABLE lev number
SQL> SET AUTOPRINT ON
SQL> EXECUTE sys.dbms_system.read_ev(10046, :lev)
PL/SQL procedure successfully completed.
       LEV
----------
         0
SQL> EXEC dbms_monitor.session_trace_enable
PL/SQL procedure successfully completed.
SQL> SELECT sql_trace, sql_trace_waits, sql_trace_binds FROM v$session
WHERE sid=userenv('sid')
SQL_TRACE  SQL_TRACE_WAITS SQL_TRACE_BINDS
---------- --------------- ---------------
ENABLED    TRUE            FALSE
SQL> EXECUTE sys.dbms_system.read_ev(10046,:lev)
PL/SQL procedure successfully completed.
       LEV
----------
         8
```

SET_INT_PARAM_IN_SESSION Procedure

This procedure sets an integer parameter in a foreign database session.

Syntax

```
DBMS_SYSTEM.SET_INT_PARAM_IN_SESSION(
    sid IN NUMBER,
    serial# IN NUMBER,
    parnam IN VARCHAR2,
    intval IN BINARY_INTEGER);
```

Parameters

Parameter	Description
sid	Session identifier; corresponds to V$SESSION.SID
serial#	Session serial number; corresponds to V$SESSION.SERIAL#
parnam	Parameter name; corresponds to V$PARAMETER.NAME
intval	Integer value to assign to a parameter

Usage Notes

No exception is raised when an incorrect SID or SERIAL# are passed.

Examples

The following example shows how to increase the setting of the parameter SORT_AREA_SIZE in a session, e.g. when sorts are slow due to an insufficient default value of the parameter SORT_AREA_SIZE[1]. First, start a session and retrieve the current setting of SORT_AREA_SIZE by calling the package DBMS_UTILITY[2].

```
$ sqlplus hr/hr
SQL> VARIABLE result NUMBER
SQL> VARIABLE sort_area_size NUMBER
SQL> VARIABLE dummy VARCHAR2(255)
SQL> BEGIN
   :result:=dbms_utility.get_parameter_value(parnam=>'sort_area_size',
      intval=>:sort_area_size, strval=>:dummy);
END;
/
PL/SQL procedure successfully completed.
SQL> PRINT sort_area_size
SORT_AREA_SIZE
--------------
         65536
```

Next, start another SQL*Plus session as user SYS, retrieve the SID and SERIAL# of the session you want to modify, and increase SORT_AREA_SIZE to 1048576 bytes by calling the package DBMS_SYSTEM:

```
$ sqlplus "/ as sysdba"
SQL> SELECT sid, serial# FROM v$session WHERE username='HR';
       SID    SERIAL#
---------- ----------
         9         19
SQL> EXEC sys.dbms_system.set_int_param_in_session(9, 19, 'sort_area_size', 1048576);
PL/SQL procedure successfully completed.
```

Now, back in the first session by HR, verify that the parameter SORT_AREA_SIZE has actually changed:

```
SQL> BEGIN
   :result:=dbms_utility.get_parameter_value(parnam=>'sort_area_size',
   intval=>:sort_area_size, strval=>:dummy);
END;
/
PL/SQL procedure successfully completed.
```

---

1. Under most circumstances SORT_AREA_SIZE and other *_AREA_SIZE parameters should no longer be used in favor of PGA_AGGREGATE_TARGET. SORT_AREA_SIZE cannot be modified with ALTER SYSTEM.
2. Retrieval of parameter settings with DBMS_UTILITY works in any session, whereas access to V$PARAMETER requires the role SELECT_CATALOG_ROLE or other suitable privilege.

```
SQL> PRINT sort_area_size
SORT_AREA_SIZE
--------------
       1048576
```

SET_BOOL_PARAM_IN_SESSION Procedure

This procedure sets a boolean parameter in a foreign session.

Syntax

```
DBMS_SYSTEM.SET_BOOL_PARAM_IN_SESSION(
    sid IN NUMBER,
    serial# IN NUMBER,
    parnam IN VARCHAR2,
    bval IN BOOLEAN);
```

Parameters

Parameter	Description
sid	Session identifier; corresponds to V$SESSION.SID
serial#	Session serial number; corresponds to V$SESSION.SERIAL#
parnam	Parameter name; corresponds to V$PARAMETER.NAME
bval	Boolean value, i.e. TRUE or FALSE

Usage Notes

No exception is raised when an incorrect SID or SERIAL# are passed.

Examples

Setting the boolean parameter TIMED_STATISTICS to TRUE in a session with SID=12 and SERIAL#=16 is accomplished as follows:

```
SQL> EXEC dbms_system.set_bool_param_in_session(12, 16, 'timed_statistics', TRUE);
```

SET_EV Procedure

This procedure sets a numeric event in a session or generates a dump of information contained in the SGA or PGA by specifying the name of the dump (i.e. SYSTEMSTATE dump[1]). It is commonly used to enable tracing of SQL statements, wait events, and binds in a session that exhibits performance problems and is foreign to the callers session. Note that tracing wait events (event 10046 at levels 8 and 12) and/or binds is highly recommended. Use of DBMS_SYSTEM.SET_SQL_TRACE_IN_SESSION is discouraged, since it enables SQL trace at level 1, i.e. without bind variables and wait events.

Syntax

```
DBMS_SYSTEM.SET_EV(
    si IN BINARY_INTEGER,
    se IN BINARY_INTEGER
    ev IN BINARY_INTEGER
    le IN BINARY_INTEGER
    nm IN VARCHAR2);
```

---

1. A SYSTEMSTATE dump reveals the current state of an instance and may be used by Oracle Support to diagnose hanging issues.

Parameters

Parameter	Description
si	Session identifier; corresponds to V$SESSION.SID
se	Session serial number; corresponds to V$SESSION.SERIAL#
ev	Event number between 10000 and 10999 for numeric events such as 10053 (optimizer trace). If nm is not NULL and ev is an ORACLE error number outside of the range 10000 to 10999, the dump named by nm is taken when the session throws the error specified. If ev=65535 and nm is not NULL, an immediate dump of the type specified by nm is taken. This is equivalent to ALTER SESSION SET EVENTS 'IMMEDIATE TRACE NAME *event_name* LEVEL *level*', where *event_name* is the name of the dump to take, e.g. SYSTEMSTATE, PROCESSSTATE or ERRORSTACK, and *level* is the event level. Named dumps are only possible within the session of the caller, i.e. they cannot be taken in a foreign session.
le	Level of the event; 0=disable event. Each event supports certain levels. The maximum level is usually 10.
nm	Name, e.g. for taking diagnostic dumps. A list of permissible dump names is available by calling ORADEBUG DUMPLIST as user SYS in SQL*Plus. If nm is an empty string (' ', i.e. two single quotes without any characters in between), the call to DBMS_SYSTEM.SET_EV is equivalent to ALTER SESSION SET EVENTS '*event* TRACE NAME CONTEXT FOREVER, LEVEL *level*', where *event* is a numeric event such as 10046 and *level* is the event level.

Usage Notes

When using a numeric event such as 10046, set nm to an empty string (passing NULL does not work, although the DBMS normally treats empty strings as NULL). If SET_EV is used incorrectly or with an si or se that does not exist, the procedure call does not have any effect and no exception is thrown.

Examples

The following examples illustrate both uses of DBMS_SYSTEM.SET_EV:

- setting an event at session level (recommended for Shared Server database sessions)
- taking a named dump

Enabling SQL Trace with SET_EV

Let's assume that the session of user HR is a resource hog. So we need to trace SQL statements and wait events to figure out what's going on. The example below shows how to retrieve the SID and SERIAL# from V$SESSION to enable tracing with DBMS_SYSTEM.SET_EV.

```
SQL> CONNECT / AS SYSDBA
Connected.
SQL> SELECT sid, serial# FROM v$session WHERE username='HR';
       SID    SERIAL#
---------- ----------
       140        862
SQL> EXECUTE dbms_system.set_ev(140, 862, 10046, 8, '')
PL/SQL procedure successfully completed.
```

Taking Named Dumps

Named dumps may only be taken in the same session that calls DBMS_SYSTEM.SET_EV. To take an immediate ERRORSTACK dump in a foreign session, use ORADEBUG (see Chapter 37). The following anonymous block takes an ERRORSTACK dump at level 3:

```
SQL> VARIABLE sid NUMBER
SQL> VARIABLE serial NUMBER
SQL> BEGIN
   SELECT sid, serial# INTO :sid, :serial
```

```
      FROM v$session
      WHERE sid=(SELECT sid FROM v$mystat WHERE rownum=1);
      sys.dbms_system.set_ev(:sid, :serial, 65535, 3, 'errorstack');
  END;
  /
```

The same result is attained by a much simpler ALTER SESSION statement:

```
SQL> ALTER SESSION SET EVENTS 'IMMEDIATE TRACE NAME ERRORSTACK LEVEL 3';
```

An error stack dump shows which subroutine a program was executing at the time the dump was taken. It also lists the entire call stack, i.e. in what sequence subroutines called each other. The currently executed subroutine is at the top of the call stack. ORACLE call stacks are similar to call stacks obtained by reading core files with debuggers, such as adb, sdb, or gdb. Taking an ERRORSTACK dump does not terminate an ORACLE process. However, you should expect the process to become unresponsive while it writes the trace file.

A level 3 error stack dump includes open cursors and is thus useful to find the SQL statement text corresponding to a certain cursor number, in case the PARSING IN CURSOR entry for a specific cursor is missing in a SQL trace file. In Oracle10g, cursors are dumped as in the example below:

```
Cursor#1(07470C24) state=BOUND curiob=07476564
  curflg=4c f12=0 par=00000000 ses=6998B274
  sqltxt(66F31AA0)=ALTER SESSION SET EVENTS 'IMMEDIATE TRACE NAME ERRORSTACK LEVEL 3'
```

SET_SQL_TRACE_IN_SESSION Procedure

This procedure enables SQL trace in a database session.

Syntax

```
DBMS_SYSTEM.SET_SQL_TRACE_IN_SESSION(
    sid IN NUMBER,
    serial# IN NUMBER,
    sql_trace IN BOOLEAN);
```

Parameters

Parameter	Description
sid	Session id; corresponds to V$SESSION.SID
serial#	Session serial number; corresponds to V$SESSION.SERIAL#
sql_trace	TRUE turns tracing on, FALSE turns tracing off

Usage Notes

No exception is raised when one of the parameters SID or SERIAL# are incorrect. Use the packaged procedure DBMS_SYSTEM.SET_SQL_TRACE_IN_SESSION only if you are sure that you don't need to trace wait events and bind variables.

Examples

```
SQL> SELECT sid, serial# FROM v$session WHERE username='NDEBES';
       SID    SERIAL#
---------- ----------
        35        283
SQL> EXEC dbms_system.set_sql_trace_in_session(35, 283, true);
```

WAIT_FOR_EVENT Procedure

This procedure causes the calling session to artificially wait for a certain amount of seconds for the event specified. The event must be a wait event from V$EVENT_NAME.NAME. If SQL trace at level 8 or 12 is enabled, artificially generated wait events are emitted to a trace file. WAIT_FOR_EVENT is useful for developers of extended SQL trace profilers who need to make sure that their profiler software understands all the wait events that might be emitted to a trace file. It would be hard to write software that is able to cause all of the 872 wait events in Oracle10g for the purpose of testing a profiler. Even more so, since Oracle10g wait events are logged with various meaningful parameter names instead of p1, p2, p3 in Oracle9*i* and earlier releases.

Syntax

```
DBMS_SYSTEM.WAIT_FOR_EVENT(
    event IN VARCHAR2,
    extended_id IN BINARY_INTEGER,
    timeout IN BINARY_INTEGER);
```

Parameters

Parameter	Description
event	Name of a wait event; corresponds to V$EVENT_NAME.NAME
extended_id	Additional information on the event
timeout	Time to wait for an event (in seconds)

Usage Notes

The session waits for the time–out period specified and populates the column V$SESSION_WAIT.EVENT with the value of the parameter EVENT and V$SESSION_WAIT.P1 with the value of the parameter EXTENDED_ID. For wait events that have more than just one parameter, the remaining parameters are set to default values, which limits the usefulness of the procedure for testing extended SQL trace profilers. In Oracle9*i*, EXTENDED_ID is emitted to a trace file in the format p1=*extended_id*, whereas in Oracle10g the format is *field_name=extended_id*, where *field_name* may be retrieved from V$EVENT_NAME.PARAMETER1 as shown in the next section. If *event* is not a valid event from V$EVENT_NAME, the exception "ORA-29352: event '*event_name*' is not an internal event" is raised.

Examples

```
SQL> CONNECT / AS SYSDBA
Connected.
SQL> ALTER SESSION SET EVENTS '10046 TRACE NAME CONTEXT FOREVER, LEVEL 8';
Session altered.
SQL> EXECUTE dbms_system.wait_for_event('db file scattered read', 1, 1);
PL/SQL procedure successfully completed.
SQL> EXECUTE dbms_system.wait_for_event('index block split', 204857603, 1);
PL/SQL procedure successfully completed.
SQL> ORADEBUG SETMYPID
Statement processed.
SQL> ORADEBUG TRACEFILE_NAME
/opt/oracle/admin/ten/udump/ten_ora_2928.trc
SQL> !egrep 'scattered|split' /opt/oracle/admin/ten/udump/ten_ora_2928.trc
BEGIN dbms_system.wait_for_event('db file scattered read', 1, 1); END;
WAIT #1: nam='db file scattered read' ela= 993052 file#=1 block#=0 blocks=0 obj#=-1
tim=456558169208
BEGIN dbms_system.wait_for_event('index block split', 204857603, 1); END;
WAIT #1: nam='index block split' ela= 994057 rootdba=204857603 level=0 childdba=0
obj#=-1 tim=456559821542
SQL> SELECT parameter1 FROM v$event_name WHERE name='db file scattered read';
PARAMETER1
----------
file#
```

Chapter 21

DBMS_UTILITY

Status: Most of the functions and procedures in the package DBMS_UTILITY are sufficiently documented. The procedure NAME_RESOLVE accepts the name of a database object and decomposes the name into its constituent parts, such as a schema, an object name, and potentially a database link. According to *Oracle Database PL/SQL Packages and Types Reference 10g Release 2*, the procedure supports the four object types synonym, procedure, function, and package. Actual testing reveals that it supports a total of eight object types, thus extending its usefulness.

Benefit: DBMS_UTILITY.NAME_RESOLVE is useful for applications that deal with database object names. It removes the burden of translating a name into a fully qualified database object designation from applications. SQL identifiers are not case sensitive, unless surrounded by double quotes. Considering that identifiers may be case sensitive or contain spaces and punctuation characters, it is clear that it makes sense to reuse existing functionality.

NAME_RESOLVE Procedure

This chapter discusses undocumented aspects of the packaged procedure DBMS_UTILITY.NAME_RESOLVE. This procedure resolves a name that may include quotes, spaces, and mixed case to an unambiguous designation of a database object. The return parameter values have the same spelling as the schema and object names in the data dictionary. The object identifier, which corresponds to DBA_OBJECTS.OBJECT_ID, is returned along with the type of object resolved.

Syntax

```
DBMS_UTILITY.NAME_RESOLVE (
    name IN VARCHAR2,
    context IN NUMBER,
    schema OUT VARCHAR2,
    part1 OUT VARCHAR2,
    part2 OUT VARCHAR2,
```

```
dblink OUT VARCHAR2,
part1_type OUT NUMBER,
object_number OUT NUMBER);
```

Parameters

Parameter	Description
name	Name of a database object in the format [*schema.*]*identifier1*[*.identifier2*][*@database_link*], where all placeholders are valid SQL identifiers. All components except *identifier1* are optional.
context	The context in which to resolve a name. An integer between 1 and 7 (not 0 and 8 as stated in the documentation)[a]. Names of different object types must be resolved in the correct context. See Table 33 for the mapping from object type to context.
schema	Schema containing the resolved object.
part1	Database object name.
part2	Lower level database object name, such as a column of a table or procedure in a package. No check for correctness is performed at this level.
dblink	Database link name, if present in parameter name.
part1_type	Numeric code representing the object type of part1. See Table 34 for mapping type codes to object types.
object_number	The unique numeric object identification from DBA_OBJECTS.OBJECT_ID. If name contains a database link, then object_number is zero.

a. Values outside of the range 1–7 cause "ORA-20005: ORU-10034: context argument must be 1 or 2 or 3 or 4 or 5 or 6 or 7"

If the type of an object is unknown, all contexts must be tried in an attempt to resolve a name. Table 33 lists the supported object types and the corresponding context numbers. Clusters, database links (by themselves), directories, indexes, LOB column names, queues, rule names, and rule sets cannot be resolved. Use the packaged procedure DBMS_UTILITY.NAME_TOKENIZE to decompose names of such objects for easier lookup in the data dictionary.

Table 33: Context Parameter vs. Object Type

Object Type	Context Parameter
Package	1
Sequence	2
Synonym	2
View	2
Table	2
Trigger	3
Type	7

The range of values pertaining to the OUT parameter PART1_TYPE is in Table 34.

Table 34: Mapping from PART1_TYPE to Object Type

PART1_TYPE	Object Type
0	Object name followed by database link
2	Table
4	View
6	Sequence
7	Procedure
8	Function
9	Package
12	Trigger
13	Type

Usage Notes

The name to resolve may include three identifiers as in *schema.table_name.column_name* or *schema.package_name. subroutine_name*. These types of expressions are resolved to *schema.table_name* and *schema.package_name* respectively. Neither *column_name* nor *subroutine_name* are checked for correctness. When a database link is detected, PART1_TYPE=0 is returned and no checking of object names occurs. To resolve such names, connect to the database where the remote object resides and repeat name resolution there or perform a remote procedure call by using the database link.

Exceptions

If a name cannot be resolved in the specified context, "ORA-06564: object *object_name* does not exist" is raised, where *object_name* is the value of parameter NAME passed to the procedure NAME_RESOLVE. If an existing object is resolved in the wrong context, the exception "ORA-04047: object specified is incompatible with the flag specified" is thrown.

Examples

In Oracle10g, the public synonym PRODUCT_USER_PROFILE points to a table with SQL*Plus configuration data in schema SYSTEM. The example below resolves this public synonym and displays the table it refers to (see file name_resolve_table.sql in the source code depot):

```
SQL> VARIABLE name VARCHAR2(100)
SQL> VARIABLE context NUMBER
SQL> VARIABLE schema VARCHAR2(30)
SQL> VARIABLE part1 VARCHAR2(30)
SQL> VARIABLE part2 VARCHAR2(30)
SQL> VARIABLE dblink VARCHAR2(30)
SQL> VARIABLE part1_type NUMBER
SQL> VARIABLE object_number NUMBER
SQL> BEGIN
   :context:=2; -- 1: package, 2: table
   :name:=' "SYSTEM" . Product_User_Profile '; -- name to resolve
   DBMS_UTILITY.NAME_RESOLVE (
      name => :name,
      context => :context,
      schema => :schema,
      part1 => :part1,
      part2 => :part2,
      dblink => :dblink,
```

```
        part1_type => :part1_type,
        object_number => :object_number
    );
end;
/
PL/SQL procedure successfully completed.
```

After a successful call to DBMS_UTILITY.NAME_RESOLVE, the bind variables contain the constituent parts of the referenced database object:

```
SQL> SELECT -- resolved_name
'"' || :schema|| '"' || nvl2(:part1,'."'||:part1 || '"', null)||
nvl2(:part2,'."'||:part2 || '"',NULL) ||
nvl2(:dblink,'@"'||:dblink || '"' ,NULL) || ' is ' ||
-- translate part1_type to object type
decode(:part1_type, 0, 'an object at a remote database',
2, 'a table',
4, 'a view',
6, 'a sequence',
7, 'a procedure',
8, 'a function',
9, 'a package',
12, 'a trigger',
13, 'a type') ||
' (PART1_TYPE=' || :part1_type || ', OBJECT_NUMBER=' ||
:object_number || ')' AS detailed_info
FROM dual;
DETAILED_INFO
--------------------------------------------------------------------------------
"SYSTEM"."SQLPLUS_PRODUCT_PROFILE" is a table (PART1_TYPE=2, OBJECT_NUMBER=10209)
```

The OUT parameter OBJECT_NUMBER may be used to retrieve additional information on a database object from the dictionary view DBA_OBJECTS:

```
SQL> SELECT owner, object_name, object_type, status, created
FROM all_objects
WHERE object_id=:object_number;
OWNER   OBJECT_NAME              OBJECT_TYPE STATUS  CREATED
------  -----------------------  ----------- ------- ---------
SYSTEM SQLPLUS_PRODUCT_PROFILE TABLE          VALID   30.Aug.05
```

The result of the query on ALL_OBJECTS at the very end of the script confirms that the name was correctly resolved. Thus, the public synonym PRODUCT_USER_PROFILE resolves to the table SQLPLUS_PRODUCT_PROFILE. With a name containing a database link ("SYSTEM".Product_User_Profile@db_link) as a final example, the result becomes:

```
DETAILED_INFO
--------------------------------------------------------------------------
"SYSTEM"."PRODUCT_USER_PROFILE"@"DB_LINK" is an object at a remote database
(PART1_TYPE=0, OBJECT_NUMBER=0)
no rows selected
```

This time, the query on ALL_OBJECTS does not return a result, since the value of the OUT parameter OBJECT_NUMBER is zero.

Name Resolution and Extraction of Object Statistics

An ORACLE performance optimization assignment may involve the extraction of object statistics used by the cost based optimizer. I frequently use a script called statistics.sql, which reports details of the table structure, table partitions and subpartitions (if present), table and index cardinality, distinct values in columns, distinct index keys, timestamps of the last statistics gathering, indexes, tablespaces, block size, and LOB columns. The report reveals problems such as stale or missing statistics, indexes on non-selective columns, or LOBs with the NOCACHE option,

```
$ sqlplus -s hr/hr @statistics.sql employees
```

Table Owner and Name	Number of Rows	Blocks	Empty Blocks	Average Space	Chain Count	Average Row Len	Global Stats	User Stats	Sample Size	Last Analyze
HR . EMPLOYEES	107	5	0	0	0	68	YES	NO	2,000	01.Oct 07 18:09

Tablespace	Block-size	Size (MB)	Moni-toring	Buffer Pool	Degree	Cluster	IOT Type	IOT Name
EXAMPLE	8 KB	0	YES	DEFAULT	1			

Column Name	Column Details	Distinct Values	Density	Number Buckets	Number Nulls	Global Stats	User Stats	Sample Size	Last Analyze
EMPLOYEE_ID	NUMBER(6) NOT NULL	107	.0093	1	0	YES	NO	2,500	01.Oct 07 18:09
FIRST_NAME	VARCHAR2(20)	91	.0110	1	0	YES	NO	2,500	01.Oct 07 18:09
LAST_NAME	VARCHAR2(25) NOT NULL	102	.0098	1	0	YES	NO	2,500	01.Oct 07 18:09
EMAIL	VARCHAR2(25) NOT NULL	107	.0093	1	0	YES	NO	2,500	01.Oct 07 18:09
PHONE_NUMBER	VARCHAR2(20)	107	.0093	1	0	YES	NO	2,500	01.Oct 07 18:09
HIRE_DATE	DATE NOT NULL	98	.0102	1	0	YES	NO	2,500	01.Oct 07 18:09
JOB_ID	VARCHAR2(10) NOT NULL	19	.0047	19	0	YES	NO	2,500	01.Oct 07 18:09
SALARY	NUMBER(8,2)	57	.0175	1	0	YES	NO		01.Oct 07 18:09
COMMISSION_PCT	NUMBER(2,2)	7	.1429	1	72	YES	NO		01.Oct 07 18:09
MANAGER_ID	NUMBER(6)	18	.0047	18	1	YES	NO		01.Oct 07 18:09
DEPARTMENT_ID	NUMBER(4)	11	.0047	11	1	YES	NO		01.Oct 07 18:09

Index Owner and Name	Index Type	Unique	B Tree Level	Leaf Blks	Created	Last DDL	Last Analyze
HR . EMP_EMAIL_UK	NORMAL	YES	0	1	01.Oct 07 18:09	05.Oct 07 09:08	01.Oct 07 18:09
HR . EMP_EMP_ID_PK	NORMAL	YES	0	1	01.Oct 07 18:09	05.Oct 07 00:42	01.Oct 07 18:09
HR . EMP_DEPARTMENT_IX	NORMAL	NO	0	1	01.Oct 07 18:09	05.Oct 07 00:42	01.Oct 07 18:09
HR . EMP_JOB_IX	NORMAL	NO	0	1	01.Oct 07 18:09	05.Oct 07 00:42	01.Oct 07 18:09
HR . EMP_MANAGER_IX	NORMAL	NO	0	1	01.Oct 07 18:09	05.Oct 07 00:42	01.Oct 07 18:09
HR . EMP_NAME_IX	NORMAL	NO	0	1	01.Oct 07 18:09	05.Oct 07 00:42	01.Oct 07 18:09

Index Owner and Name	Index Type	Distinct Keys	Number of Rows	Average Leaf Blocks Per Key	Average Data Blocks Per Key	Cluster Factor	Global Stats	User Stats
HR . EMP_EMAIL_UK	NORMAL	107	107	1	1	19	YES	NO
HR . EMP_EMP_ID_PK	NORMAL	107	107	1	1	2	YES	NO
HR . EMP_DEPARTMENT_IX	NORMAL	11	106	1	1	7	YES	NO
HR . EMP_JOB_IX	NORMAL	19	107	1	1	8	YES	NO
HR . EMP_MANAGER_IX	NORMAL	18	106	1	1	7	YES	NO
HR . EMP_NAME_IX	NORMAL	107	107	1	2	15	YES	NO

Index Owner and Name	Column Name	Col Pos	Column Details
HR . EMP_DEPARTMENT_IX	DEPARTMENT_ID	1	NUMBER(4)
HR . EMP_EMAIL_UK	EMAIL	1	VARCHAR2(25) NOT NULL
HR . EMP_EMP_ID_PK	EMPLOYEE_ID	1	NUMBER(6) NOT NULL
HR . EMP_JOB_IX	JOB_ID	1	VARCHAR2(10) NOT NULL
HR . EMP_MANAGER_IX	MANAGER_ID	1	NUMBER(6)
HR . EMP_NAME_IX	LAST_NAME	1	VARCHAR2(25) NOT NULL
HR . EMP_NAME_IX	FIRST_NAME	2	VARCHAR2(20)

which cause direct path read and write waits. The report also makes it easy to identify columns with high selectivity, which are good candidates for indexing, given that these columns appear as predicates in where–clauses. I highly recommend using the script when investigating performance problems.

The use of DBMS_UTILITY.NAME_RESOLVE renders calling the script much more convenient, since it is sufficient to provide the name of a table (or synonym) to report on in lower case instead of the owner (or schema) and table with exactly the same spelling as in the data dictionary (usually all upper case letters). The script takes the name of a database object as input, resolves the name, and then pulls the relevant information from ALL_* dictionary views (this is serious business, not an All-star Game!), such as ALL_TABLES, ALL_INDEXES, ALL_LOBS, etc. The script works without DBA privileges, since ALL_* views and not DBA_* views are used. The syntax for running the script is:

```
sqlplus -s user/password @statistics[.sql] { [schema.]table_name | synonym }
```

Data dictionary object names that contain lower case letters must be quoted. Sample output from the script statistics.sql is on page 183.

Source Code Depot

Table 35: DBMS_UTILITY Source Code Depot

File Name	Functionality
name_resolve.sql	This script contains an anonymous block, which resolves the name of any object type supported by the procedure DBMS_UTILITY.NAME_RESOLVE.
name_resolve_procedure.sql	This script creates a stored procedure called NAME_RESOLVE. The procedure resolves all the object types supported by DBMS_UTILITY.NAME_RESOLVE. The procedure NAME_RESOLVE accepts the same parameters as the packaged procedure DBMS_UTILITY.NAME_RESOLVE, tries all contexts, and if successful, returns the same information as DBMS_UTILITY.NAME_RESOLVE. Additionally, it returns the qualified resolved name. Individual components of the resolved name are returned in double quotes, to preserve case sensitivity.
name_resolve_table.sql	Example of name resolution of a table with DBMS_UTILITY
statistics.sql	This script reports optimizer statistics for table and index columns. Used for checking column selectivity and indexing when tuning SQL statements.

Part VII

Application Development

Chapter 22

Perl DBI and DBD::Oracle

Status: The documentation does not mention the fact that each Oracle10*g* and Oracle11*g* ORACLE_HOME contains a Perl installation, which includes the Perl modules DBI and DBD::Oracle for access to an ORACLE DBMS instance.

Benefit: There is no need to install Perl, DBI, and DBD::Oracle[1], which requires a C compiler and a scarce resource called time. Perl and the DBI may be used to write your own monitoring and benchmarking tools, to extract data (including LOBs) to flat file for long term archival, and to insert or update LOBs from operating system files. Furthermore, Perl DBI is an excellent prototyping tool. The Perl subdirectory plus several directories within ORACLE_HOME can be copied to create a small footprint Perl DBI Oracle client for machines that do not require a full RDBMS server installation.

Circumnavigating Perl DBI Pitfalls

Except pointing out that Perl DBI is sitting in each Oracle10*g* ORACLE_HOME ready for use and how to use it, what benefit could I possibly provide in this chapter? In my experience, users of the Perl DBI struggle with the many ways of connecting to an ORACLE instance and how to implement them in Perl DBI scripts, since the Perl DBI and DBD::Oracle documentation at the Comprehensive Perl Archive Network (CPAN; http://www.cpan.org) does not provide all the details.

The goal of this chapter is to provide the reader with a comprehensive source of Perl programming in an ORACLE environment. The following ORACLE–specific material is addressed:

- named bind variables
- connecting via the TCP/IP, bequeath, and IPC protocols

---

1. The Tk package, which is needed to build graphical user interfaces with Perl, is not included.

- connecting with SYSDBA and SYSOPER privileges
- using connect strings with and without Net service names

Basically any book should be able to speak for itself. However, including in–depth coverage of Perl, the DBI, and DBD::Oracle would be off–topic for this book. Not to mention that it would not fit the page count. By addressing the ORACLE–specific issues of connecting in great detail and providing an example Perl script that does SELECT, INSERT, calls PL/SQL, and includes transaction as well as exception handling, I hope to instill enough confidence in the novice Perl DBI user for him or her to begin coding Perl DBI scripts.

Personally, I strongly endorse the use of Perl with DBI over scripting with SQL*Plus and a shell such as Bourne or Korn shell. For example, error handling in Perl is much better, several database sessions may be opened simultaneously, file operations are much more sophisticated, etc. Once you have some practice programming the Perl DBI, development time will be reduced significantly. I encourage any DBA, even DBAs without prior knowledge of Perl, to accept the challenge of learning the language. Once proficient, you will discover that there is plenty of low–hanging fruit for its application.

A Brief History of Perl and the DBI

The inventor of Perl is Larry Wall. Perl was first released in 1987. Today it is distributed under the GNU General Public License and the Perl Artistic License. Can you keep a secret? Larry Wall said that Perl actually stands for *Pathologically Eclectic Rubbish Lister*, but don't tell anyone else he said that!

The truth is that the acronym Perl means Practical Extraction and Reporting Language. *Programming Perl*, coauthored by Larry Wall[1] (a.k.a. "The Camel Book" and "The Perl Bible") states that "Perl is designed to make the easy jobs easy, without making the hard jobs impossible" [WaCh 2000]. Although at first glance it may appear that Perl is an interpreted language, Perl code is actually compiled and run using virtual machine technology comparable to Java.

The Perl DBI (database independent interface) is written and maintained by Tim Bunce, author of the book *Programming the Perl DBI* [Bunc 2000]. His motto is "making simple things easy and difficult things possible". Except designing and implementing the DBI, Tim Bunce has been a Perl5 porter since 1994, contributing to the development of the Perl language and many of its core modules. He provides additional information on the Perl DBI and DBD::Oracle at http://search.cpan.org/~timb.

Setting Up the Environment for Perl and the DBI

The Perl installation distributed as part of each Oracle10*g* and Oracle11*g* ORACLE_HOME resides in the directory $ORACLE_HOME/perl. It is used by Oracle Corporation's Database Control and Grid Control administration tools. Perl DBI, being a database client, needs the ORACLE DBMS client shared library, which contains the Oracle Call Interface (OCI) routines, for communication with an ORACLE instance. The only obstacles on the way to leveraging the Perl DBI in $ORACLE_HOME are locating a suitable client shared library and setting platform specific environment variables.

UNIX Environment

Many UNIX systems already have a Perl installation. Usually, the DBI module for database access is missing in that installation and it would require a C compiler to install it. Much easier to set some environment variables for using Perl in an ORACLE_HOME by following the steps below.

PATH

First of all, the executable search path variable PATH needs to be modified, such that $ORACLE_HOME/perl/bin is searched before any directory that contains the perl interpreter shipped with the operating system:

```
$ export PATH=$ORACLE_HOME/perl/bin:$PATH
$ which perl
/opt/oracle/product/db10.2/perl/bin/perl
```

---

1. For more information on Larry Wall, see http://en.wikipedia.org/wiki/Larry_Wall.

PERL5LIB

The second step is setting the Perl module search path. Perl programs normally have extension .pl, while Perl modules have extension .pm. The DBI is implemented by a file named DBI.pm. It is this file that the Perl interpreter needs to locate. Fortunately, this variable does not depend on the word size of the platform or the version of Perl. The following setting may be used generically:

```
export PERL5LIB=$ORACLE_HOME/perl/lib:$ORACLE_HOME/perl/lib/site_perl
```

On a 32–bit Linux system, the required file is $ORACLE_HOME/perl/lib/site_perl/5.8.3/i686-linux-thread-multi/DBI.pm. Perl locates the file by also searching subdirectories of the directories specified with PERL5LIB. It starts looking in the most specific directory for the build and version of Perl, then tries directories further up in the directory tree and finally stops by searching the directory specified.

In the above example, the version of perl (perl -version) is 5.8.3 and the build is i686-linux-thread-multi (Intel x86 32–bit machine architecture with Perl multi–threading linked in). In case PERL5LIB is set incorrectly or the DBI is not present in the Perl installation (such as the one that ships with the operating system), you will get an error similar to the one below:

```
$ echo $PERL5LIB
/opt/oracle/product/db10.2/perl/lib
$ echo "use DBI;" | perl
Can't locate DBI in @INC (@INC contains: /opt/oracle/product/db10.2/perl/lib/5.8.3/
i686-linux-thread-multi /opt/oracle/product/db10.2/perl/lib/5.8.3 /opt/oracle/product/
db10.2/perl/lib) at dbi.pl line 3.
BEGIN failed--compilation aborted at dbi.pl line 3.
```

In the above example, $ORACLE_HOME/perl/lib/site_perl is missing from PERL5LIB. The fix is to add this directory to PERL5LIB. Use a colon as the separator character when setting up multiple directories for searching. If you need to use additional Perl modules not located in $ORACLE_HOME/perl/lib or even wrote your own modules (it's not that hard, trust me), you must also add their locations to PERL5LIB. The source code depot contains a Perl module, which is built on top of the DBI.

Shared Library Search Path

All current implementations of UNIX use shared libraries or runtime linking instead of static linking. With static linking, libraries such as the Standard C library are statically linked into programs at runtime. Dynamic linking adds the library to the text segment (where the machine code instructions are) of the program at runtime. This approach results in smaller executables and has the advantage that newer releases of shared libraries are picked up automatically by the executables the next time they are run. On many UNIX platforms, the command ldd may be used to find out which shared libraries an executable requires:

```
$ ldd `which perl`
        libnsl.so.1 => /lib/libnsl.so.1 (0x0551c000)
        libdl.so.2 => /lib/libdl.so.2 (0x00862000)
        libm.so.6 => /lib/tls/libm.so.6 (0x00868000)
        libcrypt.so.1 => /lib/libcrypt.so.1 (0x053f9000)
        libutil.so.1 => /lib/libutil.so.1 (0x00cd8000)
        libpthread.so.0 => /lib/tls/libpthread.so.0 (0x0097e000)
        libc.so.6 => /lib/tls/libc.so.6 (0x00734000)
        /lib/ld-linux.so.2 (0x0071a000)
```

In the output above, libc.so.6 is the Standard C library, libm.so is the math library and libdl.so is part of the dynamic linker itself.

The initial step on the way to a correct shared library search path is to determine whether $ORACLE_HOME/perl/bin/perl is a 32–bit or a 64–bit executable. This can be done using the UNIX command file. On an AIX system, this might yield:

```
$ file $ORACLE_HOME/perl/bin/perl
/opt/oracle/product/10.2.0.2.1/perl/bin/perl: executable (RISC System/6000) or object
module not stripped
```

Since there is no mention of 64–bit in the above output, perl is a 32–bit executable. On a 32–bit Linux system, it might look as below:

```
$ file `which perl`
/opt/oracle10/app/oracle/product/10.2.0.2/db_rac/perl/bin/perl: ELF 32-bit LSB
executable, Intel 80386, version 1 (SYSV), for GNU/Linux 2.2.5, dynamically linked
(uses shared libs), not stripped
```

On this Solaris 9 system, perl is a 64–bit executable:

```
$ file /opt/oracle/product/10.2.0.2.0/perl/bin/perl
/opt/oracle/product/10.2.0.2.0/perl/bin/perl:    ELF 64-bit MSB executable SPARCV9
Version 1, dynamically linked, not stripped
```

The next step consists of locating the ORACLE client shared library libclntsh.so with the same word length (32–bit or 64–bit) as perl. ORACLE installations can be 32–bit or 64–bit. ORACLE DBMS software is only available in a 64–bit version for platforms such as AIX and HP–UX, whereas 32–bit versions exist for Sparc Solaris, Solaris x86, and Linux. Matters are simple on an operating system that only supports 32–bit executables, such as Linux x86. On these platforms, $ORACLE_HOME/lib contains a suitable 32–bit client shared library.

In a 64–bit ORACLE_HOME, 64–bit shared libraries are located in $ORACLE_HOME/lib and 32–bit libraries in $ORACLE_HOME/lib32. Here's an example from an AIX system:

```
$ file $ORACLE_HOME/lib/libclntsh.so $ORACLE_HOME/lib32/libclntsh.so
/opt/oracle/product/10.2.0.2.1/lib/libclntsh.so: 64-bit XCOFF executable or object
module not stripped
/opt/oracle/product/10.2.0.2.1/lib32/libclntsh.so: executable (RISC System/6000) or
object module not stripped
```

On a Solaris system, it might look as follows:

```
$ file $ORACLE_HOME/lib/libclntsh.so $ORACLE_HOME/lib32/libclntsh.so
/opt/oracle/product/10.2.0.2.1/lib/libclntsh.so:        ELF 64-bit MSB dynamic lib
SPARCV9 Version 1, dynamically linked, not stripped
/opt/oracle/product/10.2.0.2.1/lib32/libclntsh.so:      ELF 32-bit MSB dynamic lib
SPARC Version 1, dynamically linked, not stripped
```

Finally, here's some output from a 64–bit Linux system:

```
file $ORACLE_HOME/lib/libclntsh.so* $ORACLE_HOME/lib32/libclntsh.so*
/opt/oracle10/app/oracle/product/10.2.0.2/db_rac/lib/libclntsh.so:       symbolic link
to `libclntsh.so.10.1'
/opt/oracle10/app/oracle/product/10.2.0.2/db_rac/lib/libclntsh.so.10.1:   ELF 64-bit
LSB shared object, AMD x86-64, version 1 (SYSV), not stripped
/opt/oracle10/app/oracle/product/10.2.0.2/db_rac/lib32/libclntsh.so:     symbolic link
to `libclntsh.so.10.1'
/opt/oracle10/app/oracle/product/10.2.0.2/db_rac/lib32/libclntsh.so.10.1: ELF 32-bit
LSB shared object, Intel 80386, version 1 (SYSV), not stripped
```

Now we are ready to set the platform–specific environment variable, which controls the shared library search path. Table 36 lists the most common platforms and the name of the variable on each platform.

Table 36: Shared Library Search Path Environment Variables per Platform

Operating System	*Shared Library Search Path Environment Variable*
AIX	LIBPATH
HP–UX 32–bit	SHLIB_PATH
HP–UX 64–bit	LD_LIBRARY_PATH and SHLIB_PATH
Linux	LD_LIBRARY_PATH
Mac OS X[a]	DYLD_LIBRARY_PATH
Solaris	LD_LIBRARY_PATH
Tru64 UNIX	LD_LIBRARY_PATH

a. Oracle10*g* Release 1 is available for Mac OS X. As of this writing, Oracle10*g*
   Release 2 is not planned for Mac OS X.

Perl will not be able to load the ORACLE driver module DBD::Oracle, unless the correct variable is used and the correct search path is set. The most concise test consists of running:

```
$ echo "use DBI;use DBD::Oracle" | perl
Can't load '/opt/oracle/product/db10.2/perl/lib/site_perl/5.8.3/i686-linux-thread-
multi/auto/DBD/Oracle/Oracle.so' for module DBD::Oracle: libclntsh.so.10.1: cannot open
shared object file: No such file or directory at /opt/oracle/product/db10.2/perl/lib/
5.8.3/i686-linux-thread-multi/DynaLoader.pm line 229.
 at - line 1
Compilation failed in require at - line 1.
 BEGIN failed--compilation aborted at - line 1.
```

If you get an error such as the one above, you need to fix the shared library search path. Error messages differ slightly per platform, but always mention that libclntsh.so could not be found.

The following Perl DBI program called perl-dbi-test.pl is ideal for testing connectivity to an ORACLE instance. It prompts for user name, password, and Net service name and then attempts to connect to the DBMS. If it succeeds, it selects the database login user name and prints it to the screen.

```
#!/usr/bin/env perl
# RCS: $Header: /home/ndebes/it/perl/RCS/perl-dbi-test.pl,v 1.1 2007/01/26 16:07:13
ndebes Exp ndebes $
# Perl DBI/DBD::Oracle Example

use strict;
use DBI;

print "Username: \n";
my $user = <STDIN>;
chomp $user;
print "Password: \n";
my $passwd = <STDIN>;
chomp $passwd;
print "Net Service Name (optional, if ORACLE instance runs locally and ORACLE_SID is
set): \n";
my $net_service_name = <STDIN>; # Oracle Net service name from tnsnames.ora or other
name resulution method
chomp $net_service_name;

if ($net_service_name) {
        print "Trying to connect to $user/$passwd\@$net_service_name\n";
}
else {
        print "Trying to connect to $user/$passwd\n";
}
# Connect to the database and return a database handle
my $dbh = DBI->connect("dbi:Oracle:${net_service_name}", $user, $passwd)
        or die "Connect failed: $DBI::errstr";

my $sth = $dbh->prepare("SELECT user FROM dual"); # PARSE
$sth->execute(); # EXECUTE
my @row = $sth->fetchrow_array(); # FETCH
printf ("Connected as user %s\n", $row[0]);
$sth->finish;
$dbh->disconnect; # disconnect from ORACLE instance
```

Example settings for 32–bit perl in a 64–bit ORACLE_HOME are:

```
export PATH=$ORACLE_HOME/perl/bin:$ORACLE_HOME/bin:/usr/bin:/usr/ccs/bin
export PERL5LIB=$ORACLE_HOME/perl/lib:$ORACLE_HOME/perl/lib/site_perl
export LD_LIBRARY_PATH=$ORACLE_HOME/lib32
```

Let's confirm that these settings are correct:

```
$ perl perl-dbi-test.pl
Username:
ndebes
Password:
secret
Net Service Name (optional, if ORACLE instance runs locally and ORACLE_SID is set):
ten_tcp.world
Trying to connect to ndebes/secret@ten_tcp.world
Connected as user NDEBES
```

The script ran successfully. The connection to the DBMS as well as the execution of SELECT user FROM dual completed without error.

Windows Environment

On Windows, the Oracle10g Release 2 Universal Installer (OUI) sets the system environment variables PATH and PERL5LIB. You may look these up by navigating to CONTROL PANEL > SYSTEM > ADVANCED > ENVIRONMENT VARIABLES and browsing the list box SYSTEM VARIABLES. However, it merely adds %ORACLE_HOME%\bin to PATH and in addition to correct directories in PERL5LIB also sets some non–existent directories (e.g. %ORACLE_HOME%\perl\5.8.3\lib\MSWin32-x86) and several unnecessary ones.

Figure 9: PERL5LIB System Environment Variable

On Windows, environment variables may be set system–wide, user–specifically, and in an instance of the command interpreter cmd.exe[1]. User–specific settings override system–wide settings. If an environment variable is changed in a command interpreter, the modified value is used instead of the user or system variable set using the CONTROL PANEL. On startup, command interpreters inherit user–specific and system–wide environment variables. If you do not have permission to change system–wide settings, you can still override them with user–specific settings.

Of course it's much more convenient to set variables with CONTROL PANEL > SYSTEM once and for all than to source a file with environment variables each time a command interpreter is started. A smart approach is to set environment

---

1. Click START > RUN... or hold down the Windows key (the one showing a flag) and type R, enter cmd and click OK
   to start a command interpreter

variables in a command interpreter for testing and to store them in the registry once the results are correct. This is the approach taken in the sections that follow.

First of all, we will set ORACLE_HOME, such that it may be reused when setting the remaining environment variables.

```
C:> set ORACLE_HOME=C:\ORACLE\product\db10.2
```

Next we need to add the directory where perl.exe resides to PATH. On Windows, it resides in the build–specific directory MSWin32-x86-multi-thread. The separator for specifying multiple directories is a semicolon (;):

```
C:> set PATH=%ORACLE_HOME%\perl\5.8.3\bin\MSWin32-x86-multi-thread;%ORACLE_HOME%\bin;
C:\WINDOWS\System32
```

Additional Windows–specific directories were omitted from the setting above. Now it should be possible to run perl.exe:

```
C:> perl -version
This is perl, v5.8.3 built for MSWin32-x86-multi-thread

Copyright 1987-2003, Larry Wall

Perl may be copied only under the terms of either the Artistic License or the
GNU General Public License, which may be found in the Perl 5 source kit.

Complete documentation for Perl, including FAQ lists, should be found on
this system using `man perl' or `perldoc perl'.  If you have access to the
Internet, point your browser at http://www.perl.com/, the Perl Home Page.
```

If you intend to use other components of the Perl installation apart from the Perl interpreter itself, you need to add %ORACLE_HOME%\perl\5.8.3\bin to PATH. You may then use perldoc to read the documentation library within the Perl installation or pod2html to generate HTML documentation from POD (Plain Old Documentation) statements embedded in Perl source (see perldoc perlpod):

```
C:> set PATH=%ORACLE_HOME%\perl\5.8.3\bin\MSWin32-x86-multi-thread;%ORACLE_HOME%\
perl\5.8.3\bin;%ORACLE_HOME%\bin;C:\WINDOWS\System32
C:> perldoc perltoc
NAME
    perltoc - perl documentation table of contents

DESCRIPTION
    This page provides a brief table of contents for the rest of the Perl
    documentation set. It is meant to be scanned quickly or grepped through
    to locate the proper section you're looking for.

BASIC DOCUMENTATION
  perl - Practical Extraction and Report Language
    ...
```

As it turns out, PERL5LIB does not have to be set for Perl in a Windows ORACLE_HOME to work, since perl.exe automatically searches the directory tree from which it is invoked. On Windows, there is no separate environment variable for searching dynamic link libraries (DLL), the Windows variant of shared libraries. PATH serves as the command search path as well as the DLL search path. The ORACLE DLL required to connect to a DBMS instance is OCI.DLL. Since perl58.dll, which is required to run perl.exe, is collocated with perl.exe in %ORACLE_HOME% \perl\5.8.3\bin\MSWin32-x86-multi-thread and OCI.DLL is in %ORACLE_HOME%\bin, you are all set once PATH contains these two directories.

The OUI also adds the directory %ORACLE_HOME%\sysman\admin\scripts to the setting of PERL5LIB in the CONTROL PANEL. This should be retained, to avoid impairing Database Control or Grid Control. Note that a Grid Control Management Agent installation also contains an installation of Perl including DBI and DBD::Oracle. After all, these components are built with Perl DBI. So you can actually get away with simplifying the environment variable PERL5LIB as below:

```
set PERL5LIB=<ORACLE_HOME>\sysman\admin\scripts
```

Remember though, to use the actual path of your ORACLE_HOME when adjusting the setting in the user or system environment variables via the CONTROL PANEL. %ORACLE_HOME% is not expanded when the variable is read from there.

Let's repeat the test we previously performed on UNIX, to verify that the settings are correct:

```
C:> set ORACLE_HOME
ORACLE_HOME=C:\oracle\product\db10.2
C:> set PATH
Path=C:\oracle\product\db10.2\perl\5.8.3\bin\MSWin32-x86-multi-
thread;C:\oracle\product\db10.2\bin;C:\WINDOWS\System32
PATHEXT=.COM;.EXE;.BAT;.CMD;.VBS;.VBE;.JS;.JSE;.WSF;.WSH
C:> set PERL5LIB
PERL5LIB=C:\oracle\product\db10.2\sysman\admin\scripts
C:> perl perl-dbi-test.pl
Username:
ndebes
Password:
secret
Net Service Name (optional, if ORACLE instance runs locally and ORACLE_SID is set):
TEN.oradbpro.com
Trying to connect to ndebes/secret@TEN.oradbpro.com
Connected as user NDEBES
```

Transparently Running Perl Programs on UNIX systems

Perl scripts can always be run by entering the name of the Perl interpreter (simply perl) and passing the name of the perl script to run as an argument as below:

```
$ cat args.pl
print "Script name: $0\n";
$ perl args.pl
Script name: args.pl
```

When a UNIX text file is made executable with chmod +x *filename* and executed with ./*filename*, a default shell for the UNIX system used is spawned and *filename* is passed as an argument to it. The default shell for Linux is bash, while sh (Bourne Shell) is the default shell for most other systems. The pseudo comment #!*executable* on the first line of a text file may be used to specify another program than the default shell for processing a text file. At first glance, it may be appropriate to put the absolute path name of the perl interpreter after the pseudo comment (#!):

```
$ cat args.pl
#!/usr/bin/perl
print "Script name: $0\n";
$ chmod +x args.pl
$ ./args.pl
Script name: ./args.pl
```

This works without problems, but is not portable. On another system, the Perl interpreter might reside in the directory /usr/local/bin/perl instead of /usr/bin/perl. The Perl script would not run on such a system:

```
$ ./args.pl
: bad interpreter: No such file or directory
```

A better approach is to employ a level of indirection by first using the UNIX command env, which is located in the directory /usr/bin on all UNIX systems, as the interpreter executable. It has the capability to set environment variables based on command line arguments and to run other programs. The environment variable PATH is considered when env attempts to locate the program to run. Thus, the code of the script need not be modified to run on other systems. Only the PATH variable must contain the directory where the Perl interpreter resides.

```
$ cat args.pl
#!/usr/bin/env perl
print "Script name: $0
$ ./args.pl
Script name: ./args.pl
```

Transparently Running Perl Programs on Windows

Matters are slightly more complicated on Windows. But then again, Windows offers the option to omit the extension .pl commonly used for Perl programs. You win some, you lose some, as they say. Here is the deal. First of all, you define a new file type to Windows and tell it which executable is responsible for the file type. Obviously the executable is perl.exe. Note that Windows requires the absolute path to the executable. The environment variable PATH is not considered for searching the executable, though environment variables may be used within the definition. The command FTYPE is used for defining the file type. Below, I use the file type PerlProgram:

```
C:> FTYPE PerlProgram="C:\oracle\product\db10.2\perl\5.8.3\bin\MSWin32-x86-multi-
thread\perl.exe" %1 %*
PerlProgram="C:\oracle\product\db10.2\perl\5.8.3\bin\MSWin32-x86-multi-
thread\perl.exe" %1 %*
```

Here, the installation of Oracle10*g* is in C:\oracle\product\db10.2. Assuming you have defined ORACLE_HOME as an environment variable, you may also call FTYPE like this:

```
C:> set ORACLE_HOME=C:\oracle\product\db10.2
C:> FTYPE PerlProgram="%ORACLE_HOME%\perl\5.8.3\bin\MSWin32-x86-multi-thread\perl.exe"
%1 %*
PerlProgram="C:\oracle\product\db10.2\perl\5.8.3\bin\MSWin32-x86-multi-
thread\perl.exe" %1 %*
```

The character strings %1 and %* represent the first and the second to last arguments to pass to perl.exe respectively. The former (%1) will contain the full path to the script file, while the latter (%*) will pass the remaining arguments to perl.exe.

Second, Windows requires an association, between the extension of a file name and a file type. Associations are maintained through the command ASSOC. Since the file name extension for Perl programs is .pl, we need to associate .pl with the file type PerlProgram that we defined above.

```
C:> ASSOC .pl=PerlProgram
.pl=PerlProgram
```

Now, instead of running Perl programs with perl *filename*.pl, it is sufficient to type just *filename*.pl. To demonstrate that both methods are indeed equivalent, we will use the following Perl program:

```
print "Script name: $0\n";
for ($i=0; $i < 10; $i++) {
        if (defined $ARGV[$i]) {
                printf "Argument %d: %s\n", $i, $ARGV[$i];
        }
}
```

Here's the output of running args.pl the old fashioned way, which requires slightly more typing:

```
C:> perl args.pl first second third fourth
Script name: args.pl
Argument 0: first
Argument 1: second
Argument 2: third
Argument 3: fourth
```

The directory where args.pl resides should be in the command search path variable PATH. Capitalizing on the association defined previously, you may now run:

```
C:> args.pl first second third fourth
Script name: C:\home\ndebes\it\perl\args.pl
Argument 0: first
Argument 1: second
Argument 2: third
Argument 3: fourth
```

The results of both methods are identical, except for the script name, which appears with its full path when the association is used. You may fully indulge your laziness after defining .pl as an additional extension of executable files. This is achieved by using the environment variable PATHEXT.

```
C:> set PATHEXT
PATHEXT=.COM;.EXE;.BAT;.CMD
C:> set PATHEXT=%PATHEXT%;.PL
C:> args first second third fourth
Script name: C:\home\ndebes\it\perl\args.pl
Argument 0: first
Argument 1: second
Argument 2: third
Argument 3: fourth
```

An association is removed by using a single blank as the file type as in:

```
C:> ASSOC .pl=␣
.pl=
```

The glyph ␣ represents a blank character.

Connecting to an ORACLE DBMS Instance

An area where novice Perl DBI programmers frequently have trouble is deciding which of the many ways to connect to an ORACLE DBMS instance is best suited for them. The Perl DBI documentation covers this subject only partially, so I have decided to include a complete overview of all variations extant.

Table 37 lists the most common Oracle Net TNS (Transparent Network Substrate) protocol adapters for connecting to an ORACLE instance. The option to use an Oracle Net service name description with IPC or TCP, without retrieving it from the configuration file tnsnames.ora, is ignored for the moment.

Table 37: Oracle Net Protocol Adapters

Method	Listener Required	tnsnames.ora Required	Notes
Bequeath adapter	no	no	The environment variable ORACLE_SID must be set. On UNIX systems ORACLE_HOME must be set too.
IPC adapter	yes	yes	For systems which do not have a network adapter or where the database client uses a different local ORACLE_HOME than the server
TCP/IP adapter	yes	yes	Most common method; TCP/IP network infrastructure must be in place

DBI connect Syntax

The DBI call for establishing a database session is connect. It has the following syntax:

```
$dbh = DBI->connect($data_source, $username, $auth, \%attr);
```

In Perl, names of scalar variables are prefixed by $, hashes by % (please run perldoc perlintro for an explanation of the terms scalar and hash).

Table 38: Connect Parameters

Parameter	Meaning
$dbh	Database handle for the database session
$data_source	Data source, i.e. specification for connecting to a local ORACLE instance or contacting a listener. The following formats are supported: "DBI:Oracle:", "DBI:Oracle:<Net service name>", "DBI:Oracle:host=<host_name>;port=<port_number>;sid=<ORACLE_SID>", "DBI:Oracle:<host_name>:<port_number>/<instance_service_name>"[a], or undef

Table 38: Connect Parameters

Parameter	Meaning
`$username`	Database username, "/" for OS authentication, or `undef`
`$auth`	Password or `undef`
`\%attr`	Optional reference to a hash with connect options

a. The Oracle Net easy connect format is available in Oracle10*g* and subsequent releases.

The Perl keyword `undef` represents an undefined value analogous to `NULL` in SQL. If one of `$data_source`, `$username`, or `$auth` are `undef`, then environment variables are used, if available. Table 39 lists the parameters and the corresponding environment variables.

Table 39: Perl DBI Environment Variables

Parameter	Environment Variable
`$data_source`	`DBI_DSN`
`$username`	`DBI_USER`
`$auth`	`DBI_PASS`

The value of `$data_source` must always start with the string "DBI:Oracle:". Note that the uppercase "O" in the string "Oracle" as well as the colon (:) after the string "Oracle" are mandatory. Using a lowercase "o" causes the following error:

```
DBD::oracle initialisation failed: Can't locate object method "driver" via package
"DBD::oracle"
```

DBI uses the string "Oracle" to build the case sensitive name of the driver module. The driver module for connecting to ORACLE instances is `DBD::Oracle` not `DBD::oracle`—thus the error. Other driver modules exist for most database products on the market. `DBD::ODBC` is a driver that works with any database product that supports ODBC (Open Database Connectivity.

Connecting through the Bequeath Adapter

When connecting to a DBMS instance using the bequeath adapter, make sure the environment variables `ORACLE_HOME` (mandatory on UNIX systems, optional on Windows) and `ORACLE_SID` are set. The following two lines of Perl code suffice to connect:

```
use DBI;
$dbh = DBI->connect("DBI:Oracle:", "ndebes", "secret") or die "Connect failed:
$DBI::errstr";
```

On Windows systems, the following exception is thrown when `ORACLE_SID` is not set correctly:

```
Connect failed: ORA-12560: TNS:protocol adapter error (DBD ERROR: OCIServerAttach).
```

The error indicates that the Windows service, which implements the ORACLE DBMS instance, is not running. The Windows service may be started with the command `net start OracleServiceORACLE_SID`. On UNIX, the error is different, since there are significant disparities between the architecture of the ORACLE DBMS on UNIX and Windows (multi–process architecture with shared memory on UNIX vs. single process, threaded architecture on Windows).

```
$ export ORACLE_SID=ISDOWN
$ perl dbi.pl
DBI connect('','ndebes',...) failed: ORA-01034: ORACLE not available
ORA-27101: shared memory realm does not exist
Linux Error: 2: No such file or directory (DBD ERROR: OCISessionBegin) at dbi.pl line 5
$ unset ORACLE_SID
$ perl dbi.pl
```

```
DBI connect('','ndebes',...) failed: ORA-12162: TNS:net service name is incorrectly
specified (DBD ERROR: OCIServerAttach) at dbi.pl line 5
```

By the way, V$SESSION.SERVICE_NAME always has the default value of SYS$USERS when connecting through the bequeath adapter.

Connecting through the IPC Adapter

Use of the IPC protocol implies that the DBMS instance, the listener, and the client are running on the same system. An entry in the configuration file listener.ora for a listener supporting only the IPC protocol might look as below:

```
LISTENER =
  (DESCRIPTION =
    (ADDRESS_LIST =
      (ADDRESS = (PROTOCOL = IPC)(KEY = TEN))
    )
  )
```

A Net service name definition in tnsnames.ora for connecting through the listener above might be:

```
TEN_IPC.WORLD =
  (DESCRIPTION =
    (ADDRESS_LIST =
      (ADDRESS = (PROTOCOL = IPC)(KEY = TEN))
    )
    (CONNECT_DATA =
      (SERVICE_NAME = TEN)
    )
  )
```

The only difference between connecting with bequeath vs. IPC is that the Net service name from tnsnames.ora (e.g. TEN_IPC.WORLD) is inserted in $data_source after DBI:Oracle: and there is no need to set the environment variable ORACLE_SID, since the value of the parameter SERVICE_NAME is taken from the Oracle Net service name definition instead:

```
use DBI;
my $dbh = DBI->connect("DBI:Oracle:TEN_IPC.WORLD", "ndebes", "secret") or die "Connect
failed: $DBI::errstr";
```

The Net service name definition might also contain (SID=TEN) instead of (SERVICE_NAME=TEN) in the section CONNECT_DATA. Use of SERVICE_NAME is recommended, since the service name is reflected in the view V$SESSION and may be used for tracing the subset of sessions using this service name with DBMS_MONITOR:

```
SQL> SELECT sid, service_name, module, action FROM v$session WHERE program='perl.exe';
 SID SERVICE_NAME         MODULE       ACTION
---- -------------------- ------------ ------
 137 TEN                  perl.exe
SQL> EXEC dbms_monitor.serv_mod_act_trace_enable('TEN','perl.exe','', true, true);
PL/SQL procedure successfully completed.
```

Unfortunately, with this approach, the view V$SESSION does not reflect the fact that tracing has been switched on:

```
SQL>  SELECT sql_trace, sql_trace_waits, sql_trace_binds FROM v$session WHERE sid=137;
SQL_TRACE SQL_TRACE_WAITS SQL_TRACE_BINDS
--------- --------------- ---------------
DISABLED  FALSE           FALSE
```

When the parameter SID is used in tnsnames.ora, V$SESSION.SERVICE_NAME has the rather meaningless default setting of SYS$USERS.

Connecting through the TCP/IP Adapter

Use of the TPC/IP protocol enables clients to connect to a DBMS instance from any system within a network. An example of an Oracle Net service name definition for a TCP/IP connection is:

```
TEN_TCP.WORLD =
  (DESCRIPTION =
    (ADDRESS_LIST =
```

```
      (ADDRESS = (PROTOCOL = TCP)(HOST=dbserver.oradbpro.com)(PORT = 1521))
    )
    (CONNECT_DATA =
      (SERVICE_NAME = TEN)
    )
  )
```

The listener needs to support the TCP/IP protocol too:

```
LISTENER =
  (DESCRIPTION =
    (ADDRESS_LIST =
      (ADDRESS = (PROTOCOL = IPC)(KEY = TEN))
      (ADDRESS = (PROTOCOL = TCP)(HOST=dbserver.oradbpro.com)(PORT = 1521))
    )
  )
```

The Perl code to connect using the service name TEN_TCP.WORLD is below:

```
use DBI;
my $dbh = DBI->connect("DBI:Oracle:TEN_TCP.WORLD", "ndebes", "secret") or die "Connect
failed: $DBI::errstr";
```

As you can see, the Perl code is analogous to the IPC connection. Merely the Oracle Net service name passed as part of $data_source has changed. All three arguments to connect can be undef, if the corresponding environment variables DBI_DSN, DBI_USER, and DBI_PASS are set using SET on Windows and export on UNIX:

```
my $dbh = DBI->connect(undef, undef, undef) or die "Connect failed: $DBI::errstr";
```

Two other approaches for connecting through the TCP/IP adapter without requiring Net service name resolution by a naming method, such as Local Naming (tnsnames.ora) or LDAP (Oracle Internet Directory), exist. The first has syntax similar to a Java JDBC URL and specifies host, port, and ORACLE_SID as part of the data source $dsn. Here's an example:

```
my $dbh = DBI->connect("DBI:Oracle:host=dbserver.oradbpro.com;port=1521;sid=TEN",
"ndebes", "secret")
or die "Connect failed: $DBI::errstr";
```

The port number may be omitted. If it is, both 1521 and 1526 are tried. The sequence of the fields host, port, and sid is irrelevant. Another method is to supply the full description that would otherwise be retrieved from the configuration file tnsnames.ora in the argument $dsn:

```
my $dbh = DBI->connect(
"DBI:Oracle:(DESCRIPTION=(ADDRESS_LIST=(ADDRESS=(PROTOCOL=TCP)(HOST=dbserver.oradbpro.
com)(PORT=1521)))(CONNECT_DATA=(SERVICE_NAME=TEN)))",
    "ndebes", "secret") or die "Connect failed: $DBI::errstr";
```

Again, use of SERVICE_NAME in the CONNECT_DATA section is preferred over SID.

Easy Connect

In Oracle10g and subsequent releases, Oracle Net easy connect may be used in connect strings. An easy connect specification has the format *host_name:port/instance_service_name*. All the information required to contact a listener is embedded in the connect string, such that Net service name resolution is not required. Below is an example DBI connect call, which uses easy connect:

```
my $dbh = DBI->connect("DBI:Oracle:dbserver:1521/ELEVEN", "ndebes", "secret") or die
"Connect failed: $DBI::errstr";
```

Easy connect is preferred over the old format host=*host_name*;port=*port_number*;sid=*ORACLE_SID*, since it uses an instance service name[1].

Connecting with SYSDBA or SYSOPER Privileges

Since DBMS release Oracle9i, connecting as user SYS is only possible with SYSDBA privileges. SYSDBA privileges are assigned either by means of operating system group membership or by granting SYSDBA while a password file is in

---

1. See page xiii for a definition of the term instance service name.

use (REMOTE_LOGIN_PASSWORDFILE=exclusive or shared). Care must be taken to distinguish between SYSDBA (or SYSOPER) privileges and operating system authentication, discussed in the next section. The connect string "/ AS SYSDBA" uses both. The slash (/) indicates that operating system authentication instead of a password is to be used, while AS SYSDBA signals that SYSDBA privileges are requested for the session. I will first show how to connect as SYSDBA with database password authentication. The following requirements exist:

- The DBMS instance must have been started with REMOTE_LOGIN_PASSWORDFILE=EXCLUSIVE or SHARED
- A password file, which was previously created with orapwd must exist (otherwise the instance would not start with the above parameter setting). On UNIX systems, the password file path name is $ORACLE_HOME/dbs/orapw$ORACLE_SID, on Windows it is %ORACLE_HOME%\database\pwd%ORACLE_SID%.ora.
- SYSDBA privilege must be granted to the user who wants to connect AS SYSDBA (in sqlnet.ora on Windows, SQLNET.AUTHENTICATION_SERVICES is not set or does not include NTS, otherwise operating system authentication might be used)

When these requirements are met, it is possible to connect AS SYSDBA with SQL*Plus, using any of the protocol adapters bequeath, IPC, or TCP/IP:

```
$ sqlplus "ndebes/secret@ten_tcp.world AS SYSDBA"
Connected to:
Oracle Database 10g Enterprise Edition Release 10.2.0.1.0 - Production
SQL> EXIT
Disconnected from Oracle Database 10g Enterprise Edition Release 10.2.0.1.0 -
Production
```

The connect command fails, after the SYSDBA privilege has been revoked from user NDEBES:

```
SQL> SHOW USER
USER is "SYS"
SQL> REVOKE SYSDBA FROM ndebes;
Revoke succeeded.
SQL> CONNECT ndebes/secret@ten_tcp.world AS SYSDBA
ERROR:
ORA-01031: insufficient privileges
```

Now we may test connecting in the same way with Perl DBI. So far, I have not addressed the parameter \%attr of the connect method. The backslash (\) indicates that the method expects a reference, while the percent sign (%) indicates that a Perl hash is expected. Special constants defined in the database driver module DBD::Oracle have to be passed as part of \%attr to make connecting as SYSDBA or SYSOPER possible. Thus, we can no longer rely on the DBI to automatically load the driver module DBD::Oracle for us. Instead, we must explicitly load the module with the command use DBD::Oracle and request that the constants ORA_SYSDBA and ORA_SYSOPER be loaded into the Perl symbol table. Here's the Perl code that connects in the same way as was done using SQL*Plus above:

```
use DBI;
use DBD::Oracle qw(:ora_session_modes); # imports ORA_SYSDBA and ORA_SYSOPER
my $dbh = DBI->connect("DBI:Oracle:", "ndebes", "secret", {ora_session_mode =>
ORA_SYSDBA})
    or die "Connect failed: $DBI::errstr";
```

Make sure the SYSDBA privilege is granted and the other requirements are met, before testing the Perl code.

Connecting with Operating System Authentication

On UNIX systems, the DBA group name commonly used to assign SYSDBA privilege is "dba", while the suggested group name for the OPER group and the SYSOPER privilege is "oper". These UNIX group names are merely suggestions. When installing with the Oracle Universal Installer (OUI), other group names may be chosen.

On Windows, the DBA group name for the SYSDBA privilege is always "ORA_DBA" and the OPER group name is "ORA_OPER". NTS (NT Security) must be enabled as an authentication service in sqlnet.ora for operating system authentication to work. This is done with the following line in sqlnet.ora:

```
SQLNET.AUTHENTICATION_SERVICES = (NTS) # required for connect / as sysdba
```

On UNIX systems, membership in the DBA group is sufficient to connect without a password. With default settings (REMOTE_OS_AUTHENT=FALSE), connecting as SYSDBA without providing a password is only possible with the bequeath adapter. This default behavior should not be changed, since setting REMOTE_OS_AUTHENT=TRUE is a security hazard.

As before, it is good practice to verify that CONNECT / AS SYSDBA works in SQL*Plus, before attempting the same with Perl DBI code such as this:

```
use DBI;
use DBD::Oracle qw(:ora_session_modes); # imports ORA_SYSDBA and ORA_SYSOPER
my $dbh = DBI->connect("DBI:Oracle:", "/", undef, {ora_session_mode => ORA_SYSDBA})
    or die "Connect failed: $DBI::errstr";
```

Note that the example above uses both SYSDBA privileges and operating system authentication. The latter is characterized by passing "/" as $user and undef (i.e. no password) as $auth.

Let's take a look at how a non–privileged user might connect with operating system authentication. This is useful for running batch jobs without embedding a password in scripts or passing a password on the command line, which might be eavesdropped by looking at the process list with the UNIX command ps. Let's say we want to permit the UNIX user oracle to connect without a password. The database user name required for that purpose depends on the setting of the initialization parameter OS_AUTHENT_PREFIX. In the example below, the default value ops$ is set:

```
SQL> SHOW PARAMETER os_authent_prefix
NAME                 TYPE        VALUE
-------------------- ----------- --------------
os_authent_prefix    string      ops$
```

Next, we create a database user by using ops$ as a prefix for the UNIX user name oracle.

```
SQL> CREATE USER ops$oracle IDENTIFIED EXTERNALLY;
SQL> GRANT CONNECT TO ops$oracle;
```

To test connecting as the new database user, we must be logged in as the UNIX user oracle:

```
$ id
uid=503(oracle) gid=504(oinstall) groups=504(oinstall),505(dba)
$ sqlplus /
Connected.
```

The Perl program os.pl below uses operating system authentication and retrieves the database user name by executing SELECT user FROM dual.

```
#!/usr/bin/env perl
use DBI;
my $dbh=DBI->connect("dbi:Oracle:", "/", undef) or die "Failed to connect.\n";
my $sth=$dbh->prepare("SELECT user FROM dual");
$sth->execute;
my @row=$sth->fetchrow_array;
printf "Connected as user %s.\n", $row[0];
$ chmod +x os.pl
$ ./os.pl
Connected as user OPS$ORACLE.
```

Connect Attributes

There are four additional attributes that may be passed to the connect method. They are AutoCommit, ora_module_name, PrintError, and RaiseError. Each is explained in detail below and recommendations for optimal values in conjunction with the ORACLE DBMS are given. You may pass one or more of these attributes to the connect method, by separating them with commas.

AutoCommit

The setting of the AutoCommit attribute decides whether or not each execution of an INSERT, UPDATE, DELETE, or MERGE statement is committed immediately and implicitly or explicitly at a later time by executing $dbh->commit. The default setting of AutoCommit is 1 (enabled). Since committing each change individually severely degrades the response time of any application, it is imperative that AutoCommit is explicitly set to 0 (disabled).

Module Name

The attribute `ora_module_name` may be used to set `V$SESSION.MODULE`, which is useful for letting the database administrator identify an application. The result of setting `ora_module_name` is the same as if the procedure `DBMS_APPLICATION_INFO.SET_MODULE` were called in an anonymous block, but is achieved with almost no extra coding. The default value is `perl` on UNIX and `perl.exe` on Windows. Note that module names set in this way are ignored by tracing and client statistics functionality controlled with `DBMS_MONITOR` (see also related data dictionary views `DBA_ENABLED_TRACES` and `DBA_ENABLED_AGGREGATIONS`).

PrintError

`PrintError` controls the behavior of the Perl DBI in case of an error. The default value is `1` (enabled), which means errors are printed on the standard error output. When `PrintError=0` is set, the application is responsible for printing error messages when deemed appropriate. Since not all errors may be fatal or even indicative of a problem, the recommended setting is `0` (disabled).

RaiseError

`RaiseError` controls whether or not DBI raises a Perl exception whenever an error is encountered. It applies to all DBI methods except `connect`. As an alternative, the return codes of each individual DBI call may be checked. Since it is much more convenient to embed many DBI calls in an `eval` block which catches exceptions, than coding an `if else` sequence for each DBI call based on the return code, using `eval` is the much preferred approach. The default value of `RaiseError` is `0` (disabled). When `RaiseError=1` (enabled) is set, exceptions are raised whenever a DBI call fails.

Comprehensive Perl DBI Example Program

Now it is time to put it all together. The following Perl DBI program illustrates many aspects of Perl DBI programming. It uses all four connect attributes and inserts rows into a table called CUSTOMER in a loop. The customer identification (`CUSTOMER.ID`) is generated by a sequence. The CREATE statements for the database objects needed to run the example are embedded as a POD section (Plain Old Documentation) in the Perl source. POD sections are ignored by the Perl compiler.

The number of rows to insert is passed as an argument. To ensure good performance, the program commits only once, just before exiting, parses the INSERT statement with bind variables only once before entering the loop, and merely makes execute and bind calls inside the loop. Another performance boost is achieved by using an INSERT TRIGGER with INSERT RETURNING instead of first fetching the next sequence number with a SELECT statement and then passing the sequence number back to the DBMS instance in the INSERT statement. The latter approach impairs performance, since it incurs unnecessary network round trips between client and server. The higher the network latency, the more severe the impact on response time will be.

As an aside, the fastest way to insert rows using a sequence to generate primary keys is to reference the sequence with *sequence_name*.NEXTVAL in the INSERT statement. This requires less CPU cycles than a PL/SQL trigger. Below is an example:

```
INSERT INTO customer(id, name, phone) VALUES (customer_id_seq.nextval, :name, :phone)
RETURNING id INTO :id
```

The downside is that access to the sequence must be coded in every application, whereas it would be coded centrally if a trigger were used.

The program features the ability to enable SQL_TRACE based on an environment variable setting. This is a feature any application should have, since it reduces the effort needed to compile performance diagnostic data. The DBI method `do` is used to execute ALTER SESSION statements. This method is also appropriate for executing non–reusable statements such as CREATE TABLE.

The program also shows how to call PL/SQL packages by preparing and executing an anonymous block. An alternative way to call PL/SQL routines (functions, packages, and procedures), which works with DBI, but is not used in the example below, is the SQL statement CALL (see *Oracle Database SQL Reference 10g Release 2*, page 13–53). I have added plenty of comments to point out what is happening in the Perl program `insert_perf4.pl` below:

```
1   #!/usr/bin/env perl
2
```

```
 3   =pod
 4
 5   create table customer(
 6     id number(*,0) not null,
 7     name varchar2(10),
 8     phone varchar2(30)
 9   );
10   create sequence customer_id_seq;
11   create or replace trigger ins_customer before insert on customer for each row
12   begin
13     SELECT customer_id_seq.nextval INTO :new.id FROM dual;
14   end;
15   /
16   variable id number
17   INSERT INTO customer(name, phone) VALUES ('&name', '&phone') RETURNING id INTO
:id;
18   print id
19
20   CLEANUP
21   =======
22   drop table customer;
23   drop sequence customer_id_seq;
24
25   =cut
26
27   if ( ! defined $ARGV[0] ) {
28     printf "Usage: $0 iterations\n";
29     exit;
30   }
31
32   # declare and initialize variables
33   my ($id, $name, $phone, $sth)=(undef, "Ray", "089/4711", undef);
34
35   use File::Basename;
36   use DBI; # import DBI module
37   print "DBI Version: $DBI::VERSION\n"; # DBI version is available after use DBI
38   use strict; # variables must be declared with my before use
39   my $dbh = DBI->connect("DBI:Oracle:TEN_IPC.WORLD", "ndebes", "secret",
40     # set recommended values for attributes
41     {ora_module_name => basename($0),RaiseError=>1, PrintError=>0,AutoCommit => 0})
42     or die "Connect failed: $DBI::errstr";
43   # DBD::Oracle version is available after connect
44   print "DBD::Oracle Version: $DBD::Oracle::VERSION\n";
45
46   # start eval block for catching exceptions thrown by statements inside the block
47   eval {
48     # tracing facility: if environment variable SQL_TRACE_LEVEL is set,
49     # enable SQL trace at that level
50     my $trc_ident=basename($0); # remove path component from $0, if present
51     if ( defined($ENV{SQL_TRACE_LEVEL})) {
52             $dbh->do("alter session set tracefile_identifier='$trc_ident'");
53             $dbh->do("alter session set events
54       '10046 trace name context forever, level $ENV{SQL_TRACE_LEVEL}'");
55     }
56
57     # parse an anonymous PL/SQL block for retrieving the ORACLE DBMS version
58     # and compatibility as well as the database and instance names
59     # V$ views are not used, since they may be accessed by privileged users only
```

```
60    # quoting with q{<SQL or PL/SQL statements>} is used, since
61    # it avoids trouble with quotes (", ')
62    $sth = $dbh->prepare(q{
63    begin
64            dbms_utility.db_version(:version, :compatibility);
65            :result:=dbms_utility.get_parameter_value('db_name',:intval, :db_name);
66            :result:=dbms_utility.get_parameter_value('instance_name', :intval,
67        :instance_name);
68    end;
69    });
70    my ($version, $compatibility, $db_name, $instance_name, $result, $intval);
71    $sth->bind_param_inout(":version", \$version, 64);
72    $sth->bind_param_inout(":compatibility", \$compatibility, 64);
73    $sth->bind_param_inout(":db_name", \$db_name, 9);
74    $sth->bind_param_inout(":instance_name", \$instance_name, 16);
75    $sth->bind_param_inout(":intval", \$intval, 2);
76    $sth->bind_param_inout(":result", \$result, 1);
77    $sth->execute;
78
79    $sth = $dbh->prepare(q{SELECT userenv('sid'),
80      to_char(sysdate, 'Day, dd. Month yyyy hh24:mi:ss "(week" IW")"') FROM dual});
81    $sth->execute;
82    my ($sid, $date_time);
83    # pass reference to variables which correspond to columns in
84    # SELECT from left to right
85    $sth->bind_columns(\$sid, \$date_time);
86    my @row = $sth->fetchrow_array;
87
88    printf "Connected to ORACLE instance %s, release %s (compatible=%s)",
89    $instance_name, $version, $compatibility;
90    printf "; Database %s\n", $db_name;
91    # due to bind_columns, may use meaningful variable names instead of $row[0], etc.
92    printf "Session %d on %s\n", $sid, $date_time;
93
94    $sth = $dbh->prepare("INSERT INTO customer(name, phone) VALUES (:name, :phone)
95        RETURNING id INTO :id", { ora_check_sql => 0 });
96    # loop, number of iterations is in command line argument
97    for (my $i=0; $i < $ARGV[0]; $i++) {
98      # bind_param_inout is for receiving values from the DBMS
99      $sth->bind_param_inout(":id", \$id, 38);
100     # bind_param is for sending bind variable values to the DBMS
101     # assign value to bind variable (placeholder :name)
102     $sth->bind_param(":name", $name);
103     # assign value to bind variable "phone"
104     $sth->bind_param(":phone", $phone);
105     # execute the INSERT statement
106     $sth->execute();
107     printf "New customer with id %d inserted.\n", $id;
108   }
109 };
110 # check for exceptions
111 if ($@) {
112   printf STDERR "ROLLBACK due to Oracle error %d: %s\n", $dbh->err, $@;
113   # ROLLBACK any previous INSERTs
114   $dbh->rollback;
115   exit;
116 } else {
117   # commit once at end
```

```
118     $dbh->commit;
119   }
120   $sth->finish; # close statement handle
121   $dbh->disconnect; # disconnect from ORACLE instance
```

Line 35 imports the package `File::Basename`, which contains the function `basename`. The Perl command `basename` works in the same way as the UNIX command by the same name. It returns the file component from a path name by stripping one or more directories from the string. The command `basename` is used to make sure that neither the module name nor the `TRACEFILE_IDENTIFIER` contain illegal or unwanted characters such as the directory separator (/) that may be contained in the Perl variable `$0`.

The connect statement, which sets the recommended values for `RaiseError` (1), `PrintError` (0) and `AutoComit` (0) is in line 39. An eval block used to catch exceptions from DBI method invocations encompasses lines 47 to 109. The check for the environment variable `SQL_TRACE_LEVEL` is in line 51. The range of values is the same as for event 10046 (1, 4, 8, 12, see also Chapter 24). If the environment variable is set, SQL trace is enabled in line 53 with `ALTER SESSION SET EVENTS`. The name of the Perl program is used as the `TRACEFILE_IDENTIFIER` in line 52, to facilitate locating trace files in the directory set as `USER_DUMP_DEST`.

Lines 62 to 77 show how to call PL/SQL packages by embedding them in an anonymous block. The publicly accessible package `DBMS_UTILITY` is called three times in a single anonymous block to retrieve information on the instance and database.

Lines 79 to 86 and 92 exemplify how conveniently fetching data can be coded with the DBI. With `bind_columns`, variables with meaningful names are used for accessing column values retrieved with the Perl DBI method `fetchrow_array`. Without `bind_columns`, array syntax such as `$row[column_index]` must be used, where *column_index* starts at 0 and designates columns in the `SELECT` column list from left to right.

The `INSERT` statement, which contains bind variables and is thus reusable is parsed once before entering the loop by calling `prepare` in line 94. It would be a costly mistake to place the `prepare` call inside the loop. Extra network round trips due to parse calls and excess CPU consumption due to superfluous soft parses would be incurred.

Inside the `for` loop, which stretches from line 97 to 108, the `bind_param_inout` method is used to tell the DBI which variable to use for receiving the sequence number returned to the client due to the SQL statement `INSERT RETURNING id INTO :id`. The bind variables `name` and `phone` are for sending values to the DBMS. This is accomplished with the DBI method `bind_param`.

The `eval` block is followed by an `if` statement, which checks the special Perl variable `$@` for an exception. If an exception has occurred, `$@` contains the error message. Otherwise `$@` is an empty string, considered by Perl as a boolean expression which evaluates as `FALSE`, such that the `if` branch in line 112 is not entered. In case of an exception, any rows already inserted are discarded by issuing `rollback` in line 114.

If all is well, `commit` is called once in line 118, the statement handle `$sth` is released in line 120, and the client disconnects from the DBMS in line 121. Below is a transcript of running the Perl program `insert_perf4.pl`:

```
$ ./insert_perf4.pl 3
DBI Version: 1.41
DBD::Oracle Version: 1.15
Connected to ORACLE instance ten, release 10.2.0.1.0 (compatible=10.2.0.1.0); Database
TEN
Session 145 on Thursday , 19. July      2007 21:57:54 (week 29)
New customer with id 1 inserted.
New customer with id 2 inserted.
New customer with id 3 inserted.
```

Exception Handling

Before the curtain drops, I'd like to show the exception handling with `eval` in action. Setting the tablespace where the table `CUSTOMER` resides to status read only causes the `execute` method call in line 106 to fail. Execution will continue at the `if` statement in line 111. Below is a step by step test:

```
SQL> CONNECT system
Enter password:
Connected.
SQL> ALTER TABLESPACE users READ ONLY;
```

```
Tablespace altered.
SQL> EXIT
Disconnected from Oracle Database 10g Enterprise Edition Release 10.2.0.1.0 -
Production
$ ./insert_perf4.pl 1
DBI Version: 1.48
DBD::Oracle Version: 1.16
Connected to ORACLE instance ten, release 10.2.0.1.0 (compatible=10.2.0.1.0); Database
TEN
Session 145 on Thursday , 19. July      2007 23:52:32 (week 29)
ROLLBACK due to Oracle error 372: DBD::Oracle::st execute failed: ORA-00372: file 4
cannot be modified at this time
ORA-01110: data file 4: 'F:\ORADATA\TEN\USERS01.DBF' (DBD ERROR: error possibly near
<*> indicator at char 12 in 'INSERT INTO <*>customer(name, phone) VALUES (:name,
:phone)
       RETURNING id INTO :id') [for Statement "INSERT INTO customer(name, phone) VALUES
(:name, :phone)
       RETURNING id INTO :id" with ParamValues: :name='Ray', :phone='089/4711',
:id=undef] at ./insert_perf4.pl line 106.
```

As is evident from the output above, the DBI provides a lot of information beyond the ORACLE DBMS error message "ORA-00372: file 4 cannot be modified at this time". It retrieves the second error message on the error stack (ORA-01110: data file 4: 'F:\ORADATA\TEN\USERS01.DBF'), tells us which SQL statement caused the error, the line number in the Perl source file for locating the statement, which bind variables were in use, and what their values were.

Source Code Depot

Table 40: Perl DBI Source Code Depot

File Name	Functionality
ORADBB.pm	The Perl module ORADBB.pm is required to run dbb.pl. It contains several Perl subroutines, which may be reused by any Perl DBI application (e.g. for connecting with SYSDBA or SYSOPER privileges).
args.pl	Perl program that prints command line arguments on standard output
dbb.pl	Command line utility capable of executing arbitrary SQL and PL/SQL statements. Query result column widths are adjusted automatically.
insert_perf4.pl	Perl program that demonstrates exception handling, PL/SQL execution, bind variables, ROLLBACK, and COMMIT.
os.pl	Perl program that uses operating system authentication to connect
perl-dbi-test.pl	Perl Program for testing connectivity to an ORACLE DBMS instance

Chapter 23

Application Instrumentation and End to End Tracing

Status: The *Oracle Database Performance Tuning Guide 10g Release 2* and the *Oracle Call Interface Programmer's Guide 10g Release 2* describe a feature called end to end application tracing. The *Oracle Database JDBC Developer's Guide and Reference 10g Release 2* documents end to end metrics support in JDBC. The *Oracle Database Concepts 10g Release 2* manual presents a feature called end to end monitoring. These three terms refer to the same set of tracing, monitoring, and application instrumentation features. The feature set is implemented with three application programming interfaces (OCI, PL/SQL, Java/JDBC), dictionary views, V$ dynamic performance views, and SQL trace. Instrumentation is leveraged by the Active Workload Repository, Active Session History, Statspack, Enterprise Manager, the database resource manager, and the TRCSESS utility. The undocumented aspects surrounding this set of features are so numerous that I refrain from listing them all[1]. For example, it is undocumented that a shared server process does not re–emit instrumentation entries to SQL trace files as it services different sessions. This may lead to incorrect results when a shared server process' SQL trace file, which contains several sessions, is processed with TRCSESS.

Benefit: A complete instrumentation case study, which points out the benefits seen in the aforementioned components and addresses undocumented aspects, such as the SQL trace file entries written by JDBC end to end metrics, is presented. A work–around that avoids incorrect results with TRCSESS in a Shared Server environment is suggested. An example of the integration between application instrumentation and the resource manager, which provides the undocumented syntax for assigning a resource group based on service name, module, and action, is also included. Finally, backward compatibility of TRCSESS with Oracle9*i* is discussed.

---

1. The Java source file `ApplicationInstrumentation.java` in the source code depot lists ten undocumented aspects.

Introduction to Instrumentation

According to Wikipedia "instrumentation refers to an ability to monitor or measure the level of a product's performance, to diagnose errors and write trace information. [...] In programming, instrumentation means the ability of an application to incorporate:

- Code tracing—receiving informative messages about the execution of an application at run time. [...]
- Performance counters—components that allow you to track the performance of the application.
- Event logs—components that allow you to receive and track major events in the execution of the application"[1].

In a nutshell, instrumentation enables software to measure its own performance. The ORACLE DBMS is well instrumented. It maintains hundreds of counters and timers that represent the workload executed as well as the performance of SQL statements, memory, file, and network access. Measurements are available at instance level, session level, and SQL or PL/SQL statement level. In 1999 Anjo Kolk, Shari Yamaguchi and Jim Viscusi of Oracle Corp., in their acclaimed paper *Yet Another Performance Profiling Method (or YAPP–Method)*, proposed the following formula:

Response Time = Service Time + Wait Time

Even though the paper was lacking a snapshot–based approach to measuring performance[2] and stated that the wait event *SQL*Net message from client* should be ignored at session level—a mistake which limits the explanatory power of performance diagnoses still seen in recent books[3]—it was a milestone towards a new tuning paradigm. Put simply, service time is the CPU time consumed and wait time is the time spent waiting for one of several hundred wait events related to disk access, synchronization, or network latency (see appendix *Oracle Wait Events* in *Oracle Database Reference* and the dynamic performance view V$EVENT_NAME). Instrumentation of the database server provides these measurements. Instrumentation itself has a certain impact on performance termed measurement intrusion. Theoretically, an extended SQL trace file is a microsecond by microsecond account of a database session's elapsed time.

The response time perceived by an end user is affected by additional factors such as network latency or processing in intermediate tiers such as application servers. Clearly, the database server has its own perspective on response time which is different from that of an application server, which is still different from that of the end user. For example, instrumentation in Oracle10*g* introduced time stamps for wait events (WAIT entries) in extended SQL trace files. Formerly, just the database calls parse, execute, and fetch were tagged with timestamps. From the database server's perspective, the response time of a SQL statement comprises the interval between the arrival of the statement at the database server and the response sent to the client. The former point in time is marked by the wait event *SQL*Net message from client* and the latter by the wait event *SQL*Net message to client*. Due to network latency, the client will not receive the response at the moment the wait event *SQL*Net message to client* completes. Thus the response time measured by the client is longer than that measured by the database server.

Not all code paths in the database server are thoroughly instrumented, such that further inaccuracies aside from measurement intrusion are introduced. The deviation between the elapsed time covered by trace file entries as delineated by timestamps in the file (parameter tim, see Chapter 24) and the time accounted for by CPU consumption and waiting is usually less than ten percent. In other words, the quality of instrumentation is high and measurement intrusion is low, such that it is possible to use the data for reliable performance diagnoses.

I use the term *application instrumentation* to differentiate instrumentation of the ORACLE DBMS from instrumentation within an application or database client. Basically, instrumentation of the DBMS is the core functionality, which may be leveraged to a greater degree when the application is also instrumented. This is the main theme I'm trying to bring across in this chapter. The DBMS has application interfaces which allow setting module, action, and client identifier. In this context, a module identifies a longer code path, which may correspond to a batch job, a business task, or a functional component within a larger application. For example, human resources and manufacturing might be mod-

---

1. http://en.wikipedia.org/wiki/Instrumentation_%28computer_programming%29
2. Both Statspack and AWR implement a snapshot–based approach to capturing performance data. Figures since instance or session startup are not snapshot–based.
3. Please see Chapter 27 for information on the relevance of *SQL*Net message from client* and how to derive think time from this wait event.

ules of an enterprise resource planning application. Modules consist of one or more actions, i.e. actions are at a more granular level than modules.

A client identifier serves to uniquely identify an end user. In a connection pooling environment, dedicated server processes are spawned once and reused again and again for running DML on behalf of different end users. A DBA has no way of knowing which dedicated server process services which end user, unless the application is instrumented and sets the client identifier. Since all the sessions in a connection pool are opened by the same application server and connect to a single database user, the columns USERNAME, OSUSER, and MACHINE in V$SESSION are useless. With application instrumentation in place, a DBA can identify the database session which services an end user. The DBA will also see which module and action are executed. Of course, you may wish to add a lot more instrumentation code than simply setting module, action, and client identifier. Code that has nothing to do with tracing or statistics collection in the DBMS, but instead focuses on your application's functionality or measures response time independently of the DBMS. Especially if your application includes modules that do not interact with a DBMS instance, you will need to include some kind of accounting for the time spent in those modules. After all, the DBMS can only account for the time spent in database calls and the time spent waiting to receive another database call, i.e. waiting for the event *SQL*Net message from client*.

In addition to module, action, and client identifier, the instance service name (see Instance Service Name vs. Net Service Name on page xiii) used by an application may also be used to facilitate monitoring and tracing. Separate applications (or even connection pools) running against an instance should use different service names. This opens up the possibility of tracing and monitoring by service name.

Case Study

I have chosen Java, JDBC, and the new JDBC end to end metrics introduced with Oracle10*g* for the code sample in this case study. In Oracle11*g*, the JDBC end to end metrics interface has been removed from documentation in favor of Dynamic Monitoring Service. However, the interface is still present in the JDBC driver release 11.1.0.6.0 and works exactly as in Oracle10*g*. Instrumentation with PL/SQL has been available for a number of years and works as expected. JDBC end to end metrics is a different issue in that the code sample provided by Oracle in the *Oracle Database JDBC Developer's Guide and Reference 10g Release 2* is neither a complete runnable program nor syntactically correct. The case study looks at the effects of instrumentation on V$ views as well as SQL trace files and shows how to leverage it with DBMS_MONITOR, TRCSESS, and the database resource manager.

JDBC End to End Metrics Sample Code

JDBC end to end metrics is a lightweight approach to instrumentation. Instead of immediately setting module, action, and client identifier as is done with the PL/SQL packages DBMS_APPLICATION_INFO and DBMS_SESSION, changed values are merely stored in a Java array of strings and are sent to the DBMS with the next database call. Thus, contrary to PL/SQL, no extra network round–trips are incurred. The functionality is available in the Thin JDBC driver as well as in the JDBC OCI driver. The API is only found in Oracle JDBC drivers starting with release 10.1. Third party JDBC drivers and Oracle drivers with release numbers 9.2 and earlier do not offer this functionality. Coding is quite simple. You declare an array of strings and use several constants to size the string and set the array elements, which represent module, action, and client identifier. The code excerpt below is from the Java program ApplicationInstrumentation.java, which is included in the source code depot:

```
1 DriverManager.registerDriver(new oracle.jdbc.OracleDriver());
2 java.util.Properties prop = new java.util.Properties();
3 // properties are evaluated once by JDBC Thin when the session is created. Not
suitable for setting the program or other information after getConnection has been
called
4 prop.put("user", username);
5 prop.put("password", pwd);
6 prop.put("v$session.program", getClass().getName()); // undocumented property
V$session.program works with JDBC Thin only; if specified, then set as program and
module, as expected end to end metrics overwrites the module; program is not
overwritten
7 Connection conn = DriverManager.getConnection(url, prop);
8 conn.setAutoCommit(false);
```

```
 9 // Create Oracle DatabaseMetaData object
10 DatabaseMetaData metadata = conn.getMetaData();
11 // gets driver info:
12 System.out.println("JDBC driver version: " + metadata.getDriverVersion() + "\n");
13 System.out.println("\nPlease query V$SESSION and hit return to continue when
done.\n");
14 System.in.read(buffer, 0, 80); // Pause until user hits enter
15 // end to end metrics interface
16 String app_instrumentation[] = new
String[OracleConnection.END_TO_END_STATE_INDEX_MAX];
17 app_instrumentation[OracleConnection.END_TO_END_CLIENTID_INDEX]="Ray.Deevers";
18 app_instrumentation[OracleConnection.END_TO_END_MODULE_INDEX]="mod";
19 app_instrumentation[OracleConnection.END_TO_END_ACTION_INDEX]="act";
20 ((OracleConnection)conn).setEndToEndMetrics(app_instrumentation,(short)0);
21 Statement stmt = conn.createStatement();
22 ResultSet rset = stmt.executeQuery("SELECT userenv('sid'), to_char(sysdate, 'Month
dd. yyyy hh24:mi') FROM dual");
23 while (rset.next())
24 System.out.println("This is session " + rset.getString(1) + " on " +
rset.getString(2));
25 rset.close();
26 System.out.println("\nPlease query V$SESSION and hit return to continue when
done.\n");
27 System.in.read(buffer, 0, 80); // Pause until user hits enter
28 // with connection pooling, execute this code before returning session to connection
pool
29 app_instrumentation[OracleConnection.END_TO_END_CLIENTID_INDEX]="";
30 app_instrumentation[OracleConnection.END_TO_END_MODULE_INDEX]="";
31 app_instrumentation[OracleConnection.END_TO_END_ACTION_INDEX]="";
32 ((OracleConnection)conn).setEndToEndMetrics(app_instrumentation,(short)0);
```

The connection is established by creating an instance of the class java.util.Properties, setting user name and password, and then passing the class instance to the driver manager in DriverManager.getConnection. This makes it possible to use the undocumented property v$session.program (line 6) to set the program and module names in V$SESSION for JDBC Thin connections. The default program and module name for such connections is JDBC Thin Client, which is not very telling. JDBC OCI ignores this property.

If you cannot afford to thoroughly instrument a JDBC Thin application, I recommend that you at least set this property prior to establishing a connection to the DBMS. Thus, the DBA will be able to identify which database session your Java program uses, but he will not be able to use the setting with DBMS_MONITOR, since it only honors the documented programming interfaces PL/SQL, OCI, and Java. The module name will not only appear in V$SESSION.MODULE, but also in Statspack and in AWR reports. Of course, the latter benefit applies to any program which sets V$SESSION.MODULE, irrespective of whether it is set with DBMS_APPLICATION_INFO.SET_MODULE, OCI, or JDBC. The module should also be set with JDBC OCI, but it requires a few more lines of code. The default program and module for JDBC OCI are java@*client_host_name* on UNIX and java.exe on Windows, where *client_host_name* is the system from which the JDBC OCI program connected.

On line 16, the variable app_instrumentation is declared as an array of strings. The constant OracleConnection.END_TO_END_STATE_INDEX_MAX is used to specify the array size. Client identifier, module, and action are set in lines 17 to 19. The call to ((OracleConnection)conn).setEndToEndMetrics in line 20 makes the new settings available to the end to end metrics API. The cast is mandatory to use the extension from Oracle Corp. In lines 20 to 25 a SELECT statement is executed. This statement causes parse, execute, and fetch database calls. The new settings will be sent along with the first database call, which results from the SELECT statement. Thus, while the program waits for the user to hit return in line 27, the new settings for module, action, and client identifier will be seen in V$SESSION. In lines 29 to 32 module, action, and client identifier are set to empty strings. This is done to show the integration with DBMS_MONITOR and TRCSESS.

The source code depot also includes a Java program which is instrumented with PL/SQL and is compatible with Oracle9*i* as well as Oracle10*g*. Use of an Oracle10*g* JDBC driver to connect to an Oracle9*i* instance is supported.

However, end to end metrics code has no effect when executed against an Oracle9*i* instance. Thus, at least to set module and action, PL/SQL must be used by Java applications running against Oracle9*i*. The Java class `OracleConnection` includes the method `public void setClientIdentifier(java.lang.String clientId)` to set the client identifier in Java. The Java program `JdbcInstrumentationOracle9i.java` in the source code depot is instrumented with PL/SQL only and works with Oracle9*i* and subsequent releases.

Compiling the Program

Since there is a Java Developer's Kit (JDK) in an Oracle10*g* ORACLE_HOME, there is no need to install additional software to compile the Java program. It's sufficient to set the environment variable CLASSPATH and to include the Java compiler `javac` in the command search path variable PATH. On UNIX, a colon (`:`) is used to separate individual entries in CLASSPATH, whereas on Windows a semicolon (`;`) is used. Below is an example from Windows:

```
C:> set ORACLE_HOME=C:\Oracle\product\db10.2
C:> set CLASSPATH=%ORACLE_HOME%\jdbc\lib\ojdbc14.jar;.
C:> set PATH=%ORACLE_HOME%\bin;%ORACLE_HOME%\jdk\bin;%SystemRoot%\system32
C:> javac ApplicationInstrumentation.java
```

At this point, the compiled Java program is in the file `ApplicationInstrumentation.class`, which is also included in the source code depot, such that you need not compile the source file.

Instrumentation at Work

Now it's time to run the program. Note that, since "." was used in the CLASSPATH setting in the previous section, `ApplicationInstrumentation.class` must be in the current directory to successfully run it. The program requires three arguments:

- a database user name
- the user's password
- a JDBC URL for either JDBC Thin or JDBC OCI

JDBC OCI URLs take on the form `jdbc:oracle:oci:@`*net_service_name*, where *net_service_name* is a Net service name defined in `tnsnames.ora` or by a directory service. JDBC Thin URLs for connecting to a specific instance service have the format `jdbc:oracle:thin:@//`*host_name*`:`*port*`/`*instance_service_name*, where *host_name* is the system where the DBMS instance is running, *port* is the port number used by the listener and *instance_service_name* is a service name listed with `lsnrctl services`. The old JDBC Thin URL syntax `jdbc:oracle:thin:@`*host_name*`:`*port*`:`*ORACLE_SID* should no longer be used, since it results in the default service name SYS$USERS in V$SESSION.SERVICE_NAME. This prevents the use of individual instance service names for different applications and also defeats the purpose of cluster services in RAC environments.

Setting Up Tracing, Statistics Collection, and the Resource Manager

Some preparations are needed to show the interaction of instrumentation with end to end tracing, client statistics collection, and the resource manager. The package DBMS_MONITOR may be used to enable SQL trace or client statistics for a certain combination of instance service name, module, and action. In the call to the packaged procedure DBMS_MONITOR.SERV_MOD_ACT_TRACE_ENABLE, merely the instance service name is mandatory. If the module is unspecified, then the setting affects all modules. Likewise, when service name and module are specified, the setting affects all actions. Tracing and statistics collection for a certain client identifier are also possible. Here are some examples which first enable and then disable trace and statistics collection at various levels:

```
SQL> EXEC dbms_monitor.serv_mod_act_trace_enable('TEN.oradbpro.com', 'mod', 'act')
SQL> EXEC dbms_monitor.client_id_trace_enable('Ray.Deevers')
SQL> EXEC dbms_monitor.serv_mod_act_stat_enable('TEN.oradbpro.com', 'mod', 'act')
SQL> EXEC dbms_monitor.client_id_stat_enable('Ray.Deevers')
SQL> EXEC dbms_monitor.client_id_stat_disable('Ray.Deevers')
SQL> EXEC dbms_monitor.serv_mod_act_stat_disable('TEN.oradbpro.com', 'mod', 'act')
SQL> EXEC dbms_monitor.client_id_trace_disable('Ray.Deevers')
SQL> EXEC dbms_monitor.serv_mod_act_trace_disable('TEN.oradbpro.com', 'mod', 'act')
```

Arguments to DBMS_MONITOR are case sensitive. The spelling of the service name must match the value of the column DBA_SERVICES.NETWORK_NAME. The settings are persistent in the sense that they remain in effect across instance restarts. The dictionary views DBA_ENABLED_TRACES and DBA_ENABLED_AGGREGATIONS reflect the current settings. If we wanted to trace all the sessions that use the instance service "TEN.oradbpro.com" and enable statistics collection for that same service and the module "mod", we could achieve this with the code below:

```
SQL> SELECT network_name FROM dba_services WHERE network_name LIKE 'TEN.%';
NETWORK_NAME
----------------
TEN.oradbpro.com
SQL> EXEC dbms_monitor.serv_mod_act_trace_enable(service_name=>'TEN.oradbpro.com')
SQL> SELECT trace_type, primary_id, waits, binds FROM dba_enabled_traces;
TRACE_TYPE PRIMARY_ID       WAITS BINDS
---------- ---------------- ----- -----
SERVICE    TEN.oradbpro.com TRUE  FALSE
SQL> EXEC dbms_monitor.serv_mod_act_stat_enable('TEN.oradbpro.com', 'mod')
SQL> SELECT aggregation_type, primary_id, qualifier_id1, qualifier_id2
FROM dba_enabled_aggregations;
AGGREGATION_TYPE PRIMARY_ID       QUALIFIER_ID1 QUALIFIER_ID2
---------------- ---------------- ------------- -------------
SERVICE_MODULE   TEN.oradbpro.com mod
```

Statistics for service name, module, and action may be retrieved from the dynamic performance view V$SERV_MOD_ACT_STATS, whereas statistics for a client identifier are in V$CLIENT_STATS.

The assignment of a database session to a consumer group based on instrumentation settings is a new feature of the Oracle10g database resource manager. Among others, assignments can be made for combinations of service name, module, and action or combinations of module and action, where merely the first component is mandatory. The settings in effect are available by querying the view DBA_RSRC_GROUP_MAPPINGS. This feature may be used to prioritize modules and services. The resource manager is shipped with a default plan called SYSTEM_PLAN. This plan includes the consumer groups SYS_GROUP, OTHER_GROUPS, and LOW_GROUP (see the dynamic performance view V$RSRC_CONSUMER_GROUP). As the name suggests, LOW_GROUP is the consumer group with the lowest priority. In a situation where CPU resources are scarce, the SYS_GROUP and OTHER_GROUPS will be given slices of CPU time, whereas sessions in the LOW_GROUP have to yield the CPU. Since the resource manager is disabled by default, it must be enabled to use these features. This can be done at run-time using ALTER SYSTEM:

```
SQL> ALTER SYSTEM SET resource_manager_plan=system_plan;
System altered.
```

The syntax for specifying a combination of instance service name, module, and action as a single string in a call to DBMS_RESOURCE_MANAGER.SET_CONSUMER_GROUP_MAPPING is undocumented. There is also no statement on case sensitivity. Actual testing reveals that a dot (.) has to be used to separate the service name from the module and the module from the action. Contrary to DBMS_MONITOR, capitalization is irrelevant. The code below instructs the resource manager to place a session which uses the instance service "TEN.oradbpro.com" and has set module and action to "mod" and "act" respectively into the consumer group LOW_GROUP (file rsrc_mgr.sql):

```
begin
    dbms_resource_manager.create_pending_area();
    dbms_resource_manager.set_consumer_group_mapping(
        attribute=>dbms_resource_manager.service_module_action,
        value=>'TEN.oradbpro.com.mod.act',
        consumer_group=>'LOW_GROUP'
    );
    dbms_resource_manager.submit_pending_area();
    dbms_resource_manager.clear_pending_area();
end;
/
SQL> SELECT * FROM dba_rsrc_group_mappings;
ATTRIBUTE              VALUE                    CONSUMER_GROUP STATUS
--------------------- ------------------------ -------------- ------
SERVICE_MODULE_ACTION TEN.ORADBPRO.COM.MOD.ACT LOW_GROUP
ORACLE_USER           SYS                      SYS_GROUP
ORACLE_USER           SYSTEM                   SYS_GROUP
```

The setting takes effect immediately, i.e. it is applied to sessions which are already connected. This completes the preparations. If we now run the Java program, we expect to see three things happening:

1. A SQL trace file is created.
2. Statistics are collected for service name, module, and action.
3. The session is placed in the consumer group LOW_GROUP as soon as it sets module and action to the values "mod" and "act" respectively.

Let's verify that the software responds as expected. The java program is run by starting a Java virtual machine and passing the class and parameters for the program as arguments:

```
C:> java ApplicationInstrumentation ndebes secret jdbc:oracle:thin:@//localhost:1521/
TEN.oradbpro.com
JDBC driver version: 10.2.0.3.0
Please query V$SESSION and hit return to continue when done.
```

At this point, the program has connected, but not yet made any calls to the end to end metrics interface. Now open another window and run the following query in SQL*Plus:

```
SQL> SELECT program, module, action, resource_consumer_group AS consumer_group
FROM v$session
WHERE service_name='TEN.oradbpro.com';
PROGRAM                        MODULE                          ACTION CONSUMER_GROUP
------------------------------ ------------------------------- ------ --------------
ApplicationInstrumentation     ApplicationInstrumentation             OTHER_GROUPS
```

This shows that the undocumented property for setting program and module has worked. The session is currently in consumer group OTHER_GROUPS. Next, hit return in the window where the Java program is running. This will cause the program to advance to the section where client identifier, module, and action are set. It will also execute a query that retrieves the session identifier and the current date:

```
This is session 40 on October    30. 2007 22:37
Please query V$SESSION and hit return to continue when done.
```

The program pauses again, allowing us to see the effects of the calls to the end to end metrics API in V$SESSION and V$SERV_MOD_ACT_STATS (timings are in microseconds):

```
SQL> SELECT program, module, action, client_identifier, resource_consumer_group AS
consumer_group
FROM v$session
WHERE service_name='TEN.oradbpro.com';
PROGRAM                        MODULE ACTION CLIENT_IDENTIFIER CONSUMER_GROUP
------------------------------ ------ ------ ----------------- --------------
ApplicationInstrumentation     mod    act    Ray.Deevers       LOW_GROUP
SQL>  SELECT stat_name, value
FROM v$serv_mod_act_stats
WHERE service_name='TEN.oradbpro.com' AND module='mod' AND value > 0;
STAT_NAME                      VALUE
------------------------------ -----
user calls                         2
DB time                         5555
DB CPU                          5555
parse count (total)                1
parse time elapsed                63
execute count                      2
sql execute elapsed time         303
opened cursors cumulative          1
```

Module, action, and client identifier are set, while the program name has been retained. As expected, the session has been placed into the consumer group LOW_GROUP. Statistics for service and module are collected and available by querying V$SERV_MOD_ACT_STATS. Now hit return in the window where the Java program is running one more time:

```
application instrumentation settings removed
Please query V$SESSION and hit return to continue when done.
```

At this point, the program has set module, action, and client identifier to empty strings. It pauses again to allow us to observe the effects. The previous consumer group of the session has been restored:

```
SQL> SELECT program, module, action, client_identifier, resource_consumer_group AS
consumer_group
FROM v$session
WHERE service_name='TEN.oradbpro.com';
PROGRAM                       MODULE ACTION CLIENT_IDENTIFIER CONSUMER_GROUP
------------------------- ------ ------ ----------------- --------------
ApplicationInstrumentation                                  OTHER_GROUPS
```

The program disconnects and exits as soon as you hit return one last time. There is now an extended SQL trace file, which includes wait events, but not binds, in the directory set with parameter USER_DUMP_DEST. To include binds, set the boolean parameter BINDS in the call to DBMS_MONITOR.SERV_MOD_ACT_TRACE_ENABLE to TRUE. The relevant sections of the trace file are reproduced below:

```
*** SERVICE NAME:(TEN.oradbpro.com) 2007-10-30 22:52:52.703
*** SESSION ID:(47.2195) 2007-10-30 22:52:52.703
WAIT #0: nam='SQL*Net message to client' ela= 3 driver id=1413697536 #bytes=1 p3=0
obj#=-1 tim=392092318798
...
*** 2007-10-30 22:53:03.984
WAIT #0: nam='SQL*Net message from client' ela= 11260272 driver id=1413697536 #bytes=1
p3=0 obj#=-1 tim=392103603777
*** ACTION NAME:(act) 2007-10-30 22:53:03.984
*** MODULE NAME:(mod) 2007-10-30 22:53:03.984
*** CLIENT ID:(Ray.Deevers) 2007-10-30 22:53:03.984
=====================
PARSING IN CURSOR #2 len=75 dep=0 uid=61 oct=3 lid=61 tim=392103604193 hv=536335290
ad='66afd944'
SELECT userenv('sid'), to_char(sysdate, 'Month dd. yyyy hh24:mi') FROM dual
END OF STMT
PARSE #2:c=0,e=90,p=0,cr=0,cu=0,mis=0,r=0,dep=0,og=1,tim=392103604185
EXEC #2:c=0,e=53,p=0,cr=0,cu=0,mis=0,r=0,dep=0,og=1,tim=392103608774
WAIT #2: nam='SQL*Net message to client' ela= 4 driver id=1413697536 #bytes=1 p3=0
obj#=-1 tim=392103608842
WAIT #2: nam='SQL*Net message from client' ela= 52777 driver id=1413697536 #bytes=1
p3=0 obj#=-1 tim=392103661760
WAIT #2: nam='SQL*Net message to client' ela= 4 driver id=1413697536 #bytes=1 p3=0
obj#=-1 tim=392103661904
FETCH #2:c=0,e=93,p=0,cr=0,cu=0,mis=0,r=1,dep=0,og=1,tim=392103661941
WAIT #2: nam='SQL*Net message from client' ela= 233116 driver id=1413697536 #bytes=1
p3=0 obj#=-1 tim=392103895174
*** ACTION NAME:() 2007-10-30 22:53:04.281
*** MODULE NAME:() 2007-10-30 22:53:04.281
*** CLIENT ID:() 2007-10-30 22:53:04.281
STAT #2 id=1 cnt=1 pid=0 pos=1 obj=0 op='FAST DUAL  (cr=0 pr=0 pw=0 time=14 us)'
=====================
PARSING IN CURSOR #2 len=63 dep=0 uid=61 oct=3 lid=61 tim=392103896865 hv=2359234954
ad='672f1af4'
SELECT 'application instrumentation settings removed' FROM dual
END OF STMT
```

The fact that the module and action names appear before the SELECT statement, which retrieves the session identifier, proves that the instrumentation settings were piggybacked with the network packet(s) sent to parse the SELECT statement. JDBC end to end metrics do not cause additional network round–trips. At the IP level, the extra data may necessitate an additional packet, but there will be no extra round–trips reported as the wait event *SQL*Net message from client*.

Using TRCSESS

TRCSESS is a new utility that ships with Oracle10*g* and subsequent releases. It may be used to extract relevant sections from one or more trace files into a single file based on the following criteria:

- service name (V$SESSION.SERVICE_NAME)
- session identification (V$SESSION.SID and V$SESSION.SERIAL#)
- module name (V$SESSION.MODULE)
- action name (V$SESSION.ACTION)
- client identifier (V$SESSION.CLIENT_IDENTIFIER)

One of the session identification, client identifier, service name, action, and module options must be specified. If more than a single option is used, the trace file sections, which satisfy all the criteria, are combined into an output file. All the option values are case sensitive. After TRCSESS has merged the trace information into a single output file, this file may be processed by TKPROF or the extended SQL trace profiler ESQLTRCPROF included with this book.

The TRCSESS utility prints information on its usage when it is called without any arguments:

```
$ trcsess
trcsess [output=<output file name >]  [session=<session ID>] [clientid=<clientid>]
[service=<service name>] [action=<action name>] [module=<module name>] <trace file
names>

output=<output file name> output destination default being standard output.
session=<session Id> session to be traced.
Session id is a combination of session Index & session serial number e.g. 8.13.
clientid=<clientid> clientid to be traced.
service=<service name> service to be traced.
action=<action name> action to be traced.
module=<module name> module to be traced.
<trace_file_names> Space separated list of trace files with wild card '*' supported.
```

In the dedicated server model, all trace file entries for a particular session are in a single file. Shared Server and connection pooling environments are a different matter. In the Shared Server model, trace file entries for a single session may be spread across as many files as shared server processes configured. This is due to the fact that a user session is serviced by different shared server processes from time to time. This makes it difficult to create a complete resource profile for a session. Connection pooling environments are the worst of all, since a DBA cannot form an association between an end user, who may have contacted him for support, and a database session, unless the application is instrumented and sets a client identifier, which allows the DBA to find out which database session is currently used on behalf of the end user.

To continue the example from the previous section, I will show how to extract the SQL statements issued while the session was executing module "mod" and action "act" with TRCSESS. Glancing back at the code excerpt on page 209, one would expect that merely the SELECT statement which retrieves the session identifier is contained in the resulting trace file:

```
$ trcsess module=mod action=act *.trc
*** 2007-10-30 22:53:03.984
*** 2007-10-30 22:53:03.984
=====================
PARSING IN CURSOR #2 len=75 dep=0 uid=61 oct=3 lid=61 tim=392103604193 hv=536335290
ad='66afd944'
SELECT userenv('sid'), to_char(sysdate, 'Month dd. yyyy hh24:mi') FROM dual
END OF STMT
PARSE #2:c=0,e=90,p=0,cr=0,cu=0,mis=0,r=0,dep=0,og=1,tim=392103604185
EXEC #2:c=0,e=53,p=0,cr=0,cu=0,mis=0,r=0,dep=0,og=1,tim=392103608774
WAIT #2: nam='SQL*Net message to client' ela= 4 driver id=1413697536 #bytes=1 p3=0
obj#=-1 tim=392103608842
WAIT #2: nam='SQL*Net message from client' ela= 52777 driver id=1413697536 #bytes=1
p3=0 obj#=-1 tim=392103661760
```

```
WAIT #2: nam='SQL*Net message to client' ela= 4 driver id=1413697536 #bytes=1 p3=0
obj#=-1 tim=392103661904
FETCH #2:c=0,e=93,p=0,cr=0,cu=0,mis=0,r=1,dep=0,og=1,tim=392103661941
WAIT #2: nam='SQL*Net message from client' ela= 233116 driver id=1413697536 #bytes=1
p3=0 obj#=-1 tim=392103895174
```

Note how all the application instrumentation entries including the client identifier, which came after the action and module names, have been removed from the output of TRCSESS. Unless a meaningful file name is used, it is not possible to tell how the file was processed. This also implies that it is impossible to drill down from module and action to a specific client identifier. Calling TRCSESS with the option `session`, leaves any other instrumentation entries intact. Specifying any other option removes all the instrumentation entries and merely leaves the timestamps which accompanied them in the resulting trace file. Since the session identification entry format is the only one that is identical in Oracle9*i* and Oracle10*g*, TRCSESS has limited backward compatibility to Oracle9*i* trace files. So far, everything has worked as one might expect. The next section addresses pitfalls of using TRCSESS in a Shared Server environment.

TRCSESS and Shared Server

According to the documentation, TRCSESS caters for Shared Server environments (*Oracle Database Performance Tuning Guide 10g Release 2*, page 20–6). However, there is a chance of incorrect results when using TRCSESS in a Shared Server environment with any option apart from session. When a shared server process begins servicing a session, which has SQL trace enabled, it only emits the session identifier (V$SESSION.SID) and session serial number (V$SESSION.SERIAL#). Any other instrumentation entries are not written to the trace file repeatedly. The current implementations of TRCSESS (releases 10.2.0.3 and 11.1.0.6) apparently do not keep track of which instrumentation settings were made by a session. Instead, TRCSESS includes trace file sections from other sessions in the output, merely because it does not encounter a new value for service name, module, action, or client identifier. In order to work properly, TRCSESS would need to see entries for service name, module, action, and client identifier each time a shared server process services a new session. But since these entries are written only once, the results obtained with TRCSESS may be incorrect. The test case below illustrates this. If Shared Server is not enabled in your test environment, then you may enable it like this:

```
SQL> ALTER SYSTEM SET shared_servers=1;
System altered.
SQL> ALTER SYSTEM SET dispatchers='(PROTOCOL=TCP)(DISPATCHERS=1)';
System altered.
```

By using a single shared server process, I can make sure that several sessions will be present in the same trace file. Next, logged in as a DBA, I enable tracing by service name, module, and action using DBMS_MONITOR:

```
SQL> EXEC dbms_monitor.serv_mod_act_trace_enable('TEN.oradbpro.com', 'mod', 'act');
SQL> SELECT trace_type, primary_id, qualifier_id1, qualifier_id2, instance_name
FROM dba_enabled_traces;
TRACE_TYPE           PRIMARY_ID        QUALIFIER_ID1 QUALIFIER_ID2 INSTANCE_NAME
-------------------- ----------------- ------------- ------------- -------------
SERVICE_MODULE_ACTION TEN.oradbpro.com mod           act
```

For the remainder of the test I need two sessions, with SQL trace enabled in both. The first session enables SQL trace manually:

```
$ sqlplus ndebes/secret@ten.oradbpro.com
SQL> ALTER SESSION SET sql_trace=true;
Session altered.
```

The second session uses the instance service specified with DBMS_MONITOR above and also sets module and action to the values used in the call to DBMS_MONITOR.SERV_MOD_ACT_TRACE_ENABLE. This enables SQL_TRACE. In the code below, I have changed the SQL*Plus setting for SQLPROMPT, such that the reader can easily recognize which session executes what.

```
$ sqlplus ndebes/secret@ten.oradbpro.com
SQL> SET SQLPROMPT "MOD_ACT> "
MOD_ACT> exec dbms_application_info.set_module('mod','act');
MOD_ACT> SELECT server, service_name, module, action
FROM v$session WHERE sid=userenv('SID');
```

```
SERVER       SERVICE_NAME     MODULE      ACTION
---------    ---------------- ----------  -------
SHARED       TEN.oradbpro.com mod            act
MOD_ACT> SELECT 'mod_act' AS string FROM dual;
STRING
-------
mod_act
```

Back to the first session. I select a string literal from DUAL. This serves the purpose of including a unique string in the trace file, which may be searched for later.

```
SQL> SELECT 'not instrumented' AS string FROM dual;
STRING
----------------
not instrumented
SQL> ALTER SESSION SET sql_trace=false;
Session altered.
```

SQL trace in the first session is switched off now. Back to session 2. In order to delimit the trace file section for extraction with TRCSESS and to switch off tracing, this session sets module and action to empty strings:

```
MOD_ACT> exec dbms_application_info.set_module('','');
```

You may now go to the directory specified with the parameter BACKGROUND_DUMP_DEST[1] and run TRCSESS:

```
$ trcsess output=mod_act.trc module=mod action=act ten1_s000_8558.trc
$ grep "not instrumented" mod_act.trc
SELECT 'not instrumented' AS string FROM dual
```

The output file created by TRCSESS includes the SELECT of the string literal by session 1, although session 1 did not set module and action to the option values passed to TRCSESS. This defect applies to TRCSESS releases 10.2 and 11.1. As stated earlier, the problem is that instrumentation entries are not written again when a shared server process services another session. Below is an excerpt of a shared server process' trace file that confirms this (all instrumentation entries are included):

```
 1 *** ACTION NAME:(act) 2007-09-06 20:23:52.514
 2 *** MODULE NAME:(mod) 2007-09-06 20:23:52.514
 3 *** SERVICE NAME:(TEN.oradbpro.com) 2007-09-06 20:23:52.514
 4 *** SESSION ID:(133.39) 2007-09-06 20:23:52.514
 5 =====================
 6 PARSING IN CURSOR #7 len=59 dep=0 uid=34 oct=47 lid=34 tim=1161233430189798
hv=919966564 ad='22c5ec10'
 7 BEGIN dbms_application_info.set_module('mod','act'); END;
 8 END OF STMT
 9 …
10 *** SESSION ID:(146.361) 2007-09-06 20:26:18.442
11 …
12 *** SESSION ID:(133.39) 2007-09-06 20:26:48.229
13 …
14 *** SESSION ID:(146.361) 2007-09-06 20:27:02.759
15 =====================
16 PARSING IN CURSOR #7 len=45 dep=0 uid=34 oct=3 lid=34 tim=1161233615975704
hv=2134668354 ad='2527ef28'
17 SELECT 'not instrumented' AS string FROM dual
18 …
19 *** SESSION ID:(133.39) 2007-09-06 20:27:27.502
20 …
21 PARSING IN CURSOR #2 len=53 dep=0 uid=34 oct=47 lid=34 tim=1161233640139316
hv=3853446089 ad='22c484d4'
```

---

1. The session level parameter TRACE_FILE_IDENTIFIER, which makes it easier to identify trace files, merely applies to dedicated server processes. These include the parameter's value in the trace file name. Shared server processes ignore this parameter.

```
22 BEGIN dbms_application_info.set_module('',''); END;
23 END OF STMT
24 PARSE #2:c=0,e=2,p=0,cr=0,cu=0,mis=0,r=0,dep=0,og=1,tim=1161233640139316
25 *** ACTION NAME:() 2007-09-06 20:27:27.503
26 *** MODULE NAME:() 2007-09-06 20:27:27.503
```

Lines 1 to 2 contain the module and action emitted due to the second session's call to DBMS_APPLICATION_INFO. Lines 10 to 14 show that the shared server process intermittently serviced another session with SID=146 and SERIAL#=361. Line 17 contains the string literal used to mark the SELECT executed by the first session, which was not instrumented. Lines 25 to 26 mark the end of the trace file section that pertains to the module "mod" and the action "act". At this point, the module and action names no longer matched the settings in DBA_ENABLED_TRACES made with DBMS_MONITOR, hence tracing in session 2 was switched off. In other words, end to end tracing noted the new values for module and action and then switched off SQL trace[1]. Since there are no entries for module and action between lines 10 and 19, TRCSESS included all the trace file entries between these lines, although some of them belong to a different session.

A correct implementation of TRCSESS would memorize the instrumentation settings for each combination of SID and SERIAL# and use them to omit or include the trace file section that follows a line with a new value for SID and SERIAL#. This approach may be used as a workaround. Look for the SESSION ID entry next to the module and action that we are interested in. Line 4 contains the SID and SERIAL# (133.39) that we need to pass to TRCSESS to get a correctly processed output file. If tracing had been enabled before module and action were set, you would need to look for the SESSION ID entry preceding the ACTION NAME or MODULE NAME entry. Instead of passing module and action to TRCSESS, we now pass the SID and SERIAL# that we identified in the trace file:

```
$ trcsess output=session_133_39.trc session=133.39 ten1_s000_8558.trc
$ grep "not instrumented" session_133_29.trc
```

This time the string literal used to mark the first session is not found in the output file. This proves that TRCSESS is able to process the shared server process' input trace file correctly, as long as the option session is used.

Instrumentation and the Program Call Stack

The examples we have looked at so far are highly simplified. A real application has many routines, which call each other. The called routine does not normally know which routine it was called by and it may not always be called by the same routine. To keep track of the program call stack, each routine needs to push the current instrumentation settings on to a stack before overwriting them with its own settings. On exit from the routine, the previous settings may be fetched from the stack (pop) and restored. Care must be taken that the pop operation is also performed upon abnormal exit from a routine due to an exception or error. As far as I know, such a stack was first implemented in PL/SQL by the Hotsos ORACLE instrumentation library (ILO)[2].

Figure 10 illustrates how routines in an application call each other. Execution begins in routine A at t_1. Instrumentation settings of routine A are in effect at this point. At time t_2, routine A calls routine B. To preserve the instrumentation settings of routine A, routine B pushes them onto a stack and then puts its own settings into effect. At t_3, routine B calls routine C, which in turn saves instrumentation settings from routine B on the stack before overwriting them. At t_4, the application exits routine C, which restores the instrumentation settings of routine B by popping them off the stack, just prior to exiting. The process goes on until the program exits from routine A at some point after t_7. The axis on the right indicates which routine is executing at a certain point in time. If this approach is adhered to throughout the code path of an application, it is be possible to find out how much time is spent in each module by using DBMS_MONITOR and V$SERV_MOD_ACT_STATS. Statistics provided by the view V$SERV_MOD_ACT_STATS include "DB time", "DB CPU", "physical reads", "physical writes", "cluster wait time", "concurrency wait time", "application wait time" and "user I/O wait time".

---

1. A dedicated server process servicing an application instrumented with JDBC end to end metrics switches off SQL trace before emitting the new values for module and action that cause end to end tracing to disable SQL trace. Since a dedicated server process, re–emits module, action and client identifier each time SQL trace is enabled, this will not lead to incorrect results.

2. The Hotsos ILO library is free software and may be downloaded from http://sourceforge.net/projects/hotsos-ilo.

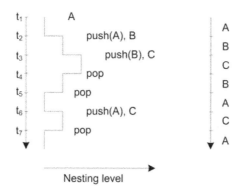

Figure 10: Program Call Stack and Instrumentation

Source Code Depot

Table 41: Application Instrumentation Source Code Depot

File Name	Functionality
`ApplicationInstrumentation.class`	Java program compiled from source file `ApplicationInstrumentation.java`
`ApplicationInstrumentation.java`	Java source file, which illustrates Oracle10*g* JDBC end to end metrics
`JdbcInstrumentationOracle9i.class`	Java program compiled from source file `JdbcInstrumentationOracle9i.java`
`JdbcInstrumentationOracle9i.java`	Java source file, which demonstrates instrumentation with PL/SQL
`rsrc_mgr.sql`	Anonymous PL/SQL block for setting up resource manager consumer group mapping by service, module, and action

Part VIII

Performance

Chapter 24

Extended SQL Trace File Format Reference

Status: The SQL trace file format is undocumented, even though the utilities TKPROF and TRCSESS are based on the analysis of SQL trace files.

Benefit: Understanding the format of extended SQL trace files is an essential skill for any DBA who is confronted with performance problems or troubleshooting tasks. Since formatting trace files with TKPROF obscures important information, such as statement hash values, timestamps, dependency levels, and SQL identifiers (emitted by Oracle11g), it is often mandatory to read and understand the trace files themselves.

Introduction to Extended SQL Trace Files

Extended SQL trace files are by and large a statement by statement account of SQL and PL/SQL executed by a database client[1]. Entries found in such files fall into four major categories:

- database calls (parse, execute, and fetch)
- wait events
- bind variable values
- miscellaneous (timestamps, session, module, action, and client identification)

Database calls, session identification, and other details from category miscellaneous are logged when tracing is enabled at the lowest level 1, e.g. with ALTER SESSION SET SQL_TRACE=TRUE, whereas recording of wait events and

---

1. Background processes may be traced too, but they are normally not responsible for performance problems.

bind variable values may be enabled independently. How to obtain trace files at various levels of detail is the topic of Chapter 28. The trace levels and the type of trace file entries they enable are summarized in Table 42.

Table 42: SQL Trace Levels

SQL Trace Level	Database Calls	Bind Variable Values	Wait Events
1	yes	no	no
4	yes	yes	no
8	yes	no	yes
12	yes	yes	yes

Sometimes extended SQL trace files are referred to as raw SQL trace files. Both terms are indeed synonymous. Since there is nothing particularly raw about the files—they are perfectly human readable—I have decided not to use the adjective raw and will stick with the term extended SQL trace file or simply trace file for the sake of conciseness.

SQL and PL/SQL Statements

The term cursor is often used in conjunction with SELECT statements and the iterative fetching of rows returned by queries. However, the ORACLE DBMS uses cursors to execute any SQL or PL/SQL statement, not just SELECT statements. SQL and PL/SQL statements in a trace file are identified by their cursor number. Cursor numbers for SQL statements sent by clients start at 1. The cursor number is the figure behind the pound sign (#) in entries such as PARSING IN CURSOR #1, PARSE #1, EXEC #1, FETCH #1, WAIT #1, and STAT #1. These examples all refer to the same cursor number 1. Each additional SQL statement run by the client receives another cursor number, unless reuse of a cursor number is taking place after the cursor has been closed. Entries relating to the same statement are interrelated through the cursor number.

Not all operations executed are assigned a proper cursor number. One notable exception is the use of large objects (LOBs) through Oracle Call Interface (OCI). When working with LOBs, you may see cursor number 0 or cursor numbers for which a parse call is missing, although tracing was switched on right after connecting. This does not apply to the PL/SQL LOB interface DBMS_LOB.

Cursor numbers may be reused within a single database session. When the client closes a cursor, the DBMS writes STAT entries, which represent the execution plan, into the trace file. At this stage, the cursor number can be reused for a different SQL statement. The SQL statement text for a certain cursor is printed after the first PARSING IN CURSOR #n entry above any EXEC #n, FETCH #n, WAIT #n, or STAT #n entries with the same cursor number n.

Dependency Level

Anyone who has worked with the TKPROF utility is presumably familiar with the concept of recursive and internal SQL statements. SQL Statements sent by a database client are executed at dependency level 0. Should a SQL statement fire other statements, such as an INSERT statement, which fires the execution of an insert trigger, then these other statements would be executed at dependency level 1. A trigger body may then execute additional statements, which may cause recursive SQL at the next higher dependency level. Below is an example of an INSERT statement executed at dependency level 0. The INSERT statement fires a trigger. Access to a sequence in the trigger body is at dependency level 1. Note how the execution of the top level INSERT statement (EXEC #3) is written to the trace file after the execution of the dependent SELECT from the sequence has completed (EXEC #2):

```
PARSING IN CURSOR #3 len=78 dep=0 uid=61 oct=2 lid=61 tim=771237502562 hv=3259110965
ad='6c5f86dc'
INSERT INTO customer(name, phone) VALUES (:name, :phone) RETURNING id INTO :id
END OF STMT
PARSE #3:c=0,e=1314,p=0,cr=0,cu=0,mis=1,r=0,dep=0,og=1,tim=771237502553
=====================
PARSING IN CURSOR #2 len=40 dep=1 uid=61 oct=3 lid=61 tim=771237506650 hv=1168215557
ad='6c686178'
SELECT CUSTOMER_ID_SEQ.NEXTVAL FROM DUAL
```

```
END OF STMT
PARSE #2:c=0,e=1610,p=0,cr=0,cu=0,mis=1,r=0,dep=1,og=1,tim=771237506643
EXEC #2:c=0,e=57,p=0,cr=0,cu=0,mis=0,r=0,dep=1,og=1,tim=771237507496
FETCH #2:c=0,e=54,p=0,cr=0,cu=0,mis=0,r=1,dep=1,og=1,tim=771237507740
EXEC #3:c=0,e=4584,p=0,cr=1,cu=3,mis=1,r=1,dep=0,og=1,tim=771237508046
```

When a client runs an anonymous PL/SQL block, the block itself is executed at dependency level 0, but the statements inside the block will have dependency level 1. Another example is auditing entries inserted into table SYS.AUD$. These are executed at one dependency level higher than the statement that triggered the auditing.

Recursive parse, execute, and fetch operations are listed before the execution of the statement that triggered the recursive operations. Statistics for SQL statements executed at dependency level 0 contain the cost of dependent statements in terms of CPU time, elapsed time, consistent reads, etc. This must be taken into consideration to avoid double counting when evaluating SQL trace files.

Database Calls

The database call category consists of the three subcategories parsing, execution, and fetching. Note that these entries correspond with the three stages of running dynamic SQL with the package DBMS_SQL by calling the package subroutines DBMS_SQL.PARSE, DBMS_SQL.EXECUTE, and DBMS_SQL.FETCH_ROWS.

Among other metrics, database call entries represent the CPU and wall clock time (elapsed time) a server process spends inside the ORACLE kernel on behalf of a database client. The aggregated CPU and wall clock times from database calls in a trace file are closely related to the session level statistics DB CPU and DB time in the dynamic performance view V$SESS_TIME_MODEL, which is available in Oracle10g and subsequent releases.

Parsing

Parsing involves syntactic and semantic analysis of SQL statements as well as determining a well suited execution plan. Since this may be a costly operation, the ORACLE DBMS has the capacity to cache the results of parse calls in the so called library cache within the System Global Area (SGA) for reuse by other statements that use the same SQL statement text.

The use of bind variables in SQL statements is crucial for the reuse of cached statements. Failure to use bind variables causes increased parse CPU consumption, contention for the library cache, excessive communication round–trips between client and server due to repeated parse calls of non–reusable statements with literals, and difficulties in diagnosing performance problems due to the inability of the TKPROF utility to aggregate statements, which are identical apart from literals. I recommend reading the section *Top Ten Mistakes Found in Oracle Systems* on page 3–4 of *Oracle Database Performance Tuning Guide 10g Release 2* before beginning design and coding of an application. While bind variables are mandatory to achieve scalability in high volume transaction processing (OLTP), literals are usually preferred in data warehousing applications to provide the CBO with as much information as possible and to avoid the unpredictability inherent in bind variable peeking. The CBO looks at bind variable values when it first encounters a statement, but not on subsequent executions of the same statement, such that the plan chosen may be optimal for the initial execution, but inappropriate for subsequent executions. This functionality is called bind variable peeking. It is enabled by default with the hidden parameter setting _OPTIM_PEEK_USER_BINDS=TRUE.

Parsing is usually represented by two adjacent entries in the trace file. The first is PARSING IN CURSOR, and the second is PARSE. The minimum SQL trace level for enabling parse related entries is 1. Here's an example of a PARSING IN CURSOR followed by a PARSE from an Oracle10g trace file:

```
PARSING IN CURSOR #3 len=92 dep=0 uid=30 oct=2 lid=30 tim=81592095533 hv=1369934057
ad='66efcb10'
INSERT INTO poem (author, text) VALUES(:author, empty_clob())
    RETURNING text INTO :lob_loc
END OF STMT
PARSE #3:c=0,e=412,p=0,cr=0,cu=0,mis=1,r=0,dep=0,og=1,tim=81592095522
```

Parameters associated with the PARSING IN CURSOR entry are explained in Table 43.

PARSING IN CURSOR Entry Format

Caching of SQL statements in the shared pool is based on a hash value that is derived from the SQL or PL/SQL statement text. Changes in optimizer settings have no effect on the hash value, whereas slight changes to the statement text such as insertion of a blank or tab character do. Rarely, two statements with different statements texts may have the same hash value.

The hash value may be retrieved from many V$ views such as VSQL, VSQLTEXT, V$SQLAREA, V$OPEN_CURSOR, and V$SESSION. It remains constant across instance startups, but might change after an upgrade to a new release. In fact, the algorithm for computing hash values has changed in Oracle10g. The hash value compatible with previous releases is available in the column OLD_HASH_VALUE of the views V$SQL and V$SQLAREA. Merely the hash value is emitted to trace files. Since Statspack stuck with the "old school" hash value but merely the new hash value is emitted to trace files, this adds the complexity of translating from the new hash value to the old hash value when searching a Statspack repository for information pertinent to statements in a trace file (more on this in Chapter 25).

Oracle10g introduced the new column SQL_ID to some of the aforementioned V$ views. The value of this new column is not written to SQL trace files in releases prior to Oracle11g, but is used in Active Workload Repository reports, such that translation from the new hash value (column HASH_VALUE) to the SQL_ID may be required when looking up information on a statement in AWR. For cached SQL statements, translation among SQL_ID, HASH_VALUE, and OLD_HASH_VALUE may be performed using V$SQL. For statements that are no longer cached, but were captured by a Statspack snapshot, STATS$SQL_SUMMARY serves as a translation table (the Rosetta stone of SQL statement identifiers). AWR has no facility for translating the hash value found in trace files to the corresponding SQL_ID. In releases prior to Oracle11g, matching the statement text between both types of capture is the only time consuming approach for extracting historical information on a statement, such as past execution time and plan, from AWR (see Chapter 26). Considering that Statspack requires no extra license and includes session level capture and reporting (watch out for bug 5145816; see Table 60 on page 273), this shortcoming of AWR might be another reason for favoring Statspack.

Oracle11g is the first DBMS release that emits the SQL identifier (V$SQL.SQL_ID) in addition to the hash value to trace files. Hence the statement matching issue between extended SQL trace and AWR is a thing of the past for users of Oracle11g. Below is an example of an Oracle11g PARSING IN CURSOR entry:

```
PARSING IN CURSOR #3 len=116 dep=0 uid=32 oct=2 lid=32 tim=15545747608 hv=1256130531
ad='6ab5ff8c' sqlid='b85s0yd5dy1z3'
INSERT INTO customer(id, name, phone) VALUES (customer_id_seq.nextval, :name, :phone)
RETURNING id INTO :id
END OF STMT
```

Table 43: PARSING IN CURSOR Parameters

Parameter	Meaning
len	Length of the SQL statement text in bytes
dep	Dependency level
uid	Parsing user identity; corresponds to ALL_USERS.USER_ID and V$SQL.PARSING_USER_ID
oct	ORACLE command type; corresponds to V$SQL.COMMAND_TYPE and V$SESSION.COMMAND
lid	Parsing schema identity; corresponds to ALL_USERS.USER_ID and V$SQL.PARSING_SCHEMA_ID; may differ from uid (see Chapter 14 on ALTER SESSION SET CURRENT_SCHEMA)
tim	Timestamp in microseconds; often slightly earlier than the value of tim in the associated PARSE entry
hv	Hash value; corresponds to V$SQL.HASH_VALUE
ad	Address; corresponds to V$SQL.ADDRESS
sqlid	SQL identifier; corresponds to V$SQL.SQL_ID (emitted by Oracle11g)

The SQL statement parsed is printed on a new line after the line starting with the string PARSING IN CURSOR. A line starting with END OF STMT marks the end of the SQL statement. The mapping from the numeric command type (parameter oct) to the command name is available by running SELECT action, name FROM audit_actions. Table

44 contains the most common command types plus some additional command types that may be used by applications. Please note that these numeric command types do not correspond with Oracle Call Interface SQL command codes (*Oracle Call Interface Programmer's Guide 10g Release 2, Appendix A*).

Table 44: SQL and PL/SQL Command Types

Numeric Command Type	SQL or PL/SQL Command
2	INSERT
3	SELECT
6	UPDATE
7	DELETE
26	LOCK TABLE
44	COMMIT
45	ROLLBACK
46	SAVEPOINT
47	PL/SQL block
48	SET TRANSACTION
55	SET ROLE
90	SET CONSTRAINTS
170	CALL
189	MERGE

PARSE Entry Format

Among other metrics, PARSE entries represent CPU and wall clock time consumed by parse operations. By looking at the parameter mis (library cache miss) it is possible to derive the library cache hit ratio from trace files. A low hit ratio usually indicates that the application does not use bind variables. Details on the parameters of the PARSE entry are in Table 45.

Table 45: PARSE Parameters

Parameter	Meaning
c	CPU consumption
e	Elapsed time
p	Physical reads
cr	Consistent reads
cu	Current blocks processed
mis	Cursor misses, 0=soft parse, i.e. statement found in library cache, 1=hard parse, i.e. statement not found
r	Rows processed
dep	Dependency level
og	Optimizer goal, 1=ALL_ROWS, 2=FIRST_ROWS, 3=RULE, 4=CHOOSE; Oracle9i default is CHOOSE; Oracle10g and Oracle11g default is ALL_ROWS
tim	Timestamp in microseconds

The following SELECT statement confirms the links between trace file entries and data dictionary views:

```
SQL> SELECT s.sql_text, u1.username user_name, u2.username schema_name, optimizer_mode
FROM v$sql s, all_users u1, all_users u2
WHERE hash_value='1369934057'
AND address=upper('66efcb10')
AND u1.user_id=s.parsing_user_id
AND u2.user_id=s.parsing_schema_id;
SQL_TEXT                             USER_NAME  SCHEMA_NAME  OPTIMIZER_MODE
-------------------------------- --------- ----------- --------------
INSERT INTO poem (author, text)  NDEBES     NDEBES       ALL_ROWS
VALUES(:author, empty_clob())
RETURNING text INTO :lob_loc
```

PARSE #*n* may be missing, such that PARSING IN CURSOR #*n* is followed directly by EXEC #*n*, such as in this trace file excerpt from a call to the $dbh->do function of the Perl DBI (more on Perl DBI in Chapter 22):

```
PARSING IN CURSOR #4 len=69 dep=0 uid=30 oct=42 lid=30 tim=81591952901 hv=3164292706
ad='67339f7c'
alter session set events '10046 trace name context forever, level 12'
END OF STMT
EXEC #4:c=0,e=68910,p=0,cr=0,cu=0,mis=1,r=0,dep=0,og=1,tim=81591952889
```

PARSE ERROR Entry Format

Failing parse calls due to incorrect syntax or insufficient privileges result in errors such as "ORA-00942: table or view does not exist" or "ORA-00904: invalid identifier". Such errors are marked by PARSE ERROR entries. Here's an example of a parse error due to an incorrectly spelled column name:

```
PARSING IN CURSOR #6 len=93 dep=0 uid=30 oct=2 lid=30 tim=170048888062 hv=986445513
ad='676bb350'
INSERT INTO poem (author, txt) VALUES(:author, empty_clob()) RETURNING ROWID INTO
:row_id
END OF STMT
PARSE #6:c=0,e=457,p=0,cr=0,cu=0,mis=1,r=0,dep=0,og=1,tim=170048888050
====================
PARSING IN CURSOR #7 len=198 dep=1 uid=0 oct=3 lid=0 tim=170048915712 hv=4125641360
ad='67b0c8d4'
...
PARSE ERROR #6:len=93 dep=0 uid=30 oct=2 lid=30 tim=170048972426 err=904
INSERT INTO poem (author, txt) VALUES(:author, empty_clob()) RETURNING ROWID INTO
:row_id
```

As in the example above, the DBMS may need to run recursive SQL statements (dep=1) to process the parse call in order to load the dictionary cache. Abbreviations used are analogous to PARSE entries, except for the last field err, which indicates the ORACLE error number. On UNIX systems, the error message text can be retrieved by calling oerr ora *error_number* from a shell command line. Where appropriate, the output of oerr also includes a probable cause of the error and suggests an action. The same information is available by looking up the error number in the *Oracle Database Error Messages* manual.

```
$ oerr ora 942
00942, 00000, "table or view does not exist"
// *Cause:
// *Action:
```

EXEC Entry Format

EXEC entries, have the same format as PARSE entries. EXEC is short for execution. The minimum SQL trace level for enabling EXEC entries is 1. INSERT, UPDATE, DELETE, MERGE, PL/SQL, and DDL operations all have an execution stage, but no fetch stage. Of course, recursive fetches at a higher dependency level may occur on behalf of these operations. When formatting a trace file containing a large number of these operations with TKPROF, you might want to sort the statements with the option exeela (execute elapsed time). Execute elapsed time includes the CPU time consumed by EXEC entries, though occasionally higher values of CPU than elapsed time are reported.

FETCH Entry Format

FETCH entries adhere to the same format as PARSE and EXEC entries. The minimum SQL trace level for enabling FETCH entries is 1. When formatting a trace file where fetching contributes most to elapsed time with TKPROF, you might want to sort the statements with the option fchela (fetch elapsed time). Fetch elapsed time includes fetch CPU time.

COMMIT and ROLLBACK

The ORACLE DBMS does not require clients to explicitly start a transaction. The DBMS automatically opens a transaction as soon as the first data item is modified or a distributed operation, such as a SELECT from a table via a database link is performed. The latter operation takes a TX and a DX enqueue, which are released when COMMIT is issued. Transaction boundaries in a trace file are marked by XCTEND entries. The minimum SQL trace level for enabling XCTEND entries is 1. Their format is:

```
XCTEND rlbk=[0-1], rd_only=[0-1]
```

Parameters used in XCTEND entries are explained in Table 46.

Table 46: XCTEND Parameters

Parameter	Meaning
rlbk	Short for rollback, rlbk=0: COMMIT, rlbk=1: ROLLBACK
rd_only	Read only transaction, rd_only=0: read/write operations have occurred, rd_only=1: read only—no data changed

The two parameters of the XCTEND entry allow four combinations. These are summarized in Table 47. Note that rd_only=1 does not imply that the session previously issued the statement SET TRANSACTION READ ONLY.

Table 47: XCTEND Parameter Combinations

XCTEND Parameters	Client Operation	Example
rlbk=0, rd_only=1	COMMIT, no data modified	COMMIT after SELECT from remote table to release locks
rlbk=0, rd_only=0	COMMIT, data modified	COMMIT after INSERT/UPDATE/DELETE of one or more rows
rlbk=1, rd_only=1	ROLLBACK, no data modified	ROLLBACK after SELECT from local tables, e.g. to increment the snapshot SCN after SET TRANSACTION READ ONLY
rlbk=1, rd_only=0	ROLLBACK, data modified	ROLLBACK after changing data, e.g. through a MERGE statement

UNMAP

When interrupting ongoing disk sorts with Ctrl+C in Oracle10g, UNMAP entries are written to the trace file irrespective of the setting of the parameter WORKAREA_SIZE_POLICY. These are apparently related to cleanup of the sort segment observed in V$SORT_USAGE. In all my testing with Oracle9i and Oracle10g I have never seen an UNMAP entry when a SELECT statement that triggered a disk sort ran to completion. My conclusion is that UNMAP entries are not part of normal operations and do not merit further investigation. Here's an example:

```
FETCH
#3:c=1972837,e=30633987,p=4725,cr=4405,cu=25,mis=0,r=1,dep=0,og=1,tim=185499193369
FETCH #3:c=0,e=3113,p=0,cr=0,cu=0,mis=0,r=15,dep=0,og=1,tim=185499197879
...
UNMAP #3:c=0,e=136661,p=0,cr=0,cu=0,mis=0,r=0,dep=0,og=0,tim=185552120691
```

UNMAP parameters are the same as those of PARSE entries.

Execution Plans, Statistics, and the STAT Entry Format

Execution plans and statistics are reported by STAT entries. Each line of a group of STAT entries represents a row source that contributed to the result of a statement. The term row source designates either data retrieved from a table or index or an intermediate result within a larger execution plan. Since no more than two tables can be joined simultaneously, a three way join includes a row source that is the intermediate result of joining the other two tables. The minimum SQL trace level for enabling STAT entries is 1. STAT entry parameters are summarized in Table 48.

Table 48: STAT Parameters

Parameter	Meaning
id	Identifier, which denotes the order of row sources in the execution plan; normally id=1 on the first STAT line of an execution plan
cnt	Number of rows processed
pid	Parent identifier; normally pid=0 on the first STAT line of an execution plan. TKPROF and ESQL-TRCPROF use id and pid to generate properly indented execution plans with dependent steps of a plan indented by one more level than their parent steps.
pos	Position of a step within the parent step
obj	Object identifier; corresponds to ALL_OBJECTS.OBJECT_ID and V$SQL_PLAN.OBJECT#
op	Row source operation performed, such as table access, index scan, sort, union, etc.; corresponds to V$SQL_PLAN.OPERATION. In Oracle10g, op contains actual statement execution metrics in parentheses after the row source information.

STAT Entry Format in Oracle9i

The only difference between Oracle9i and Oracle10g STAT entries is the amount of information conveyed with the parameter op. The inclusion of actual execution metrics in op is not implemented in Oracle9i. Below is an example of a hash join, which is the parent row source of two full table scans.

```
STAT #3 id=1 cnt=106 pid=0 pos=1 obj=0 op='SORT ORDER BY '
STAT #3 id=2 cnt=106 pid=1 pos=1 obj=0 op='HASH JOIN    '
STAT #3 id=3 cnt=27 pid=2 pos=1 obj=6764 op='TABLE ACCESS FULL DEPARTMENTS '
STAT #3 id=4 cnt=107 pid=2 pos=2 obj=6769 op='TABLE ACCESS FULL EMPLOYEES '
```

The above STAT entries would be formatted by TKPROF as below:

```
Rows      Row Source Operation
-------   ------------------------------
    106   SORT ORDER BY
    106   HASH JOIN
     27    TABLE ACCESS FULL DEPARTMENTS
    107    TABLE ACCESS FULL EMPLOYEES
```

STAT Entry Format in Oracle10g and Oracle11g

In Oracle10g and Oracle11g, as opposed to Oracle9i, STAT entries are only written when TIMED_STATISTICS=TRUE in addition to a SQL trace level of at least 1. Note that setting STATISTICS_LEVEL=BASIC (default is TYPICAL) in Oracle10g and Oracle11g implicitly sets TIMED_STATISTICS=FALSE. This behavior may be overridden by explicitly setting TIMED_STATISTICS=TRUE. Except for some additional statistics in parentheses at the end of the operation (bold below), STAT entries in Oracle9i and subsequent releases have the same format:

```
STAT #4 id=3 cnt=107 pid=2 pos=1 obj=16496 op='TABLE ACCESS FULL EMPLOYEES (cr=7 pr=0
pw=0 time=725 us)'
```

The additional information, which is useful for identifying expensive row sources in the execution plan, depends on the DBMS release and is summarized in Table 49. Oracle11*g* STAT entries have the most verbose format.

Table 49: STAT Execution Statistics

Parameter	Meaning
cr	Consistent reads
pr	Physical reads
pw	Physical writes
time	Estimated elapsed time in microseconds
cost	Cost of the execution plan calculated by CBO (requires Oracle11*g*)
size	Estimated data volume in bytes (requires Oracle11*g*); the estimate is based on object statistics (DBA_TABLES, etc.); information from the segment header is used, if object statistics are not available
card	Estimated cardinality, i.e. number of rows processed (requires Oracle11*g*); the estimate is based on object statistics

The example below (trace file excerpt) shows how the execution plan of a two–way join is represented by STAT entries in an Oracle10*g* trace file.

```
PARSING IN CURSOR #4 len=140 dep=0 uid=5 oct=3 lid=5 tim=105385553438 hv=782962817
ad='670e3cf4'
SELECT e.last_name, e.first_name, d.department_name
FROM hr.employees e, hr.departments d
WHERE e.department_id=d.department_id
ORDER BY 1, 2
END OF STMT
...
STAT #4 id=1 cnt=106 pid=0 pos=1 obj=0 op='SORT ORDER BY (cr=115 pr=0 pw=0 time=5720
us)'
STAT #4 id=2 cnt=106 pid=1 pos=1 obj=0 op='NESTED LOOPS  (cr=115 pr=0 pw=0 time=7302
us)'
STAT #4 id=3 cnt=107 pid=2 pos=1 obj=16496 op='TABLE ACCESS FULL EMPLOYEES (cr=7 pr=0
pw=0 time=725 us)'
STAT #4 id=4 cnt=106 pid=2 pos=2 obj=16491 op='TABLE ACCESS BY INDEX ROWID DEPARTMENTS
(cr=108 pr=0 pw=0 time=4336 us)'
STAT #4 id=5 cnt=106 pid=4 pos=1 obj=16492 op='INDEX UNIQUE SCAN DEPT_ID_PK (cr=2 pr=0
pw=0 time=1687 us)'
```

When formatting execution plans, TKPROF preserves the additional information provided by the parameter op:

```
Rows     Row Source Operation
-------  ---------------------------------------------------
    106  NESTED LOOPS  (cr=223 pr=0 pw=0 time=166 us)
    107   TABLE ACCESS FULL EMPLOYEES (cr=11 pr=0 pw=0 time=1568 us)
    106   TABLE ACCESS BY INDEX ROWID DEPARTMENTS (cr=212 pr=0 pw=0 time=4747 us)
    106    INDEX UNIQUE SCAN DEPT_ID_PK (cr=106 pr=0 pw=0 time=2151 us)(object id 51906)
```

The trace file excerpt below shows the more verbose format of Oracle11*g*:

```
STAT #4 id=1 cnt=106 pid=0 pos=1 obj=0 op='MERGE JOIN  (cr=19 pr=0 pw=0 time=0 us cost=6
size=3604 card=106)'
STAT #4 id=2 cnt=27 pid=1 pos=1 obj=16967 op='TABLE ACCESS BY INDEX ROWID DEPARTMENTS
(cr=12 pr=0 pw=0 time=26 us cost=2 size=432 card=27)'
STAT #4 id=3 cnt=27 pid=2 pos=1 obj=16968 op='INDEX FULL SCAN DEPT_ID_PK (cr=6 pr=0
pw=0 time=11 us cost=1 size=0 card=27)'
```

```
STAT #4 id=4 cnt=106 pid=1 pos=2 obj=0 op='SORT JOIN (cr=7 pr=0 pw=0 time=24 us cost=4
size=1926 card=107)'
STAT #4 id=5 cnt=108 pid=4 pos=1 obj=16970 op='TABLE ACCESS FULL EMPLOYEES (cr=7 pr=0
pw=0 time=4 us cost=3 size=1926 card=107)'
```

Wait Events

Capturing wait events is essential for solving performance problems due to waiting for resources such as disk access, latches, locks, or inter–instance communication in RAC. Oracle10g is the first release that has a documented interface for tracing wait events—the PL/SQL package DBMS_MONITOR.

WAIT Entry Format

The minimum SQL trace level for enabling WAIT entries is 8. Never use a SQL trace level below 8 when investigating performance problems. Otherwise the contribution of wait events to response time will be unknown, thus preventing diagnosis of performance problems where waiting and not CPU consumption is the most important contribution to response time.

Each wait event is associated with up to three parameters that provide more detail on the event. Many wait events are documented in the *Oracle Database Reference* (e.g. *Appendix C* of *Oracle Database Reference 10g Release 2*). The full listing of wait events and their parameters is available by querying the view V$EVENT_NAME like this:

```
SQL> SELECT name, parameter1, parameter2, parameter3 FROM v$event_name ORDER BY 1;
```

Some example rows from the result of the query are shown below:

NAME	PARAMETER1	PARAMETER2	PARAMETER3
SQL*Net message from client	driver id	#bytes	
SQL*Net message from dblink	driver id	#bytes	
SQL*Net message to client	driver id	#bytes	
SQL*Net message to dblink	driver id	#bytes	
db file parallel write	requests	interrupt	timeout
db file scattered read	file#	block#	blocks
db file sequential read	file#	block#	blocks
direct path read	file number	first dba	block cnt
direct path write	file number	first dba	block cnt
enq: MR - contention	name|mode	0 or file #	type
enq: ST - contention	name|mode	0	0
enq: TM - contention	name|mode	object #	table/partition
enq: TX - allocate ITL entry	name|mode	usn<<16 | slot	sequence
enq: TX - contention	name|mode	usn<<16 | slot	sequence
enq: TX - index contention	name|mode	usn<<16 | slot	sequence
enq: TX - row lock contention	name|mode	usn<<16 | slot	sequence
enq: UL - contention	name|mode	id	0
enq: US - contention	name|mode	undo segment #	0
latch free	address	number	tries
latch: gcs resource hash	address	number	tries
latch: ges resource hash list	address	number	tries
latch: library cache	address	number	tries
latch: library cache lock	address	number	tries
latch: library cache pin	address	number	tries
latch: redo allocation	address	number	tries
latch: redo copy	address	number	tries
latch: shared pool	address	number	tries

Parameters of WAIT entries relate to data dictionary or V$ views. For example, the parameters "file#" and "file number" both correspond to V$DATAFILE.FILE#, the parameter "object#" refers to DBA_OBJECTS.OBJECT_ID, and the parameter "address" of latch waits corresponds to V$LATCH.ADDRESS. Since latch and enqueue wait event names are more specific in Oracle10g, the need to drill down to the referenced enqueue or latch through the parameters of a wait event has been greatly reduced compared to Oracle9i.

WAIT in Oracle9*i*

WAIT entry parameters in Oracle9*i* are called p1, p2, and p3 generically. The meaning of the parameters is not evident from their names as in Oracle10*g*. Instead, the meanings of the parameters must be derived from the wait event name using the documentation or V$EVENT_NAME. The parameters of Oracle9*i* WAIT entries are in Table 50.

Table 50: Oracle9*i* WAIT Parameters

Parameter	*Meaning*
ela	Elapsed time in microseconds (centiseconds in desupported releases such as Oracle8*i* and earlier).
p1	First parameter of the wait event. The meaning of the parameter is to be found in V$EVENT_NAME.PARAMETER1. The value corresponds to V$SESSION_WAIT.P1.
p2	Second parameter of the wait event, analogous to p1, i.e. look at V$EVENT_NAME.PARAMETER2 for the meaning of the parameter.
p3	Third parameter of the wait event, analogous to p1.

Below is an example WAIT entry due to a single block disk read associated with cursor 4:

```
WAIT #4: nam='db file sequential read' ela= 19045 p1=1 p2=19477 p3=1
```

In the above wait event, p1 is the data file number (V$DATAFILE.FILE#), p2 is the block within the data file, and p3 specifies the number of blocks read. As you will see shortly, wait entries in Oracle9*i* trace files lack the timestamp (tim) that Oracle10*g* wait entries have.

WAIT in Oracle10*g* and Oracle11*g*

Oracle10*g* has 872 wait events (Oracle11*g* has 959). This is partly due to the fact that the single wait event *enqueue* in Oracle9*i* has been replaced by 208 individual wait events for each kind of enqueue. Similarly, Oracle10*g* has 27 wait events for latches whereas Oracle9*i* has only two.

Oracle10*g* and Oracle11*g* wait entries have meaningful parameter names instead of the generic p1, p2, and p3 parameters in Oracle9*i*. A timestamp has also been added. Here's an example:

```
WAIT #3: nam='db file scattered read' ela= 22652 file#=4 block#=253 blocks=4 obj#=14996
tim=81592211996
```

A total of 276 different wait event parameters exist in Oracle10*g* (293 in Oracle11*g*). Of these, a significant portion has different spelling, but identical meaning, such as "retry count" and "retry_count". Another example is the parameters "obj#", "object #", and "object_id". The parameters may be retrieved by running the following query:

```
SQL> SELECT PARAMETER1
FROM v$event_name
UNION
SELECT PARAMETER2
FROM v$event_name
UNION
SELECT PARAMETER3
FROM v$event_name
ORDER BY 1;
```

Bind Variables

To obtain the maximum amount of diagnostic data, tracing of bind variables should be enabled. Details on bind variables include the data type and value of a bind variable. Without this information, it is impossible to find out whether an index was not used due to a mismatch between the data type of an indexed column and the bind variable data type, e.g. an indexed DATE column and a bind variable with type TIMESTAMP. A bind data type mismatch may also cause increased CPU usage due to conversion from one data type to another. Bind variable values may be used to tune queries under the exact same conditions that they were captured. Without bind variable values, example values for query tuning must be retrieved from the tables. This is a very tedious and time consuming process. Better to accept the additional file size and higher measurement intrusion incurred with bind variable tracing than waste time on finding sample values.

BINDS Entry Format

The minimum SQL trace level for enabling BINDS entries is 4. The structure of a BINDS entry consists of the word BINDS followed by the cursor number and a separate subsection (bind *n* or BIND #*n*) for each bind variable:

```
BINDS #m:
 <subsection 0>
  <details of bind variable 0>
 ...
 <subsection n>
  <details of bind variable n>
```

Bind variables are numbered from left to right within the statement text starting at zero. When associating bind variables with subsections, do not pay attention to numerals, which may be included in the name of a bind variable (e.g. :B1). As you will see in the examples that follow, the bind variable name :B<*n*+1> may appear before :B*n*, where *n* is an integer. This is indeed confusing. The correct association is formed by reading the statement text from left to right and top to bottom. Subsection 0 provides details on the first bind variable thus encountered, subsection 1 on the second, and so on.

Bind in Oracle9*i*

The following anonymous PL/SQL block will serve as an example for examining BINDS entries:

```
DECLARE
    sal number(8,2):=4999.99;
    dname varchar2(64):='Shipping';
    hired date:=to_date('31.12.1995','dd.mm.yyyy');
BEGIN
    FOR emp_rec IN ( SELECT e.last_name, e.first_name, e.salary, d.department_name
    FROM hr.employees e, hr.departments d
    WHERE e.department_id=d.department_id
    AND e.salary > sal
    AND e.hire_date > hired
    AND d.department_name=dname) LOOP
        null;
    END LOOP;
END;
/
```

Tracing this block at SQL trace level 4 or 12 yields the trace file entries including a BINDS section below:

```
PARSING IN CURSOR #2 len=209 dep=1 uid=0 oct=3 lid=0 tim=118435024029 hv=3341549851
ad='19cf2638'
SELECT e.last_name, e.first_name, e.salary, d.department_name
    FROM hr.employees e, hr.departments d
    WHERE e.department_id=d.department_id
    AND e.salary > :b3
    AND e.hire_date > :b2
    AND d.department_name=:b1
END OF STMT
PARSE #2:c=15625,e=75118,p=2,cr=150,cu=0,mis=1,r=0,dep=1,og=0,tim=118435024022
...
BINDS #2:
 bind 0: dty=2 mxl=22(21) mal=00 scl=00 pre=00 oacflg=03 oacfl2=1 size=64 offset=0
   bfp=05babee8 bln=22 avl=04 flg=05
   value=4999.99
 bind 1: dty=12 mxl=07(07) mal=00 scl=00 pre=00 oacflg=03 oacfl2=1 size=0 offset=24
   bfp=05babf00 bln=07 avl=07 flg=01
   value="12/31/1995 0:0:0"
 bind 2: dty=1 mxl=32(08) mal=00 scl=00 pre=00 oacflg=03 oacfl2=1 size=0 offset=32
```

```
bfp=05babf08 bln=32 avl=08 flg=01
value="Shipping"
```

Bind variable values are printed as strings, instead of an internal representation. Thus, it is easy to reproduce a traced statement by using the captured bind variable values. Subsection 0 (bind 0) is associated with bind variable :b3. Subsection 1 (bind 1) is associated with bind variable :b2. Oracle9*i* uses 14 parameters to convey detailed information on bind variables.

Table 51: Oracle9*i* BIND Parameters

Parameter	Meaning
dty	Data type code
mxl	Maximum length of the bind variable value (private maximum length in parentheses)
mal	Array length
scl	Scale
pre	Precision
oacflg	Special flag indicating bind options
oacflg2	Second part of oacflg
size	Amount of memory to be allocated for this chunk
offset	Offset into this chunk for this bind buffer
bfp	Bind address
bln	Bind buffer length
avl	Actual value length
flg	Bind status flag
value	Value of the bind variable

The *Oracle Database SQL Reference* manual contains a table for translating the numeric data type codes to the corresponding data type name. The table is in section *Oracle Built–in Datatypes* in Chapter 2 of the manual and lists 18 different type codes for the 21 data types implemented in Oracle9*i* (the national character set types NCHAR, NVARCHAR2 and NCLOB use the same type code as CHAR, VARCHAR2 and CLOB respectively). The most common data type codes and names are summarized in Table 52.

Table 52: Data Type Codes vs. Names

Data Type Code	Data Type Name
1	VARCHAR2, NVARCHAR2
2	NUMBER
12	DATE
96	CHAR, NCHAR
112	CLOB, NCLOB
113	BLOB
180	TIMESTAMP

The built–in SQL function DUMP (*expr* [, *format* [, *position* [, *length*]]]) may be used to display the data type code of a column along with the internal representation of the column's value. The first argument to DUMP is the format for displaying the internal representation. The formats supported are octal (*format*=8), decimal (default or *for-*

mat=10), hexadecimal (*format*=16), and individual single–byte characters (*format*=17). Information on the character set is included, if 1000 is added to one of the three aforementioned format settings (*format=format*+1000). When *position* and *length* are omitted, the entire internal representation is returned. Otherwise, merely the portion starting at offset *position* having *length* bytes is considered. Here's an example:

```
SQL> SELECT dump(employee_id, 16, 1, 1) empid_dmp, dump(last_name, 1017,1,2) name_dmp,
dump(hire_date,10,1,1) date_dmp
FROM hr.employees
WHERE rownum=1;
EMPID_DMP        NAME_DMP                                        DATE_DMP
---------------  ----------------------------------------------- -----------------
 Typ=2 Len=3: c2 Typ=1 Len=8 CharacterSet=WE8MSWIN1252: O,C Typ=12 Len=7: 119
```

As one might expect, the values of Typ in the example correspond with the data type codes in Table 52.

Bind in Oracle10g and Oracle11g

An Oracle10g and Oracle11g Bind#*n* section is different from an Oracle9i Bind#*n* section. Oracle10g and Oracle11g use 17 parameters to convey detailed information on bind variables. There is currently no information on three of the new parameters. Some of the parameters that were also present in Oracle9i have been renamed. Taking this into account, Table 53 presents the available information.

Table 53: Oracle10g and Oracle11g BINDS Parameters

Parameter	*Meaning*
oacdty	Data type code
mxl	Maximum length of the bind variable value (private maximum length in parentheses)
mxlc	Unknown
mal	Array length
scl	Scale
pre	Precision
oacflg	Special flag indicating bind options
fl2	Second part of oacflg
frm	Unknown
csi	Unknown
siz	Amount of memory to be allocated for this chunk
off	Offset into this chunk for this bind buffer
kxsbbbfp	Bind address
bln	Bind buffer length
avl	Actual value length
flg	Bind status flag
value	Value of the bind variable

Here's an example of an Oracle10g BINDS section. It is the result of tracing the same SQL statement that was used in the previous example for Oracle9i.

```
PARSING IN CURSOR #1 len=205 dep=1 uid=67 oct=3 lid=67 tim=8546016035 hv=3746754718
ad='2548145c'
SELECT E.LAST_NAME, E.FIRST_NAME, E.SALARY, D.DEPARTMENT_NAME FROM HR.EMPLOYEES E,
HR.DEPARTMENTS D WHERE E.DEPARTMENT_ID=D.DEPARTMENT_ID AND E.SALARY > :B3 AND
E.HIRE_DATE > :B2 AND D.DEPARTMENT_NAME=:B1
```

```
END OF STMT
PARSE #1:c=0,e=96,p=0,cr=0,cu=0,mis=0,r=0,dep=1,og=1,tim=8546016029
BINDS #1:
kkscoacd
 Bind#0
  oacdty=02 mxl=22(21) mxlc=00 mal=00 scl=00 pre=00
  oacflg=03 fl2=1206001 frm=00 csi=00 siz=160 off=0
  kxsbbbfp=07d9e508  bln=22  avl=04  flg=05
  value=4999.99
 Bind#1
  oacdty=12 mxl=07(07) mxlc=00 mal=00 scl=00 pre=00
  oacflg=03 fl2=1206001 frm=00 csi=00 siz=0 off=24
  kxsbbbfp=07d9e520  bln=07  avl=07  flg=01
  value="12/31/1995 0:0:0"
 Bind#2
  oacdty=01 mxl=128(64) mxlc=00 mal=00 scl=00 pre=00
  oacflg=03 fl2=1206001 frm=01 csi=178 siz=0 off=32
  kxsbbbfp=07d9e528  bln=128  avl=08  flg=01
  value="Shipping"
```

Oracle10g introduced two additional data types. These are BINARY_FLOAT and BINARY_DOUBLE. Their data type codes (oacdty) are 21 and 22 respectively.

Statement Tuning, Execution Plans, and Bind Variables

When tuning a statement that was captured with SQL trace and includes bind variables, do not replace bind variables with literals. In doing so, the optimizer might make different decisions. Instead, when tuning the statement in SQL*Plus, declare SQL*Plus bind variables matching the data types of the bind variables in the trace file (parameter dty or oacdty). Since SQL*Plus variables do not support all data types, e.g. DATE and TIMESTAMP are not provided, you may have to resort to an anonymous PL/SQL block to replicate the data types exactly. The use of conversion functions, such as TO_DATE or TO_TIMESTAMP with a SQL*Plus variable of type VARCHAR2 when the original data type is not available, is another option, but this too might affect the plan chosen by the optimizer. Even if you do reproduce the bind data types exactly, you may still get a plan which is different from a previous execution, since the previous execution may have reused a plan that was built based on different peeked bind variable values. If that plan has meanwhile been aged out of the shared pool, you may get a different plan based on peeking the current bind variable values. Thus, it's a good idea to capture plans with AWR snapshots or level 6 Statspack snapshots.

The SQL statement EXPLAIN PLAN may be used to generate an execution plan for SQL statements that include bind variables. However, EXPLAIN PLAN knows nothing about the bind variable data types and values. You need not even declare SQL*Plus variables to successfully use EXPLAIN PLAN on a statement that includes bind variables.

EXPLAIN PLAN is notoriously unreliable. It should never be used for statement tuning, since it regularly reports execution plans which are different from the actual plan used when the statement is executed. The *Oracle Database Performance Tuning Guide 10g Release 2* has this to say about EXPLAIN PLAN (page 19–4):

> Oracle does not support EXPLAIN PLAN for statements performing implicit type conversion of date bind variables. With bind variables in general, the EXPLAIN PLAN output might not represent the real execution plan.

SQL trace files, VSQL_PLAN, VSQL_PLAN_STATISTICS_ALL, AWR, and the Statspack Repository table STATS$SQL_PLAN, which contains snapshots of V$SQL_PLAN, are reliable sources for execution plans. Be warned that V$SQL_PLAN may hold several plans for the same HASH_VALUE or SQL_ID and there is no easy way of figuring out which plan was used. To avoid this pitfall, it is possible to run tail -f on the trace file to display the tail of the file as it grows. The unformatted execution plan in STAT entries is rather awkward to read. The Oracle10g pipelined table function DBMS_XPLAN.DISPLAY_CURSOR has the most sophisticated solution to date. Its syntax is:

```
dbms_xplan.display_cursor(
    sql_id IN VARCHAR2 DEFAULT NULL,
    child_number IN NUMBER DEFAULT NULL,
    format IN VARCHAR2 DEFAULT 'TYPICAL')
RETURN dbms_xplan_type_table PIPELINED;
```

When `DBMS_XPLAN.DISPLAY_CURSOR` is called without passing a `sql_id` and `child_number`, the plan of the last cursor executed by the session is displayed, making the function an ideal replacement for SQL*Plus `AUTOTRACE`. The format argument allows precise control of the output. The most verbose output pertaining merely to the last execution of a statement is obtained by using the format `'ALL ALLSTATS LAST'`. To collect memory and I/O statistics, `STATISTICS_LEVEL=ALL` must be set at session level. The columns "A-Rows" (actual rows), "A-Time" (actual time), "Buffers", and "Reads", which are present in the example that follows, are missing at the default `STATISTICS_LEVEL=TYPICAL`. The subsequent example illustrates several points:

- Flushing the buffer cache to provoke disk reads, which affects the values reported in column "Buffers" of the execution plan generated with `DBMS_XPLAN.DISPLAY_CURSOR`.
- The use of SQL*Plus variables as bind variables in SQL statements.
- The impact of the optimizer environment, specifically the parameter `OPTIMIZER_INDEX_COST_ADJ` on execution plans.
- How to retrieve filter and access predicates along with an execution plan. Columns in a `WHERE`-clause are called predicates.
- How to retrieve query block names, which may be useful for tuning with optimizer hints.

The example consists of running a two–way join on the tables `EMPLOYEES` and `DEPARTMENTS` with varying optimizer parameter settings. The first iteration runs in the default optimizer environment and results in a nested loops join, a full scan on `DEPARTMENTS`, and an index access to `EMPLOYEES`. The smaller table `DEPARTMENTS` is used as the driving table in the join.

For the second iteration, `OPTIMIZER_INDEX_COST_ADJ` was set to its maximum value of 10000, provoking full table scans by tagging index accesses with a higher cost. This latter setting results in a hash join and full table scans on both tables. Let's walk through the example step by step. First, the buffer cache is flushed[1] and `STATISTICS_LEVEL` is changed:

```
SQL> ALTER SYSTEM FLUSH BUFFER_CACHE;
System altered.
SQL> ALTER SESSION SET statistics_level=all;
Session altered.
```

Next, we declare three SQL*Plus bind variables to mimic the bind variables `:B1`, `:B2`, `:B3` that we saw in the SQL trace file reproduced earlier in this section (page 236) and assign the bind variable values reported in the trace file. Since SQL*Plus does not support variables with data type `DATE`, `VARCHAR2` is used for the variable `HIRED` and the function `TO_DATE` is applied to convert from `VARCHAR2` to `DATE`.

```
SQL> VARIABLE sal NUMBER
SQL> VARIABLE hired VARCHAR2(10)
SQL> VARIABLE dname VARCHAR2(64)
SQL> EXEC :sal :=4999.99; :hired:='31.12.1995'; :dname:='Shipping'
PL/SQL procedure successfully completed.
```

Except for more readable bind variable names than `:B`n and the addition of `TO_DATE`, the statement text found in the trace file is used.

```
SQL> SELECT e.last_name, e.first_name, e.salary, d.department_name
FROM hr.employees e, hr.departments d
WHERE e.department_id=d.department_id
AND e.salary > :sal
AND e.hire_date > to_date(:hired, 'dd.mm.yy')
AND d.department_name=:dname;
LAST_NAME                 FIRST_NAME               SALARY DEPARTMENT_NAME
------------------------- -------------------- ---------- ----------------
Weiss                     Matthew                    8000 Shipping
Fripp                     Adam                       8200 Shipping
Vollman                   Shanta                     6500 Shipping
Mourgos                   Kevin                      5800 Shipping
```

---

1. Flushing the buffer cache requires at least release Oracle 10g.

Next, DBMS_XPLAN is called to retrieve the execution plan of the last statement executed. I have split the execution plan output in two parts, to make it more readable. The uppercase "E" in the columns "E-Time", "E-Bytes", and "E-Rows" is short for estimated. Note that this first iteration reports on child cursor number 0.

```
SQL> SELECT * FROM table (DBMS_XPLAN.DISPLAY_CURSOR(null, null, 'ALL ALLSTATS LAST'));

PLAN_TABLE_OUTPUT
--------------------------------------
SQL_ID  b70r97ta66g1j, child number 0
--------------------------------------
SELECT e.last_name, e.first_name, e.salary, d.department_name FROM hr.employees e,
hr.departments d WHERE e.department_id=d.department_id
AND e.salary > :sal AND e.hire_date > to_date(:hired, 'dd.mm.yy') AND
d.department_name=:dname

Plan hash value: 2912831499
```

Id	Operation	Name	Starts	E-Rows
* 1	TABLE ACCESS BY INDEX ROWID	EMPLOYEES	1	3
2	NESTED LOOPS		1	3
* 3	TABLE ACCESS FULL	DEPARTMENTS	1	1
* 4	INDEX RANGE SCAN	EMP_DEPARTMENT_IX	1	10

E-Bytes	Cost (%CPU)	E-Time	A-Rows	A-Time	Buffers	Reads
90	1 (0)	00:00:01	4	00:00:00.03	13	15
138	4 (0)	00:00:01	47	00:00:00.02	10	7
16	3 (0)	00:00:01	1	00:00:00.01	8	6
	0 (0)		45	00:00:00.01	2	1

```
Query Block Name / Object Alias (identified by operation id):
-------------------------------------------------------------
   1 - SEL$1 / E@SEL$1
   3 - SEL$1 / D@SEL$1
   4 - SEL$1 / E@SEL$1
Predicate Information (identified by operation id):
--------------------------------------------------
   1 - filter(("E"."SALARY">:SAL AND "E"."HIRE_DATE">TO_DATE(:HIRED,'dd.mm.yy')))
   3 - filter("D"."DEPARTMENT_NAME"=:DNAME)
   4 - access("E"."DEPARTMENT_ID"="D"."DEPARTMENT_ID")
Column Projection Information (identified by operation id):
----------------------------------------------------------
   1 - "E"."FIRST_NAME"[VARCHAR2,20], "E"."LAST_NAME"[VARCHAR2,25],
"E"."SALARY"[NUMBER,22]
   2 - "D"."DEPARTMENT_NAME"[VARCHAR2,30], "E".ROWID[ROWID,10]
   3 - "D"."DEPARTMENT_ID"[NUMBER,22], "D"."DEPARTMENT_NAME"[VARCHAR2,30]
   4 - "E".ROWID[ROWID,10]
```

Projection information lists the subset of columns accessed by the query for each step in the execution plan. The word projection is an academic term from relational algebra. For the second iteration, let's change the optimizer environment and see how this affects the execution plan:

```
SQL> ALTER SESSION SET optimizer_index_cost_adj=10000;
Session altered.
SQL> SELECT e.last_name, e.first_name, e.salary, d.department_name
FROM hr.employees e, hr.departments d
WHERE e.department_id=d.department_id
```

```
AND e.salary > :sal
AND e.hire_date > to_date(:hired, 'dd.mm.yy')
AND d.department_name=:dname;
LAST_NAME                     FIRST_NAME                SALARY DEPARTMENT_NAME
------------------------      --------------------   --------- ----------------
Weiss                         Matthew                     8000 Shipping
Fripp                         Adam                        8200 Shipping
Vollman                       Shanta                      6500 Shipping
Mourgos                       Kevin                       5800 Shipping
```

Note that the child cursor number reported below is 1. This is due to the different plan, which results from a changed optimizer environment. The plan hash value has also changed, while the SQL_ID has remained the same. It is undocumented which parameter changes force the optimizer to consider a new plan. When tuning a statement, it is wise to add a unique comment to the statement text before each execution. This forces a hard parse and ensures that the optimizer considers all aspects of the current environment, which may include updated object and system statistics as well as modified initialization parameters.

Due to caching, a single disk read occurred when the statement was run the second time (column "Reads"). This time, I have split the execution plan into three parts for better readability, since memory usage statistics from the hash join made it even wider.

```
SQL> SELECT * FROM table (DBMS_XPLAN.DISPLAY_CURSOR(null, null, 'ALL ALLSTATS LAST'));
PLAN_TABLE_OUTPUT
----------------------------------------
SQL_ID  b70r97ta66g1j, child number 1
----------------------------------------
SELECT e.last_name, e.first_name, e.salary, d.department_name FROM hr.employees e,
hr.departments d WHERE e.department_id=d.department_id AND e.salary
> :sal AND e.hire_date > to_date(:hired, 'dd.mm.yy') AND d.department_name=:dname

Plan hash value: 2052257371
```

Id	Operation	Name	Starts	E-Rows	E-Bytes
* 1	HASH JOIN		1	3	138
* 2	TABLE ACCESS FULL	DEPARTMENTS	1	1	16
* 3	TABLE ACCESS FULL	EMPLOYEES	1	31	930

Cost (%CPU)	E-Time	A-Rows	A-Time
7 (15)	00:00:01	4	00:00:00.01
3 (0)	00:00:01	1	00:00:00.01
3 (0)	00:00:01	45	00:00:00.01

Buffers	Reads	OMem	1Mem	Used-Mem
12	1	887K	887K	267K (0)
7	0			
5	1			

```
Query Block Name / Object Alias (identified by operation id):
-------------------------------------------------------------
   1 - SEL$1
   2 - SEL$1 / D@SEL$1
   3 - SEL$1 / E@SEL$1
Predicate Information (identified by operation id):
-------------------------------------------------------------
```

```
    1 - access("E"."DEPARTMENT_ID"="D"."DEPARTMENT_ID")
    2 - filter("D"."DEPARTMENT_NAME"=:DNAME)
    3 - filter(("E"."SALARY">:SAL AND "E"."HIRE_DATE">TO_DATE(:HIRED,'dd.mm.yy')))
Column Projection Information (identified by operation id):
-----------------------------------------------------------
    1 - (#keys=1) "D"."DEPARTMENT_NAME"[VARCHAR2,30], "E"."FIRST_NAME"[VARCHAR2,20],
"E"."LAST_NAME"[VARCHAR2,25], "E"."SALARY"[NUMBER,22]
    2 - "D"."DEPARTMENT_ID"[NUMBER,22], "D"."DEPARTMENT_NAME"[VARCHAR2,30]
    3 - "E"."FIRST_NAME"[VARCHAR2,20], "E"."LAST_NAME"[VARCHAR2,25],
"E"."SALARY"[NUMBER,22], "E"."DEPARTMENT_ID"[NUMBER,22]
```

Tracing the SQL*Plus session at level 4 or 12 proves that the data types of the bind variables (parameter oacdty) match the data types in the original trace file with the exception of the bind variable with data type DATE (oacdty=12), which cannot be reproduced with a SQL*Plus variable. Below is the relevant section of an Oracle10*g* trace file:

```
BINDS #3:
kkscoacd
 Bind#0
  oacdty=02 mxl=22(22) mxlc=00 mal=00 scl=00 pre=00
  oacflg=03 fl2=1000000 frm=00 csi=00 siz=184 off=0
  kxsbbbfp=04d99cb0  bln=22  avl=04  flg=05
  value=4999.99
 Bind#1
  oacdty=01 mxl=32(10) mxlc=00 mal=00 scl=00 pre=00
  oacflg=03 fl2=1000000 frm=01 csi=178 siz=0 off=24
  kxsbbbfp=04d99cc8  bln=32  avl=10  flg=01
  value="31.12.1995"
 Bind#2
  oacdty=01 mxl=128(64) mxlc=00 mal=00 scl=00 pre=00
  oacflg=03 fl2=1000000 frm=01 csi=178 siz=0 off=56
  kxsbbbfp=04d99ce8  bln=128  avl=08  flg=01
  value="Shipping"
```

The example has pointed out how to leverage information from BINDS entries in trace files by reproducing the statement as closely as possible in respect to the data types of bind variables and their values. Such precise reproduction of traced statements is the optimal starting point for tuning.

To use the DISPLAY_CURSOR functionality, the calling user must have SELECT privilege on VSQL, VSQL_PLAN and V$SQL_PLAN_STATISTICS_ALL. The role SELECT_CATALOG_ROLE may be granted to ensure these privileges are available. The previous example showed that calling DBMS_XPLAN.DISPLAY_CURSOR without arguments retrieves the plan of the previous statement from V$SQL_PLAN, even when several execution plans for a single statement (i.e. several child cursors) exist. This functionality cannot be replicated in Oracle9*i*, since the column V$SESSION.PREV_CHILD_NUMBER is not available[1].

Even in Oracle10*g*, SQL*Plus AUTOTRACE uses EXPLAIN PLAN, such that it suffers from the same deficiencies of EXPLAIN PLAN mentioned earlier. This also applies to the TKPROF option EXPLAIN=*user/password*, which also runs EXPLAIN PLAN, this time even in a different database session from the one that generated the trace file supplied to TKPROF, such that the chances of getting incorrect results are even greater. Of course, you should never use this TKPROF switch, but instead allow TKPROF to format the STAT lines in the trace file. In case a cursor was not closed while tracing was active, there won't be any STAT lines for that particular cursor in the trace file. Under such circumstances, you need to query V$SQL_PLAN (using DBMS_XPLAN in Oracle10*g*), which succeeds only if the statement in question is still cached. If the statement in question is no longer cached, access the Statspack repository using the script $ORACLE_HOME/rdbms/admin/sprepsql.sql or the AWR using DBMS_XPLAN.DISPLAY_AWR.

---

1. In Oracle9*i*, the underlying X$ fixed table X$KSUSE does not hold the child cursor number of the previous statement either.

Miscellaneous Trace File Entries

The miscellaneous category consists among others of entries that document which session, module, or action generated trace file entries. Some of these entries are written automatically, while others require application coding.

Session Identification

Session identification is always emitted to SQL trace files. In contrast to module or action identification, it does not require any application coding. The format of the session identification is identical in Oracle9*i* and Oracle10*g*, such that the Oracle10*g* TRCSESS utility can be used to extract trace information for a single session from multiple Oracle9*i* or Oracle10*g* shared server trace files.

Irrespective of the server model used (dedicated or shared) each session is uniquely identified by a combination of two figures during the lifetime of the instance. That is, the same combination of figures will not be reused, unless the DBMS instance is shut down and restarted. Contrast this with V$SESSION.AUDSID which is unique for the lifetime of the database, used for auditing purposes, and available by calling USERENV('SESSIONID'). Speaking of USERENV, Oracle10*g* and subsequent releases finally provide access to V$SESSION.SID to non–privileged users through the undocumented option SID of the function USERENV as in USERENV('SID')[1]. Non–privileged in this context means that access to V$ views has not been granted, for example through SELECT_CATALOG_ROLE.

As an aside, the most appropriate general way to figure out the SID in Oracle9*i* is to run SELECT sid FROM v$mystat WHERE ROWNUM=1. Here, general means that this works for non–privileged sessions as well as sessions with SYSDBA and SYSOPER privileges. The query SELECT sid FROM v$session WHERE audsid = userenv ('sessionid') is inappropriate for getting the SID of privileged sessions, since these are not assigned a unique auditing session identifier (V$SESSION.AUDSID). Privileged sessions have AUDSID=0 in Oracle9*i* and AUDSID=4294967295 in Oracle10*g*. This fact is undocumented in the Database Reference (Oracle9*i* and Oracle10*g*).

The first figure of the session identification is the session identifier, while the second is the session serial number. The former is found in V$SESSION.SID, whereas the latter is accessible through V$SESSION.SERIAL# and is incremented each time the SID is reused. The format of the entry is:

```
*** SESSION ID:(sid.serial#) YYYY-MM-DD HH24:MI:SS.FF3
```

The time stamp at the end of the line is depicted using ORACLE date format models (see *Oracle Database SQL Reference 10g Release 2*, page 2–58). *FF3* represents three fractional seconds. An actual entry written on February 6th, 2007 on behalf of a session with V$SESSION.SID=147 and V$SESSION.SERIAL#=40 is below:

```
*** SESSION ID:(147.40) 2007-02-06 15:53:20.844
```

Service Name Identification

Service name identification is always emitted to Oracle10*g* and Oracle11*g* SQL trace files. Oracle9*i* does not have this feature. Service names in trace files refer to instance service names. Do not confound these with Oracle Net service names defined in tnsnames.ora or a directory service (see *Instance Service Name vs. Net Service Name* on page xiii for disambiguation). The service name of a session established using the bequeath adapter—such sessions are always running on the same machine as the DBMS instance, do not go through the listener, and require setting ORACLE_SID to the same value the instance was started with—is "SYS$USERS". Such sessions do not provide an Oracle Net service name in the connect string. The connect string merely contains username and password such as in:

```
$ sqlplus ndebes/secret
```

Sessions established through a listener by specifying an Oracle Net service name in the connect string can have any service name known to the listener, provided that the Net service name definition contains the specification SERVICE_NAME=*instance_service_name* instead of SID=*oracle_sid*. The format of the entry is:

```
*** SERVICE NAME:(instance_service_name) YYYY-MM-DD HH24:MI:SS.FF3
```

Instance_service_name can be any of "SYS$USERS", "SYS$BACKGROUND" (trace is from a background process) or any instance service name known to a listener serving that particular instance. Examples are below:

```
*** SERVICE NAME:(SYS$USERS) 2007-06-12 08:43:24.241
*** SERVICE NAME:(TEN.world) 2007-06-13 17:38:55.289
```

---

1. The documented alternative is SELECT sys_context('USERENV', 'SID') FROM dual.

For mandatory background processes of the instance, such as CKPT (checkpointer), SMON (system monitor), and LGWR (log writer) service name is an empty string such as in this example:

```
$ grep "SERVICE NAME" ten_lgwr_3072.trc
*** SERVICE NAME:() 2007-06-13 17:37:04.830
```

When creating services with the packaged procedure DBMS_SERVICE.CREATE_SERVICE, the value of the parameter network_name (not service_name) is registered as an instance service name with the listener (requires at least Oracle10g). Thus, the network_name needs to be used in Net service name definitions in tnsnames.ora and will appear in the SERVICE NAME entry. The same applies to RAC Cluster Database Services created with the Database Configuration Assistant or srvctl, since these are based on the functionality of the package DBMS_SERVICE.

Application Instrumentation

The term application instrumentation refers to a programming technique, whereby a program is capable of producing an account of its own execution time. The ORACLE DBMS is heavily instrumented (wait events, counters), however this instrumentation may be leveraged to a greater degree when a database client informs the DBMS of the tasks (module and action) it is performing. This section discusses trace file entries that are related to application instrumentation. The format of these entries has changed considerably from Oracle9i to Oracle10g, so the material is presented by release. The minimum SQL trace level for enabling entries discussed in this section is 1.

Application Instrumentation Entries in Oracle10g and Oracle11g

Table 54 lists the instrumentation entries of Oracle10g and Oracle11g in alphabetical order along with the PL/SQL and OCI interfaces to generate them. Note that Oracle JDBC drivers have Java instrumentation interfaces which are more efficient than calling PL/SQL from Java (see Chapter 23). At the lowest level, application instrumentation is achieved with the Oracle Call Interface (OCI) function OCIAttrSet (see *Oracle Call Interface Programmer's Guide*).

Table 54: PL/SQL and OCI Interfaces for Instrumentation Entries

Trace File Entry	*PL/SQL Interface*	*OCIAttrSet Attribute*
ACTION NAME	DBMS_APPLICATION_INFO.SET_MODULE, DBMS_APPLICATION_INFO.SET_ACTION	OCI_ATTR_ACTION
CLIENT ID	DBMS_SESSION.SET_IDENTIFIER	OCI_ATTR_CLIENT_IDENTIFIER[a]
MODULE NAME	DBMS_APPLICATION_INFO.SET_MODULE	OCI_ATTR_MODULE

a. DBMS_APPLICATION_INFO.SET_CLIENT_INFO and the OCI attribute OCI_ATTR_CLIENT_INFO set V$SESSION.CLIENT_INFO. This setting is not emitted to trace files and cannot be used in conjunction with the package DBMS_MONITOR.

When running code such as the following in SQL*Plus, all three types of instrumentation entries are written to a trace file.

```
C:> sqlplus ndebes/secret@ten_g.oradbpro.com
Connected.
SQL> BEGIN
   dbms_application_info.set_module('mod', 'act');
   dbms_session.set_identifier(sys_context('userenv','os_user') ||
   '@' || sys_context('userenv','host') || ' (' ||
   sys_context('userenv','ip_address') || ')' );
END;
/
PL/SQL procedure successfully completed.
SQL> ALTER SESSION SET sql_trace=TRUE;
Session altered.
```

The resulting trace file contains lines such as these:

```
*** ACTION NAME:(act) 2007-08-31 18:02:26.578
*** MODULE NAME:(mod) 2007-08-31 18:02:26.578
```

```
*** SERVICE NAME:(orcl.oradbpro.com) 2007-08-31 18:02:26.578
*** CLIENT ID:(DBSERVER\ndebes@WORKGROUP\DBSERVER (192.168.10.1)) 2007-08-31
18:02:26.578
*** SESSION ID:(149.21) 2007-08-31 18:02:26.578
```

The value `orcl.oradbpro.com` of `SERVICE NAME` stems from the use of this string as the `SERVICE_NAME` in the definition of the Net service name `ten_g.oradbpro.com`.

These are the kinds of trace file entries that the Oracle10g TRCSESS utility searches for when used to extract relevant sections from one or more trace files. The sections that follow provide additional detail on the individual entries. For detailed information on TRCSESS, see Chapter 23.

Module Name

The module name is intended to convey the name of an application or larger module to the DBMS. The default setting is `NULL`. SQL*Plus and Perl DBI automatically set a module name. The example below is from a SQL*Plus session:

```
*** MODULE NAME:(SQL*Plus) 2007-02-06 15:53:20.844
```

Action Name

An action name represents a smaller unit of code or a subroutine. A module might call several subroutines, where each subroutine sets a different action name. The default setting `NULL` results in a zero length action name:

```
*** ACTION NAME:() 2007-02-06 15:53:20.844
```

Client Identifier

Performance problems or hanging issues in three tier environments, where the application uses a database connection pool maintained by an intermediate application server layer, can be extremely cumbersome to track down. Due to the connection pool in the middle tier, performance analysts looking at V$ views or extended SQL trace files cannot form an association between an application user reporting a slow database and the database session or server process within the ORACLE instance serving a particular user. There is no way to find out which SQL statements are run on behalf of the complaining end user. Unless the application is properly instrumented, which is something that has eluded me in my career as a DBA.

The client identifier is the answer to this dilemma. The package `DBMS_SESSION` provides a means for an application to communicate an identifier that uniquely designates an application user to the DBMS. This identifier becomes the value of the column `V$SESSION.CLIENT_IDENTIFIER`. If SQL trace is enabled, this same identifier is also embedded in the SQL trace file. The format is:

```
*** CLIENT ID:(client_identifier) YYYY-MM-DD HH24:MI:SS.FF3
```

Client_identifier is the client identifier set by calling the procedure `DBMS_SESSION.SET_IDENTIFIER` from the application code. To extract trace information for a certain client identifier from one or more SQL trace files, `trcsess clientid=client_identifier` can be used. The line below shows an actual entry from a trace file. The client identifier used was ND. The entry was written on February 6th, 2007.

```
*** CLIENT ID:(ND) 2007-02-06 15:53:20.844
```

The maximum length of a client identifier is 64 bytes. Strings exceeding this length are silently truncated. When instrumenting applications with `DBMS_SESSION`, consider that the procedure `DBMS_SESSION.CLEAR_IDENTIFIER` does not write a `CLIENT ID` entry into the trace file, leaving the client identifier in effect until it is changed with `DBMS_SESSION.SET_IDENTIFIER`. When connection pooling is used, this may result in trace files where sections pertaining to different client identifiers are not delineated. The solution consists of setting an empty client identifier by passing `NULL` to the packaged procedure `DBMS_SESSION.SET_IDENTIFIER` instead of calling the procedure `DBMS_SESSION.CLEAR_IDENTIFIER`.

Application Instrumentation Entries in Oracle9*i*

Running the same application instrumentation code as in the section on Oracle10g (page 243) against Oracle9*i*, results in far fewer entries being written to the trace file. The instance service name is neither available in `V$SESSION` nor in the trace file. An Oracle9*i* trace file contains lines such as these:

```
*** SESSION ID:(10.697) 2007-08-31 18:19:10.000
APPNAME mod='mod' mh=781691722 act='act' ah=3947624709
```

Obviously, the format for module and action is different in Oracle9*i*. Module and action are always logged on a single line after the keyword APPNAME, even when just the action is set with DBMS_APPLICATION_INFO.SET_ACTION. Abbreviations used in the APPNAME entry are explained in Table 55. In Oracle9*i*, the client identifier is not written to

Table 55: Oracle9*i* APPNAME Parameters

Parameter	Meaning
mod	Module; corresponds to V$SESSION.MODULE
mh	Module hash value; corresponds to V$SESSION.MODULE_HASH
act	Action; corresponds to V$SESSION.ACTION
ah	Action hash value; corresponds to V$SESSION.ACTION_HASH

the trace file. It is merely set in V$SESSION.CLIENT_IDENTIFIER[1]:

```
SQL> SELECT client_identifier FROM v$session WHERE sid=10;
CLIENT_IDENTIFIER
----------------------------------------------------------
ndebes@WORKGROUP\DBSERVER
```

ERROR Entry Format

Errors during execution of SQL statements are marked by ERROR entries. These may occur for statements that were parsed successfully, but failed to execute successfully. The minimum SQL trace level for ERROR entries is 1. An example is below:

```
PARSING IN CURSOR #6 len=94 dep=0 uid=30 oct=2 lid=30 tim=171868250869 hv=3526281696
ad='6778c420'
INSERT INTO poem (author, text) VALUES(:author, empty_clob()) RETURNING ROWID INTO
:row_id
END OF STMT
PARSE #6:c=0,e=150,p=0,cr=0,cu=0,mis=0,r=0,dep=0,og=1,tim=171868250857
EXEC #6:c=10014,e=52827,p=0,cr=2,cu=5,mis=0,r=0,dep=0,og=1,tim=171868303859
ERROR #6:err=372 tim=17186458
```

The figure after the pound sign (#) is the cursor number of the failed statement. The reason for the failing INSERT statement in the above example was "ORA-00372: file 4 cannot be modified at this time". The tablespace containing the table POEM had status read only. The parameters of the ERROR entry are in Table 56.

Table 56: ERROR Parameters

Parameter	Meaning
err	Error number
tim	Timestamp in centiseconds (appears to be 0 at all times in Oracle9*i*, but has a meaningful value in Oracle10*g*)

Sometimes applications do not report ORACLE error numbers or error messages. Under such circumstances, it is very worthwhile to do a level 1 SQL trace, to discover which error the DBMS throws. It is even possible to find out when an error occurred by looking at timestamps and tim values in the trace file. Near the header of each trace file is a timestamp such as this:

```
*** SESSION ID:(150.524) 2007-06-22 15:42:41.018
```

After periods of inactivity, the DBMS automatically writes additional timestamps with the following format into the trace file:

---

1. Strangely, the IP address was silently truncated from the client identifier by the Oracle 9.2.0.1.0 instance used.

```
*** 2007-06-22 15:42:51.924
```

Intermittent timestamps can be forced by calling DBMS_SYSTEM.KSDDT. Running the following script will generate two errors which are 10 seconds apart, due to a call to DBMS_LOCK.SLEEP.

```
SQL> ALTER SESSION SET sql_trace=TRUE;
SQL> ALTER TABLESPACE users READ WRITE /* is read write, will fail */;
SQL> EXEC dbms_lock.sleep(10) /* sleep for 10 seconds */
SQL> EXEC dbms_system.ksddt /* write timestamp to trace file */
SQL> ALTER TABLESPACE users READ WRITE /* is read write, will fail */;
```

The resulting Oracle10g trace file is shown below (excerpted):

```
1  *** SESSION ID:(150.524) 2007-06-22 15:42:41.018
2  PARSING IN CURSOR #1 len=55 dep=1 uid=0 oct=3 lid=0 tim=176338392169 hv=1950821498
ad='6784bfac'
...
3  EXEC #1:c=20028,e=208172,p=0,cr=0,cu=0,mis=0,r=0,dep=0,og=1,tim=176339220462
4  ERROR #1:err=1646 tim=17633550
...
5  PARSING IN CURSOR #1 len=33 dep=0 uid=0 oct=47 lid=0 tim=176339264800 hv=2252395675
ad='67505814'
6  BEGIN dbms_lock.sleep(10); END;
7  END OF STMT
8  PARSE #1:c=0,e=140,p=0,cr=0,cu=0,mis=0,r=0,dep=0,og=1,tim=176339264790
9  *** 2007-06-22 15:42:51.924
10 EXEC #1:c=0,e=9997915,p=0,cr=0,cu=0,mis=0,r=1,dep=0,og=1,tim=176349294618
...
11 EXEC #1:c=70101,e=74082,p=0,cr=2,cu=0,mis=0,r=0,dep=0,og=1,tim=176349582606
12 ERROR #1:err=1646 tim=17634587
```

The first tim value after the timestamp in the header will serve as a reference. In the example "2007-06-22 15:42:41.018" in line 1 is approximately the same as 176338392169 microseconds in line 2. The nearest tim value above the ERROR entry in line 4 is 176339220462 microseconds in line 3. So between line 2 and 3, (176339220462–176338392169) / 1000000 or 0.82 seconds have passed. The nearest tim value above the second ERROR entry is 176349582606 in line 11. Between line 3 and line 11 (176349582606–176339220462) / 1000000 or 10.36 seconds have passed. This is reasonable, since the session was put to sleep for 10 seconds. The intermittent timestamp in line 9 forced with DBMS_SYSTEM.KSDDT confirms this. Timestamp (tim) values of ERROR entries only have centisecond resolution. This is apparent when subtracting 17633550 (ERROR entry in line 4) from 17634587 (ERROR entry in line 12), which yields 10.37 seconds ((17634587–17633550) / 100).

Using the same approach, we can compute that the second error in line 12 occurred (176349582606–176338392169) / 1000000 or 11.190 seconds after 15:42:41.018. So the second error occurred at 15:42:52.208, which is about ten seconds after the trace file header was written and about 0.3 seconds after the timestamp written by DBMS_SYSTEM.KSDDT. Of course this approach works for any trace file entry that has a tim field and not just ERROR entries. Why there is an offset—about 3.7 seconds in my testing—between centisecond resolution tim values in ERROR entries and microsecond resolution tim values in other entries is a question for Oracle development.

I remember an assignment due to an escalated service request. It was believed that the DBMS was erroneously throwing "ORA-06502: PL/SQL: numeric or value error". By taking a level 1 trace and looking for ERROR entries, I was able to prove that there were no errors in the communication between the DBMS instance and the client. It turned out that it was an application coding error with a buffer which was too small. The ORA-06502 was thrown by the PL/SQL engine of the Oracle Forms runtime environment, not the PL/SQL engine within the ORACLE DBMS. Thus, there was no ERROR entry in the SQL trace file.

Application Instrumentation and Parallel Execution Processes

Among the three kinds of application instrumentation entries, solely the client identifier is emitted to trace files from parallel execution processes. These trace files are created in the directory assigned with the parameter BACKGROUND_DUMP_DEST and follow the naming scheme *ORACLE_SID*_p*nnn*_*spid*.trc in Oracle10g, where *n* is a digit between 0 and 9 and *spid* corresponds to V$PROCESS.SPID.

The term query coordinator refers to a process which controls parallel execution slaves. The slaves perform the actual work. The query coordinator is the same process that serves the database client. Since resource consumption, such as CPU time and I/O requests by parallel execution slaves, is not rolled up into the statistics reported for the query coordinator, the client identifier may be used in conjunction with the TRCSESS utility to get a full account of the resources consumed by the query coordinator and the parallel execution processes it recruited.

The subsequent example shows how to use the TRCSESS utility to combine the trace file from the query coordinator and four trace files from parallel execution processes into a single trace file for formatting with TKPROF. A user with SELECT ANY DICTIONARY privilege might use the table SYS.SOURCE$ for testing parallel query. Both a FULL and a PARALLEL hint are necessary to scan the table in parallel. Event 10046 is used to enable tracing, since the procedure DBMS_MONITOR.SESSION_TRACE_ENABLE has no effect on parallel execution processes. Embedding the auditing session identifier in the client identifier guarantees a unique client identifier.

```
SQL> ALTER SESSION SET EVENTS '10046 trace name context forever, level 8';
Session altered.
SQL> VARIABLE client_identifier VARCHAR2(64)
SQL> EXEC :client_identifier:='pqtest_' || userenv('sessionid')
PL/SQL procedure successfully completed.
SQL> PRINT client_identifier
CLIENT_IDENTIFIER
-----------
pqtest_1894
SQL> EXEC dbms_session.set_identifier(:client_identifier)
PL/SQL procedure successfully completed.
SQL> SELECT /*+ FULL(s) PARALLEL (s ,4) */ count(*) FROM sys.source$ s;
  COUNT(*)
----------
    298767
SQL> SELECT statistic, last_query FROM v$pq_sesstat WHERE statistic='Queries
Parallelized';
STATISTIC                       LAST_QUERY
------------------------------- ----------
Queries Parallelized                     1
SQL> EXEC dbms_session.set_identifier(NULL)
PL/SQL procedure successfully completed.
```

The query on V$PQ_SESSTAT confirms that the SELECT statement ran in parallel. At this point, the client identifier has been emitted to four trace files from parallel execution processes:

```
C:\oracle\admin\orcl\bdump> grep pqtest_1894 *.trc
orcl_p000_5412.trc:*** CLIENT ID:(pqtest_1894) 2007-08-31 23:14:38.421
orcl_p001_2932.trc:*** CLIENT ID:(pqtest_1894) 2007-08-31 23:14:38.421
orcl_p002_4972.trc:*** CLIENT ID:(pqtest_1894) 2007-08-31 23:14:38.421
orcl_p003_1368.trc:*** CLIENT ID:(pqtest_1894) 2007-08-31 23:14:38.421
```

TRCSESS is used to combine the trace files of the four parallel execution processes and the trace file of the query coordinator into a single trace file called pqtest_1894.trc. The client identifier is passed to TRCSESS with the option clientid. Since TRCSESS supports wildcards and scans all files that match, it is sufficient to pass *.trc for the local directory bdump and ..\udump*.trc for the directory where the query coordinator trace file resides as the input file specification:

```
C:\oracle\admin\orcl\bdump> trcsess output=pqtest_1894.trc clientid=pqtest_1894 *.trc
..\udump\*.trc
```

The output file is a trace file that contains the database calls and wait events of all processes involved in the parallel execution. The combined trace file may be processed with TKPROF:

```
C:\oracle\admin\orcl\bdump> tkprof pqtest_1894.trc pqtest_1894.tkp
```

Whereas the trace file of the query coordinator reports zero disk reads as well as zero consistent reads[1], the combined formatted trace file gives an accurate account of the resource consumption.

---

1. FETCH #2:c=15625,e=1875092,p=0,cr=0,cu=0,mis=0,r=1,dep=0,og=1,tim=108052435005

```
OVERALL TOTALS FOR ALL NON-RECURSIVE STATEMENTS
call      count       cpu    elapsed      disk     query  current     rows
-------  ------   --------  ---------  --------  --------  --------   ------
Parse         7      0.00       0.00         0         0         0        0
Execute       7      0.18       7.05      5209      5368         0        1
Fetch         4      0.01       1.87         0         0         0        2
-------  ------   --------  ---------  --------  --------  --------   ------
total        18      0.20       8.93      5209      5368         0        3
```

Disk reads are due to direct path reads performed by the parallel execution processes, which do not use the buffer cache in the SGA. Since parallel execution circumvents the buffer cache, it benefits from caching at the file system level by the operating system.

Chapter 25

Statspack

Status: Statspack is documented in the *Oracle9i Database Performance Tuning Guide and Reference* manual as well as in the file `$ORACLE_HOME/rdbms/admin/spdoc.txt` on both UNIX and Windows[1]. The latter document is significantly more detailed than the *Performance Tuning Guide and Reference*. Due to the introduction of the Active Workload Repository in Oracle10g, Statspack documentation has been removed from the *Oracle Database Performance Tuning Guide 10g Release 2* manual.

Benefit: This chapter covers advanced aspects of Statspack usage, such as undocumented report parameters and how to relate SQL statements identified by hash value found in SQL trace files to information in Statspack reports and the Statspack repository. Furthermore it presents the mostly undocumented repository structure and explains how to find used indexes as well as current and past execution plans for statements in SQL trace files. It also looks at how to identify periods of high resource consumption among a large amount of Statspack snapshots, by using the analytic function `LAG`.

Introduction to Statspack

Introductory documentation on Statspack is in *Oracle9i Database Performance Tuning Guide and Reference Release 2*. The chapter on Statspack has been removed from Oracle10g documentation. *Oracle Database Performance Tuning Guide 10g Release 2* merely states that Statspack has been replaced by the Automatic Workload Repository, which is not really true, since Statspack is still available in Oracle10g as well as Oracle11g.

I will not provide a thorough introduction to Statspack here, but for the novice Statspack user some minimal instructions on how to get started with the package are in order. These are reproduced in Table 57. The default file name extension `.sql` for SQL*Plus scripts is omitted in the table.

---

1. `%ORACLE_HOME%\rdbms\admin\spdoc.txt` in Windows syntax.

The installation of Statspack into the schema PERFSTAT must be performed as SYS. All other actions except truncation of Statspack tables may be run by any user with DBA privileges. Statspack is implemented by a number of scripts named sp*.sql in $ORACLE_HOME/rdbms/admin:

```
$ ls sp*.sql
spauto.sql      spcusr.sql    sppurge.sql    sprepsql.sql    spup816.sql
spcpkg.sql      spdrop.sql    sprepcon.sql   sprsqins.sql    spup817.sql
spcreate.sql    spdtab.sql    sprepins.sql   sptrunc.sql     spup90.sql
spctab.sql      spdusr.sql    spreport.sql   spup10.sql      spup92.sql
```

Note that setting ORACLE_HOME as part of the SQL script directory search path with environment variable SQLPATH removes the necessity to supply the full path name of Statspack SQL scripts and any other scripts in the directories thereby specified. On UNIX use a colon (:) as a separator between multiple directories:

```
$ export SQLPATH=$ORACLE_HOME/rdbms/admin:$HOME/it/sql
```

On Windows, use a semicolon (;):

```
C:> set SQLPATH=%ORACLE_HOME%\rdbms\admin;C:\home\ndebes\it\sql
```

Table 57: Statspack Quick Reference

Action	*Command to enter in SQL*Plus*	*Run as user*
Installation	SQL> @spcreate	SYS
Manual snapshot of performance data with optional session level snapshot and comment	SQL> EXEC statspack.snap(i_snap_level=>*snapshot_level* [, i_session_id=>*sid_from_v$session*] [, i_ucomment=>'*comment*'])[a]	DBA
Automatic snapshots every hour on the hour taken by job queue processes (DBMS_JOB)	SQL> @spauto	DBA
Reporting	SQL> @spreport	DBA
Purge obsolete Statspack data by snapshot id range to prevent default the tablespace of user PERFSTAT from overflowing[b]	SQL> @sppurge	DBA
Truncate tables containing snapshot data	SQL> @sptrunc	PERFSTAT
Deinstallation	SQL> @spdrop	DBA

a. *Snapshot_level* is an integer in the range 1..10; *sid_from_v$session* is V$SESSION.SID of a session for which CPU consumption, wait events, and session statistics are captured; *comment* is a comment, which will be reproduced along with the snapshot id, time, and level when spreport.sql is run.
   Statspack releases including Oracle10g Release 2 have a software defect concerning the generation of the session–specific report. Wait events which occurred solely in the end snapshot, but not in the begin snapshot, are omitted from the report due to a missing outer join. I reported this issue, which is tracked by bug 5145816. The bug is fixed in Oracle11g. There is no backport of the fix to earlier releases, but you can use my fixes in the source code depot.
b. In Oracle10g, the purge functionality is also available as part of the Statspack package (STATSPACK.PURGE). The source code depot contains a backport of the procedure to Oracle9i (see Table 60).

I urge the reader to capture at least one snapshot per hour. When no performance snapshots are captured on a regular basis, you will be at a loss when database users call and state they had a performance problem at some point in the recent past. You won't be able to answer the request to figure out why, except by shrugging your shoulders. With historical performance data, you ask at what time it happened, generate the Statspack reports for snapshots taken before and after that time, possibly drill down by looking at the execution plan of an expensive statement with script sprepsql.sql (requires snapshot level 6 or higher[1]), identify the cause of the problem, and solve it.

Retrieving the Text of Captured SQL Statements

Statspack is a tremendous improvement over its predecessor bstat/estat. However, it is annoying that all SQL statements are reproduced with forced line breaks as in V$SQLTEXT.SQL_TEXT. Additionally, statements with more than five lines of text are truncated. Below is an excerpt of a Statspack report that contains a truncated statement:

```
SQL ordered by CPU  DB/Inst: ORCL/orcl  Snaps: 2-3
-> Resources reported for PL/SQL code includes the resources used by all SQL
   statements called by the code.
-> Total DB CPU (s):           11
-> Captured SQL accounts for    48.4% of Total DB CPU
-> SQL reported below exceeded  1.0% of Total DB CPU


  CPU              CPU per        Elapsd                   Old
Time (s) Executions Exec (s) %Total Time (s) Buffer Gets Hash Value
-------- ---------- -------- ------ -------- ----------- ----------
   10.34         11     0.94   12.3    31.65     162,064 1455318379
SELECT emp.last_name, emp.first_name, j.job_title, d.department_
name, l.city, l.state_province, l.postal_code, l.street_address,
 emp.email, emp.phone_number, emp.hire_date, emp.salary, mgr.las
t_name FROM employees emp, employees mgr, departments d, locatio
ns l, jobs j WHERE emp.manager_id=mgr.employee_id AND emp.depart
```

Let's assume that the statement is consuming too many resources and should be tuned. But how do you tune a SQL statement when you don't have the complete text? At the time of creating the Statspack report, the application may long have terminated. If it has, it is too late to capture the statement with SQL trace.

To show the reader what the original formatting of the example statement was, I have captured it with SQL trace:

```
*** SERVICE NAME:(SYS$USERS) 2007-07-28 13:10:44.703
*** SESSION ID:(158.3407) 2007-07-28 13:10:44.703
...
*** ACTION NAME:(EMPLIST) 2007-07-28 13:10:57.406
*** MODULE NAME:(HR) 2007-07-28 13:10:57.406
...
PARSING IN CURSOR #8 len=416 dep=0 uid=0 oct=3 lid=0 tim=79821013130 hv=3786124882
ad='2d8f5f1c'
SELECT emp.last_name, emp.first_name, j.job_title, d.department_name, l.city,
        l.state_province, l.postal_code, l.street_address, emp.email,
        emp.phone_number, emp.hire_date, emp.salary, mgr.last_name
FROM hr.employees emp, hr.employees mgr, hr.departments d, hr.locations l, hr.jobs j
WHERE emp.manager_id=mgr.employee_id
AND emp.department_id=d.department_id
AND d.location_id=l.location_id
AND emp.job_id=j.job_id
END OF STMT
PARSE #8:c=46875,e=42575,p=0,cr=4,cu=0,mis=1,r=0,dep=0,og=1,tim=79821013122
```

The developer nicely formatted the statement, placing each clause of the SELECT statement on a separate line and indenting the long select list with tab stops. As we saw above, all of this is lost in the Statspack report. Active Workload Repository (AWR) HTML formatted reports do contain the complete text of SQL statements (text reports don't), but AWR is bundled with the Database Diagnostics Pack, which has a price tag of 3000$ per processor or 60$ per named user (see http://oraclestore.oracle.com). Some DBAs mistakenly assume that AWR may be used at no additional charge, since it is installed and enabled (STATISTICS_LEVEL=TYPICAL) by default.

---

1. The job created with the script spauto.sql does not call the STATSPACK package with a specific snapshot level. It uses the default snapshot level in STATS$STATSPACK_PARAMETER, which can be modified by calling the procedure STATSPACK.MODIFY_STATSPACK_PARAMETER(i_snap_level=>6). Snapshot level 6 may cause STATSPACK.SNAP to fail, due to an internal error when selecting from V$SQL_PLAN. Try flushing the shared pool with ALTER SYSTEM FLUSH SHARED_POOL in case this problem manifests itself. If this does not prevent an internal error from recurring, reduce the snapshot level to 5 and restart the instance during the next maintenance window.

The Database Diagnostics Pack includes AWR, the DBMS_WORKLOAD_REPOSITORY package for taking AWR snapshots and AWR administration, AWR reports (awrrpt.sql), the DBA_HIST_* and DBA_ADVISOR_* views, Active Session History (V$ACTIVE_SESSION_HISTORY), and ADDM (Automatic Database Diagnostic Monitor). Of course, without proper licensing, these features may not be accessed through Enterprise Manager Grid Control or Database Control either. Speaking of AWR and Statspack, AWR snapshots cannot include session specific data in the same way that Statspack snapshots can (see *i_session_id* in Table 57). Active Session History samples metrics of all sessions, whereas a session–level Statspack snapshot saves accurate, non–sampled metrics of a single session.

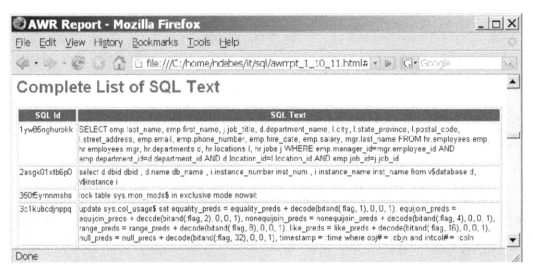

Figure 11: AWR Report Section Showing Unabridged Text of SQL Statements

If you have read the Oracle10*g* Statspack documentation in spdoc.txt then you might know that in Oracle10*g* the file sprepcon.sql (Statspack report configuration) contains a number of parameters that control the appearance of Statspack reports as well as which statements make it into the report[1]. Here's the relevant excerpt from spdoc.txt:

```
SQL section report settings - num_rows_per_hash
~~~~~~~~~~~~~~~~~~~~~~~~~~~~~~~~~~~~~~~~~~~~~~~~~
This is the upper limit of the number of rows of SQL Text to print for
each SQL statement appearing in the SQL sections of the report.  This
variable applies to each SQL statement (i.e. hash_value).  The default value
is 4, which means at most 4 lines  of the SQL text will be printed for
each SQL statement.  To change this value, change the value of the variable
num_rows_per_hash.
e.g.
     define num_rows_per_hash = 10;
```

And this is the relevant excerpt of sprepcon.sql:

```
-- SQL related report settings

-- Number of Rows of SQL to display in each SQL section of the report
define top_n_sql = 65;

-- Number of rows of SQL Text to print in the SQL sections of the report
-- for each hash_value
define num_rows_per_hash = 4;
...
define top_pct_sql = 1.0;
```

---

1. In Oracle9*i*, sprepcon.sql does not exist and num_rows_per_hash is undocumented.

Thus, the solution for getting the full text of the poorly performing SQL statement is to increase the value of num_rows_per_hash. Since the documentation does not reveal how Statspack stores captured SQL statements, we simply set num_rows_per_hash to an arbitrarily large value such as 1000 and run the Statspack report again (script $ORACLE_HOME/rdbms/admin/spreport.sql). This time, the complete SQL statement text is in the report:

```
    CPU                 CPU per         Elapsd                    Old
   Time (s) Executions Exec (s) %Total Time (s) Buffer Gets Hash Value
   -------- ---------- -------- ------ -------- ----------- ----------
      10.34         11     0.94   12.3    31.65     162,064 1455318379
   SELECT emp.last_name, emp.first_name, j.job_title, d.department_
   name, l.city, l.state_province, l.postal_code, l.street_address,
    emp.email, emp.phone_number, emp.hire_date, emp.salary, mgr.las
   t_name FROM employees emp, employees mgr, departments d, locatio
   ns l, jobs j WHERE emp.manager_id=mgr.employee_id AND emp.depart
   ment_id=d.department_id AND d.location_id=l.location_id AND emp.
   job_id=j.job_id
```

Unfortunately it's still not in a format that adheres to correct SQL syntax. The remaining task consists of copying the statement from the report and editing it, such that line breaks in the middle of identifiers, SQL reserved words, and literals are removed. This procedure can be quite annoying—especially for statements that exceed 50 lines or so.

The more elegant approach, which will pay off sooner or later, is to go directly to the Statspack repository in the PERFSTAT schema and to retrieve the statement from there. Note however that Statspack copies SQL statement texts from V$SQLTEXT instead of from V$SQLTEXT_WITH_NEWLINES. Only the latter view contains the statement with line breaks and tab stops in the original positions where the developer placed them preserved. If you're dealing with a more complex statement, proper formatting may significantly ease the process of finding out what the statement does. SQL statement texts retrieved from V$SQL and V$SQLTEXT have been subjected to an undocumented normalization procedure which removes line breaks as well as tab stops.

In Oracle10g, the column SQL_FULLTEXT was added to V$SQL to provide SQL statements with intact formatting as a CLOB:

```
SQL> DESCRIBE v$sql
 Name                                  Null?    Type
 ------------------------------------- -------- -------------
 SQL_TEXT                                       VARCHAR2(1000)
 SQL_FULLTEXT                                   CLOB
 SQL_ID                                         VARCHAR2(13)
 ...
```

When working with Oracle10g, given that the statement text is still cached in the shared pool within the SGA, the following SQL*Plus script retrieves the statement text with intact formatting:

```
$ cat sql_fulltext.sql
-- pass old_hash_value as the single argument to the script
define old_hash_value='&1'
set verify off
set long 100000
set trimout on
set trimspool on
set feedback off
set heading off
set linesize 32767
col sql_fulltext format a32767
spool sp_sqltext_&old_hash_value..lst
SELECT sql_fulltext FROM v$sql WHERE old_hash_value=&old_hash_value;
spool off
exit
```

Let's test the script sql_fulltext.sql with the SELECT statement that needs tuning:

```
$ sqlplus -s system/secret @sql_fulltext.sql 1455318379
SELECT emp.last_name, emp.first_name, j.job_title, d.department_name, l.city,
```

```
              l.state_province, l.postal_code, l.street_address, emp.email,
              emp.phone_number, emp.hire_date, emp.salary, mgr.last_name
       FROM hr.employees emp, hr.employees mgr, hr.departments d, hr.locations l, hr.jobs j
       WHERE emp.manager_id=mgr.employee_id
       AND emp.department_id=d.department_id
       AND d.location_id=l.location_id
       AND emp.job_id=j.job_id
```

This time, the tab stops in lines 2 and 3 as well as the line breaks in the original positions have been preserved. Do not despair, even if the statement has been aged out of the shared pool or the DBMS instance restarted. The next section will show how pipelined table functions introduced in PL/SQL with Oracle9*i* may be used to solve the problem.

Accessing STATS$SQLTEXT

A closer look at the main Statspack report file `sprepins.sql` soon reveals that the full statement text is stored in the table STATS$SQLTEXT, while the measurement data of the statement are in table STATS$SQL_SUMMARY. The source code of the package STATSPACK in `spcpkg.sql` reveals that STATS$SQLTEXT copies statement texts from V$SQLTEXT. Both V$ views split SQL statements into several VARCHAR2 pieces with a maximum length of 64 characters:

```
SQL> DESCRIBE v$sqltext
 Name                             Null?    Type
 ------------------------------- -------- ----------------------------
 ADDRESS                                   RAW(4)
 HASH_VALUE                                NUMBER
 SQL_ID                                    VARCHAR2(13)
 COMMAND_TYPE                              NUMBER
 PIECE                                     NUMBER
 SQL_TEXT                                  VARCHAR2(64)
SQL> DESCRIBE perfstat.stats$sqltext
 Name                             Null?    Type
 ------------------------------- -------- ----------------------------
 OLD_HASH_VALUE                   NOT NULL NUMBER
 TEXT_SUBSET                      NOT NULL VARCHAR2(31)
 PIECE                            NOT NULL NUMBER
 SQL_ID                                    VARCHAR2(13)
 SQL_TEXT                                  VARCHAR2(64)
 ADDRESS                                   RAW(8)
 COMMAND_TYPE                              NUMBER
 LAST_SNAP_ID                              NUMBER
```

This explains why it is impossible to obtain statement texts with original formatting in Statspack reports. The table STATS$SQLTEXT may be queried as follows:

```
SQL> SELECT sql_text
 FROM perfstat.stats$sqltext
 WHERE old_hash_value=1455318379
 ORDER BY piece;
SQL_TEXT
-----------------------------------------------------------------
SELECT emp.last_name, emp.first_name, j.job_title, d.department_
name, l.city, l.state_province, l.postal_code, l.street_address,
 emp.email, emp.phone_number, emp.hire_date, emp.salary, mgr.las
t_name FROM employees emp, employees mgr, departments d, locatio
ns l, jobs j WHERE emp.manager_id=mgr.employee_id AND emp.depart
ment_id=d.department_id AND d.location_id=l.location_id AND emp.
job_id=j.job_id
7 rows selected.
```

Due to the maximum piece length, there is no way to remove the forced line break after 64 characters. There is no SQL*Plus formatting option which glues consecutive lines together. However, with some background in PL/SQL programming, creating the glue to solve the issue at hand is straightforward.

The algorithm is:

1. Create an abstract data type that holds the hash value of the statement and the statement itself as a CLOB. Remember, a single CLOB can hold at least 2 GB whereas VARCHAR2 columns are limited to 4000 bytes.
2. Create a pipelined table function that selects rows from STATS$SQLTEXT piece by piece.
3. Append each piece to a temporary CLOB using DBMS_LOB.WRITEAPPEND, i.e. glue the pieces together eliminating the forced line breaks.
4. When all pieces for a single SQL or PL/SQL statement have been exhausted, use row pipelining (PIPE ROW (*object_type_instance*)) to pass an instance of the abstract data type to the caller of the function.
5. Call the pipelined table function from SQL*Plus or any other database client with the TABLE clause of the SELECT statement (SELECT * FROM TABLE (*function_name* (*optional_arguments*))).

Pipelined table functions require the keyword PIPELINED after the RETURN clause. This keyword indicates that the function returns rows iteratively. The return type of the pipelined table function must be a collection type. This collection type can be declared at the schema level with CREATE TYPE or inside a package. The function iteratively returns individual elements of the collection type. The elements of the collection type must be supported SQL data types, such as NUMBER and VARCHAR2. PL/SQL data types, such as PLS_INTEGER and BOOLEAN, are not supported as collection elements in a pipelined table function. We will use the following object type for pipelining:

```
CREATE OR REPLACE TYPE site_sys.sqltext_type AS OBJECT (
    hash_value NUMBER,
    sql_text CLOB
);
/
CREATE OR REPLACE TYPE site_sys.sqltext_type_tab AS TABLE OF sqltext_type;
/
```

The code of the pipelined table function SP_SQLTEXT is reproduced below. Objects are created in schema SITE_SYS, since SYS is reserved for the data dictionary and objects in schema SYS are not covered by a full export. Some extra work is required to obtain compatibility of the function with both Oracle9*i* and Oracle10*g*. In Oracle10*g* and subsequent releases, the column HASH_VALUE in the table STATS$SQLTEXT was renamed to OLD_HASH_VALUE due to a likewise rename in the views V$SQL and V$SQLAREA. For Oracle9*i* a synonym is used, whereas a view is created to compensate for the renamed column in Oracle10*g* and subsequent releases. Thus the code of the function SITE_SYS.SP_SQLTEXT can remain constant for both releases and dynamic SQL with DBMS_SQL must not be used.

```
$ cat sp_sqltext.sql
-- run as a DBA user
CREATE USER site_sys IDENTIFIED BY secret PASSWORD EXPIRE ACCOUNT LOCK;
/* note that show errors does not work when creating objects in a foreign schema. If you
get errors either run this script as SITE_SYS after unlocking the account or access
DBA_ERRORS as below:
col text format a66
SELECT line,text from dba_errors where name='SP_SQLTEXT' ORDER BY line;
*/
-- cleanup, e.g. for database upgraded to 10g
begin
    execute immediate 'DROP SYNONYM site_sys.stats$sqltext';
    execute immediate 'DROP VIEW site_sys.stats$sqltext';
exception when others then null;
end;
/
GRANT SELECT ON perfstat.stats$sqltext TO site_sys;
/* for 9i CREATE OR REPLACE SYNONYM site_sys.stats$sqltext FOR perfstat.stats$sqltext;
for 10g, create this view:
CREATE OR REPLACE VIEW site_sys.stats$sqltext(hash_value, piece, sql_text) AS
SELECT old_hash_value, piece, sql_text FROM perfstat.stats$sqltext;
*/
declare
    version varchar2(30);
    compatibility varchar2(30);
```

```
begin
    dbms_utility.db_version(version, compatibility);
    if to_number(substr(version,1,2)) >= 10 then
        execute immediate 'CREATE OR REPLACE VIEW site_sys.stats$sqltext
            (hash_value, piece, sql_text) AS
            SELECT old_hash_value, piece, sql_text
            FROM perfstat.stats$sqltext';
    else
        execute immediate 'CREATE OR REPLACE SYNONYM site_sys.stats$sqltext
            FOR perfstat.stats$sqltext';
    end if;
end;
/
/*
    p_hash_value is either the hash value of a specific statement in
    STATS$SQLTEXT to retrieve or NULL.
    When NULL, all statements in the Statspack repository are retrieved.
    The column is called old_hash_value in Oracle10g
*/
CREATE OR REPLACE function site_sys.sp_sqltext(p_hash_value number default null)
RETURN sqltext_type_tab PIPELINED
AS
    result_row sqltext_type:=sqltext_type(null, empty_clob);
    cursor single_stmt(p_hash_value number) is
    select hash_value, piece, sql_text from stats$sqltext
    where p_hash_value=hash_value
    order by piece;

    cursor multi_stmt is
    select hash_value, piece, sql_text from stats$sqltext
    order by hash_value, piece;
    v_sql_text stats$sqltext.sql_text%TYPE;
    v_piece binary_integer;
    v_prev_hash_value number:=NULL;
    v_cur_hash_value number:=0;

BEGIN
    dbms_lob.CREATETEMPORARY(result_row.sql_text, true);
    IF p_hash_value IS NULL THEN
        open multi_stmt; -- caller asked for all statements
    ELSE
        open single_stmt(p_hash_value); -- retrieve only one statement
    END IF;
    LOOP
        IF p_hash_value IS NULL THEN
            FETCH multi_stmt INTO v_cur_hash_value, v_piece, v_sql_text;
            EXIT WHEN multi_stmt%NOTFOUND;
        ELSE
            FETCH single_stmt INTO v_cur_hash_value, v_piece, v_sql_text;
            EXIT WHEN single_stmt%NOTFOUND;
        END IF;
        IF v_piece=0 THEN -- new stmt starts
            IF  v_prev_hash_value IS NOT NULL THEN
                -- there was a previous statement which is now finished
                result_row.hash_value:=v_prev_hash_value;
                pipe row(result_row);
                -- trim the lob to length 0 for the next statement
                dbms_lob.trim(result_row.sql_text, 0);
```

```
                    -- the current row holds piece 0 of the new statement - add it to CLOB
                    dbms_lob.writeappend(result_row.sql_text, length(v_sql_text), v_sql_text);
            ELSE
                    -- this is the first row ever
                    result_row.hash_value:=v_cur_hash_value;
                    dbms_lob.writeappend(result_row.sql_text, length(v_sql_text), v_sql_text);
            END IF;
        ELSE
            -- append the current piece to the CLOB
            result_row.hash_value:=v_cur_hash_value;
            dbms_lob.writeappend(result_row.sql_text, lengthb(v_sql_text), v_sql_text);
        END IF;
        v_prev_hash_value:=v_cur_hash_value;
    END LOOP;
    -- output last statement
    pipe row(result_row);
    dbms_lob.freetemporary(result_row.sql_text);
        IF p_hash_value IS NULL THEN
            CLOSE multi_stmt;
        ELSE
            CLOSE single_stmt;
        END IF;
    return;
END;
/
GRANT EXECUTE ON site_sys.sp_sqltext TO dba;
```

The following SQL script retrieves the statement text without forced line breaks and save it in a spool file named sp_sqltext_*hash_value*.lst, where *hash_value* is the argument passed to the script:

```
$ cat sp_sqltext_get.sql
define hash_value=&1
set verify off
set long 100000
set trimout on
set trimspool on
set feedback off
set heading off
set linesize 32767
col sql_text format a32767
spool sp_sqltext_&hash_value..lst
select sql_text from table(site_sys.sp_sqltext(&hash_value));
spool off
exit
```

Let's test the script with the hash value 1455318379 of the statement in question:

```
$ sqlplus -s system/secret @sp_sqltext_get.sql 1455318379

SELECT emp.last_name, emp.first_name, j.job_title, d.department_name, l.city,
l.state_province, l.postal_code, l.street_address, emp.email,  emp.phone_number,
emp.hire_date, emp.salary, mgr.last_name FROM hr.employees emp, hr.employees mgr,
hr.departments d, hr.locations l, hr.jobs j WHERE emp.manager_id=mgr.employee_id AND
emp.department_id=d.department_id AND d.location_id=l.location_id AND
emp.job_id=j.job_id
```

The entire statement is now on a single line of text[1] (SQL*Plus inserts a blank line at the beginning of the file, such that the total line count amounts to 2):

```
$ wc -l sp_sqltext_1455318379.lst
2 sp_sqltext_1455318379.lst
```

We finally achieved our goal of retrieving the statement text with correct SQL syntax. When called without an argument or a NULL argument, the function SP_SQLTEXT retrieves all statements from STATS$SQLTEXT.

Capturing SQL Statements with Formatting Preserved

We have already come a long way, yet we could go one step further by enabling Statspack to save SQL statements with line breaks and tab stops preserved. If you don't have any apprehensions about changing a single line in the package body of the STATSPACK package, please follow suit.

Remember, V$SQLTEXT_WITH_NEWLINES preserves line breaks and tab stops, whereas V$SQLTEXT, which is queried by Statspack, does not. First of all, we need to authorize the user PERFSTAT to access the dynamic performance view V$SQLTEXT_WITH_NEWLINES:

```
SQL> CONNECT / AS SYSDBA
SQL> GRANT SELECT ON v_$sqltext_with_newlines TO PERFSTAT;
```

I used the Revision Control System[2] (RCS) to save the original version of spcpkg.sql, which contains the STATSPACK package body, as version 1.1. Since V$SQLTEXT is referenced only once in this file, it's sufficient to change a single line as below (the line number is from an Oracle10g version of spcpkg.sql):

```
$ rcsdiff spcpkg.sql
===============================================================
RCS file: RCS/spcpkg.sql,v
retrieving revision 1.1
diff -r1.1 spcpkg.sql
4282c4282
<                       , v$sqltext  vst
---
>                       , v$sqltext_with_newlines  vst
```

Please note that the change made only has an effect on new SQL statements captured by Statspack. Any statement with a hash value already present in STATS$SQLTEXT.(OLD_)HASH_VALUE will not be captured again. To recapture existing statements, export the schema PERFSTAT to save past snapshots and run sptrunc.sql to purge all snapshots. This removes all data from STATS$SQLTEXT. Don't worry, Statspack configuration data in the tables STATS$STATSPACK_PARAMETER and STATS$IDLE_EVENT is preserved in spite of the warning which appears when running sptrunc.sql and claims that it "removes ALL data from Statspack tables".

After editing spcpkg.sql, recreating the package STATSPACK, rerunning the application, and capturing its SQL statements with Statspack, we can finally view the statement with all formatting fully preserved:

```
$ sqlplus -s system/secret @sp_sqltext_get.sql 1455318379
SELECT emp.last_name, emp.first_name, j.job_title, d.department_name, l.city,
       l.state_province, l.postal_code, l.street_address, emp.email,
       emp.phone_number, emp.hire_date, emp.salary, mgr.last_name
FROM hr.employees emp, hr.employees mgr, hr.departments d, hr.locations l, hr.jobs j
WHERE emp.manager_id=mgr.employee_id
AND emp.department_id=d.department_id
AND d.location_id=l.location_id
AND emp.job_id=j.job_id
```

---

1. The UNIX command wc counts lines and characters in files. If working on Windows, install the complimentary UNIX–like environment Cygwin from http://www.cygwin.com to get access to wc and many other UNIX utilities such as awk, grep, and find.
2. RCS is open source software. Precompiled executables for Windows ship with Cygwin and most Linux distributions. The command rcsdiff displays differences between releases of a file.

This change does not harm the appearance of the Statspack report. The section with our problem statement now becomes:

```
    CPU             CPU per      Elapsd                    Old
 Time (s) Executions Exec (s) %Total Time (s) Buffer Gets Hash Value
 -------- ---------- -------- ------ -------- ----------- ----------
    10.34         11     0.94   12.3    31.65     162,064 1455318379
 SELECT emp.last_name, emp.first_name, j.job_title, d.department_
 name, l.city,
        l.state_province, l.postal_code, l.street_address
 , emp.email,
        emp.phone_number, emp.hire_date, emp.salary, mgr.l
 ast_name
 FROM hr.employees emp, hr.employees mgr, hr.departments
  d, hr.locations l, hr.jobs j
 WHERE emp.manager_id=mgr.employee_
 id
 AND emp.department_id=d.department_id
 AND d.location_id=l.loc
 ation_id
 AND emp.job_id=j.job_id
```

Undocumented Statspack Report Parameters

As we saw in the previous sections, an important undocumented Statspack report parameter in Oracle9*i* is num_rows_per_hash. This parameter is documented in Oracle10*g*, however there are still a number of old and new undocumented report parameters in Oracle10*g*. I consider none of them as important or useful as num_rows_per_hash. Perhaps top_n_events, which is undocumented in both releases, is the most interesting. It controls how many lines are shown in the "Top Timed Events" section near the beginning of the report. Often the lowest contribution to total elapsed time (Oracle9*i*: "Total Ela Time"; Oracle10*g*: "Total Call Time") in this section is less than 2–3 percent and thus marginally relevant. It's only worth increasing top_n_events if the lowest contributor has consumed 5 percent or more of the total elapsed time. Of course, any such contributor would also appear in the *Wait Events* section of the report[1], but the percentage of total elapsed time is only reported in the *Top Timed Events* section. Below is an example "Top Timed Events" section from an Oracle10*g* Statspack report:

```
Top 5 Timed Events                                      Avg %Total
~~~~~~~~~~~~~~~~~~                                      wait   Call
Event                             Waits    Time (s)     (ms)   Time
--------------------------------- ------------ ----------- ------ ------
CPU time                                            671            90.2
db file sequential read           1,525,262         36        0    4.9
db file scattered read              138,657         16        0    2.1
latch: library cache                      7         15     2086    2.0
log file parallel write               5,187          3        1     .4
```

The lowest contribution to elapsed time comes from log file parallel write and is less than one percent, so in this case there is no need to change top_n_events. Table 58 lists the undocumented Statspack report parameters of Oracle10*g* Release 2.

Table 58: Undocumented Oracle10*g* Statspack Report Parameters

Statspack report parameter	*Purpose*	*Default Value*
avwt_fmt	Displayed precision of average wait time	1 ms
cache_xfer_per_instance	Report per instance cache transfer statistics	Y

---

1. Except if the contribution of CPU time had been so low that it was not reported in the *Top Timed Events* section, which is unlikely.

Table 58: Undocumented Oracle10*g* Statspack Report Parameters

Statspack report parameter	*Purpose*	*Default Value*
`display_file_io`	Report file–level I/O statistics	Y
`display_undostat`	Report undo segment statistics	Y
`linesize_fmt`	Controls the line size of SQL*Plus output and should be increased if any columns are made wider.	80
`streams_top_n`	Number of lines in Oracle Streams related statistics (e.g. capture, propagation, and apply statistics)	25
`top_n_events`	Number of lines in Top Timed Events report section[a]	5
`top_n_undostat`	Number of lines in undo statistics	35

a. The variable `top_n_events` is defined in `sprepins.sql` not in `sprepcon.sql`.

Statspack Tables

In Oracle10*g*, the Statspack schema PERFSTAT contains 67 tables. Among these, only STATS$ENQUEUE_STAT and STATS$STATSPACK_PARAMETER are documented in the file `spdoc.txt`. A Statspack schema contains a wealth of information on a database and the instance that opens the database (or multiple instances in case of RAC). When troubleshooting performance problems or malfunctions, it may be useful to query these tables directly to detect snapshots with high resource utilization or to figure out when a problem occurred for the first time. Table 59 contains a list of all tables, the V$ views used to populate each table, if any, and a short explanation on the purpose of the table.

Table 59: Oracle10*g* Statspack Repository Tables

Statspack Table	*Underlying V$ View(s)*	*Purpose*
`STATS$BG_EVENT_SUMMARY`	`V$SESSION_EVENT`	Wait events of background sessions
`STATS$BUFFERED_QUEUES`	`V$BUFFERED_QUEUES`	Statistics on Streams buffered queues (messages processed, messages spilled to disk, etc.)
`STATS$BUFFERED_SUBSCRIBERS`	`V$BUFFERED_SUBSCRIBERS`	Statistics on subscribers of Streams buffered queues
`STATS$BUFFER_POOL_STATISTICS`	`V$BUFFER_POOL_STATISTICS`	Buffer pool statistics per buffer pool name (DEFAULT, KEEP, RECYCLE) and block size (2 KB up to 32 KB) in the database buffer cache
`STATS$CR_BLOCK_SERVER`	`V$CR_BLOCK_SERVER`	Statistics concerning RAC consistent read block server processes (Global Cache Service)
`STATS$CURRENT_BLOCK_SERVER`	`V$CURRENT_BLOCK_SERVER`	Global Cache Service current block server statistics
`STATS$DATABASE_INSTANCE`	`V$INSTANCE`	DBMS instances for which Statspack has captured snapshots
`STATS$DB_CACHE_ADVICE`	`V$DB_CACHE_ADVICE`	Sizing advice for the database buffer cache per buffer pool name and block size
`STATS$DLM_MISC`	`V$DLM_MISC`	Real Application Clusters Global Enqueue Service and Global Cache Service statistics
`STATS$DYNAMIC_REMASTER_STATS`	`X$KJDRMAFNSTATS`	RAC Global Cache Service resource remastering

Table 59: Oracle10g Statspack Repository Tables

Statspack Table	Underlying V$ View(s)	Purpose
STATS$ENQUEUE_STATISTICS	V$ENQUEUE_STATISTICS	Enqueue statistics
STATS$EVENT_HISTOGRAM	V$EVENT_HISTOGRAM	Histogram statistics on wait events
STATS$FILESTATXS	X$KCBFWAIT, V$FILESTAT, V$TABLESPACE, V$DATAFILE	I/O statistics per data file
STATS$FILE_HISTOGRAM	V$FILE_HISTOGRAM	Histogram statistics on single block physical read time. Statistics are reported per file and per read time range (0–2 ms, 2–4 ms, 4–8 ms, etc.).
STATS$IDLE_EVENT	V$EVENT_NAME	Events considered idle waits by Statspack[a].
STATS$INSTANCE_CACHE_TRANSFER	V$INSTANCE_CACHE_TRANSFER	RAC cache transfers
STATS$INSTANCE_RECOVERY	V$INSTANCE_RECOVERY	Statistics on estimated mean time to recover in case crash recovery is needed due to instance, operating system, or hardware failure (parameter FAST_START_MTTR_TARGET)
STATS$JAVA_POOL_ADVICE	V$JAVA_POOL_ADVICE	Advice for sizing the java pool (parameter JAVA_POOL_SIZE)
STATS$LATCH	V$LATCH	Latch statistics
STATS$LATCH_CHILDREN	V$LATCH_CHILDREN	Child latch statistics
STATS$LATCH_MISSES_SUMMARY	V$LATCH_MISSES	Latch misses
STATS$LATCH_PARENT	V$LATCH_PARENT	Parent latch statistics
STATS$LEVEL_DESCRIPTION	n/a	Descriptions for snapshot levels 0, 5, 6, 7, and 10.
STATS$LIBRARYCACHE	V$LIBRARYCACHE	Shared pool statistics, including RAC specific statistics
STATS$MUTEX_SLEEP	V$MUTEX_SLEEP	Mutex statistics
STATS$OSSTAT	V$OSSTAT	Operating system statistics, such as idle time, busy time, I/O wait, and CPUs in the system
STATS$OSSTATNAME	V$OSSTAT	Lookup table for STATS$OSSTAT.OSSTAT_ID. Avoids redundant storage of V$OSSTAT.STAT_NAME.
STATS$PARAMETER	V$PARAMETER	Captured values of initialization parameters
STATS$PGASTAT	V$PGASTAT	Program global area (PGA) statistics for Automatic PGA Memory Management
STATS$PGA_TARGET_ADVICE	V$PGA_TARGET_ADVICE	Advice for setting PGA_AGGREGATE_TARGET when using Automatic PGA Memory Management
STATS$PROCESS_MEMORY_ROLLUP	V$PROCESS_MEMORY	Allocated PGA memory per category (Freeable, Other, PL/SQL, and SQL)
STATS$PROCESS_ROLLUP	V$PROCESS	Allocated PGA memory per process

Table 59: Oracle10*g* Statspack Repository Tables

Statspack Table	Underlying V$ View(s)	Purpose
STATS$PROPAGATION_RECEIVER	V$PROPAGATION_RECEIVER	Streams buffered queue propagation statistics on the receiving (destination) side
STATS$PROPAGATION_SENDER	V$PROPAGATION_SENDER	Streams buffered queue propagation statistics on the sending (source) side
STATS$RESOURCE_LIMIT	V$RESOURCE_LIMIT	Resource limit statistics on processes, sessions, enqueues, parallel execution, and undo (or rollback) segments
STATS$ROLLSTAT	V$ROLLSTAT	Rollback segment statistics
STATS$ROWCACHE_SUMMARY	V$ROWCACHE	Data dictionary cache (a.k.a. row cache) statistics per category (e.g. segments, sequences, and users)
STATS$RULE_SET	V$RULE_SET	Statistics on rule set evaluations
STATS$SEG_STAT	V$SEGMENT_STATISTICS	Segments with high physical reads or contention including RAC–specific statistics
STATS$SEG_STAT_OBJ	V$SEGMENT_STATISTICS	Lookup table for the columns DATAOBJ#, OBJ# and TS# in STATS$SEG_STAT
STATS$SESSION_EVENT	V$SESSION_EVENT	Statistics on session–specific wait events
STATS$SESSTAT	V$SESSTAT	Session–specific statistics captured if the parameter I_SESSION_ID was used with STATSPACK.SNAP
STATS$SESS_TIME_MODEL	V$SESS_TIME_MODEL	Session–specific time model statistics
STATS$SGA	V$SGA	SGA sizing information pertaining to these SGA components: database buffers, redo buffers, variable size, and fixed size
STATS$SGASTAT	V$SGASTAT	Statistics on individual pools and free memory in the shared pool
STATS$SGA_TARGET_ADVICE	V$SGA_TARGET_ADVICE	SGA sizing advice if Automatic SGA Memory Management is enabled (parameter SGA_TARGET)
STATS$SHARED_POOL_ADVICE	V$SHARED_POOL_ADVICE	Shared pool sizing advice
STATS$SNAPSHOT	V$INSTANCE, V$SESSION	Stores detailed data on each snapshot, such as snapshot id, instance number, startup time, snapshot level, session id passed to STATSPACK.SNAP with parameter I_SESSION_ID, comment, and thresholds
STATS$SQLTEXT	V$SQLTEXT	Normalized SQL statement texts split into pieces of at most 64 characters
STATS$SQL_PLAN	V$SQL_PLAN	Execution plans of captured SQL statements
STATS$SQL_PLAN_USAGE	V$SQL_PLAN	Snapshot id, date, and time when an execution plan was used
STATS$SQL_STATISTICS	V$SQL	Memory consumption by all SQL statements and non–sharable SQL statements

Table 59: Oracle10*g* Statspack Repository Tables

Statspack Table	Underlying V$ View(s)	Purpose
STATS$SQL_SUMMARY	V$SQLSTATS	Performance metrics, such as elapsed time, CPU usage, disk reads, direct path writes, and buffer gets for captured SQL statements
STATS$SQL_WORKAREA_HISTOGRAM	V$SQL_WORKAREA_HISTOGRAM	Histogram statistics for work area sizes of 0–1 KB, 1–2 KB, 2–4 KB, 4–8 KB, etc.
STATS$STATSPACK_PARAMETER	n/a	Statspack parameters such as default snapshot level and thresholds
STATS$STREAMS_APPLY_SUM	V$STREAMS_APPLY_SERVER, V$STREAMS_APPLY_READER	Statistics for Streams apply processes
STATS$STREAMS_CAPTURE	V$STREAMS_CAPTURE	Statistics for Streams capture
STATS$STREAMS_POOL_ADVICE	V$STREAMS_POOL_ADVICE	Streams pool sizing advice (parameter STREAMS_POOL_SIZE)
STATS$SYSSTAT	V$SYSSTAT	Instance–wide statistics, such as total CPU consumption, recursive cpu usage, parse calls (hard/total), number of trans-actions, etc.
STATS$SYSTEM_EVENT	V$SYSTEM_EVENT	Instance–wide wait event statistics
STATS$SYS_TIME_MODEL	V$SYS_TIME_MODEL	Instance–wide time model statistics
STATS$TEMPSTATXS	V$TABLESPACE, V$TEMPFILE, V$TEMPSTAT, X$KCBFWAIT	Statistics on sorting in temporary seg-ments
STATS$TEMP_HISTOGRAM	V$TEMP_HISTOGRAM	Histogram statistics on the number of sin-gle block read operations from temporary segments in buckets of 0–1, 1–2, 2–4, 4–8, 8–16, etc. milliseconds read duration
STATS$THREAD	V$THREAD	Information on online redo log threads
STATS$TIME_MODEL_STATNAME	V$SYS_TIME_MODEL	Lookup table for the column STAT_ID in the tables STATS$SYS_TIME_MODEL and STATS$SESS_TIME_MODEL
STATS$UNDOSTAT	V$UNDOSTAT	Undo segment statistics
STATS$WAITSTAT	V$WAITSTAT	Block contention statistics for data blocks, extent maps, file header blocks, free lists, undo blocks, undo headers, etc.

a. In Oracle10*g*, STATS$IDLE_EVENT contains 41 events from wait class "Idle", two from wait class "Network", three from wait class "Other" and 24 events which no longer exist in Oracle10*g*. STATS$IDLE_EVENT has occasionally been of concern (see bug database on Metalink), since several releases of Statspack did not insert all the wait events considered as idle in the table. For example the RAC idle wait event *ges remote message* was missing in Oracle9*i*. Thus, an idle event could make it into the report section entitled "Top 5 Timed Events" and render the calculations unusable. The solution consists of inserting missing idle wait events into the table and regenerating the Statspack report. In Oracle10*g*, 21 events from wait class Idle are not registered in STATS$IDLE_EVENT. In my view, this is rightfully so for the event *SQL*Net message from dblink*, but *PL/SQL lock timer*, which occurs when a session is put to sleep by a call to DBMS_LOCK.SLEEP, should be present in STATS$IDLE_EVENT.

Finding expensive Statements in a Statspack Repository

To get a quick overview of expensive statements in an entire Statspack repository, the result of the function SP_SQLTEXT from the previous section may be joined to STATS$SQL_SUMMARY, which contains the measurement data of all the SQL statements captured. If the figures are normalized by how many times a statement was executed (STATS$SQL_SUMMARY.EXECUTIONS), an initial overview of slow statements results.

Below is the script sp_sqltext_join.sql, which accomplishes this. It reports elapsed time in seconds (STATS$SQL_SUMMARY.ELAPSED_TIME is in microseconds). Disk reads and buffer gets are normalized by the execution count of the statement. The script restricts the result set to statements that completed after more than one second. Of course, before starting a tuning session, you should confirm that statements found in this way impair business processes.

```
$ cat sp_sqltext_join.sql
set long 1000000
col module format a6
col snap_id format 9999999
col sql_text format a80 word_wrapped
SELECT s.snap_id, s.old_hash_value,
    round(s.elapsed_time/s.executions/1000000, 2) ela_sec_per_exec,
    floor(s.disk_reads/s.executions) read_per_exec,
    floor(s.buffer_gets/s.executions) gets_per_exec,
    s.module, t.sql_text
FROM stats$sql_summary s,
(SELECT hash_value, sql_text from table(site_sys.sp_sqltext())) t
WHERE s.old_hash_value=t.hash_value
AND s.elapsed_time/s.executions/1000000 > 1
ORDER BY s.elapsed_time, s.disk_reads, s.buffer_gets;
```

Running the above query yields the well known statement that was used as an example throughout this chapter:

```
 SNAP_ID OLD_HASH_VALUE ELA_SEC_PER_EXEC READ_PER_EXEC GETS_PER_EXEC MODULE
-------- -------------- ---------------- ------------- ------------- ------
SQL_TEXT
-------------------------------------------------------------------------
      33     1455318379             2.87          2380         14733 HR
SELECT emp.last_name, emp.first_name, j.job_title, d.department_name, l.city,
l.state_province, l.postal_code, l.street_address, emp.email,  emp.phone_number,
emp.hire_date, emp.salary, mgr.last_name FROM hr.employees emp, hr.employees
mgr, hr.departments d, hr.locations l, hr.jobs j WHERE
emp.manager_id=mgr.employee_id AND emp.department_id=d.department_id AND
d.location_id=l.location_id AND emp.job_id=j.job_id
```

The above SELECT statement retrieves captured measurements since instance startup. It does not take the snapshot interval into account, such that it may miss statements which were slow intermittently, but performed acceptably on average.

Identifying Used Indexes

Statspack snapshots at level 6 or higher capture execution plans in addition to the usual measurement data. Since index usage monitoring with ALTER INDEX MONITORING is somewhat intrusive (see Chapter 4), one might consider examining index usage by accessing the Statspack repository (script sp_used_indexes.sql).

```
SQL> SELECT DISTINCT o.owner, o.object_name index_name
FROM dba_objects o, stats$sql_plan p
WHERE o.object_id=p.object#
AND o.object_type='INDEX'
AND o.owner='HR';
OWNER         INDEX_NAME
------------- -------------
HR            JOB_ID_PK
HR            LOC_ID_PK
HR            EMP_EMP_ID_PK
HR            DEPT_ID_PK
```

Execution Plans for Statements Captured with SQL Trace

When tracing applications with SQL trace, it may happen that execution plans for certain statements are absent in the trace file and as a consequence also in the TKPROF formatted report. Under these circumstances, do not use TKPROF with the option EXPLAIN or execute EXPLAIN PLAN manually, since this runs the risk of producing an execution plan which differs from the plan used by the application. Instead, use Statspack or AWR (see Chapter 26) to retrieve the execution plan, which was actually used, from the repository of the respective tool. The process is somewhat easier with Statspack, since the hash value emitted to the trace file can be used to get the desired information. In Oracle9*i*, there is a single hash value in V$SQL and it is this hash value which is also emitted to trace files. In Oracle10*g*, matters are more complicated, since there are now two hash values: V$SQL.OLD_HASH_VALUE as well as V$SQL.HASH_VALUE. Merely the latter is written to SQL trace files. Oracle10*g* Statspack uses the old hash value, which is calculated with the algorithm used by Oracle9*i*, for its SQL report. The translation from the HASH_VALUE found in the trace file to the OLD_HASH_VALUE needed to run the Statspack SQL report may be accomplished with the query below (script sp_translate_hv.sql):

```
SQL> SELECT p.snap_id, s.snap_time, p.sql_id, p.hash_value, p.old_hash_value,
p.plan_hash_value, p.cost
FROM stats$sql_plan_usage p, stats$snapshot s
WHERE p.snap_id=s.snap_id
AND p.hash_value=3786124882
ORDER BY p.snap_id;
SNAP_ID SNAP_TIME   SQL_ID        HASH_VALUE OLD_HASH_VALUE PLAN_HASH_VALUE COST
------- ---------- ------------- ---------- -------------- --------------- ----
    493 13. Oct 07 1yw85nghurbkk 3786124882     1455318379      4095786543    9
    502 13. Oct 07 1yw85nghurbkk 3786124882     1455318379      4095786543    9
    582 15. Oct 07 1yw85nghurbkk 3786124882     1455318379      3985860841   17
    602 15. Oct 07 1yw85nghurbkk 3786124882     1455318379      4095786543    9
```

The query result contains several values for the column PLAN_HASH_VALUE. Hence different execution plans were used over time. To generate the Statspack SQL report, run the script sprepsql.sql (or sprsqins.sql if Statspack data from another database was imported) and enter any adjacent snapshot identifiers from the query result above:

```
SQL> @sprepsql
…
Specify the Begin and End Snapshot Ids
~~~~~~~~~~~~~~~~~~~~~~~~~~~~~~~~~~~~~~~~
Enter value for begin_snap: 582
Begin Snapshot Id specified: 582

Enter value for end_snap: 602
End   Snapshot Id specified: 602
```

At the point where the script asks for the statement's hash value, make sure you enter the OLD_HASH_VALUE if you are using Oracle10*g*:

```
Specify the old (i.e. pre-10g) Hash Value
~~~~~~~~~~~~~~~~~~~~~~~~~~~~~~~~~~~~~~~~~~~
Enter value for hash_value: 1455318379
Hash Value specified is: 1455318379
…
Known Optimizer Plan(s) for this Old Hash Value
~~~~~~~~~~~~~~~~~~~~~~~~~~~~~~~~~~~~~~~~~~~~~~~~~~~~~~
Shows all known Optimizer Plans for this database instance, and the Snap Id's
they were first found in the shared pool.  A Plan Hash Value will appear
multiple times if the cost has changed
-> ordered by Snap Id

   First      First           Last            Plan
   Snap Id    Snap Time       Active Time     Hash Value      Cost
--------- --------------- --------------- ------------ ----------
      493 13-Oct-07 21:41 15-Oct-07 15:38    4095786543          9
```

```
     502 13-Oct-07 21:47 15-Oct-07 15:14   3985860841        17
```

Plans in shared pool between Begin and End Snap Ids
~~~~~~
Shows the Execution Plans found in the shared pool between the begin and end
snapshots specified. The values for Rows, Bytes and Cost shown below are those
which existed at the time the first-ever snapshot captured this plan - these
values often change over time, and so may not be indicative of current values
-> Rows indicates Cardinality, PHV is Plan Hash Value
-> ordered by Plan Hash Value

Operation	PHV/Object Name	Rows	Bytes	Cost
SELECT STATEMENT	----- 3985860841 ----			17
HASH JOIN		105	17K	17
TABLE ACCESS FULL	JOBS	19	513	3
HASH JOIN		105	14K	14
TABLE ACCESS FULL	EMPLOYEES	107	1K	3
HASH JOIN		106	13K	10
HASH JOIN		27	1K	7
TABLE ACCESS FULL	LOCATIONS	23	1K	3
TABLE ACCESS FULL	DEPARTMENTS	27	513	3
TABLE ACCESS FULL	EMPLOYEES	107	6K	3
SELECT STATEMENT	----- 4095786543 ----			9
NESTED LOOPS		105	17K	9
NESTED LOOPS		105	12K	7
NESTED LOOPS		105	9K	6
NESTED LOOPS		106	8K	4
TABLE ACCESS FULL	EMPLOYEES	107	6K	3
TABLE ACCESS BY INDEX ROWID	DEPARTMENTS	1	19	1
INDEX UNIQUE SCAN	DEPT_ID_PK	1		0
TABLE ACCESS BY INDEX ROWID	EMPLOYEES	1	12	1
INDEX UNIQUE SCAN	EMP_EMP_ID_PK	1		0
TABLE ACCESS BY INDEX ROWID	JOBS	1	27	1
INDEX UNIQUE SCAN	JOB_ID_PK	1		0
TABLE ACCESS BY INDEX ROWID	LOCATIONS	1	48	1
INDEX UNIQUE SCAN	LOC_ID_PK	1		0
```

The script retrieves all the execution plans for the statement with the old hash value specified. Since execution plans may change when upgrading the DBMS software to Oracle10*g*, I recommend capturing Statspack snapshots at level 6 or higher prior to an upgrade.

Oracle Corp. provides the script spup10.sql for upgrading a Statspack repository to Oracle10*g*, but states that the upgrade is not guaranteed to work. My limited experience with this script and Oracle10*g* release 2 is that repository upgrades do not succeed. To preserve Statspack snapshots captured with Oracle9*i*, export the schema PERFSTAT using the export utility (exp), before upgrading to Oracle10*g*. If necessary, an Oracle9*i* export dump may be imported into an Oracle9*i* test database to run reports (see Importing Statspack Data From Another Database on page 271).

## Finding Snapshots with High Resource Utilization

As part of my consulting work, I was occasionally asked to scrutinize an entire Statspack repository. A client would create a schema level export of the PERFSTAT schema in his production database and I would import it into a test database (more on importing Statspack data in a moment). This is a situation where initially you don't have any idea which snapshots are worth investigating.

Since a Statspack repository contains snapshots of performance data from V$ views, the Statspack report must subtract the measurements taken at the beginning of the snapshot interval from the measurements taken at the end of the
```

snapshot interval to arrive at the resource consumption during the interval. The report script `spreport.sql` is passed the beginning and end snapshot numbers as input. Hence a simple join (or outer join where necessary) is sufficient.

Matters are more complicated when all the snapshots must be investigated. This task is a case for the analytic function LAG, which maps column values of a previous row visited by a SELECT statement into the current row without a self join, such that a window containing two rows is available simultaneously. At this point the attentive reader will rightfully object that there is no previous row in a relational database. This is why an ordering must be defined using the SQL keywords OVER and ORDER BY. Below is an example of a query on STATS$SNAPSHOT using LAG:

```
SQL> SET NULL <NULL>
SQK> SELECT LAG(snap_id) OVER (ORDER BY snap_id) AS start_snap_id,
    snap_id AS end_snap_id
FROM stats$snapshot;
START_SNAP_ID END_SNAP_ID
------------- -----------
<NULL>                 33
           33          34
           34          35
```

Note that the start snapshot identifier in the first row is NULL, since it is outside of the window. For details on LAG, please consult the *Oracle Database SQL Reference* manual.

A view that yields successive snapshot identifiers and verifies that the interval is valid may be created as the basic building block for analysis. The check for interval validity is performed by comparing the values in the column STATS$SNAPSHOT.STARTUP_TIME. If the startup time does not match, then the instance was restarted in between snapshots and the measurements are not usable. In a RAC environment, matters get even more intricate. Since a single repository might contain measurements from several RAC instances, the instance numbers of the start and end snapshots must also match. This is accomplished by using the columns INSTANCE_NUMBER and SNAP_ID in the ORDER BY supplied with the function LAG. The view, which retrieves identifiers of valid consecutive begin and end snapshots, is called SP_VALID_INTERVALS (script sp_valid_intervals.sql):

```
CREATE OR REPLACE VIEW site_sys.sp_valid_intervals AS
SELECT *
FROM (
    SELECT lag(dbid) over (order by dbid, instance_number, snap_id) AS start_dbid, dbid
AS end_dbid,
    lag(snap_id) over (order by dbid, instance_number, snap_id) AS start_snap_id,
snap_id AS end_snap_id,
    lag(instance_number) over (order by dbid, instance_number, snap_id) AS
start_inst_nr, instance_number AS end_inst_nr,
    lag(snap_time) over (order by dbid, instance_number, snap_id) AS start_snap_time,
snap_time AS end_snap_time,
    lag(startup_time) over (order by dbid, instance_number, snap_id) AS
start_startup_time, startup_time AS end_startup_time
    FROM perfstat.stats$snapshot
) iv
WHERE iv.start_snap_id IS NOT NULL
AND iv.start_dbid=iv.end_dbid
AND iv.start_inst_nr=iv.end_inst_nr
AND iv.start_startup_time=iv.end_startup_time;
```

Below is a query, which accesses the view SP_VALID_INTERVALS:

```
SELECT start_snap_id, end_snap_id, start_inst_nr, start_snap_time,
trunc((end_snap_time-start_snap_time)*86400) AS interval
FROM site_sys.sp_valid_intervals;
START_SNAP_ID END_SNAP_ID START_INST_NR START_SNAP_TIME       INTERVAL
------------- ----------- ------------- ------------------- ----------
           87          88             1 15.08.2007 06:06:04       1898
           88          89             1 15.08.2007 06:37:42       2986
           90          91             1 15.08.2007 09:35:21       1323
```

High CPU Usage

High CPU usage might be an indication of a performance problem, such that snapshot intervals exhibiting high CPU usage may warrant further investigation. CPU usage is usually expressed as a percentage of available CPU resources. Applied to Statspack, this means that we need to look at CPU utilization during consecutive snapshot intervals. The algorithm for computing CPU usage from Statspack repository tables is:

1. Get the CPU consumption (in centiseconds) during the snapshot interval by subtracting the value captured by the start snapshot from the value captured by the end snapshot. This value is part of each Statspack report and is calculated by the STATSPACK package. CPU consumption since instance startup is represented by the statistic "CPU used by this session" in STATS$SYSSTAT.
2. Divide the value by 100 for conversion from centiseconds to seconds.
3. Divide the CPU consumption by the snapshot interval in seconds. The length of the interval may be derived from STATS$SNAPSHOT using the analytic function LAG.
4. Divide the result by the number of CPUs (parameter CPU_COUNT) captured at the beginning of the snapshot interval (STATS$PARAMETER) to get average CPU utilization as a percentage of CPU capacity. The CPU capacity of a system is 1 second of CPU time per CPU per second.

Let's look at an example. We will use the excerpts from the Statspack report below to provide sample figures for the calculation. The relevant figures are reproduced in bold font:

```
                Snap Id     Snap Time        Sessions Curs/Sess Comment
                -------  ------------------  --------  --------- -------
Begin Snap:         90  15-Aug-07 09:35:21     215      11.9
  End Snap:         91  15-Aug-07 09:57:24     177      10.6
  Elapsed:                  22.05 (mins)
...
Statistic                                       Total    per Second   per Trans
---------------------------------------    --------------  -----------  ---------
CPU used by this session                        82,337       62.2         23.0
```

The value of the parameter CPU_COUNT is captured, but not printed at the end of the Statspack report, since it has a default value, so we need to retrieve the value from STATS$PARAMETER:

```
SQL> SELECT value FROM stats$parameter WHERE name='cpu_count' and snap_id=90;
VALUE
-----
4
```

If we translate the above algorithm into a formula, it becomes:

$$\text{CPU usage (\%)} = \frac{\text{CPU consumption during snapshot interval (s)} \cdot 100}{\text{snapshot interval (s)} \cdot \text{CPU\_COUNT}}$$

Using the sample figures yields:

$$\frac{823.37 \cdot 100}{1323 \cdot 4} = 15.56\,\%$$

The following query automates this calculation (script snap_by_cpu_util.sql):

```
SELECT i.start_snap_id, i.end_snap_id,
i.start_snap_time, i.end_snap_time,
(i.end_snap_time - i.start_snap_time) * 86400 AS interval,
round((( (s2.value - s1.value)/ 100 / ((i.end_snap_time - i.start_snap_time) * 86400 ) /
p.value) * 100,2) AS cpu_utilization
FROM site_sys.sp_valid_intervals i, stats$sysstat s1,
stats$sysstat s2, stats$parameter p
WHERE i.start_snap_id=s1.snap_id
AND i.end_snap_id=s2.snap_id
AND s1.name='CPU used by this session'
AND s1.name=s2.name
AND p.snap_id=i.start_snap_id
AND p.name='cpu_count'
```

```
ORDER BY cpu_utilization DESC;
```

Running the query confirms the result of the manual calculation for the interval between snapshots 90 and 91:

Start SnapID	End SnapID	Start Time	End Time	Interval (s)	CPU Utilization (%)
90	91	15.08.2007 09:35:21	15.08.2007 09:57:24	1323	15.56
88	89	15.08.2007 06:37:42	15.08.2007 07:27:28	2986	7.14
87	88	15.08.2007 06:06:04	15.08.2007 06:37:42	1898	5.28

This query quickly identifies periods of high load which may merit drilling down by generating Statspack reports for the start and end snapshots with the highest CPU usage.

High DB Time

What if a performance problem is due to waiting and does not manifest itself through high CPU usage? Then the approach shown in the previous section fails. Waiting might be due to contention for latches, locks, or other resources such as slow disks. Oracle10*g* offers so called time model statistics which consider CPU consumption and waiting. These are available at instance (V$SYS_TIME_MODEL) and session level (V$SESS_TIME_MODEL). In essence, time spent within the database instance is accounted for. According to the *Oracle10g Database Reference*:

> *DB Time is the amount of elapsed time (in microseconds) spent performing database user–level calls. This does not include the time spent on instance background processes such as PMON.*

The manual further states that the metric "DB time" includes the following:

- DB CPU
- connection management call elapsed time
- sequence load elapsed time
- sql execute elapsed time
- parse time elapsed
- PL/SQL execution elapsed time
- inbound PL/SQL rpc elapsed time
- PL/SQL compilation elapsed time
- Java execution elapsed time

Not a single word about wait time here. However, considering that wait time is rolled up into the elapsed time of database calls in SQL trace files, it would be surprising if time model statistics followed a different approach. A quick proof may be built by leveraging the undocumented PL/SQL package DBMS_SYSTEM and generating some artificial wait time. At the beginning of a new database session, all values in V$SESS_TIME_MODEL are nearly zero:

```
SQL> SELECT stat_name, value/1000000 time_secs FROM v$sess_time_model
WHERE (stat_name IN ('sql execute elapsed time','PL/SQL execution elapsed time')
   OR stat_name like 'DB%')
AND sid=userenv('sid');
STAT_NAME                                                        TIME_SECS
---------------------------------------------------------------- ----------
DB time                                                            .018276
DB CPU                                                             .038276
sql execute elapsed time                                          .030184
PL/SQL execution elapsed time                                     .007097
```

Next, we generate some wait time, by artificially waiting one second for the event *db file scattered read*, which otherwise occurs when a SELECT statement causes a full table scan. Although in reality the wait happens in a PL/SQL procedure, it is accounted for as if a full table scan due to a SQL statement had occurred.

```
SQL> EXECUTE dbms_system.wait_for_event('db file scattered read', 1, 1);
PL/SQL procedure successfully completed.
```

Note how the metrics "sql execute elapsed time" and "PL/SQL execution elapsed time" both have increased by almost one second. Obviously, due to the artificial nature of this test, the elapsed time is accounted for twice. The metric "DB CPU" has risen only slightly and "DB time" has also increased by one second, since it aggregates sql and PL/SQL elapsed time[1].

```
SQL> SELECT stat_name, value/1000000 time_secs FROM v$sess_time_model
WHERE (stat_name IN ('sql execute elapsed time','PL/SQL execution elapsed time')
   OR stat_name like 'DB%')
AND sid=userenv('sid');
STAT_NAME                                                      TIME_SECS
-------------------------------------------------------------- ----------
DB time                                                          1.030818
DB CPU                                                            .045174
sql execute elapsed time                                        1.017276
PL/SQL execution elapsed time                                    .987208
```

The test shows that waiting on events, which occur as part of SQL execution, is rolled up into the metric "sql execute elapsed time". Wait time, except for wait events in wait class Idle[1], is also rolled up into "DB time".

Just like with CPU usage, we need to somehow normalize "DB time". Computer systems have a more or less unlimited capacity for wait time. The more processes run on a system and compete for the same resources, the more wait time is accumulated at a system level. When ten processes each wait one second for the same TX enqueue, ten times the total wait time of a single process results. The metric "DB time" may be normalized by the snapshot interval. I shall call this metric *relative DB time*. We will again start with a manual calculation. The relevant excerpts of an Oracle10g Statspack report are below. Figures required for the calculation of relative DB time are in bold font:

```
Snapshot        Snap Id    Snap Time           Sessions Curs/Sess Comment
~~~~~~~~        ---------- ------------------- -------- --------- -------------------
Begin Snap:        83 06-Sep-07 17:04:06          24       3.3
  End Snap:        84 06-Sep-07 17:09:54          24       3.3
  Elapsed:                5.80 (mins)
```

```
Time Model System Stats  DB/Inst: TEN/TEN1  Snaps: 83-84
-> Ordered by % of DB time desc, Statistic name


Statistic                                    Time (s) % of DB time
------------------------------------ -------------------- ------------
sql execute elapsed time                        319.3          100.0
PL/SQL execution elapsed time                   316.7           99.2
DB CPU                                          301.4           94.4
...
DB time                                         319.3
```

Expressed as a formula, relative DB time is:

$$\text{relative DB time (s)} = \frac{\text{DB time (s)}}{\text{snapshot interval (s)}}$$

Using the sample figures yields:

$$\frac{319.3}{5.8 \cdot 60} = 0.92$$

The query, which automates the calculation, is once again based on the view SP_VALID_INTERVALS (file snap_by_db_time.sql):

```
SQL> SELECT i.start_snap_id, i.end_snap_id,
i.start_snap_time, i.end_snap_time,
(i.end_snap_time - i.start_snap_time) * 86400 AS interval,
round((s2.value - s1.value) / 1000000 /* convert from microsec to sec */
/ ((i.end_snap_time - i.start_snap_time) * 86400 ), 2) /* normalize by snapshot
interval */
AS db_time_per_sec
```

---

1. Interestingly, the one second waited is not accounted for twice in the metric "DB time".
1. To retrieve all events in wait class Idle, run the following query on an Oracle10g instance:
   SELECT name FROM v$event_name WHERE wait_class='Idle'.

```
FROM site_sys.sp_valid_intervals i, stats$sys_time_model s1, stats$sys_time_model s2,
stats$time_model_statname n
WHERE i.start_snap_id=s1.snap_id
AND i.end_snap_id=s2.snap_id
AND n.stat_name='DB time'
AND s1.stat_id=n.stat_id
AND s2.stat_id=n.stat_id
ORDER BY db_time_per_sec DESC;
 Start    End
SnapID SnapID Start Time       End Time        Interval (s) DB time/s
------ ------ -------------- -------------- ------------ ---------
    83     84 06.09.07 17:04 06.09.07 17:09          348       .92
    49     50 05.09.07 07:45 05.09.07 08:00          850       .02
    25     26 25.07.07 19:53 25.07.07 20:00          401       .01
```

The highest relative DB time occurred in the interval between snapshots 83 and 84.

Importing Statspack Data From Another Database

As stated earlier, it may be desirable to import Statspack data from a database into a different database for analysis. Let's say that the schema PERFSTAT of a production database is exported once per month, backed up to tape, and then the Statspack tables are truncated to conserve space. The deleted snapshots may be imported into another database, should the need arise to investigate past snapshots, e.g. to retrieve last month's execution plan of a particular statement. Obviously, the production database cannot be the target of the import, since this might interfere with the ongoing snapshot capture process.

The procedure shown below takes into account that the Statspack table STATS$IDLE_EVENT might contain additional wait events that were missing in a particular Statspack release. The brute force approach of dropping all tables owned by PERFSTAT and letting import create them, would remove this customizing. This is why the approach shown below does not drop any of the Statspack tables. Instead, it disables referential integrity constraints, truncates the tables with sptrunc.sql[1], and uses the import setting IGNORE=Y to import data into existing tables.

As a starting point, a test database where Statspack has been installed with spcreate.sql is required. The version of Statspack installed must match the version contained in the export dump. Any automatic snapshot captures should be disabled. First of all, existing snapshots need to be removed from the Statspack repository by running the script sptrunc.sql:

```
$ sqlplus perfstat/secret @sptrunc
Connected to:
Oracle9i Enterprise Edition Release 9.2.0.1.0 - Production
Warning
~~~~~~~
Running sptrunc.sql removes ALL data from Statspack tables.  You may
wish to export the data before continuing.

About to Truncate Statspack Tables
~~~~~~~~~~~~~~~~~~~~~~~~~~~~~~~~~~~~
If you would like to continue, press <return>

Enter value for return:
Entered - starting truncate operation
Table truncated.
...
Truncate operation complete
SQL> EXIT
```

Next, referential integrity constraints are disabled, since these would be violated during the import process. The imp utility re–enables them at the end of the import run. Disabling constraints is achieved by generating a SQL script,

---

1. The script sptrunc.sql does not truncate the table STATS$IDLE_EVENT.

which contains ALTER TABLE DISABLE CONSTRAINT statements with SQL*Plus. The SQL script is named gen_disable_sp_constr.sql and its contents are below:

```
set linesize 200
set trimout on
set trimspool on
set heading off
set pagesize 0
set feedback off
set heading off
spool disable.sql
select 'ALTER TABLE perfstat.' || table_name || ' DISABLE CONSTRAINT ' ||
constraint_name || ';'
from dba_constraints
where owner='PERFSTAT' and constraint_type='R';
prompt exit
exit
```

Next, run the script as user PERFSTAT:

```
$ sqlplus -s perfstat/secret @gen_disable_sp_constr.sql
ALTER TABLE perfstat.STATS$BG_EVENT_SUMMARY DISABLE CONSTRAINT
STATS$BG_EVENT_SUMMARY_FK;
...
ALTER TABLE perfstat.STATS$WAITSTAT DISABLE CONSTRAINT STATS$WAITSTAT_FK;
```

SQL*Plus writes the generated ALTER TABLE statements to the file disable.sql. Running disable.sql disables all referential integrity constraints in schema PERFSTAT:

```
$ sqlplus -s perfstat/secret @disable
Table altered.
...
Table altered.
```

At this point, the schema is ready for importing past snapshot data. Note that the import option IGNORE=Y is used to import into existing tables. Import will signal several ORA-00001 and ORA-02264 errors. These are irrelevant and should be ignored.

```
$ imp system/secret file=perfstat.dmp full=y ignore=y log=imp.log
Import: Release 9.2.0.1.0 - Production on Wed Sep 19 18:09:00 2007
. importing PERFSTAT's objects into PERFSTAT
...
ORA-00001: unique constraint (PERFSTAT.STATS$IDLE_EVENT_PK) violated
Column 1 smon timer
...
. . importing table     "STATS$STATSPACK_PARAMETER"          1 rows imported
IMP-00017: following statement failed with ORACLE error 2264:
 "ALTER TABLE "STATS$STATSPACK_PARAMETER" ADD CONSTRAINT "STATS$STATSPACK_P_P"
 "IN_CK" CHECK (pin_statspack in ('TRUE', 'FALSE')) ENABLE NOVALIDATE"
IMP-00003: ORACLE error 2264 encountered
ORA-02264: name already used by an existing constraint
...
. . importing table               "STATS$WAITSTAT"          126 rows imported
...
About to enable constraints...
Import terminated successfully with warnings.
```

Now we are ready to run Statspack reports. Note that the script spreport.sql cannot be used, since it only considers snapshots taken by the current instance. Instead, its companion script sprepins.sql must be used. This latter script is called by spreport.sql once it has determined the database identifier and instance number. With sprepins.sql, setting both of these figures is a manual process. When sprepins.sql is run, it lists the database instances in STATS$DATABASE_INSTANCE. Select the desired instance, preferably by copying and pasting.

```
SQL> @sprepins
Instances in this Statspack schema
~~~~~~~~~~~~~~~~~~~~~~~~~~~~~~~~~~~

    DB Id    Inst Num DB Name      Instance     Host
----------- -------- ------------ ------------ -----------
 4273840935        1 PRODDB        IPROD        dbserver3
Enter value for dbid: 4273840935
Using 4273840935 for database Id
Enter value for inst_num: 1
Using 1 for instance number
Completed Snapshots
                              Snap                 Snap
Instance      DB Name          Id  Snap Started   Level Comment
------------ ------------ ----- ---------------- ----- -------------
PR02          PROD           104 15 Aug 2006 16:30   10
...

                             202 22 Aug 2006 09:15   10
                             203 22 Aug 2006 09:30   10
```

At this point, the script asks for the beginning and end snapshot identifiers and the report file name in the usual manner. Once instance name and instance number have been entered, there is no difference between reporting on snapshots captured by the current instance and imported snapshot data.

Source Code Depot

Table 60: Statspack Source Code Depot

File Name	Functionality
gen_disable_sp_constr.sql	Generates a SQL script, which disables all referential integrity constraints in schema PERFSTAT
snap_by_cpu_util.sql	Lists snapshot intervals with high CPU usage
snap_by_db_time.sql	Lists snapshot intervals with high DB time
sp_sqltext.sql	PL/SQL pipelined table function for retrieval of syntactically correct (i.e. no forced line breaks) SQL statements from the Statspack repository
sp_sqltext_get.sql	SQL script which calls the pipelined table function SITE_SYS.SP_SQLTEXT
sp_sqltext_join.sql	Retrieves statements which had an elapsed time of more than one second per execution from a Statspack repository
sp_translate_hv.sql	Translates an Oracle10*g* hash value from a SQL trace file to the old hash value for use with Statspack and to the SQL identifier (SQL_ID) for use with AWR by querying STATS$SQL_PLAN_USAGE
sp_used_indexes.sql	Identifies used indexes in a schema; requires snapshot level 6 or higher
sp_valid_intervals.sql	View for retrieving valid snapshot intervals using the analytic function LAG
sprepins_fix_10g.sql	Fix for incorrect session level reports in Oracle10*g* (bug 5145816); replaces the original file sprepins.sql
sprepins_fix_9i.sql	Fix for incorrect session level reports in Oracle9*i* (bug 5145816); replaces the original file sprepins.sql
sql_fulltext.sql	SQL*Plus script for retrieving a SQL statement identified by hash value from V$SQL (requires at least Oracle10*g*)
statspack_purge.sql	Snapshot purge PL/SQL procedure for Oracle9*i*

Chapter 26

Integrating Extended SQL Trace and AWR

Status: The Active Workload Repository (AWR) and SQL trace files both capture performance–relevant data on SQL and PL/SQL execution. It is undocumented that both data sources may be linked to answer questions which frequently arise during investigations of performance problems.

Benefit: By integrating SQL trace data with AWR, it is possible to find out whether different execution plans were used for a particular statement and at what time. Furthermore, contrary to EXPLAIN PLAN, the AWR is a reliable source for execution plans when plans for certain statements are absent from SQL trace files.

Retrieving Execution Plans

Unlike Statspack release 10.2, which captures the SQL_ID as well as the old (V$SQL.OLD_HASH_VALUE) and new hash value (V$SQL.HASH_VALUE) for SQL statement texts, AWR captures merely the SQL_ID from V$SQL. In Oracle10g, this poses a slight problem for the retrieval of past execution plans and statistics for statements captured by SQL trace files. The reason is that Oracle10g trace files do not include the SQL_ID from V$SQL. Oracle11g SQL trace files include the new parameter sqlid (see section PARSING IN CURSOR Entry Format on page 225), which corresponds to the SQL_ID from V$SQL. Thus, the issue of mapping a SQL statement text to the SQL_ID has been resolved in Oracle11g.

Note that execution plans are only emitted to SQL trace files when cursors are closed, such that it is possible to encounter trace files that do not contain execution plans for certain statements. If such statements have been aged out of the shared pool by the time the absence of an execution plan becomes evident, then AWR or Statspack (see page 265) are the only options for retrieving the plan. Occasionally the optimizer chooses different plans for the same statement over time. One execution plan might result in a very poor response time while another may cause an appropriate response time. The procedure presented below shows how to retrieve all plans for a SQL statement captured by SQL trace and AWR. The five–way join of tables in the sample schema HR depicted on page 251 is used as an example. In releases prior to Oracle11g, we need to start by determining the SQL_ID for a statement, since those releases do not emit it to the SQL trace file. Since AWR captures the SQL statement text as a character large object (CLOB) from V$SQL.SQL_FULLTEXT, this is accomplished by searching for the statement text or portions of it with DBMS_LOB. Statements captured by AWR are stored in the data dictionary base table WRH$_SQLTEXT and may be accessed through the view DBA_HIST_SQLTEXT (script awr_sqltext.sql):

```
SQL> SET LONG 1048576
SQL> COLUMN sql_text FORMAT a64 WORD_WRAPPED
SQL> SELECT sql_id, sql_text
FROM dba_hist_sqltext
WHERE dbms_lob.instr(sql_text, '&pattern', 1, 1) > 0;
Enter value for pattern: FROM hr.employees emp, hr.employees mgr


SQL_ID        SQL_TEXT
------------- ----------------------------------------------------------------
1yw85nghurbkk SELECT emp.last_name, emp.first_name, j.job_title,
              d.department_name, l.city,
              l.state_province, l.postal_code, l.street_address, emp.email,
              emp.phone_number, emp.hire_date, emp.salary, mgr.last_name
              FROM hr.employees emp, hr.employees mgr, hr.departments d,
              hr.locations l, hr.jobs j
              WHERE emp.manager_id=mgr.employee_id
              AND emp.department_id=d.department_id
              AND d.location_id=l.location_id
              AND emp.job_id=j.job_id
```

Having retrieved the SQL_ID, we may now search for AWR snapshots, which captured the statement. The view DBA_HIST_SQLSTAT not only contains the snapshot identifiers, but also gives access to execution statistics, hash values of execution plans, and the optimizer environment used (script awr_sqlstat.sql):

```
SQL> SELECT st.snap_id, to_char(sn.begin_interval_time,'dd. Mon yy hh24:mi')
begin_time,
st.plan_hash_value, st.optimizer_env_hash_value opt_env_hash,
round(st.elapsed_time_delta/1000000,2) elapsed,
round(st.cpu_time_delta/1000000,2) cpu,
round(st.iowait_delta/1000000,2) iowait
FROM dba_hist_sqlstat st, dba_hist_snapshot sn
WHERE st.snap_id=sn.snap_id
AND st.sql_id='1yw85nghurbkk'
ORDER BY st.snap_id;
```

SNAP_ID	BEGIN_TIME	PLAN_HASH_VALUE	OPT_ENV_HASH	ELAPSED	CPU	IOWAIT
72	13. Oct 07 21:39	4095786543	611815770	1.28	.05	1.21
73	13. Oct 07 21:42	4095786543	611815770	.32	.06	.27
73	13. Oct 07 21:42	3985860841	3352456078	1.82	.38	1.60
81	15. Oct 07 11:24	4095786543	611815770	.16	.06	.10

The fact that the columns PLAN_HASH_VALUE and OPT_ENV_HASH in the query result are not unique for the single SQL_ID "1yw85nghurbkk" proves that multiple plans for the same statement have been used and that the statement was run with different optimizer parameter settings. Actually, a single parameter used by the optimizer, namely OPTIMIZER_INDEX_COST_ADJ, which was varied between 100 (default) and 10000, is responsible for the effect shown. The increase of OPTIMIZER_INDEX_COST_ADJ caused the optimizer to consider index access as 100 times more expensive. As a consequence, the optimizer chose a plan with full table scans and hash joins instead of index accesses and nested loops.

There are two approaches for retrieving plans from an AWR repository:

1. the pipelined table function DBMS_XPLAN.DISPLAY_AWR
2. the AWR SQL statement report script $ORACLE_HOME/rdbms/admin/awrsqrpt.sql

Unless you wish to retrieve query block names for use in hints—these are not displayed by the AWR report—the second approach is the preferred one, since it not only contains all plans for a specific SQL_ID, but also includes execu-

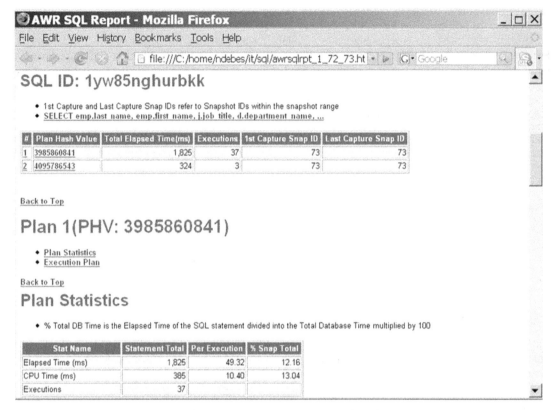

Figure 12: AWR SQL Report with Multiple Plans for a Single Statement

tion statistics. The call to DBMS_XPLAN.DISPLAY_AWR requires the SQL_ID, plan hash value, and the database identifier (V$DATABASE.DBID) as input parameters. Values for the first two parameters have already been retrieved from DBA_HIST_SQLSTAT, so solely the database identifier must be queried before DBMS_XPLAN can be called:

```
SQL> SELECT dbid FROM v$database;
      DBID
----------
2870266532
SQL> SELECT * FROM TABLE (dbms_xplan.display_awr('1yw85nghurbkk', 4095786543,
2870266532, 'ALL'));
PLAN_TABLE_OUTPUT
----------------------------------------------------------------------------
SQL_ID 1yw85nghurbkk
--------------------
SELECT emp.last_name, emp.first_name, j.job_title, d.department_name, l.city,
...
Plan hash value: 4095786543

PLAN_TABLE_OUTPUT
----------------------------------------------------------------------------
| Id  | Operation          | Name   | Rows  | Bytes  | Cost  (%CPU)| Time     |
----------------------------------------------------------------------------
|   0 | SELECT STATEMENT   |        |       |        |     9 (100)|          |
|   1 |  NESTED LOOPS      |        |   105 | 18060  |     9  (12)| 00:00:01 |
...
Query Block Name / Object Alias (identified by operation id):
```

```
  -------------------------------------------------------------
    1 - SEL$1

PLAN_TABLE_OUTPUT
  -------------------------------
    5 - SEL$1 / EMP@SEL$1
  …
```

The AWR report script `awrsqrpt.sql` asks for the `SQL_ID` and the beginning and end snapshot identifiers. These values were previously retrieved from `DBA_HIST_SQLSTAT`. Figure 12 depicts an excerpt of an AWR SQL report in HTML format with two execution plans for a single `SQL_ID`.

Lessons Learned

Retrieving execution plans for SQL statements captured with SQL trace from AWR is useful for retrieving plans absent from SQL trace files or for comparisons of current and past execution plans. Execution plans may change over time for various reasons such as:

- changes in optimizer parameters
- updated optimizer statistics (`DBMS_STATS` or `ANALYZE`)
- software upgrades or downgrades
- partitioning tables or indexes, which were previously not partitioned
- bind variable peeking

The hash value calculated on the optimizer environment and stored in the AWR repository may be used as evidence that a plan may have changed due to different parameter settings at instance or session level. Since updated optimizer statistics may cause plans to change, I recommend saving statistics in a statistics table using the packaged procedure `DBMS_STATS.EXPORT_SCHEMA_STATS` before overwriting them. The package `DBMS_STATS` includes the procedure `CREATE_STAT_TABLE` for creating statistics tables. In Oracle10g, automatic statistics recalculation for a schema may be prevented with `DBMS_STATS.LOCK_SCHEMA_STATS`.

Source Code Depot

Table 61: Extended SQL Trace and AWR Source Code Depot

File Name	Functionality
awr_sqltext.sql	Retrieves the `SQL_ID` and full statement text from `DBA_HIST_SQLTEXT` based on a text subset of a SQL statement. The `SQL_ID` may be passed to the AWR script `awrsqrpt.sql` as input.
awr_sqlstat.sql	Retrieves AWR snapshots that captured a SQL statement with a certain `SQL_ID`. Execution statistics, such as elapsed time and CPU usage, are displayed along with hash values for the execution plan and the optimizer environment.

Chapter 27

ESQLTRCPROF Extended SQL Trace Profiler

Status: To the best of my knowledge ESQLTRCPROF is currently the only free profiler for Oracle9*i*, Oracle10*g*, and Oracle11*g* extended SQL trace files.

Benefit: ESQLTRCPROF is capable of parsing the undocumented extended SQL trace file format. It calculates a resource profile for an entire SQL trace file and for each cursor in the trace file. Essentially, it is a replacement for TKPROF, since it addresses several shortcomings of Oracle Corporation's own SQL trace analysis tool.

Categorizing Wait Events

The ultimate goal is to automatically create a resource profile from an extended SQL trace file. Even though the file format has been discussed in Chapter 24, some more preparations are necessary to achieve this goal. An issue that has not yet been discussed is the categorization of wait events into intra database call wait events and inter database call wait events. This is necessary for correct response time accounting. Intra database call wait events occur within the context of a database call. The code path executed to complete a database call consists not only of CPU consumption, but may also engender waiting for resources such as disks, latches, or enqueues. Time spent waiting within a database call is accounted for by intra database call wait events. Examples of such wait events are *latch free, enqueue*, *db file sequential read, db file scattered read*, and *buffer busy waits*. In fact, most wait events are intra database call wait events. Inter database call wait events occur when the DBMS server is waiting to receive the next database call. In other words, the DBMS server is idle, since the client does not send a request.

According to Millsap and Holt ([MiHo 2003], page 88), the wait events below are inter (or between) database call wait events:

- *SQL*Net message from client*
- *SQL*Net message to client*

- *pmon timer*
- *smon timer*
- *rdbms ipc message*

Of these wait events *pmon timer*, *smon timer*, and *rdbms ipc message* solely occur in background processes. Thus, the only inter database call wait events, which are relevant to tuning an application, are *SQL*Net message from client* and *SQL*Net message to client*[1].

Figure 13 is a graphical representation of database calls, wait events, and transaction entries (XCTEND) from an extended SQL trace file. The X axis represents time (t), while the Y axis represents the dependency level (dep). Inter database call wait events are depicted in white font against a dark background. Note that all of these wait events are either associated with a cursor number *n* ($n > 0$) at dependency level 0 or the default cursor 0.

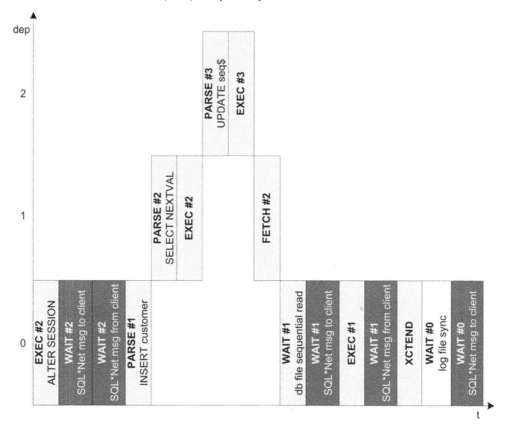

Figure 13: Dependency Levels and Inter Database Call Wait Events[a]

a. The abbreviation msg is used instead of the word message in wait event names.

---

1. The list in [MiHo 2003] also contains *pipe get* and *single-task message*. I have omitted *pipe get*, since my testing showed that this wait event occurs when an execute database call on the PL/SQL package DBMS_PIPE is made. When DBMS_PIPE.RECEIVE_MESSAGE is called with a non–zero time–out, time spent waiting for a message is accounted for with the wait event *pipe get* and is rolled up into the parameter e of the associated EXEC entry. Thus, *pipe get* is an intra database call wait event.

    All implementations of the ORACLE DBMS since Oracle9*i* are two–task implementations only, i.e. server process and client process are separate tasks, each running in their own address space. Hence the wait event *single-task message* is no longer used (see also Metalink note 62227.1).

Calculating Response Time and Statistics

According to Millsap and Holt ([MiHo 2003]), the response time R represented by a SQL trace file is defined as the sum of the elapsed time spent in database calls (e values) at dependency level 0 (dep=0) plus the sum of all ela values from inter database call wait events. The wait time (ela values) accumulated while processing a database call is rolled up into the parameter e of the database call that engendered the wait. The categorization of wait events discussed in the previous section is applied in the calculation of R. Time spent waiting for intra database call wait events must not be added to R, since this would result in double counting. The e values of a database call already contain the wait time of all intra database call wait events. Database calls are emitted to trace files upon completion. This is why WAIT entries for intra database call wait events appear before the PARSE, EXEC, and FETCH entries that engendered them.

Runtime statistics, such as consistent reads, physical writes, and db block gets at dependency levels other than zero are rolled up into PARSE, EXEC, and FETCH calls at dependency level 0. Just like ela values of intra database call wait events, these must not be double counted. To promote a thorough understanding of how an extended SQL trace profiler calculates a resource profile from a trace file, I would like to walk the reader through a manual calculation of some figures based on a small trace file.

Case Study

This case study is based on a small Perl DBI program called insert_customer.pl. The program inserts a single row into the table CUSTOMER. Each customer is identified by a unique number, which is generated by the sequence CUSTOMER_ID_SEQ. An INSERT trigger is used to assign the next value from the sequence to the column ID of the table. I have deliberately created the sequence with the NOCACHE option, since this causes recursive SQL (i.e. dep values larger than zero)[1]. The purpose of the case study is twofold:

- To demonstrate how the response time R is calculated.
- To provide evidence that runtime statistics at dependency levels larger than zero are rolled up into statistics at higher dependency levels and ultimately at dependency level 0.

Remember that statements executed directly by a database client have dependency level zero. The program pauses twice to allow the user to query the dynamic performance view V$SESSTAT, once before enabling SQL trace and once just prior to disconnection from the ORACLE instance. Since V$SESSTAT is not affected by double counting as discussed above, it holds an accurate representation of session level statistics.

Running the Perl Program

To repeat the case study, open two terminal windows. One for running the Perl program and another one for querying V$SESSTAT. Run insert_customer.pl in the first terminal window[2]:

```
$ insert_customer.pl
Hit return to continue
```

While the program waits for input, query V$SESSTAT in the second window:

```
SQL> SELECT n.name, s.value
FROM v$sesstat s, v$statname n, v$session se
WHERE s.statistic#=n.statistic#
AND n.name IN ('db block gets', 'consistent gets')
AND s.sid=se.sid
AND se.program LIKE 'perl%';
NAME                VALUE
----------------- -----
db block gets          0
consistent gets      195
```

Now hit return in the first window. The program enables SQL trace and inserts a single row. After a moment the program asks for input again:

---

1. Do not use NOCACHE in any real world applications, since it degrades performance.
2. Use the Perl DBI environment variables DBI_USER, DBI_PASS, and DBI_DSN to specify user name, password, data source, and connect string (see Chapter 22).

```
Hit return to continue
```

At this point, the INSERT statement and a subsequent COMMIT have been completed. Another query on V$SESSTAT reveals that the figures for db block gets and consistent gets have risen to 9 and 197 respectively.

```
SQL> SELECT n.name, s.value
FROM v$sesstat s, v$statname n, v$session se
WHERE s.statistic#=n.statistic#
AND n.name IN ('db block gets', 'consistent gets')
AND s.sid=se.sid
AND se.program='perl.exe';
NAME                    VALUE
------------------- -----
db block gets           9
consistent gets       197
```

You may now hit return for the second time. The program disconnects and terminates. Subtracting the initial figures from the final figures yields 9 db block gets and 2 consistent gets. In theory, the extended SQL trace file should contain the same figures, however small discrepancies are in order.

The trace file, which results from this test, is small enough to evaluate manually. Note that the trace file which results the first time you run the test may be larger than the file reproduced below, since the dictionary cache and the library cached need to be loaded. Except for some header information, the complete trace file (with line numbers added) is depicted below:

```
 1 Oracle Database 10g Enterprise Edition Release 10.2.0.3.0 - Production
 2 With the Partitioning, Oracle Label Security, OLAP and Data Mining options
 3
 4 *** ACTION NAME:() 2007-11-20 15:39:38.546
 5 *** MODULE NAME:(insert_customer.pl) 2007-11-20 15:39:38.546
 6 *** SERVICE NAME:(TEN.oradbpro.com) 2007-11-20 15:39:38.546
 7 *** SESSION ID:(44.524) 2007-11-20 15:39:38.546
 8 =====================
 9 PARSING IN CURSOR #2 len=68 dep=0 uid=61 oct=42 lid=61 tim=789991633616 hv=740818757
ad='6be3972c'
10 alter session set events '10046 trace name context forever, level 8'
11 END OF STMT
12 EXEC #2:c=0,e=98,p=0,cr=0,cu=0,mis=0,r=0,dep=0,og=1,tim=789991633607
13 WAIT #2: nam='SQL*Net message to client' ela= 5 driver id=1413697536 #bytes=1 p3=0
obj#=-1 tim=789991638001
14 WAIT #2: nam='SQL*Net message from client' ela= 569 driver id=1413697536 #bytes=1
p3=0 obj#=-1 tim=789991638751
15 =====================
16 PARSING IN CURSOR #1 len=87 dep=0 uid=61 oct=2 lid=61 tim=789991639097 hv=2228079888
ad='6cad992c'
17 INSERT INTO customer(name, phone) VALUES (:name, :phone)
18         RETURNING id INTO :id
19 END OF STMT
20 PARSE #1:c=0,e=84,p=0,cr=0,cu=0,mis=0,r=0,dep=0,og=1,tim=789991639091
21 =====================
22 PARSING IN CURSOR #2 len=40 dep=1 uid=61 oct=3 lid=61 tim=789991640250 hv=1168215557
ad='6cbaf25c'
23 SELECT CUSTOMER_ID_SEQ.NEXTVAL FROM DUAL
24 END OF STMT
25 PARSE #2:c=0,e=72,p=0,cr=0,cu=0,mis=0,r=0,dep=1,og=1,tim=789991640243
26 EXEC #2:c=0,e=62,p=0,cr=0,cu=0,mis=0,r=0,dep=1,og=1,tim=789991641167
27 =====================
28 PARSING IN CURSOR #3 len=129 dep=2 uid=0 oct=6 lid=0 tim=789991641501 hv=2635489469
ad='6bdb9be8'
```

```
29 update seq$ set
increment$=:2,minvalue=:3,maxvalue=:4,cycle#=:5,order$=:6,cache=:7,highwater=:8,audit$
=:9,flags=:10 where obj#=:1
30 END OF STMT
31 PARSE #3:c=0,e=68,p=0,cr=0,cu=0,mis=0,r=0,dep=2,og=4,tim=789991641494
32 EXEC #3:c=0,e=241,p=0,cr=1,cu=2,mis=0,r=1,dep=2,og=4,tim=789991642567
33 STAT #3 id=1 cnt=1 pid=0 pos=1 obj=0 op='UPDATE  SEQ$ (cr=1 pr=0 pw=0 time=195 us)'
34 STAT #3 id=2 cnt=1 pid=1 pos=1 obj=102 op='INDEX UNIQUE SCAN I_SEQ1 (cr=1 pr=0 pw=0
time=25 us)'
35 FETCH #2:c=0,e=1872,p=0,cr=1,cu=3,mis=0,r=1,dep=1,og=1,tim=789991643213
36 WAIT #1: nam='db file sequential read' ela= 33297 file#=4 block#=127140 blocks=1
obj#=54441 tim=789993165434
37 WAIT #1: nam='SQL*Net message to client' ela= 5 driver id=1413697536 #bytes=1 p3=0
obj#=54441 tim=789993165747
38 EXEC #1:c=1500000,e=1525863,p=1,cr=2,cu=8,mis=0,r=1,dep=0,og=1,tim=789993165858
39 WAIT #1: nam='SQL*Net message from client' ela= 232 driver id=1413697536 #bytes=1
p3=0 obj#=54441 tim=789993166272
40 XCTEND rlbk=0, rd_only=0
41 WAIT #0: nam='log file sync' ela= 168 buffer#=5320 p2=0 p3=0 obj#=54441
tim=789993166718
42 WAIT #0: nam='SQL*Net message to client' ela= 2 driver id=1413697536 #bytes=1 p3=0
obj#=54441 tim=789993166829
43 *** 2007-11-20 15:39:49.937
44 WAIT #0: nam='SQL*Net message from client' ela= 9864075 driver id=1413697536
#bytes=1 p3=0 obj#=54441 tim=790003031019
45 XCTEND rlbk=0, rd_only=1
46 STAT #2 id=1 cnt=1 pid=0 pos=1 obj=53073 op='SEQUENCE  CUSTOMER_ID_SEQ (cr=1 pr=0
pw=0 time=1878 us)'
47 STAT #2 id=2 cnt=1 pid=1 pos=1 obj=0 op='FAST DUAL  (cr=0 pr=0 pw=0 time=15 us)'
```

Calculating Statistics

Database call statistics at dependency levels other than zero are rolled up into the statistics at dependency level 0. To calculate the total number of db block gets in the trace file, we must consider only cu parameter values of PARSE, EXEC, and FETCH entries with dep=0. The database call parameter cu (for current read) corresponds to the statistic db block gets. The only cu value at dependency level 0, which is larger than zero, is in line 38 (cu=8). This is off by one from the db block gets value retrieved from V$SESSTAT. Note that three db block gets have occurred at dependency level 1 and below (line 35). Two db block gets were recorded at dependency level 2 (line 32). The fact that the total number of db block gets as determined by querying V$SESSTAT was 9, confirms that database call statistics at lower levels are rolled up into statistics at dependency level 0. The sum of cu values at any dependency level is 13. If the cu values at dependency level n did not include the cu values at dependency level $n+1$, we would see at least 13 db block gets in V$SESSTAT.

Calculating Response Time

The response time R is defined as the sum of all e values at dep=0 plus the sum of all ela values from inter database call wait events ([MiHo 2003], page 94):

$$R = \sum_{dep = 0} e + \sum_{inter\ db\ call} ela$$

The sum of all e values at dep=0 is derived from lines 12, 20, and 38:

$$\sum_{dep = 0} e = 98 + 84 + 1525863 = 1526045$$

SQL*Net message from client and *SQL*Net message to client* are the inter database call wait events present in the trace file. The sum of all `ela` values of inter database call wait events is derived from lines 13, 14, 37, 39, 42, and 44:

$$\sum_{\text{inter db call}} ela = 5 + 569 + 5 + 232 + 2 + 9864075 = 9864888$$

Since `e` and `ela` values are in microseconds, R expressed in seconds is:

$$R = \frac{(1526045 + 9864888)}{1000000} = 11.390 \text{ s}$$

To check that the code path measured is sufficiently instrumented, it is always a good idea to calculate the elapsed time covered by the trace file from the first and last `tim` values. The lowest timestamp at the beginning of the trace file is 789991633616. The highest timestamp in line 44 is 790003031019. Thus, the interval in seconds covered by the trace file is:

$$\frac{790003031019 - 789991633616}{1000000} = 11.397 \text{ s}$$

If there is a large discrepancy between R and the elapsed time covered by the trace file, then the ORACLE kernel does not have instrumentation for part of the code path in place.

The elapsed time spent in database calls consists of CPU consumption and waiting. Ideally `e` for each database call at dependency level 0 would equal the CPU usage (`c`) plus the intra db call wait time (`ela`):

$$\sum_{dep = 0} e = \sum_{dep = 0} c + \sum_{\text{intra db call}} ela$$

In practice, there is usually a difference between these two values. It is unknown where time not accounted for by `c` and `ela` was spent. The unknown contribution to response time (U) within an entire trace file may be calculated as:

$$U = \sum_{dep = 0} e - \sum_{dep = 0} c - \sum_{\text{intra db call}} ela$$

In the example, the difference is very small, slightly more than 7 ms:

$$\frac{(98 + 84 + 1525863) - 1500000 - 33297}{1000000} = -0.007252 \text{ s}$$

Of course it is much more convenient to automate the calculation of these figures with an extended SQL trace profiler such as ESQLTRCPROF. This is the subject of the next section.

ESQLTRCPROF Reference

ESQLTRCPROF is an extended SQL trace profiler written in Perl by the author. It has the following features:

- calculation of a resource profile for an entire SQL trace file
- calculation of a resource profile for each SQL or PL/SQL statement in a trace file
- categorization of the inter database call wait event *SQL*Net message from client* into unavoidable latency due to network round–trips and think time
- sorting of statements by total elapsed time (the sum of parse, execute, and fetch elapsed time plus inter database call wait time except think time)
- extraction of execution plans from STAT entries
- calculation of various statistics, such as physical reads, consistent gets, db block gets, transactions per second, and buffer cache hit ratio
- apportionment of enqueue waits by individual enqueue
- breakdown of latch waits by individual latch
- inclusion of SQL statement hash values in the report for quickly locating statements in trace files and integration with Statspack
- inclusion of SQL statement identifiers (`sqlid`) in the report for quickly locating statements in trace files and integration with AWR (requires Oracle11g trace files as input)
- inclusion of module, action, and dependency level in the report

From the perspective of the database server, think time is elapsed time that a database client accumulates without making any demands on the DBMS. In other words, the client is not sending any requests to the DBMS server. By default, ESQLTRCPROF classifies any waits of more than 5 ms for *SQL*Net message from client* as the pseudo wait event *think time*. For such waits, think time will be displayed as a contributor to response time in resource profiles.

Command Line Options

ESQLTRCPROF accepts three options that modify its processing. When called without any arguments, it prints information on its usage, supported options, and their meaning:

```
$ esqltrcprof.pl
Usage: esqltrcprof.pl -v -r <ORACLE major release>.<version> -t <think time in
milliseconds> <extended sql trace file>
-v verbose output; includes instances of think time
-r value must be in range 8.0 to 10.2
```

The threshold beyond which *SQL*Net message from client* is classified as think time is configured in milliseconds with the option -t (for threshold). The default threshold (5 ms) is usually appropriate for local area networks (LAN), but needs to be increased for trace files from database clients that connect over a wide area network (WAN). To suppress the categorization of *SQL*Net message from client*, e.g. for the sake of comparing figures with a TKPROF report or other tools, set the think time threshold to an arbitrarily large value such as ten hours (36000000 ms). This will make the pseudo wait event think time disappear from resource profiles.

The option -v (for verbose) is for printing instances of think time. When -v is used, each time ESQLTRCPROF encounters an instance of think time in a trace file, it prints a message with the length of the think time and the position in the trace file. Module and action are also included in the message, to point out where in the code path think time was detected:

```
Found 9.864 s think time (Line 64, Module 'insert_customer.pl' Action 'undefined')
```

Since ESQLTRCPROF also supports Oracle8, which merely had centisecond resolution of e, c, and ela values, it determines the unit of timing data from the trace file header. The mapping of latch numbers to latch names is also release dependent. Thus, ESQLTRCPROF refuses to process trace files, which lack release information in the header. The TRCSESS utility shipped with Oracle10g creates trace files which lack a header. When ESQLTRCPROF is passed such a file as input, it exits with the error message below:

```
$ esqltrcprof.pl insert_cust.trcsess
No trace file header found reading trace file up to line 9. ORACLE release unknown.
Please use switch -r to specify release
Usage: esqltrc_profiler.pl -v -r <ORACLE major release>.<version> -t <think time in
milliseconds> <extended sql trace file>
-v verbose output; includes instances of think time
-r value must be in range 8.0 to 10.2
```

The option -r (for release) is provided to let ESQLTRCPROF know the release of the ORACLE DBMS that created the trace file:

```
$ esqltrcprof -r 10.2 insert_cust.trcsess
Assuming ORACLE release 10.2 trace file.
Resource Profile
================

Response time: 11.391s; max(tim)-min(tim): 11.397s
...
```

ESQLTRCPROF Report Sections

ESQLTRCPROF reports consist of a resource profile at session level, statistics at session level, statement level resource profiles, and statement level statistics for each statement encountered in the trace file. The report starts with the session level section entitled "Resource Profile".

Session Level Resource Profile

The resource profile for the trace file used in the previous case study is reproduced below. The R and db block gets figures that were calculated manually are identical to the figures reported by ESQLTRCPROF. The 7 ms of unknown time also matches the manual calculation. The report includes the difference between the maximum and minimum timestamp (tim) value found as "max(tim)–min(tim)" next to the response time.

```
$ esqltrcprof.pl ten_ora_6720_insert_customer.pl.trc
ORACLE version 10.2 trace file. Timings are in microseconds (1/1000000 sec)
Warning: WAIT event 'log file sync' for cursor 0 at line 61 without prior PARSING IN
CURSOR #0 - all waits for cursor 0 attributed to default unknown statement with hash
value -1
Resource Profile
================


Response time: 11.391s; max(tim)-min(tim): 11.397s
Total wait time: 9.898s
----------------------------


Note: 'SQL*Net message from client' waits for more than 0.005s are considered think
time
Wait events and CPU usage:
 Duration     Pct        Count    Average Wait Event/CPU Usage/Think Time
 --------     ------    ---------- --------- -------------------------------------------
   9.864s    86.59%         1    9.864075s think time
   1.500s    13.17%         8    0.187500s total CPU
   0.033s     0.29%         1    0.033297s db file sequential read
   0.001s     0.01%         2    0.000400s SQL*Net message from client
   0.000s     0.00%         1    0.000168s log file sync
   0.000s     0.00%         3    0.000004s SQL*Net message to client
  -0.007s    -0.06%                         unknown
 --------    ------    -------------------------------------------------------------------
  11.391s   100.00%  Total response time


Total number of roundtrips (SQL*Net message from/to client): 3


CPU usage breakdown
-----------------------
parse CPU:     0.00s (3 PARSE calls)
exec  CPU:     1.50s (4 EXEC calls)
fetch CPU:     0.00s (1 FETCH calls)
```

The session level resource profile ends with detailed information on the apportionment of CPU usage. Sessions that modify many rows have the highest CPU consumption in the "exec CPU" category, whereas sessions that are mostly reading will have most of the CPU usage accounted for as "fetch CPU".

Session Level Statistics

The next report section contains statistical information. Transactions per second are calculated based on R and XCTEND entries. Entries of the form XCTEND rlbk=0, rd_only=0 are used as transaction end markers. The division of the number of transaction end markers encountered by R yields transactions per second. What is a transaction? Of course, this is entirely dependent on the application. Different applications perform different types of transactions. This figure may only be used to compare the performance of the same application before and after tuning. Note that the response time of a code path may be much improved after optimization, while transactions per seconds may have dropped. This would happen after the elimination of unnecessary commits. All the statistics calculated and their sources are summarized in Table 62.

```
Statistics:
-----------
COMMITs (read write): 1 -> transactions/sec 0.088
COMMITs (read only): 1
ROLLBACKs (read write): 0
ROLLBACKs (read only): 0
rows processed: 1
```

```
cursor hits (soft parses): 3
cursor misses (hard parses): 0
consistent gets: 2
db block gets: 8
physical reads: 1
buffer cache hit ratio: 90.00%

Physical read breakdown:
-----------------------
single block: 1
multi-block: 0

Latch wait breakdown
-----------------------

Enqueue wait breakdown (enqueue name, lock mode)
------------------------------------------------
```

Table 62: Statistics

Statistic	Source
Buffer cache hit ratio	cr, cu, and p in PARSE, EXEC, and FETCH entries
Consistent gets	cr in PARSE, EXEC, and FETCH entries
Cursor hits and misses	parameter mis in PARSE entries
Db block gets	cu in PARSE, EXEC, and FETCH entries
Enqueue waits	WAIT entries with nam='enqueue' or 'enq: *enqueue_details*', where *enqueue_details* contains the name of an enqueue and a short description (e.g. nam='enq: TX - contention').
Latch waits	WAIT entries with nam='latch free' or 'latch: *latch_details*', where *latch_details* contains the name of a latch and a short description (e.g. nam='latch: cache buffers chains').
Physical reads	p in PARSE, EXEC, and FETCH entries
Rows processed	r in PARSE, EXEC, and FETCH entries
Single block and multi block reads	p3 (Oracle9*i* and prior releases) or blocks (Oracle10*g*) of the wait events *db file sequential read* and *db file scattered read*
Transactions per second	R and XCTEND rlbk=0, rd_only=0

The small trace file used in the previous case study did not contain any waits for enqueues or latches. Hence the latch wait and enqueue wait sections above are empty. Below is an excerpt of an ESQLTRCPROF report, which resulted from tracing database sessions that were concurrently enqueuing messages into an Advanced Queuing queue table. The excerpt illustrates that the sessions were contending for both latches and enqueues:

```
Latch wait breakdown
-----------------------
row cache objects              waits:    1 sleeps:    0
library cache pin              waits:    2 sleeps:    0
commit callback allocation     waits:    1 sleeps:    0
cache buffers chains           waits:    2 sleeps:    1
dml lock allocation            waits:    1 sleeps:    0
library cache                  waits:    9 sleeps:    4
enqueue hash chains            waits:    1 sleeps:    0
```

```
Enqueue wait breakdown (enqueue name, lock mode)
-------------------------------------------------
HW,X  waits:          4
TX,S  waits:          7
```

The enqueue HW was requested in exclusive mode (X), whereas the enqueue TX was requested in shared mode (S). The enqueue HW (high water mark) is requested when a segment needs to grow, while the enqueue TX is used to serialize write access to rows and the interested transaction list (ITL) at the beginning of a database block.

In Oracle10g, the fixed view V$ENQUEUE_STATISTICS may be used to generate a list of 208 enqueue types and names along with descriptions and one or more reasons why each enqueue may be requested. Table 63 contains such a list for some of the more common enqueue types. The table's rows were generated by the following query:

```
SQL> SELECT eq_type, eq_name, req_description, req_reason
FROM v$enqueue_statistics
WHERE eq_type IN ('CF', 'CI', 'DX', 'HV', 'HW', 'JQ', 'JS', 'SQ', 'SS', 'ST', 'TM',
'TS', 'TX', 'UL', 'US')
ORDER BY eq_type;
```

If you encounter an enqueue that is neither documented nor listed in Table 63, then querying V$ENQUEUE_STATISTICS will give you a first impression of what the enqueue is used for and why the application you are optimizing may have requested the enqueue. Many enqueue types are identical in Oracle9i and Oracle10g. So there is a good chance that you may find information that also applies to Oracle9i.

Table 63: Enqueue Types

Enqueue Type	Name	Description	Reason for Getting Enqueue
CF	Controlfile Transaction	Synchronizes accesses to the control file	contention
CI	Cross–Instance Call Invocation	Coordinates cross–instance function invocations	contention
DX	Distributed Transaction	Serializes tightly coupled distributed transaction branches	contention
HV	Direct Loader High Water Mark	Lock used to broker the high water mark during parallel inserts	contention
HW	Segment High Water Mark	Lock used to broker the high water mark during parallel inserts	contention
JQ	Job Queue	Lock to prevent multiple instances from running a single job	contention
JS	Job Scheduler	Lock to prevent job from running elsewhere	job run lock–synchronize
JS	Job Scheduler	Lock to recover jobs running on crashed RAC inst	job recov lock
JS	Job Scheduler	Lock on internal scheduler queue	queue lock
JS	Job Scheduler	Scheduler non–global enqueues	sch locl enqs
JS	Job Scheduler	Lock obtained when cleaning up q memory	q mem clnup lck
JS	Job Scheduler	Lock got when adding subscriber to event q	evtsub add
JS	Job Scheduler	Lock got when dropping subscriber to event q	evtsub drop
JS	Job Scheduler	Lock got when doing window open/close	wdw op
JS	Job Scheduler	Lock got during event notification	evt notify
JS	Job Scheduler	Synchronizes accesses to the job cache	contention

Table 63: Enqueue Types

Enqueue Type	Name	Description	Reason for Getting Enqueue
SQ	Sequence Cache	Lock to ensure that only one process can replenish the sequence cache	contention
SS	Sort Segment	Ensures that sort segments created during parallel DML operations aren't prematurely cleaned up	contention
ST	Space Transaction	Synchronizes space management activities in dictionary—managed tablespaces	contention
TM	DML	Synchronizes accesses to an object	contention
TS	Temporary Segment	Serializes accesses to temp segments	contention
TX	Transaction	Lock held on an index during a split to prevent other operations on it	index contention
TX	Transaction	Lock held by a transaction to allow other transactions to wait for it	contention
TX	Transaction	Lock held on a particular row by a transaction to prevent other transactions from modifying it	row lock contention
TX	Transaction	Allocating an ITL entry in order to begin a transaction	allocate ITL entry
UL	User–defined	Lock used by user applications[a]	contention
US	Undo Segment	Lock held to perform DDL on the undo segment	contention

a. Waits for the enqueue UL occur when an application implements synchronization with the package DBMS_LOCK.

Statement Level Resource Profiles

The last section of an ESQLTRCPROF report contains the SQL statements encountered, statement level resource profiles, statement level statistics, and execution plans. Each statement is depicted in a separate subsection, which begins with the statement's hash value and the statement's total elapsed time. The hash value is normally unique and is useful for quickly locating a statement in a trace file. Furthermore, the hash value may be used to retrieve current and past execution plans of a particular statement from a Statspack repository (see Chapter 25).

Statement Sort Order

Unlike TKPROF, ESQLTRCPROF does not have any command line options for sorting. At first glance, this may seem like a disadvantage, however this is one of the strengths of ESQLTRCPROF. ESQLTRCPROF always sorts statements by the *total elapsed time* attributed to each statement. At the extended SQL trace file level, this means that ESQLTRCPROF calculates the total elapsed time by summing up the e values of PARSE, EXEC, and FETCH entries of a certain cursor and adds the ela values of inter database call wait events except for *SQL*Net message from client* waits, which are classified as think time. Think time is ignored, since it is not indicative of a problem with the DBMS instance. This approach is superior to the way TKPROF sorts statements on three counts:

- TKPROF sorts either by executed elapsed time (exeela) or fetch elapsed time (fchela), but not by the entire elapsed time of PARSE, EXEC, and FETCH entries. For the purpose of sorting, it is irrelevant where the time was spent, since response time is what matters.
- TKPROF ignores inter database call wait events when sorting statements.
- TKPROF subtracts the recursive resource utilization (dep values larger than zero) when reporting on statements at dependency level 0. This makes it impossible to sort by the most expensive statements executed by the client.

In my view, it is more appropriate not to subtract recursive resource utilization. Then a statement sent by a client (dep=0) appears higher in the sort order than recursive statements engendered by that same statement. Thus, it is evident which statements merit a closer look and are candidates for drilling down to higher dependency levels. Ideally, ESQLTRCPROF would create a separate report section that depicts the recursive relationship among statements, but this is beyond the capabilities of the current version.

ESQLTRCPROF has a peculiar feature for dealing with trace file entries that relate to cursor number 0 as well as for cursors that lack a PARSING IN CURSOR entry. The latter phenomenon may be seen when tracing is begun while an application is in mid–flight. There may be EXEC, FETCH, and WAIT entries for a cursor without a corresponding PARSING IN CURSOR entry. Thus, the SQL statement text for such a cursor cannot be determined[1]. There is never a PARSING IN CURSOR entry for cursor 0. LOB access with OCI may also be attributed to cursor 0. Instead of ignoring entries pertaining to such cursors, which is what TKPROF does in the section on individual statements, ESQL-TRCPROF defines a default cursor with the impossible "hash value" –1 to account for any such trace file entries. The ESQLTRCPROF report based on the trace file from the previous section's case study is continued below. Note that even this short trace file contained almost ten seconds of think time and a log file sync, which were attributed to cursor 0.

```
Statements Sorted by Elapsed Time (including recursive resource utilization)
================================================================================

Hash Value: 2228079888 - Total Elapsed Time (excluding think time): 1.526s

INSERT INTO customer(name, phone) VALUES (:name, :phone)
        RETURNING id INTO :id
```

DB Call	Count	Elapsed	CPU	Disk	Query	Current	Rows
PARSE	1	0.0001s	0.0000s	0	0	0	0
EXEC	1	1.5259s	1.5000s	1	2	8	1
FETCH	0	0.0000s	0.0000s	0	0	0	0
Total	2	1.5259s	1.5000s	1	2	8	1

Wait Event/CPU Usage/Think Time	Duration	Count
total CPU	1.500s	2
db file sequential read	0.033s	1
SQL*Net message from client	0.000s	1
SQL*Net message to client	0.000s	1

```
Hash Value: 1168215557 - Total Elapsed Time (excluding think time): 0.002s

SELECT CUSTOMER_ID_SEQ.NEXTVAL FROM DUAL
```

DB Call	Count	Elapsed	CPU	Disk	Query	Current	Rows
PARSE	1	0.0001s	0.0000s	0	0	0	0
EXEC	1	0.0001s	0.0000s	0	0	0	0
FETCH	1	0.0019s	0.0000s	0	1	3	1
Total	3	0.0020s	0.0000s	0	1	3	1

Wait Event/CPU Usage/Think Time	Duration	Count
total CPU	0.000s	3

1. The measurement scripts sp_capture.sql and awr_capture.sql presented in Chapter 28 create a level 2 error stack dump, since this dump may contain the missing SQL statement texts.

```
Execution Plan:
Step Parent      Rows Row Source
---- ------ -------- --------------------------------------------------------------
   1      0        1 SEQUENCE  CUSTOMER_ID_SEQ (cr=1 pr=0 pw=0 time=1878 us)
(object_id=53073)
   2      1        1  FAST DUAL   (cr=0 pr=0 pw=0 time=15 us)
```

Hash Value: 740818757 - Total Elapsed Time (excluding think time): 0.001s

alter session set events '10046 trace name context forever, level 8'

DB Call	Count	Elapsed	CPU	Disk	Query	Current	Rows
PARSE	0	0.0000s	0.0000s	0	0	0	0
EXEC	1	0.0001s	0.0000s	0	0	0	0
FETCH	0	0.0000s	0.0000s	0	0	0	0
Total	1	0.0001s	0.0000s	0	0	0	0

Wait Event/CPU Usage/Think Time	Duration	Count
SQL*Net message from client	0.001s	1
SQL*Net message to client	0.000s	1
total CPU	0.000s	1

Hash Value: 2635489469 - Total Elapsed Time (excluding think time): 0.000s

update seq$ set
increment$=:2,minvalue=:3,maxvalue=:4,cycle#=:5,order$=:6,cache=:7,highwater=:8,audit$
=:9,flags=:10 where obj#=:1

DB Call	Count	Elapsed	CPU	Disk	Query	Current	Rows
PARSE	1	0.0001s	0.0000s	0	0	0	0
EXEC	1	0.0002s	0.0000s	0	1	2	1
FETCH	0	0.0000s	0.0000s	0	0	0	0
Total	2	0.0003s	0.0000s	0	1	2	1

Wait Event/CPU Usage/Think Time	Duration	Count
total CPU	0.000s	2

```
Execution Plan:
Step Parent      Rows Row Source
---- ------ -------- --------------------------------------------------------------
   1      0        1 UPDATE  SEQ$ (cr=1 pr=0 pw=0 time=195 us)
   2      1        1  INDEX UNIQUE SCAN I_SEQ1 (cr=1 pr=0 pw=0 time=25 us)
(object_id=102)
```

Hash Value: -1 - Total Elapsed Time (excluding think time): 0.000s

Cursor 0 - unknown statement (default container for any trace file entries relating to
cursor 0)

DB Call	Count	Elapsed	CPU	Disk	Query	Current	Rows
PARSE	0	0.0000s	0.0000s	0	0	0	0

```
EXEC            0    0.0000s    0.0000s        0        0        0        0
FETCH           0    0.0000s    0.0000s        0        0        0        0
-------  -------  ---------  ---------  -------  -------  -------  -------
Total           0    0.0000s    0.0000s        0        0        0        0
```

```
Wait Event/CPU Usage/Think Time            Duration   Count
----------------------------------------  ---------  --------
think time                                   9.864s         1
log file sync                                0.000s         1
SQL*Net message to client                    0.000s         1
total CPU                                    0.000s         0
```

SQL Identifiers and Oracle11g Trace Files

The latest release of ESQLTRCPROF supports Oracle11g extended SQL trace files. It includes the SQL identifier, module, action, and dependency level in the header of each statement–level resource profile. SQL identifiers were introduced with Oracle10g, but are not emitted to SQL trace files prior to Oracle11g. Thus, merely ESQLTRCPROF reports based on Oracle11g trace files contain SQL identifiers. Below is an example:

```
Statements Sorted by Elapsed Time (including recursive resource utilization)
================================================================================

Hash Value: 1256130531 - Total Elapsed Time (excluding think time): 0.102s
SQL Id: b85s0yd5dy1z3 Module 'insert_perf5.pl' Action 'undefined' Dependency Level: 0

INSERT INTO customer(id, name, phone) VALUES (customer_id_seq.nextval, :name, :phone)
        RETURNING id INTO :id
```

```
DB Call    Count    Elapsed        CPU     Disk    Query  Current     Rows
-------  -------  ---------  ---------  -------  -------  -------  -------
PARSE          1    0.0002s    0.0000s        0        0        0        0
EXEC          10    0.0956s    0.0313s        5       27       36       10
FETCH          0    0.0000s    0.0000s        0        0        0        0
-------  -------  ---------  ---------  -------  -------  -------  -------
Total         11    0.0958s    0.0313s        5       27       36       10
```

```
Wait Event/CPU Usage/Think Time            Duration   Count
----------------------------------------  ---------  --------
total CPU                                    0.031s        11
db file sequential read                      0.021s         3
SQL*Net message from client                  0.006s        10
SQL*Net message to client                    0.000s        10
```

```
Execution Plan:
Step Parent     Rows Row Source
---- ------  ------- ------------------------------------------------------------
   1      0        0 LOAD TABLE CONVENTIONAL   (cr=3 pr=4 pw=4 time=0 us)
   2      1        1 SEQUENCE  CUSTOMER_ID_SEQ (cr=3 pr=1 pw=1 time=0 us)
(object_id=15920)
```

The SQL identifier in reports allows for easy integration with AWR. It may be used as input to the AWR SQL report script awrsqrpt.sql or DBMS_XPLAN:

```
SQL> SELECT * FROM TABLE (dbms_xplan.display_awr('b85s0yd5dy1z3'));
PLAN_TABLE_OUTPUT
--------------------------------------------------------------
SQL_ID b85s0yd5dy1z3
--------------------

INSERT INTO customer(id, name, phone) VALUES (customer_id_seq.nextval,
:name, :phone)           RETURNING id INTO :id
```

```
Plan hash value: 2690979981

---------------------------------------------------------
| Id  | Operation                | Name          | Cost  |
---------------------------------------------------------
|  0  | INSERT STATEMENT         |               |   1   |

PLAN_TABLE_OUTPUT
---------------------------------------------------------
|  1  |  LOAD TABLE CONVENTIONAL |               |       |
|  2  |    SEQUENCE              | CUSTOMER_ID_SEQ |     |
---------------------------------------------------------
Note
----
   - cpu costing is off (consider enabling it)
```

Module and action are extracted from application instrumentation entries. If no such entries are present in a trace file, both module and action are reported as "undefined". The Oracle9*i* APPNAME entry format is used to extract module and action from Oracle9*i* trace files. The dependency level is taken from the parameter dep of PARSING IN CURSOR entries.

Lessons Learned

The ESQLTRCPROF profiler accepts an extended SQL trace file as input and calculates session level and statement level resource profiles. To the best of my knowledge, it is the only profiler which categorizes *SQL*Net message from client* into *think time* and unavoidable network round–trips between client and database server. The pseudo wait event *think time* is defined as a WAIT entry with nam='SQL*Net message from client' where the ela value exceeds a configurable threshold. Remember that a DBA does not stand any chance to reduce think time accumulated by a database client. Occasionally the DBMS is not to blame for performance problems that end users or developers perceive as database performance problems. If you encounter a resource profile with very prominent think time, say 50% or more, the average duration of think time is more than several hundred milliseconds and there are no expensive SQL statements in the statement level ESQLTRCPROF report, this is probably such a case. If you do encounter such a case, average think time will usually be in the range of several seconds. You should check the average duration of think time to safeguard against erroneous classification of *SQL*Net message from client* as think time due to a threshold that is too low. Of course it is also important to pay attention to the measurement interval. It would be inappropriate to choose a period of inactivity by a database client as the measurement interval.

ESQLTRCPROF tries to address some shortcomings of TKPROF. Given that Millsap and Holt's book [MiHo 2003] has been available since 2003, it is somewhat astonishing that the TKPROF release shipped with Oracle11g still does not contain a resource profile, nor does it sort wait events by contribution to response time. TKPROF also fails to report average durations of database calls and wait events.

ESQLTRCPROF takes into account that inter database call as well as intra database call wait events affect a statement's contribution to response time. A statement that is executed many times at dependency level 0 incurs a network round–trip for each execution. Thus, a statement that executes in a fraction of a second, but is executed many times, may contribute more to response time than a slower statement, which is executed merely a few times. For the purpose of sorting SQL or PL/SQL statements in a trace file by their actual contribution to response time, inter database call wait events must be considered too. This is why ESQLTRCPROF defines total elapsed time for a statement as the sum of all e values plus the sum of all ela values for inter database call wait events that are associated with a statement. Total elapsed time is used to sort statements in the ESQLTRCPROF statement level report section. Due to this novel approach, ESQLTRCPROF does not need sort options in the way that TKPROF does.

Source Code Depot

Table 64: ESQLTRCPROF Source Code Depot

File Name	Functionality
esqltrcprof.pl	This Perl program creates a session level resource profile as well as statement level resource profiles from an extended SQL trace file. It classifies the wait event *SQL*Net message from client* into think time and genuine network latency. It also computes transactions per second and other metrics and breaks the wait events *latch free* and *enqueue* down to individual latches and enqueues.
insert_customer.pl	Perl program that inserts a row into a table with INSERT RETURNING. DDL for creating database objects referenced by the program is included in the Perl source code.
insert_customer.trc	Extended SQL trace file from a run of insert_customer.pl.

Chapter 28

The MERITS Performance Optimization Method

Status: The MERITS performance optimization method is built around a sophisticated assessment of extended SQL trace files. The extended SQL trace profiler ESQLTRCPROF, which is capable of parsing the undocumented trace file format, is used in the assessment phase of the method. The MERITS method uses undocumented features predominantly in the assessment, reproduction, and extrapolation phases.

Benefit: The MERITS method is a framework for solving performance problems. The goal of the method is to identify the root cause of slow response time and to subsequently modify parameters, database objects, or application code until the performance goal is met.

Introduction to the MERITS Method

The MERITS performance optimization method is an approach to performance optimization that consists of six phases and relies on undocumented features in several phases. MERITS is a designed acronym derived from the six phases of the method, which are:

1. **M**easurement
2. **A**ssessment
3. **R**eproduction
4. **I**mprovement
5. **E**xtrapolation
6. **I**nstallation

The first step in any performance optimization project should consist of measuring the application or code path that is too slow (phase 1). Measurement data are assessed in the second phase. In some cases this assessment may already reveal the cause of the performance problem. More intricate cases need to be reproduced by a test case, potentially on a test system (phase 3). If a SQL statement takes excessive time to execute, then the test case consists of reproducing the response time of the SQL statement. The fourth phase is concerned with improving the response time of the application, code path, or test case. This may involve creating a new index, changing optimizer parameters, changing the SQL statement, changing database objects with DDL, introducing previously unused features (e.g. Partitioning option, stored outlines, SQL profiles), etc. This is phase 4. Effects of the improvement are measured in the same way as the original code path. Comparing the measurement data of the original code path with the measurement data of the improvements achieved in phase 4 may be used to extrapolate the magnitude of the performance improvement (phase 5). In other words, it is possible to forecast the effect of an improvement in a test case on the code path that was measured in phase 1. If the improvement is deemed sufficient, the necessary changes need to be approved and installed on the target (production) system at some point. Discussing each phase of the MERISTS method in full detail is a subject for a separate book. However, I provide enough information on each phase to allow the reader to use the method as a framework for performance optimization tasks.

Measurement

Since extended SQL trace is the most complete account of where a database session spent its time and a resource profile may be compiled from extended SQL trace data, this data source is at the core of the measurements taken. However, an extended SQL trace file does not provide a complete picture of an application, system, or DBMS instance. Some aspects which are not covered by an extended SQL trace file are:

- load at the operating system level (I/O bottlenecks, paging, network congestion, waiting for CPU)
- ORACLE DBMS parameters
- session statistics (V$SESSSTAT)
- contending database sessions

To capture a complete picture of the system, I recommend using tools such as sar, iostat, vmstat, and top to record activity at the operating system level. Concerning the DBMS, I advocate taking a Statspack or AWR snapshot, which spans the same interval as the extended SQL trace file. The Statspack snapshot should include the traced session (STATSPACK.SNAP parameter i_session_id). If AWR is preferred, an active session history report may be used to get additional information on the session. It may be necessary to take several measurements and to compute an average to compensate for fluctuations in response time. Both AWR and Statspack reports contain a list of all initialization parameters with non–default values. An ASH report contains a section on contending sessions entitled "Top Blocking Sessions".

Measurement Tools

This section presents two SQL scripts, which may serve as measurement tools at session and instance level. The script awr_capture.sql is based on AWR and ASH, while sp_capture.sql is based on Statspack. Both scripts require SYSDBA privileges. The scripts do not invoke any operating system tools to collect operating system statistics. Yet, an Oracle10g Statspack report includes CPU and memory statistics at operating system level in the "Host CPU" and "Memory Statistics" sections and an AWR report includes a section titled "Operating System Statistics".

Both AWR and ASH are included in the extra–cost Diagnostics Pack. The downside of ASH is that it does not provide a resource profile, since it is built with sampling. A session–level Statspack report does include a rudimentary resource profile, although the report does not use the term resource profile. Session level data are based on V$SESSION_EVENT and V$SESSTAT, which afford the calculation of a resource profile. Interesting sections from an ASH report, which a session–level Statspack as well as a TKPROF report lack, are "Top Service/Module", "Top SQL using literals", "Top Blocking Sessions", and "Top Objects/Files/Latches".

Extended SQL Trace, AWR, and ASH

The script awr_capture.sql temporarily sets the hidden parameter _ASH_SAMPLE_ALL=TRUE to cause ASH to sample idle wait events for improved diagnostic expressiveness. Then the script takes an AWR snapshot and enables level 12 SQL trace for the session which exhibits a performance problem. Next, the script asks the user for how long it should trace the session. There are two ways of using the script:

- Tracing the session for a predetermined interval, such as 300 or 600 seconds. This is achieved by entering the desired length of the interval. The script calls DBMS_LOCK.SLEEP to pause for the specified number of seconds, takes another AWR snapshot, and disables SQL trace.

- Using an event–based approach to control the measurement interval. With this approach, type 0 in response to the question concerning the length of the interval, but do not yet hit return. Wait until an event, such as an end user calling to report that the session you are tracing has returned a result set, occurs, then hit return. Due to the zero–length wait interval, the script immediately takes another AWR snapshot and disables SQL trace.

At the end of the measurement interval, the script automatically creates both an AWR and an ASH report in HTML format by calling the package DBMS_WORKLOAD_REPOSITORY. The files are created in the current directory. Note that the documented ASH script does not have the capability to report solely on a specific session. Below is an example of the script in operation:

```
SQL> @awr_capture
Please enter SID (V$SESSION.SID): 143
Please enter a comment (optional): slow-app
SPID  SID SERIAL# USERNAME MACHINE     SERVICE_NAME
----- --- ------- -------- ---------- --------------
18632 143     333 NDEBES   WORKGROUP\ TEN.oradbpro.com
                           DBSERVER
PROGRAM  MODULE    ACTION CLIENT_IDENTIFIER
-------- -------- ------ -----------------
perl.exe perl.exe NULL    NULL
Oracle pid: 20, Unix process pid: 18632, image: oracleTEN1@dbserver1.oradbpro.com
Statement processed.
Extended SQL trace file:
/opt/oracle/obase/admin/TEN/udump/ten1_ora_18632.trc
Begin snapshot: 95
Please enter snapshot interval in seconds (0 to take end snapshot immediately): 300
End snapshot: 96
Begin time: 07.Sep.2007 03:51:33; End time: 07.Sep.2007 03:56:39; Duration (minutes):
5.1
ASH Report file: slow-app-SID-143-SERIAL-333-ash.html
AWR Report file: slow-app-SID-143-SERIAL-333-awr.html
```

Extended SQL Trace and Session Level Statspack Snapshot

The measurement script for Statspack is very similar to the AWR variant. It also asks for a session to trace and enables level 12 SQL trace for that session. Instead of taking AWR snapshots, this script takes Statspack snapshots, which include session level data. The script uses ORADEBUG to retrieve the extended SQL trace file name. The example below illustrates the event based approach to determining the capture interval. This means that the capture does not last for a predetermined interval.

```
SQL> @sp_capture
Please enter SID (V$SESSION.SID): 139
SPID          SID SERIAL# USERNAME    MACHINE     SERVICE_NAME
------------ ----- ------- ---------- ---------- ----------------
19376         139   41757 NDEBES     WORKGROUP\ TEN.oradbpro.com
                                      DBSERVER
PROGRAM      MODULE          ACTION     CLIENT_IDENTIFIER
----------- --------------- ---------- -----------------
perl.exe     insert_perf5.pl NULL       NULL

Oracle pid: 16, Unix process pid: 19376, image: oracleTEN1@dbserver1.oradbpro.com
Extended SQL trace file:
/opt/oracle/obase/admin/TEN/udump/ten1_ora_19376.trc
Begin snapshot: 291
```

At this point, the script waits for input. If you wish to end the capture interval as soon as an event occurs, wait for the event and enter zero:

```
Please enter snapshot interval in seconds (0 to take end snapshot immediately): 0
End snapshot: 301
```

Begin time: 07.Sep.2007 06:20:07; End time: 07.Sep.2007 06:24:44; Duration (minutes):
4.6

As soon as the capture is over, a Statspack report for the beginning and end snapshot numbers may be generated by running the script $ORACLE_HOME/rdbms/admin/spreport.sql. Below is an excerpt of a report that includes session level data captured with the script sp_capture.sql. The session specific sections are "Session Wait Events", "Session Time Model Stats" (Oracle10g and later releases only) and "Session Statistics"[1]:

```
Snapshot          Snap Id     Snap Time         Sessions Curs/Sess Comment
~~~~~~~~          ----------  ------------------ -------- --------- ------------------
Begin Snap:          291 07-Sep-07 06:20:07        21        6.7 SID-139-perl.exe-in
  End Snap:          301 07-Sep-07 06:24:44        21        6.7 SID-139-perl.exe-in
   Elapsed:               4.62 (mins)
Session Wait Events  DB/Inst: TEN/TEN1  Snaps: 291-301
Session Id:       139  Serial#:     41757
-> ordered by wait time desc, waits desc (idle events last)
                                                   Total Wait
Event                         Waits  Timeouts  Time (s)          WT
----------------------------- ------------ ---------- ---------- ----------
   Waits
    /txn
 --------
log file switch completion        3        1       1 345.605667
     3.0
db file sequential read          13        0       0 4.61123077
    13.0
control file sequential read     26        0       0 .954307692
    26.0
control file parallel write       6        0       0 2.56516667
     6.0
db file scattered read            4        0       0     3.045
     4.0
log file sync                     2        0       0    5.1105
     2.0
latch: library cache              1        0       0         0
     1.0
SQL*Net message from client  283,496       0      72 .254345627
########
SQL*Net message to client    283,496       0       1 .004825056
########


Session Time Model Stats  DB/Inst: TEN/TEN1  Snaps: 291-301
Session Id:       139  Serial#:     41757
-> Total.Time in Database calls      182.9s (or  182854062us)
-> Ordered by % of DB time desc, Statistic name


Statistic                               Time (s) % of DB time
--------------------------------------- -------------------- ------------
DB CPU                                      179.2         98.0
sql execute elapsed time                    176.1         96.3
sequence load elapsed time                   32.1         17.6
PL/SQL execution elapsed time                 6.7          3.7
parse time elapsed                            1.4           .8
hard parse elapsed time                       0.4           .2
hard parse (sharing criteria) elaps           0.0           .0
repeated bind elapsed time                    0.0           .0
DB time                                     180.6
```

1. Per transaction statistics have been omitted in the "Session Statistics" section.

```
Session Statistics  DB/Inst: TEN/TEN1  Snaps: 291-301
Session Id:       139  Serial#:     41757


Statistic                                  Total         per Second
--------------------------------     ------------------   ------------------
active txn count during cleanout              948                  3
consistent gets                            31,335                113
cpu used by this session                   18,117                 65
parse time cpu                                 30                  0
physical read total bytes                 655,360              2,366
redo size                              92,965,180            335,614
session pga memory max                  4,718,592             17,035
sql*net roundtrips to/from client         283,503              1,023
workarea executions - optimal                  56                  0
```

A resource profile may be derived from the session specific sections by using the DB CPU from the "Session Time Model Stats" section and the wait events from the "Session Wait Events" section. In Oracle9i, CPU consumption is represented by the statistic "CPU used by this session". The response time equates the interval covered by the begin and end snapshots (value "Elapsed" at the beginning of the report). The difference between the measurement interval and total wait time plus DB CPU is calculated and reported as "unknown". A large portion of "unknown" time may mean that the session did not get the CPU or that the code path captured is incompletely instrumented. There may also have been a long ongoing wait such as *SQL*Net message from client*, which has not yet been incorporated into V$SESSION_EVENT. Table 65 displays the resource profile calculated with this approach.

Table 65: Resource Profile Derived from a Session Level Statspack Report

Response Time Contributor	*Time*	*Percentage*
DB CPU	179.2 s	64.64%
SQL*Net message from client	72.0 s	26.97%
unknown	24.0 s	8.66%
log file switch completion	1.0 s	0.03%
SQL*Net message to client	1.0 s	0.03%
Response time	**277.2 s**	**100.00%**

You may compare the resource profile in Table 65 to the resource profile for the same session, which was calculated from the extended SQL trace file that spanned (almost[1]) the same interval using ESQLTRCPROF. The latter resource profile is reproduced below. The CPU usage (179.2 vs. 218.31) differs significantly between the two reports, whereas figures for the wait events are nearly identical.

```
ORACLE version 10.2 trace file. Timings are in microseconds (1/1000000 sec)
Resource Profile
================
Response time: 239.377s; max(tim)-min(tim): 271.173s
Total wait time: 74.080s
----------------------------
Note: 'SQL*Net message from client' waits for more than 0.005s are considered think
time
Wait events and CPU usage:
  Duration     Pct      Count     Average Wait Event/CPU Usage/Think Time
  --------   ------   ------------   ---------- ------------------------------------
  218.316s   91.20%    904144   0.000241s total CPU
   70.953s   29.64%    282089   0.000252s SQL*Net message from client
```

---

1. Since it takes a few seconds (usually less than three), to take a Statspack snapshot, the interval covered by the beginning and end snapshots will never have exactly the same duration as that captured by the SQL trace file.

```
 1.349s   0.56%     282092  0.000005s SQL*Net message to client
 1.037s   0.43%          3  0.345606s log file switch completion
 0.419s   0.18%         16  0.026201s KSV master wait
 0.092s   0.04%          8  0.011520s Data file init write
 0.062s   0.03%          2  0.030860s log file switch (checkpoint incomplete)
 0.060s   0.03%         13  0.004611s db file sequential read
 0.025s   0.01%         26  0.000954s control file sequential read
 0.023s   0.01%          3  0.007810s think time
 0.016s   0.01%          2  0.007905s rdbms ipc reply
 0.015s   0.01%          6  0.002565s control file parallel write
 0.012s   0.01%          4  0.003045s db file scattered read
 0.010s   0.00%          2  0.005110s log file sync
 0.005s   0.00%          2  0.002479s db file single write
 0.001s   0.00%          2  0.000364s latch: library cache
 0.000s   0.00%          2  0.000243s latch: shared pool
-53.019s -22.15%                      unknown
--------- -------  ------------------------------------------------------------
239.377s 100.00% Total response time
```

Assessment

Asking for the goal of the performance optimization should be the first step in the assessment phase. If the goal is unrealistic, then expectations need to be corrected. Having a goal is also important for deciding whether or not the goal is attainable. As you assess the data collected in the measurement phase, you will be able to decide whether the goal might be attainable or not. Often managers or other contacts will simply say "make it as fast as possible". Alright, at least you've asked.

The second question to ask is whether the issue faced is truly a database performance problem. This is done by looking at the think time figure ESQLTRCPROF derives from extended SQL trace files. If, say 90% of the response time is think time and all the SQL statements which were executed intermittently completed reasonably quickly, then there is no database problem. Think time indicates that the database client did not ask the server to process any requests. The application is either idle or busy processing instructions that do not make demands on the DBMS instance. Since it's impossible for a DBA to reduce think time in an application, the application developer must find out what is taking too long.

The next classification to make, is whether the slow response time is due to excessive CPU usage or high wait time. The statistic CPU used by this session or DB CPU in Oracle10g indicate CPU usage. If waiting is the main issue, the resolution depends on the kinds of wait events. Waiting might be due to a slow I/O system (e.g. *db file sequential read*), contention (e.g. *enqueue*, *latch free*) or lack of CPU resources. The latter cause may be reflected in wait events if the database resource manager is enabled. How to reduce wait time depending on which wait events are most prominent (Oracle10g has 878 different wait events) is a subject for a separate performance tuning book. Shee et al. ([ShDe 2004]) do a good job of addressing this topic in their book.

Resource Profiles and Performance Assessment Tools

The main goal of the assessment phase is to generate a resource profile from the data captured in the preceding measurement phase. The concept of a resource profile has been made popular by the work of Cary Millsap and Jeff Holt as published in the book *Optimizing Oracle Performance* ([MiHo 2003]). My extended SQL trace profiler ESQL-TRCPROF is strongly influenced by this publication. Yet, the addition of think time to resource profiles is my own invention. The research done by Millsap and Holt has lead to the development of a commercial profiler for extended SQL trace files, which is offered by Hotsos Enterprises, Ltd. Other tools for obtaining a resource profile are TKPROF and ESQLTRCPROF, which is described in detail in Chapter 27.

TKPROF vs. ESQLTRCPROF

TKPROF does not really report a resource profile. Nonetheless, a TKPROF report does contain enough information to calculate a resource profile from it. The same approach as with session level Statspack data may be used. The response time R consists of the sum of the elapsed times for non–recursive and recursive statements plus the wait time of the inter database call wait events *SQL*Net message from client* and *SQL*Net message to client*. Overall totals for non–recursive and recursive statements need to be added to get the totals for both CPU usage and wait events. The measurement interval is reported as "elapsed seconds in trace file" in the last line of the report by TKPROF release 10.2. Once these figures are calculated for CPU usage and all wait events, they need to be sorted and arranged as a resource profile. Much easier to use ESQLTRCPROF, which does it all automatically. Another disadvantage of TKPROF is the omission of hash values, which identify SQL statements, from the report. Hash values might be used to correlate the SQL statements with instance level (spreport.sql) and SQL statement level (sprepsql.sql) Statspack reports or V$ views (V$SQL.HASH_VALUE).

Both TKPROF and ESQLTRCPROF report CPU usage. Often high CPU usage is associated with SQL statements that access thousands or millions of blocks in the buffer cache. If this is the case, a poor execution plan, which includes unnecessary full scans, has an inappropriate join order, or uses the wrong index, might be the culprit. SQL statements with high CPU usage must be identified and their execution plans checked. TKPROF provides the sort options fchela and exeela, which may be combined. If you suspect that a SELECT statement is the most expensive statement in a trace file, use sort=fchela,exeela. Otherwise use sort=exeela,fchela. TKRPOF cannot sort by total elapsed time, which comprises elapsed time from the three stages parse, execute, and fetch. Furthermore it does not consider inter database call wait events attributed to a cursor when sorting. ESQLTRCPROF always sorts by total elapsed time and considers in between database call wait events such as *SQL*Net message from/to client* while ignoring think time. This makes sure that a SQL statement which causes many round–trips and thus incurs a lot of network latency is ranked as more expensive than a statement that is responsible for the same amount of elapsed time within database calls, but does not accumulate as much network latency.

Reproduction

Before the actual performance optimization may begin, a way to reproduce the problem at hand must be found. It is crucial to reproduce the problematic code path as closely as possible. Depending on the kind of performance problem, to reproduce an issue, the following factors may need to be identical between the original environment and the test environment:

- hardware capability
- operating system and release
- ORACLE DBMS release
- initialization parameters (documented and hidden), especially optimizer parameters
- database object statistics (a.k.a. optimizer statistics)
- database block size
- bind variables and bind data types in SQL statements which are optimized
- stored outlines
- SQL profiles (Oracle10g and later releases only)

When creating database objects, make sure you create them with the same DDL in tablespaces with the same block size as the original application. The package DBMS_METADATA may be used to extract DDL for database objects. When reproducing SQL statements with bind variables, it's important to use bind variables with the same data type as the original statement. Level 12 SQL trace files contain bind variable values as well as bind variable data types in the BINDS section (see Chapter 24). SQL*Plus or PL/SQL variables may be used to reproduce the bind data types. Last but not least, make sure no other users are running stress tests or other resource intensive programs on your test system, since this may lead to contradictory results of your tests.

Improvement

Improving performance is a vast subject. If we ignore the use of more powerful hardware, which might not even solve the problem, the following procedures may result in better performance:

- parameter changes (e.g. DB_CACHE_SIZE, PARALLEL_EXECUTION_MESSAGE_SIZE)
- adding an index to avoid full table scans
- dropping unnecessary indexes
- partitioning of tables and/or indexes
- materialized views

- use of bind variables instead of literals in SQL statements
- correction of bind data type mismatches
- calculation of more accurate optimizer statistics with DBMS_STATS
- use of system statistics, given that the cost–based SQL optimizer chooses better execution plans than without them (DBMS_STATS)
- use of cached sequences instead of counters implemented with tables
- adding hints to SQL statements (as a last resort to improve execution plans)
- stored outlines
- supplying hidden hints with stored outlines (see Metalink note 92202.1)
- SQL profiles (Oracle10g and subsequent releases)
- SQL plan management (requires Oracle11g)
- use of array inserts or bulk load programming interfaces
- reduction of network round–trips, e.g. with INSERT RETURNING
- PL/SQL native compilation
- changes in application coding to reduce contention, parse overhead, polling, etc.

Performance improvements should be documented with additional measurements. You should not rely on a single measurement, but instead take several measurements and calculate the average.

Extrapolation

By the time a substantial performance improvement has been achieved with the test case, it is important to extrapolate the effect of the improvement on the original application. This is to decide whether the tuning effort can be stopped or not. In case tests in the previous phase were run with instrumentation or SQL trace enabled, these should be switched off now. Measurement intrusion is undesirable when trying to get reliable figures to base a forecast on. After all, the original application usually runs without measurement intrusion through instrumentation or tracing. On the other hand, if the original application runs with instrumentation enabled, so should your test case.

Installation

Usually, changes are made in test and quality assurance systems first before they are allowed to go into production. If the root cause was inefficient SQL coding or application coding in general, it may take quite a while before the software manufacturer incorporates the necessary changes and releases a new version of the software. In addition to approval, changes which require reorganization of database objects need to wait for a sufficiently large maintenance window. If there is no budget for an extra–cost feature that was used in the improvement phase (e.g. partitioned tables), then it may be hard to get approval for the suggested changes. Furthermore it may require additional downtime to install the feature.

MERITS Method Case Study

This section presents the application of the MERITS method to a real world performance problem. A digital imaging company accepts JPEG image files for printing and archival from customers. A routine within the company's Web application, which is implemented in Perl, reads the EXIF image metadata in the digital still camera files and loads the image metadata along with the images themselves into an ORACLE database. The EXIF data are used by search functionality provided on the web site. The image data is stored as a BLOB, since this provides full recoverability in case of disk failure. The average size of the JPEG files loaded is 1 MB. The contact says that the application is capable of loading 68 files per minute. The goal is to at least triple the number of files loaded per minute.

I have chosen this example, since it highlights some limitations of extended SQL trace. The striking discrepancy between the response time calculated from the extended SQL trace file and the actual elapsed time you will see shortly, should not lead you to believe that analysis of extended SQL trace files is generally inaccurate. Such a high discrepancy is the exception, rather than the rule. In this case it is due to incomplete instrumentation of LOB access with OCI. The lack of accuracy observed in the response time profile for this case provides the opportunity to endow the reader with additional tools and knowledge to overcome such situations. In this particular case, I show how instrumentation combined with statistics collection at the action level offered by Oracle10g results in an accurate representation of response time per action (V$SERV_MOD_ACT_STATS). In case you were still running Oracle9*i*, you would be able to derive the elapsed time per action from the SQL trace file by looking at the timestamps which are written with the module and action entry in Oracle9*i* (see page 244). This is not as good as the data provided by the view V$SERV_MOD_ACT_STATS in Oracle10*g*, which include DB time, DB CPU, and other statistics, but it's sufficient to find out where an application spends most of the time.

Phase 1—Measurement

I sent the file awr_capture.sql to the client and asked the DBA to capture 60 seconds of activity from the image loading routine. I also asked the DBA to run the script statistics.sql to create a report on the structure of the tables involved.

Phase 2—Assessment

I received a SQL trace file as well as the AWR and ASH reports created by awr_capture.sql. The statistics.sql report showed that LOBs are stored in a tablespace with default block size. Storage of LOB data in row was enabled:

LOB Column Name	Segment Name	Tablespace	Block-size	Chunk	Pct-version	Retention	Cache	In Row
IMAGE_DATA	IMAGES_IMAGE_DATA	USERS	8 KB	8192	10		NO	YES

I processed the SQL trace file with TKPROF. Since it was likely that EXEC calls rather than FETCH calls would contribute most to response time, I used the sort options exeela, fchela:

```
$ tkprof ten_ora_3172_img_load.trc ten_ora_3172_img_load.tkp sort=exeela,fchela
```

An excerpt of the TKPROF report for the trace file is below:

```
OVERALL TOTALS FOR ALL NON-RECURSIVE STATEMENTS
```

call	count	cpu	elapsed	disk	query	current	rows
Parse	213	0.01	0.00	0	0	0	0
Execute	213	0.07	0.14	1	71	495	71
Fetch	142	0.00	0.01	0	142	0	142
total	568	0.09	0.16	1	213	495	213

```
Elapsed times include waiting on following events:
```

Event waited on	Times Waited	Max. Wait	Total Waited
direct path read	8010	0.27	13.23
SQL*Net more data from client	32182	0.00	0.43
direct path write	45619	0.01	0.69
SQL*Net message to client	8578	0.00	0.02
SQL*Net message from client	8578	0.03	4.91
db file sequential read	7130	0.25	26.11
log file sync	86	0.05	0.51
log file switch completion	5	0.99	3.23
latch: shared pool	10	0.00	0.00
latch: library cache	1	0.00	0.00
log file switch (checkpoint incomplete)	8	0.99	1.76

```
OVERALL TOTALS FOR ALL RECURSIVE STATEMENTS
```

call	count	cpu	elapsed	disk	query	current	rows
Parse	100	0.00	0.03	0	0	0	0
Execute	166	0.14	0.18	0	230	46	46
Fetch	199	0.01	0.04	5	449	0	489

```
total      465      0.15      0.27        5       679        46       535
```
Elapsed times include waiting on following events:

```
  Event waited on                          Times   Max. Wait  Total Waited
  -------------------------------------    Waited  ---------  -----------
  db file sequential read                     5       0.01         0.03
```

```
   213  user  SQL statements in session.
   166  internal SQL statements in session.
   379  SQL statements in session.
****************************************************************************
Trace file: ten_ora_3172_img_load.trc
Trace file compatibility: 10.01.00
Sort options: exeela  fchela
         1  session in tracefile.
       213  user  SQL statements in trace file.
       166  internal SQL statements in trace file.
       379  SQL statements in trace file.
        12  unique SQL statements in trace file.
    128315  lines in trace file.
        72  elapsed seconds in trace file.
```

Note the large discrepancy between total (recursive and non–recursive) elapsed time (0.43 s) and the value for *elapsed seconds in trace file* (72 s). According to TKPROF, the following recursive statement had the highest elapsed time:

```
update seg$ set type#=:4,blocks=:5,extents=:6,minexts=:7,maxexts=:8,extsize=
  :9,extpct=:10,user#=:11,iniexts=:12,lists=decode(:13, 65535, NULL, :13),
  groups=decode(:14, 65535, NULL, :14), cachehint=:15, hwmincr=:16, spare1=
  DECODE(:17,0,NULL,:17),scanhint=:18
where
 ts#=:1 and file#=:2 and block#=:3
```

```
call     count      cpu    elapsed     disk      query    current       rows
-------  ------  --------  ---------  --------  ---------  ---------  ---------
Parse       46    0.00       0.03        0          0          0          0
Execute     46    0.09       0.10        0        230         46         46
Fetch        0    0.00       0.00        0          0          0          0
-------  ------  --------  ---------  --------  ---------  ---------  ---------
total       92    0.09       0.13        0        230         46         46
```

I also processed the SQL trace file with ESQLTRCPROF. It gave hundreds of warnings like the following:

```
Warning: WAIT event 'direct path read' for cursor 4 at line 5492 without prior PARSING
IN CURSOR #4 - ignored for per statement response time accounting
Warning: WAIT event 'direct path write' for cursor 4 at line 5497 without prior PARSING
IN CURSOR #4 - ignored for per statement response time accounting
```

The warning indicates that there is a problem with response time accounting for cursor 4. The resource profile from ESQLTRCPROF is below:

```
ORACLE version 10.2 trace file. Timings are in microseconds (1/1000000 sec)
Resource Profile
================
Response time: 5.627s; max(tim)-min(tim): 74.957s
Total wait time: 50.974s
----------------------------
Note: 'SQL*Net message from client' waits for more than 0.005s are considered think
time
Wait events and CPU usage:
 Duration    Pct     Count    Average  Wait Event/CPU Usage/Think Time
 --------  ------  ---------  --------  --------------------------------------
  26.153s 464.76%     7135   0.003665s db file sequential read
  13.234s 235.17%     8010   0.001652s direct path read
```

```
   3.232s   57.43%              5  0.646382s log file switch completion
   2.604s   46.28%           8507  0.000306s SQL*Net message from client
   2.312s   41.08%             71  0.032562s think time
   1.768s   31.41%              8  0.220956s log file switch (checkpoint incomplete)
   0.690s   12.27%          45619  0.000015s direct path write
   0.516s    9.18%             86  0.006004s log file sync
   0.434s    7.72%          32182  0.000013s SQL*Net more data from client
   0.313s    5.55%           1033  0.000303s total CPU
   0.030s    0.53%           8578  0.000003s SQL*Net message to client
   0.001s    0.02%             10  0.000109s latch: shared pool
   0.000s    0.00%              1  0.000207s latch: library cache
 -45.659s -811.39%                           unknown
 ---------  ------- -------------------------------------------------------------
   5.627s  100.00% Total response time

Total number of roundtrips (SQL*Net message from/to client): 8578


CPU usage breakdown
-----------------------
parse CPU:     0.05s (313 PARSE calls)
exec  CPU:     0.25s (379 EXEC calls)
fetch CPU:     0.02s (341 FETCH calls)
```

The difference between the response time of 5.627 s and the elapsed time covered by the trace file (max(tim)-min(tim): 74.957s) is just as prominent as in the TKPROF report. Contrary to TKPROF, the ESQLTRCPROF report points out that there are 45 seconds which are not accounted for (*unknown*). The total wait time of 50.974 s proves that the application was interacting with the DBMS most of the time, but the wait time should be rolled up into parse, execute, and fetch calls.

According to ESQLTRCPROF, the highest contributor to response time was associated with a cursor that does not have a SQL statement text associated with it:

```
Statements Sorted by Elapsed Time (including recursive resource utilization)
===============================================================================
Hash Value: -1 - Total Elapsed Time (excluding think time): 2.976s


Cursor 0 - unknown statement (default container for any trace file entries relating to
cursor 0)
DB Call     Count    Elapsed        CPU     Disk    Query   Current    Rows
-------  --------  ----------  ----------  -------  -------  --------  --------
PARSE          0    0.0000s     0.0000s         0        0         0         0
EXEC           0    0.0000s     0.0000s         0        0         0         0
FETCH          0    0.0000s     0.0000s         0        0         0         0
-------  --------  ----------  ----------  -------  -------  --------  --------
Total          0    0.0000s     0.0000s         0        0         0         0


Wait Event/CPU Usage/Think Time                  Duration     Count
---------------------------------------------  ----------  --------
SQL*Net message from client                       2.431s      8081
think time                                        2.312s        71
log file sync                                     0.516s        86
SQL*Net message to client                         0.028s      8152
latch: shared pool                                0.001s         6
latch: library cache                              0.000s         1
total CPU                                         0.000s         0
```

TKPROF does not have a sort option which incorporates wait time between database calls. Hence it did not report this unknown statement as the highest contributor to response time.

What's wrong? Cursors without associated SQL statements? Wait time from intra database call waits such as *direct path read* and *direct path write*, which is not rolled up into database calls? Do both tools report incorrect results? A look at the extended trace file reveals that there were 92956 wait events pertaining to cursor 4. However, the trace file did not contain a single PARSING IN CURSOR, PARSE, EXEC, or FETCH entry for cursor 4. The level 2 ERRORSTACK dump taken by the script awr_capture.sql contained the rather strange sqltxt value "table_e_a_d21e_a_0_0" for cursor 4. Clearly, this was not an issue of a missing PARSING IN CURSOR entry due to the fact that tracing was switched on in the midst of a running application. There simply did not exist a proper SQL statement for this cursor.

```
Cursor#4(09050CE4) state=NULL curiob=090C2054
 curflg=1044 fl2=0 par=00000000 ses=6CD86754
 sqltxt(6AAAA544)=table_e_a_d21e_a_0_0
```

As pointed out in Chapter 24, the PARSE, EXEC, and FETCH entries are the only ones which report CPU usage. Furthermore, the elapsed time reported by these entries includes the wait events caused by parse, execute, and fetch operations. Since there were no such entries for cursor 4, the wait time could not be rolled up. The response time R is defined as the sum of the elapsed time of parse, execute, and fetch calls plus the sum of wait time between database calls. The reason why R differs tremendously from the interval recorded by the trace file is now clear. Theoretically, the elapsed time of all database calls should equal CPU usage plus wait time caused by the database calls. The difference is reported as "unknown". The contribution of "unknown" in this resource profile is so large, since the wait time from cursor 4 is not rolled up into any database calls. So what is it that cursor 4 is responsible for? Here are some lines from the trace file:

```
WAIT #4: nam='db file sequential read' ela= 2926 file#=4 block#=90206 blocks=1
obj#=53791 tim=19641952691
WAIT #4: nam='db file sequential read' ela= 1666 file#=4 block#=90221 blocks=1
obj#=53791 tim=19641954572
WAIT #4: nam='direct path read' ela= 275 file number=4 first dba=90206 block cnt=1
obj#=53791 tim=19641964448
WAIT #4: nam='direct path write' ela= 3 file number=4 first dba=90174 block cnt=1
obj#=53791 tim=19641955477
```

Translation of file#=4 and block#=90206 by querying DBA_EXTENTS yields:

```
SQL> SELECT segment_name, segment_type, extent_id
FROM dba_extents
WHERE file_id=4 AND 90206 BETWEEN block_id AND block_id + blocks - 1;
SEGMENT_NAME      SEGMENT_TYPE EXTENT_ID
---------------- ------------ ---------
IMAGES_IMAGE_DATA LOBSEGMENT         40
```

Obviously cursor 4 is related to LOB loading. This finding is corroborated by the fact that the Active Session History (ASH) report also lists a cursor that has caused direct path read and write operations, but lacks a SQL statement text. This information is found in the "Top SQL Statements" section of the ASH report (see Figure 14) created by the script awr_capture.sql. The "Top DB Objects" section indicates a LOB as the top object. At this point we may conclude that loading LOB data with Oracle Call Interface (OCI), which is used internally by Perl DBI, is poorly instrumented. The extended SQL trace file does not report the CPU usage of loading LOBs at all.

According to the ESQLTRCPROF report, 71 rows were inserted into the table IMAGES:

```
Hash Value: 3858514115 - Total Elapsed Time (excluding think time): 0.146s


INSERT INTO images (id, date_loaded, exif_make, exif_model, exif_create_date, exif_iso,
exif_f_number, exif_exposure_time, exif_35mm_focal_length, image_data) VALUES (:id,
sysdate, :exif_make, :exif_model, to_date(:exif_create_date, 'yyyy:mm:dd hh24:mi:ss'),
:exif_iso, :exif_f_number, :exif_exposure_time, :exif_35mm_focal_length, empty_blob())
```

DB Call	Count	Elapsed	CPU	Disk	Query	Current	Rows
PARSE	71	0.0026s	0.0156s	0	0	0	0
EXEC	71	0.1203s	0.0781s	1	71	495	71
FETCH	0	0.0000s	0.0000s	0	0	0	0
Total	142	0.1229s	0.0938s	1	71	495	71

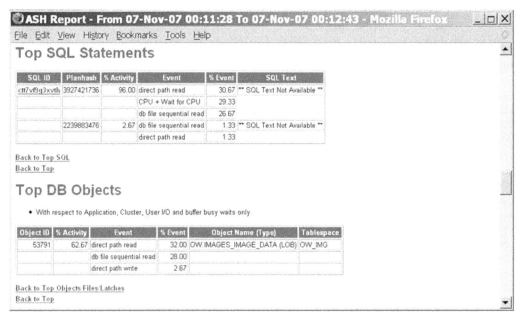

Figure 14: Top SQL Statements section of an Active Session History report

Since the interval covered by the trace file was 74.9 seconds, 56 LOBs were inserted per minute. What struck me was that there were also 71 parse calls for this INSERT statement. This was an indication that the parse call for the INSERT statement was done in a loop instead of just once before entering the loop.

It was also worth noting that 71 updates of the table SYS.SEQ$, the data dictionary base table which holds sequences, had occurred:

```
Hash Value: 2635489469 - Total Elapsed Time (excluding think time): 0.082s

update seq$ set
increment$=:2,minvalue=:3,maxvalue=:4,cycle#=:5,order$=:6,cache=:7,highwater=:8,audit$
=:9,flags=:10 where obj#=:1
```

DB Call	Count	Elapsed	CPU	Disk	Query	Current	Rows
PARSE	71	0.0026s	0.0000s	0	0	0	0
EXEC	71	0.0790s	0.0781s	0	71	142	71
FETCH	0	0.0000s	0.0000s	0	0	0	0
Total	142	0.0815s	0.0781s	0	71	142	71

This probably meant that a sequence, which was not cached, was incremented 71 times. To verify this assumption, I searched the trace file for the hash value 2635489469 in the ESQLTRCPROF report[1] and retrieved the bind variable value for column obj#. Since the script awr_capture.sql enables SQL trace at level 12, the trace file does contain bind variables. Counting from left to right, the tenth bind variable was applicable to obj#. Since bind variable values are numbered from 0, I needed to look for Bind#9:

```
Bind#9
  oacdty=02 mxl=22(22) mxlc=00 mal=00 scl=00 pre=00
  oacflg=08 fl2=0001 frm=00 csi=00 siz=24 off=0
  kxsbbbfp=0915bf8c  bln=22  avl=04  flg=05
  value=53740
```

---

1. TKPROF omits the hash values for SQL statement texts

This yielded the object identifier of the sequence, which I then used to retrieve information on the object from DBA_OBJECTS. It turned out that object 53740 was indeed a sequence and that it was not cached:

```
SQL> SELECT object_name, object_type FROM dba_objects WHERE object_id=53740;
OBJECT_NAME    OBJECT_TYPE
------------- -------------------
IMAGE_ID_SEQ  SEQUENCE
SQL> SELECT cache_size
FROM dba_objects o, dba_sequences s
WHERE o.object_id=53740
AND o.owner=s.sequence_owner
AND o.object_name=s.sequence_name;
CACHE_SIZE
----------
         0
```

All the other statements with the same hash value also had 53740 as the bind variable value for Bind#9. The update of SYS.SEQ$ did not contribute significantly to the total response time. However it was unnecessary overhead and very easy to fix with an ALTER SEQUENCE statement.

Another issue I noticed in the ESQLTRCPROF report, were 71 commits:

```
Statistics:
-----------
COMMITs (read write): 71 -> transactions/sec 12.617
COMMITs (read only): 0
ROLLBACKs (read write): 0
ROLLBACKs (read only): 0
```

Apparently, each row inserted and LOB loaded was committed separately, adding overhead. Each commit may cause waiting for the wait event *log file sync*.

Reproduction

The client agreed to provide the Perl subroutine used for loading LOBs as a standalone Perl program for further investigation on a test system. The DDL was also provided. It showed that both the LOB and the sequence did not have caching enabled.

```
CREATE TABLE images(
    id number,
    date_loaded date,
    exif_make varchar2(30),
    exif_model varchar2(30),
    exif_create_date date,
    exif_iso varchar2(30),
    exif_f_number varchar2(30),
    exif_exposure_time varchar2(30),
    exif_35mm_focal_length varchar2(30),
    image_data BLOB,
    CONSTRAINT images_pk PRIMARY KEY(id)
)
LOB (image_data) STORE AS images_image_data;

CREATE SEQUENCE image_id_seq NOCACHE;
```

The first thing I did was to instrument the Perl program with the Hotsos instrumentation library for ORACLE[1] (ILO). Instrumentation with ILO is straight forward. The procedure HOTSOS_ILO_TASK.BEGIN_TASK is used to start a new task with a certain module and action name. BEGIN_TASK pushes the previous module and action on a stack as discussed in Chapter 23. The procedure HOTSOS_ILO_TASK.END_TASK terminates a task and restores the previous mod-

---

1. ILO is free software and may be downloaded from http://sourceforge.net/projects/hotsos-ilo. The download package includes documentation in HTML format.

ule and action. Both module and action are reflected in V$ views such as V$SESSION and V$SQL. To enable SQL trace as soon as the first task is begun, the package HOTSOS_ILO_TIMER is called by the application itself as below:

```
begin
    hotsos_ilo_timer.set_mark_all_tasks_interesting(mark_all_tasks_interesting=>true,
    ignore_schedule=>true);
end;
```

I used the module name "img_load" for the entire program and defined two actions:

- The action "exif_insert" encompassed the generation of a new primary key for the next row and the retrieval of the LOB locator, which was then used to load the LOB data with the Perl DBI function ora_lob_append.
- The action "lob_load" comprised reading the JPEG file from disk and loading it into the BLOB column. Due to the average image file size of 1 MB, the LOB was loaded piece–wise.

I assumed that the file system access to read the JPEG file did not cause a lot of overhead. If this assumption had turned out to be wrong, I would have instrumented the file system access in Perl, in addition to instrumenting database access with Hotsos ILO.

The test program allowed me to indicate how many LOBs it should load. For the sake of simplicity, a single JPEG file was loaded again and again, although this would reduce the impact of reading the image file due to file system caching, whilst the original application needed to read separate image files each time.

I set up the database to collect statistics on the service, module, and actions of interest as below:

```
SQL> EXEC dbms_monitor.serv_mod_act_stat_enable('TEN.oradbpro.com','img_load',
'exif_insert')
SQL> EXEC dbms_monitor.serv_mod_act_stat_enable('TEN.oradbpro.com','img_load',
'lob_load')
```

I measured the response time of a load run comprising ten LOBs with the UNIX utility time[1]:

```
$ time perl img_load.pl 10 sample.jpg
real    0m9.936s
user    0m0.015s
sys     0m0.015s
```

Then I retrieved the relevant statistics on service, module, and action from V$SERV_MOD_ACT_STATS:

```
SQL> SELECT action, stat_name, round(value/1000000, 2) AS value
FROM v$serv_mod_act_stats
WHERE service_name='TEN.oradbpro.com'
AND module='img_load'
AND action IN ('exif_insert','lob_load')
AND stat_name in ('DB time', 'DB CPU', 'sql execute elapsed time',
'user I/O wait time')
ORDER BY action, stat_name;
ACTION       STAT_NAME                VALUE
----------- ------------------------ -----
exif_insert DB CPU                    .02
exif_insert DB time                   .02
exif_insert sql execute elapsed time  .01
exif_insert user I/O wait time          0
lob_load    DB CPU                    2.7
lob_load    DB time                   8.75
lob_load    sql execute elapsed time    0
lob_load    user I/O wait time       5.85
```

The total "DB time", which does not include network latency and think time (*SQL*Net message from client*), for both actions was 8.77 seconds. This was reasonably close to the response time reported by the UNIX utility time (9.9 s). Since the latter measurement includes compilation of the Perl program and connecting to the DBMS instance, some

---

1. A time utility for Windows ships with Cygwin.

discrepancy had to be expected. Thanks to instrumentation, it is very obvious that the bulk of response time is due to the action "lob_load", which deals with loading the BLOB column.

Whereas the extended SQL trace file failed to account for CPU usage due to LOB loading, V$SERV_MOD_ACT_STATS reported 2.7 seconds of CPU usage for loading 10 LOBs. The bulk of the response time was attributed to user I/O wait time. This correlated with the large amount of *db file sequential read* and *direct path read* as well as *direct path write* operations associated with cursor 4 of the SQL trace file. Since at least 8.77 seconds (total "DB time" for both actions) out of 9.93 seconds (response time measured by the UNIX utility time) or 88% are spent in the DBMS instance, the assumption that reading the JPEG file does not contribute significantly to response time had proven to be correct.

Figures in V$SERV_MOD_ACT_STATS are cumulative since instance startup. To disable statistics collection, these calls to DBMS_MONITOR need to be used:

```
SQL> EXEC dbms_monitor.serv_mod_act_stat_disable('TEN.oradbpro.com','img_load',
'exif_insert')
SQL> EXEC dbms_monitor.serv_mod_act_stat_disable('TEN.oradbpro.com','img_load',
'lob_load')
```

Disabling statistics collection in this way does not clear the statistics. If statistics collection on the same module and action is re–enabled at a later time, the measurements taken before are made available again, unless the instance has been restarted.

For the sake of comparing measurements taken before and after improving the response time, I recorded another run with level 8 SQL trace enabled through event 10046, since I did not want the additional executions and round–trips caused by ILO to impact the results. The resulting ESQLTRCPROF report is reproduced below:

```
ORACLE version 10.2 trace file. Timings are in microseconds (1/1000000 sec)
Resource Profile
================


Response time: 0.779s; max(tim)-min(tim): 8.902s
Total wait time: 6.012s
---------------------------


Note: 'SQL*Net message from client' waits for more than 0.005s are considered think
time
Wait events and CPU usage:
 Duration      Pct        Count      Average Wait Event/CPU Usage/Think Time
 --------    ------    ----------   ---------- -------------------------------------
   3.834s  491.92%         1160     0.003305s db file sequential read
   1.259s  161.54%         1120     0.001124s direct path read
   0.350s   44.96%         1191     0.000294s SQL*Net message from client
   0.346s   44.40%           10     0.034603s think time
   0.090s   11.60%         6227     0.000015s direct path write
   0.068s    8.72%           23     0.002954s log file sync
   0.060s    7.66%         4500     0.000013s SQL*Net more data from client
   0.004s    0.52%         1201     0.000003s SQL*Net message to client
   0.000s    0.00%          119     0.000000s total CPU
  -5.232s -671.32%                            unknown
 --------  -------  --------------------------------------------------------------
   0.779s  100.00% Total response time


Total number of roundtrips (SQL*Net message from/to client): 1201


CPU usage breakdown
-----------------------
parse CPU:     0.00s (46 PARSE calls)
exec  CPU:     0.00s (47 EXEC calls)
fetch CPU:     0.00s (26 FETCH calls)
```

```
Statistics:
-----------
COMMITs (read write): 10 -> transactions/sec 12.830
```

Note that there are ten instances of think time. This makes sense, since ten iterations were performed. This means that the profiler has correctly classified the time it takes to access the JPEG file as think time.

Phase 4—Improvement

It was very obvious that the loading of LOB data needed improvement. From other projects involving LOBs, I knew that access to LOBs, which are not cached, is quite slow. I also knew that LOBs, which are significantly larger than a few database blocks, benefit from a larger block and chunk size. The database block size of both the client's database and my test database was 8 KB. I configured a separate buffer pool with 16 KB block size, restarted the test instance, and created a tablespace for LOB storage with 16 KB block size. These are the SQL statements involved in the task:

```
SQL> ALTER SYSTEM SET db_16k_cache_size=50m SCOPE=SPFILE;
SQL> CREATE TABLESPACE lob_ts DATAFILE '&data_file_path' SIZE 1G BLOCKSIZE 16384;
```

For a production system one would use a much larger value of DB_16K_CACHE_SIZE than just 50 MB. Next, I moved the LOB segment into the new tablespace, increased the LOB chunk size to the maximum value 32768, and disabled the storage of LOB data in row with the other columns of the table:

```
SQL> ALTER TABLE images MOVE LOB (image_data) STORE AS (TABLESPACE lob_ts DISABLE
STORAGE IN ROW CACHE RETENTION CHUNK 32768);
```

Since moving a table makes indexes unusable (an INSERT would cause ORA-01502), the primary key index had to be rebuilt:

```
SQL> ALTER INDEX images_pk REBUILD;
```

The package DBMS_REDEFINITION, which supports online reorganization of tables and associated indexes, may be used to reduce the downtime incurred by this operation.

After applying these changes, I ran another load of 10 rows with instrumentation enabled and SQL trace disabled:

```
$ time perl img_load.pl 10 sample.jpg
real    0m2.550s
user    0m0.045s
sys     0m0.061s
```

The response time had come down to only 2.5 seconds. This was more than I had expected, so I repeated the run another 9 times. The average response time of ten runs was 3.02 seconds. The above changes alone more than halved the previous response time.

Next I took a closer look at the Perl code. Apart from parsing inside a loop, which was already evident from the SQL trace file and the resource profiles, I saw that the LOB was read from the file system and sent to the DBMS instance in 8 KB pieces. This seemed small, since I had increased the block size to 16 KB and the LOB chunk size to 32 KB. Here's an excerpt of the code that shows how the LOB column was loaded:

```
do {
    $bytes_read=sysread(LOBFILE, $data, 8192);
        $total_bytes+=$bytes_read;
    if ($bytes_read > 0) {
        my $rc = $dbh->ora_lob_append($lob_loc, $data);
    }
} until $bytes_read <=0;
```

I decided to try the extreme and used a piece size of 1048576 (1 MB) instead of 8192 (8 KB). The average of another 10 runs was 1.71 seconds. Another 43% reduction in response time. The two changes tested so far already more than met the goal set by the client, so I could have stopped the optimization at this point. However, I wished to show the benefits of parsing once and executing many times. Furthermore, I wanted to point out how INSERT RETURNING may be used to reduce the number of round–trips between client and database server.

The original algorithm of the application was:

1. Increment and retrieve the sequence used for numbering the primary key with the SQL statement SELECT image_id_seq.NEXTVAL FROM dual.

2. Insert a row into the table IMAGES using the sequence value as the key for column ID. The INSERT statement also initialized the BLOB with empty_blob().

3. Retrieve the LOB locator using the index on column ID with SELECT image_data FROM images WHERE id=:id.

This required parsing and execution of three separate statements. However, the three steps may be combined into a single step by using INSERT RETURNING as below:

```
INSERT INTO images (id, date_loaded, exif_make, exif_model, exif_create_date, exif_iso,
exif_f_number, exif_exposure_time, exif_35mm_focal_length, image_data)
VALUES(image_id_seq.NEXTVAL, sysdate, :exif_make, :exif_model,
to_date(:exif_create_date, 'yyyy:mm:dd hh24:mi:ss'), :exif_iso,
:exif_f_number, :exif_exposure_time, :exif_35mm_focal_length, empty_blob())
RETURNING id, rowid, image_data INTO :id, :row_id, :lob_loc
```

Unfortunately this crashes the release of Perl which ships with Oracle10g Release 2 (DBI version: 1.41 DBD::Oracle version: 1.15[1]), but works with more recent releases. As a workaround, the LOB locator may be fetched separately. With this workaround in place, the average response time of ten runs was reduced further to 1.11 seconds.

Three issues remained to be fixed:

- the sequence, which was not cached
- the superfluous parse calls inside the loop which loaded the images
- frequent commits inside the loop instead of once after finishing the load process (or at least intermittently, say after 10000 rows when loading a large number of images)

I assigned the sequence a cache of 1000 numbers with the following DDL statement:

```
SQL> ALTER SEQUENCE image_id_seq CACHE 1000;
```

Caching more sequence numbers does not increase the memory usage by the shared pool. Unused sequence numbers are noted in the data dictionary when an instance is shut down with SHUTDOWN NORMAL or IMMEDIATE. Sequence numbers are lost only when an instance crashes or is shut down with the ABORT option. Note that rolling back a transaction which has selected NEXTVAL from a sequence also discards sequence numbers. Consequently, there is no reason not to use a large sequence cache.

Finally, I modified the Perl program in such a way that both the INSERT and the SELECT statements were parsed only once. To confirm that the statements were indeed parsed only once, I enabled SQL trace with event 10046, ran the trace file through ESQLTRCPROF, and looked at the parse calls. The figures for the INSERT statement are below:

DB Call	Count	Elapsed	CPU	Disk	Query	Current	Rows
PARSE	1	0.0002s	0.0000s	0	0	0	0
EXEC	10	0.0459s	0.0156s	4	15	75	10
FETCH	0	0.0000s	0.0000s	0	0	0	0
Total	11	0.0460s	0.0156s	4	15	75	10

The numbers show that the statement was parsed once and executed ten times. Of course, the assignment of values to bind variables remained in the loop. Merely the parse call (prepare in Perl DBI) was moved outside the loop. This kind of benefit is not available when using literals in statements, since the statement text changes for each loop iteration, such that the statement must be parsed each time. Reducing parse overhead is one of the reasons why bind variables should be used. Another is the reduction of contention for the library cache. The entire resource profile is below:

```
ORACLE version 10.2 trace file. Timings are in microseconds (1/1000000 sec)
Resource Profile
================
Response time: 0.269s; max(tim)-min(tim): 0.582s
Total wait time: 0.320s
--------------------------
```

---

1. Oracle11g ships with the same DBI and DBD::Oracle releases, such that it's not an option to use an Oracle11g Perl client.

```
Note: 'SQL*Net message from client' waits for more than 0.005s are considered think
time
Wait events and CPU usage:
 Duration     Pct        Count   Average Wait Event/CPU Usage/Think Time
 --------   ------  -----------  --------- -----------------------------------------
   0.215s   80.10%           10  0.021544s think time
   0.056s   20.93%         4620  0.000012s SQL*Net more data from client
   0.035s   13.11%            1  0.035251s log file sync
   0.013s    4.94%           33  0.000403s SQL*Net message from client
   0.000s    0.06%           43  0.000004s SQL*Net message to client
   0.000s    0.00%           41  0.000000s total CPU
  -0.051s  -19.13%                          unknown
 --------   ------  -----------------------------------------------------------------
   0.269s  100.00% Total response time

Total number of roundtrips (SQL*Net message from/to client): 43

CPU usage breakdown
-----------------------
parse CPU:      0.00s (5 PARSE calls)
exec  CPU:      0.00s (24 EXEC calls)
fetch CPU:      0.00s (12 FETCH calls)

Statistics:
-----------
COMMITs (read write): 1 -> transactions/sec 3.718
```

In this resource profile, the response time R accounted for 46% of the 0.582 seconds captured by the trace file. This time, the unknown portion of response time was only 19%.

I once again measured the actions with V$SERV_MOD_ACT_STATS and DBMS_MONITOR. Since there is no way to clear statistics in V$SERV_MOD_ACT_STATS, I used the action names "exif_insert_imp" and "lob_load_imp" this time. Certainly, it would have been possible to take two snapshots of V$SERV_MOD_ACT_STATS and to calculate the differences, but changing the module and action names made more sense, since the program had changed significantly too. The necessary calls to DBMS_MONITOR are below:

```
SQL> EXEC dbms_monitor.serv_mod_act_stat_enable('TEN.oradbpro.com','img_load',
'exif_insert_imp')
SQL> EXEC dbms_monitor.serv_mod_act_stat_enable('TEN.oradbpro.com','img_load',
'lob_load_imp')
```

Now the system was ready to measure another ten iterations:

```
$ time perl img_load_improved.pl 10 sample.jpg
real    0m0.688s
user    0m0.031s
sys     0m0.000s
```

This run was so fast that I had to get the figures with millisecond resolution to prevent some values from becoming zero due to rounding:

```
SQL> SELECT action, stat_name, round(value/1000000, 3) AS value
FROM v$serv_mod_act_stats
WHERE service_name='TEN.oradbpro.com'
AND module='img_load'
AND action IN ('exif_insert_imp','lob_load_imp')
AND stat_name in ('DB time', 'DB CPU', 'sql execute elapsed time', 'user I/O wait
time')
ORDER BY action, stat_name;
ACTION          STAT_NAME                 VALUE
--------------- ----------------------- -----
exif_insert_imp DB CPU                     .003
```

```
exif_insert_imp DB time                    .003
exif_insert_imp sql execute elapsed time   .003
exif_insert_imp user I/O wait time            0
lob_load_imp    DB CPU                      .116
lob_load_imp    DB time                     .152
lob_load_imp    sql execute elapsed time   .001
lob_load_imp    user I/O wait time            0
```

The DB time for both actions, which was formerly 8.77 seconds, was reduced to a mere 0.155 seconds. This accounts for only 22% of the response time as measured by the utility time, such that it would not be a good idea to base a forecast on these figures. Note that DB time does not include wait events which occur between database calls, such as SQL*Net message from client and SQL*Net message to client.

Phase 6—Extrapolation

Since the original measurement of 68 LOBs per minute was done without instrumentation in place and without SQL trace enabled, I also needed measurements, which were not influenced by such factors as the basis for my extrapolation. I did another series of ten measurements with instrumentation and SQL trace disabled. The average elapsed time to insert 10 LOBs was 0.931 seconds. Based on this figure, the application should be able to load almost 645 LOBs per minute. Use of the elapsed time (0.582 s) covered by the level 8 SQL trace file would result in about 1030 LOBs per minute. The actual figure will probably lie somewhere in between these two values.

Table 66 summarizes some of the differences between the original test case and the optimized test case. Figures are from a load run of 10 LOBs. Elapsed time was reduced to less than one tenth of the original value.

Table 66: Measurements Before and After Optimization

Metric	Original Test Case	Optimized Test Case
Elapsed time covered by trace file	8.90 s	0.58 s
Total wait time	6.01 s	0.32 s
SQL*Net round–trips	1201	43
Parse calls	46	5
Executions	47	24
Fetch calls	26	12
Think time	0.34 s	0.21 s

Phase 5—Installation

The one significant obstacle, which had to be overcome, was the reorganization of the LOB segment, since it required downtime. Other than that, the changes were approved quickly. New measurements were taken after the table had been reorganized during a maintenance window. The measurements were taken with instrumentation and SQL trace disabled. Throughput varied between 640 and 682 LOBs per minute. This was reasonably close to the extrapolated value of 645 LOBs per minute. Compared to the original throughput, the speedup was more than tenfold.

Lessons Learned

The case study has emphasized that it's not always possible to rely on instrumentation of the DBMS, since some code paths may not be sufficiently instrumented. Even under such aggravating circumstances, it is fairly easy to determine where an application spends most of the time when instrumentation is used. For optimum performance, both database structure and application coding must leverage the rich features offered by the ORACLE DBMS, such as caching of LOBs and sequences, reduction of parse overhead with bind variables and diminution of network round–trips with INSERT RETURNING. The default settings of LOBs are inapt to achieve good performance.

Source Code Depot

Table 67: MERITS Method Source Code Depot

File Name	*Functionality*
awr_capture.sql	Script for capturing performance data with extended SQL trace and AWR. Temporarily sets _ASH_SAMPLE_ALL=TRUE to cause ASH to sample idle wait events for improved diagnostic expressiveness. Automatically generates an AWR report and an ASH report for the traced session. Both reports are generated in HTML format in the current directory.
ilo_test.sql	This SQL script enables extended SQL trace with Hotsos ILO, runs SELECT statements, begins tasks, and terminates tasks. It may be used to learn what kind of trace file entries are written by application instrumentation.
img_load.pl	Original suboptimal LOB loading test case. Contains DDL statements for the table and sequence used. To run the program, include the path to the installation directory of the Perl package Image::ExifTool in the environment variable PERL5LIB.
img_load_improved.pl	Optimized LOB loading test case
sp_capture.sql	Script for capturing performance data with extended SQL trace and Statspack. Includes taking a session level Statspack snapshot. Make sure you install the fix for the bug which causes incorrect session level reports (see source code depot of Chapter 25).

Part IX

Oracle Net

Chapter 29

TNS Listener IP Address Binding and IP=FIRST

Status: The *Oracle Database, Oracle Clusterware and Oracle Real Application Clusters Installation Guide 10g Release 2 for AIX* contains an example TNS Listener configuration, that makes use of IP=FIRST in the configuration file listener.ora, but does not explain its meaning. This option is not documented in *Oracle Database Net Services Reference 10g Release 2*. IP=FIRST is incorrectly documented in *Oracle Database Net Services Reference 11g Release 1*.

Benefit: On systems which have more than one network adapter, the default behavior of the TNS Listener is to bind to all network adapters. In Oracle10g and subsequent releases IP=FIRST may be used to prevent the Oracle Net Listener from binding to more network adapters than configured in listener.ora.

Introduction to IP Address Binding

Internet protocol network addresses may be classified into three functional categories:

- boot IP addresses
- common (non–boot) IP addresses and
- service IP addresses

Each system in a network is identified by a unique host name. The IP address assigned to such a unique host name is called the boot IP address. This IP address is bound to a network adapter during the boot process. The unique host name of a system is returned by the command hostname on both UNIX and Windows. The host name thus returned maps to the boot IP address. No additional software except the operating system itself is required for the availability of the boot IP address. Common (non–boot) addresses are addresses used by adapters other than the boot adapter (the adapter which was assigned the boot address). Of course, the latter adapters are normally assigned addresses during the boot process as well. Any system has exactly one boot IP address. To obtain the boot IP address of a UNIX system, you might `ping` the system itself:

```
$ ping -c 1 `hostname`
PING dbserver1.oradbpro.com (172.168.0.1) 56(84) bytes of data.
64 bytes from dbserver1.oradbpro.com (172.168.0.1): icmp_seq=0 ttl=64 time=0.029 ms

--- dbserver1.oradbpro.com ping statistics ---
1 packets transmitted, 1 received, 0% packet loss, time 0ms
rtt min/avg/max/mdev = 0.029/0.029/0.029/0.000 ms, pipe 2
```

On Linux, the switch `-c` instructs `ping` to send a single packet. Use `ping` *host_name packet_size count* with a *count* of 1 on Solaris.

The term service address is used to refer to IP addresses, which applications use to provide certain services. Often, service addresses are not assigned to a separate physical network adapter, but are added as an alias address to a network adapter that already has a boot address or a non–boot address. This approach is called IP aliasing. A service address is also a non–boot address, the difference being that the former is assigned to a virtual adapter whereas the latter is assigned to a physical adapter.

Within a single operating system instance, each network adapter is identified by a unique name. AIX uses ent$N$, Solaris hme$N$ (hme=hundred megabit ethernet) or ge$N$ (ge=gigabit ethernet), whereas Linux uses eth$N$, where N is an integer that distinguishes several adapters of the same type. Additional adapter names are required for use with IP aliasing. The adapter name for adding the alias IP is formed by adding a colon and a digit to the physical adapter's name. For instance, the physical adapter might be called eth0 and the adapter for IP aliasing eth0:1. The alias IP address cannot be chosen arbitrarily. It must reside within the same network as the IP address of the associated physical adapter. The network mask must be taken into consideration too (Mask:255.255.255.0 in the example below). These topics are well beyond the scope of this book[1].

Clustering software relocates service addresses from a failed node of a cluster to a surviving node in the same cluster. Service IP addresses assigned by Oracle10*g* Clusterware are called virtual IP addresses (VIP). This is just another term for the same IP aliasing concept. In a RAC cluster, the VIP of a failing node is assigned to a surviving node. The implementation of virtual IP addresses uses IP aliasing. IP aliasing can easily be done manually by the UNIX user root using the command `ifconfig`. Here's an example that adds a service IP address to adapter eth1 on a Linux system:

```
# ifconfig eth1
eth1      Link encap:Ethernet  HWaddr 00:0C:29:07:84:EC
          inet addr:172.168.0.1  Bcast:172.168.0.255  Mask:255.255.255.0
          inet6 addr: fe80::20c:29ff:fe07:84ec/64 Scope:Link
          UP BROADCAST RUNNING MULTICAST  MTU:1500  Metric:1
          ...
# ifconfig eth1:1 inet 172.168.0.11 # IP aliasing on adapter eth1
# ifconfig eth1:1
eth1:1    Link encap:Ethernet  HWaddr 00:0C:29:07:84:EC
          inet addr:172.168.0.11  Bcast:172.168.255.255  Mask:255.255.0.0
          UP BROADCAST RUNNING MULTICAST  MTU:1500  Metric:1
          Interrupt:169 Base address:0x2080
# ping -c 1 172.168.0.11
PING 172.168.0.11 (172.168.0.11) 56(84) bytes of data.
64 bytes from 172.168.0.11: icmp_seq=0 ttl=64 time=0.072 ms

--- 172.168.0.11 ping statistics ---
1 packets transmitted, 1 received, 0% packet loss, time 0ms
rtt min/avg/max/mdev = 0.072/0.072/0.072/0.000 ms, pipe 2
```

---

1. For a discussion of subnetting, see http://en.wikipedia.org/wiki/Subnetwork.

Multihomed Systems

Systems where ORACLE database software is installed may have more than a single network interface controller (NIC). A machine might belong to different LAN segments or it might have a separate network adapter for backup and restore traffic. Clustered systems running Real Application Clusters (RAC) have a separate private network called *interconnect* for communication between individual RAC DBMS instances. Machines with several network interface controllers (a.k.a. network adapters) are sometimes referred to as *multihomed*, since they are "at home" in more than just one network. If only we as humans were as fortunate as computer systems and did not have to pay an extra rent for multiple homes.

The term multihomed is somewhat ambiguous. It may be used in a broad sense where it describes any machine that has several network adapters connected to one or more networks or in a narrow sense where it only applies to Internet access via more than a single network for higher reliability[1].

It may be the intention of a network administrator to allow clients on a certain LAN segment access to a DBMS instance on a multihomed system, but deny access to clients on another LAN segment. To achieve this, the DBA needs to make sure that the TNS Listener can be reached from one LAN segment but not the other. Technically speaking, the TNS Listener should bind to the IP address of one adapter, but not the other.

Now it's time to finally fill you in on the rather awkward acronym INADDR_ANY, that was mentioned in the status section at the beginning of this chapter. It is a constant used in the C language programming interface for sockets. On POSIX compliant systems, TCP/IP as well as UDP networking is implemented using sockets (see man socket). The socket programming paradigm for a server process such as the TNS Listener is to:

1. create a socket.
2. bind the socket to an address, potentially using INADDR_ANY.
3. listen for incoming connections.
4. accept incoming connections (or maybe not as in valid node checking discussed in Chapter 30).

The C language routines for these four steps are socket, bind, listen, and accept. The use of INADDR_ANY tells the operating system that the creator of the socket is willing to communicate with any outside system that may contact it. The Solaris documentation describes INADDR_ANY as follows ([Sol8 2000]):

> By using the special value INADDR_ANY with IP, or the unspecified address (all zeros) with IPv6, the local IP address can be left unspecified in the bind() call by either active or passive TCP sockets. This feature is usually used if the local address is either unknown or irrelevant. If left unspecified, the local IP or IPv6 address will be bound at connection time to the address of the network interface used to service the connection.

The opposite would be to allow connections from hosts residing in a certain network only. The value of INADDR_ANY is an IP address which consists of all zeros (0.0.0.0). Three tools are suitable for verifying that the TNS Listener behaves as expected:

- telnet, to establish a connection to the TNS Listener and verify that it is actually listening on a port
- netstat, to list network connections (generic) as well as related processes (some operating systems only)
- A UNIX system call tracing utility such as strace (Linux), truss (Solaris, AIX), or tusc (HP–UX)

UNIX system calls are the interface to the UNIX operating system kernel. The POSIX (Portable Operating System Interface) standard is a specification for UNIX system calls. It is maintained by The Open Group[2]. Of course tnsping could also be used, but according to the documentation (*Oracle Database Net Services Administrator's Guide 10g Release 2*) it requires a Net service name as an argument. Fortunately, the undocumented feature of supplying an address specification on the command line as in the example below is a big time saver:

```
$ tnsping '(ADDRESS=(PROTOCOL=TCP)(Host=172.168.0.1)(Port=1521))'
TNS Ping Utility for Linux: Version 10.2.0.3.0 - Production on 22-JUL-2007 20:13:38
Copyright (c) 1997, 2006, Oracle.  All rights reserved.
Attempting to contact (ADDRESS=(PROTOCOL= TCP)(Host=172.168.0.1)(Port=1521))
OK (10 msec)
```

---

1. The latter definition is found on Wikipedia at http://en.wikipedia.org/wiki/Multihoming.
2. See http://www.pasc.org

The address specification follows the same syntax as a full–fledged DESCRIPTION in tnsnames.ora, but omits sections such as CONNECT_DATA or FAILOVER_MODE which are irrelevant to tnsping. On UNIX systems, quotes around it are necessary since parentheses have special meaning to shells. From Oracle10*g* onward, tnsping also supports the easy connect format *host_name:port/instance_service_name*, which also does not require Net service name resolution:

```
C:> tnsping dbserver:1521/ten.oradbpro.com
TNS Ping Utility for 32-bit Windows: Version 10.2.0.1.0 - Production on 14-DEC-2007
18:58:59
Copyright (c) 1997, 2005, Oracle.  All rights reserved.
Used parameter files:
C:\oracle\admin\network\admin\sqlnet.ora
Used HOSTNAME adapter to resolve the alias
Attempting to contact
(DESCRIPTION=(CONNECT_DATA=(SERVICE_NAME=ten.oradbpro.com))(ADDRESS=(PROTOCOL=TCP)
(HOST=169.254.212.142)(PORT=1521)))
OK (10 msec)
```

When using the easy connect format with tnsping, the *instance_service_name* is optional. If specified, it is not verified by tnsping.

IP=FIRST Disabled

Let's investigate what happens when IP=FIRST is disabled. The tests below were performed with Oracle10*g*, since Oracle9*i* does not support IP=FIRST. However, an Oracle9*i* TNS Listener has the same behavior as an Oracle10*g* or Oracle11*g* TNS Listener without IP=FIRST. The test system's host name is dbserver1.oradbpro.com. This host name maps to the boot IP address 172.168.0.1:

```
$ ping -c 1 `hostname`
PING dbserver1.oradbpro.com (172.168.0.1) 56(84) bytes of data.
64 bytes from dbserver1.oradbpro.com (172.168.0.1): icmp_seq=0 ttl=64 time=0.011 ms
```

Host Name

For this demonstration, the TNS Listener configuration in listener.ora contained the host name of the test system:

```
LISTENER=
  (DESCRIPTION =
      (ADDRESS_LIST =
         (ADDRESS = (PROTOCOL = TCP)(HOST=dbserver1.oradbpro.com)(PORT=1521))
      )
   )
)
```

Coming back to the digression on UNIX network programming with sockets, let's take a look at the bind calls the TNS Listener makes when IP=FIRST is disabled. On Linux, strace may be used to trace the bind system calls the TNS Listener makes. The basic syntax for starting and tracing a process with strace is:

```
strace -f -o output_file command arguments
```

The switch -f tells strace to trace across forks (creation of a child process) and -o is for specifying the output file where strace writes the system calls it captured. So let's start a TNS Listener under the control of strace:

```
$ strace -f -o /tmp/strace_no_ip_first.out lsnrctl start
```

Without IP=FIRST, the trace output contains a bind call, which uses an incoming address of all zeros (INADDR_ANY):

```
$ grep "bind.*1521" /tmp/strace_no_ip_first.out
25443 bind(8, {sa_family=AF_INET, sin_port=htons(1521),
sin_addr=inet_addr("0.0.0.0")}, 16) = 0
```

Running telnet *IP_address listener_port* for all the IP addresses associated with the host, confirms that the TNS Listener accepts connections on any network. This is also evident from netstat output (multiple connections between telnet and tnslsnr must be open to get this output):

```
$ netstat -np|egrep 'Proto|telnet|tnslsnr'
Proto Recv-Q Send-Q Local Address          Foreign Address      State       PID/
```

```
                                                               Program name
tcp         0      0 192.168.10.132:50388 192.168.10.132:1521  ESTABLISHED 25610/telnet
tcp         0      0 172.168.0.1:50393      172.168.0.1:1521    ESTABLISHED 25613/telnet
tcp         0      0 127.0.0.1:50394        127.0.0.1:1521      ESTABLISHED 25614/telnet
tcp         0      0 172.168.0.1:1521       172.168.0.1:50319   ESTABLISHED 25489/tnslsnr
tcp         0      0 172.168.0.1:1521       172.168.0.1:50320   ESTABLISHED 25489/tnslsnr
tcp         0      0 192.168.10.132:1521  192.168.10.132:50388  ESTABLISHED 25489/tnslsnr
tcp         0      0 172.168.0.1:1521       172.168.0.1:50393   ESTABLISHED 25489/tnslsnr
tcp         0      0 127.0.0.1:1521         127.0.0.1:50394     ESTABLISHED 25489/tnslsnr
```

The switch -n tells netstat to use numbers instead of names for host names and ports. The switch -p (Linux specific) is for displaying process names. The INADDR_ANY value of 0.0.0.0 can be seen in the column "Local Address" of the netstat output, if the switch -1 is used. This switch restricts the report to sockets with status LISTEN, i.e. sockets, which are not yet connected to a client program:

```
$ netstat -tnlp | egrep 'Proto|tns'
Proto Recv-Q Send-Q Local Address          Foreign Address        State
PID/Program name
tcp        0      0 0.0.0.0:1521            0.0.0.0:*              LISTEN
25489/tnslsnr
```

The netstat switch -t limits the output to TCP sockets only. On Windows, you would run netstat with the switches -abno -p tcp, to get nearly the same report as on UNIX.

```
C:> netstat -abno -p tcp
Active Connections
   Proto  Local Address       Foreign Address       State         PID
   TCP    0.0.0.0:1521        0.0.0.0:0             LISTENING     4524
   [TNSLSNR.exe]
   TCP    127.0.0.1:1521      127.0.0.1:2431        ESTABLISHED   4524
   [TNSLSNR.exe]
   TCP    127.0.0.1:2431      127.0.0.1:1521        ESTABLISHED   4836
   [telnet.exe]
   TCP    192.168.10.1:1521   192.168.10.1:2432     ESTABLISHED   4524
   [TNSLSNR.exe]
   TCP    192.168.10.1:2432   192.168.10.1:1521     ESTABLISHED   4224
   [telnet.exe]
```

Loopback Adapter

You may be surprised to find that the TNS Listener may also be contacted at the IP address 127.0.0.1 of the loopback adapter. The loopback adapter provides IP networking within the boundaries of a machine for situations where a system is not connected to a network, but needs TCP/IP for applications that require it. The host name "localhost" is mapped to the IP address 127.0.0.1 in the hosts configuration file. This file is /etc/hosts on UNIX and %SYSTEM_ROOT%\system32\drivers\etc\hosts on Windows. On a laptop computer, the loopback IP address may be explicitly assigned to the TNS Listener when working offline. This will allow use of the TNS Listener over TCP/IP even when not connected to any network. Another option for local connections via the TNS Listener is the IPC protocol. To check whether a process is listening on port 1521 of the loopback address, the telnet command below may be used:

```
$ telnet localhost 1521
Trying 127.0.0.1...
Connected to localhost.
Escape character is '^]'.
```

Since telnet did not terminate with the error "Connection refused", the TNS Listener accepted the connection from telnet. The strace output contains a separate bind call for the IP address 127.0.0.1:

```
25443 bind(12, {sa_family=AF_INET, sin_port=htons(0), sin_addr=inet_addr
("127.0.0.1")}, 16) = 0
```

Boot IP Address

It is undocumented in releases prior to Oracle11g that the TNS Listener does not bind to `INADDR_ANY` if the boot IP address is used in `listener.ora`, instead of the system's host name. Below is a modified TNS Listener configuration, which uses the boot IP address:

```
LISTENER=
  (DESCRIPTION =
     (ADDRESS_LIST =
        (ADDRESS = (PROTOCOL=TCP)(HOST=172.168.0.1)(PORT=1521))
     )
  )
)
```

After restarting the TNS Listener, the local address corresponds to the configured IP address:

```
$ netstat -tnlp|grep tns
Proto Recv-Q Send-Q Local Address      Foreign Address   State     PID/Program name
tcp       0      0 172.168.0.1:1521    0.0.0.0:*         LISTEN    25630/tnslsnr
```

It is no longer possible to connect to the TNS Listener on the loopback address or any other IP address, which is not explicitly configured:

```
$ telnet localhost 1521
Trying 127.0.0.1...
telnet: connect to address 127.0.0.1: Connection refused
$ tnsping 192.168.10.132:1521
TNS Ping Utility for Linux: Version 10.2.0.3.0 - Production on 08-SEP-2007 15:47:25
Copyright (c) 1997, 2006, Oracle.  All rights reserved.
Used parameter files:
/opt/oracle/product/db10.2/network/admin/sqlnet.ora
Used HOSTNAME adapter to resolve the alias
Attempting to contact
(DESCRIPTION=(CONNECT_DATA=(SERVICE_NAME=192.168.10.132))(ADDRESS=(PROTOCOL=TCP)(HOST=
192.168.10.132)(PORT=1521)))
TNS-12541: TNS:no listener
```

With this configuration, the boot IP address is used in the bind call traced with `strace`:

```
$ strace -f -o /tmp/strace_boot_ip.out lsnrctl start
$ grep "bind.*1521" /tmp/strace_boot_ip.out
25689 bind(8, {sa_family=AF_INET, sin_port=htons(1521),
sin_addr=inet_addr("172.168.0.1")}, 16) = 0
```

Service IP Address

To complement the probe into the TNS Listener's undocumented features, let's see what happens when the TNS Listener is configured with a host name, which maps to a service IP address. The alias IP address 172.168.0.11 of adapter eth1:1 that was defined above will serve as an example. This IP address is assigned to the host name vip-dbserver1 in the configuration file `/etc/hosts`:

```
$ grep 172.168.0.11 /etc/hosts
172.168.0.11    vip-dbserver1.oradbpro.com      vip-dbserver1
```

Thus, the `ADDRESS` entry in `listener.ora` becomes:

```
(ADDRESS=(PROTOCOL=TCP)(HOST=vip-dbserver1)(PORT=1521))
```

When assigned a host name, which maps to a service IP address (i.e. not the boot IP address), the TNS Listener binds specifically to that address and does not use `INADDR_ANY`. The output from `netstat` confirms this:

```
$ netstat -tnlp|egrep 'Proto|tns'
Proto Recv-Q Send-Q Local Address      Foreign Address State     PID/Program name
tcp       0      0 172.168.0.11:1521   0.0.0.0:*       LISTEN    27050/tnslsnr
```

Further testing reveals that `INADDR_ANY` is also not used for non–boot IP addresses.

IP=FIRST Enabled

To enable `IP=FIRST`, the `ADDRESS` line in `listener.ora` must be modified as follows:

```
(ADDRESS=(PROTOCOL=TCP)(HOST=172.168.0.1)(PORT=1521)(IP=FIRST))
```

After restarting the TNS Listener (`lsnrctl reload` *listener_name* is not sufficient) with this configuration, the bind call in the `strace` output file has changed. Where previously 0.0.0.0 (`INADDR_ANY`) was used, there is now the IP address, which the system's host name resolves to:

```
bind(8, {sa_family=AF_INET, sin_port=htons(1521), sin_addr=inet_addr("172.168.0.1")},
16) = 0
```

The TNS Listener is again functional at the assigned address 172.168.0.1:

```
$ telnet 172.168.0.1 1521
Trying 172.168.0.1...
Connected to 172.168.0.1.
Escape character is '^]'.
Connection closed by foreign host.
```

The TNS Listener closes the connection to `telnet` after a few minutes. Type Ctrl+C, Ctrl+D, and hit return to abort the connection. The program `telnet` then responds with "Connection closed by foreign host." as above. Now that `IP=FIRST` is in effect, attempting to contact the TNS Listener on any address other than the boot IP address fails:

```
$ telnet 77.47.1.187 1521
Trying 77.47.1.187...
telnet: connect to address 77.47.1.187: Connection refused
$ telnet localhost 1521
Trying 127.0.0.1...
telnet: connect to address 127.0.0.1: Connection refused
# netstat -tnlp | egrep 'Proto|tns'
Proto Recv-Q Send-Q Local Address      Foreign Address    State      PID/Program name
tcp        0      0 172.168.0.1:1521   0.0.0.0:*          LISTEN     27916/tnslsnr
```

Table 68 summarizes the TNS Listener's IP address binding behavior under all situations which may arise. Note that the TNS Listener's behavior for boot IP address, non–boot IP address or host name, and service IP addresses or host name is identical, irrespective of the option `IP=FIRST`. In other words, `IP=FIRST` solely has an impact when the system's host name is used in `listener.ora`. The first row of the table represents the TNS Listener's behavior when a

Table 68: TNS Listener IP Address Binding

HOST Setting in listener.ora	IP=FIRST	Boot IP Address	Other Non–Boot IP Address or Service IP Address (IP Aliasing)	Loopback Address
System host name (maps to boot IP address)	yes	yes	no	no
System host name (maps to boot IP address)	no	yes	yes	yes
Boot IP address	no	yes	no	no
Non–Boot IP address/ host name	no	no	no	no
Service IP address/host name	no	no	no	no

system's host name is used in the configuration file `listener.ora` and `IP=FIRST` is set. Columns three to five indicate the IP address binding behavior under the settings in columns 1 and 2. The values "yes" means that the TNS Listener does bind to the type of IP address indicated in the table's column heading. Thus, the TNS listener binds solely to the boot IP address under the settings depicted in the first row.

Lessons Learned

This chapter investigated the TNS Listener's binding to IP addresses on multihomed systems as well as its use of the loopback adapter. Several undocumented aspects were found:

- When assigned a system's host name, the TNS Listener uses INADDR_ANY and thus can be reached from any network as well as via the loopback adapter, which always has the IP address 127.0.0.1.
- When assigned the boot IP address or a non–boot IP address or host name, the TNS Listener does not use INADDR_ANY, but instead binds specifically to the address assigned. It also refrains from using the loopback adapter.
- When the option IP=FIRST is enabled, the TNS Listener binds specifically to the IP address, which the configured host name resolves to and cannot be reached from any other IP address including the loopback address. This option is relevant only if the system's host name is assigned to the parameter HOST in listener.ora.

Thus, there are three solutions for TNS Listeners, which shall not be reached from any network:

- Use the boot IP address instead of the system's host name (which maps to the boot IP address).
- Use a non–boot or service IP address or host name (neither the system's host name nor a host name that resolves to the boot IP address).
- Configure the option IP=FIRST when referencing the system's host name in listener.ora (requires Oracle10g or later release).

Chapter 30

TNS Listener TCP/IP Valid Node Checking

Status: Valid node checking is documented, but it is undocumented that the parameters are fully dynamic in Oracle10*g* and Oracle11*g*, such that the configuration may be enabled, changed, and removed without stopping and restarting the TNS Listener, making the feature much less intrusive.

Benefit: Valid node checking may be used to prevent unwanted or errant Oracle Net connections to critical DBMS instances. It's a "poor man's firewall" under control of the DBA.

Introduction to Valid Node Checking

Valid node checking is an interesting security feature that protects DBMS instances from malevolent or errant Oracle Net connections over TCP/IP, without the need for a firewall or IP address filtering at the operating system level. The feature is available in Oracle9*i* and subsequent releases at no extra cost.

Here's an anecdote which illustrates why valid node checking is a worthwhile feature. A production database that had several database jobs was copied onto a test machine. The database jobs started running on the test machine. Some of these jobs were using database links. Since the database link definition contained a full Net service name definition, instead of referencing a Net service name in `tnsnames.ora` (an undocumented feature), the test system was able to access a critical production system and caused a deterioration in its performance. The administrators got off lightly, since the jobs were read only. Imagine what could have happened, had the jobs modified production data. Correctly configured valid node checking would have prevented the issue.

The feature is controlled by the three parameters `tcp.validnode_checking`, `tcp.invited_nodes` and `tcp.excluded_nodes`, which are presented in Table 69. It appears that the code path for valid node checking is always executed. As long as the feature is not in use, the lists for invited and excluded hosts are empty, thus allowing any client to connect. This assumption is based on the observation that the TNS Listener writes lines such as in the excerpt below on each connect by a client to its trace file, irrespective of the setting of `tcp.validnode_checking`:

Table 69: Valid Node Checking Parameters

Name	Purpose	Values	Default
tcp.validnode_checking	Turns valid node checking on or off	yes, no	no
tcp.invited_nodes	List of nodes which may connect to the TNS Listener	Comma separated list of host names and/or IP addresses on a single line	empty list
tcp.excluded_nodes	List of nodes which are denied a connection to the TNS Listener	Comma separated list of host names and/or IP addresses on a single line	empty list

```
[12-JUL-2007 20:03:12:268] nttcnp: Validnode Table IN use; err 0x0
[12-JUL-2007 20:03:12:268] nttvlser: valid node check on incoming node 10.6.6.64
```

Only when the TNS Listener trace level is at least at level ADMIN and tcp.validnode_checking=no is set, does the trace file contain evidence that valid node checking is switched off:

```
[12-JUL-2007 19:52:28:329] ntvllt: tcp.validnode_checking not turned on
```

Let's take a look at some examples. The prompts dbserver$ and client$ indicate where each command was run. The listener.ora and sqlnet.ora on the server are below:

```
dbserver$ head -200 listener.ora sqlnet.ora
==> listener.ora <==
LISTENER =
  (DESCRIPTION_LIST =
    (DESCRIPTION =
      (ADDRESS_LIST =
        (ADDRESS = (PROTOCOL = TCP)(HOST =dbserver.oradbpro.com)(PORT = 1521))
      )
    )
  )
trace_level_listener=admin
==> sqlnet.ora <==
NAMES.DIRECTORY_PATH= (TNSNAMES)
```

Valid node checking is currently switched off. This is evident from the configuration file sqlnet.ora reproduced above. Below is the tnsnames.ora on the client:

```
client$ cat tnsnames.ora
TEN_TCP.WORLD =
  (DESCRIPTION =
    (ADDRESS_LIST =
      (ADDRESS = (PROTOCOL = TCP)(HOST=dbserver.oradbpro.com)(PORT = 1521))
    )
    (CONNECT_DATA =
      (SERVICE_NAME = TEN)
    )
  )
```

Let's start the TNS Listener and verify that the client can connect to it. For the sake of conciseness, lsnrctl output, which does not indicate whether valid node checking is configured, is omitted:

```
dbserver$ lsnrctl start
```

Since the above sqlnet.ora file does not contain any of the three valid node checking parameters, the feature is disabled and any client can connect successfully:

```
client$ sqlplus -l ndebes/secret@ten_tcp.world
Connected to:
Oracle Database 10g Enterprise Edition Release 10.2.0.1.0 - Production
SQL> EXIT
```

```
Disconnected from Oracle Database 10g Enterprise Edition Release 10.2.0.1.0 -
Production
```

Enabling and Modifying Valid Node Checking at Runtime

I claimed that valid node checking could be enabled dynamically in Oracle10*g* and Oracle11*g*, i.e. without stopping and restarting the TNS Listener. Let's verify this by changing `sqlnet.ora` as below on the server and running `lsnrctl reload`[1]:

```
dbserver$ cat sqlnet.ora
NAMES.DIRECTORY_PATH=(TNSNAMES)
tcp.validnode_checking=yes
tcp.excluded_nodes=(client.oradbpro.com)
dbserver$ lsnrctl reload
```

The output of `lsnrctl reload` does not indicate whether valid node checking is enabled or not. Now, an attempt to connect from the client system client.oradbpro.com fails:

```
client$ sqlplus -l ndebes/secret@ten_tcp.world
SQL*Plus: Release 10.2.0.1.0 - Production on Fri Jul 13 02:06:33 2007
ERROR:
ORA-12537: TNS:connection closed
SP2-0751: Unable to connect to Oracle.  Exiting SQL*Plus
```

Of course, translation of the client host name to an IP address with DNS, NIS, or other method must be configured. IP addresses may also be used in the list of invited or excluded hosts. If the TNS Listener trace level is at least USER, an entry like the one below, which identifies the client that was denied, is written to the TNS Listener trace file:

```
13-JUL-2007 02:21:02:109] nttvlser: valid node check on incoming node 88.215.114.53
13-JUL-2007 02:21:02:109] nttvlser: Denied Entry: 88.215.114.53
```

Setting the list of invited nodes in such a way that client.oradbpro.com is included and running another `reload` enables the client to connect again:

```
dbserver$ cat sqlnet.ora
tcp.validnode_checking=yes
tcp.invited_nodes=(client.oradbpro.com)
dbserver$ lsnrctl reload
client$ sqlplus -l ndebes/secret@ten_tcp.world
Connected to:
Oracle Database 10g Enterprise Edition Release 10.2.0.1.0 - Production
```

The successful connection by the client is logged as below in the TNS Listener trace file:

```
[13-JUL-2007 02:24:44:789] nttvlser: valid node check on incoming node 88.215.114.53
[13-JUL-2007 02:24:44:789] nttvlser: Accepted Entry: 88.215.114.53
```

If `tcp.invited_nodes` is set, any node not mentioned in the list is denied access:

```
dbserver$ cat sqlnet.ora
tcp.validnode_checking=yes
tcp.invited_nodes=(192.168.0.1)
dbserver$ lsnrctl reload
client$ sqlplus -l ndebes/secret@ten_tcp.world
SQL*Plus: Release 10.2.0.1.0 - Production on Fri Jul 13 02:06:33 2007
ERROR:
ORA-12537: TNS:connection closed
SP2-0751: Unable to connect to Oracle.  Exiting SQL*Plus
```

Of course, the denied hosts also include the system where the TNS Listener is running, such that subsequent LSN-RCTL commands over TCP/IP fail. You need to include the local system in `tcp.invited_nodes` to allow LSN-RCTL commands over TCP/IP. Another method is to use an IPC protocol entry as the first ADDRESS of the TNS Listener. This tells the LSNRCTL utility to communicate with the TNS Listener using IPC, which is obviously

---

1. It appears that the LSNRCTL utility caches the TNS Listener configuration. When testing, you should always run `lsnrctl` from the command line, instead of leaving the utility open and running multiple commands at the LSN-RCTL prompt. The latter approach may not pick up changes to `listener.ora`.

exempt from TCP/IP valid node checking. The next example shows a TNS Listener definition, which uses the IPC protocol in the first ADDRESS entry.

```
LISTENER =
  (DESCRIPTION_LIST =
    (DESCRIPTION =
      (ADDRESS_LIST =
       (ADDRESS = (PROTOCOL = IPC)(KEY = TEN))
       (ADDRESS = (PROTOCOL = TCP)(HOST =dbserver.oradbpro.com)(PORT = 1521))
      )
    )
  )
```

By default, an Oracle9*i* TNS Listener is unprotected against STOP commands from remote nodes. Instead of using a TNS Listener password to prevent someone from another host within the network from shutting down the TNS Listener, you could also use valid node checking. The downside is that the list of invited nodes has to include all the machines, which may access the TNS Listener. These could still be used to remotely stop the TNS Listener, but might be trusted systems. This is interesting news for installations that run clustering software, which protects the ORACLE TNS Listener against node failure, but does not support TNS Listener passwords (e.g. VERITAS Cluster Server prior to release 4).

If you want to take a more relaxed approach, you may set only tcp.excluded_nodes and list systems that you are certain may not connect to the TNS Listener, and thus the instance(s) served by the TNS Listener. All nodes not mentioned will be able to connect. Host names and IP addresses may be used at the same time.

There's no sense in setting both tcp.invited_nodes and tcp.excluded_nodes at the same time, since even nodes not mentioned explicitly as excluded nodes will still be excluded when tcp.invited_nodes is set. If a node name is contained in both tcp.excluded_nodes and tcp.invited_nodes, tcp.invited_nodes takes precedence and the node is allowed access. In Oracle9*i*, if there is a single node name that cannot be resolved to an IP address, this error is logged to the trace file:

```
[12-JUL-2007 21:25:10:162] nttcnp: Validnode Table **NOT** used; err 0x1f7
```

Valid node checking is switched off when this error occurs. Unfortunately, the Oracle9*i* LSNRCTL utility does not write an error message to the terminal. In the presence of invalid host names, Oracle10*g* lsnrctl startup fails with "TNS-12560: TNS:protocol adapter error" and "TNS-00584: Valid node checking configuration error". Using oerr on TNS-00584 gives:

```
$ oerr tns 584
00584, 00000, "Valid node checking configuration error"
// *Cause:Valid node checking specific Oracle Net configuration is invalid.
// *Action:Ensure the hosts specified in the "invited_nodes" and "excluded_nodes"
// are valid. For further details, turn on tracing and reexecute the operation.
```

If TNS Listener tracing is enabled, the trace file will contain a message similar to the following:

```
[12-JUL-2007 23:27:16:808] snlinGetAddrInfo: Name resolution failed for wrong.host.name
[12-JUL-2007 23:27:16:808] nttcnp: Validnode Table **NOT** used; err 0x248
```

A reload of configuration files with lsnrctl reload completes successfully, in spite of name resolution failures which are logged in the following format:

```
[13-JUL-2007 00:11:53:427] snlinGetAddrInfo: Name resolution failed for wrong.host.name
```

No reverse address translation is performed on IP addresses. Thus, IP addresses which cannot be translated to host names do not prevent the operation of valid node checking. The operating system utility nslookup may be used to translate between Domain Name Service (DNS) host names and IP addresses and vice versa. Keep in mind that nslookup does not read the hosts file (/etc/hosts on UNIX, %SYSTEM_ROOT%\system32\drivers\etc\hosts on Windows, where SYSTEM_ROOT is usually C:\WINDOWS). So the TNS Listener may be able to resolve a name or IP address by calling C programming language library routines (gethostbyaddr(), gethostbyname()), while nslookup may not.

I ran some tests to find out what the undocumented maximum accepted length for the invited and excluded node lists is. The maximum line length of the Vi editor I used was 2048 bytes[1]. Both parameters were still working fine at this line length. Assuming an average length of 30 bytes for a host name, this length would provide enough room for around 65 entries. If IP addresses were used, at least 128 IP addresses would fit. The list of valid nodes cannot exceed a single line, otherwise the error "TNS-00583: Valid node checking: unable to parse configuration parameters" is signaled and the TNS Listener does not start.

---

1. Other editors allow lines which are longer than 2048 bytes. Vim (Vi improved) is an enhanced implementation of Vi, which supports a line length of more than 2048 bytes. It is available for free at the URL http://www.vim.org and runs on UNIX, Windows, and Mac OS.

Chapter 31

Local Naming Parameter ENABLE=BROKEN

Status: The local naming parameter setting `ENABLE=BROKEN` is undocumented.

Benefit: This parameter may be used in a Net service name definition to switch on sending of TCP/IP keepalive packets in order to detect communication failures.

Node Failure and the TCP/IP Protocol

Before the advent of Oracle10*g* Clusterware and its support for virtual IP addresses, failure of a node in a RAC cluster would normally leave clients, which were connected to the failed node, waiting for extended periods of time, possibly up to two hours—the default period for TCP/IP connection time–out. `ENABLE=BROKEN` addresses RAC high availability environments. It can be used to reduce the interval where a client hangs due to a broken network connection to a RAC cluster node that died unexpectedly.

Syntactically, `ENABLE=BROKEN` belongs in the `DESCRIPTION` section, right where other high availability related parameters such as `FAILOVER` have to be placed. Below is an example Net service name definition for use with a two–node RAC cluster and Transparent Application Failover (TAF):

```
DBSERVER_TAF.WORLD =
  (DESCRIPTION =
    (ENABLE=BROKEN)
    (FAILOVER=ON)
    (LOAD_BALANCE=OFF)
    (ADDRESS_LIST =
      (ADDRESS = (PROTOCOL = TCP)(HOST = dbserver1.oradbpro.com)(PORT = 1521))
      (ADDRESS = (PROTOCOL = TCP)(HOST = dbserver2.oradbpro.com)(PORT = 1521))
    )
    (CONNECT_DATA =
```

```
        (SERVICE_NAME = TEN)(SERVER = DEDICATED)
        (FAILOVER_MODE=
                (TYPE=SELECT)
                (METHOD=BASIC)
                (DELAY=5)
                (RETRIES=600)
        )
    )
  )
```

The option ENABLE=BROKEN is available at least since Oracle8 and controls whether or not the keepalive option of a network connection is switched on. UNIX network programming is based on the socket interface. A socket is a communication endpoint. Again, UNIX system call tracing is the tool of choice to observe what is going on. Here's an example from a Solaris system, where ENABLE=BROKEN was not configured:

```
$ truss -o /tmp/truss-no-enable-broken.out -t so_socket,setsockopt \
-v so_socket,setsockopt sqlplus system@DBSERVER_TAF.WORLD
$ cat /tmp/truss-no-enable-broken.out
so_socket(PF_INET, SOCK_STREAM, IPPROTO_IP, "", 1) = 8
setsockopt(8, tcp, TCP_NODELAY, 0xFFFFFFFF7FFF6924, 4, 1) = 0
```

Repeating the same actions with ENABLE=BROKEN configured yields:

```
so_socket(PF_INET, SOCK_STREAM, IPPROTO_IP, "", 1) = 8
setsockopt(8, SOL_SOCKET, SO_KEEPALIVE, 0xFFFFFFFF7FFF665C, 4, 1) = 0
setsockopt(8, tcp, TCP_NODELAY, 0xFFFFFFFF7FFF6924, 4, 1) = 0
setsockopt(8, SOL_SOCKET, SO_KEEPALIVE, 0xFFFFFFFF7FFF529C, 4, 1) = 0
setsockopt(8, SOL_SOCKET, SO_KEEPALIVE, 0xFFFFFFFF7FFFDC2C, 4, 1) = 0
```

Three additional setsockopt system calls have occurred after setting ENABLE=BROKEN. The C language flag to switch on sending of keepalive packets is SO_KEEPALIVE, as is evident from the above output.

On Solaris, slightly less than 80 parameters control TCP/IP networking. The *Solaris Tunable Parameters Reference Manual* ([SoTu 2007]) has this to say about SO_KEEPALIVE (ndd is a Solaris utility for changing TCP/IP parameters):

tcp_keepalive_interval

This ndd parameter sets a probe interval that is first sent out after a TCP connection is idle on a system–wide basis.

Solaris supports the TCP keep–alive mechanism as described in RFC 1122. This mechanism is enabled by setting the SO_KEEPALIVE socket option on a TCP socket.

If SO_KEEPALIVE is enabled for a socket, the first keep–alive probe is sent out after a TCP connection is idle for two hours, the default value of the tcp_keepalive_interval parameter. If the peer does not respond to the probe after eight minutes, the TCP connection is aborted. For more information, refer to tcp_keepalive_abort_interval.

You can also use the TCP_KEEPALIVE_THRESHOLD socket option on individual applications to override the default interval so that each application can have its own interval on each socket. The option value is an unsigned integer in milliseconds. See also tcp(7P).

The Solaris manual goes on to state that the commitment level for the parameter is unstable and that it should not be changed. To the best of my knowledge, tcp_keepalive_threshold is not implemented in ORACLE DBMS software. Instead of modifying keepalive settings, the Solaris documentation recommends changing retransmit time–outs (tcp_rexmit_interval_max and tcp_ip_abort_interval).

A while back, my own testing with Oracle8*i* confirmed that ENABLE=BROKEN is functional and useful given that tcp_keepalive_interval and tcp_keepalive_abort_interval are adjusted as needed. Tracing with truss showed that it is still implemented in Oracle10*g*. Keep in mind that an appropriate test for all of these TCP/IP settings consists of either pulling the network cable (and keeping it pulled), switching off the server, or any other method of bringing down the operating system (Stop+A on Solaris), such that it does not stand a chance of sending a message to a remote system to indicate that sockets should be closed. Such a test should be performed on any RAC cluster before it moves into production.

Before I move off topic any further, let me explain why ENABLE=BROKEN should be considered an outdated feature. With Oracle10*g* Clusterware and virtual IP addresses (VIP) the IP address that went down on a failed host is brought back online on a surviving node. Retransmits by the client should then be redirected to a surviving node and fail, since it knows nothing about the sockets that were open on the failed node. As part of virtual IP address (VIP) failover, Oracle Clusterware flushes the address resolution protocol (ARP) cache, which translates between IP addresses and MAC (medium access control) addresses of ethernet adapters. This is undocumented, but is essential in accomplishing successful reconnects by database clients, which must become aware of the new mapping between IP address and MAC address. On Linux, the ARP cache is flushed by executing the command /sbin/arping -q -U -c 3 -I *adapter ip_address* in the script $ORA_CRS_HOME/bin/racgvip. The mapping between MAC and IP addresses may be displayed with the command arp -a on UNIX as well as Windows.

Additional information on the subject of TCP/IP and failover is in Metalink note 249213.1. According to the note, Sun Microsystems suggest setting tcp_keepalive_interval, tcp_ip_abort_cinterval (prevents connect attempts to the failed node from waiting up to three minutes) and tcp_ip_abort_interval (by default, a connection is closed after not receiving an acknowledgment for eight minutes). Unfortunately, the Metalink note does not state that tcp_keepalive_interval is ignored, unless SO_KEEPALIVE is set on the socket, which in turn requires ENABLE=BROKEN.

I recommend adjusting tcp_ip_abort_cinterval to prevent connections initiated before the virtual IP address has come back online on a surviving node from locking up for up to three minutes. I also suggest reducing the values of the parameters tcp_ip_abort_interval and tcp_rexmit_interval_max to 45 seconds (default: 8 minutes) and 30 seconds (default 3 minutes) respectively. These parameters must be changed on the database client machine—remember, the server is down when the reduced time–outs must be used by the client. Table 70 suggests settings which should keep the time–outs below one minute under all circumstances.

Table 70: Recommended TCP/IP Parameters

Parameter	Default	Suggested Value	Unit
tcp_rexmit_interval_max	60000 (60 seconds)	10000 (10 seconds)	ms
tcp_ip_abort_interval	480000 (8 minutes)	45000 (45 seconds)	ms
tcp_ip_abort_cinterval	180000 (3 minutes)	30000 (30 seconds)	ms

Chapter 32

Default Host Name in Oracle Net Configurations

Status: It is undocumented that the host name may be left unspecified in the configuration files `listener.ora` and `tnsnames.ora`.

Benefit: The configuration file `listener.ora` does not need to be modified in case the host name is changed. Custom scripts, that might generate a TNS Listener configuration, do not have to consider varying host names as long as the TNS Listener may use the default host name (i.e. the local system's host name, which uniquely identifies it).

Default Host Name

In a Net service name description, the host name may be omitted. The syntax for omitting the host name (or IP address) is simply `(HOST=)`. If the host name or IP address is an empty string, it defaults to the host name of the local system, which may be obtained with the command `hostname` (UNIX and Windows) or the C library routine `gethostname`. Since the latter is not a UNIX system call, it cannot be observed with system call trace utilities such as `truss`. Below is an example that passes a Net service name description to `tnsping` on the command line.

```
$ tnsping "(ADDRESS=(PROTOCOL=TCP)(Host=)(Port=1521))"
TNS Ping Utility for Linux: Version 10.2.0.3.0 - Production on 22-JUL-2007 22:13:07
Attempting to contact (ADDRESS=(PROTOCOL= TCP)(Host=)(Port=1521))
OK (0 msec)
```

The same syntax may also be used in `listener.ora`, such as in the example below:

```
LISTENER_DBSERVER1 =
  (DESCRIPTION =
    (ADDRESS_LIST =
      (ADDRESS=(PROTOCOL=TCP)(HOST=)(PORT=1521)(IP=FIRST))
    )
```

)

The UNIX command `hostname` returns the host name of the system:

```
$ ping -c 1 `hostname`
PING dbserver1.oradbpro.com (172.168.0.1) 56(84) bytes of data.
64 bytes from dbserver1.oradbpro.com (172.168.0.1): icmp_seq=0 ttl=64 time=0.072 ms

--- dbserver1.oradbpro.com ping statistics ---
1 packets transmitted, 1 received, 0% packet loss, time 0ms
rtt min/avg/max/mdev = 0.072/0.072/0.072/0.000 ms, pipe 2
```

In the absence of a host name in `listener.ora`, the TNS Listener uses the host name returned by the command `hostname`:

```
$ lsnrctl start listener_dbserver1
LSNRCTL for Linux: Version 10.2.0.3.0 - Production on 08-SEP-2007 16:32:09
Copyright (c) 1991, 2006, Oracle.  All rights reserved.
Starting /opt/oracle/product/db10.2/bin/tnslsnr: please wait...
TNSLSNR for Linux: Version 10.2.0.3.0 - Production
System parameter file is /opt/oracle/product/db10.2/network/admin/listener.ora
Log messages written to /opt/oracle/product/db10.2/network/log/listener_dbserver1.log
Listening on: (DESCRIPTION=(ADDRESS=(PROTOCOL=tcp)(HOST=172.168.0.1)(PORT=1521)))

Connecting to (DESCRIPTION=(ADDRESS=(PROTOCOL=TCP)(HOST=)(PORT=1521)(IP=FIRST)))
STATUS of the LISTENER
------------------------
Alias                     listener_dbserver1
Version                   TNSLSNR for Linux: Version 10.2.0.3.0 - Production
Start Date                08-SEP-2007 16:32:09
Uptime                    0 days 0 hr. 0 min. 3 sec
Trace Level               off
Security                  ON: Local OS Authentication
SNMP                      OFF
Listener Parameter File   /opt/oracle/product/db10.2/network/admin/listener.ora
Listener Log File         /opt/oracle/product/db10.2/network/log/listener_dbserver1.log
Listening Endpoints Summary...
   (DESCRIPTION=(ADDRESS=(PROTOCOL=tcp)(HOST=172.168.0.1)(PORT=1521)))
The listener supports no services
The command completed successfully
```

Of course, the host name could also be omitted in `tnsnames.ora`, but this is not useful except on the database server itself, since most of the time clients on remote hosts need to connect to the database server. On a client system, (`HOST=`) would be synonymous to (`HOST=client_host_name`), which will not allow the client to connect to the TNS Listener on the server.

Part X

Real Application Clusters

Chapter 33

Session Disconnection, Load Rebalancing, and TAF

Status: Neither Oracle9*i* nor Oracle10*g* manuals indicate any link between ALTER SYSTEM DISCONNECT SESSION and Transparent Application Failover (TAF). This is also true for a transactional shutdown of an instance, i.e. a shutdown operation, which is deferred until all clients have committed or rolled back their work, with the command SHUTDOWN TRANSACTIONAL. A third undocumented link exists between disconnection of sessions with the package DBMS_SERVICE in Oracle10*g* and TAF.

Benefit: ALTER SYSTEM DISCONNECT SESSION, SHUTDOWN TRANSACTIONAL, and the package DBMS_SERVICE may be used to gracefully disconnect and reconnect database sessions, which have Transparent Application Failover enabled, to another instance in cases where maintenance needs to be performed. It is also useful in a scenario where load needs to be rebalanced among DBMS instances in a RAC cluster, after one or more nodes had intermittently been unavailable.

Introduction to Transparent Application Failover

Transparent Application Failover is an automatic database session reestablishment feature built into Oracle Call Interface (OCI). It is primarily intended for RAC environments to reestablish database sessions in case of cluster node failure, but the functionality as such is fully independent of RAC and may be used for single instance as well as Data Guard environments. TAF does not work with the JDBC Thin driver, since that driver is not built on top of OCI. Below is an example of a Net service name configured with Transparent Application Failover:

```
taftest.oradbpro.com =
  (DESCRIPTION =
    (ADDRESS_LIST =
      (ADDRESS = (PROTOCOL = TCP)(HOST = dbserver1)(PORT = 1521))
      (ADDRESS = (PROTOCOL = TCP)(HOST = dbserver2)(PORT = 1521))
```

```
    )
    (CONNECT_DATA =
      (SERVICE_NAME = TEN.oradbpro.com)
      (FAILOVER_MODE =
        (TYPE = select)
        (METHOD = basic)
        (RETRIES = 36)
        (DELAY = 5)
      )
    )
  )
```

The above Net service name instructs Oracle Net to do the following:

- Enable session failover (or rather reconnection to a surviving instance). As long as FAILOVER_MODE is present, it is not necessary to explicitly request reconnection by adding (FAILOVER=ON) to the DESCRIPTION section.
- Attempt to automatically and transparently re–run SELECT statements that were in progress at the time the database connection was disrupted.
- Wait five seconds before each attempt to reconnect (DELAY).
- Retry connection reestablishment at most 36 times, such that a connection must be reestablished within three minutes. After expiration of the reconnection interval (DELAY times RETRIES), Oracle Net signals the error "ORA-03113: end–of–file on communication channel" to the client, if the reason of the disconnection was a node or instance failure. If the session was disconnected and the reconnection interval expires, the error "ORA-00028: your session has been killed" is reported. If a session attempts to run SQL statements after one of these errors, it incurs the error "ORA-03114: not connected to ORACLE". At this point, it might attempt to start a new database session without the assistance of TAF.

In a RAC environment, one would usually add the directive (LOAD_BALANCE=ON) to the DESCRIPTION section. Even without this, sessions are distributed across available RAC instances. Please refer to the *Oracle Database Net Services Reference* manual for further details on local naming parameters (tnsnames.ora) related to TAF as well as load balancing.

ALTER SYSTEM DISCONNECT SESSION

TAF takes effect when node failure or instance failure occurs. The latter may be simulated with SHUTDOWN ABORT. It is undocumented that TAF may also take effect when database sessions are disconnected explicitly. The syntax for this is:

```
ALTER SYSTEM DISCONNECT SESSION 'sid, serial#' [POST_TRANSACTION] [IMMEDIATE];
```

The parameters *sid* and *serial#* correspond to the columns by the same name in V$SESSION. The keyword POST_TRANSACTION requests disconnection after the next COMMIT or ROLLBACK by the client. The keyword IMMEDIATE requests immediate termination of the database session irrespective of open transactions. At least one of these two keywords must be present. In the absence of a transaction, POST_TRANSACTION has the same effect as IMMEDIATE in terms of timing of the disconnection. However, in terms of session reestablishment, the implications are quite different. When IMMEDIATE is specified, alone or in conjunction with POST_TRANSACTION, TAF does not take effect, whereas it does when merely POST_TRANSACTION is used. By the way, TAF will also not intervene when ALTER SYSTEM KILL SESSION is issued or the client's server process is terminated with the UNIX command kill -TERM[1].

SELECT Failover

As stated before, the requirements for TAF are a properly configured Net service name (e.g. in tnsnames.ora) and a database client built on top of OCI. To avoid boring the reader by demonstrating TAF with SQL*Plus, I have chosen to use Perl DBI (see Chapter 22), which is implemented with OCI. The screen output depicted below is from the Perl

---

1. The commands kill -TERM and kill -9 are equivalent. TERM is the abbreviated name of the signal with number nine. A list of all signals is in the C language include file /usr/include/sys/signal.h.

DBI program dbb.pl[1], which is capable of executing arbitrary SQL statements and PL/SQL blocks. I wrote it after many years of annoyance due to unreadable output from SQL*Plus and time spent making obfuscated query results halfway readable with COLUMN *name* FORMAT commands.

The Program dbb.pl reads from standard input until it finds a slash (/) by itself at the beginning of a line. At this point, it prepares and executes the statement entered. If it detects a SELECT statement by checking that the DBI handle attribute NUM_OF_FIELDS is larger than zero, it fetches and displays the rows with automatically adjusted column widths! The column width is automatically made just wide enough to accommodate the larger of either column heading or column value, leading to easily readable query results. This is what makes the program a big time saver compared to SQL*Plus, which does not have such a feature. At this stage, this is pretty much all dbb.pl can do.

For the test below, I slightly modified a routine called by dbb.pl, which iteratively fetches all rows, in such a way that it pauses after each fetch. Thus, it is guaranteed that disconnection can be requested while the program is in the fetch loop. To avoid buffering effects due to bulk fetch (a.k.a. array fetch, i.e. retrieval of more than a single row with each fetch call), it is necessary that the number of rows in the table is larger than the fetch array size. If this issue is disregarded, it may happen that all the rows have already been retrieved into a client side buffer. The client then merely reads from the client–side buffer, without interacting with the DBMS instance, such that the SELECT statement does not need to be restarted. When testing TAF SELECT failover with SQL*Plus, I recommend the following settings to avoid buffering:

```
SQL> SET ARRAYSIZE 1
SQL> SET PAGESIZE 1
SQL> SET PAUSE "Hit return to continue ..."
```

SQL*Plus will then:

- Parse and execute the statement.
- Fetch a single row at a time (FETCH ... r=1 would be seen in a SQL trace file; see Chapter 24).
- Delay display of the first row until the user hits enter.
- Pause after each row until the user hits enter.

This allows the tester to interrupt an in–flight fetch loop. Without these settings, one would need to select from a large table, to allow enough time to interrupt the SELECT statement.

Back to the demonstration with dbb.pl. I opted to point out some side–effects of session reestablishment, which are often overlooked and not explicitly documented. On page 13-15, the *Oracle Database Net Services Administrators Guide 10g Release 2* states:

> *Server side program variables, such as PL/SQL package states, are lost during failures; TAF cannot recover them. They can be initialized by making a call from the failover callback.*

As the following demonstration illustrates, there is a whole lot more that TAF does not restore:

- effects of SET ROLE statements (or DBMS_SESSION.SET_ROLE), such that a reestablished session may have less privileges than the original session
- effects of enabling secure application roles
- effects of ALTER SESSION statements, such as enabling SQL trace or adjusting NLS settings
- the client identifier (V$SESSION.CLIENT_IDENTIFIER)
- the module and action for application instrumentation (see Chapter 24)

In fact, TAF cannot restore anything beyond the session itself and the previous cursor position of SELECT statements—keep in mind that the latter is not guaranteed to work[2]. Doctor ORACLE prescribes callback functions as a remedy for this situation. A callback function is a subroutine that the client registers by calling an OCI function (or JDBC method if programming in Java). OCI then assumes the task of executing the client's callback function when certain events occur. TAF callbacks may be registered for the following events:

- commencement of session failover
- unsuccessful failover attempt; the client may indicate that OCI should continue retrying

---

1. The Perl program dbb.pl (database browser) is included in the source code depot of Chapter 22.
2. SELECT failover may fail with the error "ORA-25401: can not continue fetches".

- completed successful session reestablishment
- unsuccessful failover; no retry possible

The details are documented in *Oracle Call Interface Programmer's Guide 10g Release 2* and *Oracle Database JDBC Developer's Guide and Reference 10g Release 2*. For programming languages that do not provide an interface to OCI callback functions (this includes the Perl DBI module), it is possible to detect session failover by checking for certain errors such as "ORA-25408: can not safely replay call".

Below is a demonstration of a successful session reestablishment and a restarted SELECT statement. To point out that statements were run using dbb.pl and not SQL*Plus, the prompt DBB> is used. The Perl program dbb.pl is started in much the same way as SQL*Plus by passing a connect string:

```
$ dbb.pl app_user/secret@taftest.oradbpro.com
```

Next, module, action, and client identifier are set:

```
DBB> begin
        dbms_application_info.set_module('taf_mod', 'taf_act');
        dbms_session.set_identifier('taf_ident');
end;
/
1 Row(s) Processed.
```

Since SELECT_CATALOG_ROLE is not a default role of APP_USER, it must be enabled with a SET ROLE statement before V$SESSION may be accessed. Furthermore, the NLS date format is changed:

```
DBB> SET ROLE select_catalog_role
/
0 Row(s) Processed.
DBB> ALTER SESSION SET nls_date_format='dd. Mon yy hh24:mi'
/
0 Row(s) Processed.
DBB> SELECT sid, serial#, audsid, logon_time, client_identifier, module, action
FROM v$session
WHERE username='APP_USER'
/
Row 1 fetched. Hit return to continue fetching ...
SID SERIAL# AUDSID LOGON_TIME       CLIENT_IDENTIFIER MODULE  ACTION
--- ------- ------ --------------- ----------------- ------- -------
116   23054 110007 05. Aug 07 14:40 taf_ident         taf_mod taf_act
1 Row(s) processed.
```

Take note that the client was assigned session 116, session serial number 23054 and auditing session identifier[1] 110007. The auditing identifier is formed by selecting NEXTVAL from the sequence SYS.AUDSES$ at session establishment. The auditing identifier uniquely identifies a session for the lifetime of a database and is saved in DBA_AUDIT_TRAIL.SESSIONID if any auditing on behalf of the session occurs. The date format of the session includes the month name. Client identifier, module, and action were communicated to the DBMS. Querying failover related columns in V$SESSION confirms that TAF is switched on for the session:

```
DBB> SELECT failover_type, failover_method, failed_over
FROM v$session
WHERE username='APP_USER'
/
Row 1 fetched. Hit return to continue fetching ...
FAILOVER_TYPE FAILOVER_METHOD FAILED_OVER
------------- --------------- -----------
SELECT        BASIC           NO
1 Row(s) processed.
```

---

1. The session auditing identifier V$SESSION.AUDSID may also be retrieved with the following statement:
   SELECT userenv('sessionid') FROM dual.

Next, APP_USER enters a fetch loop that retrieves rows from the table EMPLOYEES. Note how the program dbb.pl pauses after each fetch call, without displaying any data yet.

```
DBB> SELECT employee_id, first_name, last_name, email FROM hr.employees
/
Row 1 fetched. Hit return to continue fetching ...
Row 2 fetched. Hit return to continue fetching ...
```

In a different window from the one where dbb.pl is running, disconnect the session as a DBA:

```
SQL> ALTER SYSTEM DISCONNECT SESSION '116,23054' POST_TRANSACTION;
System altered.
```

Move back to the window where dbb.pl is running and keep hitting return until all rows have been fetched:

```
Row 3 fetched. Hit return to continue fetching ...
...
Row 107 fetched. Hit return to continue fetching ...
EMPLOYEE_ID FIRST_NAME  LAST_NAME   EMAIL
----------- ----------- ----------- --------
        198 Donald      OConnell    DOCONNEL
...
        197 Kevin       Feeney      KFEENEY

107 Row(s) processed.
```

The SELECT statement completed without any noticeable interruption. Now it's time to take a look at the value in the column V$SESSION.FAILED_OVER:

```
DBB> SELECT failover_type, failover_method, failed_over
FROM v$session
WHERE username='APP_USER'
/
error code: 942, error message: ORA-00942: table or view does not exist (error possibly
near <*> indicator at char 56 in 'SELECT failover_type, failover_method, failed_over
FROM <*>v$session WHERE username='APP_USER'
')
```

The SELECT from V$SESSION, which worked previously, failed. This is a strong indication that session reestablishment has occurred without restoring all the properties of the session. Let's again enable SELECT_CATALOG_ROLE:

```
DBB> SET ROLE select_catalog_role
/
0 Row(s) Processed.
DBB> SELECT failover_type, failover_method, failed_over FROM v$session WHERE
username='APP_USER'
/
Row 1 fetched. Hit return to continue fetching ...
FAILOVER_TYPE FAILOVER_METHOD FAILED_OVER
------------- --------------- -----------
SELECT        BASIC           YES
1 Row(s) processed.
```

The value of V$SESSION.FAILED_OVER was previously NO and is now YES. This confirms that TAF succeeded. How about the remaining properties of the previous database session? They are all lost. Date format, client identifier, module, and action now have default values:

```
DBB> SELECT sid, serial#, audsid, logon_time, client_identifier,
module, action
FROM v$session
WHERE username='APP_USER'
/
Row 1 fetched. Hit return to continue fetching ...
SID SERIAL# AUDSID LOGON_TIME          CLIENT_IDENTIFIER MODULE   ACTION
--- ------- ------ ------------------- ----------------- -------- ------
133   15197 110008 05.08.2007 14:49:23                   perl.exe
```

341

```
1 Row(s) processed.
```

The auditing identifier of the new session is 110008. Perl DBI automatically registers the module name `perl.exe` with the DBMS.

Failover at the End of a Transaction

While we're at it, we might also verify that DISCONNECT SESSION POST_TRANSACTION allows ongoing transactions to complete and then initiates session reestablishment through TAF. Below is a test case for such a scenario that:

- Starts a transaction by deleting a row.
- Runs another DELETE statement that blocks on a TX enqueue due to a row locked by another session.
- Gets marked for disconnection while waiting for the lock.
- Succeeds in finishing the transaction and reconnects.

The first step of the scenario is to start a transaction with DELETE:

```
DBB> DELETE FROM hr.employees WHERE employee_id=190
/
1 Row(s) Processed.
```

As a DBA using SQL*Plus (or dbb.pl, in case you appreciate its automatic column sizing feature), check that APP_USER has an open transaction and lock the row with EMPLOYEE_ID=180 in HR.EMPLOYEES[1]:

```
SQL> SELECT s.sid, s.serial#, s.event, t.start_time, t.status
FROM v$transaction t, v$session s
WHERE s.taddr=t.addr
AND s.sid=139;
      SID   SERIAL# START_TIME            STATUS
---------- ---------- -------------------- ----------------
      139        74 07/30/07 15:34:25     ACTIVE
SQL> SELECT employee_id FROM hr.employees WHERE employee_id=180 FOR UPDATE NOWAIT;
EMPLOYEE_ID
-----------
       180
```

As APP_USER, try to delete the row in EMPLOYEES with EMPLOYEE_ID=180. The session has to wait for the DBA to release the lock:

```
DBB> DELETE FROM hr.employees WHERE employee_id=180
/
```

As a DBA, mark APP_USER's session for disconnection:

```
SQL> ALTER SYSTEM DISCONNECT SESSION '139,74' POST_TRANSACTION;
System altered.
```

As a DBA, verify that the transaction is still active and that APP_USER is still waiting for the row lock, then COMMIT, thus releasing the lock on EMPLOYEES:

```
SQL> SELECT s.sid, s.serial#, s.event, t.start_time, t.status
FROM v$transaction t, v$session s
WHERE s.taddr=t.addr
AND s.sid=139;
SID SERIAL# EVENT                         START_TIME        STATUS
--- ------- ----------------------------- ----------------- ------
139      74 enq: TX - row lock contention 07/30/07 15:34:25 ACTIVE
SQL> COMMIT;
Commit complete.
```

In the other window, dbb.pl displays the number of rows processed, which we respond to with a COMMIT statement:

```
1 Row(s) Processed.
DBB> COMMIT
/
0 Row(s) Processed.
```

---

1. An export dump containing the sample schema HR is included in the source code depot.

Right after the COMMIT, the DBMS disconnects APP_USER's session. The reconnect due to TAF starts a new session:

```
DBB> SET ROLE SELECT_CATALOG_ROLE
/
0 Row(s) Processed.
DBB> SELECT sid, serial#, logon_time, client_identifier, module, action, failed_over
FROM v$session
WHERE username='APP_USER'
/
Row 1 fetched. Hit return to continue fetching ...
SID SERIAL# LOGON_TIME CLIENT_IDENTIFIER MODULE   ACTION FAILED_OVER
--- ------- ---------- ----------------- -------- ------ -----------
139     76 30-JUL-07                     perl.exe        YES
1 Row(s) processed.
```

The above output shows that session failover has occurred (FAILED_OVER=YES). The question is, whether or not the transaction completed successfully?

```
DBB> DELETE FROM hr.employees WHERE employee_id IN (180, 190)
/
0 Row(s) Processed.
```

As implied by the lack of any errors, the transaction did complete successfully and the rows were truly deleted, since rerunning the identical DELETE statement did not find any matching rows.

The exact same functionality demonstrated is available at instance–level with SHUTDOWN TRANSACTIONAL. Thus, at the beginning of a maintenance window, all database sessions connected to an instance may be shifted to other instances providing the service requested by the client. The optional keyword LOCAL to SHUTDOWN TRANSACTIONAL applies to distributed database environments, not RAC environments. When LOCAL is specified, the instance waits only for local transactions to complete, but not for distributed transactions.

Session Disconnection and DBMS_SERVICE

Oracle10g and Oracle11g include the package DBMS_SERVICE for managing instance services and TAF. For the first time, this package allows the configuration of TAF on the server–side instead of the client–side configuration file tnsnames.ora. DBMS_SERVICE is the most sophisticated approach to services so far. In a RAC cluster, it is called behind the scenes when cluster services are created with the Database Configuration Assistant (DBCA), but it may be used directly in both RAC and single instance environments. In a RAC environment, cluster database services should be configured with DBCA, since it sets up the integration between Oracle Clusterware and DBMS_SERVICE. Services created with DBMS_SERVICE do not restart automatically on instance startup. Oracle Clusterware performs this task, given that the appropriate cluster resources were created by DBCA.

Setting up Services with DBMS_SERVICE

To create a service, at least a service name and a network name must be provided. The service name is an identifier, which is stored in the data dictionary. The network name is the instance service name (see *Instance Service Name vs. Net Service Name* on page xiii), which is registered with the listener and needs to be referenced as the SERVICE_NAME in a client–side Net service name description in tnsnames.ora.

DBMS_SERVICE.CREATE_SERVICE inserts services into the dictionary table SERVICE$, which underlies the view DBA_SERVICES. The procedure DBMS_SERVICE.START_SERVICE adds the network name to the initialization parameter SERVICE_NAMES, such that the service is registered with the listener. When registering the service with the listener, the value of the initialization parameter DB_DOMAIN is appended to the network name, unless it is already present. Instance service names specified with the parameter NETWORK_NAME are not case sensitive. The service name as well as the network name must be unique. Otherwise the error "ORA-44303: service name exists" or "ORA-44314: network name already exists" is raised. Below is sample code that creates and starts a service with the TAF settings used in the previous examples:

```
SQL> BEGIN
   dbms_service.create_service(
      service_name=>'TAF_INST_SVC',
      network_name=>'taf_inst_svc_net_name',
```

```
      failover_method=>dbms_service.failover_method_basic,
      failover_type=>dbms_service.failover_type_select,
      failover_retries=>36,
      failover_delay=>12
    );
    dbms_service.start_service('TAF_INST_SVC', DBMS_SERVICE.ALL_INSTANCES);
END;
/
PL/SQL procedure successfully completed.
```

The new service is now present in DBA_SERVICES:

```
SQL> SELECT name, network_name, failover_method method, failover_type type,
failover_retries retries, failover_delay delay
FROM sys.dba_services;
NAME                    NETWORK_NAME            METHOD TYPE   RETRIES DELAY
-----------------       ----------------------  ------ ------ ------- -----
SYS$BACKGROUND
SYS$USERS
TEN.oradbpro.com        TEN.oradbpro.com
TAF_INST_SVC            taf_inst_svc_net_name   BASIC  SELECT     36    12
```

Since the service was started, it's also registered as an active service in GV$ACTIVE_SERVICES. This view lists active services for all instances:

```
SQL> SELECT inst_id, name, network_name, blocked
FROM gv$active_services
WHERE name NOT LIKE 'SYS$%';
INST_ID NAME             NETWORK_NAME         BLOCKED
------- ---------------- -------------------- -------
      1 TAF_INST_SVC     taf_inst_svc_net_name NO
      1 TEN.oradbpro.com TEN.oradbpro.com      NO
      2 TAF_INST_SVC     taf_inst_svc_net_name NO
      2 TEN.oradbpro.com TEN.oradbpro.com      NO
```

The database domain name (DB_DOMAIN) "oradbpro.com" was appended to the network name, since it lacked a domain suffix. The network name was also added to the list of instance service names in the parameter SERVICE_NAMES:

```
SQL> SELECT name, value FROM v$parameter
WHERE name in ('db_domain', 'service_names');
NAME          VALUE
------------- ---------------------
db_domain     oradbpro.com
service_names taf_inst_svc_net_name
```

Each instance service name set with the parameter SERVICE_NAMES is registered with one or more listeners. Note that in a RAC cluster, you need to set the parameter REMOTE_LISTENER to a Net service name, which references all remote nodes in the cluster, such that an instance can register instance service names with the remote nodes. In case the local listener is not running on the default port 1521, you must also set the parameter LOCAL_LISTENER. The output of the command lsnrctl below indicates that the new instance service names were registered with the listener by both instances, since the constant DBMS_SERVICE.ALL_INSTANCES was used as the second argument to the procedure DBMS_SERVICE.START_SERVICE:

```
$ lsnrctl services listener_dbserver1
...
Services Summary...
...
Service "taf_inst_svc_net_name.oradbpro.com" has 2 instance(s).
  Instance "TEN1", status READY, has 1 handler(s) for this service...
    Handler(s):
      "DEDICATED" established:0 refused:0 state:ready
          LOCAL SERVER
```

```
Instance "TEN2", status READY, has 1 handler(s) for this service...
  Handler(s):
    "DEDICATED" established:0 refused:0 state:ready
      REMOTE SERVER
```

With this configuration, there is no need to enable TAF on the client side in the configuration file `tnsnames.ora`. TAF has already been enabled for the instance service name `taf_inst_svc_net_name.oradbpro.com`, such that the Net service name `taf_net_svc.oradbpro.com` shown below does not contain a `FAILOVER_MODE` section. Server–side TAF settings override client–side TAF settings. Note that the network name, which was passed to `DBMS_SERVICE` (suffixed by the database domain name), is used as the `SERVICE_NAME` in `tnsnames.ora`:

```
taf_net_svc.oradbpro.com =
  (DESCRIPTION =
    (ADDRESS = (PROTOCOL= TCP)(Host=dbserver1)(Port= 1521))
    (CONNECT_DATA = (SERVICE_NAME = taf_inst_svc_net_name.oradbpro.com))
  )
```

Session Disconnection with DBMS_SERVICE and TAF

Now it's time to test session disconnection with `DBMS_SERVICE` for the purpose of maintenance or load rebalancing. Connect as APP_USER, using the Net service name in the previous section, and run a `SELECT` statement:

```
$ sqlplus app_user/secret@taf_net_svc.oradbpro.com
SQL> SET PAUSE "Hit return to continue ..."
SQL> SET PAUSE ON
SQL> SELECT * FROM audit_actions;
Hit return to continue ...
    ACTION NAME
---------- ----------------------------
        0 UNKNOWN
        1 CREATE TABLE
...
```

As a DBA, verify that the TAF settings are in effect:

```
SQL> SELECT inst_id, sid, serial#, audsid, logon_time, service_name,
    failover_type, failover_method, failed_over
FROM gv$session
WHERE username='APP_USER';
INST_ID SID SERIAL# AUDSID LOGON_TIME          SERVICE_NAME FAILOVER_TYPE
------- --- ------- ------ ------------------- ------------ -------------
2       143    4139 120036 05.08.2007 19:27:58 TAF_INST_SVC SELECT
FAILOVER_METHOD FAILED_OVER
--------------- -----------
BASIC           NO
```

Now stop the service on instance 2, which hosts the client (`INST_ID=2` in the result of the above `SELECT`). The name of instance 2 is TEN2. A service may be stopped from any instance in the cluster:

```
SQL> EXEC dbms_service.stop_service('TAF_INST_SVC', 'TEN2')
PL/SQL procedure successfully completed.
```

This removes the service from instance 2 in `GV$ACTIVE_SERVICES`:

```
SQL> SELECT name FROM gv$active_services WHERE inst_id=2;
NAME
------------------
TEN.oradbpro.com
SYS$BACKGROUND
SYS$USERS
```

It also removes the instance TEN2 from the listener's services summary:

```
$ lsnrctl services listener_dbserver1
...
Service "taf_inst_svc_net_name.oradbpro.com" has 1 instance(s).
  Instance "TEN1", status READY, has 1 handler(s) for this service...
```

```
    Handler(s):
      "DEDICATED" established:0 refused:0 state:ready
        LOCAL SERVER
The command completed successfully
```

DBMS_SERVICE.DISCONNECT_SESSION affects all sessions of the local instance using a certain service, such that you need to connect to the instance hosting the client in order to disconnect all sessions. This procedure has an undocumented parameter DISCONNECT_OPTION. The default value for this parameter is the numeric constant DBMS_SERVICE.POST_TRANSACTION. It can also take the value DBMS_SERVICE.IMMEDIATE. These constants have the same meaning as the keywords POST_TRANSACTION and IMMEDIATE supported by the SQL statement ALTER SYSTEM DISCONNECT SESSION. Let's disconnect all the sessions, which were established via the service TAF_INST_SVC:

```
SQL> EXEC dbms_service.disconnect_session('TAF_INST_SVC')
```

Beware that DBMS_SERVICE.DISCONNECT_SESSION completes successfully, even when a non–existent service name is passed. Session disconnection takes effect immediately, except for sessions which have an open transaction.

```
SQL> SELECT inst_id, sid, serial#, audsid, logon_time, service_name, failover_type,
failover_method, failed_over
FROM gv$session
WHERE username='APP_USER';
INST_ID SID SERIAL# AUDSID LOGON_TIME          SERVICE_NAME
------- --- ------- ------ ------------------- ------------
      2 143    4139 120036 05.08.2007 19:27:58 TAF_INST_SVC
FAILOVER_TYPE FAILOVER_METHOD FAILED_OVER
------------- --------------- -----------
SELECT        BASIC           NO
```

Once APP_USER attempts to retrieve the remaining rows from his SELECT statement, the disconnection is detected and a new connection to an instance, which still offers the requested service, is opened. Repeating the SELECT from GV$SESSION yields:

```
INST_ID SID SERIAL# AUDSID LOGON_TIME          SERVICE_NAME
------- --- ------- ------ ------------------- ------------
      1 151    1219 130018 05.08.2007 19:31:35 TAF_INST_SVC
FAILOVER_TYPE FAILOVER_METHOD FAILED_OVER
------------- --------------- -----------
SELECT        BASIC           YES
```

APP_USER's session has been reconnected to instance 1, as evidenced by INST_ID=1, a different AUDSID, and a later LOGON_TIME. The value of AUDSID must not necessarily increment after a reconnect due to sequence caching in all instances. TAF also reconnects disconnected sessions that had open transactions. For such sessions, disconnection takes place when they commit or roll back. The procedure DBMS_SERVICE.DISCONNECT_SESSION behaves in the same way as ALTER SYSTEM DISCONNECT SESSION POST_TRANSACTION, in that it allows open transactions to complete before disconnecting the session. In fact, it is no more than a layer on top of ALTER SYSTEM DISCONNECT SESSION. This undocumented fact is given away by the source file $ORACLE_HOME/rdbms/admin/dbmssrv.sql.

Integration between the new features of DBMS_SERVICE and the vintage features associated with the parameter SERVICE_NAMES is not anywhere near seamless. The statement ALTER SYSTEM SET SERVICE_NAMES adds a service to DBA_SERVICES, whereas removal of the same service from SERVICE_NAMES does not remove it from DBA_SERVICES. It merely stops the service and removes it from V$ACTIVE_SERVICES.

To delete a service, it must be stopped on all instances. The default service, which matches the name of the database suffixed by the database domain, cannot be deleted. It appears as though it could be stopped with DBMS_SERVICE.STOP_SERVICE, which completes without error, but crosschecking with the services summary from lsnrctl services *listener_name* and V$ACTIVE_SERVICES reveals that it was not stopped. It would have been more appropriate to introduce a new error message such as "default service cannot be stopped". For example, my DBMS instance with the settings db_name=TEN and db_domain=oradbpro.com automatically has an instance service name TEN.oradbpro.com in DBA_SERVICES and V$ACTIVE_SERVICES, which can neither be stopped nor deleted.

Lessons Learned

Disruptions in database service due to scheduled maintenance or manual load rebalancing may be much ameliorated by configuring TAF and disconnecting sessions gracefully. Session disconnection can occur on three levels: instance level, service level, and session level. The commands and levels are summarized in Table 71.

Table 71: Statements for Session Disconnection

Level	SQL Statement or PL/SQL Procedure Call	Client Program
Instance	`SHUTDOWN TRANSACTIONAL`	SQL*Plus, Oracle11g JDBC

Service	`DBMS_SERVICE.DISCONNECT_SESSION(`
	`    SERVICE_NAME=>'name',`
	`    DISCONNECT_OPTION=>option);`[a]
		Any

Session	`ALTER SYSTEM DISCONNECT SESSION 'sid, serial#' POST_TRANSACTION;`	Any

a. The parameter `DISCONNECT_OPTION` is not available in release 10.2.0.1. The default value of this parameter is `DBMS_SERVICE.POST_TRANSACTION`. The disconnect option `DBMS_SERVICE.IMMEDIATE` disconnects sessions immediately.

While graceful disconnection at instance and session level were already implemented in Oracle9i, disconnection at service level was first introduced in Oracle10g. The features may even be used to hide an instance restart from database clients, given that the clients are configured and known to work with TAF. In Oracle10g and subsequent releases, TAF should be configured on the server–side with `DBMS_SERVICE`.

Source Code Depot

Table 72: Session Disconnection, Load Rebalancing, and TAF Source Code Depot

File Name	Functionality
`hr.dmp`	Oracle10g export dump file. Contains the database objects in sample schema HR.
`tnsnames.ora.smp`	Sample Net service name definition, which configures TAF on the client–side

Chapter 34

Removing the RAC Option without Reinstalling

Status: It is undocumented how to remove the option Real Application Clusters from an ORACLE installation. Removal of this option renders an ORACLE RAC DBMS instance independent of Oracle Clusterware, i.e. it can open a database in exclusive mode, when Oracle Clusterware cannot start, e.g. due to hardware failure.

Benefit: In cases of an emergency, such as the loss of all voting disks or the failure of all devices holding copies of the Cluster Registry, Oracle Clusterware cannot be started. In such a severe fault scenario, it might take hours or even days to attach new SAN (Storage Area Network) storage to the system, create logical units (LUN) in the SAN disk array, and configure zoning to make the LUNs visible to the database server. Oracle Clusterware may cause unjustified node reboots and thus unplanned downtime, although it has matured tremendously since the early days. This might be another reason for disabling RAC. This chapter explains how to use an undocumented `make` command to remove the RAC option from the `oracle` executable. Since ASM cannot run at all without Oracle Clusterware infrastructure, a procedure which converts an Oracle Clusterware installation for RAC to a local–only Oracle Clusterware installation for use with single–instance ASM is shown. Thus, a system running RAC can quickly be converted to a system running single instance ORACLE without reinstalling any software with Oracle Universal Installer, greatly reducing downtime incurred by such a severe outage.

Linking ORACLE Software

When ORACLE Server software is installed on a UNIX system by the Oracle Universal Installer (OUI), many programs, including `$ORACLE_HOME/bin/oracle`, which implements the database kernel, are linked with static and shared libraries on the system. OUI calls the utility `make` and passes it the makefile `$ORACLE_HOME/rdbms/lib/ins_rdbms.mk` as an argument. Other makefiles, such as `$ORACLE_HOME/network/lib/ins_net_server.mk` are used to link Oracle Net components and still others to link SQL*Plus, etc.

Similar steps occur when a patch set (OUI) or interim patch (OPatch) is applied. Most patches modify a static library in $ORACLE_HOME/lib by replacing an object module with a newer version, which includes a bug fix. The executable oracle must be relinked to pick up a changed object module in a static library. For someone who knows how to use the commands ar and make, it is fairly easy to manually apply an interim patch. This is useful when OPatch fails for whatever reason. For example, newer releases of OPatch (starting in versions 1.0.0.0.54 and 10.2.0.x) are able to verify that a new object module (extension .o, e.g. dbsdrv.o) was correctly inserted into a static library (extension .a, e.g. libserver10.a) by extracting the object module and comparing it to the one shipped with the patch. This very reasonable test failed on Solaris 64–bit ORACLE installations, since Solaris 10 pads object files with newline characters (use od -c *filename* to check this). OPatch complained with a message that said "Archive failed: failed to update" and backed out the interim patch. Setting the environment variable OPATCH_DEBUG=TRUE, which is documented in *Oracle Universal Installer and OPatch User's Guide 10g Release 2*, revealed that it was not the ar command that was failing, but instead the verification. Meanwhile this issue has been taken care of (see Metalink note 353150.1 for details).

The same approach of exchanging object modules is used to add or remove ORACLE server options. Options can only be purchased with the Enterprise Edition of the ORACLE DBMS. Currently, ten options exist, among them are:

- Label Security
- Partitioning
- Real Application Clusters
- Spatial
- Data Mining

The Oracle10*g* OUI has a bug that causes Data Mining to be installed unconditionally, i.e. even when it was deselected on the relevant OUI screen. The approach to add and remove options, which will be presented shortly, may be used to work around this bug.

Which options are installed becomes evident when SQL*Plus is started:

```
$ sqlplus ndebes/secret
SQL*Plus: Release 10.2.0.3.0 - Production on Thu Jul 26 02:21:43 2007
Copyright (c) 1982, 2006, Oracle.  All Rights Reserved.
Connected to:
Oracle Database 10g Enterprise Edition Release 10.2.0.3.0 - Production
With the Partitioning, Real Application Clusters, Oracle Label Security and Data Mining
options
```

SQL*Plus takes this information from the view V$OPTION:

```
SQL> SELECT parameter, value FROM v$option
WHERE parameter IN ('Partitioning','Real Application Clusters',
'Oracle Label Security','Data Mining')
PARAMETER                              VALUE
------------------------------------   ------
Partitioning                           TRUE
Real Application Clusters              TRUE
Oracle Label Security                 TRUE
Data Mining                            TRUE
```

As an option is added or removed by linking, V$OPTION.VALUE becomes TRUE or FALSE.

Case Study

In this section we will simulate the failure of all voting disks in a RAC environment, in order to create a scenario for the removal of the RAC option. Did you know that an ORACLE instance, which uses an oracle executable with RAC linked in, cannot be started irrespective of the value of the CLUSTER_DATABASE parameter when cluster group services—a component of Oracle Clusterware—on the local node is not functional? This is true for ASM as well as RDBMS instances (parameter instance_type={ASM|RDBMS}).

Simulating Voting Disk Failure

Voting disks are devices that Oracle Clusterware uses to ensure the integrity of the database in case of an interconnect failure. Say you lose all the voting disks configured for use with Oracle Clusterware. This causes Oracle Clusterware to abort. Below is a quick test that simulates the failure of all voting disks. In this case, all voting disks means just one, since external redundancy, i.e. redundancy in the storage subsystem is used instead of triple mirroring by Oracle Clusterware. The test was performed on Red Hat Advanced Server 4.

Linux does not have proper raw devices. Instead the command `raw` must be used to bind raw devices to block devices[1]. Failure of a voting disk may be simulated by binding the voting disk device to an unused block device. On the test system, /dev/md1 was such a device. It could be opened without error, but 0 bytes were returned. The individual steps to simulate voting disk failure are reproduced below:

```
 1 # wc -c /dev/md1
 2 0 /dev/md1
 3 # crsctl query css votedisk # ask Clusterware for configured voting disks
 4  0.      0    /opt/oracle/votedisk
 5 located 1 votedisk(s).
 6 # ls -l /opt/oracle/votedisk # character special device with major nr. 162
 7 crw-r--r--  1 oracle oinstall 162, 1 Jul 20 22:40 /opt/oracle/votedisk
 8 # raw -q /opt/oracle/votedisk # which block device is it bound to?
 9 /dev/raw/raw1:  bound to major 8, minor 8
10 # ls -l /dev/sda8 # major device number 8 and minor 8 is sda8 (SCSI disk)
11 brw-rw----  1 root disk 8, 8 Jul 24 03:15 /dev/sda8
12 # raw /opt/oracle/votedisk /dev/md1 # rebind to the wrong device
13 /dev/raw/raw1:  bound to major 9, minor 1
14 # crsctl start crs
15 Attempting to start CRS stack
16 The CRS stack will be started shortly
17 # crsctl check crs
18 Failure 1 contacting CSS daemon
19 Cannot communicate with CRS
20 Cannot communicate with EVM
```

As the output of the command `crsctl check crs` in line 18 suggests, Oracle Clusterware cannot be started without any voting disks available. Let's take a detailed look at the commands by line number:

- Line 1: the command `wc` (word count) reads from /dev/md1 and succeeds, but cannot read anything from the device. This device file will be used to simulate a failed voting disk.
- Line 3: the list of configured voting disks is retrieved with `crsctl query css votedisk`.
- Line 4: the only voting disk configured is /opt/oracle/votedisk. This is not the device itself, but merely a character special (a.k.a. raw) device file that points to the block device representing the disk.
- Line 7: the major and minor numbers of /opt/oracle/votedisk are 162 and 8 respectively. On Linux, all raw devices have major number 162. The major number identifies an entire devices class. The minor number identifies device instances within a device class. On Linux, raw devices instances have minor numbers between 1 and 255.
- Line 8: the current binding of /opt/oracle/votedisk is queried with `raw -q` *raw_device_file*
- Line 9: the `raw` command does not take into account that raw devices might have more meaningful names than raw*n*. The raw device /opt/oracle/votedisk is bound to a block device with major number 8 (SCSI disks) and minor number 8.
- Line 11: major number 8, minor number 8 is /dev/sda8, i.e. partition 8 of the first SCSI disk in the system.
- Line 12: the raw device /opt/oracle/votedisk is rebound to /dev/md1. This succeeds, since Oracle Clusterware was shut down and the character special file is not accessed.
- Line 14: an attempt is made to start Oracle Clusterware.

---

1. ASM instances in Oracle10*g* Release 2 for Linux also support block devices, since the implementation of raw devices is deprecated. Red Hat encourages software vendors to modify their applications to open block devices with the `O_DIRECT` flag instead of requiring raw devices.

- Line 17: the status of Oracle Clusterware processes is queried.
- Line 18: Oracle Clusterware did not start, since no voting disk is available.

Surprisingly, no error message is written to any of the documented log files (test performed with 10.2.0.3.0). On Linux, CRS writes log messages to `/var/log/messages` using `/bin/logger`[1]. It's a good idea to check this file, if you cannot diagnose a problem from `$ORA_CRS_HOME/log/`*nodename*`/alert`*nodename*`.log` or other log files in `$ORA_CRS_HOME/log`, where *nodename* is the host name of the system. CRS is not available, since it is waiting for voting disks to become available:

```
Jul 26 20:54:44 dbserver1 logger: Cluster Ready Services waiting on dependencies.
Diagnostics in /tmp/crsctl.30644.
```

The reason for the failure is in `/tmp/crsctl.30644`:

```
# more /tmp/crsctl.30644
Failure reading from offset 2560 in device votedisk
Failure 1 checking the CSS voting disk 'votedisk'.
Not able to read adequate number of voting disks
```

There is a loop in `/etc/init.d/init.cssd` which calls `crsctl check boot` until it returns exit code 0. With all voting disks offline, this will never happen, so CRS loops forever[2]:

```
# crsctl check boot
Failure reading from offset 2560 in device votedisk
Failure 1 checking the CSS voting disk 'votedisk'.
Not able to read adequate number of voting disks
# echo $?
6
```

Another way to simulate the failure of voting disks as well as any other files like the Oracle Cluster Registry, ASM disks, or data files, is to overwrite the first few blocks with binary zeros. This can be done with the command `dd` (device dump):

```
dd if=/dev/zero bs=8192 count=2 of=voting_disk_file
```

Obviously this is a destructive test, so you need to take a backup of your voting disks with `dd`, before you attempt this. However, it has the advantage that it can be performed while Oracle Clusterware is running, whereas the `raw` command cannot remap a device that is in use[3]. Errors caused by this latter test are properly reported in the documented log files below `$ORA_CRS_HOME/log/`*nodename*.

Back to my initial claim that an `oracle` executable with RAC linked in cannot be used to start a DBMS instance, unless Oracle Clusterware is functional. In case ASM is used, an ASM instance must be started before the DBMS instance. Here's some evidence (run SQL*Plus as the owner of the ORACLE installation):

```
$ env ORACLE_SID=+ASM1 sqlplus / as sysdba
SQL*Plus: Release 10.2.0.3.0 - Production on Thu Jul 26 02:35:22 2007
Copyright (c) 1982, 2006, Oracle.  All Rights Reserved.
Connected to an idle instance.
SQL> STARTUP
ORA-29701: unable to connect to Cluster Manager
```

For completeness, let's confirm that a similar error is reported by an RDBMS instance:

```
$ env ORACLE_SID=TEN1 sqlplus / as sysdba
SQL> STARTUP NOMOUNT
ORA-29702: error occurred in Cluster Group Service operation
```

Even STARTUP NOMOUNT does not work when Cluster Group Services are unavailable.

---

1. The command `/bin/logger` is a shell command interface to the syslog system log module.
2. The same happens when all copies of the OCR are unavailable. The error reported in my test was OCR initialization failed accessing OCR device: PROC-26: Error while accessing the physical storage Operating System error [Success] [0].
3. The error thrown is: Error setting raw device (Device or resource busy)

Removing the RAC Option with the Make Utility

As long as ASM is not in use, it is very easy to convert the `oracle` executable from RAC to single instance and to get one instance in the cluster running. Calling `make` as the owner of the ORACLE installation (usually oracle) and specifying the undocumented `make` target `rac_off` does the job:

```
$ cd $ORACLE_HOME/rdbms/lib
$ make -f ins_rdbms.mk rac_off ioracle
...
/usr/bin/ar d /opt/oracle/product/db10.2/rdbms/lib/libknlopt.a kcsm.o
/usr/bin/ar cr /opt/oracle/product/db10.2/rdbms/lib/libknlopt.a /opt/oracle/product/
db10.2/rdbms/lib/ksnkcs.o
 - Linking Oracle
gcc  -o /opt/oracle/product/db10.2/rdbms/lib/oracle ... -lknlopt ...
...
mv /opt/oracle/product/db10.2/rdbms/lib/oracle /opt/oracle/product/db10.2/bin/oracle
chmod 6751 /opt/oracle/product/db10.2/bin/oracle
```

The most interesting part are the `ar` commands. First `ar` is used to remove the object file `kcsm.o` from `libknlopt.a` (kernel options library), then the object file `ksnkcs.o` is added to `libknlopt.a`. This removes the RAC option. Another startup attempt yields:

```
$ env ORACLE_SID=TEN1 sqlplus / as sysdba
SQL> STARTUP
ORA-00439: feature not enabled: Real Application Clusters
```

The reason for ORA-00349 is that DBMS instances in a RAC environment are run with the parameter setting `CLUSTER_DATABASE=TRUE`. But this parameter can only have the value `TRUE`, if RAC is linked in. So we need to set `CLUSTER_DATABASE=FALSE`. In case you're using an `SPFILE`, you won't be able to modify it without starting an instance, which is currently impossible. So you need to transform the `SPFILE` by removing the binary contents, such that you get a plain text file, and remove the parameter `CLUSTER_DATABASE`, which defaults to `FALSE`. The next attempt then yields:

```
$ cd $ORACLE_HOME/dbs
$ strings spfileTEN1.ora | grep -v cluster > pfileTEN1.ora
$ env ORACLE_SID=TEN1 sqlplus / as sysdba
SQL> STARTUP NOMOUNT PFILE=pfileTEN1.ora
ORACLE instance started.
Total System Global Area  314572800 bytes
Fixed Size                  1261564 bytes
Variable Size             201326596 bytes
Database Buffers          104857600 bytes
Redo Buffers                7127040 bytes
SELECT value FROM v$option WHERE parameter='Real Application Clusters';
VALUE
--------------------------------------------------------------
FALSE
```

Finally the RDBMS instance has started. As long as it does not use ASM storage you are all set. But what if ASM is used? Let's attempt to start an ASM instance with CRS down, the RAC option removed, and the initialization parameter setting `CLUSTER_DATABASE=FALSE`:

```
$ strings spfile+ASM1.ora|grep -v cluster > pfile+ASM1.ora
$ env ORACLE_SID=+ASM1 sqlplus / as sysdba
SQL> STARTUP NOMOUNT PFILE=pfile+ASM1.ora
ORA-29701: unable to connect to Cluster Manager
```

No progress here. This is because ASM instances depend on the Oracle Cluster Synchronization Service Daemon (OCSSD) of Oracle Clusterware for communication with RDBMS instances.

Conversion of a CRS Installation to Local–Only

ASM does not require the full CRS stack. A stripped down version of CRS, which runs no daemons except OCSSD, is sufficient. OCSSD implements the Cluster Synchronization Service, which monitors node health through third party cluster software, or in its absence makes its own determination. It also provides notifications to ORACLE instances about cluster membership and notifies CRSD and EVMD of the health of the cluster. The latter two daemons are not mandatory for ASM instance operations.

A local–only installation of CRS does not require any voting disks. After all, there is just a single node that could cast a vote. A file system file is used as the Oracle Cluster Registry, so raw devices are not needed at all. The conversion consists of backing up the Cluster Registry (OCR) as well as other configuration files and running a few shell scripts located in $ORA_CRS_HOME/install and $ORA_CRS_HOME/bin.

A CRS installation for RAC is marked by three entries in /etc/inittab:

```
$ grep '^h' /etc/inittab
h1:35:respawn:/etc/init.d/init.evmd run >/dev/null 2>&1 </dev/null
h2:35:respawn:/etc/init.d/init.cssd fatal >/dev/null 2>&1 </dev/null
h3:35:respawn:/etc/init.d/init.crsd run >/dev/null 2>&1 </dev/null
```

The parameter local_only in /etc/ocr.loc[1] has the value FALSE:

```
$ cat /etc/oracle/ocr.loc
ocrconfig_loc=/opt/oracle/ocr
local_only=FALSE
```

A local–only CRS installation has but one entry in /etc/inittab and the parameter local_only is set to TRUE. Other differences in the directory structure below /etc/oracle/scls_scr exist. We will first back up the current configuration of CRS. This involves taking a backup of the cluster registry with dd, backing up configuration files and shell scripts and preserving the entries for CRS in /etc/inittab. These steps need to be performed as root:

```
# dd if=/opt/oracle/ocr bs=1048576 of=ocr.bin
258+1 records in
258+1 records out
# ocrdump ocr.txt
tar cvfP crs_local_only_false.tar /etc/oracle /etc/init.d/init.crs  /etc/init.d/
init.crsd  /etc/init.d/init.cssd  /etc/init.d/init.evmd /etc/rc0.d/K96init.crs /etc/
rc1.d/K96init.crs /etc/rc2.d/K96init.crs /etc/rc3.d/S96init.crs /etc/rc4.d/K96init.crs
/etc/rc5.d/S96init.crs /etc/rc6.d/K96init.crs
/etc/oracle/
...
/etc/rc6.d/K96init.crs
# grep '^h[1-3]' /etc/inittab > inittab.crs
```

Now that the current configuration is saved, let's dare to change it. The script rootdelete.sh removes CRS entries from /etc/inittab, notifies init of the changes, removes files from /etc/init.d as well as /etc/rc[0-6].d, and deletes /etc/oracle/scls_scr while retaining /etc/oracle/ocr.loc. In case CRS is running in the endless loop mentioned before, kill the shell scripts which were called with the argument startcheck by init.cssd. Otherwise stop CRS with crsctl stop crs and then run rootdelete.sh as root:

```
# ps -e -o pid,ppid,comm,args|fgrep init.|grep -v grep
 4584     1 init.evmd      /bin/sh /etc/init.d/init.evmd run
 4877     1 init.cssd      /bin/sh /etc/init.d/init.cssd fatal
 4878     1 init.crsd      /bin/sh /etc/init.d/init.crsd run
 8032  4584 init.cssd      /bin/sh /etc/init.d/init.cssd startcheck
 8194  4878 init.cssd      /bin/sh /etc/init.d/init.cssd startcheck
 8247  4877 init.cssd      /bin/sh /etc/init.d/init.cssd startcheck
# kill 8032 8194 8247
# $ORA_CRS_HOME/install/rootdelete.sh
Shutting down Oracle Cluster Ready Services (CRS):
Stopping resources. This could take several minutes.
```

---

1. The file ocr.loc is located in /var/opt/oracle on some platforms.

```
Error while stopping resources. Possible cause: CRSD is down.
Shutdown has begun. The daemons should exit soon.
Checking to see if Oracle CRS stack is down...
Oracle CRS stack is not running.
Oracle CRS stack is down now.
Removing script for Oracle Cluster Ready services
Updating ocr file for downgrade
Cleaning up SCR settings in '/etc/oracle/scls_scr'
```

Now that the CRS configuration for RAC has been removed, we can install a local–only CRS configuration for use by ASM with the documented script localconfig:

```
# $ORA_CRS_HOME/bin/localconfig add
Successfully accumulated necessary OCR keys.
Creating OCR keys for user 'root', privgrp 'root'..
Operation successful.
Configuration for local CSS has been initialized
Adding to inittab
Startup will be queued to init within 30 seconds.
Checking the status of new Oracle init process...
Expecting the CRS daemons to be up within 600 seconds.
CSS is active on these nodes.
        dbserver1
CSS is active on all nodes.
Oracle CSS service is installed and running under init(1M)
```

The stripped down CRS stack is now up and running. You may query its status with crsctl check css:

```
$ crsctl check css
CSS appears healthy
$ crsctl check crs
CSS appears healthy
Cannot communicate with CRS
Cannot communicate with EVM
$ ps -ef|grep ocssd |grep -v grep
oracle   14459    1  0 01:42 ?        00:00:00 /opt/oracle/product/crs10.2/bin/
ocssd.bin
```

The command crsctl check crs fails to contact CRSD and EVMD, which are now disabled. The value of the parameter local_only in ocr.loc is now TRUE and only a single entry for OCSSD is in /etc/inittab:

```
# cat /etc/oracle/ocr.loc
ocrconfig_loc=/opt/oracle/product/crs10.2/cdata/localhost/local.ocr
local_only=TRUE
# grep 'h[1-3]' /etc/inittab
h1:35:respawn:/etc/init.d/init.cssd run >/dev/null 2>&1 </dev/null
```

The ASM instance can be started and any RDBMS instance using ASM storage can mount and open the database:

```
$ env ORACLE_SID=+ASM1 sqlplus / as sysdba
SQL> STARTUP PFILE=$ORACLE_HOME/dbs/pfile+ASM1.ora
ASM instance started
Total System Global Area   83886080 bytes
Fixed Size                  1260216 bytes
Variable Size              57460040 bytes
ASM Cache                  25165824 bytes
ASM diskgroups mounted
SQL> EXIT
$ env ORACLE_SID=TEN1 sqlplus / as sysdba
SQL> ALTER DATABASE MOUNT;
Database altered.
SQL> ALTER DATABASE OPEN;
Database altered.
SQL> SELECT name FROM v$datafile WHERE file#=1;
```

```
NAME
----------------------------------------
+DG/ten/datafile/system.259.628550039
```

Startup and shutdown of OCSSD is performed with `/etc/init.d/init.cssd {start|stop}`:

```
# /etc/init.d/init.cssd stop
Stopping CSSD.
Shutting down CSS daemon.
Shutdown request successfully issued.
Shutdown has begun. The daemons should exit soon.
```

Reenabling CRS for RAC

As soon as the voting disks are available again, the RAC option can be linked back in and the CRS configuration for RAC can be restored. Make sure any RDBMS and ASM instances are shut down before you run `make`:

```
$ cd $ORACLE_HOME/rdbms/lib
$ make -f ins_rdbms.mk rac_on ioracle
```

As root, run `localconfig delete` to remove the current CRS configuration:

```
# $ORA_CRS_HOME/bin/localconfig delete
Stopping CSSD.
Shutting down CSS daemon.
Shutdown request successfully issued.
Shutdown has begun. The daemons should exit soon.
```

As long as the script `$ORA_CRS_HOME/install/rootdeinstall.sh`, which overwrites the OCR with binary zeros has not been used, there is no need to restore the backup of OCR. Considering that a local–only configuration does not access the raw device holding the OCR, the backup is just a precaution. The final steps consists of restoring the CRS scripts, adding entries in `/etc/inittab`, and notifying the init process of the changes to `inittab`:

```
# tar xvfP crs_local_only_false.tar # -P extracts with absolute path
/etc/oracle/
…
/etc/rc6.d/K96init.crs
# cat inittab.crs >> /etc/inittab # append CRS entries to inittab
# telinit q # notify init of changes to inittab
```

After a few moments, the CRS processes are running:

```
# ps -ef|grep d\\.bin
root     319 31977 1 02:21 ? 00:00:01 /opt/oracle/product/crs10.2/bin/crsd.bin reboot
oracle   738 32624 0 02:22 ? 00:00:00 /opt/oracle/product/crs10.2/bin/ocssd.bin
oracle 32577 31975 0 02:21 ? 00:00:01 /opt/oracle/product/crs10.2/bin/evmd.bin
# crsctl check crs
CSS appears healthy
CRS appears healthy
EVM appears healthy
```

CRS automatically starts the local ASM and RDBMS instances, given that cluster resources are configured correctly. Multiple RAC instances are again able to open the same database.

```
$ env ORACLE_SID=TEN1 sqlplus / as sysdba
SQL> SELECT inst_number, trim(INST_NAME) inst_name FROM v$active_instances;
INST_NUMBER INST_NAME
----------- ------------------------------
          1 dbserver1.oradbpro.com:TEN1
          2 dbserver2.oradbpro.com:TEN2
```

Lessons Learned

This chapter discussed an emergency procedure for quickly bringing up a single node in a RAC cluster in case of failure of all voting disks or OCR devices. The same procedure may be applied to other severe error scenarios, which prevent Oracle Clusterware from functioning. The procedure modifies the configuration of Oracle Clusterware, ASM, and RDBMS instances. It is not destructive, i.e. the changes made may be reversed quickly, as soon as the underlying problem, which caused the outage of Oracle Clusterware, has been resolved.

Part XI

Utilities

Chapter 35

OERR

Status: The OERR script is mentioned in Oracle10*g* documentation in conjunction with TNS errors (see *Oracle Database Net Services Administrator's Guide*). It is undocumented that OERR supports additional categories of errors except TNS. The *SQL*Plus User's Guide and Reference Release 9.2* states that "the UNIX oerr script now recognizes SP2- error prefixes to display the Cause and Action text", but does not explain how to use OERR. It is undocumented that most events (e.g. 10046 for extended SQL trace) known by the DBMS instance are also represented in the message files read by OERR and that a short description on each event is available.

Benefit: OERR provides quick access to ORACLE DBMS error message texts based on error message code (number). Furthermore, the cause and action sections retrieved by OERR along with the error message may help in solving a problem at hand.

Introduction to the OERR Script

Occasionally, software running against the ORACLE DBMS server only reports an error code in case of a failure and omits the associated error message. In such a situation, the OERR script comes in handy, since it retrieves the error message associated with the error code. But it doesn't stop there. Where available, it also prints probable causes of and remedies for the error. Too bad it can't be persuaded to fix the problem, given that it knows what's wrong and how to fix it! Here's an example of OERR in action:

```
$ oerr ora 2292
02292, 00000,"integrity constraint (%s.%s) violated - child record found"
// *Cause: attempted to delete a parent key value that had a foreign
//        key dependency.
// *Action: delete dependencies first then parent or disable constraint.
```

OERR ships with each ORACLE DBMS software distribution for UNIX systems. It is implemented by the Bourne shell script `$ORACLE_HOME/bin/oerr`. Since the script is located in `$ORACLE_HOME/bin`, there is no need to add additional directories to the PATH variable to use it. When called without arguments, OERR prints its usage:

```
$ oerr
Usage: oerr facility error

Facility is identified by the prefix string in the error message.
For example, if you get ORA-7300, "ora" is the facility and "7300"
is the error. So you should type "oerr ora 7300".

If you get LCD-111, type "oerr lcd 111", and so on.
```

OERR reads the plain text error message files shipped with UNIX distributions of the ORACLE DBMS. Windows distributions merely contain binary error message files. Plain text error message files have the extension `.msg`, whereas binary error message files have the extension `.msb`. Error message files are located in the directory `$ORACLE_HOME/component/mesg/facilityus.msg`. With the help of the file `$ORACLE_HOME/lib/facility.lis`, OERR translates the facility name into the corresponding component name. It uses the UNIX utility `awk` to extract the requested portions from a message file.

Many DBAs are already familiar with OERR. It is known to a lesser degree that it supports many more facilities than just "ORA". If, for example, you were running Oracle Clusterware to support RAC and received the error message "CLSS-02206: local node evicted by vendor node monitor", then OERR would have the following advice for you:

```
$ oerr clss 2206
2206,  1, "local node evicted by vendor node monitor"
// *Cause:  The Operating System vendor's node monitor evicted the local node.
// *Action: Examine the vendor node monitor's logs for relevant information.
```

Some common facility codes and component names are listed in Table 73. The compilation in the table is by no means complete. Oracle10g boasts a total of 174 facilities.

Table 73: Facility Codes

Facility	Description
CLSR	Message file for Oracle Real Application Clusters HA (RACHA)
CLSS	Message file for Oracle Cluster Synchronization Services
CLST	Message file for modules common to Cluster Ready Services
DBV	Database Verification Utility (DBVERIFY)
DGM	Oracle Data Guard broker command line utility DGMGRL
EXP	Export Utility
IMP	Import Utility
LDAP	OiD LDAP Server
LPX	XML parser
LRM	CORE error message file for the parameter manager
LSX	XML Schema processor
NID	New Database Id (NID Utility)
OCI	Oracle Call Interface
ORA	ORACLE DBMS Server
PCP	Pro*C/C++ C/SQL/PLS/DDL Parser
PLS	PL/SQL
PLW	PL/SQL Warnings

Table 73: Facility Codes

Facility	Description
PROT	Oracle Cluster Registry (OCR) Tools
RMAN	Recovery Manager
SP2	SQL*Plus
TNS	Oracle Net Services (Transparent Network Substrate)
UDE	Data Pump Export
UDI	Data Pump Import
UL	SQL*Loader

Retrieving Undocumented Events

In addition to the documented error messages, ORACLE error message files also contain event numbers of undocumented events. These are handled as if they were error codes and most are in the range between 10000 and 10999. Just like with true error codes, there's a message associated with them. Some of the events are described further in the cause and action sections of `oerr` output.

The following shell script (file `oerr.sh`) retrieves all the events of a particular ORACLE DBMS release:

```
event=10000
counter=0
while [ $event -lt 11000 ]
do
        text=`oerr ora $event`
        if [ "$text" != "" ]; then
                counter=`expr $counter + 1`
                echo "$text"
        fi
        event=`expr $event + 1`
done
echo "$counter events found."
```

Running this shell script against Oracle9*i* yields 623 events, while Oracle10*g* has 713 events. Oracle11*g* has 761 events. Below is a small excerpt of the output generated by the script `oerr.sh`, which contains some of the better known events such as 10046 and 10053.

```
10046, 00000, "enable SQL statement timing"
// *Cause:
// *Action:
10047, 00000, "trace switching of sessions"
// *Cause:
// *Action:
10048, 00000, "Undo segment shrink"
// *Cause:
// *Action:
10049, 00000, "protect library cache memory heaps"
// *Cause:
// *Action: Use the OS memory protection (if available) to protect library
//          cache memory heaps that are pinned.
10050, 00000, "sniper trace"
// *Cause:
// *Action:
10051, 00000, "trace OPI calls"
// *Cause:
// *Action:
10052, 00000, "don't clean up obj$"
```

```
// *Cause:
// *Action:
10053, 00000, "CBO Enable optimizer trace"
// *Cause:
// *Action:
10056, 00000, "dump analyze stats (kdg)"
// *Cause:
// *Action:
10057, 00000, "suppress file names in error messages"
// *Cause:
// *Action:
```

Instead of `oerr` on UNIX, you can use the following anonymous PL/SQL block on any platform, where an ORACLE client is available (file `oerr.sql`):

```
SET SERVEROUTPUT ON SIZE 1000000
DECLARE
    err_msg VARCHAR2(4000);
    counter number:=0;
BEGIN
    FOR err_num IN 10000..10999
    LOOP
        err_msg := SQLERRM (-err_num);
        IF err_msg NOT LIKE '%Message '||err_num||' not found%' THEN
            DBMS_OUTPUT.PUT_LINE (err_msg);
            counter:=counter+1;
        END IF;
    END LOOP;
    DBMS_OUTPUT.PUT_LINE (counter || ' events found.');
END;
/
```

Unfortunately it is impossible to access the additional information reported by `oerr` in the sections *Cause* and *Action* with PL/SQL. However, the additional information is in the *Oracle Database Error Messages Guide*. Below is an example of running the script `oerr.sql`:

```
$ sqlplus system/manager@ten.oradbpro.com @oerr.sql
Connected to:
Oracle Database 10g Enterprise Edition Release 10.2.0.3.0 - Production
With the Partitioning, Real Application Clusters, Oracle Label Security and Data Mining
options

ORA-10000: control file debug event, name 'control_file'
ORA-10001: control file crash event1
ORA-10002: control file crash event2
ORA-10003: control file crash event3
ORA-10004: block recovery testing - internal error
ORA-10005: trace latch operations for debugging
...
ORA-10998: event to enable short stack dumps in system state dumps
ORA-10999: do not get database enqueue name
713 events found.
```

The source code depot includes a full list of events in the range 10000 to 10999 for releases Oracle9*i*, Oracle10*g*, and Oracle11*g*.

Source Code Depot

Table 74: OERR Utility Source Code Depot

File Name	Functionality
events_10g.txt	List of Oracle10g events in the range 10000 to 10999
events_11g.txt	List of Oracle11g events in the range 10000 to 10999
events_9i.txt	List of Oracle9i events in the range 10000 to 10999
oerr.sh	Retrieves and counts all events (event numbers) of a DBMS release.
oerr.sql	PL/SQL script which retrieves and counts all events.

Chapter 36

Recovery Manager Pipe Interface

Status: The Recovery Manager (RMAN) pipe interface is documented. It is also documented that all message content sent to and received from RMAN with DBMS_PIPE must consist of VARCHAR2 data. However, all the details on how to pack VARCHAR2 data into pipe messages (one or multiple VARCHAR2 items per message) and how error stacks are packaged into messages are undocumented. Furthermore, the behavior of RMAN in case of an error (termination or continuation) is undocumented.

Benefit: The RMAN pipe interface is ideally suited to integrate RMAN into portable third party backup and restore tools. It is also very well suited to implement robust scripts, which can handle catalog instance failures, block corruptions, and internode parallel backup and restore for Real Application Clusters installations.

Introduction to Recovery Manager

Anyone who has worked with RMAN, the backup and recovery utility of choice since the release of Oracle8, knows that it can be used interactively in a terminal window. RMAN can also read commands from a script (e.g. rman CMDFILE *script_name*.rvc). Success or failure of RMAN can be determined by examining the exit code it passes to the calling program or shell. Exit code zero means success, whereas a nonzero exit code means failure. RMAN can write a transcript of its operations to a log file (parameter LOG, previously MSGLOG).

The trouble begins when more advanced features are required. For example, when a recovery catalog is used and RMAN is started with the command line option CATALOG or there is a CONNECT CATALOG statement in a script, RMAN exits with an error, if the catalog is unavailable. Thus, no backup is taken, even though it would have been perfectly feasible to backup the database in NOCATALOG mode and then resynchronize the control file with the catalog, once the catalog instance becomes available again. Resynchronization happens automatically, the next time RMAN executes a backup, restore, or list command while connected to the catalog. Manual resynchronization is accomplished with the command RESYNC CATALOG. This command may also be used to synchronize a control file with multiple RMAN catalogs on independent systems for increased catalog availability, dispelling the need to protect the catalog with Data Guard or clustering.

The risk incurred due to a missing backup as a consequence of a catalog outage could easily be avoided. The problem is that a utility, which tells RMAN to run a whole sequence of commands in a script, has no way of knowing why RMAN failed and at what point it failed. The same applies to block corruptions, which also cause RMAN to abort without completing the backup. Backups may be completed in spite of block corruptions by telling RMAN how many block corruptions in a data file to tolerate. The command SET MAXCORRUPT FOR DATAFILE is provided for this purpose. A program controlling RMAN via the pipe interface could easily examine the error stack RMAN returns when a backup fails due to a block corruption. If it finds the error message "ORA-19566: exceeded limit of 0 corrupt blocks for file *filename*", it could detect which data file is affected by the corruption and reattempt the backup with a suitable MAXCORRUPT setting.

When passing scripts to RMAN, it is also good practice to use two different scripts—one for backing up the database and another one for backing up archived redo logs—to make sure an error while backing up the database does not cause RMAN to abort and thus omit the execution of the BACKUP ARCHIVELOG command. Since everything including starting an instance of RMAN can be done through PL/SQL (using DBMS_SCHEDULER and external jobs; see Chapter 19), a third party tool built with the pipe interface would be highly portable.

Introduction to DBMS_PIPE

DBMS_PIPE is a package that enables asynchronous message passing between database clients. In contrast to advanced queuing, persistence of messages is not implemented. Messages are lost on instance shutdown. The package DBMS_PIPE may be used to give a database client access to functionality of an application that is primarily unrelated to an ORACLE database, but can handle requests through pipe messages. Since the introduction of the external procedure agent, an alternative paradigm for accessing services external to the DBMS instance is available.

Pipe messages consist of one or more items, where each item is one of the fundamental ORACLE DBMS data types such as CHAR, DATE, NUMBER, RAW, or VARCHAR2. Messages are unaffected by transactions and are composed by adding items using DBMS_PIPE.PACK_MESSAGE and sent using DBMS_PIPE.SEND_MESSAGE. To receive a message, the function DBMS_PIPE.RECEIVE_MESSAGE is called. Items in a message may be retrieved with the procedure DBMS_PIPE.UNPACK_MESSAGE.

There are two classes of pipes. Private pipes and public pipes. While public pipes may be used by any database client, private pipes are reserved for use by sessions with SYSDBA privilege. RMAN uses private pipes to ensure that only privileged database clients can send commands to it.

Use the option PIPE to instruct RMAN to read commands from a private pipe:

```
$ rman target / pipe  '"PIPE"'  log rman.log
```

When started in this way, RMAN creates two private pipes—one for receiving messages and another one for sending replies. The suffix "_IN" is used for the input pipe and the suffix "_OUT" for the output pipe. The prefix "ORA$RMAN_" applies to both pipes. Thus, for the above example, the following private pipe names are reported when querying the view V$DB_PIPES:

```
SQL> SELECT * FROM v$db_pipes;
   OWNERID NAME                    TYPE     PIPE_SIZE
---------- ---------------------- ------- ----------
         0 ORA$RMAN_PIPE_OUT       PRIVATE       354
         0 ORA$RMAN_PIPE_IN        PRIVATE       353
```

RMAN_PIPE_IF Package

In the source code depot, I provide a PL/SQL package that shields a lot of the intricacies of using DBMS_PIPE and interpreting the messages RMAN sends. The name of the package is RMAN_PIPE_IF (IF for interface). Writing the package, I learned the following lessons:

- RMAN normally sends one line of output per pipe message.
- RMAN error stacks consists of several lines (VARCHAR2 items) in a single message.
- Commands sent to RMAN may consist of one item per pipe message and may contain newlines.

- In pipe mode, RMAN does not echo the commands it received to a log file as it does when executing a script. The backup utility controlling RMAN in pipe mode should compensate for this, by first writing the command it is about to send to RMAN to a log file, and then sending the command to RMAN through DBMS_PIPE.
- When RMAN is ready to process the next command, it sends "RMAN-00572: waiting for dbms_pipe input" as the single item of a pipe message.
- RMAN does not terminate on error, instead it keeps running and signals through RMAN-00572 that it is ready to receive the next command.

Except handling all of the aspects mentioned above, the package RMAN_PIPE_IF also probes the pipe messages sent by RMAN and provides the following additional functionality:

- It indicates when RMAN is ready to receive the next command by detecting "RMAN-00572: waiting for dbms_pipe input".
- It concatenates RMAN error stack messages consisting of multiple VARCHAR2 items in a single message into a single VARCHAR2 string and returns it to the caller.
- It returns the RMAN error code (RMAN-*nnnnn*) and error message from the top of the error stack in case of a command failure.
- It returns the ORACLE DBMS error code (ORA-*nnnnn*) and error message from the top of the error stack in case of a command failure and the presence of an ORACLE DBMS error.
- When called to receive a message, after a time-out period of one second, the package returns an empty message and a line count of 0, if no message could be retrieved from the RMAN output pipe.

RMAN_PIPE_IF Package Specification

The source code of the package specification of RMAN_PIPE_IF is below. I have added numerous comments to the code to explain the purpose of the package's functions and their arguments. Since the schema SYS is reserved for the data dictionary, the package is created in schema SITE_SYS with AUTHID CURRENT_USER, such that clients with SYSDBA privileges may execute the package while retaining the SYSDBA privilege. Otherwise the package would be executed with the privileges of its owner SITE_SYS and it would fail to access private pipes used by RMAN.

```
create or replace package site_sys.rman_pipe_if authid current_user as
    -- send: return codes identical to DBMS_PIPE.SEND_MESSAGE: 0 on sucess
    function send(pipe_arg varchar2, -- same as argument to RMAN command line option
PIPE
        msg varchar2) return number; -- message to send to RMAN via DBMS_PIPE, may
contain several lines
    -- receive: returns 0 when pipe empty, otherwise items (one or more lines) received
    function receive(pipe_arg varchar2,
        msg out varchar2, -- message received from RMAN via DBMS_PIPE
        -- wait_for_input: 0: RMAN not ready for next command
        -- 1: RMAN ready for next command after RMAN sent RMAN-00572: waiting for
        -- dbms_pipe input
        wait_for_input out number,
        rman_error out number, -- RMAN-nnnnn error from RMAN errorstack, 0 if no error
        rman_msg out varchar2, -- RMAN-nnnnn error message, NULL if no RMAN error
        ora_error out number,  -- ORA-nnnnn error from RMAN errorstack, 0 if no error
        ora_msg out varchar2   -- ORA-nnnnn error message, NULL if no ORA error
    ) return number;
end;
/
```

Since the package is owned by SITE_SYS, EXECUTE permission on DBMS_PIPE must be granted to user SITE_SYS. The file rman_pipe_if.sql in the source code depot contains the package body, which is too large to reproduce here.

Using the Package RMAN_PIPE_IF

In this section, I show the intended use of the package RMAN_PIPE_IF with SQL*Plus. A backup and recovery tool, which leverages the pipe interface, would make exactly the same calls that I show in SQL*Plus from a programming language such as PL/SQL, C (with Pro*C), or Perl (with DBI and DBD::Oracle). The sections below address both examples of failure mentioned at the beginning of this chapter:

- failure to connect to the catalog, causing RMAN to abort the script executed
- data file corruption, causing RMAN to abort the BACKUP command and the script executed

First, RMAN needs to be started with the pipe interface option. Note that the double quotes around the word "PIPE" prevent RMAN from interpreting this string as a keyword. The single quotes make sure that the shell does not remove the double quotes around the string "PIPE":

```
$ rman TARGET / PIPE  '"PIPE"' LOG rman.log
```

After initialization, RMAN indicates that it is ready to receive commands. Let's receive the messages it sends after startup. Calling the package RMAN_PIPE_IF requires a number of SQL*Plus bind variables. Most of them correspond to arguments of functions in the RMAN_PIPE_IF package, so they should be self-explanatory. The variable msg is used for messages received, whereas cmd holds the text of a command or script sent to RMAN. The variable rv holds return values from calls to RMAN_PIPE_IF.

```
SQL> VARIABLE rv NUMBER
SQL> VARIABLE msg VARCHAR2(4000)
SQL> VARIABLE cmd VARCHAR2(4000)
SQL> VARIABLE rman_error NUMBER
SQL> VARIABLE ora_error NUMBER
SQL> VARIABLE rman_msg VARCHAR2(4000)
SQL> VARIABLE ora_msg VARCHAR2(4000)
SQL> VARIABLE pipe_arg VARCHAR2(1000)
SQL> VARIABLE wait_for_input NUMBER
```

Next, we need to set the identifier that was used as the argument to the PIPE option when RMAN was started. It will be incorporated into the names of the private pipes. As above, the word "PIPE" is used.

```
SQL> SET NULL <NULL>
SQL> BEGIN
SQL>     :pipe_arg:='PIPE';
SQL> END;
SQL> /
```

Now we may attempt to receive a message from the private pipe called "ORA$RMAN_PIPE_OUT":

```
SQL> EXEC :rv:=site_sys.rman_pipe_if.receive(:pipe_arg, :msg, :wait_for_input,
:rman_error, :rman_msg, :ora_error, :ora_msg)
PL/SQL procedure successfully completed.
SQL> COL msg FORMAT a90
SQL> COL rv FORMAT 99
SQL> SET LINESIZE 130
SQL> COL wait_for_input HEADING "Wait|for|input" FORMAT 99999
SQL> COL rman_error HEADING "RMAN|Error" FORMAT 99999
SQL> COL ora_error HEADING "ORA|Error" FORMAT 99999
SQL> SELECT :rv rv, :msg msg, :wait_for_input wait_for_input FROM dual;
 RV MSG                                                         Wait for input
 --- -------------------------------------------------------- --------------
   1 connected to target database: TEN (DBID=2848896501)                    0
```

RMAN sent a message with a single item (or line). This is indicated by the return value RV=1. The message from RMAN indicates that it connected to the target database. At this point, RMAN is not ready to receive a command, which is indicated by WAIT_FOR_INPUT=0. Let's retrieve the next message.

```
SQL> EXEC :rv:=site_sys.rman_pipe_if.receive(:pipe_arg, :msg, :wait_for_input,
:rman_error, :rman_msg, :ora_error, :ora_msg)
PL/SQL procedure successfully completed.
```

```
SQL> SELECT :rv rv, :msg msg, :wait_for_input wait_for_input FROM dual;
 RV MSG                                                      Wait for input
 --- -------------------------------------------------- --------------
   1 RMAN-00572: waiting for dbms_pipe input                           1
```

Now RMAN is ready to accept a command (WAIT_FOR_INPUT=1), so let's tell RMAN to connect to the catalog database:

```
SQL> BEGIN
   :cmd:='CONNECT CATALOG rman/rman@ten_tcp.world;';
   -- send a message
   :rv:=site_sys.rman_pipe_if.send(:pipe_arg, :cmd);
END;
/
PL/SQL procedure successfully completed.
SQL> PRINT rv
 RV
 ---
   0
```

Let's find out whether the CONNECT CATALOG command completed successfully (for the sake of conciseness, the call to site_sys.rman_pipe_if.receive has been omitted):

```
SQL> SELECT :rv rv, :msg msg FROM dual;
 RV MSG
 --- ------------------------------------------------------------------------------
   4 RMAN-00571: ===========================================================
     RMAN-00569: =============== ERROR MESSAGE STACK FOLLOWS ===============
     RMAN-00571: ===========================================================
     RMAN-04004: error from recovery catalog database: ORA-12170: TNS:Connect timeout
       occurred
```

An error, which prevented RMAN from connecting to the catalog database, occurred. Yet, RMAN is still running and ready to receive further commands as we will see shortly. But first, let's look at the additional information, such as the RMAN error code, returned by RMAN_PIPE_IF:

```
SQL> SELECT :rman_error rman_error, :rman_msg rman_msg, :ora_error ora_error,
:wait_for_input wait_for_input
FROM dual;
                                                               Wait
 RMAN                                                   ORA    for
 Error RMAN_MSG                                         Error  input
 ------ ----------------------------------------------- ------ ------
  4004 RMAN-04004: error from recovery catalog database: ORA-12170:    0      0
        TNS:Connect timeout occurred
```

The package extracted the error RMAN-04004 from the top of the error stack. There was no separate ORA-*nnnnn* error on the error stack (it was included in the RMAN-04004 error message). RMAN is not yet ready to receive the next command (WAIT_FOR_INPUT=0). Let's receive another message:

```
SQL> EXEC :rv:=site_sys.rman_pipe_if.receive(:pipe_arg, :msg, :wait_for_input,
:rman_error, :rman_msg, :ora_error, :ora_msg)
PL/SQL procedure successfully completed.
SQL> SELECT :rv rv, :msg msg FROM dual;
 RV MSG
 --- ------------------------------------------------------------------------------
   1 RMAN-00572: waiting for dbms_pipe input
```

Again, RMAN is ready to receive a command. Next, we send a BACKUP command, even though RMAN failed to connect to the catalog:

```
SQL> BEGIN
   :cmd:='run {
     backup format "DB-%d-%u.bkp" tablespace appdata;
     }';
```

```
     -- send a message
     :rv:=site_sys.rman_pipe_if.send(:pipe_arg, :cmd);
END;
/
PL/SQL procedure successfully completed.
SQL> PRINT rv
  RV
  ---
   0
```

Let's find out how RMAN responds:

```
SQL> EXEC :rv:=site_sys.rman_pipe_if.receive(:pipe_arg, :msg, :wait_for_input,
:rman_error, :rman_msg, :ora_error, :ora_
msg)
PL/SQL procedure successfully completed.
SQL> SELECT :rv rv, :msg msg FROM dual;
  RV MSG
  --- ---------------------------------
   1 Starting backup at 18.07.07 16:54
```

RMAN did start backing up tablespace APPDATA. Next, RMAN sends some messages to state what is going on as it takes the backup. Below, I only show two of the messages and omit the code used to receive the messages.

```
SQL> SELECT :rv rv, :msg msg FROM dual;
  RV MSG
  --- ---------------------------------------------------------------
   1 using target database control file instead of recovery catalog
...
SQL> SELECT :rv rv, :msg msg FROM dual;
  RV MSG
  --- ---------------------------------------------------------------
   1 input datafile fno=00007 name=F:\ORADATA\TEN\APPDATA01.DBF
```

After receiving some more messages, it turns out that the backup failed due to a block corruption. Of course I deliberately corrupted a segment in tablespace APPDATA[1]. Below is the message RMAN sent when it encountered the corruption:

```
SQL> SELECT :rv rv, :msg msg FROM dual;
  RV MSG
  --- ---------------------------------------------------------------------
   6 RMAN-00571: ===========================================================
     RMAN-00569: =============== ERROR MESSAGE STACK FOLLOWS ===============
     RMAN-00571: ===========================================================
     RMAN-03009: failure of backup command on ORA_DISK_1 channel at 07/18/2007 17:01:59
     ORA-19566: exceeded limit of 0 corrupt blocks for file F:\ORADATA\TEN\APPDATA01.DBF
     RMAN-10031: RPC Error: ORA-19583
```

Let's take a look at the remaining information on the error:

```
SQL> SELECT :rman_error rman_error, :rman_msg rman_msg, :ora_error ora_error,
:wait_for_input wait_for_input
FROM dual;
```

| | | | Wait |
| RMAN | | ORA | for |
Error	RMAN_MSG	Error	input
3009	RMAN-03009: failure of backup command on ORA_DISK_1 channel	19566	0
	at 07/18/2007 17:13:55		

---

1. A block corruption may be created with the UNIX command dd, (also ships with Cygwin) after a tablespace or data file is set offline. The command below overwrites the tenth 8 KB block in a data file with binary zeros:

   ```
   dd bs=8192 if=/dev/zero of=data_file_name count=1 seek=9 conv=notrunc
   ```

The RMAN error at the top of the stack is RMAN-03009. This time, there is also an ORA-19566 error. The text of the ORA-*nnnnn* error is in the bind variable ORA_MSG:

```
SQL> SELECT :ora_msg "ORA-nnnnn error" FROM dual;
ORA-nnnnn error
--------------------------------------------------------------------------------
ORA-19566: exceeded limit of 0 corrupt blocks for file F:\ORADATA\TEN\APPDATA01.DBF
```

The error message in bind variable ORA_MSG contains the name of the data file affected by the block corruption. Retrieval of the data file name can easily be implemented by extracting the string at the end of the error message. Knowing the name of the corrupted file, it is a breeze to rerun the backup with a SET MAXCORRUPT setting that will allow the DBMS instance to complete the backup.

```
SQL> BEGIN
    :cmd:='run {
        set maxcorrupt for datafile "F:\ORADATA\TEN\APPDATA01.DBF" to 10;
        backup format "DB-%d-%u.bkp" tablespace appdata;
        }';
        :rv:=site_sys.rman_pipe_if.send(:pipe_arg, :cmd);
END;
/
PL/SQL procedure successfully completed.
SQL> PRINT rv
 RV
 ---
  0
```

Since there is only a single corruption in the data file, RMAN now signals success and returns the name of the backup piece created:

```
SQL> SELECT :rv rv, :msg msg FROM dual;
 RV MSG
 --- --------------------------------------------------------------------------
  1 piece handle=DB-TEN-JHIN5G18.BKP tag=TAG20070718T172808 comment=NONE
```

After the successful backup, an entry describing the corruption is created in V$DATABASE_BLOCK_CORRUPTION:

```
SQL> SELECT * FROM v$database_block_corruption;
     FILE#     BLOCK#     BLOCKS CORRUPTION_CHANGE# CORRUPTION_TYPE
---------- ---------- ---------- ------------------ ---------------
         7         20          1                  0 FRACTURED
```

Note that rows are not added to V$DATABASE_BLOCK_CORRUPTION after a *failed* backup due to one or more corruptions. To repair the corruption, perform block media recovery by running the RMAN command BLOCKRECOVER (e.g. BLOCKRECOVER DATAFILE 7 BLOCK 20).

To terminate RMAN, send a message containing the command EXIT as below:

```
SQL> BEGIN
    :cmd:='exit;';
    :rv:=site_sys.rman_pipe_if.send(:pipe_arg, :cmd);
    END;
/
```

RMAN responds with another message and exits:

```
SQL> EXEC :rv:=site_sys.rman_pipe_if.receive(:pipe_arg, :msg, :wait_for_input,
:rman_error, :rman_msg, :ora_error, :ora_msg)
 RV MSG
 --- -------------------------
  1 Recovery Manager complete.
```

Since RMAN has terminated, any subsequent attempts to read from the pipe fail with "ORA-06556: the pipe is empty, cannot fulfill the unpack_message request". For the convenience of users of the RMAN_PIPE_IF package, this exception is caught and the package returns a line count of 0 and an empty message. Note that this behavior is not necessarily an indication that RMAN has terminated. While RMAN, or rather the DBMS instance, is working hard to complete the commands initiated, there may not be any messages over long stretches of time. The package

RMAN_PIPE_IF waits one second for a message to arrive and returns a line count of 0, if no message arrived during the time-out period.

```
SQL> EXEC :rv:=site_sys.rman_pipe_if.receive(:pipe_arg, :msg, :wait_for_input,
:rman_error, :rman_msg, :ora_error, :ora_msg)
PL/SQL procedure successfully completed.
SQL> SELECT :rv rv, :msg msg FROM dual;
  RV MSG
 --- ----------------------------------------------------------------------
   0 <NULL>
```

Validating Backup Pieces

Another interesting feature, that could easily be implemented, would be to check the backup pieces created for consistency with the command VALIDATE. VALIDATE reads backup pieces and verifies them block by block without restoring any files. VALIDATE CHECK LOGICAL performs more thorough tests than VALIDATE alone.

When RMAN is started with the MSGNO option, each item (or line) it packs into a pipe message is prefixed by the string "RMAN-*nnnnn*" (with the exception of the termination message "Recovery Manager complete."). Messages concerning backup pieces are prefixed by RMAN-08530 as below:

```
  RV MSG
 --- ----------------------------------------------------------------------
   1 RMAN-08530: piece handle=A16J2S5GD.BKP tag=TAG20071205T194829 comment=NONE
```

This feature could be used to extract the backup piece name and to run a VALIDATE command on the backup set containing the backup piece. The backup set key may be retrieved from the view V$BACKUP_PIECE:

```
SQL> SELECT recid, piece#, tag, status
FROM V$backup_piece
WHERE handle='A16J2S5GD.BKP';
RECID PIECE# TAG                STATUS
----- ------ ------------------ ------
   31      1 TAG20071205T194829 A
```

The column RECID contains the backup set key for the VALIDATE command:

```
$ rman target / msgno
Recovery Manager: Release 10.2.0.1.0 - Production on Wed Dec 5 19:39:27 2007
RMAN-06005: connected to target database: TEN (DBID=2870266532)
RMAN> validate backupset 31;
RMAN-06009: using target database control file instead of recovery catalog
RMAN-08030: allocated channel: ORA_DISK_1
RMAN-08500: channel ORA_DISK_1: sid=32 devtype=DISK
RMAN-08097: channel ORA_DISK_1: starting validation of archive log backupset
RMAN-08003: channel ORA_DISK_1: reading from backup piece A16J2S5GD.BKP
RMAN-08023: channel ORA_DISK_1: restored backup piece 1
RMAN-08511: piece handle=A16J2S5GD.BKP tag=TAG20071205T194829
RMAN-08182: channel ORA_DISK_1: validation complete, elapsed time: 00:00:07
```

If the backup set contains a corrupt backup piece, the VALIDATE command fails, but RMAN does not write an error stack:

```
RMAN> VALIDATE BACKUPSET 31;
RMAN-12016: using channel ORA_DISK_1
RMAN-08097: channel ORA_DISK_1: starting validation of archive log backupset
RMAN-08003: channel ORA_DISK_1: reading from backup piece A16J2S5GD.BKP
RMAN-01005: ORA-19870: error reading backup piece A16J2S5GD.BKP
ORA-19587: error occurred reading 0 bytes at block number 1
```

The corrupt backup piece is also reported in the alert log of the instance:

```
Wed Dec 05 19:59:41 2007
Corrupt block 1 found during reading backup piece, file=A16J2S5GD.BKP, corr_type=1
```

Internode Parallel Backup and Restore

Backup and recovery operations by RMAN may be parallelized within a single DBMS instance by allocating several channels. Parallelization across several RAC instances is possible by explicitly allocating channels and supplying a connect string, which resolves to individual instances. Yet, this kind of hard coded internode parallel backup is not robust. The backup would fail, if one of the RAC instances were not available.

Usually, each RAC node has one or two Fibre Channel host bus adapters to connect it to a SAN storage array, and one or more public LAN (local area network) adapters. Irrespective of the data path used by backup or restore—LAN or LAN–free over Fibre Channel—I expect backup operations to scale with the number of LAN or fiber channel adapters used, given that there is no other bottleneck elsewhere in the system.

The single missing piece is a coordinator process, which can receive commands like BACKUP DATABASE, RESTORE DATABASE, RESTORE TABLESPACE in whatever format, break down the task into smaller units and assign these to multiple instances of RMAN. Note that it is irrelevant where in the cluster (or even outside of the cluster) instances of RMAN are running, as long as the proper connect string is supplied with the command CONNECT TARGET. When backing up, one tape drive might be assigned per RAC node. Matters are more complicated during a restore, since there is no easy way to ensure that the files needed are not accidentally located on the same tape. When disk pools are used instead of or in addition to tape drives, the concurrency issues arising with tape drives are mitigated.

The RMAN pipe interface offers a solid foundation for implementing a coordinator process for internode parallel backup and restore. For example, when such a coordinator process receives the command BACKUP DATABASE, it might retrieve the list of data files from V$DATAFILE and assign data files for backup to multiple RMAN instances in a round robin fashion. Whenever an instance of RMAN finishes backing up a data file, it would send "RMAN-00572: waiting for dbms_pipe input" via DBMS_PIPE to the coordinator process. The coordinator could then assign the next data file to back up by sending another BACKUP DATAFILE command to the RMAN process. This *divide and conquer* style algorithm would also provide a rudimentary form of load balancing, since less loaded nodes would have higher I/O bandwidth and could thus handle more data files (given standard sizing of data files).

The package RMAN_PIPE_IF presented in the previous section provides the infrastructure for sending and receiving messages to and from RMAN instances on different RAC nodes. Since database pipes are local to an instance, it is not possible to write to pipe P on RAC instance 1 and to read from the same pipe P on RAC instance 2. In a multi–instance RAC environment, the package RMAN_PIPE_IF (and thus DBMS_PIPE) needs to be called via database links from a single database session or the coordinator process needs to open several database sessions, one per instance. The first method must be used when implementing the coordinator with PL/SQL, whereas the latter would be preferred when using Perl DBI or another programming language, which supports several concurrent database sessions. I provide a prototype of a serial backup implemented with PL/SQL in the source code depot of Chapter 19. For an initial assessment of speedup attainable by internode parallel backup it would suffice to manually run several instances of RMAN, which back up different parts of the same database concurrently.

Source Code Depot

Table 75: Recovery Manager Source Code Depot

File Name	Functionality
rman_pipe_if.sql	Contains the PL/SQL package RMAN_PIPE_IF for sending commands to and receiving replies from Recovery Manager via DBMS_PIPE.

Chapter 37

ORADEBUG SQL*Plus Command

Status: The manual *Oracle9i Real Application Clusters Administration Release 2* contains an example of an ORADEBUG DUMP command. *Oracle9i Database Administrator's Guide Release 2 (9.2) for Windows* contains a section entitled *Using ORADEBUG Utility*. Yet, the information provided is very fragmentary, since the requirement to attach to a process before running any further commands is undocumented. In Oracle10g and Oracle11g, the only hints on the existence of ORADEBUG are in the *Error Messages Guide*.

Benefit: ORADEBUG is very useful for diagnosing performance and hanging issues. Among other things, it may be used to verify that the correct IP addresses are used for Real Application Clusters inter–instance communication. In releases prior to Oracle11g, ORADEBUG TRACEFILE_NAME is the only way to determine the name of the trace file a process is writing to[1].

Introduction to ORADEBUG

Since ORADEBUG is primarily intended for use by Oracle Support personnel, it has remained largely undocumented since its introduction with SQL*Plus release 7.3. However, many ORADEBUG commands are very useful even for novice DBAs.

As the name suggests, ORADEBUG functionality serves debugging and tracing purposes. ORADEBUG is a SQL*Plus command, which may be entered at the SQL*Plus prompt without any special requirements, except a connection to a DBMS instance with SYSDBA privileges. It may be used to:

- Enable SQL trace in your own server process or a foreign server process.
- Figure out which trace file a process is writing to.

---

1. In Oracle11g, the column TRACEFILE has been added to the V$ fixed view V$PROCESS.

- Dump internal ORACLE structures for diagnosing database hangs or memory corruptions.
- Dump information from data file headers or undo segments headers.
- Determine which shared memory segments and semaphores a DBMS instance uses.
- Find out which interconnect address and protocol RAC instances use.
- Modify data structures in the SGA.

In all likelihood, the last item will be relevant only to Oracle Support personnel.

ORADEBUG Workflow

When using ORADEBUG, the basic workflow is:

1. Start SQL*Plus and connect as SYSDBA.
2. Attach to a process of an ORACLE instance.
3. Issue one or more ORADEBUG commands.
4. Examine screen output or trace files.
5. Detach from the process (occurs automatically when exiting from SQL*Plus or attaching to another process).

ORADEBUG Command Reference

The SQL*Plus help facility does not cover ORADEBUG, but the command itself has a help option which prints all available commands:

```
SQL> ORADEBUG HELP
HELP            [command]                  Describe one or all commands
SETMYPID                                   Debug current process
SETOSPID        <ospid>                    Set OS pid of process to debug
SETORAPID       <orapid> ['force']         Set Oracle pid of process to debug
SHORT_STACK                                Dump abridged OS stack
DUMP            <dump_name> <lvl> [addr]   Invoke named dump
DUMPSGA         [bytes]                    Dump fixed SGA
DUMPLIST                                   Print a list of available dumps
EVENT           <text>                     Set trace event in process
SESSION_EVENT   <text>                     Set trace event in session
DUMPVAR         <p|s|uga> <name> [level]   Print/dump a fixed PGA/SGA/UGA variable
DUMPTYPE        <address> <type> <count>   Print/dump an address with type info
SETVAR          <p|s|uga> <name> <value>   Modify a fixed PGA/SGA/UGA variable
PEEK            <addr> <len> [level]       Print/Dump memory
POKE            <addr> <len> <value>       Modify memory
WAKEUP          <orapid>                   Wake up Oracle process
SUSPEND                                    Suspend execution
RESUME                                     Resume execution
FLUSH                                      Flush pending writes to trace file
CLOSE_TRACE                                Close trace file
TRACEFILE_NAME                             Get name of trace file
LKDEBUG                                    Invoke global enqueue service debugger
NSDBX                                      Invoke CGS name-service debugger
-G              <Inst-List | def | all>    Parallel oradebug command prefix
-R              <Inst-List | def | all>    Parallel oradebug prefix (return output
SETINST         <instance# .. | all>       Set instance list in double quotes
SGATOFILE       <SGA dump dir>             Dump SGA to file; dirname in double quotes
DMPCOWSGA       <SGA dump dir>             Dump & map SGA as COW; dirname in double
quotes
MAPCOWSGA       <SGA dump dir>             Map SGA as COW; dirname in double
quotes
HANGANALYZE     [level] [syslevel]         Analyze system hang
FFBEGIN                                    Flash Freeze the Instance
FFDEREGISTER                               FF deregister instance from cluster
FFTERMINST                                 Call exit and terminate instance
FFRESUMEINST                               Resume the flash frozen instance
```

```
FFSTATUS                                        Flash freeze status of instance
SKDSTTPCS        <ifname>   <ofname>            Helps translate PCs to names
WATCH            <address> <len> <self|exist|all|target>  Watch a region of memory
DELETE           <local|global|target> watchpoint <id>    Delete a watchpoint
SHOW             <local|global|target> watchpoints        Show  watchpoints
CORE                                            Dump core without crashing process
IPC                                             Dump ipc information
UNLIMIT                                          Unlimit the size of the trace file
PROCSTAT                                        Dump process statistics
CALL             <func> [arg1] ... [argn]  Invoke function with arguments
```

ORADEBUG HELP *command* displays a single line help text on a *command*. Yet, this is no more detailed than what ORADEBUG HELP provides.

Attaching to a Process

It is required to attach to a target process, before any ORADEBUG commands may be executed. Three options exist:

- Attaching to your own server process, i.e. the process serving your SQL*Plus session.
- Attaching to a foreign server process by ORACLE process identifier.
- Attaching to a foreign process by operating system process identifier.

Attaching to a process which belongs to a RAC instance on another node in the same cluster is not implemented. The commands, their arguments, and how to obtain argument values are summarized in Table 76.

Table 76: Attaching to a Process with ORADEBUG

Command	*Purpose*
ORADEBUG SETMYPID	Attach to your own server process
ORADEBUG SETORAPID *pid*	Attach to a foreign process, where *pid* equals V$PROCESS.PID
ORADEBUG SETOSPID *spid*	Attach to a foreign process, where *spid* equals V$PROCESS.SPID

SETMYPID

In case you wanted to run a few SQL or PL/SQL statements in your own session to record performance metrics and execution plans, you would use ORADEBUG SETMYPID:

```
SQL> ORADEBUG SETMYPID
Statement processed.
SQL> ORADEBUG UNLIMIT
Statement processed.
SQL> ORADEBUG EVENT 10046 TRACE NAME CONTEXT FOREVER, LEVEL 8
Statement processed.
SQL> SELECT … /* run whatever statements you want to trace */
SQL> ORADEBUG TRACEFILE_NAME
/opt/oracle/obase/admin/TEN/udump/ten1_ora_24953.trc
SQL> ORADEBUG EVENT 10046 TRACE NAME CONTEXT OFF
Statement processed.
```

The example above is a full–fledged scenario for tracing your own session. ORADEBUG UNLIMIT has the same effect as ALTER SESSION SET MAX_DUMP_FILE_SIZE=UNLIMITED, except that it affects the attached process. ORADEBUG EVENT sets an event in the attached process (see also Part III). ORADEBUG TRACEFILE_NAME retrieves the trace file name used by the attached process. Note that the trace file name is subject to change by the session–level parameter TRACEFILE_IDENTIFIER. Tracing with ORADEBUG EVENT occurs at process level, not database session level. When using dedicated server, the effect is the same. Yet, when tracing is enabled in a shared server process, all the database sessions serviced by a certain shared server process are traced. When dealing with Shared Server, use the package DBMS_SYSTEM to set events at session level (see Chapter 20).

SETOSPID

A scenario for `SETOSPID` is when you see an ORACLE process that consumes a lot of CPU with a tool such as `top` (any UNIX platform), `prstat` (Solaris), `glance` (HP-UX), or `nmon` (AIX). You would then attach to the process and enable SQL trace with event 10046 at level 8 or 12. Here's an example:

```
$ top
top - 22:04:20 up 54 min,  5 users,  load average: 0.77, 0.76, 0.83
Tasks: 149 total,   2 running, 147 sleeping,   0 stopped,   0 zombie
Cpu(s): 10.8% us, 41.0% sy,  0.0% ni, 34.9% id, 13.0% wa,  0.3% hi,  0.0% si
Mem:   1034584k total,   796000k used,   238584k free,   39272k buffers
Swap:   524280k total,        0k used,   524280k free,   502048k cached

  PID USER      PR  NI  VIRT  RES  SHR S %CPU %MEM    TIME+  COMMAND
13756 oracle    16   0  394m  68m  64m R   50  6.8  0:05.95 oracle
24887 oracle    15   0  391m  30m  27m S   14  3.0  0:21.68 oracle
SQL> ORADEBUG SETOSPID 13756
Oracle pid: 19, Unix process pid: 13756, image: oracle@dbserver1.oradbpro.com (TNS V1-
V3)
```

SETORAPID

`SETORAPID` is useful in a scenario where you already know the session identifier (`V$SESSION.SID`) of a process that exhibits performance problems or hangs. By joining `V$SESSION` with `V$PROCESS`, you obtain the ORACLE process identifier (`V$PROCESS.PID`) for attaching to the process. The operating system process identifier `SPID` for use with `SETOSPID` may also be retrieved from `V$PROCESS`. The example below assumes that the process with `V$SESSION.SID=151` is of concern:

```
SQL> SELECT pid, spid
FROM v$process p, v$session s
WHERE s.sid=151 and s.paddr=p.addr;
      PID SPID
---------- ------
       19 15365
SQL> ORADEBUG SETORAPID 19
 Unix process pid: 15365, image: oracle@dbserver1.oradbpro.com (TNS V1-V3)
```

Top Sessions in Oracle Enterprise Manager may be used to identify database sessions with high resource consumption. Once you know `V$SESSION.SID`, you may use either `V$PROCESS.PID` with `SETORAPID` or `V$PROCESS.SPID` with `SETOSPID`. The next example is from a Windows system:

```
SQL> ORADEBUG SETOSPID 4172
Oracle pid: 16, Windows thread id: 4172, image: ORACLE.EXE (SHAD)
SQL> ORADEBUG SETORAPID 16
Windows thread id: 4172, image: ORACLE.EXE (SHAD)
```

When trace data collection is complete, switch off extended SQL trace with `ORADEBUG EVENT 10046 TRACE NAME CONTEXT OFF`.

ORADEBUG IPC

`ORADEBUG IPC` may be used to find out which UNIX shared memory segment(s) an ORACLE instance uses. On platforms where ORACLE instances use semaphores for synchronization[1], information on semaphores is also included. RAC instances write information on the interconnect IP address and protocol to the trace file. This is particularly useful to verify the interconnect addresses in Oracle9*i*, since releases prior to Oracle10*g* do not write this information to the alert log.

On UNIX systems, each shared memory segment and semaphore set has a unique identifier. These identifiers are listed by the command `ipcs`. Use `ipcs -mb` to list shared memory segments along with the owner and size:

```
$ ipcs -mb
```

---

1. On AIX the postwait kernel extension is used instead of semaphores.

```
IPC status from /dev/mem as of Mon Nov 19 15:30:49 MEZ 2007
T       ID     KEY         MODE        OWNER     GROUP     SEGSZ
Shared Memory:
m        6 0x00006000 --rw-rw-rw-     root    system    1928456
m        7 0xc3f37a04 --rw-r-----     oracle     dba 5050753024
m        8 0x0d000b59 --rw-rw-rw-     root    system       1440
```

The following section shows how to dump IPC information. The trace file is from a RAC instance. Thus it contains not only shared memory identifiers, but also information on the cluster interconnect, which is marked by the string "SSKGXPT" in both Oracle9*i* and Oracle10*g*.

```
$ sqlplus "/ as sysdba"
Connected to:
Oracle9i Enterprise Edition Release 9.2.0.8.0 - 64bit Production
With the Real Application Clusters option
SQL> ORADEBUG SETMYPID
Statement processed.
SQL> ORADEBUG IPC
Information written to trace file.
SQL> ORADEBUG TRACEFILE_NAME
/var/opt/oracle/udump/fhs91_ora_1065152.trc
```

The trace file excerpts below include the relevant sections. Note how the shared memory identifier 7 matches the output of the command ipcs depicted earlier:

```
Shared Memory:
ID              KEY
7               0xc3f37a04
```

The trace file section below indicates that the IP address 172.16.0.1 is used as the RAC interconnect address. The interconnect protocol is UDP (user datagram protocol):

```
SSKGXPT 0x1028d484 flags SSKGXPT_READPENDING active network 0
info for network 0
        socket no 8     IP 172.16.0.1       UDP 52608
```

ORADEBUG may also be used with ASM instances. Below is an example that illustrates the use of semaphores by an ASM instance:

```
$ env ORACLE_SID=+ASM1 sqlplus / as sysdba
SQL> ORADEBUG SETMYPID
Statement processed.
SQL> ORADEBUG IPC
Information written to trace file.
SQL> ORADEBUG TRACEFILE_NAME
/opt/oracle/obase/admin/+ASM/udump/+asm1_ora_19685.trc
SQL> !grep -A 1 "Semaphore List" /opt/oracle/obase/admin/+ASM/udump/+asm1_ora_19685.trc
Semaphore List=
884736
$ ipcs -s
------ Semaphore Arrays --------
key         semid       owner     perms     nsems
0x2c13c9dc 884736      oracle     640      44
0xcbcd5e70 1146881     oracle     640      154
```

The smaller semaphore set with identifier 884736 was used by an ASM instance, whereas the larger set with 154 semaphores was used by an RDBMS instance[1].

In a situation where one out of several instances on a system has failed without cleaning up shared memory and/or semaphores, ORADEBUG IPC is the ideal tool to gather the information required to perform cleanup with the command ipcrm. The UNIX IPC identifiers reproduced in bold in the above examples may be used to remove shared memory

---

1. The number of semaphores allocated depends on the initialization parameter PROCESSES, which had the values 40 and 150 in the ASM and RDBMS instances, respectively.

segments and semaphore sets with `ipcrm`. IPC identifiers are not reused when an ORACLE instance is shut down and restarted. When resources on a machine are scarce, it may happen that an ORACLE instance cannot be started due to resources allocated to stale shared memory segments or semaphore sets left behind by a crashed instance. Under these circumstances, the removal of both types of IPC structures with `ipcrm` is the solution.

ORADEBUG SHORT_STACK

A program call stack represents how routines in a program call each other. If a program hangs, the program call stack shows in which routine it hangs. There are two ways of obtaining a program call stack with ORADEBUG:

- the ERRORSTACK diagnostic dump
- the SHORT_STACK command

The ERRORSTACK dump results in a large trace file. The command SHORT_STACK is well suited to quickly determine which routine is currently executed by a server process. The output of this command is sent to a terminal window and not to a trace file. It is available in Oracle10g and subsequent releases. Below is an example:

```
SQL> ORADEBUG SETOSPID 14807
Oracle pid: 34, Unix process pid: 14807, image: oracleDZAV024@l012r065
SQL> ORADEBUG SHORT_STACK
ksdxfstk()+32<-ksdxcb()+1547<-sspuser()+111<-__funlockfile()+64<-kdsgrp()+283<-
kdsfbr()+228<-qertbFetchByRowID()+889<-qergiFetch()+315<-qergiFetch()+315<-
qernsFetch()+603<-qerseFetch()+158<-subex1()+176<-subsr3()+195<-evaopn2()+4188<-
expepr..7()+470<-expeal()+82<-qerflFetchOutside()+158<-rwsfcd()+88<-insfch()+496<-
insdrv()+592<-inscovexe()+404<-insExecStmtExecIniEngine()+85<-insexe()+343<-
opiexe()+9038<-opipls()+2107<-opiodr()+984<-rpidrus()+198<-skgmstack()+158<-
rpidru()+116<-rpiswu2()+420<-rpidrv()+1519<-psddr0()+438<-psdnal()+339<-
pevm_EXIM()+216<-pfrinstr_EXIM()+53<-pfrrun_no_tool()+65<-pfrrun()+906<-
plsql_run()+841<-peicnt()+298<-kkxexe()+504<-opiexe()+9038<-opipls()+2107<-
opiodr()+984<-rpidrus()+198<-skgmstack()+158<-rpidru()+116<-rpiswu2()+420<-
rpidrv()+1519<-psddr0()+438<-psdnal()+339<-pevm_EXIM()+216<-pfrinstr_EXIM()+53<-
pfrrun_no_tool()+65<-pfrrun()+906<-plsql_run()+841<-peicnt()+298<-kkxexe()+504<-
opiexe()+9038<-kpoal8()+2280<-opiodr()+984<-ttcpip()+1235<-opitsk()+1298<-
opiino()+1028<-opiodr()+984<-opidrv()+547<-sou2o()+114<-opimai_real()+163<-
main()+116<-__libc_start_main()+234<-_start()+42
```

The current routine is at the top of the output. Of course, dumping the call stack affects the call stack itself. Presumably `ksdxcb` is a debug callback function for performing a stack dump. I assume that the routine `kdsgrp` was executed when the command SHORT_STACK was received by the attached process. The names of the routines may be used as search keywords on the Metalink support platform.

Diagnostic Dumps

Oracle9i Release 2 supports 85 different diagnostic dumps, Oracle10g supports 146, and Oracle11g 165. Due to the large amount of dumps, it's impossible to cover more than a few. To list the dump names, run ORADEBUG DUMPLIST.

CONTROLF

This option is for dumping the control file(s) at different levels of detail. Here's an example of a level 1 dump:

```
Received ORADEBUG command 'DUMP CONTROLF 1' from process Windows thread id: 3580,
image:
DUMP OF CONTROL FILES, Seq # 545 = 0x221
 V10 STYLE FILE HEADER:
        Compatibility Vsn = 169869568=0xa200100
        Db ID=1156831202=0x44f3d7e2, Db Name='ORCL'
        Activation ID=0=0x0
        Control Seq=545=0x221, File size=430=0x1ae
        File Number=0, Blksiz=16384, File Type=1 CONTROL
```

EVENTS

The EVENTS dump is not a true diagnostic dump. It merely writes the enabled events to a trace file. If you are uncertain which events are active in a session, process, or instance, this is the right way to find out. Below is an example:

```
SQL> ALTER SESSION SET EVENTS '10046 trace name context forever, level 8';
Session altered.
SQL> ALTER SESSION SET EVENTS '4031 trace name heapdump level 3';
Session altered.
SQL> ORADEBUG SETMYPID
Statement processed.
SQL> ORADEBUG DUMP EVENTS 1
Statement processed.
SQL> ORADEBUG TRACEFILE_NAME
/opt/oracle/obase/admin/TEN/udump/ten1_ora_20206.trc
```

Sample trace file contents generated by ORADEBUG DUMP EVENTS are below:

```
Dump event group for level SESSION
TC Addr  Evt#(b10)   Action   TR Addr     Arm     Life
B72DB4F4 4031        1        b72db560 0 0
         TR Name              TR level  TR address    TR arm     TR life    TR type
         HEAPDUMP                3 0           1          2 -1221853072
B72DB3F8 10046       1        b72db464 0 0
         TR Name              TR level  TR address    TR arm     TR life    TR type
         CONTEXT                8 0          -1          2 -1221853072
```

The levels supported by the EVENTS dump are listed in Table 77 along with the method for setting an event at the respective level. Note that the scope of events set with ORADEBUG EVENT is the process, which was previously attached with ORADEBUG SETORAPID or a similar command.

Table 77: ORADEBUG DUMP EVENTS Levels and Scope

Level	Event Scope	Command Used
1	Session	ALTER SESSION, DBMS_SYSTEM.SET_EV
2	Process	ORADEBUG EVENT
4	Instance	ALTER SYSTEM

ERRORSTACK

As stated earlier, a program call stack may be obtained with the ERRORSTACK diagnostic dump. Depending on the dump level, an ERRORSTACK dump contains more information than merely a call stack. Table 78 gives an overview of the trace file sections for dump levels 1, 2, and 3. The information applies to Oracle10g. Trace file contents vary from release to release.

Table 78: ERRORSTACK Trace File Contents

Trace File Sections	Level 1	Level 2	Level 3
Current SQL statement	yes	yes	yes
Call stack trace	yes	yes	yes
Process state (includes session wait history)	no	yes	yes
Enabled events at session and instance level	no	no	yes
Cursor dump	no	no	yes

Below is an example of an ERRORSTACK dump:

```
SQL> ORADEBUG SETOSPID 6524
Oracle pid: 16, Unix process pid: 6524, image: oracleTEN1@dbserver1.oradbpro.com
SQL> ORADEBUG DUMP ERRORSTACK 1
Statement processed.
```

```
SQL> ORADEBUG TRACEFILE_NAME
/opt/oracle/obase/admin/TEN/udump/ten1_ora_6524.trc
SQL> !less /opt/oracle/obase/admin/TEN/udump/ten1_ora_6524.trc
Received ORADEBUG command 'DUMP ERRORSTACK 1' from process Unix process pid: 6518,
image:
*** 2007-09-09 12:36:02.525
ksedmp: internal or fatal error
Current SQL statement for this session:
SELECT sys_context('userenv', 'sessionid'),sys_context('userenv',
'client_identifier'),sys_context
('userenv', 'client_info'),sys_context('userenv', 'host'), /* corresponds to
v$session.machine */s
ys_context('userenv', 'os_user'), /* corresponds to v$session.osuser */
sys_context('userenv', 'ter
minal')FROM dual
----- Call Stack Trace -----
calling              call      entry                argument values in hex
location             type      point                (? means dubious value)
-------------------  --------  -------------------  ---------------------------
ksedst()+27          call      ksedst1()            1 ? 1 ?
ksedmp()+557         call      ksedst()             1 ? 2A120F04 ? 76010B ?
                                                    2A11FC8E ? 0 ? BFFFB638 ?
ksdxfdmp()+1382      call      0C94496E             1 ? 83CD95B ? C816D60 ?
                                                    BFFFB7DC ? 83E55FD ?
                                                    2EAF9940 ?
ksdxcb()+1321        call      00000000             BFFFBAE8 ? 11 ? 3 ?
                                                    BFFFBA48 ? BFFFBA98 ?
sspuser()+102        call      00000000             1 ? 2000 ? 0 ? 0 ? 0 ? 0 ?
0071A7A0             signal    00000000             C ? BFFFBF70 ? BFFFBFF0 ?
nttrd()+155          call      snttread()           D ? C86BEC6 ? 810 ? 0 ?
...
```

At the time when the stack was dumped, the server process was waiting for a network packet from the client in the routine nttrd. The wait event *SQL*Net message from client* in V$SESSION confirms this:

```
SQL> SELECT p.spid, s.event, s.state
FROM v$session s, v$process p
WHERE s.username='NDEBES'
AND s.paddr=p.addr;
SPID         EVENT                          STATE
-----------  -----------------------------  -------
6524         SQL*Net message from client WAITING
```

The routine nttrd waited for the UNIX system call read to return. Using the system call tracing utility strace reveals that the read system call was done against file descriptor 13, which represents a socket connection between the traced dedicated server process and the client:

```
$ strace -p 6524
Process 6524 attached - interrupt to quit
read(13, <unfinished ...>
Process 6524 detached
$ ls -l /proc/6524/fd/13
lrwx------  1 oracle oinstall 64 Sep  9 13:08 /proc/6524/fd/13 -> socket:[4514905]
```

HANGANALYZE

The command HANGANALYZE performs a hang analysis dump. Such dumps are taken to diagnose database hanging issues. Please refer to the very extensive Metalink note 61552.1 for more information on this topic. Below is an example of a level 1 hang analysis dump. The scenario was as follows:

- Session 141 (V$SESSION.SID=141) executed LOCK TABLE IN EXCLUSIVE MODE on a table.
- Session 147 tried to insert into the same table.

- The INSERT statement executed by session 147 had to wait for session 141 to release the table lock.

The resulting hang analysis dump is below. Chains list waiting sessions. Chains that contain more than a single session indicate that the session at the head of the chain (on the left) is blocking other sessions in the same chain.

```
==============
HANG ANALYSIS:
==============
Open chains found:
Chain 1 : <cnode/sid/sess_srno/ospid/wait_event> :
    <0/141/47/3580/No Wait> -- <0/147/518/6064/enq: TM - contention>
Other chains found:
Chain 2 : <cnode/sid/sess_srno/ospid/wait_event> :
    <0/145/117/5244/jobq slave wait>
Chain 3 : <cnode/sid/sess_srno/ospid/wait_event> :
    <0/150/38/440/Streams AQ: qmn slave idle wait>
Chain 4 : <cnode/sid/sess_srno/ospid/wait_event> :
    <0/152/1/5440/Streams AQ: waiting for time man>
Chain 5 : <cnode/sid/sess_srno/ospid/wait_event> :
    <0/154/1/4584/Streams AQ: qmn coordinator idle>
Extra information that will be dumped at higher levels:
[level  4] :   1 node dumps -- [REMOTE_WT] [LEAF] [LEAF_NW]
[level  5] :   4 node dumps -- [SINGLE_NODE] [SINGLE_NODE_NW] [IGN_DMP]
[level  6] :   1 node dumps -- [NLEAF]
[level 10] :  11 node dumps -- [IGN]
```

MODIFIED_PARAMETERS

This dump records any initialization parameters that were modified with ALTER SESSION or ALTER SYSTEM in a trace file. Level 1 is sufficient. Higher levels do not produce more detailed output. In the example below, the initialization parameters PGA_AGGREGATE_TARGET and SKIP_UNUSABLE_INDEXES are modified. Thus, these parameters and their new values appear in the MODIFIED_PARAMETERS dump.

```
SQL> ALTER SYSTEM SET pga_aggregate_target=512m;
System altered.
SQL> ALTER SESSION SET skip_unusable_indexes=true;
System altered.
SQL> ORADEBUG DUMP MODIFIED_PARAMETERS 1
Statement processed.
```

The trace file contains an entry for each modified parameter:

```
Received ORADEBUG command 'DUMP MODIFIED_PARAMETERS 1' from process Windows thread id:
3580, image:
DYNAMICALLY MODIFIED PARAMETERS:
  pga_aggregate_target    = 536870912
  skip_unusable_indexes   = TRUE
```

PROCSTAT and Process–Level Operating System Statistics

Process level operating system statistics may be dumped to a trace file with the command ORADEBUG PROCSTAT. CPU usage is reported at a more granular level than by the statistic "CPU used by this session" in V$SESSTAT. Below is an example:

```
SQL> ORADEBUG PROCSTAT
SQL> ORADEBUG TRACEFILE_NAME
/opt/oracle/obase/admin/TEN/udump/ten1_ora_8739.trc
SQL> !cat /opt/oracle/obase/admin/TEN/udump/ten1_ora_8739.trc
----- Dump of Process Statistics -----
User time used = 500
System time used = 1750
...
Page reclaims = 66357
Page faults = 1
```

```
...
Voluntary context switches = 2775
Involuntary context switches = 65892
```

Lessons Learned

The ORADEBUG command in SQL*Plus is an indispensable tool for troubleshooting and diagnosing performance problems. The basic workflow consists of attaching to a process, setting an event or performing a diagnostic dump, retrieving the trace file name, and detaching. ORADEBUG provides access to information which is not available by any other means. The events set in a process or session are an example of this. This chapter covered some of the most useful and commonly used ORADEBUG commands. Many more features, such as ORADEBUG LKDEBUG for invoking the global enqueue service debugger in a RAC environment, exist.

Part XII

Appendixes

Appendix A

Glossary

Application instrumentation

Instrumentation is the ability of software to measure its own performance. An instrumented ORACLE application passes module, action, and client identifier to the DBMS, allowing a DBA to collect metrics based on this information.

Concurrency

Concurrency is a property of computer systems, which have the capability to execute multiple processes at the same time. Concurrent processes may interact with each other through interprocess communication.

Connect string

A connect string consists of a user name, password, and optionally a *Net service name* or other specification for contacting an Oracle Net Services TNS Listener, e.g. ndebes/secret@ten.oradbpro.com.

Connection pool

A *connection pool* is a set of database connections, which is usually maintained by an application server. Connections to an ORACLE instance are opened when the connection pool is initialized and remain open for the lifetime of the connection pool. Clients of

the connection pool, e.g. Java Beans, request a connection, run some SQL statements, and return the connection to the pool. Connection pooling removes the overhead of establishing a new database session for each request.

Consistent read

A *consistent read* is a snapshot of data in the database based on the System Change Number, which was current at the point in time when a SQL statement was initiated. If the data accessed by the query has changed since the cursor was opened, the old values will be reconstructed from undo segments in an undo tablespace.

Cost–based SQL optimizer (CBO)

The *cost–based SQL optimizer* is a component of an ORACLE DBMS, which scrutinizes SQL statements and searches for an optimal execution plan. It calculates a cost for feasible plans and chooses the plan with the lowest cost.

Current read

Read access to a block with current data, as opposed to a consistent read, which may not retrieve the most current data.

Cursor

Strictly speaking, a *cursor* is a control structure for the iterative traversal of rows in a query result set. In ORACLE server parlance, cursors are used to execute any SQL or PL/SQL statement.

Data Definition Language (DDL)

SQL statements that create database objects such as tables and indexes.

Database

A *database* is a structured collection of records or data that is stored on a computer system, such that a program (*Database Management System*) can consult it to answer queries. An ORACLE database consists of control file(s), redo log files, and data files.

Database Management System (DBMS)

A DBMS is a set of software programs that controls the storage, management, and retrieval of data in a *database*.

Data Manipulation Language (DML)

SQL statements that retrieve and modify database data. DML statements include SELECT, INSERT, MERGE, UPDATE, and DELETE.

Database call

A database call is a *parse*, *execute*, or *fetch* operation that an ORACLE server process performs for servicing a request from a database client.

Dynamic performance view (V$ fixed view)

Views that for the most part expose the inner workings of an ORACLE DBMS and provide access to performance metrics. The names of these views start with V$. V$ fixed views are not associated with segments in a database. Many are based on memory structures in the SGA and are thus "dynamic". Others are based on control file record sections.

End to end metrics

The term end to end metrics refers to the ability of the ORACLE DBMS to provide metrics based on *application instrumentation*.

Enqueue

Enqueues are a locking mechanism that queues up requestors and services them in a first–in–first–out (FIFO) order. Enqueues may be acquired in different modes, such as exclusive and shared.

Execute

Execution of a SQL statement or PL/SQL block. Performs the operation coded by a DDL or DML statement. For SELECT statements, places the cursor on the first row of the result set.

Fetch

Data retrieval by a SELECT statement.

Idle wait

Interval of time during which no request is made upon an ORACLE server process. As the user accumulates *think time*, the server accumulates idle wait time.

Instance (a.k.a. DBMS instance)

Collection of processes and memory structures that implement the ORACLE database server by running the program $ORACLE_HOME/bin/oracle on UNIX or %ORACLE_HOME%\bin\oracle.exe on Windows.

Instance service name

Instance service names are the service names an instance registers with one or more TNS Listeners. They are set with the initialization parameter SERVICE_NAMES. In Oracle10g, the package DBMS_SERVICE may be used to add instance services. The SERVICE_NAME setting in the body of a *Net service name* definition references an instance service name.

Instrumentation

Program code in some computer language that allows the program to measure itself and to record how much time it spends per program module.

Latch

Synchronization mechanism used by the ORACLE server to implement mutual exclusion for critical sections of program code to keep data structures consistent, by allowing only one process at a time to enter the critical section. Processes consume CPU ("spin"; the undocumented parameter _SPIN_COUNT controls how many times) as they repeatedly attempt to acquire a latch. Unlike *enqueues*, latches do not queue up requestors and have no other modes except exclusive. Latches are implemented with atomic test–and–set machine instructions.

Latency

Latency is a time delay between the moment something is initiated and the moment effects of the initiation become observable. The meaning of the word is highly context dependent. The term is frequently used in the context of performance tuning. For example, unnecessary round–trips between database server and client impose a performance penalty due to network latency.

Lock

See *enqueue*

Logical read

Reading an ORACLE block cached in the buffer cache within the System Global Area is called a logical read.

Net service name

A *Net service name* is defined in the configuration file tnsnames.ora or a directory service such as LDAP. Net service names are used in *connect strings* and with the command tnsping.

Paging

Writes of portions of virtual memory to disk by the operating system are called *paging*. Paging occurs when free physical memory (RAM) becomes scarce or is exhausted. Paging allows operating systems to execute programs which demand more virtual memory than RAM installed in a system.

Parse

Syntactical and semantic analysis of SQL statements or PL/SQL blocks. Also includes verification of applicable privileges. Each statement or block parsed is associated with a *cursor*.

Performance

Performance of a computer or software system is the amount of useful work performed compared to the time and resources used. Good performance implies short response times and adequate resource usage, whereas bad performance is associated with unacceptable *response time* and an overly high demand on resources.

Physical read

Request to the operating system by some process of an ORACLE instance to read one or more blocks from disk.

Physical write

Request to the operating system by some process of an ORACLE instance to write one or more blocks to disk. Physical writes occur for example when the database writer process (DBW*n*) writes modified blocks in the buffer cache to disk. Other examples are writes to sort or LOB segments by dedicated or shared server processes.

Polling

Active request for a resource in a tight loop. *Polling* is often responsible for large amounts of wasted CPU time. Whenever possible, processes should be *sleeping* while waiting for a resource instead of actively polling for a resource's availability.

POSIX

POSIX (Portable Operating System Interface) is the collective name of a family of related standards, which define the application programming interface (API) for software compatible with variants of the UNIX operating system.

Recursive SQL

SQL statements the ORACLE DBMS executes against the data dictionary as user SYS in order to service a request from a database client. See also *user level SQL*.

Resource profile

An apportionment of response time often presented in tabular form. Each row of a tabular *resource profile* contains a single contributor to response time, e.g. CPU consumption or a *wait event*. Ideally, the following columns are included: contributor name, percentage of response time, contribution to response time in seconds, number of times the contributor was called upon, and average time consumed by a call upon the contributor. The table should be sorted by percentage of contribution to response time in descending order.

Response time

The wall clock time an electronic system needs to fulfill a request by a user. Response time consists of CPU consumption and waiting.

Rule based SQL optimizer (RBO)

The *rule based SQL optimizer* was the simpler predecessor of the more advanced *cost–based SQL optimizer* (CBO). The RBO generated execution plans based on a fixed set of rules. It knew nothing about table sizes and column selectivities. The RBO is obsolete since the release of Oracle10*g*.

SQL (Structured Query Language)

SQL is a computer language designed for the retrieval and management of data in relational *database management systems*. Among its features are creation, modification, and removal of database schema objects (DDL), data manipulation (DML), and database object access control management.

SQL trace file, extended

An *extended SQL trace file* contains a log of the actions of one or more database clients. Actions include *parse*, *execute*, and *fetch*. The trace levels 1, 4, 8 and 12 control the amount of detail in SQL trace files.

Scalability

Scalability is a desirable property of a system, network, or application program, which indicates its ability to either handle growing workloads in a graceful manner, or to be readily enlarged.

Sleeping

Processes may be put to sleep when a requested resource is not available. Sleeping processes do not consume CPU. Thus sleeping is preferred over *polling*.

Swapping

Transfer of process virtual memory from *RAM* to disk.

System Global Area (SGA)

Memory structure containing the database buffer cache, the shared pool, java pool, large pool, Streams pool and the log buffer. On UNIX, the SGA resides in shared memory.

System Change Number

Each modification of data in an ORACLE database is stamped with a monotonically increasing number, the *System Change Number*. Backup, recovery, and consistent read are implemented based on the System Change Number.

System call

A routine at the interface between an operating system and user level programs, which run under control of the operating system. System calls execute in kernel mode, whereas application code executes in user mode. Access to devices, such as disks and network adapters, is implemented with system calls. UNIX system calls are standardized by the *POSIX* standard.

Random access memory (RAM)

Random access memory is the volatile main memory of a computer system.

Real Application Clusters (RAC)

Multi–instance variant of the ORACLE DBMS, which runs on clustered hardware to achieve scalability and high availability. RAC requires cluster software, such as Oracle Clusterware, HP–UX ServiceGuard, IBM HACMP, Veritas Cluster, Sun Cluster, or HP TruCluster.

Think time

Think time is a term from the fields of load testing and benchmarking. Humans working with an electronic information service require a certain time to assimilate information returned by the service. The interval between the end of the previous request on the server and the beginning of the next request from the user is called think time, since the human user spends that interval of time thinking about what to do next.

User level SQL

SQL statements executed directly by a database user (non–recursive SQL).

Wait event

Wait events are used for response time accounting of database sessions. Through the *wait interface* or SQL trace files, wait events externalize what a database session has been waiting on and how much wait time it has accumulated.

Wait interface

The term *wait interface* is used to refer to a set of V$ fixed views, which expose wait events that database clients are waiting for. These V$ views cover database sessions that are currently waiting as well as aggregated data on past waits. The wait interface may be used to diagnose performance problems.

X$ fixed tables

Undocumented internal structures of the ORACLE DBMS. V$ fixed views are based on X$ fixed tables. X$ fixed tables are often called just X$ tables, but they are not tables in the usual sense of the word, since they do not map to segments in a tablespace.

Appendix B

Enabling and Disabling DBMS Options

ORACLE DBMS options, which were installed by the Universal Installer (OUI) may subsequently be disabled by running certain make commands. This merely applies to UNIX systems and is a convenient way to dispel the requirement to rerun OUI, when additional functionality such as partitioned tables and indexes are needed some time after the initial installation. The idea is to install all the options with OUI and to subsequently disable those options which were not licensed. The make commands are also useful for disabling options which were not chosen during the installation process, but were nonetheless installed by OUI due to a bug. The make commands must be run with $ORACLE_HOME/rdbms/lib as the current directory and always take on the form:

```
make -f ins_rdbms.mk target1 … [ targetN ] ioracle
```

The placeholders *target1* and *targetN* are make targets from Table 79.

Table 79: Make Targets for Enabling and Disabling DBMS Options

DBMS Option	*On Switch*	*Off Switch*
Data Mining	dm_on	dm_off
Data Mining Scoring Engine	dmse_on	dmse_off
Database Vault	dv_on	dv_off
Label Security	lbac_on	lbac_off
OLAP	olap_on	olap_off

Table 79: Make Targets for Enabling and Disabling DBMS Options

DBMS Option	On Switch	Off Switch
Partitioning	part_on	part_off
Real Application Clusters	rac_on	rac_off
Spatial	sdo_on	sdo_off

Below is an example that removes the Partitioning Option and Real Application Clusters:

```
$ make -f ins_rdbms.mk part_off rac_off ioracle
```

Any DBMS instances using an ORACLE_HOME thus modified, must be shut down prior to executing make.

Appendix C

Bibliography

References

[Bunc 2000] Bunce, Tim; Carty Alistair, *Programming the Perl DBI*, O'Reilly, 2000, http://www.oreilly.com

[CPAN] Comprehensive Perl Archive Network, http://www.cpan.org

[EnGo 2004] Ensor, Dave; Gorman, Tim; Hailey, Kyle; Kolk Anjo; Lewis, Jonathan; McDonald, Connor; Millsap, Cary; Morle, James; Mogens, Nørgaard; Ruthven, David, *Oracle Insights: Tales of the Oak Table*, Apress, 2004, http://www.apress.com

[Kyte 2005] Kyte, Thomas, *Expert Oracle Database Architecture: 9i and 10g Programming Techniques and Solutions*, Apress, 2005, http://www.apress.com

[Lewi 2005] Lewis, Jonathan, *Cost–Based Oracle Fundamentals*, Apress, 2005, http://www.apress.com

[MiHo 2003] Millsap, Cary; Holt, Jeff, *Optimizing Oracle Performance*, O'Reilly, 2003, http://www.oreilly.com

[OJ10 2005] *Oracle Database 10g Release 2 (10.2.0.3) JDBC Drivers JavaDoc*, Oracle Corp., http://download.oracle.com/otn/utilities_drivers/jdbc/10201/javadoc.zip

[OJ92 2002] *Oracle9i 9.2.0.8 JDBC Drivers JavaDoc*, Oracle Corp., http://download.oracle.com/otn/utilities_drivers/jdbc/9205/javadoc.tar

[OL92 2002] *Oracle9i Release 2 Documentation Library*, Oracle Corp., 2002, http://www.oracle.com/pls/db92/db92.homepage

[OL10 2005] *Oracle10g Release 2 Documentation Library*, Oracle Corp., 2005, http://otn.oracle.com

[OL11 2007] *Oracle11g Release 1 Documentation Library*, Oracle Corp., 2007, http://otn.oracle.com

[ShDe 2004] Shee, Richmond; Deshpande, Kirtikumar; Gopalakrishnan, K, *Oracle Wait Interface: A Practical Guide to Performance Diagnostics and Tuning*, McGraw–Hill/Osborne, 2004, http://www.oraclepress.com

[Sol8 2000] *Solaris 8 Reference Manual Collection*, Sun Microsystems, Inc., 2000, http://docs.sun.com

[SoTu 2007] *Solaris Tunable Parameters Reference Manual*, Sun Microsystems, Inc., 2007, http://docs.sun.com

[VaDe 2001] Vaidyanatha, Gaja Krishna; Deshpande, Kirtikumar; Kostelac, John A., *Oracle Performance Tuning 101*, McGraw–Hill Osborne Media, 2001, http://www.oraclepress.com

[WaCh 2000] Wall, Larry; Christiansen Tom; Orwant, John, *Programming Perl*, O'Reilly, 2000, http://www.oreilly.com

Index

Symbols

_ALLOW_RESETLOGS_CORRUPTION 38
_ASM_ALLOW_ONLY_RAW_DISKS 39
_ASM_AUSIZE 40, 43
_ASM_STRIPESIZE 40
_ASM_STRIPEWIDTH 40, 112
_OFFLINE_ROLLBACK_SEGMENTS 38
_OPTIM_PEEK_USER_BINDS 225
_PGA_MAX_SIZE 29
_SMM_MAX_SIZE 29
_SMM_PX_MAX_SIZE 30
_SPIN_COUNT 386
_TRACE_FILES_PUBLIC 38

A

abstract data type 130
action
    and DBMS_MONITOR 211
    and instrumentation 119, 208
    instrumentation and TAF 339
Active Session History 252
Active Workload Repository 226, 251, 274, 291

adb 177
address resolution protocol 332
Advanced Queuing 123, 130
Advanced Replication 130
Advanced Security Option 85
AIX
    and Perl 189
alert log
    parsing by monitoring tools 172
allocation unit
    and ASM 109
ALTER SESSION SET EVENTS 117
ALTER SYSTEM DISCONNECT SESSION 337
ALTER SYSTEM KILL SESSION 338
ALTER SYSTEM REGISTER xiv
ALTER SYSTEM SET EVENTS 117
ANALYZE 277
ANALYZE INDEX 55
ANALYZE TABLE 55
application instrumentation 243
application server 244
arp
    UNIX command 332

ARP cache 332
arping
    UNIX command 332
array insert 103
ARRAYSIZE
    in SQL*Plus 339
ASM 377
    and Clusterware 348
ASM_DISKSTRING 41
assoc
    Windows command 195
AUD$ 21
AUDIT_ACTIONS 22
AUDIT_FILE_DEST 20
AUDIT_SYSLOG_LEVEL 19
AUDIT_TRAIL 19, 128
auditing 20, 128, 242
AutoCommit
    Perl DBI attribute 201
automatic control file backup 145
Automatic Database Diagnostic Monitor 252
Automatic PGA Memory Management 23
Automatic Shared Memory Management 23
Automatic Storage Management 109
automatic undo management 48
AUTOTRACE
    in SQL*Plus 27
AUX_STATS$ 67

B

BACKGROUND_DUMP_DEST
    and failed jobs 153
backup and recovery 364
backup metadata 144
batch jobs
    running without using a password 201
bc
    UNIX command 134
bequeath protocol adapter xiv, 196
bind data type mismatch 233
bind variable
    use in SQL*Plus 133
bind variable peeking 71, 225
bind variables
    and avoiding parse overhead 202
    and BINDS entry in SQL trace files 233
    and cursor misses 227
    and EXPLAIN PLAN 237
    and statement reuse 225
    tracing with DBMS_SYSTEM 175
bind_columns
    Perl DBI command 205

bind_param_inout
    Perl DBI command 205
BINDS
    SQL trace file entry 234
block corruption
    creating with dd 369
BLOCKRECOVER
    RMAN command 370
boot IP addresses 317
bstat/estat 251
buffer busy waits
    wait event 278
Bunce, Tim 188

C

C programming language 89, 319
call stack 177
call stack trace 379, 380
callback function 339
cardinality
    in execution plan 81
CASE WHEN
    SQL CASE statement 49
CBO 66
CBO hint 68
client identifier
    and DBMS_MONITOR 211
    and instrumentation 119, 208
    instrumentation and TAF 339
cluster database service 343
Cluster Group Services 351
CLUSTER_DATABASE 349
clustering factor 77
Clusterware 349
    setup for ASM 40
collection type 25
COMMIT 229
compulsive tuning disorder 100
connect
    DBI call 196
connect string xiv
CONNECT_DATA xiv
connection pool 244
contention 269
CONTROLF
    ORADEBUG dump 378
CONTROLFILE_RECORD_KEEPTIME 144
COPY DATAFILE
    RMAN command 90
core file 177
corruption 367
    creating 369
cost based optimizer 66

CPU Usage 268
CPUSPEED 67
CPUSPEEDNW 67
CREATE DATABASE 47
CREATE USER
    unencrypted password 86
crsctl 40
cursor dump 379
CV_$SESSION_WAIT 107
Cygwin 157, 258, 369

D

data dictionary 47
Data Pump Export 122
Data Pump Import 122
data warehousing
    and bind variables 225
database call 225
database link
    and DX enqueue 229
    creating in foreign schema 124
DB CPU
    time model statistic 269
db file sequential read
    wait event 278
DB Time
    time model statistic 269
DB time
    statistic 308
DB_BLOCK_SIZE 23, 113
DB_FILE_MULTIBLOCK_READ_COUNT 67
DBA group 200
DBA_AUDIT_OBJECT 21
DBA_AUDIT_SESSION 22
DBA_AUDIT_STATEMENT 21
DBA_ENABLED_AGGREGATIONS 202, 212
DBA_ENABLED_TRACES 202, 212
DBA_EXTENTS 109
DBA_HIST_SQLSTAT 275
DBA_HIST_SQLTEXT 275
DBA_LOBS 48
DBA_RSRC_GROUP_MAPPINGS 212
DBA_SCHEDULER_JOB_RUN_DETAILS 161
DBA_SERVICES xiv
DBA_VIEWS 90
DBD::Oracle 187
DBI_DSN 27, 199
DBI_PASS 27, 199
DBI_USER 27, 199
DBMS_AQ 130
DBMS_AQADM 131
DBMS_BACKUP_RESTORE 143
DBMS_IJOB 150

DBMS_JOB 150
DBMS_LOB 275
DBMS_LOCK 138, 288
DBMS_LOCK.SLEEP 246
DBMS_METADATA 300
DBMS_MONITOR 118, 173, 211, 232, 243
    and ora_module_name Perl DBI attribute 202
    and parallel execution 247
DBMS_PIPE 364
DBMS_PIPE.PACK_MESSAGE 365
DBMS_PIPE.SEND_MESSAGE 365
DBMS_RANDOM 25
DBMS_ROWID 112
DBMS_SCHEDULER 156, 365
DBMS_SERVICE xiv, 337, 343
DBMS_SESSION 117, 244
DBMS_SESSION.SET_ROLE 85
    and TAF 339
DBMS_SQL 225
DBMS_STATS 66, 277, 301
DBMS_SUPPORT 118, 167, 171
DBMS_SYSTEM 118, 167, 246, 269, 375
DBMS_UTILITY 174, 205
DBMS_UTILITY.NAME_RESOLVE 179
DBMS_UTILITY.NAME_TOKENIZE 180
DBMS_WORKLOAD_REPOSITORY 252
DBMS_XPLAN 237
DBMS_XPLAN.DISPLAY_AWR 241, 275
DBMS_XPLAN.DISPLAY_CURSOR 68, 82
dd
    UNIX command 41, 111, 369
deadlock 61
debugger 177
dedicated server
    and SQL trace files 215
DELAY
    and TAF 338
diagnostic dumps
    taking with ORADEBUG 378
Diagnostics Pack 251
dictionary cache 48
DLL search path 193
Domain Name Service 328
double counting
    and response time calculation 280
DUMP
    ORADEBUG command 374
DX enqueue 229
DYLD_LIBRARY_PATH 190
dynamic linker 189
dynamic sampling 78

E

effective table selectivity 78
ENABLE=BROKEN
    in tnsnames.ora 330
enq: UL - contention
    wait event 139
enqueue 134
    wait event 278
enqueue name
    internal representation 134
enqueue wait 232
Enterprise Manager 172
env
    UNIX command 194
environment variables
    and DBMS_SYSTEM.GET_ENV 167
    on Windows operating system 192
ERROR
    SQL trace file entry 245
error message file 360
ERRORLEVEL
    Windows variable 157
ERRORSTACK dump 176, 305
ESQLTRCPROF 299
ethernet 332
eval
    Perl command 205
EVENT 119
    ORADEBUG command 374
event
    and ERRORSTACK dump 379
    retrieval with oerr 361
event 10027 61
event 10046 64, 101, 117, 118, 281, 376
event 10053 66, 118
event 10079 84
event 10231 119
EVENTS
    ORADEBUG dump 378
exception
    handling in Perl 205
execution plan 81, 96
execve
    UNIX system call 161
expdp 122
EXPLAIN PLAN
    and SQL statement tuning 237
    risk of using 265
exponential backoff
    and DBMS_JOB 154
externaljob.ora 163

F

failgroup 111
failover cluster
    and job scheduling 157
FAILOVER_MODE 331, 345
    and TAF 338
fetchrow_array
    Perl DBI command 205
file
    UNIX command 189
File::Basename
    Perl module 205
filemon 165
FIXED TABLE FULL
    row source 90
ftype
    Windows command 195
full table scan 77, 230, 238, 269, 275, 300
    and skipping corrupt blocks 119

G

gdb 177
gethostname 333
glance 376
global cache 105
GV$ views 89
GV$ACTIVE_SERVICES 344
GV$SESSION 104

H

HANGANALYZE
    ORADEBUG command 374, 380
hash value
    for SQL statements 225
    of cached SQL in Oracle9i vs. Oracle10g 265
HASH_AREA_SIZE 23, 72
hidden hints 301
high water mark 287
hint
    and CBO 68, 82
    IGNORE_OPTIM_EMBEDDED_HINTS 82
    INDEX 82
    LEADING 82
    OPT_PARAM 75
    OPTIMIZER_FEATURES_ENABLE 82
    USE_NL 82
hosts file 328
Hotsos 172
Hotsos ILO instrumentation library 218
HTML
    generating from Perl POD 193
HW enqueue 287

I

I/O service time peaks 105
I/O wait 261
IGNORE_OPTIM_EMBEDDED_HINTS hint 82
ILO 172
impdp 122
index
    identifying used indexes 264
index fast full scan 77
INDEX hint 82
index rebuild 54
index selectivity 78
INSERT RETURNING 301
instance service name xiii
INSTANCE_TYPE 41
instrumentation 243
inter database call wait event 278
interconnect 319
    IP address and protocol 376
interested transaction list 287
intra database call wait event 278
IOSEEKTIM 67
IOTFRSPEED 67
IP aliasing 318
IP=FIRST 317
IPC
    ORADEBUG command 375, 376
    UNIX interprocess communication 377
IPC adapter 196
IPC protocol
    and TNS Listener configuration 327
ipcrm 378
    UNIX command 377
ipcs
    UNIX command 376

J

JDBC Thin
    and TAF 337
JOB_QUEUE_PROCESSES 150
JOB$
    dictionary base table 150
join order 79

K

keepalive
    and TCP/IP 331
kernel options library 352

L

LAG
    analytic function 267

LARGE_POOL_SIZE 23
Larry Wall 188
latch 98
latch free
    wait event 278
latch wait 232
latency 283
LD_LIBRARY_PATH 190
ldd 189
LEADING hint 82
libclntsh.so 190
LIBPATH 190
library cache 225
linking 348
Linux
    and Perl 189
literals
    in SQL statements 225, 301
LOB segment 48
LOB$ 49
LOCAL_LISTENER xiv, 344
localconfig 40
    Clusterware script 354
Log Miner 130
LOGOFF
    audit action 22
LOGON
    audit action 22
logon trigger 118
lsnrctl xiv
LSNRCTL utility 327

M

Mac OS X 190
make
    UNIX utility 352
materialized view 300
MAX_DUMP_FILE_SIZE 375
MAXCORRUPT
    RMAN setting 365
MAXTHR 67
MBRC 67
medium access control address 332
memory mapping 23
MERITS method 294
messaging service 130
metadata 47
    and DBMS_JOB 154
    on RMAN backups 144
metadata attribute
    of database scheduler 160
mirroring
    and ASM 111

mmap 23
MODIFIED_PARAMETERS
    ORADEBUG command 381
module
    and DBMS_MONITOR 211
    and instrumentation 119, 208
    instrumentation and TAF 339
MONITORING_PROFILE
    and failed logins 128
MREADTIM 67
MSGNO
    RMAN option 371

N

Net service name xiii
NetBackup 144
netstat 319
network mask 318
NLS_DATE_FORMAT
    and RMAN 161
nmon 107, 376
NOCATALOG
    RMAN option 144
noworkload statistics 66, 75
NT security
    and CONNECT AS SYSDBA 200
num_rows_per_hash 252

O

OBJ$ 47
object statistics 66, 76
OCI.DLL 193
OCIAttrSet 243
OCR 40
OCSSD 40
ODBC 197
oerr 228, 328, 360
OERR utility 359
OmniBack 144
OPatch 349
Open Database Connectivity 197
OPER group 200
operating system authentication 200
OPT_PARAM hint 71, 75
optimizer environment 240
optimizer hint 68
optimizer statistics 77
optimizer trace 66, 176
OPTIMIZER_DYNAMIC_SAMPLING 78
OPTIMIZER_FEATURES_ENABLE 72
OPTIMIZER_INDEX_CACHING 72
OPTIMIZER_INDEX_COST_ADJ 72, 238, 275, 300
OPTIMIZER_MODE 72

ORA_DBA
    Windows group 166, 200
ora_module_name
    Perl DBI attribute 202
ORA_OPER
    Windows group 200
ORA-00054 62
ORA-00060 61
ORA-00439 352
ORA-00821 110
ORA-01078 110
ORA-04021 89
ORA-04031 120
ORA-04047 181
ORA-06564 181
ORA-12537 327
ORA-25401 339
ORA-25408 340
ORA-27369 161, 163
ORA-28000 128
ORA-32028 21
Oracle Call Interface 188, 337
    and instrumentation 243
ORACLE client shared library 190
Oracle Net packet dump 85
Oracle Net traffic 85
Oracle Secure Backup 144
Oracle Universal Installer
    and X client 157
ORACLE_HOME
    retrieving setting with DBMS_SYSTEM 167
Oracle11g 26, 47, 104, 109, 117, 187, 209, 216, 223, 226, 233, 236, 283, 317
OracleCSService 40
OracleJobScheduler service 166
ORADEBUG 373
ORADIM utility 41, 166
orapwd 200
OS_AUTHENT_PREFIX 33, 201

P

parallel execution 30, 246
PARALLEL_EXECUTION_MESSAGE_SIZE 300
PARSE 227
PARSE ERROR 228
parse overhead
    avoiding 205
PARSING IN CURSOR 225
    Oracle11g format 226
part_off
    make target 390
Partitioning 300

PASSWORD
    SQL*Plus command 85, 127
password
    and encryption 127
password authentication 33, 200
password encryption 85, 128
password file 199
passwords
    unencrypted in Oracle9*i* LINK$ 91
PATH
    and UNIX environment 188
PATHEXT 195
PCTVERSION 48
Perl DBI 187
Perl documentation library 193
PERL5LIB 189
perldoc 193
PGA_AGGREGATE_TARGET 23, 72
pipe get
    wait event 279
pipelined table function 25, 255
Plain Old Documentation 202
pmap
    UNIX command 23, 24
pmon timer
    wait event 279
POD 202
pod2html 193
POSIX 319
postwait kernel extension 376
predicate 238
prepare
    Perl DBI command 205
PrintError
    Perl DBI attribute 202
private network 319
private pipe 365
process explorer 165
process state dump 379
PROCESSSTATE dump 176
PROCSTAT
    ORADEBUG command 381
program global area 23
proxy authentication 86
prstat 107, 376

Q

query block 68
query block name 82
query coordinator 247
queue 131
queue table 131

R

rac_off
    make target 352, 390
RaiseError
    Perl DBI attribute 202
rdbms ipc message
    wait event 279
Real Application Clusters 105, 319, 348, 376
    and job scheduling 157
Recovery Manager 143, 364
Recovery Manager pipeline interface 364
regmon 165
REMOTE_LISTENER xiv, 344
REMOTE_LOGIN_PASSWORDFILE 200
REMOTE_OS_AUTHENT
    and database security 201
Resource Manager 211
resource manager 207
resource profile 299
response time 208
RESYNC CATALOG 364
RETENTION 48
retransmit time–out
    and TCP/IP 331
RETRIES
    and TAF 338
Revision Control System 258
RMAN_PIPE_IF package 365
role
    protected by password 85
ROLLBACK 229
row cache 48
row pipelining 255
row source 230

S

S.A.M.E. 39
sampling
    of performance diagnostic data 89
SBT interface 143
sdb 177
secure application roles 86
SELECT FOR UPDATE SKIP LOCKED 130
SELECT_CATALOG_ROLE 107, 242
self–tracing capability 64, 118
semaphores 376
SERVERERROR trigger 172
server–side TAF 343
service IP address 317
service name
    and DBMS_MONITOR 211
service time 208

SERVICE_NAME xiv
SERVICE_NAMES 344
session wait history 379
SESSION_EVENT
    ORADEBUG command 374
SET DBID 145
SET ROLE
    and TAF 339
SET TRANSACTION 229
SETMYPID
    ORADEBUG command 374
SETORAPID
    ORADEBUG command 374
SETOSPID
    ORADEBUG command 374
setsockopt 331
SGA sampling tools 89
SGA_TARGET 23
shared library search path 189
shared memory 376
shared pool 48, 225
Shared Server 23, 30
    and SQL trace files 215
SHLIB_PATH 190
SHUTDOWN TRANSACTIONAL 337
SHUTDOWN TRANSACTIONAL LOCAL 343
single instance 352
single–task message
    wait event 279
SITE_SYS 107
SLAVETHR 67
smon timer
    wait event 279
socket 319, 380
Solaris
    and Perl 190
SORT_AREA_SIZE 23, 30, 72, 174
SPFILE
    and RMAN backup 146
    retrieval from ASM storage 110
sql execute elapsed time
    statistic 269
SQL profile 301
SQL trace 265, 274
    and Perl DBI 202
    enabling 118
sql.bsq 47
SQL*Net message from client
    wait event 278
SQL*Net message to client
    wait event 278
sqlid
    and Oracle11g SQL trace 65

SQLNET.AUTHENTICATION_SERVICES 200
sqlnet.ora 85
    and valid node checking 327
SQLPATH 250
SREADTIM 67
STAT
    SQL trace file entry 230
STATISTICS_LEVEL 238, 251
STATS$IDLE_EVENT 261
Statspack 249
    default snapshot level 251
    identifying used indexes 264
    importing PERFSTAT schema dump 271
    upgrade to Oracle10g 266
stored outline 82, 125
strace 23, 161
Streams AQ 130
synchronization 376
SYSDBA privilege 20, 200
    and Perl DBI 199
syslog 19, 351
SYSOPER
    privilege 20
SYSOPER privilege 200
    and Perl DBI 199
system statistics 66, 75, 301
SYSTEMSTATE dump 63, 118, 175

T

TAB$ 47
table selectivity 78
tcp_ip_abort_interval 331
tcp_keepalive_interval 331
tcp_keepalive_threshold 331
tcp_rexmit_interval_max 331
tcp.excluded_nodes 325
tcp.invited_nodes 325
tcp.validnode_checking 325
TCP/IP adapter 196
telnet 319
think time 283
three tier environment 244
Tim Bunce 188
time
    UNIX utility 308
time model statistics 269
Tivoli Data Protection for Oracle 147
Tivoli Storage Manager 144, 147
TKPROF 225, 228, 230, 231, 241, 247, 292, 299
    EXPLAIN option 265
TNS Listener 317, 325
    and valid node checking 325
TNS_ADMIN 85

TNS-00583 329
TNS-00584 328
TNS-12560 328
tnsnames.ora 85
    and Perl DBI 199
tnsping xiv, 319
top 107
    UNIX command 376
top_n_events 259
total elapsed time
    and ESQLTRCPROF 288
TRACE
    exp/imp, expdp/impdp parameter 122
trace_directory_client 85
trace_level_client 84, 85
TRACEFILE_IDENTIFIER 205, 375
TRACEFILE_NAME
    ORADEBUG command 374, 375
transaction 285
Transparent Application Failover 330, 337
Transparent Network Substrate 196
TRCSESS 215, 242, 244
    and Shared Server 216
    and tracing parallel execution 247
    compatibility with Oracle9i 216
truss 23, 161, 319, 331
tusc 319
TX enqueue 229, 287
TX lock 134

U

UDP 377
UNDO_RETENTION 48
unencrypted passwords 128
UNIX IPC 377
UNLIMIT
    ORADEBUG command 375
UNMAP 229
USE_NL hint 82
user datagram protocol 377
user global area 23
user lock 139
USER$ 126
USERENV 242

V

V$ views 89
V$ACTIVE_SESSION_HISTORY 252
V$BACKUP_PIECE 371
V$CLIENT_STATS 212
V$CONTROLFILE_RECORD_SECTION 90
V$DATABASE_BLOCK_CORRUPTION 370
V$DB_PIPES 365

V$ENQUEUE_STATISTICS 287
V$EVENT_NAME 232
V$FIXED_VIEW_DEFINITION 93
V$LOCK 134
V$MYSTAT
    and getting session id 242
V$OBJECT_USAGE 51, 90
V$OPEN_CURSOR 226
V$OPTION 349
V$PGASTAT 24
V$PROCESS 24, 104
V$SERV_MOD_ACT_STATS 212, 213
V$SESS_TIME_MODEL 225, 269
V$SESSION 213, 226, 338
    and client identifier 244
V$SESSION_WAIT 104, 134
V$SESSTAT 381
V$SORT_USAGE 229
V$SQL 226
V$SQL_PLAN 96, 237
    and failure of STATSPACK.SNAP 251
V$SQL_WORKAREA 24
V$SQL_WORKAREA_ACTIVE 24, 26
V$SQLAREA 226
V$SQLTEXT 226, 253
V$SQLTEXT_WITH_NEWLINES 253, 258
V$SYS_TIME_MODEL 269
valid node checking 325
VALIDATE
    RMAN command 371
virtual IP address 332
voting disk 348

W

WAIT
    SQL trace file entry 232
wait event
    and microsecond resolution 104
wait events
    artificially generated with DBMS_SYSTEM 177
    tracing with DBMS_SYSTEM 175
wait time 208
    capacity for 270
Wall, Larry 188
Windows event viewer 20
workload statistics 75
worldwide number 43

X

X Window System 157
X$ fixed tables 89
X$BH 89
X$KCBFWAIT 92

X$KCCDC 90
X$KFFIL 109
X$KFFXP 109
X$KGLLK 89
X$KSLED 104
X$KSPPCV 92
X$KSPPI 92
X$KSPPSV 92
X$KSUPR 105
X$KSUSE 105
X$KSUSECST 104
XCTEND 229
    and transactions per second 285